TECHNOLOGY UPDATE

Diversity/Multicultural Resources on the World Wide Web

Would you like to establish e-mail connections between your classroom and a partner classroom in another country? If so, contact the Intercultural E-Mail Classr... of St. ...

Or ... versity ... sampl... contac... tained... sity of...

http://curry/edschool/Virginia.EDU/go/
multicultural/sites/education.html

TECHNOLOGY UPDATE

Standards for Social Studies, History, and Social Sciences

This is the first Technology Update, each of which is keyed to the content of the fourteen chapters in this book. Most of the Updates usually require access to the Internet, and will direct you to additional resources and materials related to teaching elementary and middle school social studies. In this instance, we provide more detailed sources for standards that apply to teaching social studies. Note that the Internet addresses listed in the

Internet Resources Related to Educational Standards

An excellent source for any standards-related materials is:

http://putwest.boces.org/StSu/Social.html

The site noted above (which you can also reach from the Cal State, Northridge address) provides links to ... organiza-

TECHNOLOGY UPDATE

So All Can See

Asking your class to crowd around one 14-inch computer screen is probably inviting problems. Someone is almost sure to step on someone else's foot or someone's elbow is almost certain to hit someone else's stomach, whether intentionally or not. How then do you use computer-based technology so that everyone can see, but without having to crowd around a single monitor?

There are at least four possible solutions to this problem. One is to use a liquid crystal display (LCD) device that fits on an overhead projector and that projects the computer-driven image on a screen. The image is not always as bright as you might hope for, and special overhead projectors that don't produce too much heat are required.

A second option is to get a device that projects the computer-driven image on a screen. Computer projectors are expensive, ($450 and up), but they permit large groups to view the image simultaneously. A third option is to get one of the "black boxes" that will project computer images through a TV set. This is a less costly option ($100 or so) than the others because most schools already have the TVs available. A fourth option is to download the files images onto a disk and then allow children to view them when it is their turn to use the computer. The disk option is the least costly, but it does not permit the entire class to view the images simultaneously. Nevertheless, it is a plausible alternative until schools are able to acquire the resources to use computer-based technology effectively.

Children and Their World

Children and Their World

Strategies for Teaching Social Studies

6th edition

David A. Welton   Texas Tech University

John T. Mallan   Syracuse University

Houghton Mifflin Company   Boston   New York

To . . .

David Jr., Stephen, Christopher, Lynda, and Shawn

. . . as they encounter their world.

Senior Sponsoring Editor: Loretta Wolozin
Associate Editor: Lisa Mafrici
Editorial Assistant: Jean Zielinski DeMayo
Project Editor: Elena Di Cesare Montillo
Editorial Assistant: Chrissy Lee
Senior Production/Design Coordinator: Sarah Ambrose
Senior Manufacturing Coordinator: Marie Barnes
Marketing Manager: Pamela Laskey

Cover design: Rebecca Fagan

Cover image: Kamil Vojnar/Photonica

Printed in the U.S.A.

Library of Congress Catalog Card Number: 98-72091

ISBN: 0-395-90415-3

123456789-QH-02 01 00 99 98

Contents

Part 2: Building a Framework for Teaching Social Studies

Part 3:   Instruction

9. Additional Strategies for Active Learning

12. Nurturing Critical and Reflective Thinking   282

Preface

Among the changes we considered making in this edition of *Children and Their World* was altering the title to better reflect the fact that a child's world is actually many worlds—the adult world, the television world, the peer world, the fantasy world, and so forth. Children are constantly bombarded with lessons from all of these worlds, lessons which they somehow sort out and make sense of, or in other cases ignore. No longer do children sit at one end of a log with the teacher at the other end, as they supposedly did in the "good old days." Children today are more apt to be sitting next to you, the teacher, on the greatest of all roller coasters—a world where change is a constant. As teachers, we know that teaching is future-oriented and should be aimed at preparing children for the future. Yet in a world that is constantly changing, it is challenging indeed to prepare children for a world that we cannot predict with any certainty.

Instead of changing the title of this book, we have opted to make clear that the children's world—"their world"—is actually many worlds. In addition, as authors we recognize that we face many of the same problems a teacher faces when starting out in the teaching profession. For example, it is one thing to appreciate the art and craft of teaching social studies from afar, but it is a different matter when one comes close enough to note things that one might be happier not seeing. Some of the problems we see—like the fact that every 26 seconds a child runs away from home, or every 12 seconds a child drops out of school (Children's Defense Fund, 1997)—sometimes seem almost insurmountable. Then too, beginning teachers often feel they are expected to know all the content, yet in reality no one does. No matter how desirable it might seem to have everything mastered before they start, beginning teachers will undoubtedly discover one of the beauties of teaching is that one learns as one teaches. It is among the best of all fringe benefits.

Underlying Assumptions of This Book

Each time we write a new edition, we reflect on the basic premises that underlie the entire book. Here, in summary form, are some fundamental ideas that are reflected throughout this edition:

* The world of teaching elementary and middle-school social studies is not a world of gimmicks and neat little recipes for activities. Yet neither is it a chaotic world that somehow, somewhere, sometime becomes clear and understandable if only students are given set clusters of information and set systems of prescriptive ideas.

- All teaching is future-oriented. This is difficult to do well when it is all but impossible to envision what the future will be.
- Children come in many different sizes, shapes, forms, and cultural packages. From the moment of birth onward, they live in a number of competing worlds and encounter/learn many lessons not found in the classroom. They bring these lessons with them.
- A fundamental part of the activities that take place in classrooms involves the social and cultural context the children bring to school.
- Teaching and learning are social activities.
- Social studies is complex partly because of its field of knowledge, and partly because some of its purposes may be in conflict. Consider that social studies is the only subject area in the school curriculum that publicly substitutes citizenship education for academic achievement as an educational goal. Although physical education is sometimes said to build health and character, citizenship education is almost never mentioned in mathematics or sciences classes.
- Teaching elementary and middle-school social studies often demands a willingness to live with a degree of bewilderment, even confusion.

Audience and Purpose

Children and Their World: Strategies for Teaching Social Studies, Sixth Edition, is intended for preservice students taking a first course in teaching elementary and middle-school social studies. By condensing several sections that typically appear in generic methods courses, as described below, this edition is shorter than previous editions. Our goal was to make this edition more compatible with the growing number of field-based courses where students' time is at a premium. At the same time, in-service and graduate students should continue to find this edition as useful, or even more so, than previous editions.

A continuing purpose of this book is to help prospective teachers understand the complex nature of elementary and middle-school social studies. We take exception to the contention that "anyone can teach social studies," because it too often ignores the complexities that a subject area that bridges the social sciences and the humanities imposes on teachers. In addition, and as much as we advocate a hands-on approach to teaching social studies, we also point out the problems that can befall teachers who adopt that approach simplistically, and who, for example, have their students spend two weeks building igloos out of sugar cubes. Our focus here is on helping prospective teachers build a perspective for judging the appropriateness of teaching activities for social studies, a perspective that recognizes the uniqueness and potential of the underlying subject matter.

This book is also based on the premise that learning is an active, constructivist process. That premise is hardly new or earthshaking—indeed, it is an approach that the late Hilda Taba advocated over thirty years ago (although she called it a "spiral" curriculum)—yet it applies equally to students in elementary or middle-school classrooms and to the students who read this book. For prospective teachers especially, our purpose is to suggest that successful social studies teaching depends on the teacher's ability to relate the three elements that form the triumvirate of teaching: the ability to correlate 1.) social studies content, 2.) teaching methods, and 3.) the application of content and methods in classrooms. Content and methods are certainly essential, but they are not sufficient in and of themselves. The key to effective instruction lies, we believe, in *application,* and, thus, we make every effort to relate subject-matter content to teaching methods, and teaching theory to practice.

Revisions in This Edition

The entire text has been extensively revised and updated throughout to incorporate the most recent research in social studies education and to reflect emerging changes and emphases in the field. At the same time, readers familiar with previous editions will find that many sections, such as questioning strategies, that are often included in generic methods courses have been substantially condensed in this edition. Without such condensations, it would have been impossible to add the new features and expanded coverage described below.

New Technology Updates

Each chapter in this edition contains a new user-friendly (no computer jargon) feature that correlates technological resources and opportunities with the content of that chapter. In Chapter 1, for example, the Technology Update identifies resources related to standards for social studies and related social science—a voluminous topic to say the least. Although many Updates provide Internet addresses, most of them go well beyond a simple list of addresses. For example, some Updates consist of mini-vignettes that show how teachers use CD-ROMs as vehicles for enhancing literacy, or how teachers can take their students on virtual tours of far-flung locations like Plimoth Plantation, the twelfth-century Durham Castle (in Durham, United Kingdom), or even the Egyptian Museum of Antiquities in Cairo, Egypt. Still other Updates provide directions and sources for downloading lesson plans or other teaching resources. So if you want copies of Matthew Brady's photographs to accompany a unit on the Civil War, check out the Technology Updates.

Significant New Coverage

Several new topics have been added to this edition. These include the following:

* **Standards** for social studies, history, geography, and civics. The standards literature in social studies comes in volumes, many of which are longer than this book. We have incorporated a major new section on standards in Chapter 1. More detailed treatments, including the Standards for Historical Thinking and the Standards for Geography, are included in the *Resource Handbook*. In addition, and because national standards and state

mandates can have a major impact on instructional planning, a significant new section has been added to Chapter 10, "Planning and Orchestrating Instruction."

* **Literacy-Related Strategies.** The literacy chapter was new to the fifth edition, but we have added expanded treatments of treating critical and noncritical vocabulary, word maps, and contextual redefinition.
* **Assessment Rubrics**. The design and construction of assessment rubrics is new to this edition.
* **Hypermedia and Integrated Application Software**. In addition to the Technology Updates, we have expanded the treatment of computer-based programs, especially hypermedia and integrated applications packages.

Other Current Features

Two major emphases begun in the fifth edition carry through in this edition. These include the following:

* **Exemplary Classroom Practices.** Vignettes of exemplary classroom practices are in effect mini–case studies of how real (or composite) teachers elect to approach social studies in their classrooms. For example, the literacy chapter begins with a vignette of how a second-grade teacher in Arizona integrates social studies and language experiences with her students, for many of whom English is their second language. Other vignettes illustrate how teachers can use historical documents as a springboard, how they integrate environmental education and social studies, and how they use a K-W-L chart with their students.
* **Integrating Children's Literature.** Opportunities for integrating children's literature into social studies were initiated in the fifth edition and have been expanded even more throughout this edition. Likewise, the already extensive bibliography of children's books in the *Resource Handbook* has been expanded to include trade books that address reducing violence.

Organization and Coverage

This edition of *Children and Their World* is organized into a Prologue, three major sections, and a brief Epilogue. The Prologue is designed to draw on readers' beliefs and prior experiences with social studies as a means for setting the stage for what is to come.

Part One, "Contexts for Social Studies," contains three chapters that examine the nature of social studies and how it impacts diverse learners. Chapter 1 has been revised to incorporate standards-related materials and to emphasize the relationship between social studies and citizenship education. Chapter 2 examines the nature of history and the social science disciplines, the knowledge base from which social studies is drawn. Chapter 3, "The Dimensions of Diversity," examines the interaction between culturally and educationally diverse learners and social studies, and it includes a brief new section on accommodating religious diversity.

Part Two, "Building a Framework for Teaching Social Studies," is a three-chapter section designed to help prospective teachers understand how social studies programs are organized and factors that can influence them. Chapter 4 addresses the question "how are social studies programs conceived?" as a means for examining how social studies can be organized for instruction. Chapter 5 considers how special topics, such as global education and environmental education, can be treated in social studies programs. Chapter 6 reflects the contemporary emphasis on character education, and it also contains a reduced treatment of traditional values education techniques, such as values clarification, moral development, and values analysis.

Part Three, "Instruction," is an eight-chapter section that focuses on the nitty-gritty elements associated with teaching social studies. Chapter 7, "Social Studies: Gateway to Literacy," treats the different dimensions of literacy and problems students often encounter in constructing meaning from social studies materials. Chapter 8 focuses on the different approaches teachers can use to teach social studies. Chapter 9 is an extension of Chapter 8 that focuses on a variety of activities that actively engage children. Chapters 10 and 11 focus on planning and assessment strategies respectively. Chapter 12, "Nurturing Critical and Reflective Thinking," examines a variety of approaches to helping students process information. Chapter 13 and 14 focus on instructional tools. Chapter 13 examines techniques for helping students to use maps, globes, and other graphic materials, while Chapter 14 is a survey of print and multimedia materials and community resources that teachers can draw upon. The book ends with a brief Epilogue in which we identify our perceived priorities for social studies in the future. The *Resource Handbook,* described below, follows the Epilogue.

Special Pedagogical Aids

To make this text easy to study, appealing to use, and a valuable teaching resource, we have included the following features:

* **Key Questions and Key Ideas** at the beginning of each chapter that serve as advance organizers for the content to be covered.
* **Introductions** that provide an overview of what is to come.
* **Technology Updates** that provide technological resources for contemporary social studies programs.
* **Model Student Activities** that illustrate model lesson formats that can be adapted to other social studies topics or content.
* **Commentaries** in which we extend ideas previously introduced or offer our point of view on various problems and issues.
* **Vignettes of exemplary practice** that demonstrate how various teachers approach social studies with their students.
* **Marginal notes** that highlight key ideas within the text.
* **Summaries** that synthesize the major concepts presented in each chapter.
* **Suggested Activities** that are designed to stimulate further thought or provide opportunities for students to apply the concepts treated within the chapter.

* **Suggested Readings** that list, with annotations, additional sources for students to locate detailed information on topics considered with the chapter.
* **A Resource Handbook** that provides additional sources and materials related to social studies teaching. The four parts of the Handbook include: (1) instructional materials relating to text activities, (2) planning aids, (3) additional instructional resources, and (4) annotated bibliographies of children's books that are keyed to common social studies topics.

Acknowledgments

We are keenly aware of our indebtedness to the many people who helped to make this book possible. Countless elementary and middle-school students helped us to learn what it means to teach a subject like social studies and, collectively, played a significant though immeasurable role in shaping this book. Equally important are the college students and in-service teachers with whom we have been privileged to work, and whose questions (and responses to our answers) have indicated directions in which we need to go and areas where we needed to be clearer than we were. We are also grateful to our colleagues, both at Texas Tech and Syracuse University, who have influenced and inspired us in so many ways.

We gratefully acknowledge the contributions of the following reviewers for the thoughtful advice and criticism they offered at various stages in the development of this book:

Robert D. Cason, *Northeastern Oklahoma State University*
Thomas B. Goodkind, *University of Connecticut*
M. Gail Hickey, *Indiana University–Purdue University Fort Wayne*
Margaret Johnson, *Texas Tech University*
Carol Sue Marshall, *University of Texas at Arlington*
Saundra J. McKee, *Clarion University of Pennsylvania*
F. Gene Miller, *Western Illinois University*
Jay A. Monson, *Utah State University*
Robert Otto, *Western Kentucky University*

We also extend special thanks to our talented developmental editors, Elaine Silverstein, Jean Zielinski DeMayo, and Lisa Mafrici; to our superb production editor, Elena Di Cesare Montillo; and to the rest of the editorial staff at Houghton Mifflin who were our partners in this endeavor.

Finally, we owe special acknowledgment to our wives, Kathy and Janet, who have come to understand the trials and joys associated with producing a book such as this, and with whom we intend to become reacquainted.

DAVID A. WELTON   JOHN T. MALLAN

Prologue:
Reflecting on What's Ahead

Remember when you

* couldn't understand why Australia was a continent but Greenland wasn't?
* thought Paris, Boston, and Chicago were states?
* spent hours building a model igloo from sugar cubes?
* had current events every Friday?
* memorized the Preamble to the Constitution, the Gettysburg Address, or the presidents of the United States, in order?
* were taught that "milk trucks carry milk" when you already knew it?
* made the outline for your report on Greece, "the South," or Andrew Jackson *after* you had written the report?

Introduction

Some things about social studies you may remember fondly, and others you've long since forgotten. From time to time, you may have asked yourself why it was necessary to learn certain things, like the states and capitals (assuming you know them), when that kind of information is so readily available. There are a variety of reasons why things like the states and capitals are often taught in social studies, and we will explore these throughout this book.

You may also be aware that some of what you studied in social studies might not have been taught at all were it not for the "Joan of Arc" syndrome. In this phenomenon, which is illustrated in the following conversation, the most important qualification is that at least one of the speakers has spent time studying about Joan of Arc, the national heroine of France.

The Joan of Arc syndrome

"I've heard they're taking Joan of Arc out of social studies. Children won't be studying her anymore."

"What! What are they doing that for?"

"I guess it's because they can't figure out why they should keep her in."

"Why they should keep her in? Isn't it obvious? I learned about Joan of Arc—you did too. Joan of Arc is someone everyone should know about. . . . I mean, well . . . look what it's done for us! We'd never have gotten where we are today if we hadn't learned about things that every child should know—including Joan of Arc.

"You're saying that because *we* learned it when we were in school, students today should learn it too."

"Exactly! We learned it, they should learn it too!"

There's probably a little "Joan of Arc" in each of us—a reluctance to reflect on some of the things we have done in the past. By no means are we suggesting that everything about the past is "bad" or outdated, or that every new idea that comes along is worthwhile and is the kind of thing that schools should move toward immediately. Our point is that the force of tradition, which is what the Joan of Arc syndrome represents, is so potent that trying to remove almost any topic from the school curriculum can elicit howls of protest. In many cases, the protestors may not remember much about the topic—whether it's Joan of Arc or whatever—all they must remember is having studied it. As long as people perceive certain topics as useful, those topics tend to remain in the curriculum, which then grows larger with every passing day.

Tradition plays a role in keeping the curriculum as large as it is, but there is another side to this coin: that is, there are some things that could be included in the curriculum but usually are not. For example, do you recall some questions that occurred to you during your school experience that you thought were important, but that were almost never considered at school? These may have included questions like the following:

Is it O.K. to lie sometimes? If so, when?
How do other people feel about me, and how can I know for sure?
If cooperation is so important, why don't you get graded on it?
Why are the best movies almost always rated "R"?
Must I like everybody? What happens if I don't?
Why doesn't everyone have all the money he or she needs?

Underlying questions like these are genuine human and social concerns that students think about and sometimes worry about. Some people argue that such questions involve things that students will learn—or should learn—from their parents or from everyday life. For schools to get involved in such matters, they argue, is either unnecessary or an invasion of parental rights and responsibilities, sometimes both. We disagree. Such questions and concerns cannot and indeed should not be the sole basis for elementary and middle-school social studies programs, but we will explore some legitimate roles they can play.

An inquiry

After spending a dozen or so years watching social studies teachers in action, you already have some beliefs, assumptions, and impressions about what social studies is and about what it means to teach it. In the next section, you have the opportunity to clarify what you believe about elementary and middle-school social studies and then compare your beliefs with ours. It is not important that we agree on everything, because our purpose is simply to establish a point of departure.

Social Studies Inventory

Please select the response that best reflects your impressions of your elementary and middle-school social studies experience by circling the appropriate number.

Comparing beliefs about social studies

	Agree	Uncertain	Disagree
1. Social studies is too often dull and boring.	1	2	3
2. What children learn in social studies is useful in their everyday lives.	1	2	3
3. Teaching social studies is not as important as teaching reading or mathematics.	1	2	3
4. The main purpose of social studies is teaching history and geography.	1	2	3
5. Most social studies teachers put about the right emphasis on teaching thinking skills.	1	2	3
6. Many social studies teachers place too much emphasis on textbooks.	1	2	3
7. Social studies involves everyday classroom behaviors, such as lining up properly to walk through the hall or learning to obey classroom rules.	1	2	3
8. Small-group work in social studies often uses time that could be better spent learning things that are really important.	1	2	3

Our Responses

Our responses in this section are geared to traditional social studies programs, and not to one-of-a-kind programs you are unlikely to encounter.

1. *Social studies is too often dull and boring.* Our response: Agree.

   Content that deals with people—which is what social studies focuses on—should never be dull and boring, yet too often that's what seems to happen. As Alter and Denworth (1990, p. 31) noted, "History itself isn't boring; it's just taught that way." As much as we are inclined to agree with Alter and Denworth, some related problems play a role here. First, many textbooks present materials in ways that are—well—less than thrilling. Second, the vast amount of material that many teachers (and textbooks) are expected to cover during a year can be almost overwhelming.

   We believe that a major part of the problem here is the so-called survey course. Many sixth-grade teachers, for example, are expected to deal with content ranging from prehistoric times to the atomic age. The scope is so broad that they and their students find themselves rushing through historic eras so quickly that students often have difficulty differentiating one era from another. Trying to cover so much material in so little time inevitably

The coverage problem

results in superficial exposure as opposed to in-depth understanding (see Newmann, 1988).

"Less is more"

Many states and local schools are addressing the problems associated with survey courses by adopting an approach that is sometimes referred to as "less is more." The premise is that by studying fewer ("less") topics in greater depth, teachers can spend the time necessary to develop ("more") in-depth understanding. This approach should help reduce the extent to which social studies may have been dull and boring in the past.

2. *What children learn in school studies is useful in their everyday lives.* Our response: Uncertain.

Relevance

Because the relevance of social studies often hinges on how teachers approach it, it is difficult to generalize here. Some portions of social studies—especially history—are taught because they represent bodies of knowledge that children are expected to learn and know, regardless of any direct relevance to their day-to-day lives. Still other segments of social studies can be taught in ways that have immediate relevance to children and to their actions as future citizens. We will consider both portions throughout this book.

3. *Teaching social studies is not as important as teaching reading or mathematics.* Our response: Disagree.

Priorities

The conventional wisdom in many elementary and middle schools holds that teaching reading and mathematics is more important than almost everything else. That's why social studies is often taught in the afternoon—if there's time to get to it. We believe that thought-provoking social studies programs can incorporate elements that are just as important as reading and mathematics, possibly more so.

4. *The main purpose of social studies is teaching history and geography.* Our response: Disagree.

History and geography are so prominent in many social studies programs that other social sciences, like anthropology, often fade into the background. Then, too, many people think that social studies is simply another name for history and geography. Common as such thinking is, it is much too limited. Social studies deals with the human experience, with human beings and human behavior in every sense of those terms.

Goal: To produce good citizens

The main purpose for teaching social studies is to produce thoughtful, competent, well-informed, and responsible citizens. In other words, the purpose for teaching social studies parallels the purpose for which schools exist—to produce good citizens. Not every child will become an engineer, a doctor, or a scientist, but everyone will be a citizen; it's an office that every one of us occupies. We think that Walter Parker (1990, p. 17) put it best when he stated that social studies

The knowledge base for citizenship

is where, if anywhere, the core knowledge base for citizenship will be developed. Social studies is the only place in the school curriculum where focused inquiry on democratic ideals and practices might be located. It is where the tragedies and victories of "liberty and justice for all" can be laid out for study. It is where students encounter models of civic courage—Abraham Lincoln and Sojourner Truth [a freed slave who lived in the same era as Lincoln], for example. *And* it is where students stand the best chance of being introduced systematically to popular sovereignty—participating in decision making and grappling with enduring public issues.

5. ***Most social studies teachers put about the right emphasis on teaching thinking skills.*** Our response: Disagree.

Teaching Thinking

We think that most traditional social studies programs place too much emphasis on learning names, dates, and other information and too little emphasis on using social studies as a vehicle for teaching critical thinking and problem solving. Throughout this book we will focus on *using* social studies content—the stuff of which history, geography, and other social sciences are made—for a variety of teaching purposes. Among the most important of those purposes is helping students to become skillful thinkers.

6. ***Many social studies teachers place too much emphasis on textbooks.*** Our response: Agree.

Texts as teaching tools

Some teachers apparently feel that skipping one or more chapters in a textbook will leave irreparable gaps in their students' education. Those teachers often rely on textbooks exclusively, perhaps because they are not aware of how to use alternative data sources. Still other teachers feel compelled to emphasize the textbook because of state or school board mandates or other forces beyond their control. All of this notwithstanding, we endorse an approach to elementary and middle-school social studies in which textbooks serve as teaching tools but do not become the program itself.

7. ***Social studies involves everyday classroom behaviors, such as lining up properly to walk through the hall or learning to obey classroom rules.*** Our response: Uncertain.

Classrooms as caring communities

We are not weaseling out here, because our response depends on the context in which the behaviors take place. In schools and classrooms that employ "developmental discipline" (see Schaps and Solomon, 1990), where students are treated as valued and participating members of a learning community, behaviors such as lining up to go to the cafeteria can be an integral part of social studies. However, this occurs only when students play an active role in classroom governance and decision making. That role includes participating in the development of classroom rules—through which students begin to understand what rules are for—and working collaboratively with teachers to solve problems. Classrooms and schools that function as caring democratic communities—as microcosms of the larger society in which students actually "do" democracy—can provide a part of citizenship education.

We disagree with teachers who claim that training children to walk down the hall properly, silently, and in single file, is necessarily a part of social studies. Training students to conform to expected behaviors through the imposition of adult authority is obviously one approach to classroom management, and classroom management is clearly something that every teacher must be concerned with. Nevertheless, we question whether teachers who adopt this approach are teaching social studies.

8. ***Small-group work in social studies often uses time that could be better spent learning things that are really important.*** Our response: Agree.

Group work

Small-group work in traditional social studies programs sometimes seems to be included as a respite from normal classroom routines, almost as a way to make the regular work more palatable. This is why we agreed with the statement. At the same time, the most common reason that people are fired from their jobs is their inability to get along with others in the workplace. Social studies can provide a context for small-group work, which helps children learn to work effectively with one another.

The key to small-group work and most of the other items on this inventory is how teachers use them. Small-group work can be a raging success, a disaster, or something in between. Likewise, you've had teachers who could somehow make the dullest, most lifeless material become interesting and worthwhile. Clearly, teachers hold the key to a vibrant and appealing social studies program.

Building on what children already know

The other key ingredient is the children. Some problems that children experience with social studies—like confusing cities, states, and countries—are simply a result of their lack of experience with the world as we know it. Young children often view their world from a highly personal perspective that, even in this age of advanced technology, may not extend beyond their immediate neighborhood. At the same time, young children are often fascinated with our world and the people who inhabit it. Our intent throughout this book is to provide the basis for developing elementary and middle-school social studies programs that capitalize on children's inherent interest in their world and that add depth and richness to what they already know.

Part 1

Contexts for Social Studies

Part One examines three contextual factors that influence how and why social studies is taught. The first of these is the nature of social studies itself and the purposes for which it is taught, which are the focus of Chapter 1, The Dynamics of Social Studies. The second contextual factor is history and the social sciences, the knowledge base from which social studies is drawn, which we examine in Chapter 2. The third contextual factor is the increasingly diverse audience that your social studies teaching will be aimed toward. We consider this element in Chapter 3, The Dimensions of Diversity.

The overarching purpose for teaching social studies, which we address in Chapter 1, can be captured in two words: citizenship education. That purpose has remained constant over the years, but as our society has changed and continues to change, the demands of citizenship education have also changed. Our society is made up of a number of overlapping cultures—national, regional, ethnic, and so forth—that can sometimes have conflicting and contending demands. We suggest that responsible citizenship in our society requires at least three complementary literacies: multicultural literacy, civic literacy, and community literacy.

Chapter 2, History and the Social Sciences: The Knowledge Base for Social Studies, is a survey of the disciplines on which social studies is based. Because history plays such a major role in most social studies programs, we devote special attention to problems associated with teaching history in both Chapters 1 and 2.

Diverse student populations can play such an important role in classrooms today that Chapter 3 is devoted to that topic. A significant section of Chapter 3 deals with multicultural education as a means for addressing cultural diversity. Sections of Chapter 3 also address other forms of diversity that can affect what you do in your classroom.

1 The Dynamics of Social Studies

Key Questions

* What is social studies, and why is it an integral part of elementary and middle-school programs?
* What is citizenship education?
* How does social studies lend itself to multiple objectives?

Key Ideas

* Social studies is a multidisciplinary school subject based primarily on history and the social science disciplines.
* Social studies is characterized by multiple goals and purposes, some of which it shares with other subject areas.
* The overarching aim of social studies is citizenship education, but how this relates to the selection and use of content in instruction has not been settled.
* The purpose of social studies is to provide children and youth with the knowledge, skills, values, and dispositions that permit them to participate actively in a democratic society.

Introduction: In the Beginning

How social studies evolved

In the beginning there was history. People had to be around before there could be history, of course, and the histories those individuals created were much more personal than the formalized record of the past that most of us know. Nevertheless, history began soon after our ancestors became aware of their past.

Almost immediately thereafter came geography. It wasn't called "geography" until much later, of course, and it was really rudimentary, focusing on things like locating good hunting and fishing areas, and avoiding places where the water sources—the springs and rivers—dried up in hot weather. Knowing what resources were available in the immediate environment was often essential to survival.

The history and geography that our ancestors dealt with were basic and important. Their history helped them identify who they were, individually and collectively, and where they had come from. Their geography helped them survive what otherwise had to have been a harrowing existence. Yet an equally important aspect of our ancestors' lives dealt with determining how they would conduct relationships between and among individuals and groups. They had to deal with questions like: Was it O.K. to take another family's food or belongings (against their wishes), simply because someone felt the urge to do so? Because safe and orderly societies cannot exist when everyone is free to "do his or her own thing," they also had to decide what would happen to those who violated the "rules." Without clear moral and ethical standards, daily life would be chaotic, and the survival of individuals and the society itself would be questionable. In many respects, creating a moral code to live by was as important to our ancestors' survival as was their knowledge of geography—sometimes more so.

Our ancestors obviously learned to cope with their physical and social environments, or we wouldn't be here today. Likewise, when some of our ancestors grew skilled enough that they no longer needed to spend every waking minute worrying about their survival, they were able to formalize their history, expand their geographical horizons, and codify their moral and ethical principles as laws. And so it went through various civilizations—the ancient Egyptians, the Greeks, the Romans, and so forth. Adults in these societies passed on their histories, their geographies, and their codes of ethics to their children so that they too would become aware of their heritage and their responsibilities to others—a challenge that remains to this day.

After they had satisfied their survival needs, some of our ancestors were able to study more specialized aspects of human behavior. For example, some individuals began to explore why corn and wheat were more costly when rainfall was sparse, but were cheaper when rainfall was plentiful. This marked the beginning of what eventually became the discipline of economics. Other specialized studies followed. Some individuals began to study cultures, both past and present, thus providing the beginnings of anthropology. Others began to explore how societies govern themselves, which provided the basis for political science (or government). Still others investigated how groups of people interact, which ultimately led to the discipline of sociology. Even more recently, some individuals began to examine everyday human behaviors, such as how we learn and how we develop our beliefs and attitudes, which are part of the discipline of psychology.

From these beginnings, the school subject called social studies emerged. History is a major component of social studies, as are the social science disciplines of geography, economics, political science, anthropology, sociology, and psychology. Morals and ethics, which we include as part of philosophy, also play a role in social studies, as do elements from the humanities and the fine arts. These components and others are reflected in the National Council for the Social Studies's (NCSS; 1994) definition of social studies. It states:

> Social studies is the integrated study of the social sciences and humanities to promote civic competence. Within the social program, social studies provides coordinated, systematic study drawing upon such disciplines as anthropology, archaeology, economics, geography, history, philosophy, political science, psychology, religion, and sociology, as well as appropriate content from the humanities, mathematics, and natural sciences.

A composite subject

The common focus of social studies is human behavior. In one form or another, all the components of social studies deal with how we interact with each other, both past and present, how we interact with our environment, and on the myriad ways in which we organize, govern, and trade among ourselves. That focus on human (social) behavior led John Dewey (1938) to suggest the shortest definition for social studies that we know of. He said: "Social studies is the study of things social."

This chapter focuses on the dynamic nature of elementary and middle-school social studies. Some of its aspects are steeped in tradition, but other elements are changing more than you might imagine. Today, for example, you are apt to find teachers using more narrative history and many more biographies and informational books, at lower grades especially, than was true only ten years ago. You may also find more schools using the "less is more" approach that we noted earlier: that is, studying fewer topics in greater depth instead of trying to squeeze all of American or world history into a 180-day school year.

In the balance of this chapter we explore some of the current debates about whether social studies should remain a multidisciplinary subject or be taught as separate disciplines, and about what standards should be applied to judge social studies programs. Finally, we consider the relationship between social studies and its major purpose, preparing future citizens to live in a democracy.

Dynamic Social Studies: The Continuing Debates

Studying the disciplines separately or as a unified subject

After the years you've spent sitting in social studies classrooms, you surely have an idea of what social studies is and how it is organized. Yet Americans (and Canadians, and Australians) are often surprised to learn that people in most parts of the world have never heard of "social studies." People almost everywhere study history, geography, and the other social sciences, but in most parts of the world these disciplines are studied as separate subjects, in much the same way as they are taught in most American high schools and colleges. That is why elementary students in England, for example, study English history and English geography separately, sometimes at different grade levels.

Intermingling several separate disciplines into a single course of study, which is sometimes referred to as a unified or *multidisciplinary studies* approach to curriculum, is common among elementary and middle-school programs. Most language arts, science, and social studies programs are organized on this basis. Elementary science programs, for example, typically include elements from botany, zoology, geology, and meteorology, each of which is a separate dis-

Multidisciplinary studies

cipline in its own right. Although the disciplines are different, both language arts and social studies also follow a similar pattern.

The following Model Student Activity shows how data from history can be used for different purposes. This activity, the first of many model activities in this book, also illustrates how students can use historically accurate materials as a basis for realistic decision making. Note also that all the model activities in this book are presented as models, that is, as exemplary lesson formats that can be adapted for other topics or content areas.

MODEL STUDENT ACTIVITY

Who Is Qualified for the Presidency?

Overview

In this activity you are asked to identify which one of eight potential candidates is the best qualified and which is the least qualified to be president of the United States. The biographical data on the candidates are presented on separate cards—a procedure usually referred to as a Q-sort. All the candidates are (or were) real people who meet (or met) the three constitutional qualifications for the presidency; that is, they (1) are natural-born citizens, (2) are at least thirty-five years old, and (3) have resided in the United States for at least fourteen years prior to a presidential election. To ensure that the candidates are judged on their qualifications—and not your prior knowledge of them—their names and gender have been omitted. The candidates' identities appear in the Resource Handbook.

Recommended Procedure

Phases One and Two of this activity should be done in small groups. The discussion questions in Phase Three can also be considered in small groups and then summarized in a large-group discussion.

Phase One—Additional Qualifications

Before considering the candidates, identify any additional qualifications (beyond those identified in the Constitution) that you think a president of the United States should possess. For example, should a president be a college graduate? Should he or she have had prior political experience?

Phase Two—Selection

Use the data cards to select the two individuals, one of whom you feel would be (1) best qualified and the other (2) least qualified to be president of the United States.

[Note: "Age as of this date" on the data cards refers to the point in each candidate's career at which he or she had accomplished all the activities listed on the card. For the candidates who actually served as president, the date used was just prior to their election to office.]

CARD 1

College Attended: None

Religion: Protestant

Career (Major Occupations): Investor, Druggist, Bookseller, Brigadier General in U.S. Army

Married: 1st spouse: 5 years until spouse's death, 2nd spouse: 1 year   **Children:** 3 by first marriage

Age as of This Date: 38

SOURCE: *Dictionary of American Biography*, Charles Scribner's Sons, 1928, pp. 362–67.

CARD 2

Colleges Attended: Harvard University, Columbia University

Religion: Protestant

Career (Major Occupations): Farmer, Lawyer, State Senator, Assistant Secretary of Navy, Governor, Vice-Presidential candidate

Married: 27 years   **Children:** 6

Age as of This Date: 50

SOURCE: *The National Cyclopaedia of American Biography*, XXXVII, University Microfilms, A Xerox Company, 1967, pp. 1–3.

CARD 3

Colleges Attended: Morehouse College, A.B. and L.H.D.; Crozer Theological Seminary, B.D.; University of Pennsylvania; Boston University, Ph.D., D.D.; Harvard University, L.L.D.; Central State College; Morgan State College

Religion: Protestant

Career (Major Occupations): Protestant minister, Teacher of Philosophy at Harvard, President of a civil rights organization, 1 of 10 outstanding men for the year according to *Time* magazine, Nobel Prize winner, Noted public speaker

Married: 15 years   **Children:** 4

Age as of This Date: 37

SOURCE: *Current Biography Yearbook 1965*, H. W. Wilson Co., 1966, pp. 220–23; *Current Biography Yearbook 1968*, H. W. Wilson Co., 1969, p. 457.

CARD 4

College Attended: None

Religion: No specific denomination

Career (Major Occupations): Land speculator and farmer, Lawyer, Member of U.S. House of Representatives, U.S. Senator, U.S. Judge, Commander of U.S. Armed Forces

Married: 38 years   **Children:** none

Age as of This Date: 62

SOURCE: *Dictionary of American Biography*, IX, Charles Scribner's Sons, 1932, pp. 526–31.

CARD 5

College Attended: Columbia University

Religion: No specific denomination

Career (Major Occupations): Writer, Served as Lieutenant Colonel in Army, Lawyer, Member of a congress, Member to a constitutional convention, Secretary of the Treasury

Married: 24 years   **Children:** 8

Age as of This Date: 47

SOURCE: *Dictionary of American Biography*, VII, Charles Scribner's Sons, 1932, pp. 171–79.

CARD 6

College Attended: None (private secondary school in England)

Religion: Protestant

Career (Major Occupations): Teacher, Journalist, Member of a labor union (trade union league), United States delegate to the United Nations Commission on Human Rights, Endorsed by a President for the Nobel Peace Prize, Noted public speaker

Married: 27 years   **Children:** 6

Age as of This Date: 65

SOURCE: *Current Biography*, Who's News and Why, 1949, H. W. Wilson Co., 1950, pp. 528–32.

CARD 7

College Attended: None

Religion: Roman Catholic

Career (Major Occupations): Director for a community service organization, Founder and director of a farm worker's organization, Served in the United States Navy, Honored for distinguished public service by the American Institute for Public Service, Second recipient of the Martin Luther King Jr. Nonviolent Peace Prize

Married: 29 years   **Children:** 8

Age as of This Date: 47

SOURCE: *Who's Who in America*, Marquis Who's Who, Inc., 1972, p. 550; *Current Biography Yearbook 1969*, H. W. Wilson Co., 1970, pp. 86–89.

CARD 8

College Attended: None

Religion: No specific denomination

Career (Major Occupations): Postmaster, Lawyer, U.S. Representative, Store owner, State congressman, Served as Captain in U.S. Army, Noted public speaker

Married: 19 years   **Children:** 4

Age as of This Date: 51

SOURCE: *Dictionary of American Biography*, XI, Charles Scribner's Sons, 1933, pp. 242–49.

Phase Three—Summary

Questions:

1. To what extent did your choices reflect the qualifications you listed in Phase One? Would you modify your list in any way?
2. Determine whether any of the following factors should be considered in selecting a presidential candidate.

   2.1. Age
   2.2. Religion
   2.3. Gender
   2.4. Educational background
   2.5. Number of children
   2.6 Character

   2.7. Previous occupation
   2.8. Personal appearance
   2.9. Personality
   2.10. Ethnic background
   2.11. Marital status
   2.12 Physical health

3. Should any other factors be considered?

4. How did your group decide what qualifications were most important? Least important?

Optional Extending Activities

1. Examine the candidate's identities as shown in the Resource Handbook. Would you change your selection? Why or why not? Does the new information influence your conclusions about the necessary qualifications?

2. Do your qualifications reflect the beliefs of most individuals in your community? in your class? Identify a plan for determining how you could find out.

Source: Adapted from Marsha Hobin, "Clarifying What Is Important," in Allan O. Kownslar, Ed., *Teaching American History: The Quest for Relevancy*. Copyright 1974 by National Council for the Social Studies. Reprinted by permission of Allan O. Kownslar and NCSS.

COMMENTARY: On Using Model Activities with Children

A key question for "Who Is Qualified for the Presidency?" or any instructional activity is: "What should students learn from having done it?" It's doubtful, for example, that students will remember much about the constitutional qualifications for the presidency, primarily because that information is almost incidental to the activity. On the other hand, students are likely to remember some of the biographical information about the candidates because the format of the activity requires them to work with that information. However, expecting students to commit the biographical information to memory, such as which college Alexander Hamilton attended, seems very questionable at best. The biographical information serves a legitimate and necessary purpose in the activity, but in the sweep of human events it is on the same level as the name of Robert E. Lee's horse (Traveler): historical trivia.

The biographical information in the "Presidency" activity serves as a vehicle to help students consider factors that influence the election of a president. In that context, an appropriate learner objective for the *content focus* of this activity would be: "Upon completion of this activity, learners will identify at least seven factors that could influence voters in their decisions about a candidate's qualifications for the presidency."

In the activity, students are also asked to identify the best- and least-qualified presidential candidate, and then reach group consensus about their choices. The students' involvement in a group decision-making process, as well as their responses to questions like "What process did the group use in reaching its decision?" and "Did some factors weigh more heavily in that decision than others?" are just as instructionally significant as whichever candidates the group selects. The point is that the group's decision-making process reflects a *process/skills focus* for this activity that deserves as much attention as their final decisions. A sample learner objective for the process/skills emphasis of the activity would be: "Given the constitutional qualifications for president, students will (a) identify additional qualifications (for the presidency) that they feel are appropriate, (b) determine if these qualifications are acceptable to a group of peers, and (c) defend or modify the selection of potential candidates to reach group consensus." In other words, the "Presidency" activity could serve as a vehicle for (1) identifying and learning about factors that may influence the selection and election of a presidential candidate, which is its content focus, and for (2) analyzing and learning about a group decision-making process, which is its process focus.

The NCSS Standards

Orchestrating subject matter

Social studies teachers have several sets of standards available to inform their teaching. These include the NCSS standards for social studies, standards for history and the social science disciplines developed by other organizations, and standards (sometimes called outcomes) adopted by the states. With so many standards to choose from, the question becomes: Where does a teacher begin? The NCSS suggests that teachers use the social studies standards, which are organized around broad themes, to address overall curriculum design and comprehensive student performance expectations. Teachers can then use standards for individual disciplines (for civics and government, economics, geography, and history) to provide focused content for grade-level strands and specific courses. Sometimes a discipline such as history will take the lead, while other disciplines, such as geography and economics will play supporting roles. At other times, disciplines such as history, geography, and economics will be equally involved, thus reflecting the multidisciplinary nature of social studies.

The basic themes for the NCSS standards (as detailed in the Resource Handbook) are as follows:

NCSS Themes

Culture
Time, Continuity, and Change
People, Places, and Environment
Individual Development and Identity
Individuals, Groups, and Institutions
Power, Authority, and Governance
Production, Distribution, and Consumption
Science, Technology, and Society
Global Connections
Civic Ideals and Practices

Performance Expectations

Performance expectations for each of the NCSS themes are presented in three clusters: (1) for the early grades, (2) for the middle grades, and (3) for high school. The following example for the early grades reflects performance expectations for the theme, Culture.

Social studies programs should include experiences that provide for the study of culture and cultural diversity, so that the learner can

a. explore and describe similarities and differences in the ways groups, societies, and cultures address similar human needs and concerns.

What children are expected to do

b. give examples of how experiences may be interpreted differently by people from diverse cultural perspectives and frames of reference.
c. describe ways in which language, stories, folktales, music, and artistic creations serve as expressions of culture and influence the behavior of people living in a particular culture.
d. compare ways in which people from different cultures think about and deal with their physical environment and social conditions.
e. give examples and describe the importance of cultural unity and diversity within and across groups.

Classroom Examples

Most of the standards documents include examples of classroom activities that illustrate how learning experiences can be designed to help students meet performance expectations. For example, a classroom activity for the NCSS theme of culture describes the experiences of a teacher, Carlene Jackson, who uses a

Examples from the standards

new program to develop geographic understanding among students in her first-grade class. Upon examining her class list, (before the first day of school), Ms. Jackson determines that she might have students of Mexican, Vietnamese, and Korean ancestry, as well as of African-American and European-American backgrounds. Jackson and her students decide to study how families meet their basic needs of food, clothing, and shelter in five places: their own community;

Juarez, Mexico; Hanoi, Vietnam; Lagos, Nigeria; and Frankfurt, Germany. The students read books and stories, look at photos and slides, watch videos, and talk to speakers from their cities. Students sharpen their reading, writing, and speaking skills and learn new geography skills such as map reading. For each city, they read and discuss something about its location, climate, region, and people. This activity addresses performance expectations a, b, and d.[1]

The NCSS standards document clearly identifies what content should be taught, and then provides examples of how to teach it. However, the document does not deal with, nor should it necessarily, the question *why?* Why, for example, should children study any of the ten themes? Thus, the basic question that we focus on in the next section is: "Why should children study social studies?"

---

[1]Abridged from the Executive Summary, *Expect Excellence: Curriculum Standards for Social Studies.* Copyright 1994 by the National Council for the Social Studies. Reprinted by permission.

Why Teach Social Studies?

PERSON ONE: What are you going to school for?

PERSON TWO (patiently): To get an education

PERSON ONE: What do you need an education for?

PERSON TWO (impatiently): To get a better-paying job, of course!

Everyone knows, or at least used to know, that getting more education can lead to a better-paying job—which is why some people spend years sitting in classrooms. What often gets lost in this line of thinking is the main reason that democratic nations support a school system. It is *not* so their citizens can get better-paying jobs, although almost no one objects if they do. In our society and others like ours, schools exist because representative democracies cannot function effectively without enlightened and responsible citizens.

Democracy demands an educated citizenry

Our democracy was still in its infancy when the French observer, Alexis de Tocqueville (ed. Commager, 1947), wrote, "The Americans are hardly more virtuous than others, but they are infinitely better educated (I speak for the mass) than any other people of my acquaintance." De Tocqueville went on to say that "the mass of those possessing an understanding of public affairs, a knowledge of laws and precedents, a feeling for the best interest of the nation, and a faculty of understanding them, is greater in America than any other place in the world." De Tocqueville wrote these words almost two centuries ago, when democracies were rare and most of the world was ruled by kings and emperors. Whether his words would still apply today is debatable.

When governing power is vested in a single individual, such as an absolute monarch, there is little need to educate the masses; the monarchs make all the decisions and the people simply follow. But when governing power is vested in the people, as in a democracy, and when people participate in determining whether something is or is not the common good, new expectations arise. As citizens in a democracy, all of us have a right—even a duty—to expect our citizen colleagues to be knowledgeable, to deal morally and ethically with others, to challenge and critically question ideas and proposals, to make good and defensible decisions, and to be concerned about the welfare of others and the common good (see Gross and Dynneson, 1991; Engle and Ochoa, 1988). A representative democracy is a fragile form of government, or what Parker and Kaltsounis (1986) have described as "unfinished business" that is continually in need of maintenance and improvement. In representative democracies, where the power of government is vested in the people, every citizen must be conversant in the basic literacies of citizenship.

"Unfinished business"

The Literacies of Citizenship

There are different kinds of literacy, including cultural literacy, historical literacy, scientific literacy, mathematical literacy, and even plain old literacy—the ability to read, write, speak, and use language effectively. Nevertheless, *literacy* is an inherently vague term. For example, determining when a child's ability to speak, read, and write moves beyond adequate and becomes "effective" is a question that people have been debating for years.

In this section we recommend three literacies, Multicultural, Civic, and Community, that we believe are essential and unique to citizens who live in a democracy.

Multicultural Literacy.

This form of literacy reflects the unique nature of American society. As MacIntyre (1990) suggested in "How To Be a North American," those of us who live in a nation of immigrants must be able to deal effectively with two cultures: one based on our common "American" heritage, and the other based on the particular ethnicities from which we derive. All of us contribute to the common American culture, and, as MacIntyre points out, if we were to lose the contributions that our ethnicities afford us, we would have nothing to bring and nothing to give. However, MacIntyre also warns that "if each of us dwells too much, or even exclusively, upon his or her own ethnic particularity, then we are in danger of fragmenting or even destroying the common life" (p. 5). More recently, Salins (1997) warned that if we as a nation are unable to maintain a reasonable balance between loyalty to individual ethnicities and loyalty to a larger American culture, we will soon join the ranks of the world's other multiethnic nations—the Bosnias and Serbias of the world—as a battleground of perpetual ethnic discord.

The goal of multicultural literacy is to develop citizens who have the knowledge and ability to understand events and experiences from different viewpoints and perspectives. This "understanding" derives from the ancient Greeks, who, according to Arendt (1961), "sought not to understand one another as individual persons, but to look upon the same world from another's standpoint, to see the same in very different and frequently opposing aspects" (p. 51). In this context, for example, it is as important for white, Anglo students to understand how slavery was viewed from the perspective of an enslaved person, as it is for African-American students to understand how slavery was viewed from the perspective of white persons living in the seventeenth and eighteenth centuries, and much of the nineteenth century. Those two views will obviously be quite different.

A second but vitally important element of multicultural literacy—the willingness to suspend judgment—may be equally difficult to achieve. In the context of slavery, for example, it is one thing to say that "I understand where they (either slaves or slave owners) were coming from." However, it is quite another to accuse contemporary Americans of being "wrong" because they reflect the ethnicity of either slave or slaveowner. It is also one thing to judge the rightness or wrongness of activities in their historical perspective, but another to transfer those judgments to modern-day activities.

Multicultural literacy should be the end product of a *multicultural education*. Both concepts share a common goal: enabling students to view concepts and issues from more than one ethnic perspective, and from the points of view of the cultural, ethnic, and racial groups that were most intimately involved in the event or issue (see Banks, 1989, 1997). In other words, it is not essential that students understand every possible point of view on every possible issue, but everyone needs to understand that any question or issue has at least two sides. We provide a short vignette later in this chapter in which one of the teacher's purposes is to illustrate this point.

A common culture or a common society?

The concept of multicultural education has been around for at least two decades, but it—like most of the topics we've discussed in this chapter—is still a matter of continuing debate. For example, some people argue that there is no common American culture, and hence no beliefs that unite us; rather, there is just a common American society in which all of us live (see Asante and Ravitch, 1991). Others argue that the current curriculum is biased toward our European origins—or what is sometimes called a "Eurocentric" curriculum. Some individuals believe that the Eurocentric curriculum should be replaced by infusing African-American studies into every course. Those who make such claims are referred to as Afrocentrists, and the resulting curriculum is referred to as Afrocentric.

Bias in the curriculum

We agree that there's a Eurocentric bias in the existing curriculum. As just one example, too many Americans are unaware that Sante Fe (New Mexico) was a thriving community before the Pilgrims ever stepped onto Plymouth Rock (and despite the fact that the Spanish who controlled Mexico at the time were of European origin). The question here is: Should a curriculum that is biased in one direction be replaced by a curriculum biased in another direction? In her response to a controversial proposal for a new social studies program for New York State, Ravitch (1990) noted that "you can't have a curriculum opposed to bias that is itself biased" (p. B4).

We deal with other potentials associated with multicultural education in more detail in Chapter 3, but from this limited treatment it should be clear that we do not yet have a multicultural curriculum that effectively addresses the goals of multicultural literacy.

Civic Literacy.   Civic literacy refers to a form of political socialization that ensures that future citizens develop knowledge, attitudes, and values that are consistent with the society's political system. This is obviously a much smaller body of information than multicultural literacy. Developing civic literacy is something that many schools already do, at least up to a point. It involves understanding the following:

Elements of civic literacy

* The political principles on which our government is founded
* Our political system and how it *really* works
* The functions of government, both real and perceived
* That a democracy places more responsibilities on individual citizens than do most other forms of government
* That political liberty hinges on the level and quality of civic and civil discourse, which also depends largely on the extent to which citizens participate and are willing to reason together

The students you encounter, including even kindergartners, will have already begun to acquire some of the attitudes and values associated with civic literacy. For example, most young children usually have a highly developed sense of "fair play." At the same time, some of their attitudes, like "the government is responsible for taking care of everyone," will be simplistic if not inconsistent with democratic citizenship. It can be difficult to determine where the citizen's responsibilities end and the government's take over, as in matters related to welfare or health care. Developing civic literacy means that citizens are aware of the different points of view on issues, not that they adopt a liberal or conservative stance. Many younger children will neither care about nor be able to understand some of the elements listed above, especially theoretical or complex explanations of the role and functions of government. As a consequence, the development of civic literacy clearly extends throughout the entire school (K–12) experience and beyond.

Going beyond traditional government classes

Civic literacy extends beyond the narrower notion of "government" that most of us were exposed to in schools—such as the idea that there are 435 members of the House of Representatives—and focuses on helping children understand and develop the abilities that will be expected of them as citizens. This can mean helping children understand the need for rules and laws, and how the two are different. It also extends to helping children understand those things for which they as individuals are responsible, which includes the respect of self and others, as well as things for which the government is responsible, such as defense from foreign invasion. It also extends to elements for which the individual and the government share mutual responsibility, such as the safety of the neighborhood.

Community Literacy.

The "spirit of community": acting together

In some parts of this country, people are virtual prisoners in their own homes. Some of them keep their window shades down at all times and dare not sit on their porches for fear of being killed in a drive-by shooting or drug-related gun battle. In this kind of environment, it is heartening to read about neighbors who band together in a spirit of community to rid their neighborhoods of criminal elements. Those neighbors' efforts do not reflect a return to the days of vigilante justice, because they almost always work in cooperation with the police. Important as it is to rid neighborhoods of criminal elements, the key here is to ensure living situations for all people that do not compromise the quality of daily life. All of us depend on each other to provide positive and supportive living environments, and by working together in a spirit of community, citizens in a democracy can influence the moral, social, and physical environments in which they live.

Individual rights and the common good

You may have read newspaper stories about the juveniles who randomly shot seven other children at a roller skating rink. According to Barnicle (cited in Martin, 1995), the mother of one accused juvenile claimed that "the police should have been there to take the gun away from my son before he went inside" (p. 356). It is common for parents to defend their children, but for the mother to argue that the police, not she or her son, were responsible for the shootings illustrates one aspect of the problem. In this instance and others like it, it is the social environment—or more precisely a failure in the social environment, in the "community" of morally responsible citizens—that permits the wanton taking of human life, often without remorse. The dilemma results when an unwritten rule of modern life, "Keep your nose out of other people's business," conflicts with the community's responsibility to control its members. It's a matter of determining where an individual's rights end so that the group's continuing survival is not threatened. As Bell (1990) suggested, the corruption of society occurs when self-centered individualism runs rampant and without regard for social costs or moral consequences, a situation that can ultimately lead to self-destruction of the environment itself.

Reciprocal relationships

The community in a democracy (and in community literacy) exists to provide the broadest and most effective environment for people to develop as citizens and as individuals. Our relationship with that community is reciprocal: The social environment affects the kinds of things that we as citizens can do, just as we, as individuals, influence the environment itself. The responsibility for a safe and effective social environment does not rest solely with Congress, which has passed crime bill after crime bill, nor with the City Council, the police, or the schools. It is a societal responsibility that rests with all of us, as citizen members of a democratic community. The point is that citizens in a democratic society, working together in a spirit of community and for the common good, can reflect Abraham Lincoln's famous words—"government of the people, by the people, and for the people." And this, after a somewhat convoluted journey, is the goal of community literacy.

These literacies of citizenship—multicultural, civic, and community—suggest multiple goals for social studies education.

Why Teach Social Studies—Revisited

In the everyday demands of teaching, it's easy to overlook the fact that schools everywhere are charged with producing responsible citizens. A related problem is that not all nations define "good citizenship" in the same way. As Kaltsounis (1994) noted, "No one would deny that Fidel Castro provides citizenship education to Cuba's youth, but his type of citizenship education is diametrically opposed to the one we would advocate" (p. 178).

Competing concerns

A problem that teachers often face in teaching citizenship is the tendency to get caught up in more immediate concerns, such as their students who cannot read on grade level, cannot divide fractions, or whatever else a student's immediate problem might be. Teaching citizenship is a long-range matter, whereas students' problems often need to be dealt with immediately. The tendency to focus on short-run concerns is very human, and as someone once said, "When you're up to your neck in alligators, it's difficult to remember you came to drain the swamp." Yet it was in this context that Brophy and Alleman (1993) suggested that too often teachers may lose sight of what social studies is all about. By no means are we suggesting that teachers ignore students' learning problems, but at the same time they cannot lose sight of the basic purposes for teaching social studies (or anything else, for that matter). Schools in general and social studies in particular share the common goal of training the young to be responsible citizens, which, in a more condensed form, is referred to as *citizenship education*. The schools' mission of citizenship education is broad and en-

Citizenship education: a common goal

compassing, whereas social studies shares a somewhat smaller piece of the action. Yet the relationship between social studies and citizenship is reflected in the NCSS's (1994) definition of social studies, which states that a major purpose of social studies is "to help young people develop the ability to make informed and reasoned choices as citizens of a culturally diverse, democratic society in an interdependent world" (p. 2).

Social Studies and Democratic Citizenship Education

Some things are taught as social studies simply because they are matters of habit or tradition (see Saxe, 1992); it's the Joan of Arc syndrome that we referred to earlier. As a result, the connection between topics like ancient Greece or China, and the goal of citizenship education can sometimes get a little fuzzy. It is reasonable, for example, to expect responsible citizens to be knowledgeable about world affairs. And to the extent that China is emerging as a major player in world affairs today, it is equally reasonable to expect responsible citizens to understand how the Chinese view the world. So far, so good . . . we hope. Problems usually arise when some people go the next step and claim that to understand how the Chinese view the world today, it's necessary to study Chinese history, including prehistoric China and the invention of gunpowder and spaghetti.

When citizenship is defined broadly

Part of the problem we are dealing with here is that citizenship education can be defined so broadly that you could justify almost anything. The rationale for virtually all the history and geography you studied in elementary and middle school was undoubted broadly stated and nonspecific: history and geography were identified as things that every citizen should know. This is essentially the argument that E. D. Hirsch, Jr., posed in *Cultural Literacy*: history and geography are part of the common core of knowledge that all of us share. That line of reasoning was also reflected in recommendations from the Bradley Commission on History in the Schools (1988) and the National Commission on Social Studies in the Schools (1989; see also Whelan, 1992). Both groups recommended (1) that history become the core of social studies programs, and (2) that, as the core discipline, the amount of curricular time devoted to teaching history should be increased. The Bradley Commission stated: "History provides the only avenue we have to reach an understanding of ourselves and of our society, in relation to the human condition over time" (1988, p. 5). Unfortunately, such reasons are not likely to satisfy a group of complaining sixth graders who want to know why you're making them study ancient Chinese history.

Selecting topics to study in social studies because they reflect what future citizens need to know and ought to know is often associated with a humanities approach to history and social studies, which we consider in the next section.

Social Studies and the Humanities

The *humanities* refer to bodies of knowledge—like history, literature, philosophy, religion, and the fine arts—that deal with people and their culture. Collectively, the humanities are sometimes called "the arts and humanities," which is merely a way to distinguish them from other bodies of knowledge like the sciences and technical crafts. The humanities deal with things human—which is a very broad category of knowledge indeed. Some people also contend that studying the humanities makes people "more human," or at least more humane. It is not always clear what that means, but this line of reasoning is one of several that may be used to support a humanities approach to social studies.

The humanities defined

Somewhere in your educational career you undoubtedly had teachers who approached social studies with a humanities focus. In practical terms, this means that they approached social studies in much the same way that many English teachers deal with literature—as content or knowledge that children should be exposed to. In a humanities approach to social studies, a discipline like history is treated as social literature in much the same way that conventional literature—*The Scarlet Letter, Silas Marner,* etc.—are treated in English classes: that is, as material that students are expected to read, understand, and hopefully love.

In a humanities approach to social studies, the relevance or immediate utility of a topic is a secondary concern—sometimes a distant second. Ask yourself, for example, how your life today would be different had you *not* studied the pharaohs of ancient Egypt, life in Imperial Rome, or the Middle Ages. Because immediate relevance is *not* an issue, the reasons for studying the humanities are usually stated in very broad terms. These may include the following:

Relevance is not a concern

* The topic—whether it be history, geography, or whatever— is something that all people must know to be culturally literate.
* Studying the topic will do one or more of the following:

Expand the student's fund of general knowledge
Provide a broader understanding of the human condition
Influence how students view the world
Affect the attitudes that students hold toward their fellow human beings

Rationale for studying the humanities

The bottom line is that when teachers adopt a humanities approach to history and the social sciences, the content is often regarded as knowledge that students are expected to know.

Promoting Democracy in the Classroom

Most schools today have vision statements, campus-based improvement plans, and social studies curriculum documents that talk about the roles and responsibilities of citizens in a democracy. However, when it comes to what actually goes on in classrooms, democracy often takes a back seat. In this section, we explore how teachers can begin to "do" democracy in their classrooms.

The major premise here is that students cannot learn the responsibilities of democratic citizenship while sitting in classrooms run by dictators. The two formats are incompatible. At the same time, however, everyone knows that teachers must deal with a host of constraints that operate against the creation of a pure classroom democracy. First, teachers have legal and ethical responsibilities for the safety, welfare, and learning of their students, and thus they cannot relinquish their overall authority as teachers. In addition, and because teachers seldom have had much experience with democratic classrooms as students, we

Constraints on doing democracy

suspect that "doing democracy" in the classroom is something that evolves over time, as opposed to something that teachers jump into immediately.

A key element in moving toward a democratic classroom is your students' prior classroom experience. Most of them will not have experienced many of the responsibilities that the role of classroom citizen demands. Some of your students may find it is easier to be a spectator or a follower, which requires only simple obedience, than it is to participate in self-governance. Be advised that helping students become accustomed to the more demanding role of participant can be fraught with problems.

A long-term enterprise

A growing body of research suggests that it is impossible to teach children the moral and ethical behaviors associated with democratic citizenship—things like respecting the right of others to voice their opinions even if they differ from yours—in twenty-minute lessons taught on every other Thursday. Teaching ethics, morals, and values must be part of a whole-school enterprise, not something that individual teachers do in isolation (*Educational Leadership,* November 1993) which we explore in more detail in Chapter 6.

Recognize that even in the most democratic, student-focused classrooms, the students are not and cannot be the primary source of curriculum. Even though asking students a question like "What would you like to study today (or this week, or month)?" would seem to reflect the epitome of a child-centered classroom, it fails to recognize that children do not know what they do not know. In other words, students cannot indicate the desire to study something they have never heard of. The point is that even in democratic classrooms, some elements always remain the teacher's prerogative.

A focus on the common good

A final element critical to operating a democratic classroom is the need to maintain an unswerving focus on the common good. No matter how much individual students may wish to follow their whims and impulses, the criterion for determining whether or not behavior is acceptable is the extent to which it reflects a shared conception of justice based on the common good. It is not your responsibility as teacher to be the sole determiner of the common good, even though that may be the case from time to time; all students should participate in that determination. In group situations, our right to do our own thing must be tempered by a concern for others, by the common good.

What does a democratic classroom look like? The following vignette, which is drawn from Van Sledright and Grant (1994), provides a specific example.

Democracy in Action

A teaching vignette

Sara Atkinson teaches fifth grade in a small midwestern city. Most of her twenty-six students are middle- to upper-middle-class, and about 12 percent are minorities. Sara has clarified her expectations as follows:

> We have a *democratic classroom* from day one. Hopefully, I'm giving examples from day one of what a democratic classroom is like by giving them some responsibilities for the way this class runs. Also . . . they understand when they have the prime responsibility for something, and times when I have prime responsibility for something, so it's not always a democracy in this room.
>
> The first rule in this room is respect. Respect is the only rule I've got, and everything kind of generates from it. If I'm respecting your point of view, I'm

Students in democratic classrooms share responsibility for
maintaining safe and caring
learning environments.
(© *Michael Zide*)

Building respect

going to give you time to generate that with me. We're not going to interrupt people, and we're going to give people time to have their say and . . . welcome their point of view. It may not be my point of view, but you are welcome to yours.

We make a lot of decisions here together. A lot of decisions that don't work originally are when people don't voice how they really feel. You might end up with a decision based on how your friend voted, and then you have to live with a decision that in reality wasn't yours. . . . It doesn't take them long to figure out it's okay to have a diverse opinion in here. So, they've got a feeling for how this classroom works long before you get into the kinds of democracy in social studies. Hopefully [they learn] this through participation. (p. 323)

Decision making

The social studies content in Sara's classroom is American history, which is true for most fifth grades across the country. In teaching the revolutionary period, for example, her purpose is to enhance students' ideas about decision making and participatory involvement. Sara argues that her overall goal involves making historical events problematic, inducing students to grapple with how decisions are made and how consequences are experienced. The following excerpt shows how Sara does this, and how she tries to teach her students that "there are always at least two sides to every issue."

An afternoon late in November marked the beginning of study about the American Revolution. Sara had been preparing her students to study this period in U.S. history for some time. She made allusions to the growing tension between the colonists and their British rulers throughout the preceding topic, the study of colonial expansion.

She began the lesson by telling students to bring out their social studies textbooks, but not to open them. She wondered aloud about why she enjoyed the topic of the American Revolution so much, and concluded that it was based on the idea of misrepresentation. She asked her students rhetorically what comes to mind when she mentioned the Boston Tea Party or the French and Indian War. She queried, "Who was fighting?"

Several students responded in unison, "The French and the Indians."

Sara's eyes sparkled and the corner of her mouth turned up wryly as she feigned success in conveying how the title of this war misrepresents the combatants, especially the British, who won the war.

Ms. Atkinson shifted quickly to the word *massacre*. "What does this mean?" "What comes to your mind when I say massacre?"

A girl called out, "Like a riot or something. . . ."

A boy followed with, "Oh, lots of killing and blood!"

Misleading terms

With a tinge of irony in her voice, Sara claimed that she had trouble imagining why anyone would call such events a Boston Tea Party or a French and Indian War or a Boston Massacre. She then went on to note that early colonial life, while both rugged and dangerous, could be characterized by relative peacefulness between British control from afar and colonial self-rule.

Sara asked Lisa to read an account beginning with a crowd gathered at the Old South Meeting House in Boston, then stopped her after the first paragraph. Sara commented on how the term *tea party* seemed misleading. She asked why such misleading terms were necessary, who intended to misrepresent events, and for what purpose. "Clearly," she admitted, "something is wrong! Our goal today is to figure out what went wrong and why."

Sara Atkinson proceeded to explain the nature of colonial "propaganda." She discussed with her students how point of view and interpretation of events bear importantly on reading and understanding this period of history. In short, she prepared her students for at least two sides of the issue, complementing her goal to get her students to listen and read arguments carefully before they voted (both figuratively and literally) to accept or reject a perspective.

Making informed choices

Sara's goal was to teach her students how to interpret history (and link it to newspapers, a topic she teaches in language arts) in order to build a type of understanding upon which to base their decisions. Teaching them how to be inquirers and careful readers served her goal of teaching them how to make informed decisions, a goal that requires much more time than simply covering content or having the teacher, as the knowledge authority, supply the correct answers.

An imperfect example

Sara Atkinson's classroom is not perfect. Were we teaching in her place, we would make some minor adjustments, such as doing more modeling and asking fewer questions. But then for all the other things that Sara has to contend with—things like the amount of time it takes to go into depth, and a school district policy that mandates subject-matter coverage—our classroom probably wouldn't be perfect either. Nevertheless, Sara knows where she wants to go and is clearly moving toward a democratic classroom—a place that, as Boyer (1990) noted, actively helps students develop responsible ways of thinking, believing, and *acting*.[2]

---

[2]Abridged from Bruce A. VanSledright & S.G. Grant, *Theory and Research in Social Education*. Copyright 1994 by the National Council for the Social Studies. Reprinted by permission.

Contexts and Purposes for Social Studies

Sara Atkinson's classroom provides the context for all the subjects she teaches. In addition, how she has elected to approach social studies reflects, to varying degrees, the four basic reasons why social studies is taught. Those purposes are the following:

Goals for teaching social studies

* Teaching young citizens about our collective cultural heritage—about where we as world cultures have come from, where we are, and where we may be going
* Teaching young citizens to think and process information skillfully and intelligently
* Teaching young citizens about human behavior
* Teaching young citizens to act morally and ethically in accordance with what they know

Transmitting the human story

Teaching about our cultural heritage usually means learning history, as it did in Sara's classroom, but it also includes related disciplines such as anthropology. Our cultural heritage extends to the origins of human civilization, the development of cultures throughout the world, literary and technological achievements, and the different ways we humans have devised for explaining our place in the universe. The mission is to transmit that "story"—that knowledge and its associated attitudes and values—to students.

Thinking critically

It was equally clear that Sara wanted her students to read carefully, to make connections, and to think skillfully and intelligently. In other words, Sara's intent was to help her students develop information-processing skills they could use with any kind of data they encounter. These include skills such as hypothesizing, identifying relevant and irrelevant information, hypothesis testing, and generalizing. Processing information is also referred to by a variety of other terms, such as *critical thinking, reflective inquiry, problem solving* or, simply, *inquiry*. There are subtle differences between these terms, but they are more similar than they are different; all of them involve doing something with information.

The questionable role of background information

One of the most widely accepted but highly questionable assumptions in social studies (and elsewhere) is that thinking cannot take place until students have accumulated a sufficient body of background information to think with, an assumption noted by one of the most influential advocates for using social studies to teach thinking skills, the late Hilda Taba (1967). All of us have encountered teachers who said something like "First, we need some background information about 'X'," but after, when they finished presenting the information, there was seldom time left to do anything with it. In this context, Taba noted that teaching that follows this assumption stresses coverage of factual knowledge, and can burden the student's memory with an unorganized, perishable, and obsolescent assemblage of facts.

Few people will argue against teaching children to think skillfully and make intelligent decisions. Nevertheless, this is an area where teachers like Sara may encounter criticism because the time it takes to teach thinking might otherwise be spent transmitting factual knowledge. When the Joan of Arc syndrome makes its appearance, Sara and teachers like her must be prepared for possible criticism if their students cannot name Belgium's major export, the geographic regions of Mexico, or all the state capitals.

Multiple purposes

Like most social studies teachers, Sara Atkinson sometimes dealt simultaneously with two or more purposes for teaching social studies. For example, when Sara's students analyzed the motives that led to the Revolutionary War, they were applying information-processing skills. At the same time they were studying a war that is a significant event in our cultural heritage. At times you may find yourself emphasizing one purpose for teaching social studies over others, as Sara did, but it is unlikely that you will treat any one of them in isolation. The first point here is that social studies often serves multiple objectives. The second point is that determining where to place one's emphasis is a basic decision that every social studies teacher must make.

COMMENTARY: **Is Thinking Really Valued?**

Although few people argue against teaching children to think skillfully, traditional social studies programs don't always devote much attention to thinking skills. We think there are some important though usually unstated reasons for this. What do you think?

1. *Thinking skills are not really valued (despite what people may say to the contrary).* Imagine yourself in the following situation: You have been accused of a crime and have been offered two methods of trial. One is by a jury of your peers; the other is by a computer that is accurately programmed to analyze all the available information and to render a verdict wholly consistent with the data.

   Which option would you choose—the jury of your peers or the computer? Would it make a difference if you were guilty? Or innocent?

2. *Thinking skills are difficult; they are too much work, and besides, the children can't do them.* If students could apply thinking skills prior to instruction, there would be little need to teach them. But because children may have difficulty recognizing an underlying assumption or distinguishing between a fact and an opinion, for example, is not a sufficient basis

for avoiding such skills. Applying thinking skills is sometimes difficult; it can be hard work. It's a curious logic that uses this as a basis for not teaching such skills.

The situation is further complicated by a comment that you've undoubtedly heard from time to time: "Don't bother me with all that, just tell me the answer." Our concern for getting answers—the quicker the better—and our corresponding lack of concern for the processes used to produce those answers, may help to explain why thinking skills don't get more attention than they do.

3. *Thinking skills are cold, abstract, and impersonal.* Thinking is one of the few quiet activities (sleeping is another one) children engage in. You can't necessarily tell when it is taking place. Although thinking can be a very personal kind of thing, it's doubtful that thinking skills are any more abstract than, say, the skills involved in long division. They may be more difficult at times, but are not inherently "colder" or lacking in emotion. Were some people more intimate with thinking skills, perhaps they would become more personal and less "distant."

Summary

Social studies is a composite subject created for teaching purposes that draws its content from history and the social science disciplines—geography, sociology, political science, economics, anthropology, and psychology—and to a lesser extent from philosophy, religion, and the fine arts. The main purposes for teaching social studies include (1) teaching children about our cultural heritage, (2) teaching children to think skillfully, (3) teaching about human (social) behavior, and (4) teaching children to act morally and ethically according to what they know. Because these purposes are not mutually exclusive, teachers will often deal with two or more of them simultaneously.

The overarching goal of social studies is citizenship education: that is, training students to be effective participants in a democratic society. Of course, educating responsible citizens is one of the main reasons that schools exist, so citizenship education is an all-school enterprise, not the responsibility of social studies alone.

Citizens in democratic societies have special responsibilities that are often denied their counterparts in totalitarian societies, where leaders make the decisions and citizens merely follow. For example, citizens in democratic societies must be able to strike a balance between the common heritage that all of us enjoy and the contributions that individual ethnicities make to our cultural mosaic—what we have referred to as multiethnic literacy. At the same time, citizens in a democratic society must recognize their responsibilities for maintaining a civic environment that welcomes their voice in determining how government will function—what we have referred to as civic literacy. And finally, citizens in a democratic society must recognize their responsibilities for maintaining secure living environments that ensure the continuing safety of one's family and community, yet still enable individuals to achieve their aspirations—or what we have referred to as community literacy. We contend that these literacies of citizenship are essential to nurturing and maintaining a representative democracy. As such, they reflect an ongoing challenge that all of us share.

Suggested Activities

1. Is there a common culture, a cluster of beliefs and values that all Americans share? Or is there, as some individuals argue, simply an American society? Which way do you lean?
2. Stuart Chase has said that "formal history, with its Caesars and Napoleons, tends to be a record of the abnormal, the geniuses, sports, freaks, and misfits; the glandular cases of mankind" (*The Proper Study of Mankind,* 1963, p. 65). How would you react to Chase's contention in light of your experience?
3. In his article "The Futility of Trying to Teach Everything of Importance," Grant Wiggins (1989) argues that when teachers claim that everything they teach is important, then nothing will seem important to students. The ultimate test, Wiggins claims, comes when students say "*This* is important," and when the teacher is silent on the matter. How do you respond to Wiggins's claim?
4. Some people suggest that most teachers don't know enough about different ethnic perspectives to teach multicultural education with any assurance. Others suggest that many individuals resist a multicultural approach because it threatens the Anglo mainstream power structure that dictates what is or is not taught in American schools. Decide the extent to which either of these contentions reflects your personal position.

Suggested Readings

Robert D. Barr, James L. Barth, & S. Samuel Shermis. (1977). *Defining the social studies.* Bulletin 51. Washington, DC: National Council for the Social Studies. Shirley Engle (1965) has noted that this classic book has clarified "the lines of battle between the competing philosophies of the social studies and [has pointed] up the irreconcilable nature of the issues that separate them" (p. 103).

Jere Brophy & Bruce VanSledright. (1997). *Teaching and learning history in the elementary schools.* New York: Teachers College Press. Most of this book focuses on three fifth-grade teachers and the very different ways they teach fifth-grade American history. However, the first two chapters also present an excellent overview of recent research.

Theodore Kaltsounis. (Spring, 1994). Democracy's challenge as the foundation for social studies. *Theory and Research in Social Education.* 22, 176–193. In this brief but excellent article, Kaltsounis argues that citizenship education is too vague and ill-defined to serve as the foundation for social studies. He argues, instead, that social studies programs should be guided by democracy-related knowledge, values, and practices.

Peter D. Salins. (1997). *Assimilation, American style*. New York: Basic Books. In this short (259 pages) but brilliant work, Salins argues that in the past thirty years we have moved toward a policy of enhancing ethnic consciousness, but at the expense of America's historic commitment to assimilation. If you read Salins, you should also read Nathan Glazer's (1997) *We Are All Multiculturalists Now* (Cambridge, MA: Harvard University Press), to get the other side of the coin.

Grant Wiggins. (1989). The futility of trying to teach everything of importance. *Educational Leadership* (November), 44–51. This wonderful article explores the fallacious assumptions we make about schooling, and points out the futility of trying to teach children everything they will need to know before they leave school.

2 History and the Social Sciences: The Knowledge Base for Social Studies

Key Questions

* What is the academic knowledge base for social studies?
* How has the human experience influenced what we think, do, and value?
* What is science, and what is its relationship to social studies programs?
* How does social science differ from history?
* On what areas of the human experience do the social science disciplines focus?
* How does one teach history and the social sciences to young children?

Key Ideas

* Individually and collectively, all of us learn from past experience.
* History and the various social sciences study different aspects of the human experience. Collectively they are sources of content for social studies programs.
* History has a history, as do the each of the social science disciplines. What they study and how they study the human experience have changed over time.
* Science, as in social *science* discipline, refers to a rigorous process for producing and validating knowledge.
* Findings from the social sciences are usually stated as tendencies or probabilities, not absolutes.

Introduction: On Waiting in Line

Have you ever found yourself waiting in line at a bank, post office, or supermarket, only to discover that all the other lines are moving faster than yours? Which of the following describes your reaction when this happens?

a. Do you think about changing lines?
b. Do you scowl at the person causing the delay?

c. Do you continue waiting impatiently until it is your turn?

d. Do you do all of the above?

In these situations, our response would be "All of the above." To avoid these kinds of responses, many businesses—airports, banks, and fast-food restaurants especially—have shifted to "snake lines." This is where all the windows or stations are served from a single-file line. Snake lines are no more efficient than separate lines, but they are much fairer, because you cannot get stuck in a line that's moving slower than all the others.

Snake lines

In some nations, waiting in line is referred to as "queuing up." New Yorkers call it "waiting on line." Yet regardless of what it is called, social scientists have found that "queuing up" is part of a complex social system that involves culturally specific principles of fairness and justice. This means that some cultures know how to line up properly and others don't. For example, when the Walt Disney Corporation opened Euro-Disney in France, they had expected ticket buyers to line up in the same orderly way they do at Disney locations in California and Florida. But to Disney's dismay, the lines for both rides and tickets at Euro-Disney were chaotic. Disney's experience was consistent with what social scientists had noted previously: the more a society values equality, the more fairly its members will queue up.

Lining up is culturally related

Social scientists have found that it's not how long people actually wait in line that matters, but their *perception* of how long they *think* they had to wait. People often felt that they had waited 30 percent longer than they actually had. A similar phenomenon occurred when high-rise office buildings and hotels were first constructed and workers began complaining about long waits for the elevators. The researchers suspected that instead of installing more new elevators or speeding up the existing ones, there might be a less costly solution: provide something for the people to do that would influence their perception of the time they spent waiting. The researcher's recommendation was to install mirrors in the elevator lobbies. The complaints declined markedly. The next time you're in a major hotel or high-rise office building, take notice of the decor in the elevator lobbies.

How perceptions influence reality

Researching how we humans respond to waiting in line may seem like pretty banal stuff. You might even want to ask, "Shouldn't those researchers be studying something more significant?" But imagine that you are the architect of a high-rise building and you are confronted by an angry chief executive officer (CEO) who says, "Look at all these complaints! You didn't install enough elevators." Do you install more elevators, which is an expensive proposition? Or tell the CEO to ignore the complaints? If you are aware of the social science findings, you could propose a far less expensive alternative that CEOs and many other people would probably never think of: mirrors.

Significance?

Most of us are not architects (or CEOs) who might reap direct benefits from this research. So the next question is: Should students be expected to study these findings as a part of social studies? In addition to offering some insights into human behavior, the findings about waiting in line could reflect persistent behavior patterns that may emerge in other settings. Students could investigate questions such as: In what ways (besides waiting in line) does perception influence our view of reality? Or, in what other ways besides waiting in line do cultures that place less value on equality differ from ours? The waiting-in-line findings are insignificant and almost trivial by themselves, yet they could serve as a vehicle for reaching other more significant ideas about human behavior. We'll show you how information can serve as a vehicle for developing ideas in other contexts throughout the balance of this book.

This chapter focuses on history and the social sciences, both of which reflect the largest portion of the knowledge base from which social studies is drawn. First we consider history as a field of study and look at some of the problems associated with teaching history to young children. We then examine the individual social science disciplines and what it means to be historically, geographically, and politically literate. Finally, we consider what all of this means in terms of those portions of the human experience that we as teachers pass on to the young in the form of social studies.

History and the Human Experience

Many of the things that affect our lives today are of comparatively recent origin, historically speaking. Laptop computers, pagers, fax machines, and cellular phones are just a few that come to mind, but consider that, in the perspective of historical time, even things like the printing press are relatively recent innovations. This becomes especially evident when historical time is depicted through the metaphor of a clock. Imagine the face of a clock on which every minute represents fifty years—a substantial part of anyone's lifetime. On that basis, the entire clock face represents 3,000 years—or from about 1000 B.C.E. (before the Christian Era) to A.D. 2000 (see Figure 2.1). (Portions of this material are based on Postman and Weingartner [1969].) On this scale, the printing press would have been invented only nine minutes ago, television about a minute ago, and fax machines and cellular phones in the last second or two. In the field of medicine, it would have only been about three minutes ago that doctors began curing more people than they harmed. Likewise, it has also been only seconds since medicine achieved some of its most significant developments—organ transplants, laser surgery, synthetic drugs, and many other things we take for granted today.

The clock metaphor illustrates that life today is much faster paced than it was in years past. An hour is still sixty minutes long, of course, but changes and innovations—particularly technological innovations—have become an accepted and even expected part of modern life. Yet as quickly as changes are occurring today, history shows that change was also a facet of life in the past, although the pace was much slower.

Two areas that have changed significantly over time are not in technology or medicine, but in how we look at ourselves as human beings, and how we regard the world in which we live. It's been only recently that we have understood our historical past well enough to realize that how we think of ourselves as human beings can differ from how members of other cultures view and think of them-

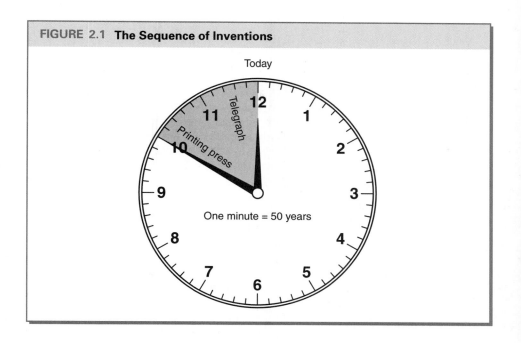

FIGURE 2.1 The Sequence of Inventions

Today

Printing press

Telegraph

One minute = 50 years

selves. And only recently have we come to understand that our definition of what it means to be human has changed over time. The information on Table 2.1 is oversimplified, but it reveals some of those changes.

History and the World Children Know

History as understanding

One of the values in teaching and studying history is the extent to which it can help young citizens view the human experience in its broader context and understand events from different perspectives (Arendt, 1961). We will use the phenomenon of slavery to illustrate how this occurs.

It is widely known that during the seventeenth and eighteenth centuries and portions of the nineteenth century, thousands of African-Americans were enslaved and brought to this country against their will. It is less widely known that during the same period slavery was also practiced elsewhere in the world, especially in parts of Asia and North Africa. Most women in harems, for example, were not there of their own free will. Even today, parents in some parts of Southeast Asia sell their daughters into virtual slavery working in the brothels of larger cities like Bangkok.

Three-corner trade

Shift now to your twentieth-century classroom. You have reached the section of every American history textbook that deals with the three-corner (or triangular) trade. This was where American ships would haul cargoes of naval stores (lumber, pitch, etc.) or other products from New England to southern Europe—the first leg of the triangle. The ships then sailed to North Africa, where the captains would purchase cargoes of slaves. The enslaved people would then be transported to ports in the southern United States or the Caribbean, where

Table 2.1 What It Means to Be Human: A Western Historical Perspective

When	Conceptual Framework	Implications
Ancient Times	Without necessarily making any reference to the real world about them, human beings were believed to be able to use their unique mind to reason about their condition.	The world was what human beings said it was. Humans were unique and set apart from the rest of the world. The concept of science at this time was the application of reason to morality and virtue.
Early Christian Era	Religious frameworks found men and women to be part of a larger scheme and to serve purposes for existence that transcended their earthly experience. The application of the human mind and reasoning ability found rational reasons for following reasoned authority and authorities.	Mind was pure and good and physical needs and desires were viewed as evil. Humans were seen as having two dimensions—the soul and the body. Men and women were born in sin, and human effort was directed toward redemption and the "other world."
Renaissance	The political framework found men and women recognizing social realities found in existing social conditions. Power, control, leadership, and forms of social organization were based on political realities. Machiavelli's precepts emerge. Note: some argue that Machiavelli was the first political *scientist*—a scientist because he built his framework by observing and generalizing from the real world.	Beginning of the nation-state and nourishment of loyalty to earthly concerns now ran parallel to religious ideals. Beginning to use observed and observable information upon which to build ideas, people started to become increasingly aware of the complexity of their world. This movement modified their "way of knowing."
18th and 19th Centuries	The economic framework emerged. The human condition began to focus on industrializing, on ideological justifications for property, and the accumulation and distribution of wealth. The industrial revolution was under way. Adam Smith, Karl Marx, and others observed and interpreted the human experience as basically economic. Economic activity was part of the "natural" world. Human behavior was subject to "laws" just as the natural world was.	There was a definite relationship between people's "daily bread" and their larger conceptual frameworks of politics and religion. Class distinctions emerged, and economic mobility was related to social mobility. The organization and rules for economic activity fed nation-state rivalry, the need for justifying imperialism, and the need for explaining differing economic "levels." Natural laws pertaining to government, economics, and social class emerged as "right" when viewed as a larger, observed pattern of human experience. This led to a view of natural progress that human beings couldn't control.

(continued on next page)

Table 2.1 **What It Means to Be Human: A Western Historical Perspective** *(continued)*

When	Conceptual Framework	Implications
Early 20th Century	The psychoanalytic conceptual framework found men and women at the mercy of their subconscious and deterministically influenced by experiences. The framework reintroduced the individual and raised concern with the ego, superego, and id. Each individual was a product of his or her environment—especially the early environment that acted in screening subsequent experiences. Freud's interpretation helped sharpen this framework.	The primary focus appeared to be on the individual, and this seemed compatible with political and economic world-views that seemed to carry weight. Emphasis was *not* on the individual deliberately interacting with experience but on the impact of early experiences that "conditioned" the psychological sets that an individual carried through life. Stress was on the inner person and the psychological impact one's life history carried.
Middle 20th Century	The physical sciences had struggled into maturity. The social sciences commenced to scientifically (empirically) study human behavior. Instead of emerging with set and unchanging "laws" of human behavior, the social sciences, through systematic research, came up with findings stated in "if-then" terms—findings stated in probability rather than certainty. Aspects of human behavior became the provinces of specific disciplines, as potential sources for understanding and explaining the human condition. The proper study of humans was humans. Previous conceptual frameworks that focused on external absolutes became challenged through the application of a maturing science to the area of human behavior.	The social science concept of human beings freed people from any sort of absolute determinism. It portrayed human beings as organisms interacting with artificial and natural environments. Rational applications of social science findings again brought focus to *Homo sapiens* as a learning/teaching and valuing species. Social concern moved from "other-worldliness" to the human condition on this planet. Ways of "knowing" shifted from logic and reason to observable human phenomena. In a continuing struggle, men and women assumed responsibility for their life choices. As John Dewey maintained, the purpose of life is life. Social science provided different information with which to help adapt and control. The choices, difficult as they are, are ours to make.
Turn of the 21st Century	Traditional ways of knowing, including the natural epistemology provided by science, as well as the notions of objectivity and rational rules for evidence, are being challenged in the academic community. The turn of the century is a time of ferment as the conceptual framework seems to be moving from a form of rationalism—rooted partly in the Enlightenment and based on the canons of science—to a form of intellectual relativism that accommodates multiple methods and procedures for knowing.	The implications of competing ways of knowing are not entirely clear. However, it appears there will no longer be a single standard, for measuring and judging what one knows and how one knows. What this will mean for the structure and nature of the school curriculum and the academic disciplines is not clear. Also unclear is the mechanism—other than sheer numbers and power—that societies will use to resolve social conflicts, or whether the courts will need to establish new rules for handling evidence. The implications are substantial.

they were sold. To complete the triangle, the ships would pick up cargoes of agricultural products—often rum, cotton, and sugar—and transport them back to New England, where their voyage had begun originally. It was a lucrative trade that made many shipowners wealthy.

Against this background, consider one of your fifth graders who asks: "How could those people buy and sell human beings? Don't they know it's wrong? Don't they have a conscience?" The student's questions are reasonable, and common. How will you respond?

In developing your response, consider that your students are products of twentieth-century thinking, and, as suggested in Table 2.1, are likely to believe in self-determination. They are also likely to believe (as your student has already indicated) that buying and selling human beings or keeping them in bondage is immoral and illegal. It has probably never occurred to most children that people in other times and places, including the seventeenth and eighteenth centuries, looked at their world quite differently than today's children do.

Different ways of viewing the world

The problem of helping children understand different views of the world is compounded because elementary textbooks almost never deal with different views. This means that you are essentially on your own. In this context, the first time you say "natural laws," you are apt to get some bewildered looks from students. Nevertheless, people in the seventeenth and eighteenth centuries who considered themselves moral individuals were able to rationalize the practice of slavery on the basis of one or more so-called laws of nature, or "natural laws." The natural law that applied to slavery was based on the notion that some human groups were ranked as "higher" or "lower" than others, usually along racial lines. By virtue of their ranking, members of lower groups were considered eligible for domination, subservience, and even enslavement.

"natural laws"

Unless you are willing to explain how people in the seventeenth and eighteenth centuries viewed the world, including the concept of natural law, providing intelligible responses to your student's question will be difficult. An adequate though not very comforting compromise is to say something like "What those people did was wrong by our standards today. I'm not trying to excuse what they did, but people at that time didn't look at their world in the same way we do." If you think that the last line is too much, you could ignore it. However, unless you've laid some preliminary groundwork with your students, they won't understand the notion of world-view any more than the notion of natural laws.

Helping Young Children Connect with the Past

Part of the dilemma arises because of the way history is often presented in schools. From your experience, you know that most history courses are organized as chronological surveys in which you begin somewhere in the past and then work slowly toward modern times. But, as Levstik and Barton (1997) noted, "Too often, history instruction is simply a march through time that never quite connects to the present" (p. 1). When history survey courses finally get to the present day—if they do—it is typically in a hurried treatment that occurs during the last week of May, when most students are looking forward to the end of school.

Chronological surveys

You may also recall that when history is taught chronologically, one event usually leads up to, or is said to "cause," a later event. The Boston Tea Party, for example, is often presented as a cause that led to the Revolutionary War, just as slavery and states' rights are usually identified as causes of the Civil War. In this context, ask yourself whether the colonists who participated in the Boston Tea Party were saying to themselves, "We are causing the Revolutionary War!" Even if most colonists wanted a war with England, which some of them did, they could not say they were causing the Revolutionary War—at least not until the war itself actually occurred. Likewise, the first enslaved person arrived in this country in 1619, but the Civil War did not occur until 1861, almost 250 years later. Is it possible that a cause existed for five generations? What actually happened, of course, is that beliefs changed over those 250 years, and the natural laws that had once made enslavement a tolerable practice were gradually replaced by even stronger beliefs in self-determination for all people. The first point here is that slavery became a cause of the Civil War, even though it didn't start out that way. The second point is that historians can look at past events, such as the Revolutionary or Civil wars, and then, with the hindsight that history permits, go back to identify what caused those events. Despite the image that many textbooks convey, children need to understand that the cause-effect nature of history always occurs after the fact. Our third point is that although historians can rightfully focus on explaining the past, they cannot predict the future. Even after analyzing events that are occurring today, no reasonable historian would say: "These events *will* cause the Caribbean War of 2008." Forecasting is the business of meteorologists, not historians.

"causes" and "effects"

History looks back, not forward

Yet another factor that influences how young children understand history is the way they perceive the passage of time. Very young children often think of time in terms of tonight, tomorrow, and perhaps next week. If you have any doubt about this, recall those holiday eves from your childhood when you wondered if it would *ever* get dark? Perhaps you've also noticed that your birthdays (and possibly the holiday seasons) come around more quickly than they used to. As adults, we know that time has not speeded up; rather it's our perception that changes. The time that once crept along so slowly when we were children somehow speeds up as we get older. The point here is that for young children who measure time past by the number of "longs" they attach to "ago"—as in "It happened a long, long time ago"—trying to instill precise historical dating is probably an exercise in futility. All of us eventually develop the ability to deal with the past, including the distant past, but expecting young children who have lived a decade or less to understand historical time is probably a case of imposing adult views onto children who look at their world quite differently.

How children perceive time

Two additional factors, one peculiar to history and the other pertaining to how we as adults expect children to deal with history and the other subjects they study, also have a bearing here. The distinguished historian Arnaldo Momigliano (1982) noted that although history has existed as a research and literary activity for at least twenty-five centuries, it has been a subject taught in schools and universities for only two or three centuries. Momigliano went on to note that in the two thousand years before it became a school subject, "history

History was originally for adults

was written for *adult* minds" (p. 245). Although young children can deal with history, teachers need to be sensitive to (1) how they approach it as a subject, and (2) the kinds of expectations that they impose on children who are expected to learn it.

History for Young Children

A growing body of research (see Brophy & VanSledright, 1997; and Levstik and Barton, 1997) indicates that young children can deal with history quite readily. However, teachers must approach history in ways that accommodate young children's abilities and prior experiences. Sometimes this can mean avoiding certain practices. For example, when history was first introduced as a school subject, the prevailing educational view was that children were "miniature adults"—individuals who needed only proper guidance and training to function effectively as adults. At that time, the dominant educational technique for providing that training was called "mental discipline" or "mind training." From this perspective, the mind was regarded as a muscle that would "strengthen" and respond to exercise, just as skeletal muscles do. The usual procedure for training children's minds, and thus building mental discipline, was by providing children with long and often onerous mental exercises—things like memorizing the presidents *and* vice presidents of the United States, in order. History and geography provided ideal subject matter for the advocates of mental discipline—just look at all the facts children could be expected to memorize.

Providing miniature adults with mental discipline

The "mental discipline" notion has died a lingering death, as did the conception of children as "miniature adults." Despite the huge body of research (e.g., Piaget, 1950; Elkind, 1982; Egan, 1979) that shows that young children do not think and reason as adults do, at least not initially, some parents today still dress their children in designer clothing and otherwise put the trappings of adulthood onto their children.

How then should you approach history with young children? Here is a brief summary of practices that are based on a growing body of research (see Brophy & VanSledright, 1997; Bruer, 1993; Bruner, 1986; Caine & Caine, 1994; Gardner, 1991; Good & Brophy, 1994; Levstik & Barton, 1997; Levstik & Pappas, 1987; Thornton & Vukelich, 1988; White, 1988).

Recommended practices

* Avoid chronological surveys designed to cover long periods of time very quickly. Focus instead on detailed narrative accounts from various eras in history, or better yet, let children become involved in those detailed accounts. With a teacher's help, young children can usually make sense of the original source materials found in journals, diaries, biographies, pictures, and historical documents—anything that personalizes history and makes it real for them.

* Avoid broad and sweeping statements such as "Reconstruction was a time of turmoil," at least until students have had experiences that permit them to know what such statements mean. Instead of painting history with a "broad brush," try focusing instead on *particular* history, that is, on narrative accounts where *a* person (or small group of persons) deals with *a* particular

problem in *a* particular place at *a* particular time, and under *a* particular set of circumstances. Note also that particular history is the kind of stuff biographies are made of.

★ Avoid outlines and timelines as introductory activities. If you remember making an outline after you had written your report (on whatever the topic), as we suggested in the Prologue, don't expect your students to approach an outline any differently. An outline of historical events that children have not yet encountered is simply a disjointed list. Outlines and timelines are excellent devices for organizing information and are also useful as concluding activities. However, neither you nor your students can organize information that you do not have (which is why you wrote your outline after you had written your report).

The research and our experience suggest that two important keys to teaching history to young children successfully are *time* and *specificity*. Let's assume that you want your students to understand the role that the Underground Railroad played before the Civil War. You could probably convey this information

---

TECHNOLOGY UPDATE

Using Search Engines to Locate Resources

The Internet contains so much material that locating specific sites would be impossible were it not for locator services, called "search engines." To use one of the search engines, you simply enter keywords for whatever information you are looking for, and the search engine then scans the Internet to find potential sites. For example, when we were seeking sites that dealt with the Plimoth Plantation, the Massachusetts settlement established in 1620, we entered *Plimoth Plantation.* We received over 10,000 possible sites, including every site that had the word *plantation* in its title. Unfortunately, we had neglected to tell the search engine to look for the two terms together instead of separately. When we changed our entry to *Plimoth,* we still had over 100 sites to deal with. When you enter keywords for search engines on the Internet, a single word, like *Egypt,* is sometimes more productive than two words, like *ancient Egypt,* unless you are able to direct the search engine to find both words together. Some search engines permit this; others do not.

Some of the widely available search engines include the following:

AltaVista:
> http://altvista.digital.com

infoseek:
> http://infoseek.com

SEARCH.COM:
> http://www.search.com

Yahoo:
> http://www.yahoo.com

Magellan:
> http://www.mckinley.com

ElNet Galaxy:
> http://www.einet.net/

WebCrawler:
> http://webcrawler.com/

Lycos:
> http://lycos.cs.cmu.edu

Switchboard:
> http://www.switchboard.com/

Four 11:
> http://www.four11.com/

in a ten- to fifteen-minute mini-lecture, or you could have students spend almost a week reading a biography of someone who lived through that period, possibly Harriet Tubman. Which would you do? Despite the time it takes, we would opt for the biography. It would personalize events surrounding the Underground Railroad in ways that children can relate to, and it would also permit you to *scaffold,* that is, to build on students' prior knowledge and experiences. A last but not insignificant reason we would use the Harriet Tubman biography specifically is that most students love it.

The issue here is not whether you could "cover the material" in less time, but whether you could do it with the specificity, immediacy, and poignancy that most biographies, picture or informational books, and original source materials do. Instead of trying to cover vast amounts of material in a hurried once-over, teachers who adopt a "less is more" approach to history will take the time necessary to study selected events or eras in depth, and in ways that permit children to participate in the human dramas that are part of every historical event. In addition, by focusing on less material but in greater depth, students should retain much more of what they study.

History, Science, and the Human Experience

Everybody knows that history and science are subjects you study in school, but not everyone recognizes that science is more than just a label for subjects like biology and chemistry. *Science* is also a way of knowing. Science refers to a set of procedures for validating information that is common to all sciences—natural, physical, and social.

There are other ways of knowing besides science, of course, some of which many of us may use from time to time. For example, we sometimes act in terms of our hunches, suspicions, or our intuition. At other times, we may accept things based on faith, that is, in the belief they are true but usually without explicit proof. Most religious beliefs, for example, are based on faith—which is probably why religious denominations are referred to as *faiths.* However, if someone were to say something like "We have a hunch that eating ten prunes a day will cure cancer," we'd be very leery. We'd probably ask, "Can you prove it?", which is another way of saying "Show me your data." Expecting scientists to publicly validate their procedures and findings *before* anyone asks them to is a legacy of science. The need to report *everything* in detail may also explain why most research reports make dull reading.

Scientists present their findings in a variety of forms, but one of the most common is the conditional "if-then," cause-and-effect format. For example, *if* you smoke, *then* your chances of getting cancer increase significantly. *If* there is freezing weather in Brazil, *then* the cost of coffee will usually increase. There is almost always an element of probability in scientific findings. No one can say that if you smoke, for example, then you *will* get cancer, just that your chances for doing so are increased. Scientific findings do not come with a 100 percent money-back guarantee, but they give a reasonably good indication of what could happen in the future.

It is not the white coats or test tubes or computers that make someone a "scientist." Rather, what all sciences have in common are the rigorous processes for producing and validating new knowledge that we mentioned earlier. Those processes are also what set science apart from mere speculation or conjecture, and what set the sciences apart from the arts and humanities.

Some people separate the natural sciences and social science into distinct categories, but the view of science in Figure 2.2 shows that the two are functionally related. Findings from the natural sciences influence social science methodologies and findings, just as findings from the social sciences can influence the methodologies and findings of the natural sciences.

FIGURE 2.2 The Fields of Science

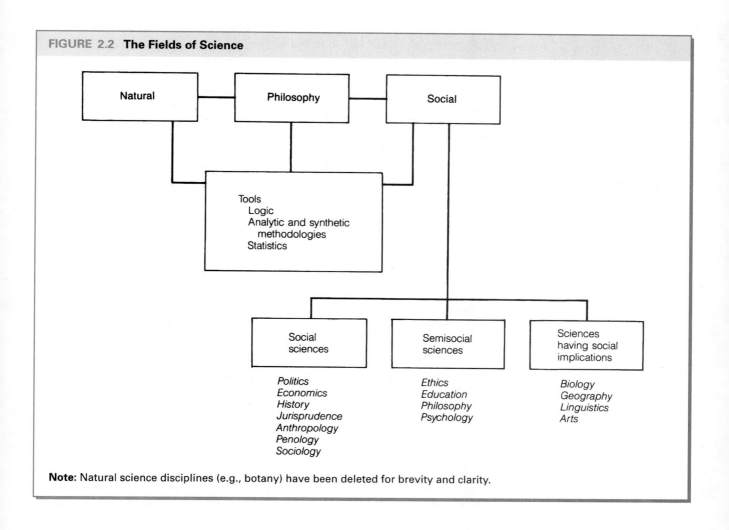

Note: Natural science disciplines (e.g., botany) have been deleted for brevity and clarity.

Consider the following ideas that derive from Figure 2.2:

Key ideas

- ★ Science is an offspring of philosophy. The ancient Greeks equated science with moral philosophy.
- ★ Natural and social sciences share the same basic tools and procedures.
- ★ The extent to which a social science discipline (1) uses the tools of science, and (2) is committed to the systematic use of observation and measurement influences its classification.
- ★ Education is classified as a semi-social science because some educational processes and procedures are based on scientific findings whereas others are based on faith, folklore, or sources unknown.

The Behavioral Sciences. There are many different ways to organize knowledge, and many different labels that could be applied to the various categories of knowledge. One term you may hear from time to time is "the behavioral sciences," which usually refers to a subset of the social science disciplines, mainly sociology, anthropology, and psychology, that focuses on human behavior directly. The waiting-in-line findings we presented in the introduction to this chapter reflect a behavioral science emphasis because they focus on what we humans do in specific situations. In other social science disciplines, such as economics and political science, the focus on human behavior is often more indirect. There is human involvement in the behaviors that economists focus on, such as determining the price of pork bellies, for example, but it tends to be more indirect than in the behavioral sciences. It's a matter of emphasis.

History and the Social Sciences

In this section we revisit history briefly to explain why most social studies educators use the expression "history and the social sciences," instead of lumping the two together. We then examine the social science disciplines, how they are organized, and areas of the human experience they usually focus on.

History

History is not a social science discipline, which is why we use the expression "history and the social sciences" throughout this book. History actually falls into a grey area that lies between the social sciences and the humanities. This is not a defect or deficiency; it simply reflects the nature of that vast and wonderful discipline.

Why history is not a social science

History differs from the social sciences in at least two significant ways. First, historians focus on the past—which is not exactly a revelation, we're sure. However, because the events of history are in the past, it is physically impossible for historians to move backward in time to control and reproduce historical events experimentally in the same way scientists can control events in a laboratory. This is why historians cannot predict future events with a reasonable degree of accuracy. Historians often reconstruct events from historical documents, but this too can pose other problems: historians cannot be certain they have all the pertinent documentation. Neither can they be certain that whatever documentation they have reflects an unbiased account of the events in question. In times of war, for example, the losing side's records are often destroyed or lost, sometimes intentionally. This situation is what possibly led the noted historian Henry Steele Commager (1980) to comment that, over the centuries, history is typically written by the victors, not the vanquished.

In most social studies programs, history is treated as a social science discipline, even though it does not meet all the procedural requirements of a science. At the factual level—the names, places, and dates that we typically associate with history—there is probably no problem in treating it that way. But if, as Momigliano noted, "we take it for granted that history can answer questions about the purpose of life or about the shape of the future—which history cannot answer—we are placing ourselves and history in a false position" (p. 495).

Historical viewpoints and objectivity

Elementary and middle-school students typically believe that everything in their history textbook is fact, an agreed-upon and unquestioningly true record of the past. It wasn't until we majored in history in college that we discovered there were different schools of history, and that historians may interpret the same events very differently. Just one example of this is the current movement to revise historical treatments of America's westward expansion during the eighteenth and nineteenth centuries. Today, the traditional view of "how the West was won" has a competing view based on "how the West was stolen." Unless children see both views, they probably won't know that they are on the receiving end of what amounts to ideological propaganda. The point is that no historical account is entirely objective. Events of history are always interpreted through human eyes, and everyone knows that if six different people observe the same event, you can get six different accounts of what occurred. Historians must decide which (of those six or more) accounts are the most plausible, but even then there is always a lingering doubt. Did the historians miss something, or overemphasize one account at the expense of others? Such questions simply reflect the often incomplete and interpretive nature of history. This also suggests why history's niche among the branches of knowledge is often more closely associated with the humanities than the sciences.

Selected Focal Areas of History

Civilization	Change	Continuity	Progress
Chronology	Bias	Invention	Leadership
Colonization	Perfectability	Historical records	Exploration

Geography

Geography is the science of place and space. Geography's two major areas of study are (1) places on the earth, and (2) the interaction between places and the people who live in them. These areas are the focus of geography's two major subdisciplines: *physical geography* and *cultural geography*.

Physical geography, which is one of the oldest of the social sciences, focuses on the physical characteristics of place. Physical geographers study place location, landforms, climate, resources, and the other facets of our habitats on earth. When you learned about the capital of Belgium (Brussels), the mountains that separate France and Spain (the Pyrenees), or the major American river that flows into the Gulf of Mexico (the Mississippi), you were studying physical geography.

The components of geography

Cultural geography focuses on the interaction between peoples and their environments, or, in other words, how people use the spaces in which they live. Cultural geographers look mainly at the effects of human intervention on the environment. These include how people are distributed on the earth's surface, how they use resources, how they develop transportation and communication systems, and so forth. If you remember studying how the scarcity of usable land forced farmers in the Orient to build terraces on the steep hillsides, you were dealing with cultural geography.

A third subdivision of geography is *cartography*—mapmaking. Maps and aerial or satellite photographs (from which most maps are made) are among geographers' most important tools for displaying and analyzing the phenomena they study.

Geographic Literacy. Although geography is second only to history as a mainstay of the social studies curriculum, most of the geography that students study occurs in elementary and middle schools, primarily in Grades 3 through 7. Rather than having students take additional courses in "pure" geography, the emerging view is that geography and history are complementary subjects that are best taught together in the social studies curriculum (see Bednarz, 1997). When you think about it, every event in history occurred somewhere on earth, and sometimes where the event occurred influenced its outcome. As Bednarz noted, there are good geographic reasons why the Revolutionary War's "Battle of Bunker Hill" was actually fought on nearby Breed's Hill (p. 140).

Complementary subjects

Most efforts to assess geographic literacy have been based almost solely on the student's knowledge of physical geography. This means that students were expected to answer questions such as "What is the capital of the Philippines?" and "What are the five major rivers of Africa?" Information of this kind is sometimes derisively called "place-name geography," but it still plays an important role in social studies programs and as a component of geographic literacy. For example, it is not unusual for fourth-grade students to be expected to do the following:

Place-name geography

* Locate the seven continents and four oceans on a world map
* Locate specific features such as the Ozark Plateau, the Susquehanna River, and Lake Okeechobee, on a map of North America
* Tell a story about what it is like to travel to or live in another region of the country or world
* Find answers to geographic questions, such as "What are the five largest cities in your state?" by using an encyclopedia, atlas, gazetteer, computer database, or other library resources

Performance standards

Five Fundamental Themes of Geography

The Joint Committee on Geographic Education (1984, pp. 3–7) identified five fundamental themes that are intended to capture the essence of geography and serve as guidelines for geographic education in the schools.

THEME ONE: *Location: Position on the Earth's Surface*

Absolute and relative location are two ways of describing the positions of people and places on the earth's surface.

THEME TWO: *Place: Physical and Human Characteristics*

All places on earth have distinctive tangible and intangible characteristics that give them meaning and character and distinguish them from other places. Geographers generally describe places by their physical or human characteristics.

THEME THREE: *Relationships within Places: Humans and Environments*

All places on the earth have advantages and disadvantages for human settlement. High population densities have developed on flood plains, for example, where people could take advantage of fertile soils, water resources, and opportunities for river transportation. However, flood plains are periodically subjected to severe damage. By comparison, population densities are usually low in deserts, yet some desert areas, such as Israel, have been modified to support large populations.

THEME FOUR: *Movement: Humans Interacting on the Earth*

Human beings occupy places unevenly across the face of the earth. Yet these people interact with each other; that is, they travel from one place to another, they communicate with each other, or they rely upon products, information, and ideas that come from beyond their immediate environment.

THEME FIVE: *Regions: How They Form and Change*

The basic unit of geographic study is the region, an area that displays unity in terms of selected criteria. We are all familiar with regions showing the extent of political power, such as nations, provinces, countries, or cities, yet there are almost countless ways to define meaningful regions, depending on the problems being considered. For example, Indiana as a state is a governmental region, Latin America as an area where Spanish and Portuguese are major languages can be a linguistic region, and the Rocky Mountains as a mountain range is a landform region.

[1]Abridged from T. Henry, Mapping out geography plans. Copyright 1994 by *USA Today*. Reprinted by permission.

* Measure the distance between two places on an interstate highway map
* Describe the relative location of your local community in terms of its situation in your state and region, such as "My town is halfway between the state capital and the largest city in the state" (Henry, 1994, p. 4D)

Selected Focal Areas of Geography

Landforms	Location	Areal specialization	Demographics
Region	Migration	Habitat	Population density
Resources	Ecosystem	Climate	Spatial interaction

Anthropology

Anthropology is the study of culture—the different ways of being human. Using artifacts, written and oral accounts, and on-site observations, anthropologists strive to develop profiles of cultures around the world. Anthropologists (and geographers) often use maps in their studies, but anthropologists' most important tools are their cameras or camcorders, tape recorders, and field notebooks.

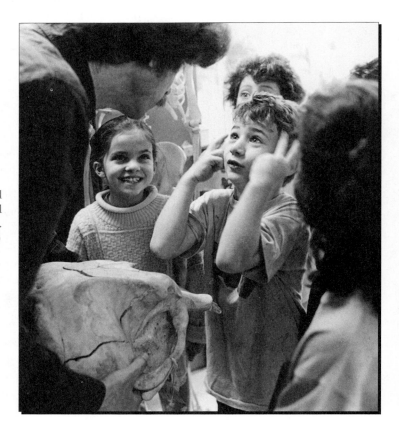

Historical and archaeological artifacts can bring the real world into the classroom.
(© *Susie Fitzhugh*)

The discipline of anthropology is organized much like geography: its two major subdisciplines are *physical anthropology* and *cultural anthropology*. Physical anthropology focuses on the physical characteristics of humans and, in some cases, animals. The fact that one branch of physical anthropology, *primatology*, focuses on the behavior of nonhuman primates—apes, baboons, and gorillas—harkens back to a time when anthropology was considered a subdiscipline of biology. Today, physical anthropologists typically seek answers to two questions: (1) What has been the course of human evolution? (2) What is the nature and significance of human physical variation? (Owen, 1986, p. 141). Anthropologists who focus on studying fossils (instead of living beings) reflect a subspeciality known as *paleoanthropology* or *paleontology*.

Cultural anthropology (or social anthropology) is the broad descriptor for the study of culture. Some cultural anthropologists employ a "cross-cultural perspective" to study the behaviors of past or present cultures. Others narrow their study to a single culture or ethnic group, such as the Hopi, the Maori of New Zealand, or former Puerto Ricans who now live in the Spanish Harlem neighborhood of New York City. Anthropologists who study single ethnic groups are called *ethnographers*, or literally, "individuals who map an ethnic (or culture)."

Selected Focal Areas of Anthropology

Culture	Acculturation	Diffusion	Customs
Ethnology	Tradition	Language	Kinship patterns
Rituals	Enculturation	Innovation	Tools

Anthropological linguistics or *linguistic anthropology*—the two terms are interchangeable—focuses on the study of language and its use in social contexts. Most anthropologists agree that the creation and use of language is one of the key elements of human adaptation. As a result, linguistic anthropologists study the structure of a group's language, how they acquire it, and what it shows about their relationship to other groups.

~~~~~~

COMMENTARY: **The Indiana Jones Syndrome**

When the Indiana Jones (*Raiders of the Lost Ark,* etc.) films were released in the late 1980s, they apparently stimulated an unusual interest in anthropology, especially archeology. The view of archeologists as people who, with cameras in hand, cross burning deserts or steaming jungles in search of lost civilizations, apparently had wide appeal. Unfortunately, the glamorized portrait of archeology that those movies presented had some significant omissions, as many Hollywood films do. Going into the field to gather artifacts is the flashy part of archaeology, but few people see the countless hours that archeologists must spend cleaning, repairing, and studying artifacts in the laboratory. The Indiana Jones films were surely exciting, but they showed only part of the picture.

~~~~~~

Archeology reflects a subspeciality of anthropology that focuses on the remains from lost or past civilizations. The materials could be a single piece of broken pottery or the contents of an entire city, as in Pompeii, Italy; but they usually fall somewhere in between. By studying these remains, the archeologist's goal is to discern the way of life of the peoples who used them.

Political Science

Political science is the study of how human beings think, organize, and act politically (Brody, 1989). However, some totalitarian societies, such as China, do not recognize political science as a legitimate area of study (Theroux, 1997). Specializations in political science include public administration, international relations, political theory, and the study of policymaking and political behavior.

Government and political behavior

All societies develop ways to maintain social order, which are usually called governments, and most societies endow their governments with power and authority over members of the society. The form of government may be very simple—a chief and a council of elders or sometimes just a chief who acts unilaterally—or it can be more complex, as in the executive, legislative, and judicial branches of the U.S. government. The authority of government may be reflected by rules, which when written are called *laws* or when unwritten are called *mores* or, more simply, *tradition*.

In our society, decisions about whether someone has violated the law are vested in the judicial branch of government. In other societies, those decisions may be vested in the same bodies or persons who make the laws—a chief, a council, or some similar individual or group. In our society, the legislative, executive, and judicial branches of government are separate, at least theoretically. Ongoing issues like the abortion question have refocused attention on the way in which the Supreme Court interprets the law, thus determining what is or is not lawful behavior.

Civics emphasis

Political science appears in most elementary and middle-school social studies as *government* (or *civics*). The major emphasis is on the law-making process and the form and structure of government at the local, state, and national levels. A second emphasis emerges at the upper elementary and middle-school grades when students study the historical evolution of the American government—from colony to confederacy to republic.

Selected Focal Areas of Political Science

Government	Authority	Power	Socialism
Citizenship	Democracy	Fascism	Monarchy
Socialism	State	Law	Judiciary
Republic	Federalism	Communism	Due process

Sociology

The study of group behavior

Many of us voluntarily join a variety of groups—school groups, the PTA perhaps, religious groups, or social or service groups such as the Lions Club or the Rotary. At the same time, all of us are members of other groups—cultural, ethnic, or age groups, such as teenagers, yuppies, or seasoned citizens—simply because of who we are. Whether one is a teenager, a young adult, or a Golden Ager is not a matter of choice. But sociologically speaking, all of the groups to which you belong influence your behavior, just as you influence the behavior of the group itself.

Sociology is the study of human groups, how they form, and how they function (Gray, 1989). During the 1800s, sociology was very broadly defined as the study of all aspects of human life and social activity (Dawson, 1929). Almost everything "social" was subsumed under either sociology or history. However, as the other social science disciplines began to carve their niches from the human experience, people tended to drop the generic "sociology" and refer to the more specialized disciplines, such as political science. *Sociology* was retained as a term, but its focus was narrowed to the discipline concerned with the study of group behavior.

Sociology has an array of subdisciplines. Some of these include economic, organizational, political, rural, and urban sociology; the sociologies of knowledge, law, religion, and medicine; human ecology; the history of social thought; sociometry and other small-group research; survey research; and special fields such as criminology and demography.

How disciplines may overlap

Sociology's focus on groups sometimes overlaps with other social science disciplines, mainly anthropology and political science, which also deal with human behavior in group settings. At times, the question becomes one of who is overlapping whom. Sociology and political science typically focus on modern, industrialized societies, whereas anthropology usually focuses on preliterate societies. Yet when sociologists, anthropologists, and political scientists all focus on a contemporary society, some overlap is probably unavoidable. However, each discipline typically examines phenomena from a different perspective and, in so doing, adds richness and depth to what we know about the human condition.

Selected Focal Areas of Sociology

Groups	Socialization	Discrimination	Stratification
Social class	Social status	Society	Norms
Role expectations	Segregation	Social mobility	Power

Economics

Economics is the study of systems for producing, distributing, exchanging, and consuming goods and services. The economy of a society may be based on trading grain or beads or tobacco or money, but regardless of its medium of exchange, an economy underlies every society. Subdisciplines in economics include economic history, agricultural economics, industrial economics, international economics, public finance, and certain aspects of business management.

Scarcity is the engine that drives economies everywhere. If we lived in a utopian world where everyone had everything that they could ever want or need, scarcity would not exist and an economy would be unnecessary. In the real world, there are more things we want and need (or think we need) than there are resources available to satisfy them. Thus we must allocate resources to balance our wants and needs with the resources available to us. In the process, we may be forced to settle for a compact Ford or Chevrolet instead of the Corvette we always dreamed of. Economics is sometimes called the science of scarcity because of the central role it plays in every economy.

Allocating resources

One of the two major areas of study within economics is *microeconomics*, which focuses on specific segments of the larger economy. These segments may include individual consumers or households, or businesses that serve a particular segment of the market, such as retail sales or medical services. The other major area of economics, *macroeconomics,* studies the economy as a whole. Macroeconomists typically study the complex web of relationships among such things as the money supply, the inflation rate, business and industrial inventories, and the unemployment rate.

The findings of macroeconomists often provide the basis for governmental intervention in the economy, whether it be to maintain lower interest rates or low inflation, or to reduce unemployment. Strictly speaking, actions designed to maintain low interest rates, low inflation, and full employment are matters of social policy, *not* economics per se. Economists do not intervene in the economy; rather, they provide the data that enable social planners—who are usually employed by government—to do the actual intervention.

Intervening in the economy

Macroeconomics focuses on economic elements, like inflation and the gross national product, that can have a profound influence on consumers. At the same time, macroeconomics can seem abstract and far removed from day-to-day living. Few of us, for example, may pay much attention to changes in the interest rate until it becomes so high that we can't afford taking out a loan to purchase something. Likewise, trying to understand abstract concepts such as inflation, much less what causes it, can be frustrating for young children and adults alike. Inflation is an abstraction that no one has ever seen, although we do see its effects in higher prices. In place of abstract concepts like inflation, the economic components of elementary and middle-school social studies programs usually focus on *consumer economics,* which aims at helping children become informed consumers. Most social studies programs also deal with basic concepts of microeconomics, such as resources, wants and needs, production, consumption, and exchange.

Consumer economics emphasis

Selected Focal Areas of Economics

Goods	Services	Production	Exchange
Resources	Profit	Scarcity	Supply and demand
Consumer	Labor	Needs and wants	Price

Psychology

Psychology is the study of behavior—animal or human, instinctive and learned. The psychologists who study rats in a maze or chickens pecking at buttons to obtain food may be interested solely in the animals' behavior or may be searching for clues to human behavior, or both. Humans are infinitely more complex than rats or chickens, of course, which is why findings based on animal behavior don't always transfer to human beings. The point is that psychology is the study of behavior, broadly speaking, not human behavior alone.

Behavior is a tremendously complex and varied subject, and so is the discipline that studies it. Some subdisciplines of psychology use procedures more common to medicine and the natural sciences, such as treating disturbing or abnormal conditions, including mental illnesses. Still others focus almost exclusively on human behavior and are clearly social sciences.

The fields of psychology most pertinent to the social studies include social psychology, which focuses on the behavior of humans in groups and group settings; cognitive psychology, which focuses on intellectual functions such as memory, perception, learning, and reasoning; and developmental psychology, which deals with the development of human behavior over the lifetime. Other related subdisciplines include personality psychology, which deals with the nature and development of personality, and psycholinguistics, which examines the development of language and language skills.

Content drawn from psychology is common in elementary and middle schools, but it is more often part of the health curriculum, not social studies. Most health programs consider topics such as the nature of thinking and learning, the stages of human development, and the influences of heredity and the environment on human behavior, all of which derive from psychology. Also common to schools is what could be called "applied psychology." This is reflected by teachers' efforts to help students (1) build their self-concept and self-esteem, (2) deal with possible feelings of inadequacy, (3) cope with physical or verbal abuse, and (4) maintain good relationships with adults and peers. Although the elements of "applied psychology" are an inescapable part of teaching, they seldom occur as a formal subject. Whether psychology is treated as health or social studies, it remains a fertile source of social content.

The study of behavior

More common in health programs

Selected Focal Areas of Psychology

Learning	Personality	Motives	Self-concept
Perception	Aggression	Attitudes	Traits
Instinct	Conditioning	Punishment	Reinforcement

Related Disciplines

Other fields of study besides the social science disciplines apply the processes of science to social phenomena. For example, the field of psychiatry, which we normally think of as part of medicine, could be considered a social science (see below). The following are related disciplines that may be incorporated into social studies programs:

Related fields of study

Law—including jurisprudence, the major legal systems, legal theory, and the relation of law to the other social sciences.

Psychiatry—including theories and descriptions of the principal mental disorders and methods of diagnosis and treatment.

Statistics—including theoretical statistics, the design of experiments, sampling errors, sample surveys, governmental statistics, and the use of statistical methods in social science research. Note that statistics are mathematical tools that scientists use to determine the probability that the phenomenon they observed in a sample of the population is an accurate reflection of the entire population. In other words, scientists use statistics to test the probability that their findings are valid and not simply random or chance occurrences.

Natural Sciences—including biology, geology, and environmental sciences.

Major Findings from the Social Sciences

Findings from the social science disciplines can take many different forms. Sometimes they are presented as generalizable statements that apply at all times and in all places. For example, all cultures develop a means for social control—that is, for governing the conduct of their members. This means that all cultures hold certain expectations of how their members should behave. Other social science findings are presented in the "if-then" format that we described earlier, and that describe how people will tend to behave. Thus, for example, the members of a group will tend to perceive the group's collective opinion as closer to their own than it really is. Such findings provide a basis for anticipating and interpreting the behavior of others, but because they are based on tendencies, not absolutes, the behaviors they predict will not always occur.

In many (some will say too many) cases, data from the social sciences consist of factual, uninterpreted, documentary information. You could, for example, find out how many acres of farmland were harvested in 1957 or how many bushels of wheat were produced in Kansas in 1994—assuming that you needed that kind of information. In still other instances, social science findings can reflect reinterpretations of previously existing information. This might include a reconsideration of the role that slavery played as a cause of the Civil War, or a new explanation for why the food problem in India might be further complicated if the Hindus were to eat their sacred cows.

Regardless of the form the data take, one of the problems we face is that social scientists are continually adding to the fund of knowledge. That's why social studies books get thicker, not thinner. The efforts of individual social scientists are usually systematic and well organized, but because there is no systematic way of managing all the information they produce, their findings are scattered throughout hundreds of sources—journals, magazines, even the Internet. Some of them, like the findings about waiting in line, eventually appear in textbooks.

Generalizations (margin note beside first paragraph)

Raw (uninterpreted) data (margin note beside third paragraph)

The following selected generalizations, which are stated in nonacademic language, are based on history and the social sciences. They apply to human activities regardless of social situation, cultural background, or geographic location, and could serve as a foundation (or part of one) for social studies programs.

Selected generalizations from A to Z

A. People all over the world are the same in some ways and different in other ways. People respond to the same problems, but the ways they respond may differ.

B. Human beings learn to behave the way they do. How humans think and act depends more on their experiences than on their being born with differences.

C. Most human beings learn social habits, some of which are performed automatically and without thought. When people behave in habitual ways, patterns in their behavior emerge, patterns that can help others predict how people will behave.

D. Most people think that their way of doing things and their ways of thinking are natural and right.

E. Every habit, pattern of behavior, and idea that people have makes "sense" to them and to their living situation. The habits, behaviors, and ideas of other people not in the same life situation may not make the same sense.

F. All people can learn from past experience, and can accept or change their ways of living.

G. When a change takes place in one part of a person's life, it often requires changes in other parts of their life. Some intended changes may cause unintended changes.

H. People usually respond to what they think things are and not to what things really are.

I. Most people live in group settings. A person may live in several different group settings simultaneously. This may cause conflict for the person, especially if different groups expect opposite kinds of behavior.

J. Most people carry a "map" of their social worlds in their mind. This helps make social living different from just being in the physical presence of others.

Most groups depend on other groups

K. Most groups in which people live are dependent upon other groups (in which they don't live). This can lead to cooperation or conflict.

L. People learn to play certain roles. Other people expect the roles to be played in certain ways. The roles a person plays (and the rewards and punishments that go with the roles) may change over time and with new situations.

M. A person seldom behaves in a certain manner for only one reason. Why individuals behave as they do usually involves several factors. Behavior is not a simple thing to understand.

Most human behavior is purposeful

N. Most human behavior satisfies some purpose. Humans behave to achieve certain goals.

O. All human beings are born with the same physical needs. Ways of satisfying these needs differ from one person to another and from one group to another.

P. A person's personality is usually made up of physical traits, life experiences, and the physical setting in which the person lives.

Q. Individual human beings differ from each other in what they value and how they behave. People living in the same group tend to share values and behaviors that are similar.

R. The groups in which people live have ways to teach group members what to think and how to behave. Most people influence others and are influenced by others.

S. Every human group has ways of handling how people work, how resources are used and distributed, and how the group's "wealth" is to be managed. All of these are related to what the group values.

T. In most groups, individual members depend upon one another for satisfying needs and wants.

U. How people use their physical environment depends on what is available, what is wanted, and how the group manages itself. How people use their physical and social environments depends on their value systems.

V. How people think and behave depends, in part, on their experiences. People can use past experience several ways: (1) to learn how and when to change, (2) to find reasons for continuing certain things, (3) to provide answers to problems, and (4) to make people feel unique yet part of a common, shared past.

All societies have rules they live by

W. All people live under some form of control. There are basic rules of behavior and basic ways of enforcing the rules. In all groups there are rules for individual behavior and rules for group behavior. How rules are made and enforced often depends upon what people value.

X. All human groups develop ways for handling disagreements.

Y. For human beings to live with one another, they need a common language that permits them to share ideas.

Z. Most people and groups of people believe in myths and legends that help them interpret and make sense of their world.

These findings could become the major ideas—the content—around which social studies instruction is organized. In this instance, content refers to two different but mutually supporting ideas: (1) the information and ideas contained in a particular subject area, such as social studies, and (2) the subjects or topics that matter in a specific field of study. If you consider the two different meanings, a significant aspect of social studies teaching may emerge: being a teacher is different from being a scholar. Teachers must identify and use specific information and ideas to ensure that their students learn to identify and use information and ideas. Scholars, on the other hand, usually identify information and ideas to be used in developing more content and more effective modes of inquiry. We are not suggesting that scholars can't teach, nor are we suggesting that teachers cannot also be scholars. The point is that although teachers have some dependency upon the scholars' work, teachers and scholars may view content from different perspectives.

The knowledge base for social studies

The social science disciplines were originally created to aid in the scholarly pursuit of knowledge. Yet the content and findings from history and the social sciences furnish the raw materials—the knowledge base—upon which social studies programs are built. How one chooses to select, organize, and use these raw materials will determine the nature of the program, which is our focus in Chapter 4.

COMMENTARY: Social Studies or Social Science Education

When most of us were in elementary and middle schools, we studied social studies, not social science. We learned the names, dates, and places of history and geography, and we occasionally sampled some of the other social science disciplines. What we did not study much about was how scientists work with information and how they validate their findings. For example, we did not receive two conflicting accounts of the same event and were then asked to judge which one was the most accurate. Occasionally we put information into chart and graph form, but it was usually decontextualized data—stuff like graphing the amount of wheat grown in Kansas from 1970 to the present. Some of us may have experienced the problems associated with polling or conducting a survey to determine the most popular soft drink or peanut butter, and whether students' taste for such products change from kindergarten to sixth grade, but such activities may have been the exception, not the rule.

When the knowledge base of history and the social sciences is drawn on to produce a social studies program, what often gets omitted are the processes of science. In other words, most social studies programs leave out the "science" part of social science. We are not suggesting that we need to put science back into social studies, because for the most part it was never there to begin with. We do suggest, however, that the information processes of science should be part of every social studies program. Helping students to gather, process, and evaluate information would be useful in its own right, and would also help move from traditional social studies toward social science education.

Summary

The human experience is that colossus from which all social studies stem. Our collective knowledge of the human experience is so all-encompassing that scholars created smaller, more manageable bodies of knowledge to organize what we know. Yet even these smaller bodies of knowledge, like geography and biology and medicine, have grown to massive proportions.

Somewhere in the human experience, scholars began referring to the smaller branches of knowledge as *disciplines.* At another point in the human experience, scholars who specialized in certain disciplines adopted rigorous (disciplined) processes and procedures, called *science,* for adding new knowledge to their fields of study. Consequently, the social science disciplines today represent organized bodies of knowledge in which scholars employ the processes of science to study selected aspects of the human experience.

The fields of study most pertinent to social studies are history and the social science disciplines of geography, political science, economics, anthropology, sociology, and psychology. Because some aspects of psychology are affiliated with the natural sciences, and others are closer to the social sciences, psychology—like history—can fall into a grey area. Psychology can provide a kind of bridge between the natural and social sciences, whereas history provides a bridge between the social sciences and the humanities. The point is that how curriculum developers and others classify the various disciplines that focus on the human experience can influence the topics that are included in a social studies program.

Recent research suggests that even young children are often able to study history and historical events, but they must do so in ways that accommodate their limited range of experiences. The key element in presenting historical events to young children is to make them as specific as possible. This means that sweeping statements, such as "The Reconstruction period (after the Civil War) was a difficult time for many people," will probably be meaningless to young children unless they have had prior experiences with the problems that people actually faced during that era. Historical narratives, including historical fiction in which someone does something to someone, can often provide the immediacy and involvement that young children require. Young children must be able to see how history relates to their lives, but the same principle is also appropriate for older students—even adults.

Suggested Activity

1. When historians write history, they look to an event and then seek out the causes for it. In other words, the Stamp Act was not a cause of the American Revolution until the revolution actually began. Prior to the Revolution, it was simply a troublesome law that the colonists had to deal with. Consider how things would be different if history were taught in reverse chronological order, beginning with the present and moving back to the past.

Suggested Readings

Stuart Chase. (1967). *The proper study of mankind: An inquiry into the science of human relations*. Rev. ed. New York: Harper & Row. This classic has long been one of our favorites. An excellent introduction to how the social sciences look at experience.

Linda S. Levstik & Keith C. Barton. (1997). *Doing history: Investigating with children in elementary and middle schools*. Mahwah, NJ: Lawrence Erlbaum Associates. This is an engaging book on teaching history in elementary and middle schools. Its 171 pages are packed with countless examples of appropriate classroom practice along with the most recent thinking on how children learn history, much of it the product of the authors' own research. This book belongs on your "must read" list.

Raymond H. Muessig (ed). (1980). *Study and teaching of social science series*. Columbus: Charles Merrill. This introductory series consists of six 100-page volumes, each of which examines a single social science discipline. The authors and volume titles are as follows:

Henry Steele Commager & Raymond H. Muessig. *The study and teaching of history*.

Jan O. M. Broek, Henry Hunker, Raymond H. Muessig, and Joseph M. Cirrincione. *The study and teaching of geography*.

Pertti J. Pelto & Raymond H. Muessig. *The study and teaching of anthropology*.

Roman F. Warnke, Raymond H. Muessig, & Stephen L. Miller. *The study and teaching of anthropology*.

John A. Straayer & Raymond H. Muessig. *The study and teaching of political science*.

James A. Kitchens & Raymond H. Muessig. *The study and teaching of sociology*.

3 The Dimensions of Diversity

Key Questions

* What kinds of diversity should you anticipate in your classroom?

* How do you accommodate diverse students' interests and abilities?

* How can teachers approach multicultural education?

Key Ideas

* Diversity is a normal part of life in classrooms today.

* The range of diversity in any given class can be astounding—religious, ethnic, cultural, physical, intellectual, and social.

* Various strategies can be used to tailor instruction to meet students' needs.

* Multicultural activities must be authentic; otherwise they can lead to inaccurate stereotyping.

Introduction: Mottoes and Metaphors

The eagle on the Great Seal of the United States, which is on the back of a dollar bill, is holding a ribbon or scroll in its beak. Inscribed there is our national motto: *E pluribus unum*—"Out of many, one." Because the notion of *E pluribus unum* is a dominant theme in the multicultural education literature, it seemed to provide an appropriate introduction to this chapter on diversity.

Are we one? or many? or both?

The current interest in *E pluribus unum* focuses not on "the many," for we are clearly a nation of immigrants, but on *unum*—the "one." As we suggested in Chapter 1, the question today is, Is the United States *one*—a nation with a common culture that binds us together? Or is our national character better described by *E pluribus pluribus*—out of many, many? As Barber (1992) suggested, the diversity of America is at once a virtue, a source of pride, a brave boast, a troubling reality, and an unsettling problem that muddles what it means to be an American.

When people try to describe the American character, they sometimes turn to metaphors. Our society, and schools especially, was once described as a "melting pot" from which recently arrived immigrants were expected to emerge as "Americans." The problem with metaphors is that they seldom "fit" perfectly. Many people's problem with the melting pot image stemmed from the belief that America is not a single culture but a multitude of cultures, each with traits and characteristics that contribute to the larger society. As the melting pot notion fell into disfavor, some people turned to a "salad bowl" metaphor, in which each ethnicity retains its separate identity but still contributes to the whole. Describing America as a salad bowl was an improvement over the melting pot, but this metaphor too has problems. Among other things, it's too easy to overemphasize the ingredients in the salad and neglect the importance of the bowl—which represents the beliefs and values that all Americans have in common.

Changing metaphors

Instead of a food-related metaphor, we prefer to describe American society as a mosaic—a work of art when it is assembled, but is simply a collection of individual pieces before it's put together. The parts-whole relationship of a mosaic captures the duality of *cultural pluralism* that we noted in Chapter 1; that is where all of us must deal with at least two cultures: the common American culture that everyone shares, and our individual ethnicities that set each of us apart from other people. If you still question whether there are beliefs and values that all of us share, consider what would likely happen if the people who argue that we have no common values were denied their right to state that position. We suspect that phrases like "freedom of speech" and "the Bill of Rights" would appear as if out of nowhere.

The American mosaic

The diversity that you and every teacher must deal with has grown tremendously in the last twenty or so years. One reason for this is *desegregation,* in the broadest sense of that term. *Brown v. Topeka Board of Education* (1954) marked the beginning of the end of racially segregated schools, although the effects of the Supreme Court's ruling were by no means immediate. In addition, *Brown v. Topeka* did not address the issue of schools that were segregated by virtue of the neighborhoods they served, which is where busing entered the picture.

Accounting for increased diversity

The end of racial segregation accounts for some of the increased diversity in classrooms, but the end of another more subtle form of segregation also had an impact. The Individuals with Disabilities Education Act of 1990, which extended Public Law 94-142, continued to reduce the number of physically and educationally disabled students who were formerly segregated into separate classrooms. The legislation did not abolish separate classes entirely, but it did require that students be placed in the *least restrictive environment:* that is, an environment that best meets the individual student's needs. That environment could be a regular classroom, a regular classroom plus special services in separate classrooms (pull-out programs), placement in a totally separate classroom, or, in the most extreme cases, institutionalization. The key point is that one effect of PL 94-142 (and subsequent legislation) was to increase the diversity in regular classrooms.

Demography, immigration, numbers . . .

Three other factors also account for the increased diversity in classrooms today: (1) demographic changes resulting from new immigration, (2) increasing minority populations, and (3) an increased recognition of the ethnicities of all students, many of whom had been in classrooms all along. For example, there is an elementary school in downtown San Francisco where students may speak one or more of twenty-seven different languages in their homes. This situation, in California and elsewhere, has resulted largely from increased immigration—some of it illegal immigration—primarily from Mexico, the Pacific Rim, and Central America. Should you elect to teach in one of the twenty-five largest school districts in America, the majority of your students will be nonwhite (Lisack, 1987). By the year 2010, it is estimated that people of color will be the majority of students in more than fifty major cities in the United States (Susuki, 1987).

Troublesome hyphens

In the days when the melting pot was the prevailing metaphor, schools often worked diligently to remove the hyphen from Irish-Americans, Japanese-Americans, and other immigrant groups. The prevailing belief was that the faster that newly arrived students dropped the hyphen and began thinking of themselves as "Americans," the better. On the other hand, expecting people to submerge their ethnicities was tantamount to asking them to deny their heritage, which was a nearly impossible request to begin with; it diminishes one of the qualities on which our nation of immigrants was built. Instead of denigrating or trying to erase individual ethnicities, more and more people have come to prize them for the contributions they make to the mosaic of life in America.

How this chapter is organized

In this chapter, we examine the educational impact that the increasingly diverse American culture has and will have on those of us who teach its future citizens. To provide a context, we first present a profile of a typical classroom that reflects at least some of the diversity you are likely to encounter in your own classroom. We then turn to ways in which you can address two of the most basic forms of diversity: (1) racial and ethnic differences, and (2) the various physical, emotional, and learning disorders that exist regardless of race and ethnicity. For lack of a better term, we will refer to the latter group as reflecting "educational" diversity.

A Classroom Profile

The following vignette illustrates the diversity you are apt to encounter, regardless of where you teach. In this vignette, we describe a fourth-grade classroom at Roscoe Hunt Elementary School, a racially and ethnically mixed magnet school located in a lower-middle-class neighborhood of a small city in the southwestern United States. Hunt Elementary serves neighborhood children as well as students from other parts of the city who want to take advantage of its enhanced programs in math and science.

Mary Jane Blanchard is in her third year of teaching fourth graders. She has between twenty-two to twenty-six students in her class—the number changes almost weekly. Every couple of weeks, a student will leave and a new student will arrive or a former student will return. For example, one former student, Tyrone, has recently returned after spending three months living with his aunt in Chicago. Only seventeen of the twenty-four currently enrolled students began the year with Ms. Blanchard.

Diversity in a sample classroom

The mobility of students in Mary Jane's classroom is high. But with only a couple of exceptions, the diversity in Mary Jane's students is not all that uncommon.

Some of Ms. Blanchard's students include the following:

Academic considerations

* Five students—Tyrone, Trisha, Jesus, Miguel, and Maria—who have reading skills that are *at least* one-half year below grade level; all of them spend a part of each day in the Resource Room, where they receive special tutoring in academic skills. Two of these students, Trisha and Miguel, have great difficulty remembering what they read but can remember almost everything they hear. Maria, especially, can repeat almost anything Ms. Blanchard says word for word.

* Six students—Juan, LaShawna, Melissa, Gina, Richard, and Chen Lee—who have reading, math, and language skills that are at the sixth-grade level or above. LaShawna, Chen Lee, and Richard are considered gifted.

* Three students—Tyrone, Richard, and Christi—who have handwriting that is often illegible.

* Three other students—Jesus, Miguel, and Maria—who come from homes where Spanish is the dominant language.

* One student, Trang, who spoke no English at the beginning of the year (and no one in the school spoke Vietnamese). With voluntary assistance from several students in the class, Trang now speaks passable English and has made remarkable progress in just four months.

Emotional considerations

* One student, Heather—an African-American girl with apparently normal intelligence and physical development—who can do fourth-grade work but prefers not to. Instead, she spends her day huddled in her seat with her coat pulled over her head, almost as if she is withdrawing from the world. Heather will answer direct questions from Ms. Blanchard, but her responses are mono-syllabic and barely audible; she will not look at the teacher, even when asked to do so. Heather has not uttered a complete sentence all year and avoids interacting with other students as much as possible. Heather has no friends in the class, but neither does she have any enemies. The other students are patiently tolerant of Heather, and some are almost protective of her.

Need for structure

* One gifted student, Chen Lee, is an extremely hard worker who places extraordinary emphasis on memorization. In math, for example, she memorizes the answers and the problems. Chen Lee also has "high structure needs"; that is, she has difficulty dealing with independent problem solving and unstructured or open-ended activities. Chen Lee often became frustrated when Ms. Blanchard gave topical assignments, such as "read the next section in the text." This is no longer the problem it was, because to accommodate Chen Lee's need for structure, Mary Jane now provides page numbers for all assignments.

Disabling conditions

* One student, James, who has muscular dystrophy and is confined to a wheelchair. The school district provides a full-time aide who assists James and helps him get from place to place. Because James is unable to write, he dictates all written assignments to his aide.

* Another student, Jason, who must take the drug Ritalin to calm his hyperactivity. The difference between Jason's pre-Ritalin behavior and his behavior today is like night and day. Jason's parents have given Mary Jane

permission to administer Jason's midday dose of Ritalin; in fact, they have asked that he take it at 11:30 sharp, so that he will be ready for his evening dose when he gets home from school. Because both Jason and Ms. Blanchard sometimes get involved and forget about Jason's medication schedule, Richard has volunteered to remind them.

Religious diversity
* Two students, Amy and Melissa, whose parents have requested that their children be excused from any lessons involving witches, ghosts, goblins, or other supernatural beings, all of which are offensive to their religious beliefs. In addition, Melissa's parents have requested that she be excused from saying the Pledge of Allegiance during the opening exercises, again because of the family's religious convictions.

* Six students—Tyrone, LaShawna, Patrick, James, DeLeon, and Charles—who come from single-parent homes. Four students live with their mother, one lives with his grandmother, and Charles lives with his father.

If you think that Mary Jane Blanchard's class is an uncommon example, consider the kinds of diversity she does not have in her classroom, at least not this year. She does *not* have students who

* have limited vision or hearing,
* are cognitively disadvantaged,
* are absent from school more than three days every week,
* have infant alcohol or "crack baby" syndrome,
* have known tobacco, drug, or alcohol addictions, or
* are abused.

All classes are diverse, some more so and some less so than Mary Jane Blanchard's. This means that all teachers need to adapt their teaching in ways that will accommodate their students' needs. Some forms of diversity may require major instructional changes, like accommodating Trang's limited ability with English or Tyrone's lack of reading skills. Other forms of diversity, like making sure that Jason gets his medication on schedule, don't require instructional modifications, but they are things that a teacher must keep in mind.

The forms of diversity and exceptionality reflected in Mary Jane Blanchard's classroom, and that we deal with in this chapter, include

Diversity summarized
* cultural and ethnic diversity. Mary Jane's class currently has eight mainstream Anglo students—including one, Ian McTavish, of Scotch-American origin—four Latinos and one Cuban-American, four African-Americans and one Haitian-American, six Asian-Americans—two from China, one from Taiwan, one of Japanese ancestry, one each from Vietnam and Laos—and one student of mixed Anglo and African-American heritage.
* religious diversity, especially as reflected by Amy and Melissa.
* physical and emotional disabilities—as reflected by James, Jason, and, apparently, Heather.
* academic diversity, which includes both students working below grade level (Tyrone, Miguel, etc.) and gifted students (Richard, LaShawna, etc.).
* learning style, as reflected by Chen Lee's need for precise directions and Trisha's preference for listening as opposed to reading activities.

* linguistic diversity, as reflected by Trang, Miguel, and Maria, for whom English is clearly a second language.

In the next section, we look at how teachers can accommodate diversity.

Responding to Cultural and Ethnic Diversity

"Being Bad is the Way We Are"

Marc Elrich (1994) teaches in a school on the outskirts of Washington, D.C. All but two of the twenty-nine students in his sixth-grade class are African-American or Hispanic, and most of them are of low socioeconomic status—in other words, they are poor. In some respects, Marc doesn't face the range of diversity that Mary Jane Blanchard must deal with, but he faces some difficult problems nonetheless.

Marc teaches in a school that offers a range of programs meant to teach children to celebrate and prize their diversity. This, in part, is one of the goals of multicultural education (which we described briefly in Chapter 1 and expand on later in this chapter). Despite the school's programs, many of Marc's students have low self-esteem, low expectations, and, by the age of ten or eleven, have opted out of the educational system.

Another classroom example

On one occasion Marc showed a film that he hoped would provoke a discussion of self-esteem. The film was based on a Langston Hughes story about an African-American youth who attempts to steal the purse of an elderly African-American lady. The youth fails, and the woman takes him into her home, where she applies a generous amount of love and understanding. The messages: love is a powerful medicine, and, with love, all of us can become better people.

In the postfilm discussion, it soon became apparent that Marc's students hadn't bought the message. For example, one student said, "As soon as you see a black boy, you know he's gonna do something bad!" Marc's reply: "Just because he's black, he's bad?" Student: "Everybody knows that black people are bad. That's the way we are." Marc: "Do you mean 'bad' like 'cool' or 'tough' or 'hot,' or do you mean 'bad' as in 'not good' or 'evil?'"(p. 12). The student meant the latter.

As the discussion continued, a disturbing picture began to emerge. Marc's students were nearly unanimous about the following comments:

Students' self-images and beliefs

* "Black people don't like to work hard."
* "Black boys expect to die young and unnaturally."
* "White people are smart and have money."
* "Asians are smart and have money."
* "Asians don't like blacks or Hispanics."
* "Hispanics are more like blacks than whites. They can't be white so they try to be black."
* "Hispanics are poor and don't try hard because, like blacks, they know it doesn't matter" (pp. 12–13).

In subsequent discussions, Marc's students indicated that people who can afford the material goods associated with the "good life" get their money through guns and dealing in drugs. They also believed that wimps die young and live in fear, whereas tough guys die young but are proud. Likewise, bosses are white and workers are black, and black people don't do important things, except in school books. "But," Marc also indicated, "my students don't lack for pride. They are, in fact, quite proud of what they are. They were good at being bad, some were excellent at it, and the badder they were, the greater their social status" (p. 14).

Good at being "bad"

Another Marc, in this case Mark Twain, once said, "I never let my schooling interfere with my education." Marc Elrich's students had obviously learned some powerful lessons, perhaps not what we might have wanted and hopefully not in school, but powerful nonetheless. In reflecting on his experience, Marc indicated:

Students' responses to special programs

> I gave a lot of thought to how we teach students to value diversity. The thoughts and words of my students make a mockery of our [school's] celebrations. Setting aside a month for black history or women's history seems strange and artificial to most students regardless of color. These children aren't naive. What are the seven other months: White Male History Months? History needs to be inclusionary, but it needs to be natural so that children come to see that there's nothing strange or odd about black people or women achieving success. I have begun to fear that singling out groups for special attention does more to foster suspicion, jealousy, and cynicism, than it does to promote understanding, empathy, and community. (p. 14)

Schools and real-life experiences

We share Marc's concerns. All children are perceptive observers of their world, and for one to believe that teachers can change those views by teaching occasional lessons on successful African-Americans, Asian-Americans, or whatever, may be naive at best. As Elrich noted, ". . . children form their own impressions early on, and they sense the dissonance between the reality of life and the pretty pictures offered in school. If we are concerned with our children genuinely valuing diversity and with all children developing high self-esteem, then we have to offer our children genuine knowledge and insight into the world in which they live. I don't think we do" (p. 15).

Powerful lessons

Whether schools can single-handedly eliminate the kinds of stereotyping that Marc Elrich's students reflect is debatable. The fact that streetwise children consider examples of successful minorities that appear in textbooks—the Jackie Robinsons and the Martin Luther King Jrs.—as exceptions, as people far removed from the life they know, suggests that the underlying problems may extend beyond what schools can influence on their own. Multicultural education programs (which we consider in the next section) may be able to address some of these problems, but for this to occur, students, teachers, and communities that schools serve must regard multicultural education as an integral part of the school program, not simply an add-on designed to placate (or mislead) minority children.

Multicultural Education

There is no single, agreed-upon definition for *multicultural education*. Both multicultural education and cultural pluralism reflect the notion that the richness of our society is rooted in every nook and cranny on the globe. This means that all peoples must be treated in ways that recognize and respect their inherent dignity and their contributions to contemporary society.

Goal

One goal of multicultural education is to help all children—regardless of ethnicity, gender, disabilities, or social class—understand and appreciate events and people from various points of view. Those points of view may reflect cultural and ethnic similarities and differences, as well as identify alternative choices for people regardless of their situation.

The literature on multicultural education is vast, and some of it reflects attempts by individuals to push a particular agenda. For example, consider the following survey of cultural awareness (Grant and Sleeter, 1989) in which you are asked to match the following individuals with their occupations. The answers are at the end of the chapter.*

Multicultural awareness?

1. _____ Richard Wright
2. _____ Mary McLeod Bethune
3. _____ Emma Tenayuca
4. _____ Patsy Takemoto Mink
5. _____ Marion [*sic*] Anderson
6. _____ Larry Itliong
7. _____ Leslie Silko
8. _____ Reies Lopez Tijerina
9. _____ Lerone Bennet
10. _____ Alvin Poussaint
11. _____ Lucy Stone
12. _____ Yoshiko Uchida
13. _____ Zora Neale Hurston
14. _____ Rudolfo Acuña

a. Mexican-American labor leader
b. African-American psychiatrist on Harvard faculty
c. Opera singer
d. Founder and former president of a college
e. Mexican-American historian
f. African-American male novelist
g. Philippino-American labor leader
h. Mexican-American political leader
i. Author of children's books
j. Indian novelist
k. African-American female novelist
l. Former member of Congress
m. African-American historian

Some people breathe a sigh of relief when they get to Marian Anderson, the acclaimed African-American opera singer. Often this is the first entry they recognize. In desperation, they sometimes turn to a process of elimination based on the perceived ethnicity of the individual's last name. They might also ask where was Ella Fitzgerald, Ernie Banks, Kathleen Battle, Joycelyn Elders, Henry B. Gonzales, and Cesar Chavez—people they had heard of.

With due respect to Grant and Sleeter, one might question whether this is a legitimate survey of cultural awareness. Or perhaps it was designed to heighten

---

*Source: From *Turning on Learning: Five Approaches for Multicultural Teaching* by Grant/Sleeter. Copyright 1989. Reprinted by permission of Prentice-Hall.

one's awareness of what one does not know. The point is that the goal of multicultural education is *not* to replace Eurocentric trivia with a different kind of more politically correct trivia. Rather multicultural education is intended to develop the knowledge, perspectives, and frames of reference that build *mutual respect* between and among all peoples.

Approaches to Multicultural Education

Multicultural education can be embraced in different ways, some more and some less effective than others. One of the best descriptions of how to approach this, we think, was described by Banks (1989) and is shown in Figure 3.1.

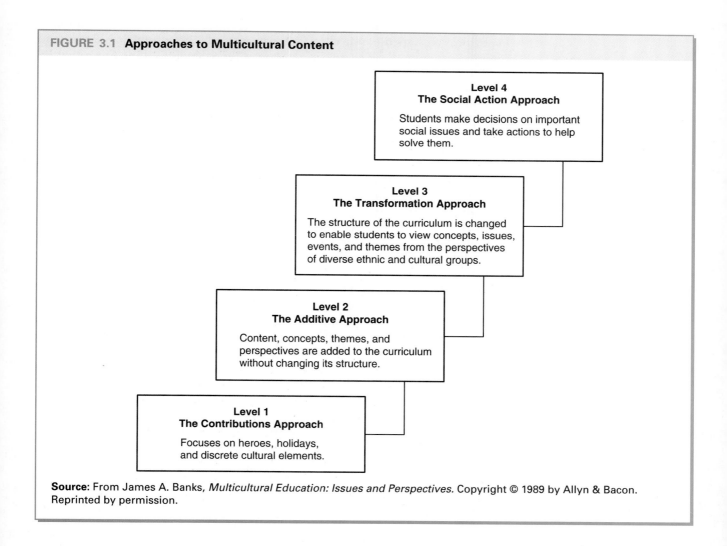

FIGURE 3.1 Approaches to Multicultural Content

Level 4
The Social Action Approach

Students make decisions on important social issues and take actions to help solve them.

Level 3
The Transformation Approach

The structure of the curriculum is changed to enable students to view concepts, issues, events, and themes from the perspectives of diverse ethnic and cultural groups.

Level 2
The Additive Approach

Content, concepts, themes, and perspectives are added to the curriculum without changing its structure.

Level 1
The Contributions Approach

Focuses on heroes, holidays, and discrete cultural elements.

Source: From James A. Banks, *Multicultural Education: Issues and Perspectives.* Copyright © 1989 by Allyn & Bacon. Reprinted by permission.

Contributions Approach. Banks suggests that the "contributions approach" to multicultural education is often the first stage that schools and teachers employ in moving toward a multicultural curriculum. Special events such as "Black History Month" or "African- or Native-American Heritage Day" characterize this approach, as do curricular insertions of ethnic heroes such as Crispus Attucks (the first African-American to die in the Battle of Concord), Cesar Chavez (the organizer of Mexican-American farm workers), or even Rosa Parks (who initiated the Montgomery bus boycott).

Stage One: Contributions

The contributions approach to multicultural education has some limitations, not the least of which is that children will see it as a curriculum add-on designed to appeal to a certain population. If there is a question about this, consider Marc Elrich's students' responses to the inclusion of certain African-American heroes in their textbooks.

A second limitation of the contributions approach is that well-intentioned activities can sometimes do as much harm as good. The special days set aside to honor certain cultural or ethnic groups, or the eating of ethnic foods that Elrich (Banks and many others) referred to, can unintentionally convey inaccurate information and create negative stereotypes. For example, serving your students tacos or tamales that were purchased at the local 7-Eleven does not help children "appreciate Hispanics" any more than eating chitterlings (deep-fried pig intestines known as "chitlins") will help them to appreciate the African-American culture. Likewise, having students line up "Indian style" can teach cultural images that are inaccurate and undesirable. As Banks (1989) noted, the essence of ethnic communities lies in their values and related lifestyles, not in chow mein, basket weaving, and soul food.

Limitations and liabilities

Arts and crafts activities must also be treated carefully, or they too can sometimes have the same effect. On one occasion, for example, we visited a kindergarten class in which the children were studying Native Americans. They had dyed elbow macaroni with red, orange, yellow, green, and blue food coloring. After the macaroni had dried and was strung on strings, the children proudly displayed their "Indian necklaces." The teacher's motives were well intended; she wanted a hands-on activity that related to the unit, preferably one the students could complete quickly. The problem here was with what the children learned from the activity: that Native Americans wear necklaces made from colored macaroni—which no self-respecting Native Americans do.

Having students create a macaroni necklace can be an engaging craft activity that may be worth doing on that basis alone. However, problems can arise if the teacher introduces it with "Today, boys and girls, we are going to make necklaces like the Native Americans used to wear." Justifying activities on a multicultural basis can easily become misleading, and can provide learnings that go beyond what the teacher intended. Multicultural education is an area where otherwise well-intended activities, like the African-American History Month that Marc Elrich referred to, could be regarded as an insult.

The context is important

Additive Approach. The additive approach to multicultural education involves the inclusion of books, units, or courses that add to the existing curriculum but do not change it substantially. It would also be reflected by a teacher who, for

Adding new elements to the existing curriculum

example, decides to teach a unit on the internment of Japanese-Americans in special camps during World War II—a topic often omitted from textbooks. The teacher might base the unit on Yoshiko Uchida's *Journey to Topaz: A Story of the Japanese-American Evacuation* (1971) and Ken Mochizuki's (1993) *Baseball Saved Us*, an easy book that traces how Japanese-Americans imprisoned in a desert internment camp built a baseball field to relieve the monotony. The teacher might also develop materials like those in the Model Student Activity "What Is an American?" (p. 70).

Limitations of the add-on approach

The add-on approach is a legitimate stage in the development of a truly multicultural curriculum, particularly for teachers working on their own. However, it has some limitations. For example, Banks (1989) noted that students may see the units as appendages rather than as an integral part of the overall course of study. Occasional add-on units can provide different cultural perspectives, but they are unlikely to show how the histories and cultures of various groups are interwoven over time.

Transformational Approach. This approach focuses on transforming the existing curriculum within and across subject areas by "the infusion of various perspectives, frames of reference, and content from various groups that will extend students' understanding of the nature, development and complexity of U.S. society" (Banks, 1989, p. 203). In other words, the transformational approach involves restructuring the existing curriculum so that it routinely provides a variety of cultural perspectives.

Transforming the existing curriculum

A transformed curriculum should, in Bank's (1989) view, reflect the process of *multiple acculturation*. Instead of focusing simply on contributions per se, the

Multicultural activities should be an ongoing part of social studies. (© *Marc W. Bernsau/The Image Works*)

MODEL STUDENT ACTIVITY

What Is an American?

This model activity shows a teacher-developed lesson that is based on historical sources.

Student Reading Material

J. Hector St. John de Crevecour was born in France, which is why he had such a long name. However, de Crevecour was an American. He came to the American colonies in 1760, long before the Revolutionary War began, and settled on a farm in New York. In 1782, and after the Revolutionary War was over, de Crevecour wrote a book called *Letters from an American Farmer*. In one of his letters he asked: "What is an American?" It's a question that Americans seem to keep asking themselves.

De Crevecour began one of his letters by telling foreigners what they would see when they came to America. First, he said that they would see a "modern society," instead of one where kings or bishops ruled over Americans. "We have no princes," de Crevecour wrote, "for whom we toil, starve, and bleed. We are the most perfect society now existing in the world."

De Crevecour then tried to answer his own question.

What is this American . . . ? He is either a European or the child of people who came from Europe. He is a strange mixture. You will not find anyone like him in the rest of the world.

The American has left behind his old ways of doing things, and all of his prejudice and customs. Americans have learned new things because they have lived in America, where people from all nations are melted into a new nation. In America, people who work hard will be rewarded as their work improves.

The American is a person who has learned new ideas, and who is able and willing to change. An American is willing to keep learning.

Over the years, America grew in the way that de Crevecour thought it would; many different groups of people came to the United States. However, in 1942,

160 years after de Crevecour had first asked, "What is an American?", the United States was at war with Japan. Some people had come to this land from Japan and had become American citizens. Some of those citizens' children and grandchildren were born here. But during World War II, some Japanese-American families were forced to leave their homes and move to camps in the desert.

How could this happen in a country like America? Most of these people were American citizens. When people began asking why Japanese-Americans were being moved to the desert camps, an American general, John DeWitt, tried to answer de Crevecour's question: What is an American? But DeWitt's answer dealt with people who had come to this country from Japan.

General DeWitt wrote:

A Jap is a Jap. It makes no difference whether they are Americans. Actually they are still Japanese. You cannot change them. You can't change them by giving them a piece of paper that says they have earned the right to be American citizens. (Wish, 1952, p. 511).

Let's compare what you think an American is with de Crevecour and Gen. DeWitt's descriptions.

Questions to Consider

* Why do you think that de Crevecour and DeWitt have different ideas about being an American?
* Almost 160 years went by between the time when de Crevecour and DeWitt tried to answer the question. What might have happened in the meantime?
* Could de Crevecour's and DeWitt's occupation have made a difference in how they felt?
* Do you agree with de Crevecour, DeWitt, or neither of them?

Note: Quoted material has been simplified somewhat for instructional purposes.

"emphasis should be on how the common U.S. culture and society emerged from a complex synthesis and interaction of the diverse cultural elements that originated within the various cultural, racial, ethnic, and religious groups that make up U.S. society" (p. 161).

Social Action Approach. This approach builds on the transformational approach by adding dimensions that ask students to make decisions and take appropriate actions in light of their decisions. Banks (1989) contends that traditional schooling often fosters political passivity and socializes students to accept existing ideologies and practices rather than helping them to become skilled participants in social change. As Banks states, "to participate effectively in democratic social change, students must be taught social criticism and must be helped to understand the inconsistency between our ideals and social realities, the work that must be done to close this gap, and how students can, as individuals and groups, influence the social and political systems in U.S. society" (p. 205).

Moving from knowledge to social action

Assessing Multicultural Activities

The four approaches to multicultural curriculum that Banks described reflect one way of looking at multicultural literacy. The key element in all of them involves the nature of culture itself.

The Cultural Pyramid. Artifacts, relics, and foodstuffs are among the most visible and readily available aspects of a culture. At the same time, they are among the *least* significant aspects of the total cultural mosaic. Figure 3.2 shows

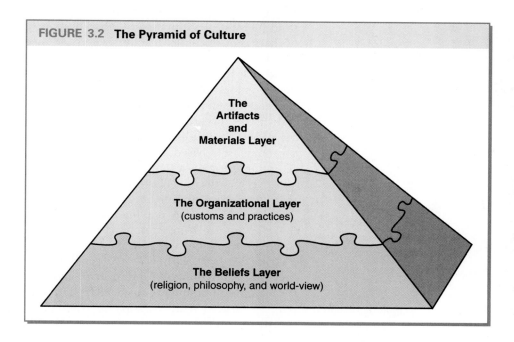

FIGURE 3.2 The Pyramid of Culture

The
Artifacts
and
Materials Layer

The Organizational Layer
(customs and practices)

The Beliefs Layer
(religion, philosophy, and world-view)

that the basis of every culture rests in its fundamental beliefs and attitudes—in its cosmology or world-view. A second component is reflected by the way the culture has organized itself—the organizational layer—and by the customs and practices the culture follows. Those customs and practices usually reflect the group's underlying beliefs. At the top of the cultural pyramid are the materials and artifacts the culture uses, including the foods it considers suitable for consumption.

Consider, for example, that Jews who follow the kosher tradition do not serve meat and dairy products on the same dish. This practice reflects the organizational layer—the middle layer—of the cultural pyramid. The reason for serving meat and dairy products separately is rooted in the Jewish faith, in the belief layer of culture. Because of their beliefs, kosher Jewish families have two sets of china and kitchen utensils, one used exclusively for dairy products and another for meat and other foods. The dishes themselves reflect the artifacts and materials layer of culture.

Considered in isolation, the two sets of china in kosher Jewish families or the practice of serving meat and dairy products separately may seem nothing more than quaint customs or religious and cultural oddities. The same would be true of the Amish's refusal to use electrically powered appliances or to drive automobiles. In any multicultural activity, it is essential that students understand how a culture's artifacts, customs, and practices are related to the underlying basis in belief. If those relationships and connections are *not* made, children can easily regard unfamiliar groups as cultural eccentrics.

Multicultural Activities with Substance

Despite some questionable activities that are passed off as multicultural education, there are legitimate and educationally defensible ways to deal with some of them. For example, teachers who have their students build a tepee or models of other cultural artifacts must make certain that students clearly understand that they are re-creating historical or cultural events, and imperfectly at that. For food-related activities, recognize that in many cultures the preparation and presentation of food is often more important than eating. For tortillas or Indian corn bread, for example, let students experience what it is like to grind the corn into flour—as some people in Mexico and some Native Americans still do today. Be advised, however, that grinding corn by hand is boring and tedious; and it takes a long time to grind enough corn to make a single tortilla. Students may become frustrated at their lack of progress, but with that frustration may come a new appreciation of what some people do to obtain food.

Likewise, instead of serving canned spaghetti, consider having your students make spaghetti from scratch, as many Italian-Americans do. All it requires is some flour, an egg, and a little water kneaded together on a clean surface, like a clean desktop. No bowls or utensils are needed except for a rolling pin, a knife to cut the dough into thin strips, and a large pot of water in which to cook it. (Note that homemade spaghetti is flat, not round like the commercially prepared product.) While their pasta is drying, one group of students can research the recipe and then prepare a tomato-based sauce characteristic of southern

Italy. Another group can research and make a clear or cream-based sauce like those served in northern Italy. In this activity, cookbooks—the Time-Life series is wonderful for this—can become reference books. There is a world of difference between what children can learn from the spaghetti activity described here, and what they can learn from heating and eating canned spaghetti.

We've dealt with food-related activities at length because this is an area in which we've seen too many abuses. The rule of thumb, we think, should be: if you wish to use food-related multicultural activities, do them in educationally defensible ways. If that takes too much time—and such activities can require a lot of classroom time—then don't do them at all. Multicultural education clearly demands unusual sensitivity to and respect for the peoples of all cultures.

Respecting Religious Diversity

Teaching *about* religions

Some public school teachers mistakenly believe they cannot mention religion in their classrooms. If that were the case, it would be impossible to teach about any of the world's religions—Islam, Hinduism, Buddhism, Shintoism, and so forth. Not only have the courts sustained teachers' (and schools') rights to teach *about* religion, but they have also indicated that information about religion is necessary to a good education. This means that you could do an in-depth analysis of Christian and non-Christian religions if you wished to, so long as it is relevant to the course of study. It also means that teaching about religion should be handled as objectively as possible, and without any suggestion that teachers are attempting to sway their students' beliefs.

You may recall that because of their religious beliefs, the parents of two students in Mary Jane Blanchard's class had requested that their children be excused from Halloween activities involving witches and goblins. In addition, Melissa's parents had requested that she be excused from saying the Pledge of Allegiance during morning exercises. In both of these instances, the underlying issue involves the parents' and childs' rights to the free exercise of their religious beliefs under the First Amendment.

How did Mary Jane Blanchard handle the parental requests? In the case of Halloween observations, the school board had previously passed a policy banning black cats, witches, and symbols of the occult from all school-based activities, including Halloween. By virtue of this policy, excusing Amy and Melissa was unnecessary; Ms. Blanchard adjusted activities for her entire class accordingly. More and more schools are adopting policies of this nature, but in schools that do not have them, we recommend that you honor the parent's request. For other questions of this nature, especially attempts to censor certain books, most schools have established procedures for determining whether the protested content or activities serve an overriding and compelling educational purpose.

Court rulings At one level, the request to excuse Melissa from saying the Pledge of Allegiance was also a kind of nonissue. Over fifty years ago the Supreme Court ruled that students cannot be compelled to say the Pledge of Allegiance. But for questions about whether teachers can ask students to stand during the Pledge (even if they do not say it)—where standing can be regarded as a means for honoring something—or whether teachers can permit the student to leave the classroom during the Pledge, the answer is: it depends. The Supreme Court has not ruled on either question, but many federal circuit and state courts have. The problem, according to our school law specialists, is that the various courts have not ruled consistently one way or the other. This effectively means that what is or is not legal depends on the rulings (or absence of rulings or local policies) in the legal jurisdiction where you teach.

Excusing Melissa from saying the Pledge was problematic for Ms. Blanchard in the sense that she pondered long about how she would present Melissa's nonparticipation to the rest of the class. She finally decided to say, "The Pledge of Allegiance is a way of showing our respect for the flag and what it stands for, but some people's religious beliefs—like Melissa's—do not permit them to say the Pledge. We are going to respect Melissa's beliefs too." It turned out that what Mary Jane had worried about was a bigger problem for her than for her students. Melissa stood for the Pledge without being asked to, but she did not speak the words. For Melissa's classmates, this procedure had been going on since they were in kindergarten and was nothing out of the ordinary.

The basic requirement for dealing with the ethnic, religious, and cultural diversity in classrooms today is a healthy respect for each individual's heritage, including the teacher's, and for the deeply held beliefs associated with that heritage. For those of us who teach, diversity in all of its forms demands that we demonstrate an honest and supportive sensitivity to what individuals bring with them to the classroom.

COMMENTARY: The Scope of Diversity

Among the myths in education is the notion that diversity occurs only in classrooms inhabited mainly by African-Americans. Lest you believe this, we suggest that plenty of diversity exists in suburbia too.

When I (Welton) first accepted the offer to teach sixth grade in the Quaker Ridge School in Scarsdale, New York—one of the wealthiest school districts in the country—I could not help but think what a delight it would be to teach those "smart little rich kids." I had from twenty-seven to thirty-six students in each class I had taught previously in rural Ohio, but in Scarsdale, my largest class had nineteen students and the smallest, nine. This, I thought, was going to be a teacher's dream, a kind of heaven on earth.

You can probably see where this is leading. It wasn't long into the school year before I found that some of my preconceived notions were incorrect. The idea that these students were "smart little rich kids" was one of the first to fall by the wayside. None of my children's parents were on welfare, and the free lunch program was nonexistent. However, I soon discovered that in wealthy communities like Scarsdale, many parents send their children to private schools. Although most of my students lived in comfortable homes, almost half of them were the children of housekeepers, chauffeurs, maids, and cooks and were often restricted to cramped "help's quarters" within the larger homes. Even though many of my students came from the higher end of the economic spectrum, an almost equal number came from the lower end; there were few middle-class students, economically speaking. In addition, and even though most of my students didn't need to worry where their next meal was coming from, they were neither smarter nor any less intelligent than the students I had taught previously.

In three years of teaching in rural Ohio, I had not encountered an African-American or an Asian-American student. This was not the case in Scarsdale. Three African-American students and four Asian-American students were among that sea of fifty or so shining faces I saw each day. One African-American student whom I especially remember was Clarence, whose parents were both prominent physicians. Clarence was among the brightest students I have ever encountered, but homework was a lost cause with him; he didn't think he needed it, and based on his performance without it, I eventually agreed.

My four Asian-American students performed as the stereotype says they will: they worked harder and more conscientiously than most of the other students that I dealt with that year. At one point I asked one of them if she ever relaxed, but the blank look suggested that I didn't understand her cultural mores.

Yet another incident indicated how provincial my perspective on diversity had been. While teaching in Ohio, I had the unenviable task of organizing the school's assemblies. We sang patriotic songs at Thanksgiving, Christmas carols at Christmas, and so forth. Upon moving to Scarsdale, I made the mistake of mentioning my prior experience handling assemblies, and they once again became my responsibility. The Thanksgiving program went as well as such programs usually do, but when I sat down with the music teacher (and pianist) to select the carols for the Christmas program, I was informed that (1) we were planning a "Winter Holiday Program," and (2) my old list of carols—which included "Oh Come All Ye Faithful" and the like—would be inappropriate in a largely Jewish community. We quickly discarded the religious carols and sang "Winter Wonderland" and "Santa Claus Is Coming to Town" instead. However, this incident caused me to reflect on how many non-Christian families in Ohio I may have unintentionally offended.

The point is that every classroom and school reflects diversity, even when you may not expect it (or should know better).

Physical and Emotional Diversity

Responding to the needs of physically and emotionally disabled students, like James and apparently Heather (from Mary Jane Blanchard's class), almost always involves additional funding, which necessarily means some form of administrative involvement. A key element for children with physical disabilities, although not those with emotional disabilities, lies in removing the barriers that

Removing barriers

hinder their physical access to buildings, classrooms, and other ancillary services. Stairways, drinking fountains, and rest room facilities can still pose problems for children with physically disabling conditions, but many schools have modified their facilities to accommodate them.

There are also some no-cost, commonsense things that teachers can do to make life easier for physically challenged students. These include things like seating sight- and hearing-impaired students toward the front of the classroom. This also includes seating students with physical disabilities near the door, so they don't have to thread their way through a roundabout route to reach their desks. Such seemingly minor accommodations can have important consequences for children with physical impairments.

Seeking help

When we talked with Ms. Blanchard about Heather, the student with the (apparent) emotionally disabling condition who we described earlier, Mary Jane said,

> I just didn't know what to do about Heather. . . . I thought about her all the time. I know that I wasn't trained to handle this kind of problem. At first, I tried creating some special assignments for Heather—really interesting activities, you know—but she would just sit there with her coat pulled over her head.
>
> I got so frustrated that I finally called the school district's Diagnostic and Counseling Center. They agreed to work with her for an hour every week, but things didn't change. Then I complained again, so the counselors began working with her for an hour every day. We were finally able to obtain some medical testing, which indicated that Heather had a chemical imbalance that had led to a form of depression. It took a while for them to get her medication adjusted correctly, but today she acts like a perfectly normal fourth grader.

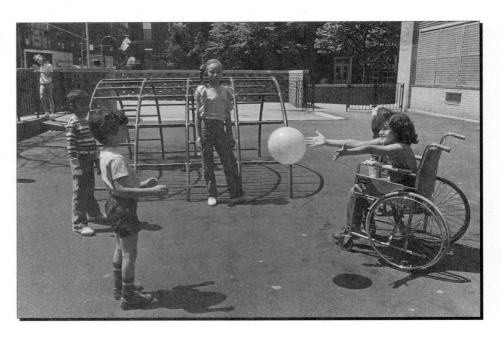

Diversity is the norm in most classrooms today. (© *Laimute E. Druskis/Stock Boston*)

Helping students with emotionally disabling conditions (including, in Heather's case, an underlying medical problem) is often difficult, in part because few teachers have the skills and training needed to cope with severe emotional disabilities. The situation can become more complicated if the children's problems are caused by child abuse. Not all learning disabilities are the result of abuse or emotional problems, of course, but sudden changes in academic performance are often symptoms of underlying emotional (or sometimes physical) problems. Because there are so few instructional options that a teacher can use, the key lies in identifying and orchestrating the school and community support services that can deal with emotional disabilities, as Ms. Blanchard did for Heather. Also, each time you encounter children with emotional disabilities, you will undoubtedly be reminded of how complex and fragile our emotions really are.

Instructional Diversity

You are almost sure to have students, like some of those in Mary Jane Blanchard's class, who are *at least* one-half year below grade level, or who have difficulty remembering what they read, but can remember almost everything they hear. You *may* also have students who excel academically and are considered gifted, but who quickly become bored with routine schoolwork. You are just as likely to have one or more students who have "high structure needs," and thus have difficulty dealing with independent problem solving and unstructured or open-ended activities. You may also have students who abhor small-group work and who cannot wait until you tell them exactly what they need to know. Then, too, you are very likely to have students who thrive on working in small-groups and who cannot wait until you stop talking. Unlike some of the preexisting disabling conditions that we dealt with in the previous sections, at least some of the expectations we have noted here can be accommodated with variations in your instructional program, as we describe in the next section.

Accommodating Educational Diversity

Educational diversity is a category we've created to include students, like some of those in Mary Jane Blanchard's classroom, who have nonethnic and nonculturally related conditions that influence what and how they learn. Those conditions can influence the kind of instruction a teacher offers, the form in which he or she offers that instruction, and the way in which students respond to it.

Cooperative Learning

Cooperative learning is an approach to instruction in which students deal with learning tasks cooperatively, usually in small groups. The teacher acts as a consultant and other students serve as resources. Each individual is accountable for the group's effort, and all group members must learn the material in question. Typically, everyone in the group receives a common grade. Students who goof off or don't contribute to the group's effort are usually subjected to intense peer pressure, which is often more effective than pressure from teachers, because the group's success (or lack thereof) depends on contributions from every member. The cumulative research findings (Johnson & Johnson, 1987) suggest that cooperative learning results in higher achievement, enhanced self-esteem, and improved attitudes toward teachers, other students, and school itself.

Cooperative learning can provide a working environment in which all students can contribute according to their abilities, but without rejecting the individual work ethic that has prevailed in classrooms for many years. Group members must still work hard, sometimes harder than they would working alone. What cooperative learning does do is reject applying the competitive, individualistic model (often associated with the work ethic) to cooperative group enterprises. It all boils down to a question of "fit." The cooperative model should be applied to tasks where students are expected to work cooperatively, and the competitive, individualistic model should be applied to tasks that students are expected to deal with on their own. Trying to mix the two gives rise to problems and probably explains why legitimate small-group work has often played second fiddle in many schools. In the final analysis, few things are more basic than working successfully with others.

The Jigsaw Method. A group-learning procedure associated with cooperative learning is called the *jigsaw method.* Its name derives from an analogy to a jigsaw puzzle, which is not complete until all the separate pieces are in place.

Imagine a situation where Mary Jane Blanchard divides her twenty-five-member class into five heterogeneous teams of five students each. She gives each team the same assignment: to produce a pictorial collage that shows examples of, and clearly distinguishes among, goods and services in five different areas—health, food, transportation, housing, and education. Each team member is responsible for one area. For example, Student A on each team has health, Student B has food, and so forth. Each task (e.g., health-related goods and services) corresponds to a separate puzzle piece, and the team assignment (the collage) corresponds to the jigsaw puzzle itself.

Each team will need to meet initially to clarify the assignment. Then the teams disband temporarily, and the members convene in task-alike groups. All the students working with health-related goods and services meet together, all food-related members meet as a group, and so forth. The task-alike groups consider such things as the kinds of pictures that would show their respective areas, and whether a picture of a nurse, for example, would show a good or a service. When the job-alike group members are certain what they are after, they can begin working either as a group or, in this instance, individually, seeking pictures from magazines supplied by Ms. Blanchard. Mary Jane can also provide guidance and support throughout the activity, because cooperative learning is not a technique in which students must work totally on their own.

After each team member has completed his or her task, the original team reassembles to complete the larger assignment, the collage. The problem the teams must deal with now, if they have not done so already, is to figure out how they can present their information so that the goods and services for each area are displayed clearly and separately from the other areas. The complete collages are hung around the room and shared during the debriefing. Also considered during the debriefing are the problems that the teams encountered in completing their tasks and how they dealt with them.

A less-structured alternative

The jigsaw method is a highly structured approach to cooperative learning. A less-structured yet equally viable approach involves assigning projects to teams of students and then allowing the teams to work out their own procedures, thus eliminating the formal task-alike groups. Regardless of the approach that a teacher takes, the problems that students encounter as they work together must be considered together with whatever content they learn.

Learning Style

When you are faced with learning new material, would you rather read a really good explanation or listen to someone explain it? Or when trying to determine the correct spelling of a word, do you write it three different ways and pick the one that looks right, or do you sound it out as best you can and let it go at that? When you study, can you have the stereo on or must you have absolute quiet? And when asked to write a paper on something, do you need precise instructions on how you should do it—absolute minimum length, including the number of paragraphs, type font, width of margins, and so on—or are you more willing "to go for it" until you think you've met the assignment? (Grading standards will make a difference, of course.)

Accommodating personal preferences in learning

Learning style is a generic term that refers to various personal preferences for the conditions under which people like to learn something (see Dunn & Dunn, 1992). The diversity in learning style can include both cultural and personal factors. Many teachers, for example, are highly visual learners; they prefer to read something as opposed to listening to a verbal explanation about it. Many highly visual learners remember where certain words appear on a page, and many use the "write the word three ways and then pick the one that looks right" approach to spelling. Fewer teachers are auditory learners, like Mary Jane Blanchard's students, Trisha and Miguel. Both students have difficulty remembering what they read but, in some cases, can recall explanations with the same precision that visual learners remember where words are on a page. Problems can arise when visually oriented teachers fail to provide the verbal explanations that sound-oriented learners rely on. As Ms. Blanchard says, "I sometimes explain stuff that seems obvious, but I know at least some of my kids need that explanation." The fine line that teachers must determine, of course, is when they have explained something in enough depth to satisfy their auditory learners but without boring their visual learners in the process.

Personal preferences related to learning style can be categorized as follows:

Factors that influence learning style

* Environmental—includes factors such as studying with music or in complete silence
* Sociological—includes factors such as working alone or in groups
* Emotional—includes factors such as working on open-ended or highly defined assignments
* Physiological—includes factors such as studying while standing, sitting, or lying on the floor

* Psychological—includes factors such as preference for visual or auditory sources.

A sample learning style inventory is presented in Part 1 of the Resource Handbook.

Multiple Intelligences

Just as some of us may have preferred learning styles, so some of us are artistically, musically, or athletically inclined and others of us are not. Why can some people play a musical instrument without lessons, whereas for others it is a lifelong struggle? These abilities or inclinations have become the focus of a growing body of theory and research related to multiple intelligences.

Traditionally intelligence has been regarded as a single, inherited entity that enabled people to learn almost anything, provided it was presented in an appropriate way (see Gardner, 1993). Anyone who has taken traditional intelligence (IQ) tests know that they place a premium on one's ability to manipulate words, what Gardner (1993) calls "linguistic intelligence," and on one's ability to solve logic or mathematical problems, or what Gardner calls "logical-mathematical" intelligence. A growing number of researchers today believe that there are multiple intelligences, each quite independent of each other and each with its own strengths and constraints. For example, in addition to linguistic and logical-mathematical intelligence, Gardner suggests that there are at least five other identifiable intelligences. These include: musical, spatial, bodily-kinetic, interpersonal, and intrapersonal intelligences.

The ancient Greeks viewed intelligence as a multifaceted phenomenon that included shrewd intelligence, analytic intelligence, aesthetic intelligence, spiritual intelligence, and others (Rosenthal, 1971). The first point is that the concept of multiple intelligences is not new, but it has been ignored or minimized until recently. The second point is that differences in learning style could reflect differences in underlying intelligences. The third point is that the diversity reflected in multiple intelligences could mean that there are multiple ways to teach something (not just one). The implications are almost mind-boggling, but much more work remains to be done before it is possible to identify teaching techniques that are appropriate for specific kinds of intelligence.

An expanded view of intelligence

Accommodating Students with High Structure Needs

Another aspect of learning style is reflected by Chen Lee, one of Mary Jane Blanchard's gifted students. You may recall that Chen Lee has what we referred to as "high structure needs." This simply means that Chen Lee and other students like her are very uncomfortable in unstructured situations. They usually want to know what task is to be done, exactly how that task should be done, when it must be done by, and in some instances, how they will know when they are finished. Children like Chen Lee stand in contrast to students who have low structure needs, who can tolerate ambiguity in the tasks they are expected to do, and who often prefer to decide things for themselves.

Two aspects about children's perceived need for structure are worth noting here. First, the need for structure is apparently not linked to intelligence (as traditionally defined). Chen Lee is a gifted student, but the same needs for structure appear among normal and low-ability students. A second aspect about the apparent need for "structure" is that it is a one-way relationship. Children with low structure needs may prefer open-ended and unstructured tasks, but they can also tolerate highly organized assignments. However, children like Chen Lee, who have high structure needs, are often frustrated with open-ended tasks. Therefore, if you are going to err, do so in favor of providing more structure, not less, to the tasks you assign. Or you may want to use your students' structure needs as a basis for creating groups (which will be heterogeneous in terms of sex, ethnicity, etc.). This will enable you to provide special guidance to your "high structure need" groups, which may really need it, but without stifling the creativity of your other groups.

Summary

Four factors have contributed to the phenomenal diversity in classrooms today: (1) desegregation, (2) increased immigration, (3) rapidly growing minority populations, and (4) growing recognition of the ethnicity of students who were in classrooms all along. Of these factors, the end of segregation has two dimensions; the first dimension involves ending the practice of segregating schools along racial lines, and the other involves removing students with handicapping conditions from separate classrooms and returning them to the mainstream of public education, regular classrooms.

Multicultural education has become the major means for recognizing the multiple cultures and ethnicities that exist in almost every classroom. Multicultural education is a multifaceted effort aimed primarily at helping all children, regardless of ethnicity, gender, disabilities, or social class, to understand and appreciate events and people from various points of view.

In this chapter, we have identified several issues related to the diversity you will face in your classroom, not the least of which is the difficulty that schools face in moving away from a one-size-fits-all educational model. Just the thought of providing instruction geared to divergent learning styles or a particular intelligence, for example, will panic some people. History suggests that in movements of this kind, there will be a series of refinements, each of which offers more specific guidance to classroom teachers. However, history also suggests that there will be some gross errors, some backtracking, and some people who go overboard or use the movement to serve their own ends. As a teacher, you will be pushed and pulled in various directions and will be told that you should do this instead of that. Surviving in this environment probably requires two things above all others: a healthy dose of thoughtfulness and common sense.

Suggested Activities

1. Design a poster or bulletin board that uses a metaphor to describe our multicultural society. Consider pizza as a possibility, but do not restrict yourself to food-related products. Then determine in what respects your description might be distorted.
2. Determine which of the following statements best describes the U.S. culture: (1) The whole is greater than the sum of its parts. (2) The whole is equal to the sum of its parts. (3) There is no whole, just parts.
3. The need for teachers to respond to diversity in their classrooms has received much attention, but there is growing concern that this emphasis may be too one-sided. Don't teachers have personal rights that should be acknowledged and respected just as much as the rights of their students? Should teachers who do not wish to celebrate holidays be forced to do so anyhow? And what about teachers who do not wish to say the Pledge? What kind of role model are they presenting to students? Either individually or in small groups, establish a clear position on these questions.
4. Obtain a fifth-grade social studies text. Using the index entries for "Native Americans" and one other

identifiable ethnic group as a guide, assess the overall balance of the way the two groups are treated.

5. There is a widespread belief that schooling should be the same everywhere, and that providing special programs for exceptional students is somehow undemocratic. To what extent, if any, does this feeling conflict with the principle that every child has the right to an education appropriate to his or her needs and abilities?

6. Teachers who use cooperative learning groups extensively often find that in a class where everyone receives the same instructions, some groups work well while others flounder helplessly. What factors may account for this, and what steps would you take to correct the problem?

Suggested Readings

James A. Banks. (1997). *Educating citizens in a multicultural society.* New York: Teachers College Press. This paperback reflects Banks's latest contribution to the multicultural education literature, and directs special attention to the relationship between multicultural education and citizenship education.

Daniel Hallahan & James Kauffman. (1997). *Exceptional learners.* Boston: Allyn & Bacon. This special education text takes the position that in dealing with exceptional children, the emphasis should be on their abilities, not their handicapping conditions.

Susan S. Ellis & Susan F. Whelan. (1990). *Cooperative learning: Getting started.* Jefferson City, Mo.: Scholastic. In less than 100 pages, a public school staff development specialist and a teacher provide a step-by-step guide to using cooperative learning techniques.

Eugene Garcia. (1994). *Understanding and meeting the challenge of student cultural diversity.* Boston: Houghton Mifflin. This book provides excellent treatments of the different types of diversity in classrooms today and ways in which teachers can respond appropriately to them.

Howard Gardner. (1993). *Frames of mind.* New York: HarperCollins Basic Books. This is the book that sparked the growing interest in multiple intelligences.

Geneva Gay. (1991). Culturally diverse students and social studies. In J. A. Shaver (Ed.), *Handbook of research on social studies teaching and learning* (pp. 157–174). New York: Macmillan. The chapter is an excellent source for recent research on multicultural education.

Answers to Cultural Awareness Activity

1. f   His most well-known novel is *Native Son*.
2. d   The college was called the Daytona Educational and Industrial School; it was for African-American girls.
3. a   She was jailed for her actions in the Pecan Shellers' strike in 1937.
4. l   She was a representative from Hawaii; the only Asian-American woman to serve in Congress.
5. c   (No answer provided in original.)
6. g   Helped organize the grape boycott with Cesar Chavez.
7. j   Best known for her recent novel, *Ceremony*.
8. h   Fought state and federal authorities for land grants to Hispanics, which were legally protected by the Treaty of Guadalupe.
9. m   Best known for his book, *Before the Mayflower*.
10. b   Publishes widely in both scholarly and popular literature, such as *Ebony*.
11. n   (No answer provided in original.)
12. i   Former Japanese-American internment camp prisoner who has published numerous stories.
13. k   Her most well-known novel is *Their Eyes Were Watching God*.
14. e   Best-known book is *Occupied America*.

Part 2

Building a Framework for Teaching Social Studies

Part Two examines three elements of the overall framework for teaching social studies. This includes how social studies programs are conceived, which we address in Chapter 4, and how special topics, such as global and environmental education, are woven into social studies programs, which we examine in Chapter 5. In Chapter 6, we explore the increasingly important task of developing character and teaching values.

There are literally hundreds of ways in which you could teach social studies, but, as we explain in Chapter 4, "How Social Studies Programs Are Organized," this variety is *not* reflected in most of the programs you are likely to encounter. Chapter 4 focuses on common social studies programs—especially the expanding environments approach, the most common program of all. It also examines alternative program formats, both past and present.

In Chapter 5, "Weaving Special Topics into Social Studies Programs," we examine how you might explore topics or themes such as global and environmental education, consumer education, law-related education, economic education, and gender equity education. Most of these topics extend across grade levels, and in almost all cases, reflect a K–12 emphasis.

In turn-of-the-century schools, *character education* was used to describe efforts to mold children into responsible citizens. Over the years that term fell into disfavor, for reasons we describe in Chapter 6, "Developing Character and Values." The major section on building character in this chapter, as well as our inclusion of the term *Character* in the title, reflects changes in the broader society that are imposing new demands on what schools and teachers do.

4 How Social Studies Programs Are Organized

Key Questions

* What topics are taught in social studies, and when?
* What are common patterns for organizing social studies programs?
* How important is sequence to a social studies program?
* How does the nature of social studies influence the creation of social studies programs?

Key Ideas

* The predominant organizational pattern for elementary social studies programs is the expanding-environments pattern.
* Developmental considerations, including how children develop concepts of time, space, and distance, influence the organization of social studies programs—or should.
* Traditional social studies programs usually examine various facets of a topic.
* Alternative social studies programs usually examine various facets of a concept or idea.
* Because social studies does not have the inherent structure of a subject like mathematics, teachers often have more flexibility in designing a social studies program than they realize.

Introduction: On Framing the Constitution

New York is one of almost twenty states, including California, Texas, and Virginia, where social studies programs are determined primarily at the state level. This sometimes means that what gets included in, or is omitted from, the state's social studies curriculum may depend on how successfully individuals or groups can lobby for their cause at the state level.

This phenomenon became apparent when the New York Board of Regents (the state board of education) was considering the adoption of a new, multicultural social studies program. As one aspect of the proposed program, students would be expected to learn that the framers of the U.S. Constitution were inspired by two factors: the European Enlightenment, and the Iroquois Confederation—the alliance of seven tribes of indigenous people from New York and the surrounding areas.

New York State experience

Most historians readily acknowledge the Enlightenment's impact on the framers of our constitution. The Enlightenment reflected the growing belief that common people were capable of deciding the common good. However, no social studies program we know of has included the Iroquois Confederacy as a contributing factor to the Constitution. Some people in New York apparently questioned this also and began asking, "How does anything—not just the Iroquois Confederation—get into the (state-mandated) social studies program?"

Jack Weatherford contends in his book *Indian Givers* (1988; see also Johansen, 1982) that the Iroquois helped the colonists resolve the dilemma of how to join the thirteen colonies into one country without each one giving up its powers. A confederacy, which is a voluntary association of separate states, does that. The United States actually operated as a confederacy during the period between the Revolutionary War in 1776 and 1789, when the Constitution was ratified. In 1988, Congress passed a joint resolution acknowledging the historical debt that the United States owed "to the Iroquois Confederacy and other Indian nations for their demonstration of enlightened democratic principles of Government."

Who's history?

Whether the Iroquois Confederacy did or did not influence the framers of the Constitution was one aspect of an often heated debate in New York between supporters of the new multicultural curriculum and others who argued that history was being rewritten to serve political purposes. The controversy grew even more heated when people learned that the Iroquois's contributions to the Constitution were included in New York's new social studies program after a delegation of Iroquois had visited Thomas Sobol, the state's commissioner of education (see Starna, 1990). Armed with the congressional resolution, the Iroquois apparently convinced the commissioner that New York's social studies program should be changed—a decision that would ultimately affect the 2.5 million school children who live in that state.

A growing trend

The issue here is: Is the failure to include the alleged Iroquois contribution to the Constitution a glaring omission that should be changed (in New York and elsewhere), or is this an instance where certain predisposed individuals are guilty of rewriting history to make it come out the way they want it to? We mean no disrespect to the Iroquois, because our purpose here is to suggest that decisions about the social studies you will be expected to teach are increasingly being made at the state level, and not in local school districts as was once the case. This incident in New York is not an exception, because similar situations (usually involving different content) have occurred elsewhere (see Cornbleth & Waugh, 1995).

In this chapter, we examine the organization of contemporary elementary and middle-school social studies programs and other factors that often influence them. Throughout the chapter, we will use *program* and *curriculum* interchangeably. Authorities sometimes distinguish between the two, usually using *curriculum* to indicate the broad framework within which teachers may develop their own *programs,* yet in many schools today you will hear expressions such as "our social studies program" or "our map skills program." Because *program* seems to be edging out *curriculum* in common usage, we follow that convention in this chapter.

In the next section, we present the predominant curriculum pattern for elementary and middle-school social studies programs. We follow that with an examination of several alternative curriculum patterns and conclude with a sampling of factors that can influence the way social studies programs are organized.

The Dominant Curriculum Pattern: Expanding Environments

Figure 4.1 illustrates the organizational approach to social studies that was created in the mid-1920s, became increasingly popular during the 1940s and 1950s, and continues to dominate programs throughout the country today. You may find occasional variations on the *expanding-environments* approach to social studies, some of which we describe later in this chapter, but for all practical purposes it is a national curriculum (see Joyce, Little, and Wronski, 1991). This organizational pattern is also known as *expanding horizons, widening horizons,* or the *expanding communities of man.*

The organizing principle

The organizing principle for the expanding-environments approach is a mixture of physical and conceptual distance. The sequence begins with the environments (or communities) that are physically closest to the child, such as the home, school, and neighborhood. It then progresses through environments that are successively more distant: the local community, the state (or region), the nation, and finally the world. Because all of us live in these environments simultaneously, the assignment of certain environments to certain grade levels is done for instructional simplicity and convenience.

FIGURE 4.1 **Expanding-Environments Approach to Social Studies (K-6)**

Grade 6: World—history, geography, cultures
Grade 5: Nation (U.S.)—geography, history, cultures
Grade 4: State history, geographic regions
Grade 3: Communities—local and regional
Grade 2: Neighborhoods
K–Grade 1: Family & school

Child

A Composite K–8 Program

When the expanding environments principle is translated into an actual curriculum, the result is similar to the composite program shown in Table 4.1. The table, which reflects the commonalities among four, widely used textbook series, shows the common topics, the typical sequence of units, and the social studies disciplines emphasized within the units.

Table 4.1 **Composite Social Studies Curriculum (K–8)**

Grade	Focus/Title	Typical Sequence/ Unit Topics	Dominant Discipline
K	*Getting Started*	Learning About My World	The social science disciplines are integrated throughout all units.
		Families	
		Community Helpers	
		Transportation and Communication	
		Weather and Seasons	(Meteorology)
		Special Days	None
1	*Families, Homes, and Neighborhoods*	Our Earth	Geography/Map Skills
		Families Meet Their Needs: Food, Clothing, Shelter	The social science disciplines are integrated throughout all units.
		Families at Work	
		The Neighborhood	
		Holidays Around the World	Anthropology/History
2	*Neighborhoods and Communities*	Exploring Our Earth	Geography/Map Skills
		Urban, Suburban, and Farm Communities	The social science disciplines are integrated throughout all units.
		Communities—Today and Yesterday	
		Transportation and Communication	
		Communities Celebrate Holidays	Anthropology/History
3	*Communities and Resources, Here and There*	Map and Globe Skills	Geography/Map Skills
		Living in Different Communities	Integrated
		Governing Communities: Making Rules and Laws	Political Science
		How Communities Change	Integrated
		Farm and Ranch Communities (Dairy Farm, Wheat Farm, etc.)	Integrated

(continued on next page)

Table 4.1   Composite Social Studies Curriculum (K–8) (*continued*)

Grade	Focus/Title	Typical Sequence/ Unit Topics	Dominant Discipline
		Communities Around the World (Desert, Forest, Grassland)	Geography/History
4	*Regions Near and Far*	Our Earth	Geography/Map Skills
		Regional Studies Emphasis:	Geography
		Units on Forest, Plains,	Geography
		Mountain, and Desert Regions, e.g., The Pacific Northwest, The Central Plains, etc.	Geography
		Working Together Around the World	Economics
		State History Emphasis:	
		Major Resources and Land Forms	Geography
		Early Settlements	History
		Governing Our State	Political Science
		Citizens Who Helped Our State Grow	History
		Our State Today	None/Integrated
5	*Our United States*	Map and Globe Skills	Geography/Map Skills
		Founding the New World	History
		Building a Nation (through the Revolutionary War)	History
		Establishing a Government	History/Political Science
		A Divided Nation (Civil War)	History
		Our Nation Expands (Westward Movement)	History
		Our Nation Today	History
		Regional Geography of the United States: Units on New England, the Mountain States, the Pacific States, etc., Canada and Latin America	Geography
			Geography/History
		Map, Globe, and Graph Skills	Geography
6	*Our World Today*	**World History Emphasis:**	
		Classical Civilizations: Egypt, Greece, Rome	History
		The Middle Ages	History

(*continued on next page*)

Table 4.1 **Composite Social Studies Curriculum (K–8)** (*continued*)

Grade	Focus/Title	Typical Sequence/Unit Topics	Dominant Discipline
		Our Changing World (Industrial Revolution through Twentieth Century)	History
		Eastern Hemisphere Emphasis: Our World Today: Units on Europe, Africa and the Middle East, Asia, and Australia	Geography and history are integrated in all units.
		Western Hemisphere Emphasis: Early Beginnings: Inca, Aztecs	History and geography are integrated in all units.
		Our Neighbors to the South: Units on Mexico, South and Central American nations, the Caribbean Basin, etc.	
		Our Neighbors to the North: Units on the St. Lawrence Seaway, the Canadian Provinces, etc.	History and geography are integrated in all units.
7	*State History, World History, or World Geography*	Early Times to the Present	History
		Selected Civilizations	History
		Regions of the World	Geography
8	*U.S. History*	See Grade 5 except for the geography	History

Scope and Sequence

Kindergarten.   Most social studies programs for kindergarten are designed to familiarize children with their developing selves and their new environment—the school. No social science discipline predominates in kindergarten programs, and the sequence of topics has no particular logic. And although the "Special Days" or holidays unit is listed last in kindergarten and in Grades 1 and 2, teachers often draw on it extensively throughout the year, in what is usually referred to as the "holiday curriculum."

Focus: Self and School

Focus: School and family

Grade 1.   First-grade programs typically focus on the family, the school, and the neighborhood. The social science disciplines are usually integrated throughout, although consumer economics often gets more attention than the others. The emphasis on holidays also continues.

Grade 2. Second-grade programs traditionally focus on neighborhoods, but this focus is often broadened to include communities and "community helpers." This broadening has occurred, in part, because of how neighborhoods have changed. Fifty years ago, the residents of a neighborhood were often ethnically similar (Polish, Italian, Chinese, etc.), and many neighborhoods had stable populations and well-established social systems; often a person was born, got married, and eventually died in the same neighborhood. As the U.S. population has become increasingly mobile, the stability of many neighborhoods—along with the social control and cohesiveness that they once enjoyed—has largely disappeared. Thus in many areas today, neighborhoods are no longer cultural enclaves but simply places where one resides.

Second-grade programs usually deal with different types of neighborhoods and communities—rural, urban, and suburban. Identifying connections between the students' local community and communities elsewhere in the nation or world is often the focus of the last unit.

Focus: Neighborhoods

Grade 3. After an obligatory first unit on maps and globes, the emphasis in third-grade programs turns to communities in the generic sense of the term. The initial focus is usually on communities in different environments, and then shifts to an emphasis on political, economic, and social aspects of community life. Selected cities, both contemporary and historic (e.g., Washington, D.C., Williamsburg, Virginia), are often presented as case studies. Third-grade programs also commonly have one or more units on the local community.

Focus: Communities

Grade 4. Most fourth-grade social studies programs focus on the geographic regions of the United States, which are often compared with similar regions

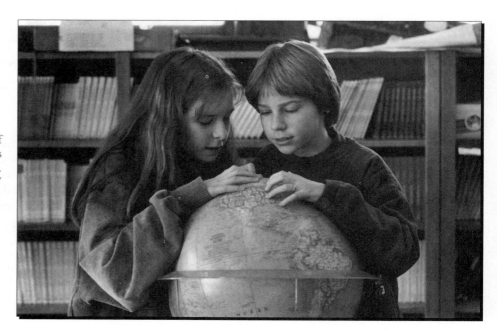

Map and globe skills are part of most social studies programs from Grade Two onward.
(© *Jean-Claude Lejeune/ Stock Boston*)

Focus: Regions/the state

elsewhere in the world. Geography—physical, social, and economic geography—is the dominant social science discipline. However, in many states, the regional geography focus is either supplemented or replaced entirely by a state history/geography emphasis.

Grade 5. The historical emphasis of fifth-grade programs is clearly evident in Table 4.1. The emphasis on geography in Grade 5 depends in part on the program for Grade 4. In areas where state history is emphasized in Grade 4, a regional geography emphasis is usually incorporated into Grade 5. However, when regional geography is treated in Grade 4, American history is the main focus in Grade 5.

Focus: U.S. history and geography

The trend toward limiting the scope of fifth- and sixth-grade programs seems to reflect a growing acceptance of the "less is more" approach that we noted earlier. Instead of trying to teach all of American history in the fifth-grade year, schools are increasingly dividing the content into two parts. For example, in the California program (which we illustrate in more detail shortly), fifth-grade history ends at 1850. Recent American history is not picked up again until Grade 8.

Grade 6. The scope of many sixth-grade programs is often even broader than for fifth grade. A common pattern is to devote the first semester to a survey of world history and the second semester to a study of the geography of nations in the Eastern Hemisphere.

Focus: World history and geography

If there is one grade where there is too much content to teach effectively, this is it. It is almost impossible to do justice to world history in a typical ninety-day semester, much less the geography of nations of the Eastern Hemisphere in a second ninety-day semester. This is why some states have split the course into two or more segments. In the California program that we referred to earlier, the sixth-grade program is limited to ancient civilizations prior to A.D. 500.

Grade 7. The guiding principle of the expanding-environments approach exhausts itself at Grade 6; it is strictly an elementary (K–6) program. The grade-to-grade sequence in secondary (7–12) social studies programs is topical, but there is no apparent guiding principle for organizing or sequencing courses or topics.

Focus: Varies considerably

Social studies programs for Grade 7 seem to have more variability than at any other grade level. Some seventh graders will study either world geography or world history, which are extensions of what they studied in Grade 6. Others will study state history, which is theoretically an extension of what they studied in Grade 4 but often has significant repetition. In still other areas, seventh-grade programs will combine both elements: one semester of world geography and one semester of state history.

Focus: U.S. history

Grade 8. In Grade 8, the study of American history is almost universal, but without the emphasis on geography that occurred in Grade 5. Significant deviations occur in schools where American history is treated over a two-year period. In those cases, the eighth-grade program may focus on American history through 1850, 1860, 1877, or another convenient date, and the "second half" is treated at another grade level (usually Grade 9 or 11).

Selected Program Features

In this section we comment on selected features from all levels of the composite program illustrated in Table 4.1.

Scope

1. *Large increases in the scope of the program from grade to grade*—Primary-level social studies programs are sometimes faulted for dealing with a limited range of material. At the same time, the scope of intermediate-grade (4–6) programs can be faulted because the scope is often very broad.

Map and globe skills

2. *A first unit on map and globe skills at most grade levels*—Map and globe skills are vital components of social studies programs, but when they are presented in isolation, they are often decontextualized and seemingly without purpose. Instead of teaching map and globe skills as a separate unit, we recommend that you integrate these skills into lessons throughout the year in contexts where those skills provide information that your students can actually use.

A global emphasis

3. *An emphasis on developing a global view*—This emphasis is reflected by units or chapters that have an "our world" perspective in their titles. The intent is to help students understand that many problems, such as providing food and shelter and maintaining world peace, are common to people around the globe. We consider global education as a theme for social studies in Chapter 5.

Holidays

4. *The continuing presence of the "holiday" curriculum*—Much of the primary (K–3) curriculum is devoted to observing and celebrating holidays and festivals throughout the year. This long-standing practice has added life and color to classrooms for many years and has been the reason for holding

---

COMMENTARY: Teaching About Birthday Parties?

In a scathing review of four primary-level social studies textbook series, Larkins, Hawkins, and Gilmore (1987) argue that "adherence to the sequence of family, neighborhood, community is in part responsible for the trivialization of social studies in the first three grades" (p. 301). The authors cite many examples that support their contention, but one involving the study of birthday parties is especially illustrative:

> [The textbook publisher] is also convinced that children must be taught about birthday parties. A Chinese-American family is shown with a birthday cake. An American-Indian family is shown with a birthday cake. And a nonminority American family is shown with a birthday cake. A superficial dribble of noninformation about the differing cultural backgrounds of the three families is thrown in to help fill out the ten pages devoted to birthday parties. Danny's Chinese-American

grandmother tells him how birthdays are celebrated in China. Unfortunately, neither she nor Danny share that information with the reader. Maria's father tells her about birthdays on the Chippewa reservation, but neglects to tell us. And Jane's mother tells her, but not us, about what it was like to grow up in West Virginia. (p. 304)

Had these texts told us how birthdays are celebrated in China, on the Chippewa reservation, or even in West Virginia, that ten-page section might have been salvaged. In the absence of such information, we find ourselves wondering (1) what it is about birthday parties that children need to learn in school, and (2) is this not the kind of knowledge children will learn without instruction? We share Larkins, Hawkins, and Gilmore's concern about the damage such treatments can do to children's, teachers', and the public's perception of the importance of social studies as a curriculum offering in the schools.

---

countless parties. We urge caution here because in some classrooms the "holiday" curriculum gets so much emphasis that it overwhelms everything else.

5. *Multidisciplinary social studies tends to diminish at the higher grades.* The multidisciplinary nature of primary social studies programs is clearly evident on Table 4.1. Also evident, however, is the emphasis on single disciplines that begins in Grade 4 and continues through the middle (and high) school years.

Expanding Environments Reconsidered

The organizing principle for the expanding-environments approach—studying nearby environments before more distant environments—seems to make eminent sense. Each environment seems to build on the previously studied environment, and in a logical sequence that's readily evident to most adults.

The expanding-environments pattern also seemingly reflects the educational principle of "beginning with the concrete and moving to the abstract." Families (Grade 1) and neighborhoods (Grade 2) are certainly more concrete and real for most children than are states (Grade 4) or the nation (Grade 5). When third graders are studying their community, they are learning about something fairly concrete, something most of them have experienced simply by having lived in a community. However, when children study "the state" in fourth grade, they move to something that is often beyond their immediate view of the world. States have physical dimensions—boundaries, a capital, and so on—of course, but the state is a phenomenon of political organization; it is lines on a map that can't be seen anywhere else.

Conceptual versus physical distance

Although states are smaller and less-distant environments than the nation (which children study in fifth grade), and although children do indeed live in a state, these factors do not make the state any less an abstraction. Likewise, fifth-grade children cannot "see" the United States, except by looking at a map that is itself an abstract representation of the country. Eventually most children gain the experience that enables them to deal with the different worlds in which they live. Our point here is that abstraction is determined by conceptual distance—the extent to which a phenomenon is within or beyond a child's realm of experience—*not by physical distance.* From this perspective, the expanding-environments approach is not so much a logical progression from concrete to abstract as a quantum leap that occurs after third grade.

Role of sequence

The sequence in which children study different environments is neither as rigid nor as important as it might seem. In more practical terms, this means that it is not necessary for primary-level children to study their families (or *the* family) before they study the (their) neighborhood, for example. Neither is it necessary for children to study the American family prior to studying Russian families or any other family around the globe. Rather, if the family is the focus of study, we think an appropriate way to study it is by examining various families in the neighborhood and in other nations.

Despite its continuing popularity, the expanding-environments approach is not without some other problems. For example, most kindergarten and first-grade children are not aware of, nor do they necessarily understand or care about, the sequence of environments they will study over the next six years. They almost never concern themselves with the "whole," with how one topic relates to other topics they will study; rather, their concern is with what they are studying today. For most young children, the future—next week perhaps—is so distant that they hardly even think about it. At the other end of the program, it is not clear whether sixth, seventh, or eighth graders necessarily understand the organizational pattern of social studies that they've been exposed to. But then, perhaps children don't need to understand the overall pattern of what they study; that's a question researchers have yet to investigate.

An important consideration in organizing any instructional program rests on the nature of the underlying subject areas. Although the expanding-environments pattern makes it seem otherwise, social studies does not have the same kind of inherent structure or prerequisites as does a discipline like mathematics. In teaching arithmetic, for example, you must begin with counting, addition, and subtraction, for these are legitimate prerequisites for other arithmetic processes. In social studies, on the other hand, it is not necessary for children to know anything about families in order to study communities, nor is it necessary for them to have studied American history before they study the history of ancient civilizations. The point is that the mathlike sequence of the expanding-environments pattern makes social studies appear to be an inherently structured subject based on prerequisite learnings when, in fact, social studies programs can be assembled in many different ways.

Variations on the source of "structure"?

You could, for example, teach first graders a unit on the Stone Age, instead of waiting until Grade 6 as called for by the expanding-environments approach. You would need to make adjustments for the children's limited reading ability,

---

COMMENTARY: **The Power of Contrast**

It may seem to be common sense to begin studying nearby environments—like the family, home, and school—before tackling more distant environments. This is also one of the basic premises of the traditional expanding-environments approach to social studies. But this is one time when common sense may fail us. Studying things that we are extremely familiar with and close to, such as our families, our language, and ourselves, is often very difficult, simply because we are too familiar with them. Our families, for example, are so much a part of our everyday lives that we often take them for granted. Likewise, each of us has a vast body of feelings and information about families in general and about our own family in particular, but because of our upbringing and prior cultural experiences, most of us (including children) have developed perceptual blinders that keep us from thinking about families objectively. Common sense notwithstanding, things that are more physically distant from us are often easier to study objectively.

When first graders study "the family," you sometimes find them studying Japanese families. They are not doing this because there are things about Japanese families that everyone should know, but because information about (or from) other cultures can provide a basis for *contrast*, that is, a way to relate the unfamiliar with phenomena that we know well. In other words, first graders can study Japanese families as a vehicle for studying American families, for learning how they are alike and how they are different. When first graders discover that Japanese children do not celebrate their birthdays every year, they simultaneously discover something about themselves and about their own culture.

---

but there is nothing so inherently complex about the Stone Age as to be beyond a first grader's comprehension. Or you could use chronology as your organizer and begin teaching first graders about ancient civilizations (Egypt, Greece, etc.) as many European nations do. The single exception to everything we've said here is the area of map skills. This is because most map skills, especially latitude and longitude, are based in mathematics, as we illustrate in Chapter 13. We examine some alternatives to the expanding-environments pattern later in this chapter.

Alternative Organizational Patterns

From time to time, various groups and individuals have proposed alternative elementary programs. Most of them are variations on the expanding-environments approach, but in other instances, they ignore the expanding-environments pattern entirely. We have used this difference as the basis for organizing this section.

Variations on the Expanding-Environments Pattern

NCSS alternatives

The National Council for the Social Studies (NCSS) (1989) has endorsed three alternative curriculum models for social studies, one of which is shown in Table 4.2. Although this proposal is not a radical departure from the expanding-environments approach, it claims different motives. Those motives, along with the other two recommended models, are included in the Resource Handbook.

Most state social studies programs are similar to the composite program we presented earlier (see Table 4.1). However, the California History–Social Science Framework represents an exception to the rule. It attempts to (1) incorporate appropriate children's literature at each grade, (2) incorporate more multicultural and historical content than do most traditional programs, at the

---

COMMENTARY: How States Affect Textbooks, and Vice Versa

Whenever states opt to change their social studies programs, they could create something that doesn't "fit" any of the current textbook series. This was potentially the case when California decided to limit its sixth-grade program to ancient civilizations prior to A.D. 500. This was not a problem in a state as large as California—which has 11 percent of the nation's schoolchildren—nor would it have been a concern in other large states like New York and Texas. In large states, the textbook market is so huge that most publishers will design materials to fit the state's program. For years, most publishers have offered specialized state history books (at Grade 4) for larger states. However, in smaller states, publishers typically offer a regional geography book that they also market nationwide. Thus if you live in states such as North Dakota or New Hampshire, and if one of the smaller publishers has not produced a book to meet your needs, you may need to settle for a generic textbook that is marketed nationwide. It is a matter of economics. Should you encounter a new, fifth-grade text that goes only to 1850, it is fairly safe to assume the book was designed for another state's program, in this case, California.

Table 4.2 NCSS Proposed Social Studies Program

Grade Level	Content
Kindergarten	Awareness of Self in a Social Setting Socialization experiences to bridge home life with life in schools
Grade 1	The Individual in Primary Social Groups: Understanding School and Family Life Specialized roles, family structure, interdependence, the need for rules and laws
Grade 2	Meeting Basic Needs in Nearby Social Groups: The Neighborhood Social functions including education, production, consumption, communication, and transportation within a neighborhood context
Grade 3	Sharing Earth Space with Others: The Community Same social functions of Grade 2 except in the context of the community in a global setting
Grade 4	Human Life in Varied Environments: The Region Geographic and cultural regions; the state as a political region, as may be required
Grade 5	People of the Americas: The United States and Its Close Neighbors Emphasis on the development of the United States, core values, significant individuals, history and geography of Canada and Mexico
Grade 6	People and Cultures: The Eastern Hemisphere Major geographical regions, historic and economic development, political and value systems

Source: NCSS Task Force on Scope and Sequence, "In Search of Scope and Sequence for Social Studies." Reprinted by permission from National Council for the Social Studies *Social Education.*

primary grades especially, and (3) at the same time reduce the scope of the history covered at the intermediate level. Table 4.3 shows the major topics and selected children's literature for each grade in the California program.

A Distinctive Variation: The CORE Curriculum

Until the early 1990s, most variations to the traditional expanding-environments approach to social studies were produced by states, like the California program we just considered. However, in 1991, a group of educators inspired by E. D.

Table 4.3 Selected Children's Literature Used in the California Social Studies Program (Abridged)

Grade	Topic	Children's Literature
K	Learning and Working, Now and Long Ago	*Jack and the Beanstalk, Goldilocks,* *Aesop's Fables*
1	A Child's Place in Time and Space	*Little Toot, Little Red Light-house,* *Mike Mulligan and His Steam Shovel*
2	People Who Make a Difference	*Johnny Appleseed* Other myths, folktales, and legends
3	Understanding Continuity and Change	*White Stallion, Wagon Wheels,* *The Drinking Gourd*
4	California: A Changing State	
5	The Making of a New Nation, to 1850	*Immigrant Kids* *Waiting for Mama*
6	Ancient Civilizations, to A.D. 500	Selections from Greek and Roman literature and the Bible
7	The Medieval World, A.D. 500 to 1789	*Pillow Book, Song of Roland* *Tale of Genji*
8	U. S. History, 1783–1914	*Huckleberry Finn, My Ántonia*

The CORE Knowledge Program

Hirsch's book *Cultural Literacy* (1988) decided to use it as the basis for an elementary curriculum that would have national circulation. The last section of *Cultural Literacy* contained an alphabetical listing of 5,000 names, dates, phrases, and concepts ranging from names such as Aaron (Hank), through colloquial sayings such as "A stitch in time saves nine" to places around the globe, such as Zurich (Switzerland), that Hirsch believed reflected the "core" knowledge that everyone should know to be considered "culturally literate." However, Hirsch did not identify his criteria for selecting the 5,000 items, and this reluctance has remained a bone of contention among his critics. Nevertheless, the educators organized those random elements into an instructional program.

The product of the group's effort is called the CORE Curriculum. In this instance, CORE is not an acronym; rather, it refers to the "core" of fundamental knowledge that we referred to above. The CORE Curriculum is a comprehensive program that was designed to comprise 50 to 60 percent of an elementary curriculum. It also covers almost every discipline of knowledge, from mathematics, fine arts, science, and language arts, to world and American civilizations. A second distinguishing feature of the CORE Curriculum is its content specificity; it lays out exactly what teachers are expected to teach in each subject and at each grade level. The Core Knowledge Foundation makes available sample units that were developed by teachers, but it does not otherwise specify how teachers should teach the material.

E. D. Hirsch, Jr., is among the individuals we identified in Chapter 1 as a critic of multidisciplinary social studies. He argued that because multidisciplinary social studies does not allow children to study history and geography in depth, it keeps them from becoming historically and geographically literate. Based on this position, it should be no surprise that the words *social studies* do not appear in the CORE materials. Instead, the CORE's "social studies" component is organized around three strands: World Civilizations, which focuses primarily on world history; American Civilizations, which includes American History and cultures of the Western Hemisphere; and Geography. Table 4.4 shows how the CORE Curriculum compares with a traditional social studies program.

The "social studies" strand of the CORE program is new to this country, but it reflects a curriculum pattern that has been used in Europe for years. In contrast to the expanding-environments pattern, its organizing variable is historical chronology. In practice this simply means that older civilizations are taught

Disciplines are taught separately

before later civilizations. This seemingly minor change also means that first graders will study ancient Egypt, and second graders will study ancient Rome, both topics that are far removed from the family, school, and neighborhood focus of traditional social studies programs at those grade levels. However, this also means that instead of an entire year of American History at Grade 5 and a similar year of World History at Grade 6, these two disciplines are spread across the seven years (K–6) of a child's elementary and middle-school career.

From 1991, when the CORE Curriculum was created, through 1997, it has been adopted by over 600 public and private schools across the country. Acceptance of the CORE Curriculum has been rapid, especially when you consider

No textbooks

that no currently available textbook series is geared to it. Teachers sometimes use one of seven books that accompany the program, variously titled *What Your Kindergartner* (First Grader, Second Grader, etc.) *Needs to Know* (Hirsch, 1991–1993), which highlight the topics taught at each grade level. In place of regular textbooks, CORE teachers usually make extensive use of informational books and whatever other resources they can lay their hands on.

The CORE Curriculum places a heavy burden on teachers, especially during their first year using the program. At the same time, comments from teachers on the Core Knowledge (Internet) Webpage (http://www.coreknowledge.org) occasionally provide glowing testimonials amid requests for resources and sporadic complaints. Data supplied by the Core Knowledge Foundation (Marshall, 1996) indicate that administrators in CORE schools credit the program with having a dramatic impact on students' performance on standardized tests.

Of course, the CORE program also has its critics. Some of that criticism stems from E. D. Hirsch's reluctance to identify the criteria he used for selecting the 5,000 elements of "cultural literacy" (see Apple, 1993). A second and

Table 4.4 Comparison of Traditional Social Studies and CORE Curriculum

| | | CORE Curriculum Strands | | |
Grade	Traditional Programs	World Civilization	American Civilization	Geography
K	Family and School	Seven Continents	American Geography Native Americans Columbus/Mayflower	Maps and globes
1	Family and Community	Early Civilizations: Egypt, etc. World Religions Mexico	Early Civilizations: Mayas, Incas, Aztecs Early Colonies to Independence	Place location for topics at left
2	Neighborhood	Ancient Civilizations: India, China, Greece Modern Civilizations: Japan	The Constitution Westward Expansion Civil War	Geography of the Americas and World Civilizations
3	Community	Ancient Rome Byzantine Civilizations	Earliest Americans The 13 Colonies	Geography of the Mediterranean
4	The State	The Middle Ages Islam and Holy Wars Medieval Africa and China	American Revolution The Constitution Presidents and Heroes	Mountains Geography of Africa
5	The Nation (U.S. History)	Meso-Americans: Mayas, Aztecs European Exploration Renaissance English Revolution Russia	Westward Expansion The Civil War Reconstruction	The Political Geography of Europe Geography of topics at left
6	The World (World History)	Lasting Ideas from Ancient Civilizations: Judaism and Christianity, Greece and Rome, Capitalism and Socialism Latin America	Immigration, Industrialization, Urbanization America as a World Power	Geography of topics at left

more fundamental issue, however, concerns whether traditional knowledge—what some critics refer to as nineteenth-century knowledge—is what students need to live in the twenty-first century. Still other criticisms have focused on the strong Euro-American bias in the literary selections. For example, Peterson (1995) noted that over 80 percent of the poetry and literature selections are Euro-American, and over one-third of the non-European selections have animals as the main characters. This, Peterson argues, sends a not-so-subtle message that stories about non-European cultures are not as serious. Then, too, the inclusion of classic tales, such as Snow White and Cinderella, where passive females are rescued by handsome princes, has raised gender equity questions that we deal with in more detail in the next chapter.

Critics' concerns

Additional information on the CORE Curriculum is available from the Core Knowledge Foundation, 801 East High Street, Charlottesville, VA 22902; 804-977-7550.

The Core Knowledge Program is a distinctive variation from traditional social studies programs that requires much more teacher planning than do most traditional programs. Other approaches that teachers can take to create distinctive variations include using a thematic-unit approach or attempting to build a spiral curriculum or a concept-based social studies program. We consider these variations in the next section.

Developing Social Studies Programs

We understand that you probably don't plan to design an entire social studies program in the next week or so, but in this section we provide an overview of program development elements that every teacher and program developer must consider.

Basic Program Design Elements

The essential aspects of creating any instructional program are captured in four little words: *what, why, when,* and *how. What* am I expected to teach? *Why* am I expected to teach "this" instead of "that"? *When* in the year am I expected to teach something? And *how* am I supposed to do that? These are the basic questions of curriculum planning that teachers usually refer to as their "scope and sequence."

What to study

Scope. The first decision in determining a social studies program involves scope. In other words, what segments of the universe of social studies knowledge will be taught? In more practical terms, the question is one of whether a unit on "the farm" or "desert communities," for example, will or will not be included in a social studies program.

Concerns related to scope, or the *what* you plan to teach, must always be considered in relation to the question of *why* (or *why not*). Answering a question like Why should we include a unit on the farm?, for example, gets into matters of the program's rationale.

Why study it? **Rationale.**   The question *why* ("this" topic instead of "that" topic) is a request for a rationale—a reasoned statement of justification about why children should be taught and expected to learn certain subject matter.

The curriculum guides that most new teachers receive seldom provide a justification for why the selected topics are worth being studied. Somewhere along the line, whoever created the program had to address that question, but the reasons why certain content was selected and other content ignored are seldom conveyed to teachers. As a result, you may find yourself wondering why you are expected to be teaching something. And if you aren't sure why you are supposed to be teaching something, it probably won't be long before your students are asking the same question.

In what order and at what grade? **Sequence.**   After determining what topics should be taught, and why, it then becomes necessary to decide *when*—at what time and in what order, or sequence—to teach them.

Sequencing subject matter has two dimensions: a "between-grades" dimension and a "within-grade" dimension. First, it's necessary to determine at which grade level something will be taught. For example, having decided that a unit on "the farm" should be included in a program, the between-grade question is, At which grade level should "the farm" be taught? Once that question has been answered, the second element involves determining when (at what time during the year) it should be taught within that grade level.

The within-grade-level question concerns the sequencing of units within a grade level. For example, having determined that Greece, Rome, and ancient Egypt should be taught at a certain grade level (probably Grade 6), the next decision is to determine the order in which those topics will be taught. Sometimes that sequence may be based on a logical progression, such as from simple to complex; in other cases it may be arbitrary. When history is involved, as in this example, the sequence is invariably based on chronology. On that basis, you will teach ancient Egypt first. But which will come next—Greece or Rome?

Making it meaningful **Synthesis.**   How will everything be pulled together into a whole that is meaningful to students? There probably isn't any one best basis for sequencing a social studies program, but the program needs to be organized around something. To illustrate the importance of the synthesis, consider a third-grade social studies program that asks you to teach the following sequence of topics:

1. explorers
2. the geography of Australia
3. community helpers
4. transportation
5. the Civil War

If there is something—a theme, an approach, anything—that can pull these topics together so that they make sense, it isn't apparent. However, young children may not care about the sequence of topics they study as long as they are interesting. In some respects, sequencing may be more of a problem for adults than for children.

Subject Matter Considerations

We suggested earlier that social studies is a subject that does not impose the kind of prerequisite prior learnings that you might associate with a subject such as mathematics. Children's vocabulary and reading ability may limit what you can teach, but this holds true for almost every subject area. The absence of a hierarchy or predetermined sequence in which history or social studies must be taught means that teachers have more latitude to use other factors, such as students' interests and abilities, as a basis for selecting content.

Alternative entry points

There are many possible entry points to studying about the human experience, and some of these possibilities are illustrated in Table 4.5. By mixing and matching items from the various columns of Table 4.5, it is possible to create hundreds of alternative configurations for social studies. Each of these will reflect a different orientation and a different blending of content and instructional purpose. When we suggested that social studies could be approached in many different ways, we doubt that you anticipated quite this many possibilities!

Table 4.5   **Alternative Ways of Looking at Social Studies**

Objects of Study	Disciplines	Major Findings and Ways of Knowing	Instructional Purposes
The community	Anthropology	Value statements	Miniature scholars
Native Americans	Economics	Descriptions	Cognitive skill development
Area studies	Geography	Nonempirically based feelings	Accumulation of knowledge
The United States	History	Principles (analytic or empirical)	Concept development and testing
Non-Western civilization	Philosophy		Creative use of individual and collective experience
The environment	Political science	Generalizations based on observations and probability	Indoctrination
Change processes	Psychology		Social control
Minorities	Sociology		
Local, state, and national government			
Citizenship			
Consumer economics			

Developmental Considerations

Creating a viable social studies program must also consider young children's abilities to deal with elements like time, space, and distance.

Children's concepts of time

Time.   It isn't entirely clear how children develop a sense of time, especially historical time. Apparently children's conceptions of time—including personal time, social time, and historical time—develop at different rates and so gradually that children are unaware of what is taking place.

When young children enter elementary school, they have a fairly secure conception of "yesterday." But events that happened to them prior to yesterday—two weeks, two months, or two years ago—are usually thought of as happening "a long time ago," somewhere in a vast and undifferentiated past. However, because young children sometimes have difficulty differentiating the time span of past events does *not* mean that they have forgotten what happened. Children can often describe past events—vacations, birthday parties, or other experiences—in excruciating detail. They can tell *what* happened, but they may be unable to provide an accurate time frame for *when* the events took place.

At about age ten or eleven, children's conceptions of time apparently permit them to feel an awareness (but not a complete understanding) of the historical past. All of this does *not* mean that history is out of the question for younger children, however. Even very young children can often relate vicariously to the individuals and events of history, particularly if those events are presented in narrative (story) form.

TECHNOLOGY UPDATE

So All Can See

Asking your class to crowd around one 14-inch computer screen is probably inviting problems. Someone is almost sure to step on someone else's foot or someone's elbow is almost certain to hit someone else's stomach, whether intentionally or not. How then do you use computer-based technology so that everyone can see, but without having to crowd around a single monitor?

There are at least four possible solutions to this problem. One is to use a liquid crystal display (LCD) device that fits on an overhead projector and that projects the computer-driven image on a screen. The image is not always as bright as you might hope for, and special overhead projectors that don't produce too much heat are required.

A second option is to get a device that projects the computer-driven image on a screen. Computer projectors are expensive, ($450 and up), but they permit large groups to view the image simultaneously. A third option is to get one of the "black boxes" that will project computer images through a TV set. This is a less costly option ($100 or so) than the others because most schools already have the TVs available. A fourth option is to download the files images onto a disk and then allow children to view them when it is their turn to use the computer. The disk option is the least costly, but it does not permit the entire class to view the images simultaneously. Nevertheless, it is a plausible alternative until schools are able to acquire the resources to use computer-based technology effectively.

Space and Distance. Children's conceptions of space—how they fit into their environment—and distance (physical remoteness) seem to develop in ways similar to their conception of time. Initially, distance is measured by the number of *fars* they attach to *away*. As any young child can tell you, "far, far away" is much farther than "far away."

Children's views of space and distance

Eventually everyone develops conceptions of time and space. It's something all of us do, simply through the process of living. Thus we question whether trying to speed up processes that will occur normally is a good investment of your time. Instead of trying to accelerate the way your students perceive time, space, or distance, we suggest that you can teach educationally valuable things that do not require them to alter the way they view their world.

Organizational Considerations

In this section, we present three distinctive ways to organize subject matter for a social studies program. These include: (1) thematic units, which integrate elements from several subject areas, (2) spiral curricula, where early learnings provide the basis for later learning, and (3) a concept-based approach, which provides a way for children to organize what might otherwise be isolated facts.

Thematic and Topical Units. The whole-language approach to reading and language arts has come under fire in some parts of the country. Nevertheless, the underlying belief that the components of language—reading, writing, spelling, handwriting, and so on—are best learned and taught in contextualized settings instead of as separate subjects makes intuitive sense. Teachers in whole-language classrooms often provide those settings by organizing units around a theme or topic, such as "desert environments," "time," or even "bears" or "dinosaurs."

Fusion

More and more teachers are recognizing that it is possible to integrate elements from several subject areas into what are sometimes called *transdisciplinary units*. It is needlessly redundant, for example, to study a unit on desert environments in science at one point in the year, and then study a unit on desert communities in social studies later in the year. By carefully selecting themes and topics, and by identifying learning experiences that seem to cluster together, teachers can integrate across subject areas.

Is it a worthwhile topic?

The potential themes for integrated units are almost endless, and we provide a detailed example of a technique for identifying potential activities for thematic units in Chapter 8. However, a word of caution is in order here: Be certain that the theme you select is worth studying. Children might very well enjoy a three-week unit on bears, for example, but you need to ask yourself just how much about bears children need to know. Does a unit on "bears" have enough substance and learning potential to warrant spending three weeks on it?

Figure 4.2 shows an abridgement of a web for a thematic approach to time that was developed by Pappas, Kiefer, and Levstik (1995). The original of this figure fills two 8½-by-11-inch printed pages.

Figure 4.2 shows that the overall theme of time was divided into several subthemes, including "Changes over Time," "Personal Time," and "Measuring Time." Instructional activities and relevant works of children's literature were then identified for each subtheme. Titles of the children's books for each sub-

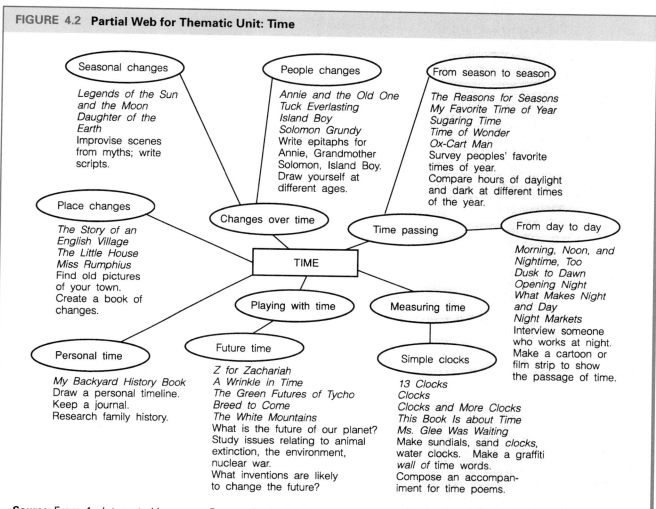

FIGURE 4.2 Partial Web for Thematic Unit: Time

Seasonal changes

Legends of the Sun and the Moon
Daughter of the Earth
Improvise scenes from myths; write scripts.

People changes

Annie and the Old One
Tuck Everlasting
Island Boy
Solomon Grundy
Write epitaphs for Annie, Grandmother Solomon, Island Boy. Draw yourself at different ages.

From season to season

The Reasons for Seasons
My Favorite Time of Year
Sugaring Time
Time of Wonder
Ox-Cart Man
Survey peoples' favorite times of year.
Compare hours of daylight and dark at different times of the year.

Place changes

The Story of an English Village
The Little House
Miss Rumphius
Find old pictures of your town.
Create a book of changes.

Changes over time

Time passing

From day to day

Morning, Noon, and Nightime, Too
Dusk to Dawn
Opening Night
What Makes Night and Day
Night Markets
Interview someone who works at night.
Make a cartoon or film strip to show the passage of time.

TIME

Playing with time

Measuring time

Personal time

My Backyard History Book
Draw a personal timeline.
Keep a journal.
Research family history.

Future time

Z for Zachariah
A Wrinkle in Time
The Green Futures of Tycho
Breed to Come
The White Mountains
What is the future of our planet?
Study issues relating to animal extinction, the environment, nuclear war.
What inventions are likely to change the future?

Simple clocks

13 Clocks
Clocks
Clocks and More Clocks
This Book Is about Time
Ms. Glee Was Waiting
Make sundials, sand *clocks*, water clocks. Make a graffiti *wall of* time words.
Compose an accompaniment for time poems.

Source: From *An Integrated Language Perspective in the Elementary School: Theory into Action* by Christine C. Pappas, Barbara Z. Kiefer, and Linda S. Levstik. Copyright © 1995, 1990 by Longman Publishing Group. Reprinted with permission.

theme are shown in italics, and complete citations are provided in the references for this chapter.

Spiral Curricula. The basic premise that underlies a spiral curriculum is that once students learn an idea, teachers can help them build on what they know by extending those ideas to new situations. It is the scaffolding process that we referred to earlier.

Scaffolding

Helping students apply ideas to new situations may seem like common sense. Yet too often, we suspect, ideas that students are expected to learn are treated in isolation, and students have nothing to connect them to. In a spiral approach to content, concepts and generalizations are introduced in the primary

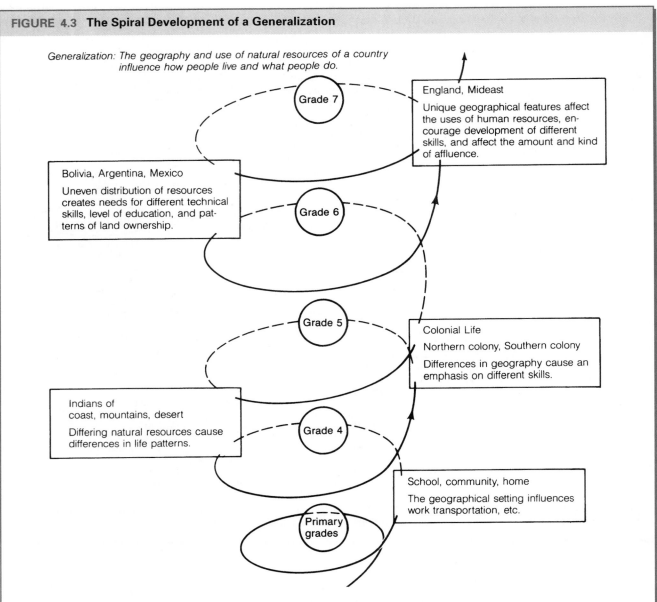

FIGURE 4.3 The Spiral Development of a Generalization

Generalization: The geography and use of natural resources of a country influence how people live and what people do.

Grade 7

England, Mideast

Unique geographical features affect the uses of human resources, encourage development of different skills, and affect the amount and kind of affluence.

Bolivia, Argentina, Mexico

Uneven distribution of resources creates needs for different technical skills, level of education, and patterns of land ownership.

Grade 6

Grade 5

Colonial Life

Northern colony, Southern colony

Differences in geography cause an emphasis on different skills.

Indians of coast, mountains, desert

Differing natural resources cause differences in life patterns.

Grade 4

School, community, home

The geographical setting influences work transportation, etc.

Primary grades

Source: *Teacher's Handbook for Elementary Social Studies* © 1967 by Taba, Durkin, et al. Copyright Addison-Wesley Publishing Company. Used by permission.

grades and then expanded upon as the children progress from grade to grade. The key in the expansion process is not simply to present new applications of the idea, lest the students treat them as totally new ideas. It's often necessary to help students understand how a new application of an idea is connected to an earlier application.

Expanding on an idea

Figure 4.3 shows an example of the spiral development of a generalization as described by Hilda Taba (1967). This spiral focuses on the development of generalizations (as opposed to a sequence of expanding environments). For example, the notion that geography and natural resources influence how people live is first introduced in the primary grades and then expanded upon in different contexts at higher grade levels.

Concept-Based Approaches.   In most traditional social studies programs, the emphasis is on learning the information associated with whatever topic is the focus. If the topic was Holland, for example, you probably learned about tulips, and chocolate, and cheese. If the topic was China, you probably studied things associated with the geography and climate of China, China's government, China's resources, and other aspects of life in that nation. If the next unit was Japan, you went through the same process again, this time studying Japanese agriculture, the climate of Japan, and so forth. This topic-by-topic approach is illustrated in Figure 4.4.

Topical and concept-based approaches

A quite different approach is based on following a single concept or idea through several different applications. In other words, the concept-based approach is premised on the idea that it is not necessary to study every country in the world to be able to say something about how nations organize their governments, practice agriculture, or use their resources, and so on. By studying only selected nations (instead of the entire universe of nations) it is possible to identify patterns among nations. Figure 4.5 illustrates that it is possible to identify *patterns* in agricultural practices by studying agriculture in China, India, Japan, Russia, and the United States.

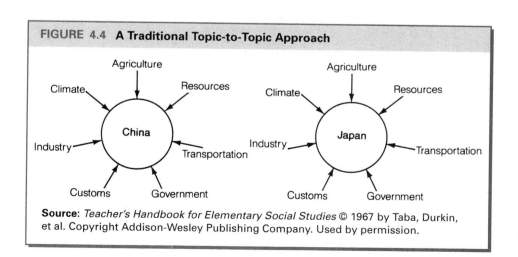

FIGURE 4.4   A Traditional Topic-to-Topic Approach

Source: *Teacher's Handbook for Elementary Social Studies* © 1967 by Taba, Durkin, et al. Copyright Addison-Wesley Publishing Company. Used by permission.

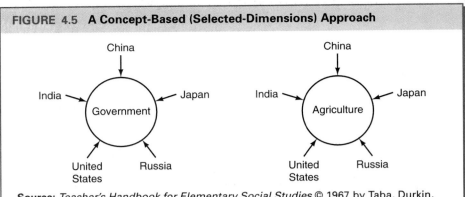

FIGURE 4.5 A Concept-Based (Selected-Dimensions) Approach

Source: *Teacher's Handbook for Elementary Social Studies* © 1967 by Taba, Durkin, et al. Copyright Addison-Wesley Publishing Company. Used by permission.

In traditional programs, students often become so concerned with the "parts"—the climate, the government, the customs, and so on—that they may not see the "whole." By focusing on agricultural practices in Thailand, in Laos, in China, and in Japan, children tend to treat each nation separately, and in that process may miss the point of agricultural practices that are common to heavily populated areas in the Pacific Rim or elsewhere.

An emphasis on the whole

In a concept-based approach, the focus shifts from the parts to the "whole." This parts/whole emphasis is illustrated by the questions associated with each approach. In a topic-by-topic approach, at least seven questions are generated, all of which follow this general form: "What is Chinese (agriculture, transportation, etc.) like?" The same questions are then asked about Japan. The result may be fourteen or so pieces of discrete data. In a concept-based approach, however, such an examination has fewer questions, and each is studied in greater depth.

When to use which approach

A concept-based approach can help students become aware of patterns that exist among cultures, but it is not appropriate for some elements, especially truly unique elements such as a culture's customs and rituals. For example, if your interest is in Japanese customs, it will be necessary to study Japan. On the other hand, if you are interested in determining whether some customs are common to nations in the Far East, you would need to study several Far Eastern nations to decide.

A concept-based approach to social control

We suspect one reason that concept-based instruction has not been more widely accepted is that most teachers lack familiarity with it. Not having experienced concept-based instruction as students, they will tend to use the topic-to-topic approach with which they are more familiar. In a concept-based program, for example, the children might study the sixteenth- and seventeenth-century Spanish monarchs, the Mayflower Compact, and the Inuit (Eskimos). From a traditional perspective, these would be seen as three separate and unrelated topics, but as Figure 4.6 illustrates, the focus for all three is the concept "social control."

You may recall that the Mayflower Compact was produced by the travelers on the good ship *Mayflower,* who agreed in writing to govern (control) themselves for the common good. The Inuit on the other hand govern themselves by elab-

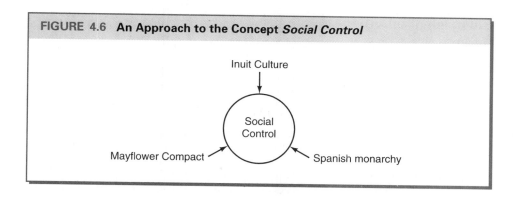

FIGURE 4.6 An Approach to the Concept *Social Control*

Inuit Culture

Social Control

Mayflower Compact

Spanish monarchy

orate but unwritten laws and traditions. The Spanish monarchy serves as an exemplar of absolute control based on the divine right of kings. The differences among these forms of social control provide the basis for contrast.

Concept-based programs may sometimes seem a little piecemeal, especially to individuals who are familiar with traditional topic-based approaches. As a result, some teachers occasionally provide in-depth case studies of a single culture, subculture, or nation. However, a concept-based approach to social studies allows children to learn about human behavior in general, as opposed to learning unrelated ideas about many different subjects.

Summary

Traditional elementary and middle-school social studies programs are based on the expanding-environments (expanding-horizons) approach, where children progress from environments they are close to—such as the home, family, school, and neighborhood—in the primary grades, to ever more distant environments—the state, nation, and world—at the intermediate grades. Although such programs may seem logical and sequential from an adult perspective, their logic and sequence may be much less evident for children.

It is sometimes more difficult for children to study objectively those things that they are very close to—like their family, language, and customs—without studying cultures that do things quite differently, which then provide a basis for contrasting unfamiliar behaviors with those children already know well. Thus, when children study the structure and daily activities of Japanese families, or families anywhere, that information can help to clarify the day-to-day activities and the structure of American families.

The CORE Knowledge Program, based on E. D. Hirsch's book *Cultural Literacy* (1988), is a recent and distinctive variation to traditional social studies programs. Because of Hirsch's philosophical differences with the notion of multidisciplinary social studies, it is based on studying elements of world history, American civilizations, and geography at each grade level. In addition, instead of using a sequence of expanding environments as its organizer, the Core Program's "social studies" strand is organized around historical chronology. As a result, children study ancient civilizations in the early grades such as Egypt, Greece, and Rome, instead of at Grade 6, as is common in traditional programs.

Other variations to traditional social studies programs include: (1) the thematic unit approach, in which content from several subject areas is integrated around a topic such as "the desert," or "time"; (2) a spiral approach to curriculum, in which new ideas and applications build on the ideas that students have learned previously, and (3) a concept-based approach, in which children look for patterns among cultures, such as how they organize their governments, practice agriculture, or exercise control over their citizens.

Suggested Activities

1. Do you think it is important for children to understand the logic (the *why*) of what they are studying? In math? In social studies? In anything?
2. Determine how the old saying "familiarity breeds contempt" might apply to the expanding-environments approach to social studies.
3. Go to your curriculum library or resource center and get three or four texts, each for the same grade level but from different textbook series. Do a content analysis, comparing the topics they cover, the approach they take, and the things they do and do not emphasize. If you work in a small group of six to eight members and each member takes a different grade level to study, you will have a composite of the similarities and variations among textbook series, any one of which you might find yourself teaching from.
4. Review the assumptions on which the expanding-environments approach to social studies is based—for example, that children should be exposed to the world by Grade 6. Then, in small groups, outline the characteristics of a K–8 social studies program that follows alternative assumptions of your choosing.

Suggested Readings

E. D. Hirsh, Jr. (Ed). (1992). *What your third grader needs to know.* New York: Doubleday. This is one book from the Core Knowledge series edited by the author of *Cultural Literacy;* other books have similar titles for different grade levels, for example, *What your first grader needs to know.* Various sections cover language arts, American and world civilization, fine arts, mathematics, and the natural sciences.

Catherine Cornbleth & Dexter Waugh. (1995). *The great speckled bird: Multicultural politics and educational policymaking.* New York: St. Martin's Press. If you are interested in exploring how political pressures can influence the curriculum, this book is where you should begin.

Stephanie Steffy & Wendy J.Hood (Eds.). (1994). *If this is social studies, why isn't it boring?* York, ME: Stenhouse. This book is just as delightful as its title. It contains fifteen first-person essays by teachers and others describing how they brought new life to social studies classes by integrating different kinds of literature.

William W. Joyce, Timothy H. Little, & Stan P. Wronski. (1991). Scope and sequence, goals, and objectives: Effects on social studies. In J. P. Shaver (Ed.), *Handbook of social studies teaching and learning* (pp. 321–331). New York: Macmillan. This section of the *Handbook* provides a good summary of recent research on social studies curriculum patterns.

5 Weaving Instructional Themes into Social Studies Programs

Key Questions

* What are instructional themes?

* When and how are instructional themes taught?

* How does a global education help students recognize the interdependence of all peoples?

* What role can narratives and case studies play in teaching social studies?

Key Ideas

The following themes and the goals associated with each of them emerge throughout the K–12 social studies curriculum:

* *Global education* is intended to help children understand the complexities of citizenship in an increasingly interdependent world community.

* *Energy and environmental education* is intended to help children understand problems related to energy and environmental issues.

* *Law-related education* is intended to help children understand the nature of law and its influence on their lives.

* *Gender-equity education* is intended to foster equality among all Americans.

Introduction: "Change Begets Change"

Harding Elementary School was built in the mid-1930s, in what was then a working-class neighborhood of Buffalo, New York. At the time, Buffalo's chemical and heavy manufacturing industries were recovering from the Depression, and much of the city was often shrouded in a pall of sulfurous yellowish grey smoke. All of that has largely changed today; the smoke and smell are gone, as are most of the heavy industries.

The neighborhood that Harding Elementary serves has also changed; it is now inner city. And despite several renovations, the school is now showing its age. Recently additional electrical outlets were added to accommodate the overhead projectors and computers, but the old yet still serviceable slate blackboards remain, as do the twelve-foot ceilings and polished hardwood floors.

During our three-day visit to Harding Elementary, we observed Shane Fielding, a former college baseball player, who is in his third year of teaching sixth grade. Here is what we saw:

Day One. Shane began the lesson by saying, "O.K. We've been talking about how when one thing changes, other things usually change too. Today we're going to look at something that happened in Borneo, a little island country in the Pacific [pointing to a world map]. Everyone needs a copy of the case study I wrote [based on a book called *Global Geography* (Backler & Hanvey, 1986, cited in Miller & Jacobson, 1994)]. It's about how they tried to stop malaria, which is a serious disease in the tropics. After you read it, try to restate what happened in your own words to your partner [in your cooperative learning group]." Shane then distributed the following case study.

Using a case study

Case Study: Conquering Malaria in Borneo

Malaria means "bad air" in Italian. That's because people used to think that you could get the disease by breathing the awful-smelling air in a swamp. About one hundred years ago, scientists found that people could get malaria if they were bitten by a kind of mosquito that lives only in warm climates.

If you get malaria, you will have a high fever and chills—like what you get with the flu sometimes, only worse. Malaria is so serious that about 2 million people around the world die from it every year. A drug called *quinine,* which is made from the bark of a tree, can help to ease the symptoms of malaria, but it does not cure it. Even today there is no cure or vaccine for the disease.

Malaria had always been a problem for the people of Borneo. Finally, the people asked the World Health Organization (WHO), a part of the United Nations, for help. The WHO agreed to spray the swamps with an insecticide called *dieldrin.* The dieldrin really worked! It killed the mosquitoes and stopped the malaria, and the villagers were overjoyed. The dieldrin also killed flies and cockroaches that lived in the villager's huts, which delighted the villagers even more. However, many of the lizards that ate the dead flies and mosquitoes also died. And unfortunately, many of the cats in the village ate the dead lizards, and they died too. Without the cats, rats from the surrounding jungle invaded some of the villages. In addition, some rats carried fleas that were infected with typhus, a disease even more deadly than malaria. So instead of worrying about getting malaria, the villagers now had to worry about getting typhus.

Unintended consequences

Besides the mosquitoes, flies, and cockroaches, the dieldrin also killed a species of wasp that eats caterpillars. However, the spray did not affect the caterpillars. Without any wasps around, the caterpillar population exploded. Soon the caterpillars began eating the leaf roofs of the villager's huts until the roofs finally fell in. When the villagers replaced their roofs, the caterpillars ate the new ones until they, too, fell in. Malaria was no longer a problem, but now the people of Borneo had new problems to worry about.

Things to think about:
1. What things resulted from killing the malaria-carrying mosquitoes?
2. What do you recommend that the villagers do now?

A lively discussion followed about whether spraying the dieldrin had helped or harmed the villagers, and what they should do now. Shane's students eventually decided that the people of Borneo should ask the WHO to supply them with new cats, which could control the rats, and thus the threat of typhus. They would also ask for new wasps that would eat the caterpillars. In the course of their discussion, the students saw that the one change—getting rid of the mosquitoes that caused malaria—had led to other changes the villagers could not ignore. As one student put it, "You need to be careful messing with Mother Nature!"

Shane summarized the lesson by suggesting that "one little change, like spraying the dieldrin, did what it was supposed to do; it killed the mosquitoes. But that change also led to other changes that the villagers were not prepared for." He ended the lesson by adding, "Tomorrow we are going to look at something a lot closer to home and see if the same principle applies here."

One change brings other changes

Day Two. Shane began by observing that "Everyone around here knows about Love Canal, right?" The Love Canal incident had occurred before most of Shane's students had been born, but most of them nodded that they were aware of the housing development that was built on what had once been the dumping ground for chemical refuse. After an unusually large number of residents had developed cancer, the entire development was abandoned. "Let's take a look at something that might have a bearing on this. All of you know that the big ol' Niagara River flows past Buffalo toward Niagara Falls and Lake Ontario. Let's look at some things that it could affect."

Shane placed a videotape of a program called *The Nature of Things,* which he had recorded earlier from the Discovery Channel, into the VCR. The episode, titled "Water, Water, Everywhere," dealt mainly with the long-term effects of pollution in rivers, lakes, and streams. A portion of the program focused on how scientists had determined what was causing the death of the white beluga whales that spent part of the year in the St. Lawrence River. Autopsies had shown that the whales' deaths were caused by chemical residues, primarily PCBs. The puzzling aspect was that both the Niagara and St. Lawrence Rivers had been the focus of intensive cleanup efforts, and dumping chemical pollutants into them had been stopped almost a decade ago.

What caused the death of the belugas turned out to be eels, which begin life in Lake Ontario and then migrate into the St. Lawrence River, where they become a staple of the whales' diet. The scientists discovered that Lake Ontario was still laced with chemical residues, which the eels absorb into their bodies. The chemicals become concentrated in the eels, then become even more concentrated in the whales when they eat the eels, and ultimately cause the whales to die. The program showed that, although many sources of pollution were halted years ago, unexpected long-term effects may still remain. "Does anyone want to try summarizing this?" Shane asked. Tyrone's hand shot up and Shane nodded. Tyrone said, "The stuff we do today could be around when we are old and grey."

The long-term effects of pollution

Day Three. To follow up on the previous lessons, Shane provided each two-student team with Xeroxed copies of topographical maps (that students could mark on) of the Buffalo area. Each group then identified a stream or river that emptied into Lake Erie, the Niagara River, or Lake Ontario. Beginning at the river's mouth, they drew a line around all of the branches and tributaries in

Mapping a watershed

their watershed and lightly shaded the entire area with colored pencils, so that the underlying map was still visible. The students also identified significant natural features (forests, grasslands, marshes, etc.) within their watershed, as well as the major land uses (industry, agriculture, residential neighborhoods, commercial developments, etc.). In the ensuing discussion, the students identified where the water in each watershed came from, some of the major land uses in the Buffalo area, and how human activities in one part of the watershed might affect other parts of the watershed.*

Global and environmental education

The lessons that Shane Fielding's students studied were far removed from the ancient civilizations that most sixth-grade programs focus on. When we asked him about this, he said, "We study ancient civilizations, but we occasionally take a break from the ancient world to look at other things. The lessons you observed focused on global and environmental education. In addition, two of the concepts that we focus on during the entire year are: 'when one thing changes, other things are likely to change,' and, 'when we humans intervene in the environment or any other system, there are often long-term results that are not immediately apparent.' We'll pick up on those ideas again when we get back to the Middle Ages."

Different approaches

The global education and environmental education that Shane referred to are two of the themes, which also include law-related and sex-equity education, that emerge from time to time and at various grade levels in social studies. The themes do not emerge consistently. Sometimes a unit on law-related education, for example, is included in the district's curriculum guide. At other times, teachers create lessons that reflect their particular interests and then weave them into their instructional programs at appropriate points—as Shane did in this example. In some cases, teachers may ignore the instructional themes entirely, especially if they do not fit into what they are doing, or because some teachers may disagree with the desirability of the view associated with a particular theme. The main point is that instructional themes are a highly variable aspect of social studies programs.

Global Education

Basic premises

We who inhabit Planet Earth face a host of problems, some unique to a few nations and some common to many: overpopulation, homelessness, pollution, the inequitable distribution of food, and the denial of basic human rights, to cite just a few. To prepare children to understand and deal effectively with such problems, schools must provide a global view that enables citizens to live in an increasingly interdependent and global society. This is the basic goal of global education.

---

*This activity was adapted from *Investigating Streams and Rivers* by M. Cromwell et al. (1992), which is associated with the Global Rivers Environmental Education Network (GREEN) project, 721 E. Huron Ave., Ann Arbor, MI 48104.

The need for a sense of world-mindedness, or a global perspective, has become apparent with the emergence of two opposing trends in American society. On the one hand, the United States is being drawn into an increasingly interdependent stance with other nations. Recently, for example, the United States has imported more products than it exports, thus contributing to trade deficits that range into the billions. In addition, the U.S. government continues to subsidize farm products to make them more competitive on the world market—an action that irritates farmers in countries like Canada, who don't enjoy such benefits. Both examples underscore the intensity of our economic relationships with other nations.

Building a global perspective

The global emphasis notwithstanding, some Americans apparently would prefer that we turn inward and become less internationally minded. Our collective focus, they argue, should be on problems we face in our own backyard. From their perspective, proposals to identify ourselves as citizens of a global society are unwise, perhaps even un-American. Some groups oppose the notion of global citizenship because they believe that it will lead to what they call "one-world government" (Jenkinson, 1987), but the supporters of a global emphasis usually respond that being citizens in the world community does not mean that we must repudiate our national identities. The point is that agreement on the desirability of a global perspective is by no means universal.

Teaching for Global Understanding

Some authorities, such as Tye and Tye (1992) and Woyach and Remy (1988), argue that global awareness is so significant that it should be incorporated into all areas of the elementary and middle-school curriculum—not just social studies. Other educators (see Kniep, 1989) urge that the entire social studies curriculum should have a strong global focus. For example, Kniep suggests that global studies focus on four persistent problems: environmental concerns, human rights, peace and security, and national/international development. To incorporate a global perspective into social studies programs, he (1986) has recommended focusing on the following four elements:

Basic elements of global education

* The study of diverse human values—with an emphasis on the commonalities (housing, food, dress, tools, etc.) that transcend the diversity
* The study of global systems—economic, political, ecological, and technological
* The study of global issues and problems—particularly problems related to peace, security, development, the environment, and human rights
* The study of global history (*not* histories of Western civilization)—which can help students understand the conditions that underlie issues and problems in the world today

The following Model Student Activity illustrates how global education can be approached in an intermediate-level classroom.

MODEL STUDENT ACTIVITY

Is It "Made in the U.S.A."?

Introduction

Most adults and some children already know that many products are made in countries where manufacturing costs are significantly lower than in the United States. This activity is designed to help children determine an approximate proportion of randomly selected clothing and apparel items that are made elsewhere.

Materials Needed

1. Data Retrieval Chart (as shown)
2. Samples of wearing apparel (in the children's closet) as determined by the child's task group

Procedure

1. Explain that the purpose of this activity is to determine how many of the clothes that the children (and their parents) wear are made in the United States.

2. Explain that small groups will be assigned to different kinds of apparel (shoes, shirts, blouses, etc.), and students will need to read the labels to determine where the objects were made.

3. Do a sample investigation:

   * Ask each student to remove one shoe, place it on the desk, and look for the label indicating where the shoe was made. The label may be inside the shoe, stamped on the tongue, or on the sole. If there is no label or it is unreadable, tell children, "That's O.K., because these are the kinds of problems we may find in our investigation."

   * Record the information for each child's shoe on an overhead transparency of the Data Retrieval Chart. A sample chart with some information filled in follows.

   * After completing the Data Retrieval Chart, do a preliminary analysis by summarizing (counting) the number of shoes manufactured in the various

Sample Data Retrieval Chart

Your Name: _____   Article: Children's shoes

Brand Name	Type	What the Label Says	Owner
Nike	Sneaker	Made in Korea	LaVonne's
Hush Puppy	Leather (brown)	Made in China	Susan H.
None	Sneaker	Unknown	Richard G.
Eddie Bauer	Shoe boot	Made in U.S.A.	Jack M.

countries. Consider problems such as what to do with the "Unknowns." Should they be in a separate category, included with U.S.A., or what?

4. Suggest that before jumping to any conclusions the class needs a larger sample of items. Explain that various task groups will investigate different types of apparel and bring their data back for analysis.

5. Divide the class into task groups to investigate three randomly selected items of apparel groups in their own or their parents' closets. The following groups are recommended: (1) children's shoes, (2) adult men's shoes, (3) adult women's shoes, (4) boys' clothes (shirts, slacks, etc.), (5) girls' clothes (blouses, skirts, etc.), (5) babies' clothes, and (6) adult casual clothes (shorts, slacks, etc.).

6. Indicate that children should not read the labels before selecting an apparel item. They should first identify the three items they intend to record, and then read the label. Also indicate that students should copy the "Made in . . ." phrase exactly as it appears on the label (see Comment).

7. Challenge each task group to present the information from their survey as interestingly and completely as they can. As part of their presentation, ask students to identify the countries and the objects made in those countries on a world map.

8. Summarize the data from each task group in an appropriate way—for example: "Here's what we found out about where adult women's shoes are made." Help the children develop generalizations based on the data they have gathered—for example: "About two-thirds of the shoes that Americans wear are made in other countries."

Comment

Recording the information from the article's label is extremely important to this activity. For example, foreign manufacturers often ship garment parts to this country separately. The bodies of sweaters are typically shipped in one carton and the finished arms of the sweater in another carton, and the two parts are sewn together here. This practice avoids the stiff import duties that are imposed on finished sweaters, but not on sweater parts. In instances like this, the label will usually read "Tailored in the United States." Be certain that students understand that "Tailored in . . ." and "Made in . . ." are not synonymous.

Resource people from the community often offer unique perspectives on special topics in social studies. *(© Joel Gordon)*

Related Issues. In the course of global education programs, children often become aware of tremendous inequities in the distribution of wealth and resources. For example, in many third world nations, there are often only two classes: a small and very wealthy elite group, and a huge group of people living in abject poverty. A middle class is almost nonexistent. Likewise, workers in foreign countries often toil under sweatshop conditions that would not be tolerated in this country (see Bigelow, 1997). Two related questions usually arise in this context: (1) Should elementary and middle-school children be exposed to activities that highlight inequities, unfairness, and injustice in the world? and (2) Should children deal with both the "good" and the "bad" in the world, or should we highlight just the "good" and de-emphasize the "bad"?

The "Doomsday" effect

Overemphasizing global problems, such as inequities in the distribution of resources, environmental pollution, or the possibility of nuclear war, can sometimes lead to what has been called the "Doomsday effect." This occurs when students come away from global education activities believing that the world is an awful place, that its problems are unsolvable, and that Doomsday is inevitable. Yet the other extreme, oversimplification, is equally undesirable. For children to say such things as "We wouldn't have homeless people if they'd just get jobs" or "We wouldn't have terrorist bombings if someone would just shoot 'X' [the leader of a nation in the Middle East]" vastly and inaccurately oversimplifies complex problems. In other words, either extreme—overemphasis or oversimplification—can be misleading.

Scope. Global education does not seek to make children into experts in world affairs by the time they leave elementary or middle school. Also, the broad perspective of global education can sometimes pose problems for young children whose perspective is so much narrower and who see themselves as members of their families and their classes at school, but who do not yet think of themselves as functioning members of other communities (the state, nation, world, etc.) in which they live. A global emphasis in elementary and middle schools can address such simple things as the ways in which people everywhere satisfy their need for food, housing, and a sense of safety.

Resources for teaching global education are located in the Resource Handbook.

Goals. The following goals for global education apply throughout the K–12 curriculum.

K–12 Goals for Global Education

Students will:

1. see themselves as members of (a) a family, (b) other groups, (c) the nation, (d) the human species, and (e) inhabitants of the planet.

The encompassing role of global education

2. identify basic human commonalities. Some of these include a common dependence on the biosphere, basic human needs and desires, similar cultural adaptations, and common problems, such as population growth, resource depletion, and pollution.

3. describe interconnections between their lives and the society in which they live, as well as their impact on global conditions, and vice versa.
4. practice the skills required to participate in and to shape a global society, including communication, problem solving and conflict resolution, and functioning in a group.
5. understand that people everywhere have overlapping membership in various social, cultural, and loyalty-demanding groups.
6. analyze events from a global perspective.
7. show empathy for the perspective from which others view the world.

Energy and Environmental Education

A subset of global education

If you had difficulty classifying Shane Fielding's lessons in our opening vignette, it is probably because global education serves as an umbrella for social, political, and environmental issues that affect people everywhere. Environmental problems—like water pollution, acid rain, and deforestation—also can be covered as part of global education or in the narrower context of energy and environmental education.

In this narrower context, we recently learned that a Dutch company has begun to ship its computers packed in popcorn—minus the salt and butter, of course—instead of Styrofoam nuggets. Likewise, as we were driving south of San Francisco not long ago, we came upon a wind farm—an area covered with hundreds, perhaps thousands, of tall, wind-driven generators. We suspect that no one needs to tell you why popcorn replaced the Styrofoam or what the windmills are used for. Information about the environment and alternative energy sources is almost inescapable in the media and elsewhere.

Examining the use of resources in a broader context

The purpose of energy and environmental education is not to indoctrinate children in a particular cause or point of view—to be for or against nuclear power, for example—but to help them examine the allocation and use of resources in relation to the total ecosystem. In this respect, Kniep (1986) noted,

> Of all the species that make up life on the planet, human beings, because of our capacity to manage and exploit, maintain or destroy, have become the most critical actors in the ecological system. A global education will . . . help students to feel part of the living world, to respect it and their unique place in it, and to undertake individual actions only after consideration of their actions on the whole ecological system. (p. 440)

K–12 Goals for Energy and Environmental Education

The students will:

1. recognize the consequences of human intervention on the total ecosystem.
2. describe the effect of different energy use on the environment.
3. practice acceptable custodianship of the Earth.
4. explain the collective role that they play in the use and abuse of the environment and of various energy forms.
5. weigh the potential benefits of technological advances against the potential dangers that such advances pose for the environment.

Law-Related Education

If your experience was anything like ours, you probably sat through your share of lessons on such topics as "How a Bill Becomes a Law" or on the legal distinction between felonies and misdemeanors. Despite the long tradition of teaching about the courts and the legal system in general, the basic question here concerns how law-related education is different from what schools have been doing all along.

Understanding the basis of law

The renewed emphasis on law-focused education is in part a response to a general ignorance of the practical operation of the legal system and a growing sense of powerlessness among people who believe that legal rights are available only to certain individuals (Wasson, 1994). It is also a reaction against the traditional approach to teaching about the law as a body of theoretical principles. Law-related education does not deny the need for students to understand traditional topics, such as the Constitution and the Bill of Rights or the structure of the legal system or the lawmaking process. However, the goal of law-related education is to help children understand the basis of law (or jurisprudence) and the role it plays in daily life.

Teaching Implications

Young children can deal with many law-related concepts, at least in part. For example, even very young students have well-developed ideas about fairness, which they are quick to demonstrate if they feel they are being treated unfairly. Initially, young children's concepts of fairness are me-oriented and egocentric: "Why can't I do what you are letting her do?" "Why does he get a candy bar but I don't?" The basic task is to extend that me-oriented sense of fairness to a "we" orientation. Other law-related concepts besides fairness that can be developed in elementary and middle schools include authority, equality, freedom, honesty, participation, property, privacy, responsibility, and tolerance.

Using Children's Literature. Children's literature often provides an excellent vehicle for examining law-related concepts. For instance, you may remember the classic tale *The Little Red Hen,* in which a hen finds several grains of wheat. Her pleas for help to plant and harvest the wheat and then grind it into flour go unheeded, and she is forced to do everything herself. But when the bread emerges from the oven, she discovers many volunteers who are willing to help her eat it. However, because nobody helped her to do the work, she decides to eat the bread herself. And she does!

Using literature for law-related education

Instead of moralizing about the story, a teacher could work toward building upon the children's concept of fairness by asking, "Was the little red hen fair to the others?" and "Was she fair to herself?" Conducting good discussions among primary-level children (to whom such stories are usually told) is often difficult, so consider using stories like *The Little Red Hen* with older students—even sixth, seventh, or eighth graders. Many of them will recall the stories, and you may be pleasantly surprised at how well they respond to them in a new context.

Using Case Studies. Law schools often use a case study approach for teaching prospective attorneys, and the technique has been refined and simplified somewhat for upper elementary and middle-school students. Case studies usually capture the essential elements of real legal cases, some of which were decided in the Supreme Court.

Few teachers have the time or the legal expertise to develop case studies on their own, so we recommend that you consult sources, such as *Cases: A Resource Guide for Teaching about the Law,* Goodyear Books, Scott, Foresman and Company, 1900 East Lake Avenue, Glenview, IL 60025, or the other resources listed in the Resource Handbook.

Law-related case studies for children must focus on significant legal questions and issues but without involving them in the courtroom posturing and legal minutiae—the kind of thing they often see on TV—that can easily become overwhelming. In using cases with children, it is also important for teachers to keep their personal views to themselves until children have shared their perspectives. The key element in any case study is not the verdict, although that can never be dismissed, but in helping children understand the important issues and questions that are involved.

Keep a focus on the issues

Using Mock Trials. Conducting mock trials of significant legal cases goes hand in hand with law-related education, but the amount of background information such trials require is far larger than you might anticipate. For example, you cannot conduct a mock trial based on a bare-bones description of an incident as simple as a car wreck and then let the witnesses imagine what each of them saw—the result would be chaos. All participants must have detailed accounts so that they are able to present their version of the incident in the trial and then withstand cross-examination. Then, too, because five witnesses may present five different accounts of the same incident, this phenomenon needs to be accommodated so that the witnesses can present themselves credibly during the trial. Because the amount of background information that mock trials require is often extensive, the materials available from commercial sources often use videocassettes to present it.

In addition to the facts of the case, most mock trial participants also need information on trial procedures. These include opening statements, the order in which witnesses are presented, how the judge charges the jury (assuming it is a jury trial), and so forth. Here, again, commercially available materials often use videocassettes to present the procedural information.

Instead of a real legal case, consider conducting a mock trial for an incident from a fairy tale. For example, was Goldilocks guilty of trespassing when she entered the home of the Three Bears? Or was Mr. MacGregor guilty of attempted assault when he attacked Peter Rabbit for eating the vegatables in his garden? In the Peter Rabbit case, the first decision is who to put on trial, Peter or Mr. MacGregor? Because most students already know the story line of most fairy tales, the amount of background information they need is almost nil. Even though the characters are mythical, these mock trials can teach important law-related concepts. Mock trial materials for fairy tale characters are often available from state or regional service centers, so be sure to check with them before setting out on your own.

Placing fairy tale characters on trial

Most mock trials usually have three phases: (1) preparation, (2) enactment, and (3) debriefing. This usually requires a substantial block of time, possibly a week or more if you are dealing with a real case and somewhat less if you are dealing with a mythical character. To justify committing that much classroom time, be certain that whatever case you deal with involves substantial and significant issues, like human rights, discrimination, or equality before the law. An excellent resource is M. Hickey, "Mock Trials for Children," *Social Education*, 54 (1990), 43–44.) Also, be sure to investigate the commercially available materials noted in the Resource Handbook.

Goals

The goals for law-related education, like those for other instructional themes presented in this chapter, should be viewed as long-term expectations. The following summary is from Anderson (1980) and presents each goal as a continuum.

K–12 Goals for Law-Related Education

Children Move Away From	*Children Move Toward*
* perceiving law as restrictive, punitive, immutable, and beyond the control and understanding of the people affected	* perceiving law as promotive, facilitative, comprehensible, and alterable
* perceiving people as powerless before the law and other socio-civic institutions	* perceiving people as having the potential to contribute to the social order
* perceiving issues of right and wrong as incomprehensible to ordinary people	* perceiving right and wrong as issues all citizens can and should address
* being impulsive decision-makers and problem solvers who make unreflective commitments	* being reflective decision-makers and problem solvers who make grounded commitments
* being inarticulate about commitments made or positions taken	* being able to give reasoned explanations about commitments made and positions taken
* being unable to manage conflict in other than a coercive or destructive manner	* being socially responsible conflict managers
* being uncritically defiant of authority	* being critically responsive to legitimate authority
* being illiterate about legal issues and the legal system	* being knowledgeable about law, the legal system, and related issues
* being egocentric, self-centered, and indifferent to others	* being empathetic, socially responsible, and considerate of others

Children Move Away From	Children Move Toward
* being morally immature in responding to ethical problems	* being able to make mature judgments in dealing with ethical and moral problems

Source: Charlotte C. Anderson, "Promoting Responsible Citizenship through Elementary Law-Related Education." Reprinted by permission from National Council for the Social Studies *Social Education.*

Gender-Equity Education

The first illustration in a first-grade social studies book from the 1960s shows a neatly dressed, aproned woman standing on the front steps waving good-bye to her children as they board the school bus. Several pages later, after the children have reached school, the pictures show that the teacher and nurse are female and the principal and custodian are male. Somewhat later in the book, a briefcase-carrying male arrives home from work (according to the text) and is then shown, his feet on the ottoman, reading the newspaper. In the same illustration, the woman (who we know by then is the wife and mother) is shown preparing dinner in the kitchen. When the family goes on trips—which families do often in first-grade books—guess who drives?

Consider the subtle messages that such illustrations can convey to children. They begin with "A woman's place is in the home" and go on from there. Such messages are simplistic and sexist, and they inaccurately depict and limit the roles and responsibilities of both women and men in modern society.

Current social studies textbooks are far less guilty of such treatments. They often show single-parent families, women in roles traditionally viewed as male, and men in roles traditionally viewed as female. In the future, we expect that such roles will be increasingly identified as gender-free and that expressions such as "traditionally viewed as male (or female)" will become meaningless. Meanwhile, teachers should be sensitive to instructional materials that may still present forms of gender-role stereotyping, or that stereotype the poor, members of different races, and so on (see Schmuck & Schmuck, 1994). The immediate goal of gender-equity education involves the equal treatment of people regardless of gender, but it is part of a broader goal that encompasses the inclusion of individuals regardless of gender, race, age, religion, or economic position.

No teaching materials focus explicitly on gender-equity education, at least none that we know of. As a result, gender-equity education places more demands on the teacher than perhaps any of the other instructional themes we have dealt with in this chapter. Gender-equity education focuses primarily on helping children develop a way of looking at the world—and at how individuals are treated within that world—not on learning a body of information. You can play a key role in that process, especially by selecting teaching materials in which the gender-role treatment is balanced and equitable (Flynn &

Use older materials cautiously

A female police officer in the classroom can speak volumes about the increasing equity among individuals of either gender. (© *Michael Zide*)

Chambers, 1994). You can also call attention to the inequitable treatment of individuals of either gender in whatever situations or materials the children encounter.

Despite significant progress in presenting gender roles equitably, even some contemporary materials may be guilty of promoting gender bias, though less blatantly than in the past. For example, Bigelow (1996) suggests that the popular computer simulation, *Oregon Trail* (MECC) can contribute to gender bias. Bigelow argues that even if students play a female character—a selection they make at the beginning of the game—most of the decisions they are asked to make are usually made by males, not females. This does not mean the *Oregon Trail* is unsuitable for children, but it does mean that some of the same cautions that apply to classic fairy tales may also apply to contemporary materials.

K–12 Goals for Gender-Equity Education

Students will:

1. identify instances of sexism in their lives.
2. describe the socialization process that initiates and maintains sexism.
3. identify gender bias in textbooks and other instructional materials.

Internet Resources for Teaching Instructional Themes

Locating teaching resources for instructional themes on the Internet sometimes requires that you look under more generic titles. For example, we found an excellent lesson plan based on the children's tradebook *Mama Is a Miner* (Lyon, 1994) that would be appropriate for gender-equity education. It was located under the category "Economics and Geography Lessons" at:

> http://www/mcps.k12.md.us/curriculum/
> socialstd/grade2/Mama_Miner.html

The Teacher Forum of the Center for Adolescent Studies at Indiana University has a large collection of on-line lesson plans for mock trials, environmental education, and most of the instructional themes in this chapter. These lessons are geared to middle-school and high-school students, but most of them are not reading intensive and can easily be adapted to the lower grades. These lessons are available at:

> http://education.indiana.edu/cas/ttforum/
> lesson.html

Additional Internet-based resources for other instructional themes are listed below.

Global/Environmental Education

A basic resource for global and environmental education is the American Forum for Global Education at:

> http://www.globaled.org/

In addition, an excellent series of lessons based on solid wastes is available from the Cornell University Solid Waste Project at:

> http://nceet.snre.umich.edu:777/11/
> activities/cornell

How to Make an Apple Pie and See the World (Priceman, 1994) is a beautifully illustrated story about a girl who gathers the ingredients for an apple pie from locations all over the world. The lesson plan is available at:

> http://www.mcps.k12.md.us/curriculum/
> socialstd/grade2/How_Make.html

Law-Related Education

Sample lesson plans for topics such as "What are the possible consequences of privacy?" and "What responsibilities accompany our rights?" are available from the Center for Civic Education at:

> http://www.primenet.com/~ccc.lesson-
> plans.html

This location also has additional teaching resources, as does the Constitutional Rights Foundation at:

> http://www.crf-usa.org/select/html

Summary

Individually and collectively, the instructional themes covered in this chapter reflect beliefs or positions that are thought to be desirable for children (and adults) to hold. For example, the goal of global education is to help children see themselves as citizens in a world community and to understand that problems in one part of that community can affect individuals in other parts of the globe.

A knowledge component and a value component are associated with each theme. The knowledge components include such things as understanding the nature of interdependence in a world community (global education), identifying contributions to society from different cultural groups (multicultural education), and understanding the pervasiveness of law in our daily life (law-related education). The value component is reflected by the fact that not everyone agrees about the desirability of all the themes. For example, opponents to gender-equity education sometimes argue that it will destroy traditional sex roles in American families and could lead to the destruction of the family as we know it. On the other hand, proponents argue that gender-equity education should reflect the changes that have already taken place or are currently under way in both families and the larger society. Whether your personal view leans toward the opponents or the proponents, the fact that you have a personal viewpoint further reflects the value base that underlies each of the themes we've dealt with in this chapter.

Suggested Activities

1. Select two social studies texts for the same grade level and examine how they treat the topic "family." Decide if the texts promote a particular bias.
2. Assume that you are teaching in a community in which a small but vocal segment of the population belongs to very conservative, fundamentalist religious groups. Classify the instructional themes treated in this chapter into one of two categories: (a) those that are likely to arouse active opposition from this segment of the population, and (b) those that are less likely to arouse such opposition.
3. Obtain a fifth-grade social studies text. Using the index entries for "Native Americans" and one other identifiable ethnic group as a guide, assess the overall balance of the way the two groups are treated.

Suggested Readings

K. Checkly. (1996). Reducing gender bias in school. *Education Update*. Association for Supervision and Curriculum Development, 38 (1). Much of the overt gender bias in schools has already been eliminated. This practical article focuses on eliminating the more subtle forms that still exist.

Anthony Fredricks. (1991). *Social studies through children's literature: An integrated approach*. Englewood, CO: Teachers Idea Press. The book provides an easy-to-follow approach for integrating children's literature into social studies lessons.

Mildred Knight Laughlin & Patricia Payne Kardaleff. (1991). *Literature-based social studies: Children's books & activities to enrich the K–5 curriculum*. Phoenix, AZ: Oryx Press. This wonderful little book presents sample literature-based lessons that are keyed to grade levels and the social studies topics typically taught at those levels.

Mary Kay Thompson Tetreault (Ed.). (1987). Women, gender, and the social studies. *Social Education*, 51 (March), 167–213. This special section takes the perspective that, by making women an integral part of social studies education, we change the way we think about both men and gender.

6 Developing Character and Values

Key Questions

* What gives schools and teachers the right to intervene in children's values and morals?

* How sensitive must teachers be to parental and community expectations?

* What are the moral implications associated with teaching or *not* teaching values and character?

Key Ideas

* The school's role in teaching values and character continues to be controversial.

* Every teacher teaches values and morals, whether explicitly or implicitly; it's an unavoidable fact of teaching . . . and living.

* Community expectations concerning values education are seldom consistent, nor are they necessarily known in advance.

* The key components of character education are (1) values themselves and (2) a process of valuing. General agreement on these components does not exist.

* Alternative approaches to values education include (1) inculcation, (2) literature-based techniques, (3) values clarification, (4) moral reasoning, and (5) values analysis.

* The "hidden curriculum" is a powerful instrument of instruction.

Introduction: The Reemergence of Character Education

Teachers cannot avoid teaching morals and values even if they want to. Everything they say and do, everything they study and discuss in class, even how they operate their classrooms, will reflect the values and standards that guide their conduct. Simply by observing your actions and deeds, children will learn what you think is important, valuable, and worth cherishing—and what is not. Without your saying a word about respecting others, for example, your students will know whether you respect them as individuals.

We're not suggesting that children will necessarily adopt your values or any teacher's values. Some children may have value systems that prompt them to reject what you hold dear. When that happens, it's difficult not to take the child's rejection of what you value as a rejection of you personally. It takes a strong person who, in the face of defiance and rejection, can still say to a child, "I care about you regardless of how you feel about me." At the same time, the child's out-of-school environments may also reflect a self-centered, "do your own thing" mentality that directly contradicts many of the behaviors you are trying to model. Nevertheless, for those of us who intervene in children's lives, teaching morals and values is an inescapable fact of life.

When we wrote the first edition of this book over twenty years ago, serious questions were being asked about the school's role in teaching morals and values. At the time, the nation was extracting itself from the war in Vietnam, and teaching even long-cherished values like patriotism had become controversial. As new faculty members, we witnessed the antiwar riots and protests on our campus and elsewhere among individuals who believed that the Vietnamese conflict was an unjust war that the United States should get out of as quickly as possible. Many of those protestors also believed that the notion of patriotism as "Our country, right or wrong," was itself wrong, and that expecting them to support an unjust war was immoral. Such antiwar views often clashed with the views of other Americans who believed that the nation was obliged to support its armed forces, regardless of whether they personally supported or opposed the war. Those were troubling times indeed.

When the United States was involved in the Korean conflict in the early 1950s, similar protests did not occur. In the time between the two wars, the moral climate had changed dramatically. Beginning after World War II and continuing into the 1960s, more and more people in America (and around the world) began to embrace a rampant form of individualism that was divorced from notions of social responsibility. Also emerging at that time was a movement toward *logical positivism:* that is, the tendency to distinguish between facts, which were scientifically verifiable, and matters involving morals and values, which were regarded as expressions of personal feelings or preferences. Thus, when someone advocated a particular course of action as "the right thing to do," the usual responses were "Says who?" and "Nobody can force me to do anything I don't want to." Values and morals were becoming personalized and privatized, and moral and value issues were increasingly seen not as matters of doing the right thing, but as matters of personal judgment. For many Americans, morality was becoming a matter of "doing one's own thing."

Lickona (1993) suggests that the era between the Korean and Vietnam wars and into the 1970s and 1980s was marked by a worldwide rise in *personalism.* This was and is a social movement that celebrates the autonomy of individuals. Personalism emphasized individual rights and freedoms. As Lickona stated, "Personalism rightly protested societal oppression and injustice, but it also delegitimized moral authority, . . . turned people inward toward self-fulfillment, weakened social commitments (for example, to marriage and parenting), and fueled the socially destabilizing sexual revolution" (p. 6).

Questioning the school's role in teaching values

President Theodore Roosevelt once said, "To educate a person in mind and not in morals is to educate a menace to society." Nevertheless, the legitimacy of teaching morals and values in the schools began to be questioned during the 1970s and 1980s. In the process, many schools and teachers began consciously avoiding explicit instruction in moral and ethical principles, at least to the extent they could (see Sizer, 1985). In place of the school's traditional role in character education, they began focusing almost exclusively on the knowledge component of education—on transmitting "smartness."

The concerns for self-fulfillment and individual rights continued through the 1980s and into the 1990s, but disheartening signs arose on the horizon. Many families were no longer the stabilizing force in society they once were; crime and corruption were increasing; everyday life was becoming increasingly uncivil; and sex, nudity, and violence were becoming commonplace on TV and in the movies.

Calls for returning to teaching morals and values

By the mid-1980s, some authorities had begun to call for a return to the school's former role of providing explicit instruction in morals and values (see Kohlberg, 1980; Shaver, 1985). For example, Ryan (1986) contended that by *not* treating values explicitly, the schools were doing only half their job. In a Gallup poll for 1990, more than half (57 percent) of the parents responding felt that schools should offer a *required* course in character education (Elam, 1990). It's apparent that many people didn't like some of the changes that they were seeing in society, and perhaps in their children.

Character education

By the mid-1990s, the occasional voices suggesting that our society was facing a growing number of problems had become a chorus. Some individuals, like William Kilpatrick (1992), suggested that in addition to persistent educational problems—like Johnny's inability to read well—an even more serious problem is that Johnny doesn't seem to know the difference between right and wrong. The contention among many observers was that schools could not remain morally and ethically neutral, but must return to their traditional role of teaching character education. In the late 1990s, character education is returning to many schools, in some cases with a vengeance.

Schools mirror the society

The schools had some valid reasons for backing off from traditional character education in the 1960s and 1970s. How, for example, could teachers continue to teach about "doing the right thing" when the larger society said, in effect, "It's O.K. to do your own thing"? Schools always tend to mirror the larger society, so to whatever extent the society says "we are going in this direction," the schools inevitably follow (see Rogers & Frieberg, 1994). When society effectively said "Back off on teaching values as moral absolutes," schools did. Today, however, more and more people are turning to schools to do something about the problems facing our society. Yet there is no clear consensus on (1) how schools should accomplish the task, or (2) whether schools have the tools and skills necessary to remedy moral problems.

Can schools do the job?

In the first part of this chapter, we examine some current attempts to reestablish character education in the schools. In the following sections, we turn to several alternative approaches for dealing with value issues.

Terminology Clarified

Ethics defined, from the Greek

The area of morals and values can easily become a morass of vague terms, so we have included the following definitions:

Ethics comes from the Greek *ethikos* and refers to norms and standards for judging behaviors as right and good or wrong and bad. In popular usage, ethics is typically used in connection with how we conduct our relationships with others; for example, persons who act unethically always do so in relationship to someone else.

Morals defined, from Latin

Morals is the Latin version of the Greek *ethikos* and carries the same meaning. In popular usage, *morals* often refers to the norms and standards that guide behavior.

Values defined

Values are ideas that serve as standards of conduct, beauty, efficiency, or worth. No one has ever seen an individual's values because they, like all ideas, are mental constructs. But we can observe how people behave, which indicates what they value.

Ethics and aesthetics

The standards we use for determining beauty are usually treated separately from standards of conduct, efficiency, and worth. For example, what we enjoy and find beautiful, such as a spectacular sunset, is said to reflect *aesthetics*. Aesthetic matters, such as whether you like or dislike modern art or classical music, seldom involve moral or ethical considerations. One way to think of this is that morality and ethics deal with "right" and "wrong," whereas aesthetics deals with what we think of as good or bad, beautiful or ugly.

Virtue defined

Virtue, a term popular in the Victorian era, is enjoying a rebirth (see Bennett, 1994; Doyle, 1997; Himmelfarb, 1995). It refers to qualities that all individuals should strive for, such as honesty, truthfulness, self-respect, and self-reliance. Himmelfarb suggests that the need to distinguish between virtues and values has come about because values in popular usage can refer to "beliefs, opinions, attitudes, feelings, habits, conventions, preferences, even idiosyncrasies—whatever any individual, group or society happens to value, at any time and for any reason" (p. 3). Some authorities use the term *core values* to describe virtues such as those noted above and to set them apart from other values.

Character

Character refers to virtuous behavior—behavior that conforms to valued norms and customs.

Building Character

When one of the school's missions was to "melt" newly arrived immigrants into the mainstream society, the teaching of values and morals was usually called *character education*. That term is enjoying a rebirth today, but you will sometimes hear it called *values education* or *moral education*. All three terms refer to what schools do to help children become ethically mature adults who are capable of practicing moral thought and action in democratic ways.

As part of their character education mission, many schools in the 1920s and 1930s devised pledges and codes of conduct. The "Children's Morality Code," for example, stressed duty, good health, good workmanship, and teamwork in addition to the core values previously noted (Leming, 1993). Teachers also used techniques that included preaching, modeling desired behaviors, and, occasionally, mocking children who deviated from what was expected. Whatever success the schools enjoyed in these efforts was judged by the extent to which the core values (or virtues) were incorporated into students' belief systems and, ultimately, their behavior.

What to teach, exactly?

Teaching character is clearly a more complex enterprise than teaching content-oriented lessons. For example, what exactly would you teach if you wanted your students to demonstrate respect for others? There is some excellent children's literature that you could use, which we will indicate shortly, but unlike conventional subjects, character traits do not have any easily defined content. You might resort to preaching platitudes like "Be nice to others," but the research indicates that such exhortations, as well as various codes and pledges, are unlikely to have any lasting effects on students' character (see Leming, 1993).

What Is Good Character?

The purpose of character education is to develop good character in the young. One authority, Thomas Lickona, suggests that "good character consists of knowing the good, desiring the good, and doing the good" (1993, p. 9). Lickona's definition, broad as it is, highlights a major difference between character and conventional knowledge-based subjects. In addition to a cognitive (or knowledge)

The multidimensional nature of character

Is this the future of teaching in the age of technology? © 1997. Reprinted courtesy of Bunny Hoest and PARADE Magazine.

"Keep your eyes on your own monitor, and don't e-mail anyone."

dimension that character traits share with conventional subjects, character also has an attitudinal (or feeling) dimension and a psychomotor (or behavioral) dimension that conventional subjects usually lack. Many children already know about values like honesty and truthfulness, for example, but nobody needs to tell you that some children (and adults) will still be dishonest or lie whenever it suits their purpose. What they may lack is an attitude, a disposition, a conscience if you will, that disposes them to do the right thing regardless of its ultimate effect on them. The affective, or dispositional, component of character provides an essential bridge between character's cognitive (or knowing) dimensions and a person's actions. The cognitive, affective, and behavioral dimensions of character, as identified by Lickona (1993), are summarized in Table 6.1.

Simply knowing about character is inadequate

Which Values Should Be Taught?

Parents who oppose character education often do so out of fear that schools will indoctrinate their children about gay rights, abortion, premarital sex, and similar matters. The issue is compounded by individuals who want schools to deal explicitly with such issues. The character education programs we know of focus not on a political agenda, but on core values, or virtues, that are (1) basic to morality and (2) that almost no one opposes. Those values include respect, the dignity of the individual, personal and civic responsibility, honesty, trustworthiness, fairness, caring, and courage. (All of these values are elements of community literacy that we referred to in Chapter 1.) Some schools integrate elements of character education into their programs without using an explicit label like *character education,* whereas other schools may use terms such as "*positive conflict resolution.*" Yet regardless of what they call it, most schools involve parents in meetings that focus on the values they intend to promote. Almost never do those schools encounter anyone who argues, for example, that lying is better than telling the truth.

Most programs focus on old-fashioned virtues

Academic Values. No one talks about them very much, but in addition to the virtues we noted above, there is also a core of values or principles that govern scholarship and academic work. These values focus primarily on procedures for working with data, and include such things as being relatively objective, having integrity in reporting one's findings, and not reporting someone else's work as one's own—as in copying a report from an encyclopedia. All of these values represent dispositions necessary to the processes of science and are reflected in the following guidelines, adapted from Bronowski (1973).

Values and procedures governing scholarship

The Procedural Values of Science
1. One should not make wild claims about human behavior or the nature of social environments.
2. One should establish "truth" based on evidence and logic, as opposed to personal hopes and feelings.
3. One should not base knowledge claims on prejudice or private authority.
4. One should use empirical (real-world) data as the basis for knowing.

Table 6.1 The Moral Components of Character

Dimension		Trait
Cognitive	1.	Awareness of the moral dimensions of a situation
	2.	Knowing moral values, like truthfulness, and what they require in concrete cases
	3.	Perspective taking, the ability to look at situations from various perspectives
	4.	Moral reasoning, the ability to differentiate among different rationales and motives for behaving in certain ways
	5.	Thoughtful decision making, the ability to assess alternative courses of action
	6.	Moral self-knowledge
Affective	1.	Conscience, the felt obligation to do what one judges is right
	2.	Self-respect
	3.	Empathy
	4.	Love of the good
	5.	Self-control
	6.	Humility, a willingness to recognize and correct our moral failings
Behavioral	1.	Competence, skills such as listening, communication, and cooperating
	2.	Will, which mobilizes judgment and energy
	3.	Moral habit, a reliable disposition to respond to situations in morally good ways

Source: Abridged from Thomas Lickona, "The Return of Character Education," *Educational Leadership,* 51, (1993), 10.

5. One should be willing to describe the processes and evidence upon which one's knowledge and findings are based.
6. One should not manipulate one's evidence to arrive at predetermined outcomes.
7. One should not attempt to persuade others at any cost.
8. One should not hide from others that which is not known.
9. One should respect and welcome individuals who challenge one's thoughts and thinking.
10. One should live with humility and in an appreciation of tolerance.

Academic values are seldom controversial, unless someone is suspected of violating one of them. At the same time, because academic values tend not to be dealt with explicitly, they often become part of the hidden curriculum.

Dealing with the Hidden Curriculum

The notion of the *hidden curriculum* has been around for years, but references to it occur increasingly throughout the character education literature (see Berreth & Scherer, 1993; Leming, 1993; Lickona, 1993; Lockwood, 1993; Ryan, 1993). This seems to reflect growing recognition that profound teachings are often conveyed by the hidden curriculum, that is, in the day-to-day schooling practices that all students experience but that are not part of the formal school curriculum. Consider, for example, teachers who talk about the importance of cooperation but then set up instructional programs in which students must compete for every reward. Other students will remember teachers for whom putting an incorrect heading on an otherwise perfect paper could produce devastating results.

Classroom Management Practices.

Many classroom management programs, including Lee Canter's popular Assertive Discipline (1989) and others like it, feature a series of systematic consequences for students who misbehave. For a first offense, the student's name goes on the board; for a second offense, the student must stay after school, and so forth. Although negative consequences can tend to reinforce the teacher role of "prison guard," they are usually only one part of such plans. As Canter notes, "The key to Assertive Discipline is catching students being good: recognizing them and supporting them when they behave appropriately" (p. 57). Rewarding students for good behavior might seem an appropriate balance for negative consequences, but as Kohn

Rewarding good behavior can have unintended consequences

COMMENTARY: **Communitarianism**

The social movements in the 1960s and 1970s that fostered the personalization and privatization of moral behavior that we see today had their roots in Europe. Perhaps it is fitting that some people are supporting a new social movement that seeks to move in the opposite direction. That movement, called *communitarianism,* was founded by Amitai Etzioni, a professor at George Washington University and author of *The Spirit of Community* (1993).

Communitarianism is rooted in two beliefs: (1) that strong individual rights presume equally strong responsibilities, and (2) that moral standards should be based on consensus, not individual choice alone. Communitar-ianism thus opposes the notion that the individual's rights must be preserved at all costs. According to Etzioni, "Society can't function if everybody takes and nobody gives, and that's happening, mainly because we uphold [individual] rights but not responsibilities" (interview in Berreth and Scherer, 1993, p. 15). We suspect that reversing the individualistic, "anything goes" mentality will be an uphill struggle and that getting people to voluntarily accept limitations on their unbounded individualism is a medicine that will not go down easily.

For information on the Communitarian Network, call 1-800-245-7460.

(1997) points out, this aspect of most management plans can sometimes undermine a character education program.

Regardless of the specific management plan teachers use, the key concern is how they reward good behavior. Providing students with tangible rewards can be an effective technique in the short run but can also have negligible or negative long-run effects. According to Kohn, questionable reward systems include (1) providing "bonus bucks" (or punching tickets or putting marbles into a jar) that can then be redeemed for an ice cream or pizza party, and (2) rewarding children with a leaf to hang in their "Forest of Virtue." Equally questionable, according to Kohn, are activities such as targeting a certain value on a particular day of the week—"If it's Thursday, this must be Respect Day"—and then rewarding children for demonstrating that day's value. One could ask, "What's wrong with respecting others on Mondays, or any other day of the week?" Even worse than tangible rewards, in Kohn's view, are awards that are so limited that only a few children can get them: "This week's winner of the Hard Worker Award is. . . ." Such awards—assuming children really value them—force children to compete with their peers and thus to regard their classmates as potential obstacles to success.

The downside of tangible rewards

Using tangible rewards for virtuous conduct is a form of extrinsic motivation that can undermine intrinsic motivation. What can children learn from such practices is not that virtuous behavior is good, desirable, and something worth doing on its own merits, but that the purpose of "being good" is to earn rewards. Frequent rewards for children who demonstrate virtuous behavior can make them *less* likely than other children to continue demonstrating those behaviors (Fabes et al., 1989; Grusec, 1991, cited in Kohn, 1997).

Extrinsic vs. intrinsic motivation

If you find yourself teaching in a school that has adopted Assertive Discipline, or a similar management plan, your options are necessarily limited. Because ignoring the school's plan would probably be unwise, you should consider modifying the plan, especially to the extent to which you provide tangible rewards for desired behaviors. In place of tangible rewards, consider using classroom meetings as they are described in William Glasser's *The Quality School* (1990) and his earlier works. From time to time, you might want to conduct classroom meetings that focus on whether it is "right" to reward people for doing what they ought to do anyhow.

An alternative to tangible rewards

The basic point here is that the hidden curriculum and classroom management practices must complement, or at least not contradict, everything else that schools and teachers do. In one study, Williams (1992) went so far as to suggest that "respect is best taught through a hidden curriculum of modeling and quality teaching" (p. 22). The hidden curriculum and questionable classroom management practices are such powerful forces that to ignore them could negate the purpose of a character education program.

Guidelines for Character Education

According to the current research (see Brooks & Kann, 1993, and Lickona, 1993), successful character education programs are comprehensive and schoolwide. For example, you may establish your classroom as a caring moral community, a

Schoolwide efforts

Many schools are including a community service component in their character education programs. *(© Grant Le Duc/Stock Boston)*

place where students respect and care about one another and feel membership in and responsibility to and for the group (Lickona, 1993). However, what you do in your classroom is more likely to have long-term results if the entire school functions as a caring moral community, where your classroom reflects the norm, not an exception, for classrooms throughout the school. Should you eventually teach in a school that does not have a schoolwide program, you can still operate your classroom as a caring, moral community, but don't be surprised if you feel like a lone voice in the wilderness.

Lickona (1993, pp. 10–11) recommends the following schoolwide actions to support character education:

Schoolwide actions

* *Fostering care beyond the classroom.* Using positive role models to inspire altruistic behavior and providing opportunities at every grade level to perform school and community service

* *Creating a positive moral culture in the school.* Developing a schoolwide ethos . . . that supports and amplifies the values taught in the classroom

* *Recruiting parents and the community as partners in character education.* Letting parents know that the school considers them their child's first and most important moral teacher, giving parents specific ways they can reinforce the values the school is trying to teach, and seeking the help of the community, churches, businesses, local government, and the media in promoting the core ethical values

Lickona also recommends the following as activities that individual teachers can use in their classrooms:

* *Acting as caregiver, model, and mentor.* Treating students with love and respect, setting a good example, supporting positive social behavior, and correcting hurtful actions through one-on-one guidance and whole-class discussions

* *Practicing moral discipline.* Using the creation and enforcement of rules as opportunities to foster moral reasoning, voluntary compliance with rules, and a respect for others

* *Creating a democratic classroom environment.* Involving students in decision making and sharing the responsibility for making the classroom a good place to be and learn

* *Teaching values through the curriculum.* Using ethically rich content of academic subjects (such as literature, history, and science) as well as outstanding programs, such as the Heartwood Ethics Curriculum for Children (which we describe shortly)

* *Using cooperative learning.* To develop students' appreciation of others, perspective taking, and ability to work with others toward common goals

* *Developing the "conscience of craft."* By fostering students' appreciation of learning, capacity for hard work, commitment to excellence, and sense of work as affecting the lives of others

* *Encouraging moral reflection.* Through reading, research, essay writing, journal keeping, discussion and debate

* *Teaching conflict resolution.* To help students acquire the essential moral skills of solving conflicts fairly and without force

The movement toward reestablishing character education will undoubtedly be challenging. If nothing else, many teachers today grew up in a cultural milieu that encouraged the personalization and privatization of moral values. Also, many questions exist for which there are no clear answers. Why, for example, do some people consistently act in morally responsible ways and others don't? And, can schools provide the same kind of moral anchors that families have provided in the past? Despite the unanswered questions, the consensus in the literature is that character education has become a moral imperative.

Other Approaches to Values Education

Most of the alternative approaches to values education we deal with in this section are amenable to ethical questions or to issues involving the moral standards or principles that influence one's behavior.

Inculcation

Throughout human history, *inculcation* (or exhortation) has been a common technique for molding human behavior. It refers to the process of making an impression on the mind through frequent repetition, insistent urging, or modeling. Inculcation, like brainwashing, is based on the premise that if you show or tell people something often enough, eventually they will behave accordingly.

Repeated telling

Whenever you hear parents (or teachers) saying things like "Good girls (or boys) don't do *that* kind of thing," they are using inculcation. Somewhere along the line, the parents identify the desired behavior, such as "Children should respect their elders." Then, over the years, they provide appropriate reinforcement—a nod or smile of approval when children demonstrate the desired behavior and a gentle reminder (or worse) when they don't.

For centuries parents have successfully inculcated desired values and behaviors in their children. And the children will usually behave as they are expected, at least when their parents are present. Even though many parents have used inculcation successfully, research suggests that it does not work equally well for teachers. The research doesn't indicate why this is so, but we suspect it has to do with contact time. Parents can consistently reinforce desired behaviors in their children from their birth onward. Teachers, on the other hand, have only a 180-day school year in which to accomplish the same thing. And children know that, come each September, they will have a different teacher who will probably hold different expectations.

Literature-Based Techniques

Most children have heard those famous lines "I think I can, I think I can, I think I can," and "I thought I could, I thought I could, I thought I could," which are from Walter Piper's (1930/1954) children's classic, *The Little Engine That Could.*

Literacy springboard to teaching values

Through diligence, perseverance, and a lot of effort, a little switch engine is able to pull a trainload of Christmas food and toys to the children who live on the other side of the mountain. If some of your students have never heard the story, you can read it again—even students familiar with the story will enjoy it another time. Children's stories like *The Little Engine That Could* can provide the basis for a follow-up discussion of how diligence, perseverance, and patience, combined with a positive attitude, can often overcome overwhelming obstacles. The children can also talk about times when positive attitudes have helped them complete challenging tasks or do things that they were afraid to do.

If you want to focus on behaving responsibly, you might consider reading Chris Van Allsburg's (1988) delightful tale, *Two Bad Ants.* This story focuses on an ant colony that sets out to retrieve a huge mound of delicious crystals

Examples

(sugar) their scouts have located. But instead of returning to the colony with all the other ants, the two bad ants decide to remain and feast for a while. The crystal pile soon becomes a dangerous place, and the two ants eventually end up in a coffee cup, are put down into the garbage disposal, and even get blown out of an electrical outlet where they are trying to hide. Needless to say, the ants suffer severe consequences for their actions.

Still in the context of responsible behavior, older students will enjoy Kate McMullan's (1991) *The Great Eggspectations of Lila Fenwick.* In this story, a librarian tries to teach sixth graders about responsibility by having them care for a hard-boiled egg as if it were a newborn baby. Lila discovers that many of her usually great ideas backfire on her as she tries to care for her egg.

So many literary works can serve as springboards for values-oriented discussions and activities that an extended listing of children's stories is included in the Resource Handbook. These stories are organized by the main values they focus on—sharing, responsibility, etc.

A literature-based approach to values education can be as organized (or unorganized) as you wish to make it. The basic procedure is to read the story to your students and then conduct a follow-up discussion or share-and-tell session. The discussion period should be regarded as a time to talk with children about the values in question, and not an opportunity to moralize.

Other literature-based programs

Two character education programs that make use of children's literature warrant special mention here. They are the Heartwood Ethics Curriculum and the Exploring Ethics through Children's Literature Program. The Heartwood program was developed by an attorney from Pittsburgh who was appalled by the lack of remorse among the young defendants she represented in court, as well as by some retired teachers from the Pittsburgh area. The Heartwood materials are based on Newbery award-winning, multicultural books (stories) that address core values such as courage, loyalty, justice, respect, hope, honest, and love. The Exploring Ethics through Children's Literature Program follows a similar format. For additional information about the Heartwood Ethics Curriculum, contact The Heartwood Institute, 12300 Perry Highway, Wexford, PA 15090 (412-934-1777). Additional information on the Exploring Ethics through Children's Literature Program is available from the Critical Thinking Press & Software, PO Box 448, Pacific Grove, CA 93950-0448 (1-800-458-4849).

Resources. Character education is such a "hot topic" that there many resources at your disposal. Some organizations offer character education programs, and others offer support services such as workshops; some offer both. A listing of character education resources is included in the Resource Handbook.

Values Clarification

Clarifying what our values are

Values clarification is one of the rare techniques whose title describes exactly what it tries to do: Help individuals *clarify* what their values really are. The underlying premise is that most individuals are not clear about what their values are until they are confronted by situations that cause them to examine their values.

Values clarification is a value-neutral approach that was created in the mid-1970s, when the explicit teaching of values was declining. Rather than trying to instill or impose certain values, values clarification is based on a seven-phase valuing process, as follows:

Choosing

The valuing process

1. Encourage children to make choices, and to make them freely.
2. Help them *discover alternatives* when faced with choices.
3. Help children weigh alternatives thoughtfully, reflecting on *the consequences* of each.

Prizing

4. Encourage children to consider what it is that they prize and *cherish*.
5. Give them opportunities to *affirm their* choices to others.

Acting

6. Encourage children to act, *behave,* and live *in accordance with their choices.*
7. Help them be aware of repeated behaviors or patterns in their life [emphasis added] (Raths et al., 1978, pp. 28, 38).

Why should people be clear about the values they hold? Raths et al. (1978, p. 10) state that "it seems to us that the pace and complexity of modern life has so exacerbated the problem of deciding what is good and what is right and what is desirable that large numbers of children are finding it increasingly bewildering, even overwhelming, to decide what is worth valuing, what is worth their time and energy."

The Clarifying Response.   A key element of values clarification is the clarifying response. This refers to how teachers respond to students, either individually or as a class, to help them identify what is important and desirable. In many instances, the exact form of the clarifying response will be situational and may take the form of a question, as illustrated in the following exchange:

TEACHER: Bruce, don't you want to go outside and play on the playground?

STUDENT: I dunno. I suppose so.

The clarifying response

TEACHER: Is there something that you would rather do?

STUDENT: I dunno. Nothing much.

TEACHER: You don't seem much to care, Bruce. Is that right?

STUDENT: I suppose so.

TEACHER: And mostly anything we do will be all right with you?

STUDENT: I suppose so. Well, not anything, I guess.

TEACHER: Well, Bruce, we'd better go out with the others now. You let me know sometime if you think of something you would like to do. (Dialogue adapted from Raths et al., 1978, p. 55.)

The intent here is not to get the student to adopt the values clarification process in a fifteen-second exchange. Clarifying responses should encourage students to examine their ideas, but without the teacher moralizing, criticizing, evaluating, or otherwise suggesting that they have a "right answer" in mind (Raths et al., 1978). If the exchange isn't genuine, it will fall flat on its face.

Productive clarifying response questions include the following:

Suggested clarifying responses

Is this important to you?
Are you happy about that?
Did you think of other (alternative) things you could do?
Would you really do that or are you just talking?
What other possibilities are there?
Would you do the same thing over again?

Is it important enough that you would be willing to share your idea (project, experiences, etc.) with the others? (Raths et al., 1978, pp. 59–63)

What Critics Say About Values Clarification.   Most criticisms of the values clarification approach have focused on techniques that (1) could jeopardize the student's right to privacy, (2) could place teachers in the role of a trained counselor (or psychiatrist), (3) fail to distinguish between moral and nonmoral issues, and (4) suggest that all value beliefs are equally valid (ethical relativism) (Lockwood, 1977). It is difficult for students to state their beliefs publicly without disclosing personal information about themselves and their relationships with others, including their families. Thus any one of the clarifying questions could lead to a potential invasion of the student's right to privacy. Invasion is even more likely if explicit questioning techniques are used, for example, if students are asked to identify who in their family brings them the greatest sadness. Then, too, the clarifying questions as shown on page 140 are much like those that trained counselors and psychologists use in group therapy sessions. For example, it is easy enough to ask a child, "Is that important to you?", but the child's responses could go beyond those you are trained to handle.

Potential to invade one's privacy

Simple questions can have hard-to-handle responses

Values clarification activities have also been criticized for failing to distinguish between moral (ethical) and nonmoral (aesthetic) value issues. There is obviously nothing immoral about asking students to identify their favorite foods, or how they would spend their allowance, both of which are largely a matter of personal priorities. However, in a popular values clarification activity called "The Bomb Shelter," students are asked to select which six of ten candidates—which include a doctor, a violinist, a police officer, and a law student

Treating aesthetic and moral issues alike

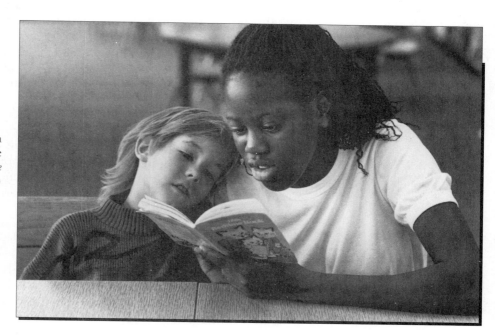

When students help each other, both may gain from the experience. (© Jean-Claude Lejeune)

and his wife—should be permitted to enter the shelter. Candidates who are not admitted will presumably die. Asking children to determine which individuals should be permitted to live and which should die, as well as whether doctors make greater contributions to society than do violinists, is a far different matter from asking about a student's favorite flavor of ice cream. We question whether children should be placed in situations where they are asked to (1) make life-or-death decisions, or (2) judge the relative merits of different occupations.

A final criticism of the values clarification approach is that it tends to promote *ethical relativism*. This means that instead of using overarching moral principles, such as the dignity of the individual and the sanctity of human life— principles that should apply in all situations—the values clarification approach seems to suggest that individuals' actions should be governed by the situations in which they find themselves, and by what is practical or expedient. This criticism arises, in part, because there is no justification phase in the seven-step valuing process (pages 139–140). Because students are not asked to justify or defend their decisions, they could come away with the impression that one person's views are as good as anyone else's, regardless of the situation.

After reviewing over seventy-five studies involving values clarification approaches, Leming (1985) found that they seldom produced the kinds of attitudinal or behavioral changes the researchers had anticipated. Leming therefore suggested that the popularity of values clarification activities may result, in part, from their widespread availability for classroom use.

Moral Reasoning

The *moral-reasoning* approach to values education is closely associated with the work of the late Harvard psychologist Lawrence Kohlberg and his associates. Kohlberg first developed a theory that dealt with how children learn to reason morally and then developed a teaching strategy to help children improve the quality of their moral reasoning. To determine what makes one kind of moral reasoning "better" than another, it's necessary to understand the moral development theory on which Kohlberg's teaching strategy is based.

Moral Development. Kohlberg's research focused on the question "How do individuals develop the ability to reason morally (to justify their actions)?" After investigating moral reasoning among individuals of various ages and from various cultures, Kohlberg identified a developmental sequence, which is shown in Table 6.2. (At one time the developmental sequence had six stages, but Kohlberg redefined his model so that Stage 5 now incorporates what was formerly in Stage 6.)

In Jean Piaget's scheme for cognitive development, sooner or later almost everyone reaches the last stage, formal operations: the ability to think and reason abstractly. However, Kohlberg found that fewer than 25 percent of American adults ever reach Stage 5 (Principled level) in the development of their moral reasoning. If you consider that the moral basis of the Bill of Rights reflects Stage 5 reasoning, Kohlberg's findings suggest that many citizens may neither understand nor appreciate the fundamental moral principles upon which the nation was founded. This also helps to explain why many fifth- and

Ethical relativism

Implications

Table 6.2 Kohlberg's Stages of Moral Development

Level	Stage	Characteristics
Principled: Concern for fidelity to self-chosen moral principles	5	*Motivator:* Internal commitment to principles of "conscience"; respect for the rights, life, and dignity of all persons. *Awareness:* Particular moral/social rules are social contracts, arrived at through democratic reconciliation of differing viewpoints and open to change. *Assumption:* Moral principles have universal validity; law derives from morality, not vice versa.
Conventional: Concern for meeting external social expectations	4	*Motivator:* Sense of duty or obligation to live up to socially defined role and maintain existing social order for good of all. *Awareness:* There is a larger social "system" that regulates the behavior of individuals within it. *Assumption:* Authority or the social order is the source of morality.
	3	*Motivator:* Desire for social approval by living up to good boy/good girl stereotype; meeting expectations of others. *Awareness:* Need to consider intentions and feelings of others; cooperation means ideal reciprocity (golden rule). *Assumption:* Good behavior equals social conformity.
Preconventional: Concern for external, concrete consequences to self	2	*Motivator:* Self-interest: What's in it for me? *Awareness:* Human relations are governed by concrete reciprocity; let's make a deal; You scratch my back, I'll scratch yours. *Assumption:* Have to look out for self; obligated only to those who help you; each person has own needs and viewpoints.
	1	*Motivator:* Fear of getting caught; desire to avoid punishment by authority. *Awareness:* There are rules and consequences of breaking them. *Assumption:* Might makes right; what's regarded by those in power is "good"; what's punished is "bad."

Source: Based on material in Thomas Lickona, "How to Encourage Moral Development," *Learning,* 5 (March 1977), 37–42.

eighth-grade teachers get frustrated teaching a required unit on "the Constitution"; the majority of their students may be operating at Stage 3, the level at which their primary interest is in gaining the social approval of others, as opposed to the Stage 5 reasoning on which the Constitution is based.

In Kohlberg's developmental scheme, each stage serves as a basis for the next. But unlike developmental schemes that link children of certain ages with

Holly and the Cat in the Tree—Procedure for Young Children

Introduce the Situation

TEACHER: One day, a little girl named Holly was walking down the street.

Role-Playing

TEACHER: We need someone to play Holly and the little boy. James? Do you want to play Holly?

JAMES: I'm not playin' no girl.

TEACHER: Sure you can, James. We're just role-playing.

JAMES: (Shakes his head no.)

TEACHER: Okay, Rosemary . . .

(Two students role-play a possible solution for the incident.)

1. Mini-discussion
   Teacher. Did they manage to solve the problem?
   (Brief discussion follows. If a child wants to suggest a different solution, move to part 2 immediately. If not, the teacher suggests another solution, secures new role players, and the incident is reenacted again.)
2. Role-play another alternative.

   Continue (1) and (2) until children are satisfied they have identified the possible alternatives.

Debriefing

1. Review briefly.

TEACHER: Let's see. In the first incident, Holly disobeyed her Daddy and climbed the tree. In the second, she went to get somebody else to help. What happened in the third incident?

LOUISE: Holly made the boy get someone else to help.

TEACHER: Thanks, Louise. Then in the fourth incident.

2. Evaluate alternatives.

TEACHER: Were some solutions better than others? And do you think Holly's father should punish her for disobeying?

(Students' responses will vary.)

TEACHER: (Summarizing) It's good to help a person in need, but we should obey our parents too. Sometimes we need to look for a way to do both things. It's hard, sometimes, isn't it? (More discussion may follow.)

The debriefing is not an opportunity for the teacher to moralize or present "right" answers, Rather, the pluses and minuses of each alternative should be summarized.

---

particular stages, Kohlberg found that the age-stage relationship is less evident in moral reasoning. As Lickona has noted, "In general . . . Stages 1 and 2 dominate in the primary school years and persist in some individuals long beyond that. Stage 3 gains ground during the upper elementary grades and often remains the major orientation through the end of high school. Stage 4 begins to emerge in adolescence. Only one in four persons moves on in later adolescence or adulthood to Stage 5" (1977, p. 39). Note also that individuals who can reason at higher levels may sometimes use lower-level reasoning to justify their actions.

75 percent don't reach Stage 5

Heinz and the Druggist

In Europe, a woman was near death from a special kind of cancer. There was one drug that the doctors thought might save her. It was a form of radium that a druggist in the same town had recently discovered. The drug was expensive to make, but the druggist was charging ten times what the drug cost him to make. He paid $200 for the radium and charged $2,000 for a small dose of the drug.

The sick woman's husband, Heinz, went to everyone he knew to borrow the money, but he could only get together about $1,000, which is half what it cost. He told the druggist that his wife was dying and asked him to sell the drug cheaper or let him pay for it later. But the druggist said, "No, I discovered the drug and I'm going to make money from it." So Heinz gets desperate and considers breaking into the man's store to steal the drug for his wife.

Question: Should Heinz steal the drug?

Procedure

1. Ask students to identify what should be done and why. "What should Heinz do?"

2. Divide the class into small groups, either in terms of those who support a particular course of action or at random. Ask them to discuss their reasons and justify the course of action they have chosen. "Why should Heinz do what you think he should do?"

3. Permit groups to summarize and clarify their positions.

4. Ask additional probing questions:

   * Is the welfare of one's relatives more important than the welfare of others?

   * Should Heinz steal the drug for a stranger? For a pet that he loves?

   * It is against the law for Heinz to steal. Does that make it morally wrong? Why or why not?

Students should be encouraged to express reasonable value positions, though it is not necessary that they arrive at consensus.

Source: From *Models of Moral Education: An Appraisal* by R. H. Hersh, J. P. Miller, and G. D. Fielding. Copyright 1980 by Longman Publishers. Reprinted with permission.

Dilemmas involve conflicting moral principles

Using Moral Dilemmas. Kohlberg's research suggests that students will be stimulated to move to the next stage of moral development upon repeated exposure to higher levels of moral reasoning. Such exposure can be gained by helping students work with moral dilemmas. These are stories or situations that involve conflicting moral principles and in which students must identify and evaluate alternative courses of action. Dilemmas necessarily involve situations in which the alternative courses of action are either desirable or undesirable, but not both. When the two elements are mixed, there is no dilemma; the individual merely follows the most desirable course of action.

A simple moral dilemma suitable for younger children might involve a seven-year-old girl named Holly who comes upon a small boy whose kitten is stranded in a tree. Tears stream down the boy's cheeks as he pleads with Holly to rescue his kitten. Although Holly is sympathetic, the last time she climbed a tree she fell and sprained her wrist. After that incident Holly promised her father she wouldn't climb any more trees. What should Holly do? (Lickona, 1977, p. 37.)

Holly could do many things, including trying to get help from an adult or breaking her promise to her father. By exploring such alternatives in group settings, moral dilemmas are intended to expose students to different and, it is hoped, higher stages of moral reasoning. For younger children, the dilemmas should involve relatively few characters and moral principles (obedience to authority versus helping a friend in need, for instance). Note also that changing just one element in the kitten moral dilemma, such as changing the kitten in a tree to a kitten trapped on a telephone pole, can alter the situation dramatically.

The Model Student Activity on page 145 is designed for older students. It is based on a classic moral dilemma involving a husband's attempt to secure a drug for his sick wife. How students justify what Heinz should or should not do will identify their level of moral reasoning, as illustrated below:

* *Stage 1:* Heinz should not steal the drug because he will be severely punished if he does.
* *Stage 2:* Heinz has the right to steal for his wife *if he wants to;* besides, a judge would understand and wouldn't punish him.
* *Stage 3:* Heinz has an obligation to help his wife, even if it means stealing for her. Besides, the druggist is being cruel and selfish; doesn't he have a heart?
* *Stage 4:* Heinz has an obligation to obey the law; by stealing the drug and thus breaking the law, he will be harming the society.
* *Stage 5:* Stealing and the law are not issues. Heinz should work to see that scarce drugs are distributed fairly, but even if that fails, the sanctity of human life exceeds everything else.

The small-group decision making and the extended discussion of complex issues associated with moral dilemmas can demand a level of experience and sophistication that some younger children cannot handle. "Heinz and the Druggist," for example, involves too many elements for young children to deal with simultaneously.

What Critics Say About Moral Reasoning. Much of the criticism directed toward the moral-reasoning approach has questioned either the adequacy of Kohlberg's theory or the contention that higher-stage reasoning is necessarily better than lower-stage reasoning. Harvard psychologist Carol Gilligan (1977, 1982), for example, contends that women tend to score lower than men on Kohlberg's scale, not because of deficiencies in women's moral reasoning, but because women often use a different basis—an ethic based on interpersonal caring—for determining morality.

Earlier questions about whether discussing moral dilemmas results in movement from one stage to the next have largely been resolved. Leming (1985) states that "unlike the values-clarification approach, the weight of the evidence supports the claim . . . that the discussion of moral dilemmas can stimulate development through the stages of moral reasoning" (p. 131). For this to occur, however, moral-dilemma discussions must take place regularly, not just once or twice during a semester.

Caring: An Alternative Ethic for Moral Reasoning. The moral-reasoning approach is based on the ethical ideal of justice. In that context, the most

Exposure to higher level reasoning

Stage level reasoning

Designing simple dilemmas

Adequacy

prized values are the equality of human rights and the dignity of human beings (Woolever and Scott, 1988). On the other hand, some authorities (Gilligan, 1977, 1982; Kohn 1997; Scott, 1987) argue that although nothing is wrong with justice as an ethic, using it as the sole defining standard for morality is too limiting. Those authorities (and others) argue that justice does not adequately reflect the caring and supportive behaviors on which human relationships should be based.

Justice is one aspect of morality

As an example of this, Brogmann (1992) suggests that the "Heinz and the Druggist" episode reflects the main point of contention between the masculine and feminine moral voice. Brogmann argues that the masculine way is to rest one's case on the universal principle that life comes before property, which means that Heinz should steal the drug. The feminine approach, Brogmann contents, is to consider the consequences that stealing would have on Heinz and his wife, and to explore alternatives to stealing; such as borrowing the money or seeing an understanding between Heinz and the druggist (see also Gilligan, 1982). The point here is that justice is only one of the principles that can be used to resolve this dilemma.

The following dilemma reflects elements inherent in an ethic of caring.

An example of caring

Bob, a top high school swimmer, was asked to teach young children with physical disabilities to swim. This would help strengthen their legs, possibly enabling them to walk. Bob was the only one in town who had the life-saving and teaching experience to do this job well. But helping these children would take most of Bob's free time after work and school, time that Bob would otherwise use to practice for some important, upcoming swimming contests. If Bob did not use his free time to practice, his chances of winning the contests, and possibly receiving a college scholarship, would be greatly lessened.

Should Bob agree to teach the disabled children? Why or why not? (Adapted from Mussen and Eisenberg-Berg, 1977, p. 121)

Prosocial behaviors

Integral to an ethic of caring are *prosocial behaviors:* that is, actions that aid other people without the expectation of direct rewards. Prosocial behaviors, such as that illustrated in the preceding dilemma, can sometimes involve personal costs or sacrifices. Prosocial behaviors, such as sharing, helping, sacrificing, and giving, are motivated by empathy, altruism, respect, sensitivity, nurturing, and a sense of caring.

Values Analysis

"Should students be permitted to go outside on the playground for recess, weather permitting?" This may seem like an innocuous question, but as more and more schools remove their playground equipment and do not permit students to leave the building during recess, it's being debated in many communities. When children ask it, it's the kind of question that also lends itself to values analysis.

Analyzing the values in an issue or question

The values-analysis approach to values education emphasizes careful, deliberate, discriminating analysis. The idea is to examine value questions as rationally and unemotionally as possible and then arrive at a decision. In contrast to moral reasoning, where students take a position and then justify it, values analysis would have students refrain from taking a position until they have analyzed the issues involved.

The following tasks are essential to the analysis of the recess question or any value question or issue:

The phases of values analysis

1. *Identifying the issue.* The underlying issues in allowing children to go out onto the playground for recess usually involve one or more of the following: (a) the children's safety, (b) the legal liability and costs that the school may face in the event of injury, and (c) teachers' distaste for playground supervision responsibilities. The issue also may involve whether the recess policy is districtwide or whether each school can establish its own.

What are the value issues?

2. *Clarifying the value question.* Dealing with this element is not as easy as it appears. Ostensibly the value question is whether children's safety is more important than their need for physical exercise. However, whether safety, the avoidance of legal liability, or some other factor or combination of factors is the main motivation must be determined.

Do we have the data we need?

3. *Gathering and organizing evidence.* See Step 4 below.

Are our data accurate and relevant?

4. *Assessing the accuracy and relevance of the evidence.* For the recess question, Steps 3 and 4 of values analysis can occur simultaneously. To facilitate this, the teacher could place the following on the board or in a more permanent location in the classroom:

   ### Reasons for children to go outside for recess

   1. Need for physical activity
   2. Need for a change of scene

   ### Reasons for children to stay inside for recess

   1. Safety
   2. Lawsuits
   3. Other??

The visual display helps children keep track of what portion of the issue they are dealing with. Various individuals can be invited to give their views: an attorney knowledgeable about school litigation, a school board member, the principal, a telephone interview with a principal whose students go outside for recess, and so on. Students could also survey teachers in the school for their opinions.

What are the alternatives?

5. *Identifying potential solutions.* The key question here is, What are the options? Are there other means for providing a break and physical activity for children?

Do our "solutions" create other problems?

6. *Identifying and assessing the possible consequences for each solution.* The children need to consider questions such as: Would running around in a crowded gym be any safer than going outside? What if the gym is already scheduled? If legal liability is the problem, can insurance cover this? And if so, is there money to pay for such insurance? And, if insurance were possible, would the administration permit going outside?

7. *Choosing among the alternatives.* Determining viable alternatives will hinge on the assessment done in Step 6 above.

8. *Deciding and taking appropriate action.* The latter phases of value analysis depend on what happens in the earlier steps. In the recess question, students may decide to petition the principal to review the current policy. This kind of action is only appropriate if the students have determined it is the kind of issue on which the principal or another administrator can act. Students may find that, in today's world, their health and safety cannot be compromised.

What is the best course of action?

As the preceding example illustrates, values analysis is not a "quickie" process. It need not be as elaborate as we have described it here, yet some steps in values analysis, including gathering and assessing evidence, can require considerable time to do well. The overall intent is to wean students from the teacher's influence so that they can follow the processes on their own.

What Critics Say About Values Analysis.

Values analysis has many supporters and few critics. Nevertheless, because some elements of values analysis are similar to the other approaches to values education, some of the same cautions may be in order. For example, elements of values analysis rely heavily on teachers asking a series of questions. Sometimes a single student may respond to a sequence of three or four questions (or more if elaboration is required). In a class of twenty-five students, a teacher could find herself engaged in a dialogue with one student. Hopefully the other twenty-four children will be interested enough to pay attention, but the longer the minidialogues go on, the more likely young children are to become disinterested. In light of this, several cautions seem prudent:

Cautions

1. Teachers should be especially sensitive to the interest level of students who are not participating actively.
2. When possible, the approaches should be used in a small-group format.
3. When student interest begins to sag, summarize and move on to something else.
4. For values analysis especially, do not begin unless the issue is sufficiently involving *and* time is available to see the matter through to resolution.

Summary

Values underlie *everything* a teacher does. It is simply impossible to sterilize lessons to make them value-free. In the 1970s and 1980s, when schools were retreating from their traditional role in building good character, moral education tended to be a hit-or-miss proposition. Teachers might occasionally employ one or more of the approaches that we presented in this chapter, but there was seldom a coherent program. To varying degrees, the approaches tend to be value-neutral; that is, they help individuals to explore what they *might* do, but they usually refrain from saying what the individual *ought* to do. This value-neutral stance was and is consistent with the privatization and personalization of values and morals that has occurred in the last half of this century.

In view of the myriad social problems the United States is facing today, and especially the inability of some children to act in morally responsible and acceptable ways, a growing number of schools are moving to reestablish character education programs. Their common goal is to produce students with good character: that is, students who know the good and feel disposed to act accordingly. Character education is a comprehensive, schoolwide effort that focuses on teaching core ethical values such as honesty, respect, responsibility, and truthfulness—values that are essential to the society's continuing survival and that almost no one opposes. Character education also extends to the hidden curriculum, the day-to-day schooling practices that can sometimes contradict, even neutralize, the values that schools and teachers espouse.

Character education is an overarching movement that sometimes incorporates one or more of the alternative strategies we identified in this chapter. Those strategies can provide excellent vehicles for raising moral and ethical questions. However, some of the alternative moral education strategies, especially values clarification, must be approached cautiously.

Character education is the focus of intense interest across the country, in part because of the growing recognition that transmitting knowledge—making students smart—does not ensure that children will act in morally acceptable ways. But whether schools can become caring moral communities remains to be seen. Equally unknown at this point is whether schools can provide moral anchors for children from families that are unable to do so. Until we get answers to such questions, the final chapter on character education cannot be written.

Suggested Activities

1. Select and examine at least one chapter in a social studies textbook for any grade level. Determine the extent to which statements within the chapter reflect a value-based agenda.
2. Select an elementary social studies text for the grade level you'd like to teach. For any section of the book you choose, show how you might incorporate values education into your approach to teaching that segment.
3. The Scout Law expected everyone to be trustworthy, loyal, helpful, friendly, courteous, kind, obedient, cheerful, thrifty, brave, clean, and reverent. Determine to what extent these expectations are consistent with the character education movement today.
4. The practice of providing tangible rewards to students for demonstrating good behavior may be successful in the short run, but over time it can undermine a child's intrinsic motivation. Determine how you might resolve this apparent dilemma.
5. Not long ago, a student teacher asked us for "the three best lessons we knew of" that would "make" her students respect each other. Why just three lessons? "Because that's all I have time for." Develop a response for this teacher.

Suggested Readings

J. S. Benninga (Ed.). (1991). *Morals, character, and civic education in the elementary school.* New York: Teachers College Press. A good collection of articles.

Educational Leadership. (November, 1993). This special issue contains several excellent articles on character education.

Linda Eyre & Richard Eyre. (1993). *Teaching your children values.* New York: Simon and Schuster. This highly practical book is designed for parents to use with their children, but it is equally useful for social studies teachers. It makes an interesting distinction between values of being, such as honesty and courage, and values of giving, such as kindness, respect, and love.

Gertrude Himmelfarb. (1995). *The demoralization of society.* New York: Knopf. This is a splendid account of the shift from Victorian virtues to the "anything goes" nature of modern values.

Phillip Jackson, R. Boostrom, & D. Hansen. (1993). *The moral life of schools.* San Francisco: Jossey-Bass. This book provides fascinating vignettes of the different kinds of moral activities that occur in everyday life in schools. Highly recommended.

Linda Leonard Lamme, Suzanne Lowell Krough, & Kathy A. Yachmetz. (1992). *Literature-based moral education.* Phoenix, AZ: Orynx. This wonderful paperback presents brief synopses and teaching suggestions for a wealth of children's literature suitable for moral education. The literary works are organized by values/traits such as self-esteem, responsibility, sharing, truthfulness, and unconditional love.

Alfie Kohn. (1997). How not to teach values. *Phi Delta Kappan* 78, 429–439. This article provides an in-depth analysis of techniques that are purported to teach values, but probably don't.

Thomas Lickona. (1991). *Educating for character: How our schools can teach respect and responsibility.* New York: Bantam Books. Lickona argues that if we care about the future of our society and our children, educating for character is a moral imperative.

E. A. Wynne & Kevin Ryan. (1992). *Reclaiming our schools: A handbook on teaching character, academics, and discipline.* New York: Merrill. The title says it all.

Part 3

Instruction

wPart Three presents the "nuts and bolts" of teaching social studies. Chapter 7, "Social Studies: Gateway to Literacy," focuses on language literacy and children's ability to encounter social studies. We are not suggesting that social studies should be taught as reading, whereby children open their textbooks and begin reading aloud. Rather, our focus is on how you can use social studies to enhance children's literacy skills without doing a disservice to either social studies or literacy.

Chapter 8, "Strategies for Effective Teaching," examines aspects of teacher- and student-directed instruction, both of which should be part of every teacher's repertoire. Also integral to Part Three are the group-management skills and teaching strategies relating to small-group instruction, which we examine in Chapter 9, "Engaging Students in Active Learning."

Chapter 10, "Planning and Orchestrating Instruction," and Chapter 11, "Assessing Learning," make up a two-chapter section that addresses these most basic elements of instruction. In Chapter 12, "Nurturing Critical and Reflective Thinking," we examine teaching activities and skills that can enable children to analyze, interpret, and otherwise deal with various kinds of social studies information. The title for Chapter 13, "Helping Students Use Maps, Globes, and Graphics," provides a clear indication of its focus, as does the title of Chapter 14, "Using Instructional Tools: Print, Multimedia, and Community Resources."

7 Social Studies: Gateway to Literacy

Key Questions

* What are the different forms of literacy?
* How can social studies serve as a gateway to literacy, and vice versa?
* What role does oral language play in building literacy?
* How do children (and adults) construct meaning?

Key Ideas

* Language literacy is the ability to use a standard form of language fluently and effectively.
* Oral language and listening provide the basis for subsequent reading and writing.
* Children (and everyone else) construct meaning by incorporating new ideas into their existing frames of reference.
* Social studies can facilitate language development.

Introduction: People, People, People

Setting the focus

For the last fourteen years, Ms. Lynda Esparza has taught second graders at Mesa Verde Elementary School in southern Arizona. Over 80 percent of her students are Hispanic. A few recently arrived from Mexico, some arrived three or four years ago, and others are native-born citizens of the United States. Another 10 percent of Lynda's students are Native American, and the balance are Anglo- and African-American.

We visited Ms. Esparza on a warm November afternoon as she and her class were beginning a social studies unit on community helpers. To find out what her children already knew about communities and community services, Ms. Esparza gathered everyone in the carpeted area. Seated on a low chair and using an overhead projector on a low cart, Lynda told her second graders, "Today, we're going to share ideas about people who work in communities. Remember our rules for brainstorming—everybody gets a chance to speak. After I put down everyone's ideas, we'll go back and work on them." The children nodded; they had apparently done brainstorming activities before. "O.K., what different jobs do people in communities do?"

Hands shot up. Carlos suggested, "police." Lynda recorded it on the transparency. Maria suggested, "store people," and Lynda asked, "What do you mean, Maria?"

"People who work in stores."

Brainstorming "What about "mall people?" asked Armondo. "Lots of people work at the mall."

Lynda turned to the class and said, "Let's decide whether we should describe some people by where they work, or whether we should list specific jobs, like clerks or cashiers." The class decided that either way was O.K.

Gracie then suggested "mail people." Because the homophone for *mail* could be confusing, Lynda asked, "Do you mean people like letter carriers, people who work for the post office?"

"Yeah, people like that," Gracie replied.

"Let's put that down as 'postal people,' and then put *mail* in parentheses just so we're sure," Lynda said, demonstrating what parentheses were as she did so. Soon the transparency was filled with a listing of various occupations, some public and some private employees, and some people listed in terms of where they worked. Lynda said, "All these people work in communities, and some of them work for communities. Right now, let's make a 'Beans' poem from our brainstorming."

From the children's expressions, it was that clear that they knew what a "Beans" poem was, and that they enjoyed doing it. A "Beans" poem is a form of structured poetry based on "Beans," by Lucia and James Hynes (1960) (shown in Figure 7.1).

FIGURE 7.1   Beans

Beans,
Beans,
Beans.
Butter beans,
Baked beans,
Big fat Lima beans,
Long thin string beans—
Those are just a few.
Green beans,
Black beans,
Big fat kidney beans,
Red hot chili beans,
Jumping beans too.
Pea beans,
Pinto beans,
Don't forget shelly beans.
Last of all, best of all,
I like jelly beans!

Source: HOORAY FOR CHOCOLATE (pp. 34–35), © 1960 by Lucia and James L. Hymes, Jr. Reprinted by permission of Addison-Wesley Publishing Company, Inc.

Lynda rose from her chair and dragged an easel filled with large chart paper to an area where everyone could see it. She flipped back the cover sheet to reveal the "Beans" poem format that she had drawn previously, but with blanks where the words had been. Taking a marker, she then said, "Because our poem will be about people, I'm going to put the word *people* where *beans* used to be. She quickly wrote "people" in the appropriate spaces, as shown in Figure 7.2.

Deciding on an ending

Lynda then said, "Remember that when we make a 'Beans' poem, one of the first things we decide is how we're going to end it. Let's think about what would make a good last line." Lynda and her students talked about different endings, and finally settled on "I like all people." Lynda then handed the marker to Maria, and said, "Why don't you write this for us?" Maria jumped up, took the marker, and filled in "i like all" in the spaces on the last line before "people." Half a dozen

FIGURE 7.2 A Writing Pattern Based on "Beans"

People,
People,
People,

_____ people,
_____ people,

_____ _____ _____ people,
_____ people,

Those are just a few.

_____ people,
_____ people,

_____ _____ _____ people,
_____ people,

_____ people too.
_____ people,
_____ people,

Don't forget _____ people.

Last of all, best of all,

I like _____ people !

hands went up. Lynda nodded to Placido, who said, "I think Maria needs a capital *I*." Turning to Maria, Lynda asked, "What do you think, Maria?" Maria thought for a moment and said, "Yes, I should have made a capital *I*." She then took her marker and neatly transformed the lower-case *i* into a capital letter.

With the ending decided, Lynda and the class then began filling in the other blanks. Lynda suggested that they put people who work for the government in the top half of the poem, and people who work in the community in the lower half. For example, when Carlos suggested "fire people," Lynda asked, "Should this go in the top half or the bottom?" Carlos responded that "fire people are city workers, so they belong in the top half." Lynda handed Carlos the marker and he wrote "Fire" in one of the empty spaces. When Armondo was writing "electricity," he spelled it

Interactive writing

"electrisity." Changing the *s* to a *c* was more difficult than changing a lower-case *i* to a capital letter, so Lynda reached for her roll of correction tape, which is similar to Post-It Notes, and handed a small piece to Armondo, who pasted it over his errant *s*, and then wrote the *c* where it belonged. The result was a product with correct spelling and grammar. If there are quite a few spelling errors or other changes, all the correction tape can create a speckled appearance on the final chart.

When all the blanks were filled in, Lynda asked, "What should we do now?"

Choral speaking

"We chorus it!" her students responded in unison. Lynda picked up a pointer with her right hand and began quietly snapping the fingers of her left hand to establish a rhythm. The students quickly joined in. In unison, and as Lynda pointed to each word, they began chorusing, "People, people, people. . . ."

When the first chorusing was completed, Lynda asked, "Let's see if there is anything we want to change?" Several students offered suggestions, including changing the last line to "*We* like all people." The group debated each suggestion, using more correction tape to make the necessary changes, until the final poem was as shown in Figure 7.3.

FIGURE 7.3 People, People, People

People,
People,
People,
Police people,
Fire people,
Electricity and water people,
Friendly, helpful postal people
Those are just a few.
Teacher people,
Principal people,
Library and cafeteria people,
Doctor and nurse people,
TV people too.
Delivery people,
Store people,
Don't forget McDonald's people.
But last of all, best of all,
We like all people!

After chorusing the revised poem another time, Lynda suggested, "Let's orchestrate this poem—any ideas?" Jason's hand waved vigorously, but his actions violated a rule the class had agreed on previously: A raised hand is sufficient to get attention. If you wave your hand too vigorously or call out "Me, me," you won't get called on. Lynda raised an eyebrow as she looked at Jason, and then called on Lucinda, who suggested, "Let's let the girls be 'people' people, and the boys say the other parts; then we can switch."

Lynda responded, "Shall we try it?" The children nodded. Lynda continued, "The boys and I will say the words until we get to the word *people*. Then we'll stop and our 'people' people (the girls) will say their word." With the same finger-snapping rhythm they had used previously, a chorus of girls' voices began, "People, people, people." A chorus of boys' voices then chimed in with "Police," "Fire." . . . Later, the boys chorused "People, people, people . . ." and the girls added the specifics. After a second time through the poem with the boys as "people" people, Lynda said, "Let's give all our choristers a round of applause." It was a fitting ending for an activity the children had clearly enjoyed.

Aside from listing public employees separately from those who work in private industry, there were no profound social studies learnings from Lynda's lesson. Neither was there any effort to determine whether these "community helpers" actually *help* the community. Those learnings would come later. At this

Determining what students already know

point in the lesson, Lynda was satisfied that her students already knew about many of the jobs available in the community. Whether the students could organ-

Planning should encompass what you as a teacher will do and what your students will be doing. (© Suzie Fitzhugh)

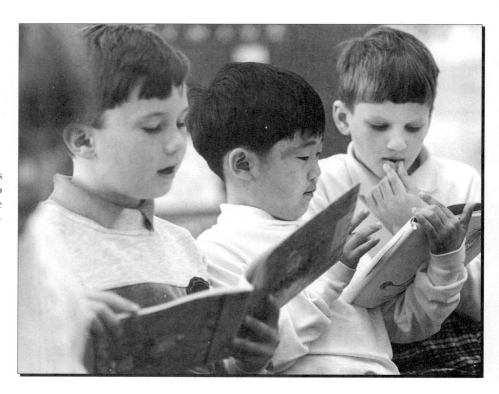

ize and classify the different occupations they had listed would become the focus for another lesson.

Lynda's students had participated in an activity that enhanced their oral fluency and that could ultimately enhance their ability to deal with language in different contexts. That, in part, is what language literacy is all about—the ability to read, write, and speak the language fluently and effectively in different situations.

Oral Language and Listening: Bases for Literacy

Developing facility with language

When Lynda Esparza and her second graders created and then chorused the "People" poem, that activity was more than a cute way to end a social studies lesson. A large body of research (see Button, Johnson, & Ferguson, 1996; Cooper, 1993; Dickinson, 1987; Flood & Lapp, 1987; Pinnell & McCarrier, 1994) indicates that both reading and writing depend, at least initially, on children's facility with speaking and listening. Children who have poor oral language and listening skills are also likely to have poor reading and writing skills. This also means that many students, especially those for whom English is their second language, can benefit from experiences in speaking and using language fluently, comfortably, and confidently.

Prior language learnings

By the time most five- and six-year-old children arrive in school, they have already acquired a vast knowledge of language, most of which they learned without formal instruction. In that process, they will have learned to distinguish separate units of sound (*phonemes*) and meaning (*morphemes*), to discover patterns and rules by which units of phonemes and morphemes are combined into sentences (*syntax, grammar,* etc.), and can identify context clues (*semantics*) that guide the social aspects of dialogue. Children don't use the kinds of labels we have here, of course, but when most of them enter school, they already have what linguists call a "fully formed grammar and language system." It matters not whether the children speak standard English, a regional dialect, Black English, or a mixture of English and another language; they will have acquired whatever language they speak through listening and observing, and then by experimenting with their language in social situations.

How do children use listening, speaking, and observing as they acquire language? Were you to observe young children over time, you would likely see them do the following:

* They rely on listening and speaking as the main channels for learning language (which is obviously true for children who are unable to read or write).

Building and testing theories about language

* They actively reflect on and analyze what they observe and hear.

* Based on what they hear and observe, children usually form theories about language and then test those theories in real situations. For example, most children learn that by adding the (bound) morpheme *ed* to certain words, they can talk about things that happened in the past. They test their theory about *ed* by using it in different situations, such as "I walked to the store." However, having discovered the marvelous power that *ed* gives them to talk

Overgeneralizing	about things that happened in the past, many children overgeneralize its application by adding *ed* to verbs of any tense, including *go* or *went*. Thus, it's common to hear young children make statements like "We *goed* to Burger King" or "I *runned* around the track." Eventually, most children discover that their new rule doesn't work all the time. They learn these language patterns without asking questions such as, "When do you add *ed* to a word or use a different word—when do you use *ran* instead of *runned*? Instead they typically look for patterns in the language to identify words that are exceptions to that rule.
The role of prior experience	✱ When children lack the correct words for describing something, they usually reflect on words that they already know and then select one or more terms that seem reasonable. This is why, upon meeting an elderly man with deep wrinkles, a child might ask, "Why does that man have *paths* all over his face?" (Morrow, 1989). It makes complete sense, at least from a child's point of view.

Clearly, children do not develop their ability to use language passively; they continually construct or reconstruct language as they learn it (Morrow, 1989). How children learn to use language correctly also transfers to the ways in which they learn (as opposed to memorize) anything. Children (and even adults) construct knowledge by overgeneralizing, by identifying and refining ideas, by testing ideas that may or may not fit their prior experiences, and then by going back through the cycle again. We'll return to this process again later.

Helping Children Develop Fluency in Standard English

Children bring their language
from home

Most children come to school fluent in the language of the home. That language may be standard English, the language of schools and textbooks, but it will often reflect at least a regional or ethnic dialect, sometimes both. In still other cases, the primary language of the home may be something other than English. Thus these children will be learning English as a second language. Either situation can pose problems for children who are becoming fluent in standard English.

English as a Second Language (ESL).   We suspect that only people who are truly bilingual can appreciate the problems associated with becoming proficient in two languages simultaneously. Children who are learning English as a second language face challenges that native English speakers seldom encounter. For example, all the children in Lynda Esparza's class know their alphabet, but students whose native language is Spanish tend to pronounce the vowels differently than English-speaking children. What English speakers say as /a/, /e/, /i/, /o/, /u/ are pronounced in Spanish as /ah/, /ey/, /ee/, /o/, /oo/. As a result, native Spanish speakers may have difficulty distinguishing between words like *cut, cat,* and *cot* (see Henning, 1994).

Even native English speakers sometimes encounter problems when they first see familiar words in written form. Because English has so many silent letters, what children know and say as /rit/, for example, seems to take on extra letters when it is written as *write*. However, because English-speaking children's pro-

Problems of second-
language learners

nunciation of the word does not change, their problem is primarily one of recognizing the word in its written form. For Spanish-speaking children, however, the problems are compounded because, except for *h*, all the written letters in Spanish are sounded. Thus, upon encountering a word like *write* in its written form, a native Spanish speaker will want to pronounce it as a two-syllable word, /wreetey/, which is something they have never heard before, even if they're familiar with the English word *write* in its spoken form. In such situations, an ESL child's ability to use context clues becomes even more important than it is for native English speakers.

In some parts of the country, Spanish-language textbooks may be available for social studies and other subjects. However, these texts typically reflect Castilian Spanish, which can be quite different from regional Spanish dialects, like Tex-Mex, that the children are accustomed to hearing in the home. This can mean that, in addition to basic structural differences in the languages, ESL students must often overcome dialectical differences. If the ESL child's native language is neither English nor Spanish, finding appropriate text materials will be almost impossible.

Dialectically Different Children.   Anyone who speaks a regional or social-group dialect exclusively can be regarded as dialectically different. For example, children from New England often add an /r/ to words that end in *a*. Thus, *Cuba* (the country) is usually pronounced /cuber/. On the other hand, children from New York City tend to drop the /r/, as in /pak da cah/ (park the car). Likewise, children in Appalachia typically say /warsh/ for *wash,* and /feeshin/ for *fishing,* whereas children who speak Black English often use expressions like "I be goin'" and "I done it." Such dialectical usages are most common in the eastern United States and diminish significantly farther west. Children who speak Cajun or Hawaiian English use still other variant speech forms.

Regional and cultural dialects

Dialectically related usages are different from standard English, but they are not substandard forms. Children from Appalachia who say /warsh/ for *wash* or "I done it," for example, are simply repeating the speech patterns they hear and use in their homes and neighborhoods. As different as their pronunciations may be, they are not doing anything "wrong." Teachers who insist on "correcting" such usages in children's oral language may very well send the message that there is something "wrong" with a language form that children feel comfortable with. As Henning notes, "Children who are made to believe there is something wrong with their speech may stop speaking in school, which is counterproductive" (1994, p. 59).

The problems that dialectically different children encounter learning standard English are similar to the problems that ESL students face but are less serious. For a child from Appalachia to discover that there is no *r* in *wash,* for example, is hardly as serious as learning that descriptive adjectives in English go before the noun, not afterwards as in Spanish.

Developing Fluency.   The techniques for helping children become fluent and effective users of standard English are similar to the techniques that children use to learn language in the first place (which is why we went into such detail on that earlier). Children need opportunities to "play" with language. They need oral activities that enable them to build on, transform, expand on, and interpret standard English sentence patterns. They also need to experience the rhythms of standard English, which is one of the reasons that Lynda Esparza had her students chorus the "People" poem in different ways. Children also need to hear standard English used in realistic settings. You may have noticed that Lynda Esparza used the word *shall* correctly during her lesson, and she did so naturally and without making a "big deal" about it. Although even some proficient users of standard English cannot distinguish between when to use *shall* or *will,* Lynda effectively modeled a usage that was not likely to be in her children's everyday language repertoire.

Additional suggestions for handling oral language and listening activities include the following:

* Model correct, standard English speech and writing to the best of your ability to do so.
* As you model the language, do it in ways that say to children, "I accept you (and the way you speak) as you are."
* Recognize that the goal is to help children use standard English effectively and fluently, *not* to denigrate the child's (and the family's) existing dialect. Literacy is not a crusade to stamp out regional or social dialects.
* Permit children to use whatever dialects they are most comfortable with in class discussions, storytelling, and creative dramatics.
* React to the message the child is trying to convey and not to the form of speech. Cursing and obscene language are obviously unacceptable.
* Resist the impulse to interrupt children to correct their vocabulary or sentence structure. As Henning notes, "Constant interruption and correction can easily turn a pleasurable sharing time into a period of discomfort that children dread" (1994, p. 60).

Listening Activities

Listening is a combination of what you hear, what you expect to hear, what you observe, and what you recall from your previous experiences. Effective listeners are aware of factors that influence listening. These include (1) thinking ahead of the reader or talker and anticipating the direction of the discourse; (2) assessing the kind(s) of evidence the reader or talker is using; (3) periodically reviewing the author's or speaker's main points; (4) "listening between the words"; (5) constructing ideas instead of just picking up facts; and (6) withholding evaluation of the message until after the reader or speaker is through talking.

Like other language-related activities, listening is probably best approached as part of other ongoing activities. We suspect that the best activity for this is reading aloud to children. What you read aloud should not be restricted to children's literature or limited to the primary grades. Sharing *brief* passages of informational content with older students can be equally appropriate.

Whenever you are reading aloud or it is possible to stop someone who is talking to the class, you might interrupt with *one* of the following questions:

1. What do you think will happen next?
2. What has the author/speaker said up to this point?

3. What is the author's/speaker's main idea?
4. What things [kind(s) of evidence] has the author/speaker used to get us to believe what he or she is saying?
5. Which parts of what the author/speaker said were opinion?
6. How would you have said what the author/speaker said?

Because students (or anyone) may resent the intrusion when their train of thought is interrupted, you must use your judgment about when such questions are appropriate. If students are bored, they probably won't mind the interruption, but then they may not have been listening well enough to answer your questions.

"Hearing" a supermarket

Cassette tape recorders have made it possible to develop homemade listening-oriented activities. By taking a tape recorder with you as you travel, for instance, you can gather interesting materials for listening activities. Consider developing a three-minute tape of sounds at a busy intersection, a shopping mall, or a supermarket. The idea, initially, is to have students *describe what they hear,* not guess what they're hearing. If a child says, "I hear a supermarket," for example, he or she is inferring something rather than describing the sounds. Inferring is a logical extension of describing—usually an inevitable extension—but the students' first focus should be on describing the sounds themselves.

Reading, Writing, and Social Studies

The focus is meaning

This section is based on two simple yet powerful ideas: Children learn to read by reading, and they learn to write by writing. Reading is that marvelous process by which children gain meaning by decoding written symbols. If children do not understand what they are decoding, they are merely *word-calling,* not reading.

Writing is the process of encoding thought and speech into written symbols. Because meaning is inherent in our every thought or utterance, we simply don't think meaningless thoughts. As a result, almost all writing is inherently meaningful, at least to the writer. Unfortunately, what some students do in school might look like writing but is likely to be *pseudowriting* (see Welton, 1982). Certainly you remember reports and term papers that you largely copied from encyclopedias or other sources. That's pseudowriting.

A different perspective on rules

Even the most basic conventions of writing can make sense to children if they are approached from the perspective of writers who are trying to convey meaning to readers, instead of as decontextualized rules that writers must follow. Consider: How do writers tell their readers that they've come to the end of an idea? They use a period. How do writers tell their readers that they're beginning a new idea? They begin with a capital letter. How do writers tell readers that they are finished with one cluster of ideas and are ready to move on to a new cluster? A new paragraph.

From thinking thoughts to writing sentences

There are surely millions of students across the country learning rules like "Always end a sentence with a period." Those students really need to understand that a sentence is a thought, an idea in written form, and that the period simply marks the end of the idea. Unfortunately, schools sometimes complicate matters by teaching rules that involve multiple abstractions. Remember, for example the countless hours you spent drawing one line under the subjects and two lines under the predicates of sample sentences? Ask yourself when was the last time you thought about predicates. The subject-predicate business may be useful if you want to talk about sentences, but you might also ask yourself how often you need to talk about sentences. Most people don't think in terms of nouns, verbs, subjects, or predicates—they think whole thoughts.

Clear thinking leads to clear writing.

Our points here are several. All of us think in terms of thoughts and ideas that have meaning to us. And when we convert an idea into spoken form, it becomes a statement. When we put a thought or idea into written form, we produce a sentence. However, if decontextualized rules and labels are introduced in the context of writing, the effect can be to make writing more difficult than it really is. All writers must deal with many things as they write, including spelling, punctuation, intended audience, tone, and organization. Yet, to the extent that writing is thinking in a written form, we suggest that the key to helping children produce clear writing is clear thinking.

The primacy of meaning

Reading and writing are complementary processes for getting and conveying meaningful ideas. So, regardless of how you feel about the "whole" language approach to literacy, one of the main contributions of that movement may be the renewed focus it has placed on meaning in all language-related activities.

Reading and Textbooks

Several factors play a role in helping or hindering children from getting meaning from the materials they read, especially social studies textbooks. You could regard the subtitle for this section as: "Why Are Social Studies Textbooks So Difficult?"

Consider the following passage from a fifth-grade social studies book. As you do so, try to (1) identify the number of ideas it presents explicitly—not those that are implied—and then (2) decide which if any of these ideas is important enough that you would ask a test question about it. If an idea is important enough to be included on a test, it is objective—something students should know and remember.

Sample textbook passage

> Little by little, Canada won its freedom from Great Britain. By 1949, Canada was fully independent. Canadians control their own country. They also choose their own leaders. (McAuley & Wilson, 1985, p. 41)

The passage, which amounts to a sweeping summary of recent Canadian history, contains only four short sentences—twenty-seven words in all. Yet the number of ideas that are packed into this space is significant. We identified the following (list continues on page 164):

Few words, but many ideas

* Canada is a country that now controls itself.
* Canada got its freedom gradually.
* Canada gained its independence from Great Britain in 1949. (This idea could be considered two separate ideas: [1]independence from Great Britain and [2]independence in 1949.)

Computers as Writing Tools

Each of the twenty-four students in Mrs. Mary Llanas's combined class of fifth and sixth graders uses one of the four computers in her room to produce a "report" on an African nation. Each report is filled with pictures that students have downloaded from the Internet or reproduced from various books or other sources. When students locate a picture they want to include, they place the book on an easel and use a video camcorder to incorporate the image into their report. Sometimes they use pictures of animals indigenous to the nation or other scenes as the background for the text they write, which appears in a contrasting color in front of the picture. In other instances, pictures are presented with accompanying text either above or below them. In either case, the students are involved with the total visual effect their reports create, not just the words they write.

Other teachers may have their students use "presentation software" as a vehicle for writing activities. The picture below is from a book on colonial occupations. It was produced by Mrs. Judy Rogers's third-grade class using the *Time Trip USA* (EdMark) presentation program. Each student wrote the text for his or her occupation and then incorporated it into the animated program. We cannot show the animation in this format, but everything moveable in this scene actually moves—the horse and carriage, the people, and so on. The children even borrowed a technique from Richard Scary's popular children's books, which include a tiny worm that peers over the activity on each page. Instead of the worm, Mrs. Rogers's children decided to include a child who pops out of a barrel, as shown in the illustration below. Such computer-based presentation programs offer an excellent medium for motivating students to write.

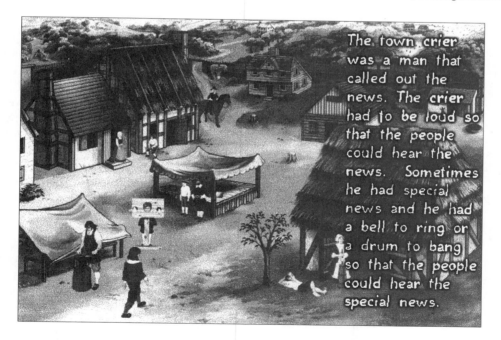

Source: Used by permission of Judy Rogers and Darlinda Rogers.

* Canada was partially independent before 1949.
* The people of Canada select their leaders.

Concept loading

This passage has more ideas than sentences. The extent to which this or any other passage contains ideas that are packed densely, sparsely, or somewhere in between is called *concept loading*. Concept loading contributes to the material's *readability*, that is, to the relative ease or difficulty of reading and gaining meaning from the material. Passages in which ideas are densely packed, and thus have a high concept load, are usually more difficult to understand than passages with a lower concept load.

There are no absolute standards for high or low concept loading, which can vary for different types of materials—novels versus textbooks, for example—so concept loading is a relative measure. However, placing ideas in short sentences does not in itself make those ideas easier to understand. Although the sentences in the sample passage are short, its concept load is fairly high.

Textbooks and Readability. According to Chall and Conard (1991) and others, the readability level of most elementary social studies texts ranges from one to two grade levels above the intended grade level. For example, most fourth-grade books have a fifth- or sixth-grade reading level. This difference tends to diminish during the middle-school years, so that by eighth grade textbooks are likely to be closer to their intended grade level.

What the research says

To understand the abstract concepts and terms that social studies texts often contain, most children usually need concrete examples that they can relate to. The more examples, the better. Yet this is where a confounding element, length, enters the picture. Every example in a book requires space, which adds to a book's length. The overall length of the text becomes a concern, primarily because of the way in which textbooks are perceived. If social studies textbooks were regarded more like dictionaries, as resources to be drawn upon as needed, their length would be irrelevant—except, perhaps, with respect to cost. However, because textbooks are often viewed as something students must "cover" by the end of the year, their length can become a significant factor. Dictionary-size textbooks would strike fear in the hearts of students and teachers alike, and their chances of being adopted are unlikely. Thus textbook authors and publishers are almost forced to maintain a reasonable length and, in the process, are denied the opportunity to clarify abstract concepts and ideas with multiple examples. Presenting large numbers of concepts on each page can make books more efficient, but doing so can also make them more difficult to read and understand.

The dilemma: Adding examples without increasing the length

In response to complaints about high concept loading, most publishers have tried to simplify their materials. However, instead of attacking concept loading directly, which would mean eliminating some abstract concepts and adding examples for others, they usually attack the problem by shortening the sentences, as we saw in the textbook passage about Canada. In theory, short sentences are easier to read than longer, more complex sentences, even though that notion has been disputed by some recent research in reading. Nevertheless, the trend in textbooks is to improve readability (and thus reduce the apparent difficulty level) by reducing sentence length.

Shorter sentences

Some people have criticized attempts to simplify textbooks—a process they refer to as "dumbing down." It has led, they claim, to textbooks that are so dull and lacking in style that they are almost simplistic (see Ravitch, 1987; Sewall, 1988). Yet even some critics acknowledge that the blame for mediocre textbooks does not rest solely with the publishers (see Sewall, 1988), who must deal with voluminous curriculum guidelines and various other factors that change from district to district and state to state.

Helping Children Handle Specialized Vocabulary

Every subject has its specialized vocabulary. Literature has its *sonnets* and *metaphors,* science has its *atoms* and *antennae,* and social studies has its *wings, steppes,* and a host of others. For most students, such vocabulary poses a twofold problem. Even though a simple word like *wash* is already part of a student's oral vocabulary and even though the student can probably spell the word correctly, he or she may
Terms with multiple meanings have never heard of a dry streambed referred to as a *wash.* Likewise, *run* is a regional expression for a brook or stream. Words with multiple meanings like these are called *polysemous,* and they make up about one-third of all commonly used words (Irvin et al., 1995). They often have meanings that are specific to particular content areas—such as *antenna* in science and *wash* in geography.

In many instances, polysemous words like *wing, class, bill, branch,* and *fork* are not particularly difficult for students if the teacher can build on the child's existing experiences. In the case of *wash* and *run,* the goal is to associate the word with the child's prior experiences with rivers and waterways, thus adding other terms to their repertoire. Other regional expressions that fit this category are *borough, county, parish; tote, carry; pop, soda, tonic.*

Two categories of terms that can pose more perplexing problems are *figurative*
Figurative expressions and *expressions,* such as *Fertile Crescent, dark horse, cold war, iron curtain, log rolling,* and
abstract concepts *corn belt,* and terms associated with *abstract concepts,* such as *ethnocentrism, nationalism, culture, temperate, democracy,* and *inflation.* Even though none of us have ever seen a belt made from corn, many children already have *corn* and *belt* in their reading and oral vocabularies. Their problem usually arises because they have never encountered these familiar words in their *corn belt* configuration. Abstract terms can pose added problems because they are often not part of the child's oral and reading vocabularies and because they, like figurative expressions, refer to phenomena that are beyond the child's realm of experience. Figurative expressions and especially abstract terms often require more comprehensive teaching strategies that we will consider in detail in the last section of this chapter.

Two final categories of specialized terminology that can affect social studies teaching include the following:

* *Proper names for historically or physically remote personages and places.* Many terms in this category do not follow familiar rules for phonic analysis. Examples: pharaoh, tsar (or czar), Hwang Ho, La Jolla, San Jose.

* *Acronyms and abbreviations.* These can present problems because they are often abbreviations for organizations with which students are not familiar. Examples: OPEC, IRS, GOP, FCC.

In helping children understand unfamiliar vocabulary, a key element to keep in mind is that not all terms are equally important (see Irvin et al., 1995). In many cases, students can get the basic thrust of a passage even if they don't understand every word. For example, consider the following sentence: "With the mechanization that accompanied the agrarian revolution, farmers were able to grow more corn, wheat, oats, and barley." Many students today have never heard of barley, a grain crop used extensively in producing beer, but this word is actually incidental to understanding the text. In addition, because *barley* is presented in association with other grains that should be more familiar to students, the context of the sentence suggests that it is one of several crops that a farmer might grow. Thus, the preteaching of *barley* is not essential, although you could make certain that students understand it in postreading follow-up.

Students are very unlikely to understand the sample sentence above unless they also understand the term *mechanization*. In this instance, *mechanization* is so critical to the meaning of this passage that teachers cannot treat it in the same way they do *barley*. The key here is to anticipate potential problems before students become frustrated. The time-honored technique for doing this is to preteach the term before students read the passage. The teacher should introduce new terms that are vital to understanding the passage—not including *barley*—by writing them on the chalkboard and then defining them before students begin reading. Although this technique tends to treat the vocabulary out of context, it is often preferable to having students look up the new terms in a dictionary, which at this stage in a lesson too often becomes a ritual in word copying. Thus teachers must be familiar enough with what their students will read that they can decide between terms that are critical to understanding the passage or lesson, and thus demand preteaching, and terms that are incidental or for which context clues will be sufficient.

A second technique that also requires preplanning involves integrating social studies vocabulary with other subject areas. Suppose, for example, that *fence* is a word in a spelling lesson. If you know that your students will encounter the figurative expression *iron curtain* in social studies one or two weeks hence, you can use the spelling lesson (and the word *fence*) for a brief foray into the realms of metaphor. You could ask, "What could we call a *wooden fence* besides a wooden fence? Any ideas? How about a wooden wall? What about a fence made of steel? A steel shield? A fence of copper? A copper curtain?" This might open the way for a *brief* explanation of the figurative meaning of *iron curtain,* which students can refer back to later. If this example seems contrived, the key to it lies in brevity; the entire episode need not take any longer than the time it has taken you to read about it.

What Do You Do for Children Who Can't Read the Text?

The commonsense solution for helping students who have reading difficulties is: get an easier textbook. Unfortunately social studies content varies so markedly from one grade level to the next that it's almost impossible to find easier texts that cover the same topics *and* are appropriate to the student's reading-skill level.

A second alternative is: don't use the book! There is a vast array of children's literature that is far more interesting than the textbook. You are more likely to find an easier literary book, even a picture book, on almost any topic, than an easier textbook. We have already suggested some children's books that you could use either in place of or in addition to the text, and additional annotated bibliographies are presented in the Resource Handbook.

If you feel that your students absolutely must have access to information in the text, you could use one of the following courses of action. Perhaps the least difficult and most readily available option is to read the passages to the students who are having difficulty. However, if you use this approach, have students point to each word in their book as you read from your book. The idea is to have students see each word as you read it, not just listen to your spoken presentation (see Clay, 1993).

The management problem associated with reading to a small group lies in finding something meaningful for the other students to do. This can be avoided if you (1) have an aide or parent volunteer read to individual children, (2) have one student read to another, or (3) have designed a section of the room as a listening center and have recorded portions of the text available on cassette tapes.

Your third and fourth options, both of which can be time-consuming, involve having small groups of children rewrite *small* portions of the text in their own language and with illustrations after they have finished a section, or rewriting the material in simpler language yourself. If you have the children do the rewriting, be sure that you (1) explain to the children why they are doing this activity, (2) have students work cooperatively in groups but on different sections, and (3) do not use this activity too often—despite its utility, it can pose problems for younger students especially.

The feasibility of the fourth option, rewriting material yourself, often depends on the kind of material you are working with. It isn't easy to simplify *statistics,* for example. For text material, this option is further complicated because most texts are written at a very simple level to begin with. Rewriting is a more viable (and necessary) option if you wish to use advanced material, especially from sources such as *Time, Newsweek,* or social science journals.

A longer-range course of action involves identifying the problem that's keeping the child from reading the text in the first place. No one needs to tell you that reading remains a problem for some students, and that we, like teachers everywhere, are looking for answers to that problem. Until those answers are found, you will undoubtedly be forced to rely on one of the preceding alternative strategies.

The Reading-Writing Connection

Few educational movements can match the revolution in writing instruction that has occurred over the last decade or so. Whereas writing was once regarded as drudgery, in some classrooms it now rivals recess as a preferred activity.

A growing body of research shows a clear reading-writing connection: improved writing skills can lead to improved reading skills, and vice versa. As young children write, they also come to understand that the words on a printed page were written by somebody—they didn't just magically appear there. As students begin to grasp the concept of author, they begin to realize that authors are responsible for communicating clearly and understandably to others—a responsibility that students assume whenever they write.

The Writing Process. One notable aspect of the ongoing revolution in teaching children to write well is the recognition that most traditional writing assignments, where children were given a topic and expected to produce a polished story in one draft, were a far cry from the way in which most authors really write. Moreover, little or no teaching was involved; rather, those assignments were actually tests of the children's existing abilities. We now recognize that instruction in writing should more closely parallel the processes that most authors follow when they write. Many teachers now follow variations of the writing model shown in Figure 7.4.

Writing Activities. The potential for realistic writing activities in social studies is almost endless. In most cases, the possible writing activities that we describe next require prior class activities or research. However, in many instances, the activities can provide a motive for doing the research.

* *"How to's"* are precise, step-by-step descriptions of how to do something. Examples:
  1. How to brand a calf
  2. How to make soap
  3. How to make a peanut butter sandwich

FIGURE 7.4 A Writing Model

What to write about. Decide on a topic that may be worth pursuing.

Research. Do you need to find out more about the topic?

Initial Draft. Write your story.

Two revisions (may be done simultaneously). Focus on (1) content and (2) mechanics.

Extend. Share your writing with others.

---

* *Diaries* or *journals,* or *anecdotes* or *stories* of real or imagined people describing a place, event, or experience. Examples:
    1. A visitor to a dairy
    2. A pioneer on the Santa Fe Trail
    3. A photojournalist in Scotland
* *Applications* for jobs, describing qualifications for the position and reasons why you would like it. Examples:
    1. A sailor on Magellan's first voyage
    2. A firefighter
    3. The king or queen of England
* *Letters* written by students themselves or as another person, either real or imagined, containing descriptions, reactions, observations, or attempts to persuade someone to take a certain course of action. Examples:
    1. A description of San Francisco (or Fairbanks, Alaska) during the Gold Rush
    2. A letter to the mayor asking that the community follow a particular course of action
    3. A letter (circa 1860) from a Northerner to a southern relative explaining why the South should not secede from the Union (or vice versa)
* *Radio scripts* describing events or conditions. Examples:
    1. A "You Are There" description of the first Thanksgiving
    2. A news broadcast from Paris during the time of Joan of Arc
    3. A news bulletin from inside the Alamo (or Nagasaki, Japan, just after the atomic bomb was dropped)
* *Pamphlets* or *brochures* (with illustrations) that describe places or events. Examples:
    1. Washington, D.C.
    2. Valley Forge
    3. The school
* *Interviews* (with real or imaginary people) in which students ask and answer questions. Examples:

What was General Lee thinking?

   1. An interview with General Lee on the eve of signing the surrender at Appomattox, Virginia, in 1865
    2. An interview with Martin Luther King, Jr., circa 1965
    3. An interview with a French fur trader, circa 1700
* *Advertisements* for inventions, places, products, and so on. Examples:
    1. The printing press
    2. The water wheel
    3. A medieval castle
* *Biographies* of imaginary children living in other times or places. Examples:
    1. A child living in ancient Sparta
    2. A child living on a plantation in Georgia in 1840
    3. A child living in Sydney, Australia, today

* *Wanted posters,* with a picture, description, crime, and so on. Examples:
  1. Benedict Arnold
  2. Jean Lafitte (pirate)
  3. Saddam Hussein
* *Itineraries* for imaginary trips through places past or present. Examples:
  1. A trip on the Underground Railroad
  2. An itinerary for Marco Polo
  3. A sightseeing trip through your community

Before using any of these writing activities, be certain to establish an authentic, purposeful context. Writing a descriptive brochure of Washington, D.C. or a wanted poster for Jesse James, for example, needs to serve a useful purpose. Otherwise, the activities could easily become "writing for the sake of writing."

Helping Children Construct Meaning

Consider the following conversation between a mother and her six-year-old daughter.

MOTHER: What did you learn at school today?

DAUGHTER: Oh, the teacher said we live in a democracy, but I told her that we live in an apartment.

MOTHER: That's nice.

DAUGHTER: What *is* a democracy anyway?

MOTHER: Why it's a form of government, dear.

DAUGHTER: What's a *form?*

Form is yet another of the polysemous (multiple-meaning) words that we noted earlier. Young children often know that *form* refers to the shape of something, and, after experiences like the one above, they may learn that *form* can also refer to a category or type of phenomenon. We used *construct* in the heading for this section because words and ideas (other than our own) are meaningful only to the extent that we can relate them to our prior experiences. For unfamiliar terms, we must rearrange the mental pigeonholes we use to organize and store our past experiences to accommodate the new ideas. That process is often called *accommodation,* although more recently the term *scaffolding,* which more clearly conveys the notion of "constructing" or "building onto," is often used.

We were reminded of the scaffolding process when we encountered the Dennis the Menace cartoon shown on page 171. We already had many ideas that we associated with Abraham Lincoln—a tall, bearded man in a stovepipe hat, the sixteenth president, the Emancipation Proclamation, teaching himself the law by candlelight, Ford's Theater, assassination, John Wilkes Booth. Each of these elements reflects an *attribute* that we associate with Lincoln. Also included among

Source: DENNIS THE MENACE ® used by permission of Hank Ketcham and © by North America Syndicate.

those attributes are our attitudes, feelings, and impressions about Lincoln, which, though more difficult to describe, are along the lines of respect for his apparent honesty and an appreciation for the dignity and bearing with which he conducted himself.

Accommodating new ideas

Dennis the Menace suggested a new attribute that we (and perhaps you) had *not* previously associated with Abraham Lincoln. We accommodated this new attribute by adding "toys" to our existing concept. However, we have since learned that Lincoln Logs were invented by Frank Lloyd Wright, the famed architect, who named them after the president who was sometimes called "the log splitter." That piece of trivia could be useful if you ever become a contestant on the TV show *Jeopardy!*, but it also suggests that the relationship between Lincoln Logs and our sixteenth president is more tangential than direct.

Testing new conceptualizations

In our earlier example in which the daughter is puzzled by the term *form*, she will probably reconstruct her existing ideas (about *form*) to accommodate the new usage. In addition, at some time in the future she will probably test her newly constructed schema for *form* by using the word in an appropriate situation (or one that she hopes is appropriate). Such testing is a normal part of the language learning process that we referred to earlier, such as when children discover that adding the bound morpheme /ed/ to certain words enables them to talk about events that happened in the past.

The problem with definitions

The old rule of thumb—"If you don't know what a word means, you look it up in a dictionary"—is not especially productive for most polysemous terms. For example, a *wing* can refer to the thing that a bird flies with or to a part of a larger building, both of which most children already know. However, *wing* can also refer to a more or less identifiable group of people who belong to an organization, often a political group called a *party*, or it can mean any one of twenty other definitions listed in our dictionary. For children who think of "party" as a kind of celebration, the dictionary definitions for *wing* can create a situation where they must cope with multiple attributes simultaneously, a potentially mind-boggling situation. There are times when using the dictionary to define new terms is appropriate, as we illustrate shortly, but this is not one of them.

Helping children understand the various attributes associated with polysemous terms like *wing* is more than simply a matter of definition learning. To approach it in that way would, we think, be a classic example of decontextualized instruction—of trying to learn things in isolation and without reference to the phenomena with which they are associated. To provide a context for *wing*, teaching needs to begin with the phenomenon it is associated with, in this case, political parties. If children have only a vague notion of what political parties (or similar organizations) are, which is more than likely, then that becomes the appropriate beginning point for instruction. In other words, trying to teach children about wings when they don't understand the nature and characteristics of political parties is putting the cart before the horse.

Coping with inclusive and narrow ideas

Part of the difficulty that both teachers and students face in understanding abstract ideas like *wing* or *democracy* is their breadth—they are broad concepts with many attributes. In contrast, nonpolysemous words like *barley*, or even a term like *pharaoh*, are often easier for children to handle. Although pharaohs were unique to ancient Egypt, the term reflects a narrower concept with relatively few attributes, as opposed to a broader and more inclusive concept such as *absolute monarch*. Eventually you might wish to help students build the broader concept of *absolute monarch*, but until they are comfortable with narrower concepts—like *pharaohs, kings,* and *emperors*—they may not know what you are talking about.

To summarize briefly, we've suggested that the process of making things meaningful for children or adults involves connecting new ideas with the individual's existing experiences. When children have no previous experiences with the phenomenon in question, like the *wing* of a political party, teachers may need to begin from scratch and provide experiences for them. We've also suggested that broad ideas that have many attributes—like *freedom, democracy, or absolute monarch*—tend to be more difficult for children than narrower concepts like *pharaoh*, which, though they may be equally abstract, have fewer attributes that children must accommodate. There are so many broad and encompassing concepts in elementary and middle-school social studies that it is often impossible to avoid them. If you find yourself in that situation, one of the strategies in the next section may be appropriate.

COMMENTARY: The Role of Details in Constructing Meaning

Obviously, students cannot move backward in time and actually participate in the events of history—actually join Christopher Columbus on his voyage, for example. And if your students saw how tiny the *Nina*, *Pinta*, and *Santa Maria* actually were, they probably wouldn't want to. In lieu of real experiences, teachers can often appeal to children's imagination in ways that support their vicarious participation in events. By using literature to create vivid mental images of historical events, it's sometimes possible to engage children as if they were witnessing the events unfold. These vivid mental images are created by *details*.

Unfortunately, the role of factual details in teaching history is among the most widely misunderstood aspects of social studies instruction. For example, consider the following statements as they might appear in a textbook: "In 218 B.C.E., Hannibal led an army of over 100,000 soldiers across the Alps. He then met and defeated the Roman legions in what is now Italy." The passage is factually accurate but so bland it fails to capture the imagination. It takes details to make the passage come alive, such as the fact that Hannibal was only eighteen years old when he gathered his huge army from various parts of Africa and Europe. Hannibal's army spoke so many different languages that often his troops could not communicate with one another. In addition to the 100,000 soldiers, Hannibal's army also included thirty-seven elephants. Thirty-six of them were African "attack" elephants that had been trained to terrorize enemy soldiers by trampling on them; the elephants practiced on prisoners at the training center in Carthage. The thirty-seventh, an Indian elephant named Syrus, was probably Hannibal's personal pet.

After a harrowing journey across the Alps, Hannibal still had to get his army, its supplies, and the elephants across the Rhone River. The army "borrowed" boats, made rafts, or used anything they could get their hands on to get across the river. But getting the elephants across was another problem; they refused to go onto the rafts that had been built for them. In desperation, Hannibal's soldiers covered the rafts with pieces of sod so that they looked like extensions of the shoreline. Apparently the elephants were deceived, because they willingly walked onto the rafts. However, when boats began towing the rafts toward the opposite shore, the elephants realized something was wrong and panicked. Some reared up, trumpeted loudly, and threw their mahouts (drivers) into the river. Many of the mahouts, who were originally from Africa, had never learned how to swim and were drowned. Some of the elephants also jumped into the river, but they swam to the opposite shore and waited there for the elephants that had remained on the rafts. All the elephants made it safely across the Rhone River.

Individually and in the sweep of human experience, most details appear small and insignificant. It is not important that students come away remembering how many elephants Hannibal had, for example, even though they often do remember such information. The point is that, collectively, details play a vital role in the creation of vicarious experience and subsequent learning. Too often, we suspect, children must deal with test questions such as "How many elephants did Hannibal have?"—questions that ultimately become part of their grade. Because teachers' test questions often define what is or is not important, we wonder how many students focus their attention on trying to learn what is actually historical trivia. Perhaps some students learn to hate history because the role of factual details continues to be misunderstood.

Examples of Instruction Designed to Construct Meaning

The following exemplars illustrate how you might go about managing the idea-building process.

Vocabulary. When you suspect that your students do not understand a narrow concept, such as *isthmus*, you have several options. First, you can *define* it for them: "An isthmus is a narrow strip of land between two bodies of water."

Building on what students know

However, because few students will have prior experience with an isthmus, your words will mean more if you use a picture or other illustration to provide a visual image of the term. You might also use an *analogy*—for example, "An isthmus is a kind of 'land bridge,' a skinny piece of land that connects two larger land masses." That analogy could be part of a larger explanation in which you use a *simile*—for example, "An isthmus is like a strait, except it's land instead of water." Your explanation for some concepts, such as *peninsula*, might include a description of the origin of the expression: "*Peninsula* comes from the Latin—*pene* for 'almost' plus *insula* for 'island.' In other words, a peninsula is almost an island."

Having students use a dictionary or glossary is another option for relatively narrow real-world concepts, such as *isthmus* and *peninsula*. But for abstract concepts such as *capitalism* or *imperialism*, dictionary definitions may lead to the situation we noted earlier—that is, where one abstraction is defined with other abstractions.

The Taba Model. The following idea-building strategy was developed by the late Hilda Taba and is based on a three-step sequence illustrated in Table 7.1 (Taba et al., 1967). In some respects, this strategy is similar to the way that Lynda Esparza began her lesson in the introduction to this chapter, although she opted not to do the entire process in a single lesson. In this strategy, students are asked first to identify and enumerate items, then to find a basis for grouping or clustering the items together, and finally to identify a label for the items they have clustered. How the three phases might be conducted for a second-grade class is illustrated in the following Model Student Activity.

An old strategy but still useful

Table 7.1 **Taba's Concept-Formation Strategy**

Phase	Overt Activity	Covert Mental Operations	Eliciting Questions
One	Enumeration and listing	Differentiation	What did you see? Hear? Note?
Two	Grouping	Identifying common properties, abstracting	What belongs together? On what criterion?
Three	Labeling and categorizing	Determining the hierarchical super- and subordination	What would you call these groups? What belongs under what?

Source: *Teacher's Handbook for Elementary Social Studies* © 1967 by Taba, Durkin, et al. Copyright Addison-Wesley Publishing Company. Used by permission.

MODEL STUDENT ACTIVITY

Taba's Concept-Formation Strategy

Phase 1: Enumeration and Listing

TEACHER: Let's start listing on the board the things that you would buy if you went to the store.

DAVID: Apples.

PAUL: I'd buy a steak.

RANDY: Shrimp.

DENNY: I'd buy a puppy.

TEACHER: A puppy is different, isn't it?

MICHAEL: Watermelon.

CARLA: Candy bar.

ANN: Scooter.

TEACHER: Scooter, that's something different again, isn't it?

TEACHER: We've almost filled up our board with things that we would buy. What can we do with these things? Do some of them belong together? Which ones belong together? Which ones could you find in the same place?

DENNY: You can buy a doll and scooter in the same place.

TEACHER: You would buy them in a toy shop, wouldn't you? Let's pick the ones that you might buy in a toy shop. What else would you buy in a toy shop?

RICKY: Squirt gun.

TEACHER: All right, we would buy a squirt gun in the toy shop. What else would we buy in the toy shop? (Taba et al., 1967, pp. 95–99).

Phase 2: Grouping

Students continue to suggest different (and multiple) groupings for some items, such as "steak and watermelon—things at a cookout" or "shrimp and steak, because both are meats." Students may or may not identify a "food" category for items such as apples, watermelon, steak, and shrimp.

Phase 3: Labeling and Categorizing

After the larger clusters have been identified, the teacher then moves to labeling and categorizing by asking, "What would you call these groups?" Responses may include "things you can buy in a store," "things we eat," and "things we use." As Taba and her colleagues (1967, p. 94) noted, it is important for students "to discover that any item has many different characteristics and therefore can be grouped in many different ways. Each of the multiple qualities can be used as a basis for grouping."

Contextual Redefinition

Helping students learn to use the context in which unfamiliar words appear is vital to the process of becoming an independent learner. We illustrated this earlier in an example involving the word *barley*, which we suggested was not important enough to the meaning of the passage that it demanded preteaching. Unlike our *barley* example, students will encounter many passages with unfamiliar words that are critical to understanding and that must be pretaught. In such cases you can use contextual redefinition, a teaching strategy that is based on making and verifying predictions. Phases of the contextual redefinition strategy are as follows:

Selecting problem terms

★ *Phase 1:* Select terms that are likely to be unfamiliar to students *and* that are critical to understanding the passage. For purposes of illustration, we will use the term *civil service* (after Irvin et al., 1995).

- ★ *Phase 2:* Using an overhead or chalkboard, present each term individually and in isolation.
- ★ *Phase 3:* Ask students to brainstorm possible definitions for each term. Accept all suggestions, including those that are wrong or "off the wall," as in "a civil service is a wedding where everyone is polite" (Irvin et al., 1995).

Deciding on a possible meaning

- ★ *Phase 4:* Help students reach a consensus on the most probable meaning.
- ★ *Phase 5:* Present a sentence or cluster of sentences that illustrates the meaning of the term. For example: "Civil service was created during the T'ang dynasty in China. Using an examination system, government officials were selected based on their qualifications instead of their noble birth."

Modify as needed

- ★ *Phase 6:* Help students modify their earlier definitions if necessary.
- ★ *Phase 7:* Ask one or two students to verify the definition in a dictionary or glossary.

Word Maps

In the example for Phase 5 above, the term *dynasty* might also be troublesome for some students. An alternative strategy to contextual redefinition involves creating a word map for the unfamiliar term, in this case *dynasty*. The emphasis in this strategy is on relating unfamiliar terms to students' prior experiences. A sample word map for *dynasty* is shown in Figure 7.5.

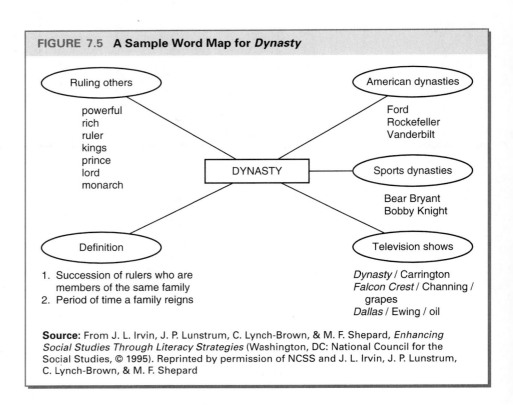

FIGURE 7.5 A Sample Word Map for *Dynasty*

Ruling others

powerful
rich
ruler
kings
prince
lord
monarch

American dynasties

Ford
Rockefeller
Vanderbilt

DYNASTY

Sports dynasties

Bear Bryant
Bobby Knight

Definition

1. Succession of rulers who are members of the same family
2. Period of time a family reigns

Television shows

Dynasty / Carrington
Falcon Crest / Channing / grapes
Dallas / Ewing / oil

Source: From J. L. Irvin, J. P. Lunstrum, C. Lynch-Brown, & M. F. Shepard, *Enhancing Social Studies Through Literacy Strategies* (Washington, DC: National Council for the Social Studies, © 1995). Reprinted by permission of NCSS and J. L. Irvin, J. P. Lunstrum, C. Lynch-Brown, & M. F. Shepard

Using Semantic (Concept) Maps.   Semantic (or concept) maps are similar to word maps but have a broader focus. Semantic maps are devices that (1) visually depict the attributes associated with an idea or concept, and (2) show the relationships among those elements.

Visualizing how elements are related

The process of making a semantic map is sometimes called "webbing," probably because the finished product can resemble a spider web. Semantic mapping uses elements that are similar to the Taba strategy, especially since students organize and cluster related elements. To illustrate the mapping process, we use the textbook passage about Canada on page 162. The steps in creating a semantic map are shown below.

The ideas

* *Step 1: Determining students' existing ideas.* Ask, "When someone says Canada (or whatever your map will focus on), what do you think of?" List the students' responses in key words on the board or an overhead projector. Their responses, which will be organized in Step 2, may include attributes such as "borders the United States to the north," "is larger than the United States," "national capital is Ottawa," and "bilingual, especially in the eastern provinces, where French is commonly spoken."

* *Step 2: Clustering related responses.* Help students identify related elements by using symbols to show each relationship—circles around items related to language, boxes around elements related to the economy, and so forth. The purpose of this step is to organize what might otherwise be a random listing of attributes.

* *Step 3: Making a preliminary concept map.* Begin the webbing process on an overhead transparency or a blank section of the board. Place "Canada" in the center; then add elements radiating outward as shown by the solid lines in Figure 7.6. Use branching to show related elements.

* *Step 4: Adding new elements to the map.* Decide with students where new elements should be placed. In this example, the new elements come from the textbook passage noted earlier:

Canada is a country that now controls itself.
Canada got its freedom gradually.
Canada gained its independence from Great Britain in 1949.
Canada was partially independent before 1949.
The people of Canada select their leaders.

Many students will treat each fact as a separate item until they see a need or reason to organize or cluster them in a different way. To stimulate clustering, ask, "Is there any pattern to these new elements?" or "Do they fit together somehow?" Multiple categories that could accommodate these elements include history, political organization, and independence. There is no best way to organize the new items, but one way needs to be agreed upon and then added to the concept map. Our treatment is shown by the broken lines in Figure 7.6.

* *Step 5 (Closure): Debriefing and reflection.* This step helps students reflect on what they have done and how they did it. The idea is to get students to think about how they dealt with the problem—to think about thinking. Ask questions such as these: "How did we deal with this?" "Is there a better way

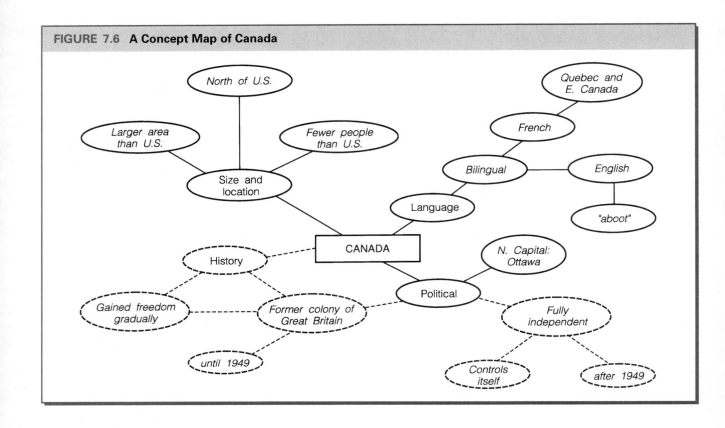

FIGURE 7.6 A Concept Map of Canada

we could have done this?" "What have we learned from doing this?" Responses will vary.

Thinking about thinking

If it seems that we have gone to a lot of trouble with a four-sentence passage about Canada, we clearly have. In one respect, it would be simpler to ask children to remember the facts within that passage and to leave it at that. However, doing so would place the burden on the students, who *might* store the information in their short-term memory—perhaps long enough to take a test—but in six months or less it will assuredly be forgotten. Even having done all this, students are still likely to forget some specifics, such as the date of Canada's independence. Whether they should be expected to remember such information to begin with is debatable. What they should learn from this activity is a process for organizing and dealing with information in ways that are personally meaningful. Without meaning, the activity would be an academic exercise.

Summary

This chapter has focused on helping children gain meaning from spoken or written words. The first premise is that in the absence of meaning, literacy is an impossibility. Meaning depends largely on the extent to which children can make connections between new ideas and their existing base of experiences. Helping children to make those connections is one of the most important roles a teacher plays.

Language literacy refers to the ability to use language—to read, write, speak, and listen—fluently and effectively in different situations. Recent research has indicated that children require opportunities to talk and play with standard English, the language of textbooks and the school, in ways that mimic how they learned their language in the first place: by listening, observing, and sometimes by testing theories about how language operates in realistic and purposeful situations. Too often, children in traditional classrooms had few opportunities to practice or demonstrate their oral language skills. When researchers discovered that children with poor oral language facility also tended to be poor readers and writers, things began to change—although slowly at first. It has become increasingly apparent that the basis for literacy is the child's facility with oral language. In slightly different terms, this means that if children cannot understand the spoken word, they will be not be able to understand those ideas when they try to read them, nor will they be able to convey those ideas in written form.

Suggested Activities

1. Select two social studies texts (from different publishers) for the same grade level. Select at least two topics common to both books—there will be many—and compare the two texts in terms of their concept loading.

2. Using one of the texts from the activity above, select one chapter at random. On a separate paper, create a two-column list with the overall heading "Potentially Troublesome Concepts." The subhead for one column should be "Concepts that lack real world referents," which will include figurative expressions and other abstract concepts described in this chapter. The subhead for the second column should be "Concepts observable in the real world." After reading the first ten pages of the chapter, place any potentially troublesome concepts in the appropriate category. Then select one of the concepts from those that lack real world referents and design a teaching activity that might help children build meaning for that idea.

3. Some teachers contend that the only way children will learn to use standard English correctly is by writing and speaking correctly in classroom discussions and writing activities. Other teachers accept dialectal usages in oral communication but insist on correct English in the children's written work. Still other teachers allow children to use whatever language they feel most comfortable with, so long as it is appropriate (no cursing, etc.). Determine where you stand on this issue.

Suggested Readings

Lucy McCormick Calkins. (1994). *The art of teaching writing*. Portsmouth, NH: Heinemann. A book with this title *must* be well written; this one is superb.

J. David Cooper. (1993). *Literacy: Helping children construct meaning* (2nd ed.). Boston: Houghton Mifflin. An excellent resource on developing literacy.

Leslie W. Crawford. (1993). *Language and literacy learning in multicultural classrooms*. Needham Heights, MA: Allyn & Bacon. This book is especially useful because of its focus on multicultural classrooms.

Donald Graves. (1983). *Writing: Teachers and children at work*. Portsmouth, NH: Heinemann. This wonderful book is written by the individual often considered to have begun the writing revolution.

8 Strategies for Effective Teaching

Key Questions

* What teaching strategies work best for which objectives?
* What's the difference between teacher-directed and student-centered teaching strategies—in action, that is?
* How do teachers manage small-group activities?

Key Ideas

* Teaching techniques—lectures, discussions, and so on—are the building blocks from which teaching strategies are created.
* Teacher-centered strategies tend to be more appropriate for conveying information; student-centered strategies tend to be more appropriate for developing information-processing skills.
* Teaching strategies reflect a system of interacting behaviors purposely designed to achieve learning goals.
* Teachers may use several teaching techniques in a single lesson.

Introduction: The "Pine Tree Shillings" Activity

Janet Jacobsen has been teaching fifth grade in the same classroom for twenty-six years in the Yakima Valley in South Central Washington State. When she began teaching, the building was a K–8 elementary. It then became a K–6 elementary, and it is now a departmentalized, 5–8 middle school. Mrs. Jacobsen, who plans to retire next year, is the head teacher for the fifth-grade teaching team and the building coordinator for social studies.

Applying "selective neglect"

We asked Mrs. Jacobsen to tell us how she approaches teaching social studies. "When I began," she said, "I went pretty much by the book, but we were always rushing to finish something so we could move on to the next chapter. Then I began to cut out things—things we'd skip. I've become a real believer in studying fewer things in more depth."

"What kinds of things did you leave out?" we asked.

"The War of 1812 was the first thing to go, because the kids can never understand what we were fighting for. I also began to leave out the Mexican War, the Spanish American War . . . and things like the Depression of the 1930s.

Changing roles "But I think the biggest change," Janet continued, "was when I decided to modify my role as teacher and help my kids become more responsible for their own learning. How do you say it—I shifted from being 'a sage on the stage' to a 'guide by the side.'"

We asked Mrs. Jacobsen to tell us more. "I use a modified cooperative-group investigation approach where the kids focus on researching and answering questions they've raised," Janet said as she walked over to her filing cabinet. She handed us a one-page handout and said, "Here's an example. This is about the 'Pine Tree Shillings' incident that I took from an old reader." Janet pointed to an obviously old book, *Stories of Our Country* (Johonnot, 1887). "I got it for 50 cents at the Salvation Army store. This is my springboard."

Pine Tree Shillings

A springboard for inquiry The Puritan colony of Massachusetts assigned John Hull to be the mint master. Using silver from old tableware, buccaneer bullion, and old European coins, he cast thousands of shillings, sixpence, and threepence. Each coin had an image of a pine tree on one side and the date 1652 on the other.

Sometime after Captain Hull had made his fortune minting coins, his plump daughter, Betsy, attracted a suitor, the young Sam Sewell. Captain Hull, recognizing that Sewell sought love and not a dowry, granted Betsy's hand in marriage.

Just after the wedding, Captain Hull instructed his servants to bring in a large set of scales. He directed his daughter to get on one side and then instructed his men to balance the scale. The servants scooped up handfuls of bright silver Pine Tree shillings into the other pan.

"There, son Sewell!" cried the honest mint master. "Take these shillings for my daughter's portion. Use her kindly, and thank Heaven for her. It is not every wife that's worth her weight in silver!"

—Hawthorne

(Johonnot, p. 81, cited in Lauritzen & Jaeger, 1994, p. 582)

Cognitive dissonance The term *buccaneer bullion* in the second line immediately caught our attention. Buccaneers were pirates, of course, but we'd never heard of pirates in New England. This was puzzling, but we decided to pursue it later. Instead we said, "This just says 'Hawthorne.' Is this *the* Nathaniel Hawthorne?"

"That's a question the kids ask," Janet responded, "except most of them don't know about Nathaniel Hawthorne, so they ask, 'Who was Hawthorne?' After we've read the vignette, I invite questions about it. Look," she said, as she pulled three overhead transparencies from the file. "I save these from year to year to remind me what I'm getting into. The kids have literally hundreds of questions."

A few of the children's questions are shown here.

Children's questions What is a mint master?
Were some mint masters dishonest?
How did a mint master make coins?
How did Captain Hull get the silver to make coins?

Did people donate old silverware? Why?

What is bullion? What is buccaneer bullion?

What is a shilling? A sixpence? A threepence? A pence?

Why was 1652 on the coins?

What did the scales look like?

How "plump" was Betsy?

What was Betsy really worth?

Is this a true story? Are the people real?

Who was Hawthorne?

What is a dowry? Do we still have dowries today? Were they common in Puritan times?

"I invite students to follow up on their most compelling questions," Janet added. "I forewarn the librarian before we get into this, and she gets a lot of books ready for us. As a matter of fact, she's purchased a lot of books on coinage and Nathaniel Hawthorne because she knows the kids are going to ask for them."

Using on-line services

"Even more than the books," Janet continued, "my kids love to get on CompuServe. [America Online and Prodigy are other computer-based information services.] I can't tell you how impressed they are when they get an E-mail answer to one of their questions. When some of them deal with English money, like shillings and pence, they sometimes get E-mail responses from England; it's fabulous."

We told Janet, "Whenever we tried this kind of inquiry approach, there were always a few kids who wouldn't get involved. They'd say there was nothing they wanted to investigate. Do you ever encounter this?"

Computers as motivators

"Sure," Janet replied. "I always have a couple of students who need some prodding, but I never realized how powerful computers are as motivational tools. Few students can resist the prospect of receiving a personal E-mail from someone somewhere in the world. Anyhow, for the kids who still won't get involved, I tell them that they must be doing something productive; they can't just sit there and do nothing."

Investigating different facets of the incident

"Most of my students," Janet continued, "read books on colonial times to research the personalities; some of them go to the coin shop in the mall and look at examples of colonial coinage; some of them study the literature of Nathaniel Hawthorne to determine if it is similar to the 'Pine Tree' story; and some of them experiment with different models for testing how many coins Sam Sewell received in the dowry. The kids also record their findings in their journals, including the feelings that this inquiry evokes."

Sharing findings

"It usually takes a week or more to deal with this activity, usually more like two to three weeks when you add in the sharing time, because some of the kids really get into it. And because everyone's following a different line of inquiry, the sharing aspect of this unit is *really* important. I have one, and only one, rule for sharing: show us, don't just tell us. Every student makes some kind of visual presentation that describes his or her investigation. To eliminate duplicate reports, we sometimes team up for the sharing time. Most of the kids use the [Microsoft] *Works* program for word-processing and *Hyperstudio* for developing graphics for their presentations. To show the similarities between Hawthorne's writing style in the 'Pine Tree Shillings' piece and his other works, they used to copy pages from Hawthorne's works onto butcher paper. But now they use the scanner in the computer lab to transfer portions of the book directly into the computer. Then they make printouts for everyone. I'm thankful the language arts teacher also buys into this because she begins a unit on style at the same time I start this activity, and she uses Hawthorne as one of her examples."

"O.K., you've hooked us," we said. "Did any of the 'Pine Tree Shillings' stuff really happen?"

The real story

"Oh, yes," Janet replied. "Captain John Hull minted Pine Tree shillings in Massachusetts Bay colony in the mid- to late-1600s. However, all the Pine Tree shillings made after 1652 carried the same date. That was because when Charles II was restored to the English throne in 1652, the Massachusetts Bay colony lost the right to mint its own coins. Despite the new regulations, the Bay colony continued to mint its own coins for the next twenty years or so, and to avoid raising Charles II's suspicions, every coin was dated 1652. A clever ploy, don't you think?"

We will return in Chapter 11

We agreed. We'll revisit Mrs. Jacobsen again (in Chapter 11) to find out about her assessment and grading strategy.

This chapter focuses on teaching strategies, those patterns of daily lessons and activities that teachers design to enable their students to reach desired learning outcomes. At one time Mrs. Jacobsen supplemented the textbook with additional activities. However, she moved toward a more student-centered, small-group investigative approach to instruction. Mrs. Jacobsen also told us (as described in the introduction to Chapter 11) that during the six-week period just before her students take standardized tests, she moves back to a very teacher-directed approach. During that time, she covers a large body of information that her students will be responsible for on the test. The point here is that Mrs. Jacobsen, and all teachers, have a range of teaching strategies at their disposal, as shown in Figure 8.1.

Using different strategies for different purposes

FIGURE 8.1   A Range of Teaching Strategies

Teacher-Centered

Direct Instruction

Mixed

Student-Centered

Inquiry / Group Investigation

When Mrs. Jacobsen is working with her students on an activity like the "Pine Tree Shillings," her basic orientation is toward the right-hand side of the range. Then, when she moves into her pretest review mode, she shifts toward the left-hand side of the range. We examine some of the options and activities associated with each of these teaching orientations in the first part of this chapter. We then turn to the skills necessary for working successfully with small groups. And finally, because teacher-centered and student-centered teachers often hold different views on how children should deal with social studies content, we consider those dimensions in the last section of this chapter.

Teaching Strategies Defined

Strategy defined

Although the term *strategy* can sometimes have manipulative overtones, a teaching strategy is simply a series of activities designed to help students reach desired learning outcomes. Individual teaching techniques—such as lecturing, modeling, role-playing, conducting group discussions, videos, possibly computer-based simulations, and others—must somehow fit together to constitute a

---

COMMENTARY: There Is Nothing like a Good Lecture

In some educational circles a notion prevails that lectures are inherently bad and that, should you ever lecture to your students, you will be committing a grievous sin. At the same time, you've undoubtedly witnessed some extremely good lectures during your career as a student, some of which made eight-o'clock classes worth getting up for. How then can it be that lecturing is such an evil?

Our experience suggests that the quality of a lecture depends heavily on the lecturer's ability. Good lecturers demonstrate the following characteristics:

1. *They must be well versed in their subject.* Good lecturers stand at the opposite end of the continuum from students, whose reports to the class often reflect the total scope of their knowledge on a topic. Subject-matter expertise is just one qualification, however, because we've heard nationally known specialists in their fields deliver some abominable lectures.

2. *They must be master communicators.* Good lecturers must be sensitive to timing, pacing, and the form and style of expression—when to raise their eyebrow, change their tone of voice, use humor, or ask a question. The importance of these so-called "show-biz" aspects of lecturing was illustrated in what has been called "The Doctor Fox Effect." To determine whether the way a lecture was

presented made any difference in how students reacted to it, two researchers hired a professional actor, whom they called Dr. Fox, to present six different types of lectures. The actor first memorized the scripts for three different lectures on the same topic. Each lecture differed in the amount of information it contained; one had a very high content, another had some content, and the third contained a lot of verbiage but little information. The actor then presented each lecture to different students in one of two ways. For one presentation of each type of lecture, Dr. Fox really hammed it up, using gestures, humor, movement, vocal inflection, and considerable enthusiasm. For the second set of lectures, all of the expressive embellishments were omitted and the actor virtually read from the prepared script.

What happened? According to Williams and Ware (1977), students who experienced the highly expressive presentations did significantly better on achievement tests than did students who experienced the less expressive presentations. In addition, the students almost always rated expressive presentations as "more effective" than the less expressive lectures, regardless of their content. The implication, then, is that even if you have little to say on a topic, you should say it with gusto!

---

teaching strategy. The relationship between a teaching strategy and the individual teaching techniques is shown in Figure 8.2.

Identifying Teaching Strategies

No one needs to tell you that teaching strategies may range from almost complete teacher domination at one extreme to almost complete student involvement at the other (refer again to Figure 8.1). Few teachers are at either extreme, because most of them use a combination of teaching techniques and thus fall into a "mixed" strategy. Then, too, every classroom is teacher-directed to some extent at least, because that's what teachers are paid to do.

Teacher-Centered Instruction

Teacher-centered instruction is usually characterized by a "telling" or "explaining" orientation. In teacher-centered classrooms, the main emphasis is on what teachers do, and to a lesser extent on what students are doing because of the teacher's actions.

Many teacher-centered strategies are variations on a Read-Recite-Lecture-Test format. The recitation phase, which is typically an oral test of retained information, is sometimes omitted, especially at the college level. Occasionally the teacher may reverse the format and talk about material prior to having students read it. And on other occasions, additional elements may be added, such as videos, discussions, demonstrations, student reports, or current events periods. Despite such variations, the goal of most teacher-centered strategies is to present information to students as quickly and as efficiently as possible.

Goal: to present information

When teachers conduct question-and-answer sessions to determine how well students have retained information, they sometimes mistakenly refer to those sessions as discussions. *Discussion* may sound less formal and imposing than the

---

FIGURE 8.2 Components of a Teaching Strategy

A teaching strategy is created from various combinations of short-term techniques, such as

- discussion
- modeling
- role-playing
- lecturing
- group projects
- individual reports
- case studies
- simulations
- decision making
- mapping
- etc.

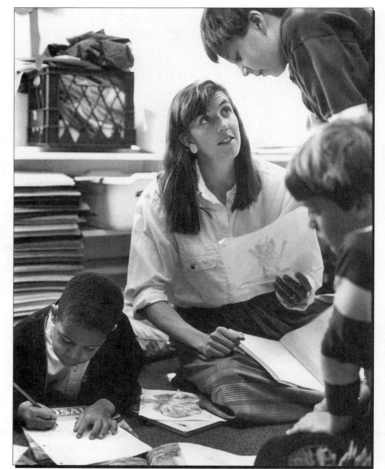

Getting down on the children's level can often enhance involvement and participation. (© *Susie Fitzhugh*)

correct term, *recitation,* but the two terms are not synonymous. The distinction between *discussion* and *recitation* is based on the purpose of the activity. Discussions can serve multiple purposes, including sharing different points of view on an issue, motivating students or developing interest in a topic, generating ideas, synthesizing ideas, or providing closure to an activity. The purpose of recitation is to test (orally) how well students have understood and retained prior information.

Despite the bad reputation sometimes associated with teacher-centered strategies, at times lecturing (or telling or explaining) and especially teacher modeling are both desirable and useful. This is often referred to as *direct instruction,* because teachers are doing something directly to students. When students are not fully aware of the issues associated with a topic, a so-called discussion can become a futile exercise in shared ignorance. At other times, students may find themselves floundering hopelessly because their teachers—who favor a student-

Direct instruction

centered approach to teaching—mistakenly believe that students can discover *everything* on their own, including the information that is essential for students to know. Given enough time, for example, students might discover how to determine the distance between two cities on a map. But it is often more efficient and effective if the teacher gives an explicit demonstration and explanation in which she or he models that process for students. Likewise, through a mini-lecture or short presentation, teachers can also bring fresh information to bear on points in question. We don't advocate a daily diet of half-hour speeches, but there are countless instances where mini-lectures are appropriate teaching activities.

A Model for Effective Instruction.

The direct instruction model

Over the last twenty years, researchers have focused intense interest on the relationship between teachers' strategies and students' academic achievement. One of the most consistently successful instructional sequences for dealing with *certain kinds of subject matter* was described by Rosenshine and Stevens (1986). This model is similar to what is sometimes referred to as the "Madeline Hunter" model, which is named after its creator. Both the Rosenshine and Stevens model, which is described next, and the Madeline Hunter model are highly sequenced, teacher-centered approaches to "direct-instruction."

Sequence of activities

Begin the lesson with a short review of the previous day's work, reteaching if necessary.

Provide an overview and a short statement of objectives for the lesson.

Present new content/skills, usually in small steps and at a rapid pace; provide opportunities for student practice after each step.

Give clear and detailed instructions and explanations.

To check for comprehension, ask a lot of questions and try to obtain responses from all students.

Provide opportunities for students to practice under the teacher's guidance.

Provide systematic feedback and correctives, reteaching if necessary.

Provide independent practice until students' responses are firm, quick, and automatic.

Provide weekly and monthly reviews. (pp. 377, 379)

Appropriate for well-structured subjects

Rosenshine and Stevens indicate that this model is most appropriate for subjects that they call "well structured," that is, subjects that have a learning hierarchy and in which later learning depends on earlier learning (p. 377). As noted earlier, few areas of social studies (except for map-reading skills) have the hierarchical structure with which this model might work well.

Major Teacher-Centered Techniques and Purposes Summarized

Technique	*Purpose(s)*
Lecture	To present information
Recitation	To test, orally, retained information

Technique	Purpose(s)
Discussion	Multiple purposes:
	To motivate or generate interest
	To share points of view on an issue
	To generate ideas or identify new applications for ideas
	To synthesize ideas
	To bring closure to an activity

Mixed Instruction

A blend of techniques

Mixed teaching strategies reflect a blend of teacher-centered and student-centered teaching techniques. Just how those techniques are blended often varies from teacher to teacher and, in some cases, from topic to topic.

The further that teachers move away from the more clearly defined roles of the teacher-centered strategy, the more difficult it becomes to describe their behavior precisely. When the focus shifts to a student-centered teaching strategy, discussed next, the attention necessarily shifts to the teacher *and* the students, and to what the students will be doing.

Student-Centered Instruction

Goal: to process information

Student-centered teaching strategies typically have a problem-solving or inquiry orientation. The goal of these teaching strategies is to help students develop the ability to manipulate and process information from various sources—academic, social, and experiential. To do this, teachers act as guides to assist students in identifying problems, generating possible answers, testing those answers in the light of available data, and applying their conclusions to new data, new problems, or new situations. In other words, the focus is on the skills of inquiring and processing information. This means that student-centered teaching strategies are more appropriate for helping students develop information-processing skills, whereas teacher-centered strategies are more appropriate for transmitting information.

Individual and Group Investigation.   Group investigations can be conducted

Three formats

in one of three ways: (1) the entire class acts as a research group in which everyone investigates aspects of the same problem simultaneously; (2) individuals or small research groups investigate one aspect or dimension of a classwide problem; or (3) individual or small research groups investigate separate problems. Mrs. Jacobsen's class used the second approach to investigate different dimensions of the "The Pine Tree Shillings" incident. The following Model Student Activity, "The Wearin' of the Green," reflects a whole-class approach to group investigation.

The Inquiry Process.   The procedures Ms. Fleury (see the Model Student Activity) and her students followed are common to many individual or group investigations. For example, after Ms. Fleury remarked that more intermediate than primary students would wear green the following day, this struck a discor-

"The Wearin' of the Green"— A Group Investigation

It was March, a time when winter seems to stretch out longer and longer. It was also the day before St. Patrick's Day.

Ms. Fleury, a fourth-grade teacher, commented to her class that although some families don't celebrate St. Patrick's Day, many students were likely to wear green clothing the following day. She added that students in the intermediate grades were more likely to wear green than primary-grade children. Her comment prompted a curious "why?" from one student, Stephen.

Ms. Fleury responded by saying that intermediate students were older and more likely to wear green clothing because many other intermediate students would be wearing green. Stephen suggested that primary children wear the clothes that their mothers lay out for them and that many of those mothers would see that their children wore something green; therefore primary children would be more likely to wear green. In other words, there were two competing views, one based on peer pressure and the other based on parental influence.

Ms. Fleury recognized that the question—who was more likely to wear green—was an opportunity for the class to gather data and to figure out which view was correct.

The students decided that they would observe each classroom in the building. Some students would be observers and others would stay in their classroom— the "control room"—to process the results. As their planning progressed, the principal came into the room.

She asked how much green someone needed to wear to be counted and whether it needed to be solid green. The students decided that someone had to have at least a sweater, shirt, blouse, skirt, slacks, scarf, or ribbon to be counted and that the dominant color had to be green. When everything seemed in place, the observers went to the different classrooms to ask permission to visit that room the next morning. The students agreed in advance to tell the teachers why they wanted to visit, but they knew that if they told each class what they were doing, it could change their results.

The next morning, the students observed their assigned classrooms and then gave the data to the student-tabulators. As Ms. Fleury had predicted, more intermediate students wore green than did primary-level students. Ms. Fleury was going to let it go at that, but one student, Christie, said she thought that there were more fourth, fifth, and sixth graders than there were students in the primary grades. This meant that there were more intermediate students who *could* wear green, and naturally they would win.

This was something Ms. Fleury hadn't anticipated. The issue involved percentages, which was something the students had not worked with yet. The talliers provided the total number of primary- and intermediate-level students and the numbers at each level who wore green, which Ms. Fleury then used to find the percentage. The new results: 76 percent of the primary children wore green clothing, compared with 64 percent of the intermediate-level children. Ms. Fleury admitted that Stephen's hypothesis seemed to be true.

dant note with Stephen, who politely disagreed by asking his question, "Why?" The difference between Stephen's views and Ms. Fleury's was a discrepant event that ultimately became the problem that the entire class investigated. The other phases of the inquiry process are discussed next.

Cognitive dissonance

1. *Awareness of a Possible Problem.* One's awareness of a discrepant event results from a kind of mental "disturbance" called *cognitive dissonance.* This

happened to us when we were visiting with Mrs. Jacobsen and encountered the phrase *buccaneer bullion,* which didn't "fit" our existing view of American history.

The awareness of the problem is critical to the inquiry process. Likewise, when students don't sense dissonance—something that doesn't fit—they have nothing to explain, and nothing to research. Therefore, teachers who wish to use investigation-oriented teaching strategies may sometimes need to structure activities in which they intentionally create cognitive dissonance that provides students with a motive for inquiry. The "Pine Tree Shillings" incident served this purpose in Mrs. Jacobsen's class.

The inquiry process

2. *Defining the Problem.* Based on the discrepancy between Ms. Fleury's and Stephen's views, the problem was: Will more or fewer primary-level students wear green clothing than intermediate-grade students?

3. *Hypothesizing.* Stephen's contention that primary children were more likely to wear green on St. Patrick's Day because their mothers usually laid their clothing out for them was a hypothesis. Likewise, Ms. Fleury's contention that intermediate children would wear green because they were more sensitive to peer pressure was a second hypothesis.

4. *Testing Modified Hypotheses.* An interesting aspect of this investigation is that it did not investigate the validity of either Stephen's or Ms. Fleury's explanations for *why* one age level was more or less likely to wear green clothing. Rather, it was restricted to the more basic problem: the age level of children who actually wore green clothing.

5. *Gathering Data.* Ms. Fleury and her students agreed on a process for collecting the information they needed—observing in other classrooms. They also defined their terms so that everyone knew what "wearing green" meant.

6. *Concluding, Tentatively.* Based on the preliminary data, it appeared that more intermediate students had worn green clothing than had primary students. Thus, Ms. Fleury was apparently correct, at least in terms of absolute numbers (though not in terms of the students' motivation).

7. *Testing the Conclusion.* Had there been no questions about the tentative conclusion, there would have been no need to test its applicability and it might have been accepted without further consideration. However, Christie raised the question about the number of students at each level who might potentially wear green, so it became necessary to reanalyze the data. That analysis showed that proportionately more primary students wore green than did intermediate students.

Based on this investigation, who was correct: Stephen or Ms. Fleury?

The phases of the inquiry/investigation process are summarized as follows:

The inquiry process

Phase 1. Becoming aware of a discrepant event, which leads to a problem to be solved.

Phase 2. Identifying hypotheses (possible explanations or tentative answers).

COMMENTARY: Inquiry, Discovery, and Problem Solving

When teachers talk about student-centered instructional strategies, they sometimes say, "I use a discovery approach"; others say, "I prefer a problem-solving approach." Because universally accepted definitions for inquiry, discovery, and problem solving don't exist, you would need to visit these teachers to find out how they actually teach. Despite the different terminology, these teachers' strategies are apt to be more similar than different.

One similarity among these approaches is their emphasis on thinking processes and skills. Literally, *discovery* refers to the moment that a student perceives a relationship among various data—when the student says "Aha, I've got it!" The teacher's role in discovery teaching is creating situations and environments where stu-

dents are encouraged to discover and test their ideas. In many respects, discovery is part of a larger process that is similar to the inquiry processes that we outlined earlier.

Problem solving can be confusing because the expression is used to refer to several different types of activities. One of these, probably the most common, refers to what students do as they complete the exercises in a math text, most of which have a right or desired answer. A second type of problem solving involves genuine investigative inquiry, such as Ms. Fleury's students experienced in the "Wearin' of the Green" activity. Ms. Fleury's students were investigating a real problem and no one, including Ms. Fleury, knew what they would find in advance.

Phase 3. Testing the hypotheses in light of the data.

    3.1. If a hypothesis is rejected, the problem may be restated for clarity, before returning to Phase 2.

    3.2. If the hypothesis is accepted (not rejected), the inquirer proceeds to Phase 4.

Phase 4. Modifying the hypothesis, which has become a tentative conclusion, in light of additional data until satisfied that it is a plausible explanation.

Phase 5. Testing the tentative conclusion (Does it fit? Does it explain the discrepant event?).

Phase 6. Knowing your limitations; becoming aware of what you don't know.

The Dynamics of Group Investigation. Not all group investigations work out as

Deciding on a hands-on activity

well as the "Wearin' of the Green" activity. For example, consider what can happen when, in the course of studying the Inuit (Eskimos), you wrack your brain for some hands-on activities that students might do. You reject the idea of written reports because students have already written about the Inuit in their journals. You also decide against building harpoons because of the potential dangers associated with overly enthusiastic role playing. You finally settle on the apparently safe idea of constructing model igloos from sugar cubes.

When you announce the igloo activity to the class, not everyone is thrilled with the prospect of model building. So you decide to make it an option, not a requirement. Next, Clarisa wants to know what kind of glue they should use to stick the sugar cubes together. Will plain paste work? Tyrone asks if he can use model airplane cement, the kind you use for plastic models. Or should he use Elmer's?

Resolving the glue problem

You have visions of half-constructed igloos collapsing if you give the wrong information, but you really don't know what will work. So you pose the question, "How do you suppose we can find out?"

Shamus claims that Elmer's works best because, well, he just *knows* it will. Shamus is usually right about such things and you are tempted to believe him this time, but Janet poses the obvious answer: "Everyone bring in the kind of glue they want to use and we'll test them." You agree, willingly and thankfully.

Still other problems

Once the glue crisis is resolved, still other questions are likely to arise. For example, will you permit your students to glue their sugar cubes to Styrofoam balls (cut in half) and then fill in the gaps with granulated sugar? Or will you have them cut off one edge of each cube so that it will lean inward properly to form the igloo's "roof"? Real igloos are hollow in the middle, not filled with Styrofoam, so cutting the sugar cubes to fit properly would be more realistic. On the other hand, cutting sugar cubes isn't easy, and you begin to wonder if this activity is any safer than the harpoon project you discarded.

Reassessing the purpose of the activity

Thus far the igloo-building project has generated more nitpicking problems than you ever anticipated, and you begin to wonder whether it is really worth it. You may also find yourself rethinking how you had originally justified the project—that by building model igloos, your students would learn about what it was like to find shelter in a land of scarce resources. You may also wonder if this activity has anything to do with life in the Arctic, or whether it is simply a lesson in construction—in learning how to cut sugar cubes without crumbling them, and in finding what kind of glue sticks them together best.

The igloo-building episode is an example of what Brophy and Alleman (1990) refer to as activities that occupy students' time but that often lack substance and fail to engage students intellectually. The moral? When you are considering group activities, such as presenting a play on Mexico or holding a Greek Olympic Day, be certain that the mechanics of collecting sombreros and serapes, making the scenery, or building chariots does not overshadow everything else.

Inquiry versus Activity.   The "Wearin' of the Green" and the igloo-building activity illustrate a key difference between genuine investigations and simple activities. In the "Wearin' of the Green," the children identified questions they wanted answered, and then did the research necessary to answer their questions. In other words, the inquiry process that the children followed was *purposeful and systematic.* For the igloo-building activity, however, the final product became the overriding concern, and the inquiry process got lost in the shuffle. An investigation is purposeful and systematic, whereas in a simple activity, the behavior is often not so systematic and organized.

Process versus product

The irony of inquiries and activities is that students often "feel good" about both. The students who conducted the "Wearin' of the Green" inquiry probably felt good about what they had accomplished. But the students who made model igloos probably felt good about their efforts too, even though they didn't learn much about their topic. Feeling good, by itself, however, is not a sufficient criterion for judging the quality of a learning experience.

The Challenge of Student-Centered Teaching.   Involving students in the inquiry process is not without some practical problems. This is especially true for primary students. Even very young children can become aware of discrepant events, but apparently because there are so many discrepant events in young children's lives, they may either become so interested that they insist on stick-

Practical problems

ing with a question until it's resolved to their satisfaction, or they dismiss it immediately and for no apparent reason. Unlike some adults, young children do not feel compelled to explain everything and can live quite happily with things that they don't understand.

Older students, on the other hand, sometimes jump on the first explanation (hypothesis) they create and cling so tenaciously to it that they ignore other possibilities or data to the contrary. It sometimes becomes a case of "I've already made up my mind, so don't bother me with information!" In a child's world, where things are often clearly "right" or "wrong," the idea of rejecting a tentative answer because the data do not support it can be construed as being *wrong* (when it is actually *right* to reject it).

Children's perceptions of what it means to teach

Another more subtle but equally important consideration in moving toward student-centered instruction is students' perceptions of what it means to teach. Children often believe that teachers are actually "teaching" only when they stand in front of the entire class and do their thing—explaining, modeling, conducting a discussion, or whatever. Based on those prior experiences, children are apt to believe that teachers who use cooperative learning and small groups extensively are, as students often put it, "not teaching very much."

Encouraging parental involvement

Such opinions are based primarily on the child's expectations (and often their parents' expectations) of teachers in general. Most children typically divorce how much they are learning, if they are even aware of it, from what student-centered teachers do to see that such learnings occur. Thus, it's wise to get parents involved from the outset—at least let them know what you are up to—before students' comments create negative perceptions that are difficult to overcome.

Managing group investigation

In terms of classroom management, involving an entire class in a single investigation, as Ms. Fleury did in the "Wearin' of the Green" activity, is a difficult task. However, because the activity occurred over a short (two-day) period, it was manageable. On the other hand, keeping an entire class involved with a single problem over a period of a week or more is difficult. Mrs. Jacobsen manages small-group investigations over a long period by having students self-select the problems they investigate. This procedure creates smaller groups that are inherently more manageable. However, having many small groups operating simultaneously also calls for some group-management skills on Mrs. Jacobsen's part, skills that would be far less important had she opted for a more teacher-centered strategy. We examine some of those group-management skills in the following section.

Managing Small-Group Instruction

Helping children learn to work productively in small groups is directly related to the overall goal of social studies teaching: promoting citizenship education. It is difficult, perhaps even impossible for students to learn to work cooperatively with others if all they experience is large-group instruction. Likewise, it's almost impossible for students to demonstrate their willingness to respect the rights and opinions of others if they seldom get the opportunity to express their opinions.

Almost everything you can do with large groups (of twenty to thirty students) can also be done in small groups; you can even lecture to two students if you want to. But the reverse does not hold true: what you can do with small groups is not always possible with large groups. Discussions that involve twenty or more students, for example, are less likely to be successful than discussions involving groups of five to seven students, simply because participants in the larger groups must wait so long before they get a chance to speak. On the other hand, good small-group discussions don't happen just because you create small groups in your class. Some special structuring is usually required, as we note later in this section.

You may remember times in the past when your small group spent thirty minutes getting organized when you could have completed the group's task yourself in half the time. Or when everyone in your group got the same grade but only one or two individuals did all the work. Or when group activities didn't make any difference because your grades were based solely on tests and individual projects. All of these experiences reflect decisions that need to be made before you undertake group work as a teacher. For example, will students' small-group work be graded and, if so, on what basis? You also need to decide how the groups will be created. Will you let children choose whom they will work with, or will you do the selecting? If you do the selecting, will you put two students who dislike each other on the same committee? Will you put a low-social-status child in the same group with high-social-status children (or vice versa)? High- and low-status children can often work successfully in the same group, but the relationship between two children who actively dislike each other is unlikely to improve if they are in the same small group, primarily because most groups don't deal with the causes of their disenchantment.

The Dynamics of Small Groups

From the moment you divide your class into small groups, the proportion of each student's responsibility to the group increases dramatically. Instead of representing one twenty-fourth of a class (of twenty-four), for example, a student could represent one-fourth of a group of four. The formula for determining the number of possible interactions (Ni) in small groups is $(NP - 1) \times NP = Ni$ (the number of persons in the group minus 1 times the number of persons in the group). This means that a group of four can have twelve possible interactions: $(4 - 1) \times 4 = 12$. If you were to create eight-person groups, the number of potential interactions increases to fifty-six: $(8 - 1) \times 8 = 56$. However, an eight-person group doing library research will probably spend as much time checking among themselves (and duplicating their efforts) as they will in doing the research itself. Thus the question of group size must be considered in relation to its purpose.

As a general rule, smaller groups have fewer problems than larger groups. But then small groups can also encounter problems. Groups of two, for example, often have a high exchange of information, but they also tend to have high tension. Likewise, one individual in a two-person group tends to be seen as the active initiator, while the other person acts as a passive controller (with a veto). In groups of three, you need to be careful that two stronger members do not

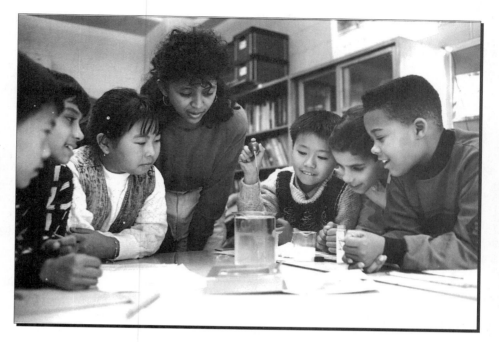

Small groups offer opportunities for hands-on experiences and increased involvement and participation. (© *Joel Gordon*)

overwhelm the weaker member, whereas four-person groups can easily deadlock, two against two. Groups of five seem to be the most personally satisfying, because they are small enough for participation yet large enough for stimulation. In addition, the possibility of a three-two split among members of a five-person group provides an ally for minority members.

Groups and Purposes

Purposes for small groups

You can establish small groups for any number of purposes, but four of the most common to social studies instruction are (1) to discuss issues or events, (2) to engage in decision-making exercises, (3) to provide small-group instruction, either remedial or enriched, and (4) to research or investigate problems or questions. Characteristics of these groups are summarized below.

Discussion Groups

Purpose. To provide children with opportunities to express and clarify their points of view on issues pertinent to their interests.

Size. Two to six (enough children to stimulate interaction but not so many as to overwhelm or restrict the flow of discussion).

Comment. Because discussion groups can easily degenerate into rap sessions, consider establishing a task for the group, such as a conclusion, a verbal report, or a summary, that will be presented after the group's deliberations. Preprinted questions or other guides to help groups structure their discussion can also be useful. Consider appointing a student discussion leader and selecting group members instead of allowing children to form their own groups.

Decision-Making Groups

Purpose.   To provide children with experience in group consensus and in considering alternatives and arriving at a decision.

Establish clear and manageable tasks

Size.   Three to seven.

Comment.   The life of most decision-making groups is short, seldom exceeding an hour and typically shorter than that. Consequently, the social status of discussion-group members is less critical than it is in longer-range tutorial or research groups. Students can form their own decision-making groups, or members can be selected at random. Also be certain that you have realistic activities or other established procedures for the early finishers.

Short duration

Tutorial Groups

Purpose.   To provide individual help or advanced work to a small group that might most need or benefit from it.

Size.   Two to nine.

Opportunities for feedback

Comment.   Tutorial groups provide opportunities for more immediate, direct feedback than is possible in large-group settings. However, the rest of the class will need meaningful activities while you work with a tutorial group.

Research Groups (Investigative)

Purpose.   To provide students with opportunities to solve problems, research questions, pursue lines of inquiry, or prepare projects.

Organization is the key

Size.   Two to four.

Comment.   The limitation on group size should be observed. Also, you may need to spend considerable time providing explicit instructions and helping the group organize itself.

Social Skills and Feedback

Some people claim that when children work together in small groups, they are learning social skills—how to cooperate, how to get along with one another, and so on. We question whether placing children in situations that require cooperation will necessarily teach them anything about cooperation per se. It may mean that students cooperated only because they were placed in a situation that demanded it.

When problems arise within small groups, it is sometimes difficult to know how to respond appropriately. For example, consider how a teacher might deal with an uncooperative student, in this instance, a student named Jamie. The first impulse is usually to say something like "Jamie, you are not cooperating," or

Beware of unwarranted assumptions

"The next time you work in a group, I want you to cooperate." The problem with such global statements is their lack of specificity. They assume that Jamie (1) is aware of how and when he has failed to cooperate and (2) is able (and wants) to do something about his apparent problem. If either of these assumptions is not valid, then simply telling Jamie to cooperate in the future is likely to be futile.

Dealing effectively with students who refuse to cooperate, who dominate groups, who don't respect the rights and opinions of others (both of which also reflect a form of noncooperation), or who refuse to accept their fair share of the work will depend in large measure on the kinds of messages you provide to them. In general, your feedback must be in a form that they, either individually or as groups, can do something with (or about).

Characteristics of Effective Teacher Feedback

Be as descriptive as possible

Specificity.   Effective feedback should identify specific behaviors that the child can modify or do something about. Statements such as "You're not smart enough to be in this group" or "You two don't care about this group" are judgments, not descriptions. Besides being unnecessarily cruel, neither statement indicates what the child should do to correct the problem. On the other hand, a statement such as "Before you proceed, you need to recheck your source of information" provides information that the child can act on.

When in doubt, add description

Positive feedback, such as "That was a good report" or "This group is really working well together," can be music to the ears of anyone—even if it is more judgmental than descriptive. However, negative feedback is another matter entirely. To say to Jamie (from our earlier example), "You are not a good group member," for example, is likely to evoke Jamie's ego-defense mechanisms, especially if you state it publicly. Perhaps the only time that such a statement will *not* cause problems is if Jamie values the fact that he is *not* a good group member. To avoid such consequences, feedback should be presented descriptively, nonjudgmentally, and as your reaction. Examples:

> *Poor:* Jamie, you are not cooperating.
> *Better:* You did not seem to listen to what the others were saying.

> *Poor:* This group does not work well together.
> *Better:* This group seems to be having difficulty deciding what information is important enough to include in the presentation.

When to give feedback

Timing.   The most useful feedback is provided immediately after the behavior in question takes place. Sometimes, of course, you may need to delay feedback until you can deal with a student individually. For example, if Jamie or another student is obviously upset about something—perhaps the death of a grandparent, or almost any of a thousand other things—it is probably not the time to criticize his unwillingness to cooperate; he's got other things on his mind. Likewise, if you are upset about something, the form of your feedback may serve your needs but not the student's. A sharp "Jamie, you should go along with the majority" may let you vent your feelings, but it could compound Jamie's problem.

Clarity. From time to time, it may be necessary to determine whether students are receiving the messages that you think you are sending: what you intend as descriptive feedback could or may be regarded by the children as criticism. At other times, a student may interpret a teacher's description of a group problem as if it were the student's own fault (when it is indeed a group problem). To determine that the communication is clear, the teacher can simply ask the receiver to rephrase the feedback.

Have students rephrase the feedback

Feedback that exhibits the characteristics we have identified here is appropriate for both small-group work and handling discipline problems in large-group settings (see, e.g., Schmidt & Friedman, 1987). In other words, a statement such as "Jamie, stop misbehaving" might be more effective if it were phrased like this: "Jamie, your persistent talking is bothering me and the people around you. Please stop." The rephrased statement identifies (1) the specific behavior in question, (2) the effects that behavior is producing in others, and (3) an appropriate course of action ("stop talking") that can eliminate the problem. Such a statement is specific, descriptive, clear, and delivered with appropriate timing—all elements of effective feedback.

Small-Group Management Practices Summarized

As you consider cooperative group work, we offer the following recommendations:

Begin with short-range tasks

1. Begin long-term group work only when you feel confident that (a) you can manage several groups operating simultaneously and (b) the individuals in each group can work together with minimal problems. You can get some idea of how individuals can work together by beginning with short-range group assignments.

Preliminary decisions

2. Decide how you plan to evaluate the group work before you begin, and then make this information known to students. If you plan to grade their reports or presentations, tell them the criteria you intend to use. They will listen intently.

Clear tasks

3. Identify clearly defined tasks and products (a report, a display, etc.) for each group. It may be necessary from time to time to remind the groups to focus on their tasks, and not on the final product.

4. Present common group tasks in a whole-class format. Presenting tasks to individual groups may invite problems among groups that have nothing to do until you get around to them.

Reasonable alternatives

5. Consider alternative ways in which groups can present the results of their efforts—videos, murals, skits, plays, charts, pictures, film. Long oral reports can leave much to be desired.

6. Make it clear that both group-process and content-related (but not interpersonal) problems are "fair game" for discussion in small groups or by the class as a whole, and allow time accordingly. Obviously, immediate intervention is recommended *before* a group begins to flounder.

Reasonable deadlines

7. Establish reasonable deadlines; you can always extend them if necessary. Without deadlines, groups working on even the simplest tasks can drag on forever. Similarly, have something prepared for groups that finish early.

Teaching Strategies Revisited

Focus on helping students use content

As you develop your repertoire of teaching strategies, you will obviously need to consider the group-management aspects of student-centered instruction that we have been dealing with here. Another more subtle but equally important consideration will involve how you perceive and approach different kinds of social studies content. Consider, for example, that when Janet Jacobsen used the "Pine Tree Shillings" handout with her students, it served as a springboard for further inquiry. It was not something every student had to memorize and learn, although they probably remember the incident well anyhow, nor were they tested on it. Although it may sound like a play on words, Mrs. Jacobsen used the "Pine Tree Shillings" incident to teach, but she did not teach it as merely something students needed to know. We elaborate on this perspective in the next section.

A Perspective on Using Social Studies Content

Mike Mulligan

You probably remember that delightful children's classic *Mike Mulligan and His Steam Shovel* (Burton, 1939), in which Mike's steam shovel, Mary Anne, is nearly sent to steam-shovel heaven because the new, engine-powered shovels are getting most of the jobs. In Burton's story, Mike and Mary Anne agree to dig the cellar for the new Popperville town hall. They also agree to complete the job in just one day; otherwise they won't get paid. By digging furiously for the entire day, Mike and Mary Anne manage to finish the job—except for one thing. In their haste, Mike forgets to leave a way to get Mary Anne out of the cellar (see Figure 8.3). So there she sits, quietly belching smoke, at the bottom of the huge hole.

Creative thinking

Henry B. Swap, a member of the Popperville town council, arrives at the construction site and argues that because Mary Anne is stuck in the cellar, the job wasn't finished within the agreed-upon time and Mike should not be paid. The day is saved when a little boy, who has been watching the whole episode, suggests that they build the new town hall around Mary Anne and make her its new furnace. And Mike? He could become the new janitor.

Structure and function

Mike Mulligan and His Steam Shovel is not the kind of content that you would normally associate with social studies. Nevertheless, a teacher could use the story to introduce the idea of structure and function. That idea reflects the fact that certain structures—like steam shovels—could be used for several functions (such as a hole digger, a *very* slow form of transportation, or even a furnace). Some of those functions, such as digging, are obviously more appropriate than others, yet all are potential functions for a steam-powered shovel.

Many teachers approach social studies subject matter as if it had only one major function, as something that "teachers teach and students are expected to know." Our purpose in this section is to show how content can serve a variety of instructional purposes and how it can become something that teachers and students *use*, not simply something that students are expected to know.

FIGURE 8.3 Children's Book Illustration

Using content as a vehicle

Content utilization refers to the notion of using content (subject matter) as a *vehicle,* as a way to help teachers and students move toward educational destinations. Using content as a vehicle is not restricted to social studies, but our main focus here is on using content in teaching social studies.

Throughout this section we use *content* and *subject matter*—the "stuff" of instruction—synonymously. It matters not whether you are using excerpts from a biography of Martin Luther King or Thomas Jefferson, or a textbook passage dealing with vital services in a community. A teacher could use ideas inherent in social studies content as the "stuff" children are supposed to know, or as a vehicle to help students identify and test hypotheses, or to distinguish

Multiple uses

between facts and opinions, or to teach countless other critical thinking skills. Students could also use the ideas inherent in social studies content as a basis for looking for recurring patterns in the human experience, to test previously identified hypotheses, as a springboard for further inquiry and research, and for many other purposes. In other words, social studies content can have a multitude of uses.

The Model Student Activity, "Who Is Qualified for the Presidency?" (from Chapter 1) reflects the nature of content utilization. In that activity, the biographical information served as a vehicle to help students identify various factors, such as age, education, marital status, and the like, that might influence the selection and election of a president. It was *not* intended to teach information about the candidates themselves. What we are driving at here is the recip-

Purpose determines use

rocal relationship between the teachers' purposes and the kind of content they use with their students:

Purposes ◄-------------► Content

If a teacher's purpose is to involve children in identifying several factors that influence the selection of a president, the teacher could use the "Presidency" activity to do that. However, instead of the "Presidency" activity, other teachers might wish to have students use a prepared list of factors that can influence presidential elections as the basis for a debate. Either approach is equally valid, although not necessarily equally effective—a situation we get to shortly.

The content can suggest potential uses.

The first point here is that the relationship between purposes and content is reciprocal, or nearly so. A teacher's purposes can dictate the content she or he needs, just as certain content, like the "Presidency" activity, can suggest some purposes for which you could use it. Our second point is that major curriculum goals are the dominant element in the purpose-content relationship. The "Presidency" activity and every other Model Student Activity in this book must fit into a larger picture. At the risk of stating the obvious, teachers should not use the "Presidency" activity in the middle of a unit on the geography of Australia if they want to maintain any sense of curricular continuity. Content vehicles can *suggest* purposes for which they can be used, but they do not *determine* what those purposes should be.

TECHNOLOGY UPDATE

Pictures Are Worth a Thousand Words

Somewhere among the Library of Congress's (LOC) 13.6 million images (photographs, pamphlets, paintings, etc.) you can surely find something that would be useful for whatever topic your students are studying. If the prospect of searching through several million images seems a little daunting, be advised that the LOC has a keyword search index that will narrow your choices considerably. Moreover, only a few thousand of the LOC's images are available for downloading on line at:

> http://lcweb.loc.gov/coll/print/guide/.

Many printers can make passable copies of downloaded images, but if you would rather have photo-quality prints, these are available at reasonable cost from the Library's Photo Reproduction Division.

The Library of Congress is only one source of downloadable images. If your topic is more subject-specific, check out one or more of the following:

The Louvre, at:
> http://www.paris.org/Musees/Louvre/

The National Museum of the American Indian, at:
> http://www.si.edu/nmai/

The Gallary of the Open Frontier, at:
> http:/www.unl.edu/UP/gof/home.html

The U.S. Holocaust Museum, at:
> http://www.ushmm.org/

The Museum of Fine Arts, at:
> http://www.mfa.org/

The Library of Congress's American Memory Page, at:
> http://lcweb2.loc.gov/ammem/ammemhome.html

If you are still unable to find what you are looking for, visit the Smithsonian Institution at:
> http://www.si.edu/

Using Unconventional Content to Teach Social Studies

Education has such a long tradition of using written or printed materials as content sources that it's easy to overlook other materials that can serve the same purposes. In this section, we illustrate how two cans of Green Giant Niblets corn might serve as a content vehicle for social studies (and other subject areas).

Why corn? Why not something more conventional? First, using corn as a content vehicle avoids the "it's something that every child should know" syndrome. There is probably nothing about two cans of corn that students must know (see Figure 8.4). Our second purpose is to illustrate how it's possible to

Purposes clarified

FIGURE 8.4 The Basis for the Corn Curriculum

NUTRITION INFORMATION PER SERVING
Serving Size: ½ cup (solids and liquid)
Servings Per Container: 2

Calories 90   Fat 0g
Protein . . . . 2g   Sodium** . . . 230mg
Carbohydrate . . 20g   Potassium . . 170mg
**Nutrition is calculated for liquids and solids together. If the liquid is removed, there will be 180mg sodium.

PERCENTAGE OF U.S. RECOMMENDED DAILY ALLOWANCES (U.S. RDA) PER SERVING:
Protein 2   Thiamine (B₁) .2   Calcium . . . . . *
Vitamin A . . . 2   Riboflavin (B₂) .4   Iron . . . . *
Vitamin C . . 10   Niacin 4   Phosphorus . .6
*Contains less than 2% of the U.S. RDA of these nutrients.
Ingredients: Golden Whole Kernel Corn, Water, Sugar, Salt.
Distributed by Green Giant Co., The Pillsbury Company, Minneapolis, MN 55402
††Weight of corn means weight before addition of liquid necessary for processing.

NUTRITION INFORMATION PER SERVING
Serving Size: ½ cup (solids & liquid)
Servings Per Container: 4

Calories 80   Fat 0g
Protein . . . . 2g   Sodium** . . . 290mg
Carbohydrate . . 18g   Potassium . . 170mg
**Nutrition is calculated for liquids and solids together. If the liquid is removed, there will be 230mg of sodium.

PERCENTAGE OF U.S. RECOMMENDED DAILY ALLOWANCES (U.S. RDA) PER SERVING:
Protein 2   Thiamine (B₁) . *   Calcium . . . . . *
Vitamin A . . . 8   Riboflavin (B₂) .2   Iron 2
Vitamin C . . . 8   Niacin 4   Phosphorus . .4
*Contains less than 2% of the U.S. RDA of these nutrients.
Ingredients: Golden Whole Kernel Corn, Water, Sugar, Salt.
Distributed by Green Giant Co., The Pillsbury Company, Minneapolis, MN 55402

---

identify and teach legitimate skills by using neutral content. Our third purpose is to illustrate that our content vehicle, mundane as it is, can also be used in subject areas other than social studies. Whether you ever use this "corny" curriculum with students would depend on your purposes, of course.

The immediate task here is to use the canned corn as a vehicle for potential questions and teaching activities. Besides posing possible research questions, you could identify potential instructional activities, such as "Design a new label" or "Try to figure out a more appealing color scheme for the existing label." Or you could do both. We find it useful to begin with a combination of questions and potential teaching activities because they provide a focus for possible lessons. A question such as "How many words can be made from the word *niblets?*," for example, clearly implies a language-related activity. In presenting the task to students, it's not essential that the teacher pose the question directly. Rather, the teacher can say something such as "Let's see how many words we can make from the letters in *niblets*," instead of posing the question directly. If you use such an activity, you could present it either as a task or as a question.

Brainstorming activity Try your hand at brainstorming three or four potential research questions or teaching activities in each of the major subject areas: language arts (including reading), mathematics, science, and social studies. We suggest some potential questions and activities to get you started. Note that as you identify potential research questions, it is *not* essential that you be able to answer them in advance. Some of your best and most interesting questions will be those you can't answer immediately. For example, questions like "Why do most cans have ridges (or rings)?" or "Is there any tin in a tin can?" can serve as things to research or inquire about. Concern for answers to those questions can come after your students (or you) have inquired.

Language Arts

Possible activities
★ Is *niblets* a real word? How could we find out?
★ Write a story in which the Green Giant comes to life.
★ Classify the words on the label beginning with *G* as naming words, action words, or describing words. Star the words that fit into more than one category. Then use at least some words from your list to create a cinquain poem.

Other Language Arts Questions/Activities

_____

_____

_____

Mathematics

★ Identify three ways to figure out the number of kernels in the large can. Then determine which way is the most accurate.
Possible activities
★ Determine how you could measure the length of the label without taking it off the can.
★ When would purchasing the large can be a bad buy?
★ Figure out three different-shaped cans that would hold the same amount of corn.

Other Math Questions/Activities

_____

_____

_____

Science

Possible activities

* What else is in these cans besides corn? How could we find out? Why would this be important to know?
* Does "net weight" include the liquid the corn is packed in? How could we find out?
* Are tin cans really made from tin? How could we find out?
* Will the canned corn grow if we plant it? How could we find out?

Other Science Questions/Activities

_____

_____

_____

Social Studies

Possible activities

* Do most people in this class prefer canned corn or frozen corn? How could we find out?
* What information on the label is there by law? When did labeling laws come into effect? Why?
* What ingredients (resources) went into growing the corn and producing the can and label?
* What role does corn play in our diet? How could we find out?
* What occupations are involved in getting corn from the Green Giant's valley to us?

Other Social Studies Questions/Activities

_____

_____

_____

Shifting to a process focus

A question such as "How could we find out?" shifts the focus of an activity from a concern for the answers to a concern for *finding* answers. Realistically, the answers to many of these questions, such as "What else is in these cans besides corn?" (water, salt, etc.), have little utility in a child's day-to-day life. However, their transfer value often lies in the processes that students use to arrive at their answers—processes that students can use to solve other problems they encounter. Indeed, how can you find out what is in these cans besides corn?

The potential questions and activities we have identified here are a nebulous collection, nothing more. And simply because we have identified potential questions and activities doesn't mean they are worth using with students; some may have very limited instructional value and should be discarded. The point is that content—even seemingly unconventional content like canned corn—can be used for a variety of teaching purposes and in different subject areas. It's all a matter of how you perceive it.

Summary

Teaching strategies are the ways in which teachers orchestrate a variety of day-to-day teaching techniques—such as discussions, lectures, case studies, and student projects—to achieve desired learning goals. How teachers do this will vary according to their philosophy of teaching and their instructional purposes. Teachers who see their role as primarily that of conveying information to students are most likely to adopt a teacher-directed "telling" or expository orientation, whereas teachers who want to foster their students' ability to engage in independent inquiry are more likely to adopt a student-centered orientation. However, many teachers adopt a mixed orientation: sometimes they play the primary role, and at other times the students play the active role.

The distinction between teacher-directed and student-directed teaching strategies is designed to highlight two different teaching orientations. Unfortunately, some people mistakenly assume that the term *student-centered* means that the teacher designs a few activities and then lets students take over. Students in a student-centered classroom usually have considerable responsibility for what they are learning, and in some cases, not all students will be learning the same things (as was evident in Janet Jacobsen's classroom at the beginning of this chapter). However, all teachers have overall responsibility for their students' activities and what they learn, regardless of their personal orientation. The skills demanded of a teacher to use a student-centered orientation successfully are equal to and often exceed the skills needed to operate a teacher-directed classroom.

When a purely teacher-centered teacher looks at a social studies textbook, he or she may regard it as four hundred pages or so of subject matter to impart to the students. However, when student-centered teachers look at the same textbook, they may say to themselves, "How can I use this information with my students?" The distinction they are making reflects the subtle yet vitally important distinction between "teaching content" and "using content to teach." In one instance, teachers may approach content as something students must know, but in other instances the content can serve as a vehicle to achieve other instructional purposes.

When students use social studies content for particular purposes—as a data source for testing hypotheses, for example—they are learning to use social studies content. Students learn to analyze social studies content by analyzing social studies content—hopefully in the presence of competent modeling and teaching. Students also learn how to generate hypotheses by generating hypotheses, and to distinguish between facts and opinions by doing so.

The essence of teaching social studies does not lie solely in *what* one knows, but also in how one *uses* what one knows. No teacher can be sure that as students use social studies content in the classroom they will automatically transfer this use to their outside activities, since factors beyond teachers' control will influence that action. However, the hope is that teachers will have provided students with the skills that enable them to make that transfer.

Suggested Activities

1. In a small group, address the question of whether children's participation in group activities should be part of their grade. In other words, should group work "count"? If you think it should, recommend some guidelines for incorporating group work in the grading procedure. If you think it should not, suggest why.
2. While students are engaged in group work many teachers find themselves confronted with an interminable line of students waiting to talk with them. How do you account for this?
3. Observe a children's television program, such as *Sesame Street*, and determine what teaching strategies are *used most often*.
4. Schools in some parts of the country periodically suspend their regular curriculum for a day. In its place, teachers develop variations on the "can of corn" curriculum described in this chapter. On those days, the entire curriculum is developed around a single vehicle—apples, pumpkins, breakfast cereals, sports, or almost anything you can imagine (including corn).

You may never be called upon to teach "apple math" or "soccer social studies," but the prospect can be intriguing. Using the procedures suggested earlier (pp. 202–205), try your hand at identifying possible questions and student activities for each subject in the curriculum for the topic/vehicle of your choice.

Suggested Readings

Linda Albert. (1989). *A teacher's guide to cooperative discipline.* Circle Pines, MN: American Guidance Service. This book provides a clear, step-by-step approach to cooperative discipline.

Bruce Joyce & Marsha Weil. (1992). *Models of teaching* (3rd ed.). Englewood Cliffs, NJ: Prentice-Hall. This volume ranks among the landmark texts in education because it was one of the first to reduce the mountain of literature dealing with teaching strategies to manageable terms.

Stephanie Steffy, & Wendy J. Hood (eds.). (1994). *If this is social studies, why isn't it boring?* York, ME: Stenhouse. The fifteen, first-person vignettes in this book describe how teachers and others modified the ways in which they taught social studies to make it more student-centered.

9 Additional Strategies for Active Learning

Key Questions

* What is dramatic play?
* Why involve students in role-playing?
* What are simulations, and how do they differ from games?

Key Ideas

* Active learning often involves bringing the real world into the classroom.
* Group-based activities provide students with common experiences that can then be analyzed.
* Most teaching techniques can be adapted to fit certain teaching objectives.
* The debriefings that should follow group activities are often as important as the activities themselves.

Introduction: The Empty-Chair and Author's Chair Techniques

Context One

Mr. Chris Huber's fifth-grade class has been studying Abraham Lincoln and his involvement in the Civil War. For this activity, Mr. Huber has placed an armchair in the front of the classroom facing the class.

MR. HUBER: Let's pretend that this chair is President Abraham Lincoln. He is a tall, bearded man with many interests and lots of problems. How might he be dressed?

CHILDREN: . . . [Fill in how you think children might respond.]

Role-playing: Example one   MR. HUBER: What do you think he is like? And with the war dragging on, how might he be feeling?

CHILDREN: . . .

MR. HUBER: Well, let's pretend that Jefferson Davis has just walked into the room. He has heard that Mr. Lincoln, here [pointing to the chair], is going to free the slaves. Does anyone want to be Mr. Davis? Okay, Gerry, you be Jefferson Davis. I'll play Mr. Lincoln's part.

ALLISON: . . .

MR. HUBER: Okay, Allison. You play Mr. Lincoln.

ALLISON: Welcome, Mr. Davis. I wish we were meeting under happier times.

GERRY: Thank you, Mr. Lincoln. I do too.

ALLISON: . . .

GERRY: . . .

Context Two

Role-playing: Example two

Ms. Lynda Esparza's second-grade classroom, which we visited earlier, is now further along in their study of communities and community helpers. An empty armchair sits at the front of the classroom.

MS. ESPARZA: Let's pretend that a police officer is sitting in this chair. How might he or she be dressed?

CHILDREN: . . . (Children describe a male police officer.)

MS. ESPARZA: What kind of person [moving toward the chair]should this police officer be? What might he be like?

CHILDREN: . . .

MS. ESPARZA: Okay. Now let's put our officer at the corner of Cactus and First [two streets the children are familiar with] directing traffic. He sees a young boy about ten or eleven years old running out of a convenience store clutching something under his jacket. Close behind him is the store owner, yelling, "Stop that child!" What do you think the police officer might be thinking?

CHILDREN: . . .

MS. ESPARZA: How do you think he might be feeling? Is he frightened?

CHILDREN: . . .

MS. ESPARZA: Does anyone want to play the police officer's role? Juan?

JUAN: . . .

MS. ESPARZA: Okay, Juan, you be the officer. And Debbi, you be the store owner. Who wants to be the boy?

Context Three

Role-playing: Example three

An empty armchair, designated as the "author's chair," is placed in the front of Janet Jacobsen's middle-school classroom. Sometimes student authors sit in the chair when they share their writings with the class. At other times, students who have studied the works of a particular author sit in the chair and role-play the author as other students interview them. On this day a fifth grader, Becky Rodgers [alias Nathaniel Hawthorne], is sitting in the chair.

BECKY: I'm pleased to be with you today.

MRS. JACOBSEN [interrupting Jason who was about to speak]: On behalf of our entire class I want to welcome you here today, Mr. Hawthorne.

JASON: Yeah. And are you the one who wrote our "Pine Tree Shillings" thing?

BECKY: What makes you ask that, sir?

JASON: 'Cuz that sheet Mrs. Jacobsen gave us said 'Hawthorne' on it.

BECKY: Well, I've written many things, like *The Scarlet Letter, Twice Told Tales, The House of Seven Gables,* and lots of others. And yes, the "Pine Tree Shillings" is from something I wrote.

AARON: Did you really see them put Becky Hull on the scales and match her weight in silver?

BECKY: No, that happened 150 years before I was born. When I was a student at Bowdoin College, I used to write articles that I sold to newspapers and magazines. That's how I got my spending money. And that's when I wrote the "Pine Tree Shillings" article.

AARON: Oh!

CINDI: You mean people back then really paid people to marry their daughters?

BECKY: Yes, ma'am. Some traditions the Puritans brought with them from England continued while they were here.

CINDI: I thought that those people came here to have . . . what do you call it, religious freedom?

BECKY (patronizingly): I think you may be confusing the Puritans and the Pilgrims, my dear.

CINDI: Oh!

The first two vignettes illustrate the introductory moments from role-playing episodes that use the "auxiliary-chair technique" originally developed by Rosemary Lippitt (1958). The third vignette illustrates the "author's chair" technique, as described by Graves and Hansen (1983). For both techniques, a chair is placed at the front of the classroom. In the first instance, the chair remains empty but is assigned human characteristics. Students then interact with the chair as they might interact with a person who has those characteristics. In the author's chair example, students who know something about whatever author they are role-playing sit in the chair and interact with other students accordingly. In cases where student authors sit in the chair (to discuss their written works with the class), there obviously is no role-playing.

A chair can serve many functions

The empty-chair technique focuses children's attention on the chair, not on the person playing the character in the chair. This helps to protect the "player" from the nervousness that occasionally accompanies drama-oriented activities. It also avoids another problem common to role-playing episodes, such as when a girl plays what may be perceived as a male role or vice versa. However, in the author's chair example, where students actually role-play a real person, advance preparation is obviously essential.

Post-role-playing activities Not illustrated in the examples here are the post-role-playing discussion, analysis, and debriefing of what took place. In the Lincoln and police officer activities, the discussion would continue with a consideration of both the portrayal itself and how the role players felt and what they were thinking at various points in the enactment. The follow-up activities may also include one or more reenactments involving different players and revised roles. That kind of follow-up is probably not as essential in author's chair activities, but without appropriate debriefing and follow-up, role-playing activities are not complete.

Role-playing and the other activities we consider in this chapter are intended to re-create reality—or a slice of reality—in the classroom. They also provide children with opportunities to "walk in someone else's shoes." Once that reality has been established, the children can then examine, analyze, and, ultimately get a handle on the "real" reality they will face outside the classroom.

Re-creating reality in the classroom

We begin this chapter with an examination of a dramatic-play activity and then move to a variety of role-playing and decision-making activities. We also look at games and simulations, and, finally, we consider expressive and enactive experiences, activities through which children express themselves through drama, etc., or projects where students construct or build things.

Dramatic Play

Dramatic play involves the spontaneous acting out of real-life situations in structured settings. The settings can involve ships in a harbor, pioneers moving westward in the 1800s, or almost any other situation. Dramatic play differs from the play that children normally engage in because it (1) occurs in a structured setting and (2) is designed to lead to educational outcomes. These elements are illustrated in the following Model Student Activity, which describes a dramatic-play activity dealing with ships and ports. Note especially the amount of attention, detail, and especially the time that was devoted to structuring the dramatic-play environment.

The author of the Model Student Activity illustrates how dramatic play can be a stimulus for raising questions. Of course, in the lower primary grades, children's reading and research skills may require that you provide some answers for them. In fact, sometimes you may need to raise *and* answer some of the questions associated with dramatic-play activities.

Cautions

Occasionally dramatic play can unintentionally convey incorrect or distorted ideas. Historical reenactments, for example, are particularly susceptible to distortion. Re-creating an 1849 westward journey in a covered wagon is unlikely to sensitize children to the problems encountered by pioneers, primarily because most classrooms are a far cry from the rugged terrain the pioneers had to cross. Far better for that purpose is a computer-based simulation, *The Oregon Trail* (MECC), or the updated and retitled version of that simulation, *Wagon Train 1848,* which is designed for a local area network of computers. In *Wagon Train 1848,* several teams interact simultaneously as they move westward. Other dramatic-play activities involving Mexican fiestas or re-creating Native American villages can also lead to some of the complications we discussed in Chapter 3. Thus, dramatic-play activities must be handled cautiously lest they be of questionable instructional value.

MODEL STUDENT ACTIVITY
Dramatic Play

Arranging the Environment

After the class leaves on a Friday afternoon, you set about creating an arranged room environment where everything will be related to ships and ports. One bulletin board is filled with pictures of ships. Underneath goes a strip of tagboard on which you have printed "What do these ships carry?"

Another, but smaller, bulletin board is covered with a chart showing signal flags. Across the bottom of the chart hang four or five flags you have made from scraps of cloth. On a small table below the flags are small heaps of scrap cloth.

You cover the library table with books. In each are two or three colored markers, each inserted at a colorful picture or an exciting passage.

You set a large fish tank on the sink counter and fill it with water. You toss in a small wooden ship. Next to it you leave two metal ships (one must be large enough so that its displacement of water can be observed). You add a sign, "Why do metal boats float?" You drop a ruler and grease pencil next to the sign.

In one corner of the room you pin up, just above floor level, 6 feet of paper that will take tempera paint. Cans of paint and brushes sit nearby. Above the paper is an accurate picture of a port. In front of the paper you drop enough scraps of lumber so breakwaters and docks can be built.

Above the science table goes a picture of a lighthouse. On the table goes a set of instructions on how to build a lighthouse. Next to the instructions are batteries, wire, wood, tacks, bulbs—everything needed to build a lighthouse.

You use masking tape to hang a display. It shows men and women at work on ships and around the port. The caption asks, "What are these workers doing?"

You drop some more scraps of wood in the construction corner. Next to them go three small, dull saws, three small hammers, and an assortment of nails. You also leave a small ship that you made.

You put a song of the sea on the record player, slip on your coat, and head for home. The trap has been baited. The quarry is the interest of your pupils.

Play, Discussion, and Research

On Monday morning your class can't miss the changes in the classroom. When school begins, tell the class they may spend a little time wandering around the room, looking at things, and playing with the objects.

Give them enough time to prowl, but not enough time to satisfy their curiosity. (The interrupted pleasure is sure to be returned to eagerly.) Then ask, "Well, what do you think this is all about?"

> "Boats!"
> "Sailing!"
> "The ocean!"

You ask, "What did you see that you liked most?"

> "The boats!"
> "The lighthouse!"
> "The tools!"

Pick out from one-third to one-half of the class (depending on the size of the class, the amount of free space you have, and the number of toy ships available). Say, "OK, each of you get a ship or boat, and you can play with it."

They play. You watch. The other pupils watch. You circulate among the watchers and ask quiet questions.

"What is Billy doing?"
"Why is Mary running her boat up the wall?"
"How would you do that?"

Then you shift the groups until everyone has had his chance to play with the toy ships. The class has finished its first session of *dramatic play*.

The next step is discussion of what went on during play. You will probably pursue several ideas that occurred to you as you observed the play, but I'll just use one example.

TEACHER: Billy, why were you and Kathy hitting your ships together?

BILLY: Because, I was sailing along, and she ran into me.

TEACHER: Why'd you run into his ship, Kathy?

KATHY: Because he was in my way. He should have let me by. He's a boy and I'm a girl, and boys are supposed to be polite to girls.

TEACHER: What happens if two ships smash into each other out in the ocean?

BILLY: They sink.

KATHY: The policeman comes out in a rowboat and gives them a ticket.

TEACHER: What policeman?

KATHY: Oh, you know. It was a joke.

TEACHER: Do ships smash into each other on the ocean?

BILLY: Sure, and some of them smash into ice cubes . . . uh, icebergers and sink.

TEACHER: Do all the ships that are on the ocean smash into each other all the time?

BILLY: . . . No.

TEACHER: Why not?

BILLY: I dunno.

TEACHER: How can you find out?

BILLY: Look it up.

TEACHER: Where?

BILLY: In the books.

TEACHER: How else?

BILLY: Ask somebody.

BILLY: Who?

BILLY: My dad.

KATHY: A sailor.

BILLY: A sixth-grader.

KATHY: The principal.

TEACHER: OK. Who wants to work with Billy and Kathy on this question?

And so it goes. A small research group is formed. You move on to another mistake or question or problem.

"Now, about that policeman in a rowboat. Do you really believe . . . ?"

And so on.

When children play, they reflect what they know. They do some things correctly, and they make some mistakes. The mistakes are used to stimulate discussion that leads to questions that can be researched.

You do not say, "Billy, you are doing that wrong. Someone show him the right way." What you want is for the pupil to find the right way by his own (or his research group's) efforts.

You keep at these questions until everyone has elected a research group. The next day, you review, with each group, what they are trying to find out. Don't tell them! Ask them.

"Everybody set? OK, how much time do you want?"

And off they go, some to the library table, some to the library. They will waste time this first time. Why not? They have to become acquainted with many new books. They have to find what will be useful. They skim and finger and look at pictures. You visit each group, praising and prodding. Research takes time. And you must be willing to let them take time.

Your responsibility is to be certain that they can find out. You have to be sure the answers are in materials available to them. Why else did you do your research and write that resource unit?

Of course, someone always comes up with a question you didn't, and couldn't, anticipate. Then you have to dig out the answer. If third-graders can't read your source, then you rewrite it as simply as you can. I don't think I ever taught a unit of any kind where I didn't have to do some rewriting for the class.

Then, after one day or three days—however long it takes to find answers or partial answers—each group makes its report. When all are armed with this new knowledge, you go back to a play session.

Let's review for a moment. You create an environment. The class explores that environment. You let the class play with the ships. You observe the mistakes in the play. The class discusses the mistakes. Research groups are formed. Research takes place. The results of research are reported. The class plays again.

SOURCE: Abridged and reprinted with the permission of The Free Press, a division of Simon & Schuster from *Teaching Social Studies in the Elementary School* by John R. Lee. Copyright © 1974 by John R. Lee.

COMMENTARY: On Structuring the Environment

Sarah Ancell teaches third grade at Bozeman Elementary School in a city in the Southwest. She's part of a three-teacher team, who plan together, correlate their units, and occasionally trade classes for various activities.

All teachers on the team—Kippy Broderson, Sharon Newsom, and Sarah—agree that third grade is the upper limit for dramatic-play activities, and even then it's borderline. Some third graders take well to dramatic play, but often the children who don't like it make fun of those who do. As Kippy says, "At this grade level, we don't think it's worth the risk." "But," Sarah adds quickly, "we think the classroom environment is *really* important, regardless of how old the kids are."

It's impossible to describe all the different ways that Sarah and the Bozeman team arrange their classroom environments, so one example will have to suffice. When the students come down the hallway one morning, they find a huge tree—made from brown and tan colored paper and covering what used to be a pillar—its branches extending most of the way across the hallway ceiling. You can tell the tree is made from paper but it is still fairly realistic.

At first the tree's branches are bare, but a couple of days later, the branches are covered with pink blossoms. The children aren't too surprised because they made the flowers in art class. A few days later, green leaves appear among the blossoms; then the blossoms disappear and

only the leaves remain. The "branches" that hang down from the classroom ceilings mimic the changes in the tree in the hallway. Soon, tiny green apples appear, then larger green apples, and finally red apples. After a day when everyone has had an apple for a snack, both the apples and the green leaves disappear, replaced by yellow, gold, and red leaves. A few days later, the colored leaves disappear, and the tree returns to its original barren state.

As the tree and the classroom go through their various stages, children record the events in their journals. The students also do an assortment of activities related to plants, trees, and apples. They determine the average number of seeds in an apple in math; they make applesauce—after which they write the directions for "How to Make Applesauce"; they read the story of Johnny Appleseed (Kellogg, 1988) and plot his travels on a map; they study—what kinds of trees grow where, what kinds of trees lose their leaves, and what kinds keep their leaves in winter; they study products made from wood; and they read Shel Silverstein's *The Giving Tree* (1964).

Lest there be any question about it, the social environment in those classrooms is as warm and supportive as the physical environment is spectacular. But are all the decorations worth the tremendous amount of time and the considerable expense they require? Are they really necessary? Obviously, Sarah Ancell and her colleagues think so.

Dramatic-play activities are best suited to children who also engage in real-play activities, which means these activities are restricted largely to the lower elementary grades. If you try the ships and harbor activity with fifth or sixth graders, most of them are likely to feel they are being treated like babies. However, dramatic activities minus the "play" components often work well with older students, as we describe later in this chapter. Structuring the classroom environment, as was done for the ships and harbor activity, can also be done in ways appropriate in the intermediate and middle-school grades.

Dramatic play often requires extensive preplanning and a lot of materials. In summary, well-planned dramatic play can have the following outcomes:

Outcomes
* Stimulate questions that children can then research
* Provide a means for children to use and understand concepts and symbols
* Reveal needs that can be addressed in subsequent instruction
* Stimulate other expressive activities (painting, models, etc.)
* Reveal new information and understandings the children have gained

Role-Playing

Three differentiating factors

In both dramatic play and role-playing, one child might play a father or mother, another child might play a store owner, someone else might play a ship's captain or an airline pilot, and so forth. The difference between the two types of activities lies in three factors: (1) *intent,* (2) teacher *structuring,* which can range from loosely organized (unstructured) to more tightly controlled (structured), and (3) *student involvement.*

The intent in dramatic play is to re-create an experience so that as the children play they will get a vicarious feel for that experience and raise questions that lead to further research and investigation. The intent in role-playing is to provide children with opportunities to experience and *analyze a problem situation.* There is not much of a problematic nature associated with ships in a harbor, for example, as opposed to, say, a situation in which a pioneer family is moving west and, because of space restrictions, must decide between taking the family Bible or a set of heirloom china. The Bible-china question *might* arise during a dramatic play involving pioneers moving westward, but as a rule, role-playing situations are more narrowly defined. To this extent, role-playing is somewhat more structured and teacher directed than dramatic play.

Analyzing alternatives

In role-playing activities a few students re-enact a situation while the rest of the class acts as observers. In dramatic play, there is usually no audience and everyone is involved in the "play." How a role-playing group resolves a problem becomes the focus for discussion and analysis after the enactment is completed. However, unlike plays in which the actors follow a script, role-playing situations are open-ended, and the role players must figure out how to resolve the situation.

Role of the audience

Role-playing activities are sometimes used to help students develop a sense of social consciousness—to help them experience what it is like to "walk in another person's moccasins," that is, to view an issue or problem from another person's perspective (see Berman, 1990). Role-playing can also help sensitize students to the idea that maintaining a win-lose posture, one in which "I am right and they are wrong," often serves only to perpetuate a problem. For example, helping children understand that the police officer in the example at the opening of this chapter is expected to act in certain ways can provide a perspective that may explain some of his or her actions. The purpose here is neither to condemn nor to exonerate certain actions but to help children say, "This is where he or she seems to be coming from." When that is said, the basis for consensus building and resolving problems may have been laid.

Walking in someone else's shoes

In *Role Playing in the Curriculum,* Shaftel and Shaftel (1982) recommend the following procedure for handling role-playing activities:

Role-playing procedures

1. "Warming up" the group (problem confrontation)
2. Selecting the participants (the role players)
3. Preparing the audience to participate as observers
4. Setting the stage
5. Role-playing (an enactment)
6. Discussing the enactment

MODEL STUDENT ACTIVITY

The Lunch Policy

Provide the following information to students.

A fast-food restaurant (e.g., McDonald's or Burger King) is to open next week across the street from Meridian Elementary School. Some students have requested permission to eat lunch there. Currently students must eat at school, or they may go home for lunch if they bring a signed permission slip from their parents. The principal has called a meeting with the following people:

A parent

A student

A cafeteria director

A teacher

Tell students that the group must decide what to do.

Procedure

Role-Playing Option

Identify students to play each of the roles, and have them try to arrive at a decision agreeable to everyone. The rest of the class should discuss and evaluate both their decision and the procedures they used in arriving at it.

Decision-Making Option

Divide the class into small groups with each student taking a role. When all groups have made their decisions, they should be reported and evaluated by the class as a whole.

7. Further enactment (replaying revised roles, suggested next steps, exploring alternative possibilities)
8. Further discussion (which may be followed by more enactments)
9. Sharing experiences (relating the role-playing to one's life experiences) and further debriefing.

Role-Playing and Decision-Making

Format

Role-playing is often a part of decision-making activities. Depending on the way you arrange the activity, you can emphasize either the role-playing dimension or the decision-making dimension. The format for role-playing and decision-making activities is illustrated in the Model Student Activity entitled "The Lunch Policy." It involves (1) an open-ended problematic situation and (2) roles for the students to play.

Options

For "The Lunch Policy" and other activities like it, you could select either the role-playing or the decision-making option. Several factors might influence that decision. For example, if you think a group could handle this activity in five to ten minutes, you might select either option or both options. If it might take longer than five to ten minutes or the role-playing enactments might drag, you might lose the observers' attention. In that event, you might select the decision-making option in which all students are involved (in small groups) in the same situation simultaneously.

Unstructured Role-Playing

In all role-playing activities, students must deal with a problematic situation. Teachers must identify the role players and be certain that everyone understands the situation. In other words, there is a certain amount of teacher direction in all role-playing activities, as well as a certain amount of spontaneity.

Unstructured: Limited teacher direction

Most of the role-playing examples we have presented thus far are unstructured; that is, the role players define their roles without specific teacher direction. In "The Lunch Policy," the teacher may have no idea how the situation will be resolved or whether the role players will become aware of all the factors that might influence the decision. In unstructured role-playing, teachers cannot be certain that a specific issue (such as safety in crossing the street) will emerge from the role-playing enactment. Of course, a teacher could introduce a neglected issue (such as the safety element) in the follow-up discussion, but teachers who want to be certain that specific issues are considered in the role-playing enactment can use a structured role-playing format.

Structured Role-Playing

Structured: Includes roles and sample positions

The element that distinguishes structured from unstructured role-playing is the addition of positions or points of view that the role players must incorporate into their enactments. For example, if you are concerned that students will not know how a cafeteria director might feel about the lunch policy question, you could structure the activity by adding position statements to the roles in the previous Model Student Activity, as illustrated below:

1. A parent wants her children eating well-balanced meals, not hamburgers every day.
2. A student feels that the school should not dictate eating habits.
3. The cafeteria director needs a full cafeteria to meet operating expenses.
4. The teacher doesn't want to be bothered with permission slips and feels it is up to the parents and children to decide where lunch will be eaten.

The modified model for structured role-playing activities reflects the following elements:

1. an open-ended problematic situation,
2. roles for the individuals involved, and
3. position statements for each role player.

You are obviously free to add other roles or positions. Or you might use a mixture of each, specifying positions for some roles while leaving others open so that players can operate according to their convictions. Your procedure should be dictated by your objectives. If you wish to heighten the sense of drama and add an element of mystery, you can distribute the role positions on separate slips of paper so that, initially, only the role players know who they are. This approach tends to heighten interest at the outset of role-playing.

Handling Conflict.   If you choose to use role-playing activities with conflicting role positions, you must be prepared to help the group cope with the disputes that are almost guaranteed to occur. Many of us have been taught that conflict is bad, something to be avoided, yet in many real-life situations, conflict is unavoidable. Acting as if conflict does not exist does not make it disappear. Students need to view conflict as a reality of human life. However, they also need to understand that conflict can be managed if it is addressed directly, and the process of doing that can often yield creative and mutually agreeable solutions to problems. In other words, part of the purpose of some role-playing activities can be to explore ways in which conflict-based win-lose situations can be converted into consensus-building win-win situations.

Helping students deal with conflict

Simulation and Gaming

Simulating reality

Simulations, which often involve elements of role-playing and decision-making, are a comparatively recent innovation in education. Games, which rarely involve role-playing, have been around much longer.

Simulations are instructional activities in which elements from the real world are re-created (or simulated) in the classroom. For example, after an experience in which the classroom is turned into a miniature factory to mass-produce valentine cards (see Resource Handbook), students have an opportunity to discuss what it is like to perform a task over and over again, as one would on a real assembly line. Likewise, in the computer simulation *Oregon Trail*, students have an opportunity to experience the tribulations of traveling west in a covered wagon during the nineteenth century. If students playing *Oregon Trail* do not plan properly, they may die before reaching their destination—as real pioneers sometimes did. If death occurs, they can try to do better in the next round.

Reality is a complex idea

In a simulation such as *Democracy,* students play the role of legislators who are seeking reelection. By negotiating with their colleagues for the passage or defeat of legislation in keeping with their constituents' interests, the student legislators may be able to win reelection. In the course of playing *Democracy,* students learn about factors that can influence the passage or defeat of legislation. In reality, however, the legislative process is so complex that were you to attempt to re-create it in a classroom, your students would be overwhelmed by the sheer number of things to consider (e.g., legislative procedure, parliamentary procedure, political parties, and lobbyists). About the only place you will find a totally realistic legislative process is in a real legislature, and that, unfortunately, cannot exist very practically in most classrooms. Thus *Democracy* and all other simulations necessarily simplify whatever real-world equivalent they represent.

Simplifying reality

Because all simulations simplify the reality they deal with, it becomes possible to analyze a situation without a lot of other elements clouding the picture. For example, students playing the first stages of *Democracy* are able to analyze the negotiation phase of the legislative process without the confounding influence of political parties or other factors. In later stages of the simulation, the legislator's convictions and the influence of political parties are added, so it more nearly reflects the real legislative process. (*Democracy* was originally developed by James S. Coleman for the 4-H Foundation and is available from Western Publishing Company, 850 Third Avenue, New York, NY 10022.)

The real world provides the model on which almost all simulations and many games are based. If you drive around Atlantic City, New Jersey, you will encounter street names such as Baltic Avenue, St. James Place, and Park Place, and the Boardwalk. Even the socioeconomic levels of the various neighborhoods roughly parallel the property values on a Monopoly board—or they did when the game of Monopoly was developed in the 1920s. That's because the model for Monopoly is based on real estate transactions in Atlantic City, New Jersey. But, to make a game of it, the Monopoly developers had to take some liberties with reality by adding more chance factors than are found in the real world. For example, you cannot buy property in Monopoly unless you land on the property, and where you land depends on the roll of the dice. Other chance factors include "Community Chest" and "Chance" cards, "Go to Jail," "Luxury Tax," and "Income Tax." All these make Monopoly fun to play, because you never know what will happen next, but the chance factor in Monopoly so exceeds reality that you can't use the game to teach the principles of real estate investment and development.

Many games are simply contests in which winning is determined by a combination of prior knowledge, luck, and skill. These include those old classroom standbys, spelling bees and Twenty Questions, and the takeoffs on TV game shows like *Jeopardy!* and *Password*. Most simulations, on the other hand, lack the contest quality of games. All simulations have an outcome—a result—but these usually lack the clear flavor of winning or losing that is typical of most games. In addition, because the chance or luck factor in simulations is usually lower than in most games, simulations tend to be more realistic. These and the other characteristics of simulations and games are shown in Table 9.1.

Table 9.1 Differences Between Simulations and Games

Characteristics	Simulations Tend To:	Games Tend To:
Size	Involve more students, often the entire class	Be limited to fewer players, typically four, seldom more than eight
Length	Be of longer duration (more than one period)	Be of shorter duration (one period or less)
Chance	More realistically reflect the real world	Contain a "chance" factor that exceeds reality
Result	Produce an outcome usually without winners or losers	Have defined winners and losers
Preparation and materials	Require considerable advance preparation and materials	Require minimal preparation and materials

Computer-Based Simulations

Computer-based simulations usually have the ability to reflect more real-world complexities than are possible through nontechnological means. For example, as pioneers journeyed westward during the nineteenth century, they encountered one set of problems as they crossed the plains and different problems as they crossed the deserts and the mountains. In the *Oregon Trail* simulation that we noted earlier, microcomputers make it possible to replicate conditions that pioneers faced at various points on their journey. A somewhat similar situation prevails for the computer-based simulation *The Golden Spike* (National Geographic Society), in which players are involved in building the transcontinental railroad. If players spend too much money purchasing rails and ties and don't allocate enough money for food and wages for workers, they too must beware. Thus computer-based simulations can take information from a player's prior decisions and incorporate it into the next decision that the player must make.

Some computer-based simulations provide excellent opportunities for children to use map skills. In the simulation *Geography Search* (McGraw-Hill), players must make navigation decisions as they sail to the New World. The computer then provides them with the precise location of their ship. Likewise, in

Computer-based simulations consider many variables

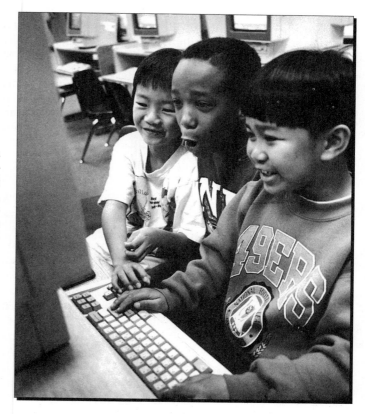

Computers offer a variety of applications in social studies classrooms, including simulations. *(© Susie Fitzhugh)*

Using Interactive CD-ROMs

The year is 1492. Your monitor is displaying an animation of Queen Isabella and King Ferdinand's throne room in Spain. The king and queen are there, along with Queen Isabella's confessor, a brown-robed Franciscan monk named Francisco Jimenez de Cisneros, and a young adventurer, Christopher Columbus, who is pleading with Ferdinand and Isabella to allow him to find a new route to the Orient. After Ferdinand and Isabella agree to fund Columbus's voyage, the scene shifts to a view from a ship just offshore from a Caribbean island. Occasionally the scene also shifts to Columbus talking with one of his officers about what they might find on the island. If you move the cursor to the brush along the island's shoreline, you can view a closeup of what Columbus and his crew will encounter when he comes ashore. Depending on where you place the cursor, you may see more junglelike terrain, and sometimes you will discover natives huddled in the underbrush. If you don't place the cursor on the different locations, you will simply follow Columbus as he lands on the island. The materials on this CD-ROM are called "interactive" because they permit viewers to examine elements they want to look at in more detail.

The above scenario is a segment from a CD-ROM called "Explorers of the New World" (Learning Company, $49). Christopher Columbus is one of several fifteenth- through seventeenth-century explorers, including Magellan, De Soto, and Henry Hudson, whose voyages are chronicled on this software. The explorers are fully animated, and some of them occasionally share their hopes and concerns with viewers. The actor who portrays Columbus reads accounts from the real journals of Columbus's voyages to the New World.

Just as impressive as "Explorers" is the CD-ROM "The Alamo: Victory or Death" (Archimedia Interactive, $140). Narrated by people like newscaster Dan Rather and with music of the period performed by contemporary country music stars like Johnny Cash and Mel Tellis, this two CD-ROM set presents more information than any teacher and class can possibly cover. Highlights include an interactive tour of the Alamo as it was before Santa Anna's attack, a recreation of the siege of the Alamo as seen from a bird's-eye view, and detailed views of weapons and materials from the period. One notable segment shows viewers how to load a flintlock musket, and then viewers practice shooting at a rabbit that runs across the screen. Because most muskets were not very accurate, the rabbit usually makes it across the screen safely.

the simulation *SimCity 2000,* players must become the planner, designer, and mayor of one or more cities.

Limitations. Although the number of computer-based simulations for social studies is increasing, there are still very few for primary-level children. The fact that children must be able to read the instructions on the computer screen (monitor) is often a limitation for very young students. In addition, some programs may require knowledge that students do not have. For example, the simulation *Rails West* is about building the transcontinental railroad. It required prior knowledge about financial markets (stocks, bonds, and debentures) that we, as adults, found taxing. Far less difficult is the simulation *Railroad Tycoon,* in which you can watch your locomotives chugging across the landscape.

Many simulations (noncomputer-based) are designed or can be adapted for an entire class. However, unless you have access to a local area network, computer-based simulations are usually limited to one or two participants. The length of time it takes for an entire class to experience a particular simulation depends on the number of computers available, of course, but restrictions on the number of players are sometimes another limitation.

Building Simulations.   Commercially produced simulations and games are available from a variety of sources, such as The Social Studies School Service (10000 Culver City Blvd., Culver City, CA 90232). However, some teachers develop their own simulations.

The first step in designing a simulation is deciding what aspects of the real world you wish to simulate. For your first effort, the rule of thumb is to keep it simple. Attempting to simulate the judicial system, for example, will prove overwhelming, but you could simulate one aspect of the judicial process, such as a jury's deliberation, as a starter. If you want to try your hand at some simulations, here are a few situations that can be used to generate simulation activities:

1. *Zoning questions.* Should a gas station, liquor store, or high-rise low-income housing be permitted in a residential neighborhood?
2. *Community priorities.* What should a community spend its money on—sewers, parks, playgrounds, more police and firefighters?
3. *Deciding what is newsworthy.* Put together the front page of a newspaper, given an assortment of articles—news, sports, features—clipped from a local paper. Which stories should be given prominence? Why?
4. *School policy questions.* Should recess be abandoned? (Or should children be permitted to go to fast-food restaurants for lunch?)

If some of these sound like decision-making activities, that's because they can be used in that form too. Decision-making and role-playing activities are often integrated into a simulation format.

Developing Board Games

Many elements of social studies, especially processes that result in products such as milk, bread, or steel, readily lend themselves to a board-game format. An example board-game format is illustrated in Figure 9.1. We developed this sample, which we call "The Milk Game," after first identifying the stages of milk production: the dairy farm, transporting the milk from farm to dairy, the dairy itself, and so on. We then outlined segments of the game-board pathway so that it corresponded, in sequence, to the different stages of milk production. Our game board uses straight pathways only because they are easy to draw neatly; curved trails would work equally well. The idea of this and similar board games is that as students move their tokens around the game board, they become familiar with the stages in the process—in this case, the process of milk production. It is possible to build more complex and thought-provoking board games, of course, but for illustrative purposes, we have restricted ourselves to a simple example.

Once we had our basic game board outlined, we needed to find a way to make the game appealing and fun for students. We did this by first determining

FIGURE 9.1   Sample Board Game

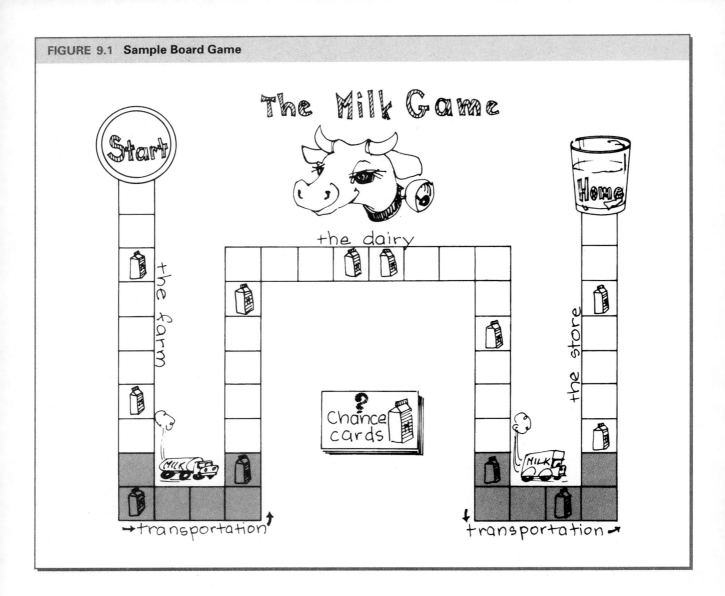

how the winner would be decided (the first student to reach "Home"). Second, we determined how the movement of tokens would be governed. We decided to use a die (one of a set of dice) that we made from a three-inch cube of foam rubber cushion filler, although regular dies or playing cards (with the number of spaces indicated on them) could work equally well. Third, we decided to add additional interest by using "Chance cards" that players draw when they land on a square marked with a tiny milk carton. We could have handled the chance element by marking directly on the squares, but we opted instead for the additional variety that the "Chance cards" provide. To make our game even more realistic, we keyed the "Chance cards" to things that might occur as milk is produced: "Your dairy farm is struck by a power failure, and you must milk the cows by hand—miss one turn." "The milk truck encounters very light traffic—move ahead two spaces."

The principles we applied in developing "The Milk Game" would be equally appropriate for other kinds of board games, including those based on the history or geography of a region. Instead of drawing the pathway on plain posterboard or oak tag, we would use a map of the region as the background, glued or dry-mounted to posterboard. We would then be ready to draw the trail (or pathway) for something like "Sherman's March Game" on a road map of Georgia or the southeastern United States. "The Santa Fe Trail" game could be done on a map of the southwestern United States.

Summary of Steps for Designing a Simulation or Game

Designing a simulation or game begins with an idea. After that, it requires some materials, a little creativity, and often more time than you might imagine. The steps for designing a simulation or game are as follows:

1. Identify the process or system that you want to simulate.
2. Identify the specific characteristics of the system or process. These include the various stages in the process or system and any human components that are involved. It may be necessary to narrow your focus; for example, simulating only part of the nineteenth-century factory system, not the entire system.
3. Decide which characteristics of the system or process you wish to emphasize and which you are willing to omit.
4. Decide which format—simulation or game—is best suited to the topic.
5. Decide what the players will be doing. Will they be making something, playing a role, moving tokens around a board, or what?
6. Decide on an outcome. When will the simulation or game end—after the players have reached a decision, been reelected, reached "home," made the most points, or after time expires?
7. Decide how you will introduce the chance element (to make the activity more interesting). Make certain that negative and positive chance factors are equally balanced.
8. Simulations only: Decide how you will get information to the players. Will each player get different roles? Separate instructions?
9. Decide if everything you have decided on thus far "fits" together. If it does, begin developing or collecting whatever materials you will need.
10. Prepare a preliminary set of written rules or directions.
11. Try out the simulation or game on a small group of "guinea pigs." (This is one of the most essential steps in the entire process—you'll be amazed at what you forgot to consider.)
12. Make necessary adjustments as indicated by the field test.

Expressive and Enactive Experiences

Terms defined

The role of problem solving

Expressive experiences are activities in which children have an opportunity to express themselves through drama—plays, skits, pageants, and so on—or through dramatic play, music, role-playing, or other forms of sociodrama. *Enactive experiences,* which are sometimes called *projects,* are activities in which students build or create something, such as models or murals. Opportunities for children to express their creative or artistic talents are common to both experiences.

Most worthwhile enactive experiences incorporate a *research* or *problem-solving* dimension. For example, before boiling the first grain of rice for a Japanese meal, students should have identified what kinds of things might be served at such a meal, what ingredients are used in the various dishes, how the foods are prepared and served, and on what occasions they are eaten. In other words, the guiding question here is, What are the components of a typical Japanese meal? Similarly, before building a model dairy farm, students should have compared a series of pictures of dairy farms (or visited dairy farms, if that is feasible) to identify their common characteristics. And before cooking that pioneer meal, students should have researched the foods available to the pioneers—for example, see *The Little House Cookbook* (Walker, 1979).

A research component is an essential part of every enactive experience. Often students are so eager to begin construction that they are reluctant to take the time needed to complete the necessary research. Failing to do the research can produce countless problems, both for students and you as the teacher. If there is any question about this, refer back to the igloo-building activity we described in Chapter 8.

Many hands-on activities require that students apply what they know in problem-solving situations. *(© Bob Daemmrich/The Image Works)*

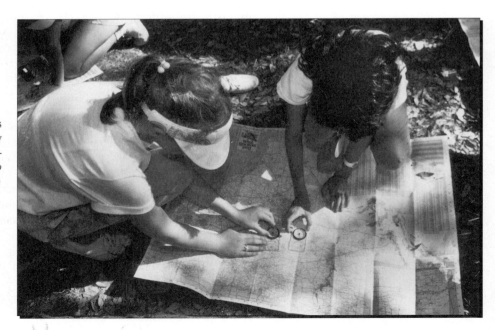

Balancing assets and liabilities

Enactive experiences often have a dimension that cannot be measured in precise educational terms. Likewise hands-on activities can permit students to contribute to class activities in ways that are denied them in more formal, reading-oriented activities. Thus the appropriate use of expressive and enactive experiences probably lies somewhere between two extremes—between teachers who are always building something or getting ready for another play or pageant and teachers who rarely use any of these experiences. We encourage you to use expressive and enactive experiences so long as they (1) are integral to whatever you are studying, (2) involve a significant inquiry or research component that engages children intellectually, and (3) are done "right"—that is, they are a genuine reflection of the culture, period, or phenomenon.

Summary

The teaching activities that we have described in this chapter range from dramatic play, in which you establish a setting and then let the students' creativity come forth, to those in which the children follow precise, step-by-step directions, as in a simulation. The basic rule here is the more teachers structure an activity, the more they may lose spontaneity and creativity. The associated tradeoff is that what is lost in spontaneity may be offset by greater assurance that students will consider the issues and questions that have been built into a more structured activity. Whichever kind of group-based strategy you use—structured or unstructured, expressive or enactive—will ultimately depend on your purposes for developing the activity in the first place. Yet regardless of which type of activity you use, a key element in all of them is debriefing students afterwards.

Suggested Activities

1. Design a board game following the suggestions in this chapter. It may take time, but your students will love it.
2. Design a dramatic-play activity following John Lee's format but involving a different content area.
3. Design an unstructured role-playing activity. Then identify the techniques you could use to add greater structure to the experience.
4. Suppose a teacher informs you that he or she plans to serve raw fish to a class so that the students will have better appreciation of Inuit life. Identify the positive and negative learning outcomes that might result from this experience.
5. In the Commentary we described the elaborate physical environment that Sarah Ancell and her colleagues established in their classrooms. Decide the extent to which such attention to the environment is necessary, desirable, or is a frill.

Suggested Readings

Fannie R. Shaftel & George Shaftel. (1982). *Role playing in the curriculum*. Englewood Cliffs, NJ: Prentice-Hall. The name Shaftel has become almost synonymous with role-playing and other group activities. This is the most complete and authoritative source. This remains the most complete and authoritative source on role playing.

10 Planning and Orchestrating Instruction

Key Questions

* How does one plan (compose) social studies lessons and units?
* What are the major components of instructional planning?
* How do teachers manage the planning process?
* How do goals and objectives differ?

Key Ideas

* Planning is a systematic process, as opposed to a series of discrete steps, in which each aspect interacts with every other aspect of instruction.
* Planning is complex only because of the number of elements that must be considered; it is not inherently complicated.
* Effective planning hinges on two elements: (1) determining what students should know and be able to do *after* instruction, and (2) orchestrating instructional activities that enable them to reach those goals.
* Learning outcomes are stated with varying levels of specificity.

Introduction: On Composing and Orchestrating

Isn't it amazing how a composer like John Williams can create the wonderful music for *Star Wars*, the *Superman* series, *Schindler's List*, and countless others? Thankfully, no one has ever asked us to do what Williams does, because we wouldn't know where to begin—or how. Yet almost as impressive as composers are arrangers, the individuals who orchestrate existing pieces of music. Compare the Mormon Tabernacle Choir's well-known arrangement of the *Battle Hymn of the Republic* with the version of that piece which you sang in elementary school, and you will know what we are talking about.

This foray into the world of music is intended to explain why we have titled this chapter as we have. In the musical world, there's usually a clear distinction between composers and arrangers, for seldom do the same people do both tasks. In the instructional world, however, teachers are regularly expected to do both—although not simultaneously. Every teacher is responsible for planning (composing) instructional sequences and then orchestrating them during instruction.

As we were composing this chapter, we considered reprinting a published unit plan, of which there are many in the literature and on the Internet. We rejected that option because completed unit plans don't reflect the processes their developers used to create them. Neither do they indicate what the developers thought about but excluded from their final plans. We think that deciding what *not* to include in a teaching unit is just as important as deciding what to include, especially if you are the one doing the including.

Instead of a finished unit, this chapter will take you through the process of planning a sample third-grade teaching unit, including the different things we considered, what we included, and what we rejected. This unit is also an extension of the "Can of Corn" curriculum development activity we presented in Chapter 8, because we wanted to show how selected elements of that activity can be incorporated into a full-blown teaching unit. We also consider some other planning-related elements, such as how you might involve students in determining what they will study, and how state and national standards have affected teachers' (and our) planning. In the next chapter, we turn to the reciprocal of planning: assessment. The focus there is on determining how well students have reached the outcomes that we created during the planning process described in this chapter.

To what extent will you allow your students to play a role in determining the kinds of things they study? Are you going to be the one who makes all the decisions? Involving students in planning is a more complex issue than it appears, primarily because, as we have indicated previously, students do not know what they do not know. In other words, students cannot suggest that they study rainforest environments if they have never heard of rainforests—jungles, yes, but not rainforests. The following vignette shows how one teacher sought to involve his students, in a limited way at least, in determining what they were going to learn.

Vignette: The K-W-L Strategy (or, Why Woodpeckers Don't Hurt Themselves)

For the last several years, Eric Cederstrom has taught third grade at Harwell Elementary, a predominantly Hispanic school in a midsized city in the Southwest. When Eric, who was born and raised in North Dakota, accepted the teaching position at Harwell, his Spanish vocabulary consisted of a few terms like *adios* and *amigos*, and some food items like *tacos* and *enchiladas*. "I still can't speak the Tex-Mex dialect fluently," he says, "but I do a lot better than I did."

When we dropped by Eric's classroom one afternoon, we noticed a huge, red paper covering one of the chalkboards. Under a large heading "Animals," the paper was divided into three columns: (1) Know, (2) Want to Know, and (3) Learned (see Table 10.1). On our first visit, the "Learned" column was still blank.

Table 10.1 K-W-L Chart for Animals

What We Know	What We Want to Know	What We Learned
1. They can be furry.	1. How do animals communicate?	1. Some lay eggs.
2. Most have four legs.	2. Can sharks jump to the sun?	2. They can have long or short tails.
3. Some animals can fly.	3. How do sharks breathe?	3. Turtles can't get out of their shells.
4. Some animals are playful.	4. Do animals have secrets?	4. Some animals are slow, some are fast.
5. Animals have insides like ours.	5. Do turtles have ears?	5. There are different types of animals.
6. Some animals are mean.	6. How do dogs bark?	6. Some animals swim a lot.
7. Some animals bite.	7. How do animals swim without hands?	7. Some eat a lot.
8. Some animals live in trees.	8. Why do animals have tails?	8. Dogs "talk" with their tails.
9. Some animals live in water or underground.	9. How do people train animals, like Flipper?	9. Some animals have hands.
10. Some animals have two feet.	10. Why don't woodpeckers hurt themselves?	10. Some animals don't have ears.
11. Some animals peck.	11. How do dogs stand?	11. Kangaroos have pockets.
12. Some animals have sharp teeth.	12. How do clown dogs jump over fire?	
13. Most animals don't talk.	13. How do turtles put their head in their shell?	

Source: Courtesy of Eric J. Cederstrom's Third-Grade Class, Harwell Elementary School, Lubbock, TX.

We said, "Oh, you're using the K-W-L strategy [developed by Ogle (1989)]."

Eric replied, "I don't know whether I'm doing it or it's doing me. We're working on an animal unit, and yesterday we brainstormed what the kids already knew about animals and what they wanted to know more about. The brainstorming is supposed to activate their prior knowledge, and the 'Want to Know' column identifies what they want to find out. Right now, the kids are at the library getting books on animals."

Unanticipated questions

"I got a lot of stuff I really didn't expect," Eric continued, "like 'Why don't woodpeckers hurt themselves?' I don't know why woodpeckers don't hurt themselves, and when I wrote that item on the chart, I told the kids that I didn't think we'd be able to answer this one—or why animals have tails or whether they have secrets. But then I didn't get the kinds of things I wanted to focus on either, like 'What do animals do in the winter?'"

"Maybe not," we answered, "but you got a good indication of what your kids are thinking about."

"That's true; . . . we'll see how it goes," Eric said hopefully.

On our return to Eric's classroom, all the columns on the K-W-L chart were filled in. "How did it go?" we asked.

Unexpected answers

"Not bad for the first time using this strategy," Eric responded. "As I expected, they couldn't answer some of their questions, but I was also surprised about some of the items, like 'Kangaroos have pockets.'. . . I thought almost everyone knew that."

We agreed. "So, would you use this activity again?" we asked.

Refining an activity for the next time

"I think so," Eric answered, "but I would do some things differently. I really need to limit the topic more, because 'animals' is way too broad. Maybe we should do reptiles and birds separately. And instead of one master chart, I'll have the kids make their own copies so they can have something to refer to. I'm also thinking about structuring the groups a little more."

Eric Cederstrom's rendition of the K-W-L strategy isn't perfect, which he readily admits. However, he's already identified some things he will do differently another time around. The same is true for Janet Jacobsen (whom we met in Chapter 8), who, after twenty-five years of teaching, continually makes modifications in preparation for next year. The first point here is that the K-W-L strategy permits students to participate, albeit in a limited way, in clarifying what they are going to learn. The second and perhaps more important point is that planning is an ongoing process that occurs before, after, and in some cases during instruction.

Managing Multiple Planning Elements

Typical expectations

Students who have studied social studies are typically expected (1) to *know* something about the facts, concepts, and generalizations of social studies; (2) to apply *skills* that enable them to use the knowledge they have acquired; and (3) to have acquired certain *attitudes* and *values* that our society feels are important for all citizens to share. These expectations are seldom as separate as we have made them appear here, because the three areas (knowledge, skills, and attitudes) often overlap.

The composing tasks of planning

Determining what children should know at the end of an instructional episode and determining what skills, attitudes, and values they should acquire along the way are the basic composing tasks of planning. Almost immediately thereafter come the tasks of identifying and designing instructional activities and then orchestrating them in ways that make sense to you and to children. All of this should ultimately lead to the outcomes identified in the composing phase. That's the simplified version of how planning is supposed to work, but other elements enter the picture. These include your students' abilities, which will influence the kinds of activities you can use with them, as well as state-mandated requirements and national standards. We will consider each of these elements as they affect the various phases of our planning.

Composing a Sample Unit: Part 1

Making certain things relate

Planning a teaching unit is like lesson planning, only on a broader scale. Instead of focusing on one lesson, unit planning focuses on creating a series of related lessons. Because teaching units have a broader focus than individual lessons, they can attend to broader learning outcomes than is possible with most lessons. In addition, unit planning offers a way of ensuring that the lessons you teach today will relate to the lessons you taught yesterday, and will also relate to the lessons you teach tomorrow. This simply means there is a flow to how students learn.

Identifying a Unit Focus

To determine what our sample unit will be about, we could simply pick a topic and "go for it." The traditional content focus of third-grade social studies is "communities," so we would surely be safe in developing one or more units on that topic. Or we might select other topics, like "transportation" or "Native Americans," especially if we have lots of teaching materials. However, few teachers today are free to teach anything they want to. They may be able to sneak in one or two units on their favorite topics over the course of a year, but most of what they teach needs to be compatible with state-mandated essential elements and national standards. Of course, teachers could ignore state mandates entirely, but no one needs to tell you that in this age of accountability doing so is ill advised. We'll come back to the impact of state and national standards momentarily.

Using corn as a vehicle

We noted earlier that we wanted portions of our sample unit to reflect the "Can of Corn" curriculum development activity we presented in Chapter 8. Our purpose in doing so is to illustrate that it's possible to design a legitimate teaching unit based on something as mundane as a can of corn. Obviously, there is nothing about canned corn that every student needs to know, but then this unit is not going to teach *about* canned corn per se. Rather, our intent is to *use* the corn as a content vehicle, as a tangible point of departure that allows us (and our students) to consider the kinds of decisions that went into producing it and other products. Why, for example, would a farmer decide to grow corn instead of another crop, such as wheat or soybeans? Land is an obvious resource for farmers, but what other factors enter into their decisions to grow one crop instead of another? And what other resources beside land would a farmer need to grow corn? Then too, what resources are used to produce the can that the corn (or any vegetable) comes in, to make and print the label, and to get the corn from the field where it was grown to the supermarket? Finally, are there some human resources (in addition to natural resources) that come into play here?

Using Questions in Planning. Most curriculum guides and published units provide (1) a statement of the unit theme or topic, (2) a list of desired learning outcomes (goals and objectives) (3) a list of suggested student activities, (4) a list of resources and materials essential to teaching this unit, (5) assessment procedures or other evaluation activities, and (6) a listing of additional resources.

The sequence of presentation sometimes leads prospective teachers to believe that instructional planning follows the same sequence, although in most instances it probably does not. We note this here, because some elements, such as some of the questions we developed earlier, may not appear in the final unit. Nevertheless, key questions such as "Why do farmers decide to grow corn instead of cotton, soybeans, wheat, or other crops?" and "What human resources are involved in producing canned vegetables?" suggest what students could be expected to know at the completion of the unit.

After identifying the unit topic, how humans use resources, we first suggest that you attempt to identify some key questions that students *could* answer at the end of the unit. The questions will lend specificity and clarity to your lessons and, perhaps more importantly, can easily be converted into learning outcomes. For example, "Why do farmers decide to grow corn instead of cotton, soybeans, wheat, or other crops?" can be restated as "Students will explain the factors that farmers consider in deciding which crops to produce." The absence of questions makes it more difficult to identify specific learning outcomes. Our second point is that, in the initial stages of instructional planning (which is where we are), everything is tentative. As we get further into our planning, we may generate more key questions and topics to pursue, but we are just as likely to discard some questions (and the topics they are associated with), especially if we cannot create reasonable teaching activities that are geared to them. We'll provide an example of this shortly.

Progress Report

Using the "can of corn" as an entry point, we have identified a unit focus, "How People Use Resources," as well as some questions and activities that are associated with that topic.

Using Webbing as a Planning Tool.   Because the relationship between canned corn and how people use resources is still fairly amorphous at this point, we have elected to use a webbing technique to get a better handle on what we are dealing with. The *webbing* process produces a kind of semantic map similar to the one for Abraham Lincoln in Chapter 6 and the thematic unit on "time" in Chapter 7, both of which show the range and scope of relationships among related elements.

There are several ways to begin the webbing process. One is to brainstorm (free-associate) by listing anything you can think of related to the theme or topic (canned corn). A second technique is to identify questions and possible teaching activities, a process that we began in Chapter 9. Or you could do either of these. Because we've already explored some aspects of our corny curriculum (in Chapter 8), we have elected to follow up on that here. Figure 10.1 shows a web that is based on and expanded from the questions and activities we developed earlier. The web and everything else we have noted thus far confirm that the notion of resources—natural and human—offers a potentially workable direction or theme for this unit. Next we need to make sure that our proposed

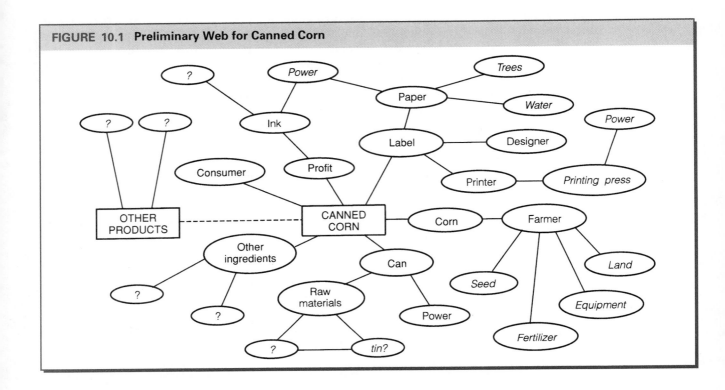

FIGURE 10.1 Preliminary Web for Canned Corn

unit will be compatible with state-mandated essential elements and/or national standards.

How State and National Standards Affect Planning

In the days before states got into the business of mandating curriculum standards, which was followed almost immediately by statewide testing programs, teachers could follow their instincts in selecting content to teach. More recently, the creation of national standards has added an additional element that teachers must consider.

The Impact of State-Mandated Standards. When the states first began mandating curriculum standards, most of the standards followed a similar format. The goals were stated as general outcomes, such as "The students will understand the interplay of economics in their daily lives." Objectives associated with each of the goals were stated more explicitly, such as "[The students will] identify the relationship between supply and demand and its effect on the price of a product," and "[The student will] identify the natural resources that determine the types of jobs in your community in the past, present, and future." These sample goals and objectives are derived from one state's core curriculum document for third-grade social studies, but they could just as easily have been from

Most state programs have similar expectations

another state because the requirements are very similar, in some cases almost identical.

State mandates would not be the imposing force they have become if the states had not created testing programs that are keyed to them. Test results are almost always released to the local media, and certain schools may be singled out as "exemplary" or, the more feared designation, "low performing." The pressures that such devices can place on teachers are significant indeed.

A change in emphasis

Over the last decade, there has been a significant change in how most states pose their curriculum mandates. Instead of narrowly defined content objectives, such as "Does the student know who fought whom in the War of 1812?" the shift has been toward more general topics and generic skills, such as the student's ability to apply reflective thinking skills to various kinds of information. Such changes may explain why Janet Jacobsen (whom we met in Chapter 8) can safely ignore the War of 1812 and other elements traditionally covered in American history. Mrs. Jacobsen's emphasis on developing her students' ability to (1) think chronologically, (2) use historical reasoning, and (3) interpret historical events in light of cause and effect are actually more consistent with most state mandates than was the case when she taught the War of 1812 and other subjects.

Determining Compatibility with State Mandates.

After identifying the key concept for this unit—"The allocation of resources, both natural and human, results from human decisions"—our next task is to determine whether it is compatible with state mandates. For illustrative purposes, here are one state's essential elements for third-grade social studies:

Sample state mandates

Goal 01—The students will practice a variety of listening, speaking, writing, and reading skills in completing social studies activities. [This goal appears in all elementary grades, but the objectives become more complex at the higher grade levels.]

Goal 02—The students will understand the cultural and historical development of their local community.

Goal 03—The students will understand that people use natural resources to meet their basic needs and these resources must be protected and conserved.

Goal 04—The students will understand geographic concepts.

Goal 05—The students will understand the interplay of economics in their daily lives.

Goal 06—The students will understand that the purpose of government is to protect and serve the needs of citizens in their community.

For brevity, we have reproduced the objectives portion for only one goal statement (05) below.

Objectives (for Goal 05)

Students should be able to:

0501—Define wages, prices, producer, consumer, specialization, division of labor, profit, loss, and productivity.

0502—Explain reasons for spending and saving money.

0503—Identify relationships between supply and demand and its effect on the price of a product.

0504—Identify an advantage of division of labor job specialization which increases productivity and creates interdependence.

0505—Identify the natural resources that determine the types of jobs in your community in the past, present, and future.

0506—Identify the role of profits as being the primary reason for production.

0507—Identify how inventions influence change in society.

The scope of these state mandates is broader than we can deal with in our unit, or any single unit for that matter. However, there seems to be a "fit" between our unit and Goal 03 and Objective 0505 (of Goal 05) of the state's essential elements. The mandates may also suggest additional elements we may want to include, which we will determine as our planning progresses.

The Impact of National Standards. There is a kind of "chicken-egg" question of whether state standards have had an impact on the creation of national standards, or vice versa. The outcomes and terminology used in the state standards are often similar to the national standards. This means that instead of assessing whether students know the combatants in the War of 1812, state testing programs are more likely to focus on behaviors such as those found in the national standards for history, geography, and the other social science disciplines.

The Standards for Historical Thinking, proposed in 1995 by the National Center for History in the School, as well as the Essential Elements (Standards) for Geography (1994), are presented in the Resource Handbook. However, we

National standards are overarching expectations

You can proceed inductively or deductively

Progress Report

When we began to design our sample unit, we did not go first to the state mandates or the geography standard noted above. Rather, we began with an idea about how people elect to use resources and identified several key questions that grew out of the "Can of Corn" curriculum development activity. Then we examined state and national standards to determine whether our potential unit would "fit."

We identified our organizing idea for this unit by moving from questions about canned corn to more general questions involving how people allocate resources. This kind of inductive approach, which moves from specific examples to general principles, is one way to approach planning. However, you may feel more comfortable by planning deductively, that is, by first identifying general concepts or principles and then identifying specific instructional activities that will be meaningful to children. Either way is wholly acceptable.

Thus far we have (1) identified a unit focus, using resources, (2) the state-mandated standards it will address (at least initially), and (3) a national geography standard that also applies. We now need to identify appropriate learning outcomes.

have reproduced one of six geography standards below, first, because it reflects the expectations common to the standards documents, and second, because our sample unit will address this standard directly.

The Fifth Essential Element of Geography: Environment and Society

The physical environment is modified by human activities, largely as a consequence of the ways in which human societies value and use Earth's natural resources. Human activities are also influenced by the Earth's physical features and processes. The geographically informed person knows and understands the following:

* How human actions modify the physical environment
* How physical systems affect human systems
* The changes that occur in the meaning, use, distribution, and importance of resources

A Perspective on Learning Outcomes

Outcomes should fit the time span

As teachers plan their courses, units, and lessons, the time span they are dealing with affects how they create and state their learning outcomes. For example, it's doubtful that any teacher can attain the goal of "producing effective citizens," because this is likely to be the desired outcome for an entire school experience. As such, it would represent the collective effort of teachers over a period of years. Still other outcomes, such as having students "understand the geography of the Western Hemisphere" or "understand the Civil War" will cover shorter periods, possibly a course, semester, or a unit of study. Daily lessons, on the other hand, almost always have more specific outcomes or objectives than units or courses.

The levels of specificity for educational outcomes are shown below:

Goals
    Level 4: Very General. Example: The student will be able to cope with the problems of life. (School or Lifelong Goal)
    Level 3: General. The student will understand how technology has influenced our way of life. (Course Goal)

Objectives
    Level 2: Specific. Given a limited amount of information about unknown nations, students will be able to identify two or more plausible hypotheses that describe life in those nations. (Unit or Course Objective)
    Level 1: Very Explicit. Example: Given a state highway map, the student will be able to use the index to locate five towns or villages. (Specific Lesson Objective)

Creating broadly stated goals, such as helping students "to understand the geography of the Western Hemisphere" or "to understand how humans use resources" indicates the overall direction that teaching should take. However, these outcomes are not specific enough to indicate what students who understand "the geography of the Western Hemisphere" or "how humans use resources" should know or be able to do. This is where more specifically stated outcomes, often called objectives, enter the picture. An objective, such as "name forty-five

Objectives are stated specifically

of the fifty state capitals," indicates exactly what students should know and thus lends precision and direction to what could otherwise be very general expectations. There are problems with an objective like "name forty-five of the fifty state capitals," which we consider shortly, but the overall point is that although goals and objectives play a role in teaching social studies, they serve different functions.

Stating Outcomes in Performance Terms

Stating expectations for units or lessons often depends on the specificity of the words you use. Of the two lists of phrases shown below, determine which one uses terminology more appropriate for units and courses, and which is more applicable to daily lessons.

List 1	*List 2*
To grasp the significance of	To write or list
To understand	To illustrate
To recognize	To define
To appreciate or to enjoy	To predict or to suggest
To believe or to have faith in	To name or identify
To comprehend or to understand	To locate or to rate
To know (or to know thoroughly)	To restate or to tell why
To be aware of	To distinguish between or to discuss

The terms in List 1 are more often associated with units or courses, whereas the more explicit terms in List 2 are typically associated with specific lessons. Learning outcomes that use the more specific format are sometimes called *performance objectives, behavioral objectives,* or *criterion-referenced objectives* and typically have four components:

Characteristics of performance outcomes

1. An *object* of instruction ("state capitals")
2. A *condition* under which the behavior will be demonstrated ("from memory")
3. A *standard* (*criterion or performance level*) that the student must demonstrate ("forty-five of fifty")
4. An identifiable *task* or *behavior* ("to name")

Judging the Appropriateness of Objectives

Although the sample objective "Students will be able to name forty-five of the fifty state capitals from memory" reflects all the criteria for precisely stated objectives, it still has some problems. Every objective must be judged in terms of (1) whether students can realistically achieve it, which may depend on students' grade level and maturity, (2) whether it is logically consistent with the purpose(s) to which it relates, *and* (3) whether the goal or objective pertains to something that children *should* attempt to do. Given enough time, for example, most first graders could probably memorize forty-five of the fifty state capitals. But simply

Criteria for judging appropriateness

because children *could* achieve that objective does not mean it is something they should strive for.

The "who cares?" test is one technique for judging the appropriateness of learning outcomes. For an objective such as "Students will identify from memory the number of horses that pulled Cinderella's coach," you need simply ask "who cares?" If your answer is "nobody," the objective should probably be discarded.

Creating Intermediate-Level Outcomes

Intermediate level outcomes—
a middle ground

Although learning outcomes should be stated as precisely as possible, this does not mean that *everything* must or can be stated in behavioral terms. For example, it's almost impossible to specify precise behavioral indicators for creative or open-ended group activities, especially when there are no right answers. The same situation can exist for objectives pertaining to attitudes or higher-level thinking skills, such as analysis and synthesis, and for works of children's literature. To accommodate situations like these, we have found it helpful to create somewhat intermediate-level goal statements, which, although they may lack the specificity of instructional objectives, are often explicit enough to guide instruction. For example, suppose you want to use a book like Bunting's (1991) *Fly Away Home* with your students. This is a moving story of a homeless boy and his father who live in an airport. Developing precise objectives for this story, such as "The student will from memory, identify at which gate the father and son most often slept" is possible, but some of them will probably be on the same level as "How many horses pulled Cinderella's coach?" Such objectives could ask students to focus on what is essentially trivia. Some intermediate-level goals you might be after using a story like *Fly Away Home* are (1) for students to appreciate what it feels like to be homeless, and (2) to be aware of the things that homeless people sometimes think about as they search for shelter. Intermediate-level goal statements can provide guidance for identifying instructional objectives, unit objectives, and even course objectives.

Goals and Objectives for Thinking and Feeling

Many of the elementary and middle-school classrooms we visit each year have a semipermanent poster or bulletin board that states:

Knowledge

Comprehension

Application

Analysis

Synthesis

Evaluation

These bulletin boards reflect the work that Benjamin Bloom and his associates did over forty years ago when they developed a system for organizing and classifying educational goals and objectives. Two major parts of this landmark work are the *Taxonomy of Educational Objectives: The Classification of Educational Goals, Handbook I: Cognitive Domain* (Bloom et al., 1956), and *Handbook II: Affective Domain* (Krathwohl et al., 1964). A *taxonomy* is simply a hierarchical classification scheme whereby each level builds upon and is more complex than the previous level.

The *cognitive domain* refers to activities that involve different kinds of thinking and remembering. The taxonomy for the cognitive domain is organized in terms of the complexity of the thinking skills involved, as shown on the sample poster above. Thus, when you hear people refer to "higher-level thinking skills," they are in all likelihood referring to skills at the higher and more complex levels of the *Taxonomy* (application, analysis, synthesis, and evaluation).

The *affective domain* includes attitudes and values, both of which involve feelings and emotions. For analytical and planning purposes, it's possible to treat the cognitive (knowing) and affective (feeling) domains separately, but in practice the two often merge together. You've seen this in instances where your teacher's attitudes and feelings about certain subject matter came across as strongly as the subject matter itself.

The part of social studies directed toward the affective domain is reflected by goals such as "Develops respect for the American way of life," "Develops an appreciation for American history," or "Becomes a responsible school citizen." It is one thing to state a desired attitude, such as "being a good classroom citizen," but it is another to identify specific behavioral indicators for that notion. Although everyone might agree that a "good school citizen" is someone who pays attention, turns in work on time and so on, it soon becomes difficult to avoid stating behaviors that students should not exhibit—does not interrupt, never gets out of seat. Unfortunately, when possible affective objectives are phrased as positive statements, such as "The student will stop interrupting the teacher whenever the teacher is talking," they can take on a "Have you stopped browbeating your spouse yet?" flavor. Our point is that developing affective objectives is a difficult task.

Content, Process, and Affective Outcomes. The reason for this detour through the various kinds of instructional outcomes is to indicate why our teaching unit will have three kinds of goals or objectives. The first type is knowledge or *content objectives,* which indicate what we expect students to know from having studied this unit. For example, after studying a unit on resources, it is reasonable to expect students to know what resources are. Thus one of the content objectives will be that the student will describe the nature of a resource. The second type of outcome is skill or *process objectives,* which indicate how students will use data. Process objectives depend largely on the kinds of activities we develop (and which we haven't done yet), but an illustrative objective is that students will generate and test three hypotheses that explain how farmers decide what crops to grow. The third type of outcome is attitudinal or *affective goals,* which indicate the attitudes and appreciations we would like students to develop from having studied this unit. We will not have many affective goals, but one exam-

Teaching Units and Lesson Plans on the Internet

So many lesson plans and units are available on the Internet that some sites have their own mini–search engines. The following is a sampling of sites that have lesson plans and units available for downloading.

Academy Social Studies Curriculum Exchange for Elementary (K–5) or Intermediate (6–8) Schools. Two sites with 130 different lesson plans. The address for elementary plans is:

> http://ofcn.org/cyber.serv/academy/ace/soc/
> elem.html

The address for intermediate (6–8) plans is:

> http://ofcn.org/cyber.serv/academy/ace/soc/
> inter.html

Columbia Education Center in Portland, Oregon. This center offers a large assortment of lesson plans for Grades K–5 and 6–8. The address for K–5 plans is:

> http://www.col-ed.org/cur/#sst1

For intermediate plans, substitute "#sst2" for "#sst1" (do not type the quotation marks) in the K–5 address.

Core Knowledge Lesson Plans and Units. All of the K–6 units and lessons available from this site correspond with the Core Knowledge program that we described in Chapter 4. Address:

> http://www.coreknowledge.org/

Education Station Lesson Plans. Uses a search engine for the 2,600 K–12 lesson plans at this site. Address:

> http://www.digicity.com/lesson/l_socstd.html

Publishers' plans and activities. Houghton Mifflin and McGraw-Hill are two of several publishers that have K–8 lesson plans available. The address for Houghton Mifflin is:

> http://www.hmco.com/school/search/activity.
> html

The address for McGraw-Hill is:

> http://www.mmhschool.com/teach/socialstud/
> socstu1.html

Lesson plans and activities that correspond with television programs. Two examples in this category are the History Channel Classroom Materials, at:

> http://www.historychannel.com/historychannel/
> class/teach/tea ch.html

and CNN (The Cable News Network) Lesson Plans and Multimedia Resources at:

> http://www.nmis.org/NewsInteractive/CNN/
> Newsroom/contents/html

Lesson plans and activities that encourage students to use the Internet are available from organizations such as IBM at:

> http://www.solutions.ibm.com/k12/teacher/
> activity.html

ple is that the student will appreciate the need to use resources wisely. We will identify additional outcomes for each category as our planning progresses.

Systematic Planning

An interactive process

As Figure 10.2 illustrates, determining your instructional intent, which means identifying your instructional goals, is the appropriate starting point in planning. Thereafter, planning usually becomes an interactive process or system in which the various elements mingle with each other and there is no predetermined order in which those elements must be considered. Sometimes you

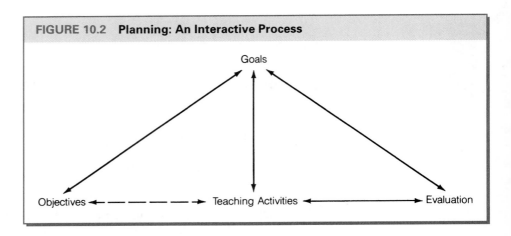

FIGURE 10.2   Planning: An Interactive Process

Goals

Objectives ← — — — → Teaching Activities ← — — → Evaluation

might focus on designing student activities for a particular goal or objective, after which you develop objectives and evaluation strategies to fit those activities. Once you are satisfied that you've covered your goals, you can then evaluate your plan in terms of its overall consistency. The key questions at this stage of unit development are "Does everything 'fit' together?" and "Will this plan do what I want it to do?" For the last question especially, the ultimate test will come when you use your plan with students.

Composing a Sample Unit: Part 2

Identifying Learning Outcomes

Our immediate planning task is to identify a preliminary set of goals for this unit. We could pull these elements out of the blue, but for our unit we will use the state-mandated competencies noted earlier. We've done this because the competencies reflect topics common to third-grade social studies programs, state-mandated or otherwise.

Briefly, the mandated goals involve (1) communication skills, (2) the local community, (3) use of natural resources, (4) geographic concepts, (5) economics, and (6) government. Trying to deal with all of these at once could be overwhelming for children, to say nothing of adults, so our next decision is to narrow them down to the point that they are more manageable.

Making things manageable

Organizing or Key Questions.   As we indicated earlier, identifying key or organizing questions can be a useful intermediate step in identifying additional learning outcomes. Those questions, some of which derive from the web we completed earlier, are as follows:

Guiding questions

1. What are resources, and where do they come from?
2. What resources (and occupations) were involved in producing the two cans of corn?
3. What resources are used to produce other common products?

4. What other products could be produced from those same resources?
5. How do human and natural resources differ?
6. How do renewable and nonrenewable resources differ?
7. How are resources allocated?
8. How do goods and services differ?

These questions are not necessarily in their final order, nor is it essential that we deal with all of them.

Relationship to Mandated Goals.

Correlating mandates and activities

If it seems that we keep moving back and forth, we are. This is the systematic nature of planning we noted earlier, where it is necessary to balance several elements simultaneously. That's why we have gone back to our state-mandated goals once again. However, this time we deal only with the goals that pertain to this unit (which is why Goals 02 and 06 do not appear here) and identify possible activities associated with each of them.

Goal 01—The students will practice a variety of listening, speaking, writing, and reading skills in completing social studies activities.

Application. Some teaching activities in our unit will have language arts–related extensions that address components of Goal 01. In one activity, for example, each child will select a simple product, such as a telephone pole, a hammer, or a wooden ruler. After he or she researches how the product is made, the child will present the results of the research in the form of an illustrated, first-person diary, for example, "Hi, I'm Teddy Telephone Pole, and I grew up on the slopes of Mount Helen. . . ." This activity will correlate with an ongoing language arts and reading activity in which the children are reading real biographies.

Goal 03—The students will understand that people use natural resources to meet their basic needs and these resources must be protected and conserved.

Application. Activities that involve identifying the occupations and resources that went into producing the canned corn—including the label, the corn, and the can itself—pertain to this goal and Goal 05. More specifically, we will create a "family tree" for a can of corn (which we describe shortly).

Goal 04—The students will understand geographic concepts.

Application. This is not a major focus of this unit, but activities pertaining to crops that farmers grow will involve elements related to terrain, weather conditions, and so on. In addition, because the canned corn can represent products produced in certain geographic regions of the country, we will undoubtedly deal with additional elements of geography.

Goal 05—The students will understand the interplay of economics in their daily lives.

Application. This will be one of the major areas of this unit. In addition, the fact that corn and other products are produced, bought, sold, and consumed can also lead to some of the objectives below.

Objective 0501: Define wages, prices, producer, consumer, specialization, division of labor, profit, loss, and productivity.

Objective 0503: Identify the relationship between supply and demand and its effect on the price of a product.

Objective 0505: Identify the natural resources that determine the types of jobs in your community in the past, present, and future.

Objective 0506: Identify the role of profits as being a primary reason for production.

Other Elements

One element we thought about including in our emerging unit focused on the different forms of transportation involved in producing and transporting canned corn. Such a topic would be within the scope of Objective 0501, and it would also add an appealing focus to our unit, especially if we could create some interesting non-reading activities dealing with trucks, trains, and other forms of transport. On the other hand, most third graders are already aware of trucks, trains, and so on, so unless we are careful we could find ourselves conducting a lesson about how milk trucks carry milk.

To pursue the transportation focus, we need to determine what the children must understand before they can deal with the role that transportation plays in any kind of trade. An obvious prerequisite is the need to understand the notion of trade as the exchange of goods and services. The students must also understand the notion of transportation in terms of its function—the movement of goods and people. In addition, to understand why things are transported, students must also understand why goods are traded, which involves concepts related to self-sufficiency, interdependence, and profit.

If this topic seems to have become very complex, you're right. The potential ideas we have identified include *trade, transportation, self-sufficiency, interdependence, goods and services, exchange,* and *communication.* Separately, none of these is beyond the grasp of third graders, but when it comes to helping them understand how these topics are interrelated, we have tackled something much more complicated than we bargained for, something unnecessarily complex for exemplary purposes. Thus, we will not include transportation as a significant element in this unit, for some of the reasons noted above. This decision illustrates a common planning phenomenon: the need to back up and either go in a different direction or, in some cases, delete or even start over. If everything went well on the first try, planning would be less exciting and time consuming.

After considering many alternatives, we have finally laid the foundation for our unit. Our planning is far from complete, but the progress report on page 243 shows the elements we have identified thus far.

Is this becoming too complex?

Backing up is not unusual

Identifying and Sequencing Instructional Activities

We have established a basic structure for this unit, but we still need to create some teaching activities. There isn't necessarily one best way to proceed from this point, but our preference is to identify a way to initiate the unit, preferably a way that grabs students' attention and establishes a direction for the activities that follow.

Planning: Progress Report

Unit Development

Unit title: How We Use Resources

Grade level: Primary (third)

Unit focus: Resource utilization

Generalization: The allocation and use of human and natural resources is based on decisions.

Major vehicle: Canned corn

Unit goals (partial listing):

Cognitive

* The child will understand what makes something a resource, either natural or human.
* The child will understand that the use of resources always involves choices and decisions. (For brevity, we have not repeated the additional goals shown earlier.)

Affective

* The child will appreciate the scarcity of resoruces, our widespread dependency on them, and the need to use resources wisely.

Topics: Resources, natural resources, human resources, wants, needs, allocation, scarcity

Objectives (tentative):

* The student will identify, from memory, three examples of natural resources.
* The student will distinguish between a human resource and a natural resource.
* The student will identify at least three alternative uses for a particular resource. (For brevity, we have not repeated the additional objectives shown earlier.)

Skill focus: To be determined in activities

Learning activities: Yet to be decided

Creating an Initiating Activity. Among the possible ways to initiate this unit, our first decision is not to begin with the usual defining of terms. We'll need to deal with definitions eventually, of course, but beginning with them is about as dull a way of starting a unit as we can think of. Our inclination is to begin the unit by identifying the resources that went into producing the cans of corn. (Note that we're using adult language here, not necessarily what we'd use with students.) Presenting a list of "things" (resources) that went into producing the canned corn is one alternative; or we could develop a kind of "family tree" for canned corn, as illustrated in Figure 10.3.

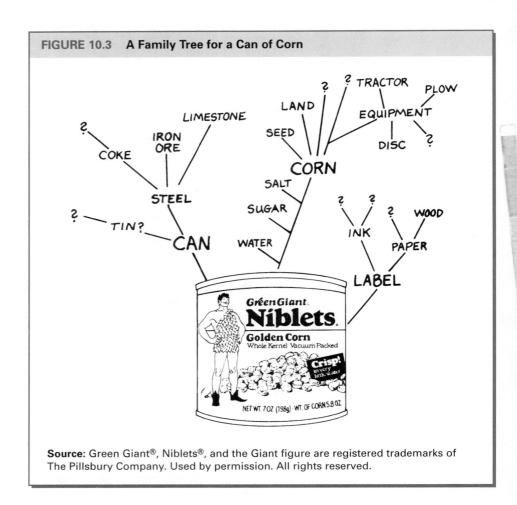

FIGURE 10.3   A Family Tree for a Can of Corn

Factors to consider

Choosing between beginning the unit with a list of resources, a family tree activity, or something else is just one of the countless decisions that planning demands. In this instance, we would opt for the family tree activity because it illustrates both the resources used in producing canned corn and their sequence of use. Also, we think it is an appealing format for presenting data. Finally, developing a family tree for canned corn in a whole-class setting could serve as a model for follow-up activities in which small groups of students could create similar charts for other familiar products—furniture, clothing, agricultural products, or almost anything else.

We have gone into such detail here to indicate some of the factors we considered in arriving at our decision. If the notion of a family tree is foreign to our students, a preliminary activity in which students learn to create their own family trees may be advisable. This decision would hinge on our awareness of our students' previous experiences with family trees, which is something teach-

COMMENTARY: All Teaching Activities Are Not Equally Effective

Brophy and Alleman (1991) have suggested an important criterion for selecting teaching activities, which they call an activity's *cognitive engagement potential*. This refers to the extent to which a teaching activity has the potential to engage the student cognitively—that is, the degree to which it gets students thinking actively.

Brophy and Alleman argue that many teaching activities have only a limited potential to engage children intellectually. Notable among these is much of the "seatwork" that students encounter—the page after page of workbook-like questions that students must complete. Such activities are sometimes called "check-ups" or "skill-builders" or some other beneficial-sounding name, but it would probably be more honest to call them what they usually

are: tests or merely busywork. Seldom will students "build a skill" simply by answering questions that test their prior knowledge.

Brophy and Alleman contend that the educational value of some long-term projects, including some hands-on activities and end-of-unit or end-of-semester activities, is also suspect. (Remember the igloo-building activity we considered in Chapter 8?) Likewise, some end-of-unit pageants or the construction of complex displays—like scale-model colonial villages—can consume vast amounts of time but have very limited instructional payoff. Students sometimes enjoy such long-term projects and may even look forward to them, but often their enjoyment may stem from the chance to avoid more seatwork.

---

ers gain simply by working with their classes. Since the students' experiences are unknown to us here, we are forced to make assumptions. If we assume incorrectly or don't make provisions for instances where we have assumed improperly, we may find ourselves in serious trouble.

Sequencing potential activities

After students have identified some natural resources used to manufacture various products, they could compare their charts to decide which, if any, resources are common among the products. They could then produce pictorial charts (pictures cut from magazines or downloaded from the Internet) or murals showing the different products produced from a particular resource, with titles such as "Things Made from Wood." So that children would not need to rely solely on their prior experiences for this, we would make available some of the vast array of videos, with titles such as *The Story of . . . (Bread, Wood, Steel)*, that focus on how we use natural resources.

Developing and sequencing learning activities is neither more nor less important than any other aspect of planning, but unfortunately, we know of no formula or procedure to help you do it. Many times it is simply a matter of what makes the most sense to you.

Determining a Culminating Activity. This stage is something teachers may think about throughout the entire planning process. In our case, we were sensitive to Brophy and Alleman's comments about end-of-unit activities that take considerable time but fail to engage students's thinking processes (see Commentary). Culminating activities should also provide opportunities to apply and extend some ideas previously dealt with in different contexts. We began the unit using canned corn as a primary vehicle and decided to return to it in the culminating activity in a slightly different context. Returning to the master family tree chart for corn, we will ask the children to identify the main decision makers and to

MODEL STUDENT TEACHER ACTIVITY

A Sample Unit Plan: Using Resources Wisely

Grade Level: Third Grade

Introductory Note: Because we have already discussed many elements of this unit plan, we have elected to refer you to relevant pages rather than repeat them again here. In addition, the following activities are described in adult terms, not necessarily as we would present them to children. In developing your units, you may wish to include key questions in the language you would use with students.

Introduction: As described on pages 243–245.

Curriculum Standards:

* **Benchmark Standard:** The Fifth Essential Element of Geography. See page 255.

* **Mandated Outcomes:** See pages 233–234.

Key Learning Outcomes: See pages 241–242.

Ongoing Activities: (1) Journals; (2) *DynoPark Tycoon* (MECC) simulation

Activity One: Initiating Activity

Objective: Working in small groups, students will identify the components of canned corn.

Description: Phase One: Divide the class into small groups and, if possible, provide each with an identical can of corn. Ask each group to identify as many "things" as possible that went into making the corn, can, and label. Gauge the time spent on this portion of the activity by the students' interest. Five minutes or less may be sufficient.

Phase Two: Have the various groups report their findings. List the components on the chalkboard as each group reports. Probe, cajole, and stimulate as necessary. After the groups have gone as far as they seem able, ask if any of the items seem to go together (following the Taba concept-building procedure, pages 245, 249). Note that some items may go into more than one category.

Skill Areas: Observing, analyzing, inferring, classifying.

Activity Two: Building a Family Tree

Overview: The teacher and students will develop a model "family tree" for canned corn.

Objective: The child will explain the process for making a family tree (pedigree) chart.

Description: Working with the list of "things" previously identified, the teacher and students will locate components on a family tree chart similar to the one illustrated in Figure 10.3. As a group, students will identify all the "things" (not yet identified as resources) they can think of that were involved in producing the cans of corn. Have one student read the label. Items the students identify should be listed on the board and may include such things as farmer, metal, paper, and ink. Don't push too far here. For example, accept paper without going into paper's components (wood, etc.) unless the children insist on it. This will be picked up again in Activity 3.

Skill Area: Recording data.

Optional Initiating Activity: If students are unfamiliar with a family tree chart, the unit could begin by having students make family tree charts of their own using snapshots if available or simply names of relatives.

Activity Three: Paper

Activities Three, Four, and Five each follow a similar format. The children should tentatively identify the resources and processes that go into producing the various components of the cans of corn—paper, metal, and others. Their suggestions should be treated as hypotheses that will then be tested against data (on paper making, etc.) provided through films, filmstrips, or other media.

The exact nature of these activities and the length of time they take will depend on the materials and resources available.

Objectives:

* The student will identify a natural resource as something from our environment that people may use.

* The student will describe the process for making paper.

Description: The intent of this activity is to test and then validate the children's ideas about the resources used in making paper. Key question: What do you think paper is made from?

Phase One: List responses to the key question on the chalkboard.

Phase Two: Make paper following the instructions in the Resource Handbook.

Phase Three: Review the elements the children hypothesized originally. Add the resources to the master family tree chart.

Skill Areas: Hypothesizing, hypothesis testing.

Activity Four: Tin Cans

Objective: The student will identify the major components in metal cans.

Description: Follows the same format as Activity Three. Key question: What are tin cans made from? Possible materials include the following:

* Films: *Tin from the Malayan Jungle* (International Film Bureau); *Steel & America* (Disney Productions)

* Filmstrip: *Rocks, Minerals, and Mining* (Encyclopaedia Britannica Films)

* *Explorapedia,* a children's interactive encyclopedia (Microsoft)

* Other encyclopedia articles

Skill Areas: Hypothesizing, hypothesis testing.

Activity Five: Corn

Objectives:

* The student will identify the major steps in the production of corn.

* The child will name at least five resources used in the production of canned corn (for Activities Three, Four, and Five collectively).

Description: Follows same format as Activities Three and Four. Key question: What elements are involved in producing corn?

Possible materials include the following:

* Filmstrips: *Farming in Indiana* (Jam Handy); *Where Food Comes From* (Encyclopaedia Britannica Films); *The Corn Belt* (Society for Visual Education)

* *Explorapedia,* a children's interactive encyclopedia (Microsoft)

* Other encyclopedia articles

Skill Areas: Hypothesizing, hypothesis testing.

Optional Activities: Children can consider and investigate the nature of salt, ink, or any other component as interest warrants. Follow same format as Activities Three, Four, and Five.

Activity Six: Where Do Things Come From?

Objective: Given a common object or article, the student will identify either (1) the components (resources) that were used to produce it or (2) the steps involved in its production.

Description: Each child (or small group) will select a common object or article and make a family tree chart for it (similar to the one done for the corn). For some materials, such as articles of clothing, this may involve identifying the steps in its production.

Children should explain and display their charts.

Skill Areas: Observing, inferring.

Activity Seven: Minisynthesis

Objectives:

* The student will identify at least five resources originating in the land.

* The student will distinguish between a human resource and a natural resource.

* The student will distinguish between wants and needs.

Description: Using the corn chart and the materials the children constructed for Activity 6, develop a discussion-oriented activity that will help the children recognize that (1) the "things" (materials) that went into making the canned corn all ultimately originated in the land, (2) all goods ultimately have their origin in the land, and (3) people are involved at every step along the way. If the occasion has not arisen previously, the term *resources* can be identified as a label for "things," and the term *goods* can be associated with objects or products produced from natural resources.

Key questions include the following: (1) Do you notice anything about those "things" that our cans of corn were made from? (2) Can you think of anything that does not come from the land?

Skill Areas: Classifying and labeling, inferring.

Activity Eight: What Would Happen If?

Objective: Students will speculate on how things might be different if certain products were not available.

Description: This discussion activity is based on the key question, "What would happen if we didn't have any wood? electricity? water? bicycles? corn?"

Skill Areas: Hypothesizing, speculating.

Activity Nine: Alternative Uses for Existing Resources

Objective: Given a picture of one product or basic natural resource, the student will identify at least seven other pictures of that resource being used in different ways.

Description: The intent of this activity, which may take several days, is to extend the idea that goods and basic resources are used in different ways. For example, a tree, while reflecting the use of the land in a particular way, can itself be used in different ways.

Provide individual students or groups with labeled pictures (cut from magazines, etc.) of various resources—land, a tree, water, and so on. The students are then asked to make a collage of pictures that illustrate different ways in which the product or resource might be used. The teacher should also make a collage showing land being used in different ways—for a playground, for growing crops, for housing, for parks, for parking lots.

Instruct students *not* to include their original picture in their collage until after the class has had an opportunity to identify what resource each collage depicts.

Skill Areas: Observing, interpreting, inferring.

Activity Ten: What Could We Do with the Playground?

Objective: The students will identify at least three factors that might influence the ways in which resources are used.

Description: This activity is intended to illustrate that people have decided to use a particular piece of land, the school playground, in a certain way. In other words, if oil were discovered beneath the playground, the land might be used for other purposes—in this case, to hold an oil well. How the playground is used is subject to certain limitations, including the presence of mineral resources.

Certain value issues also enter the picture. For example, if gold or oil were discovered on the school playground, it could be turned into a gold mine or an oil field, but *should* it? Any physical determinants—climate, for example—should be dealt with first through questions such as "Could our playground be used as an orange grove? a tree farm?"

Value considerations can then be introduced through role-playing. For example, the following situation could be presented to students.

Gold Discovered on School Playground

Gold has been discovered on the (Name) School playground. The Acme Mining Company wants to buy the playground and build a gold mine there. They are willing to pay a lot of money for the property.

The key question is, What should the school do?

Skill Areas: Inferring, identifying alternative explanations.

Culminating Activities

Objectives:

* The student will, from memory, (1) identify the primary decision makers (the farmer, the lumberman, etc.) involved in the production of the canned corn and (2) identify at least one alternative decision that those individuals might have made in terms of the way they used the resources available to them.

* Given a series of pictures of people in different occupations (a machinist, a dairy farmer, a baker, etc.), the student will identify (1) the goods or services being provided and (2) the natural resources being used.

Description: As described on pages 000–000.

identify at least one alternative decision that each individual might have made in determining how he or she would use the available resources. We would follow that by giving small groups of children pictures of someone in a particular occupation (a machinist, a diary farmer, etc.), which will serve as the centerpiece of a collage in which students pictorially identify (1) the goods and services being provided and (2) the natural resources being used.

It is not essential that we return to the canned corn in the culminating activity, but it seems to round things out rather nicely. It is also helpful, though not essential, if the culminating activity provides a bridge to the next unit, which might focus on conservation (the use and abuse of resources), the role of tools in using resources to produce goods and services, or perhaps the role of money as a medium for allocating resources.

Determining Ongoing Activities. This aspect of planning is not essential unless you will have some activities that carry on throughout the entire unit. We intend to have two ongoing activities: (1) student journals and (2) the award-winning, computer-based simulation *DinoPark Tycoon* (1995), which is available from MECC. In this engaging simulation, students must plan and operate a dinosaur theme park. In addition to meeting the needs their dinosaurs will have, such as land, fencing, and food, students must also decide how they will staff the park and make provisions for maintenance and daily operations.

Reviewing the Unit for Completeness and Consistency

In planning this unit, several stages were left partially completed. Once the unit has taken on a clearer form and direction, it is time to go back and fill in the holes. A Unit Plan Checklist that can be useful for this task is shown in Figure 10.4

The final test of any unit plan comes when you teach it with students. In the process, you will discover those activities that work well and those that don't and will make the necessary adaptations for the next time you teach it.

Lesson Planning

Detailed unit plans usually decrease the need for separate daily lesson plans. However, many prospective teachers' lesson plans are vehicles to communicate with cooperating teachers, college supervisors, and sometimes even principals (some of whom collect weekly lesson plans). As a result, your daily lesson plans may be more detailed than they would otherwise need to be for effective teaching. Thus the length and scope of your lesson plans may be a function of the dual purpose they serve: (1) as a plan for the students you teach and (2) to convey your intent to those who observe you.

Figure 10.5 shows on page 251 a template you can use to write daily lesson plans.

Figure 10.4 Unit Plan Checklist

General Elements

Yes	No	Goals
_____	_____	Have we identified what students should know at the end of this unit?
_____	_____	Have we identified the skills that students should be able to demonstrate at the end of this unit?
_____	_____	Have we identified affective goals for this unit?
_____	_____	Have we identified what should be done for students who cannot demonstrate what is indicated above?
_____	_____	Have we identified cognitive and affective objectives for this unit?

Specific Elements

Yes	No	
_____	_____	Have we identified a vehicle or focus for the unit?
_____	_____	Have we identified a main idea or generalization for the unit?
_____	_____	Have we task-analyzed the elements of this unit in terms of prerequisite understandings?
_____	_____	Have we stated instructional objectives in performance terms?
_____	_____	Have we identified and sequenced learning activities?
_____	_____	How we identified guiding (key) questions
_____	_____	a. For planning purposes?
_____	_____	b. For instructional use with students?
_____	_____	Have we identified teaching materials and resources?
_____	_____	Have we identified a way to initiate the unit?
_____	_____	Have we identified the means for student evaluation?
_____	_____	Have we identified a way to bring closure to the unit?
_____	_____	Have we devised a means for evaluating the unit for internal and external consistency (such as this checklist)?
_____	_____	a. Do the various sections of the unit "fit together"—for example, no "hidden objectives" (internal consistency)?
_____	_____	b. Is the unit, as a whole, justifiable? Can it be defended as worthy of being studied (external consistency)?

Figure 10.5 Template for Daily Lesson Plans

Put the title of the lesson here

I. Introduction/Overview

Write a brief overview of the lesson, including why it is something students should experience or learn. Also indicate how you intend to introduce (or set the stage) for the lesson.

II. Entry-Level Knowledge/Skills

Briefly describe what learners will need to know prior to this lesson (that they cannot pick up in the course of the lesson).

III. State the Task (Objectives)

Describe clearly what the end result of the learners' activities will be—answer a series of question, solve a problem, summarize what they have learned, etc.

IV. Resources/ Advanced Preparation

List the specific physical resources you need to teach this lesson. Do not include materials common to classrooms, such as chalkboard, overhead projector, etc. Attach copies of worksheets, charts, or other materials you plan to use with stud ents.

V. The Process

Describe the basic steps the learners will experience as they go through the lesson. These may include the following:

1. How you will make connections with the students' previous learning (review)

2. How you will make students aware of the objectives for the lesson

3. How you will introduce and/or model the content/skills

4. How you will provide guided practice (if applicable)

VI. Assessment/Evaluation

Describe how you will assess or evaluate students' performance or understanding.

VII. Conclusion/Closure

Briefly describe how you will bring this lesson to a close.

VIII. Follow-up Activities.

Briefly describe other activities or lessons that logically follow from this lesson, or how you would integrate the "big ideas" from this lesson into other subject areas.

Summary

For most teachers, planning is a never-ending process. It continues even as teachers are teaching, usually in the form of day-to-day adjustments. Additional planning often occurs after instruction as teachers decide what should be changed, deleted, and added to the unit when (and if) they teach it again.

In this chapter, we identified the components of planning and illustrated how those components fit together. Goals are statements of intent that show the general direction teaching should take. A sample goal for the affective domain, which pertains to feelings and attitudes, is: "Students will appreciate the contribution of

American patriots." A sample goal for the cognitive domain, which pertains to different types of thinking, is: "Students will understand the impact of technology on contemporary life." Objectives, on the other hand, describe specific behaviors that students are expected to demonstrate at the end of an instructional activity. Outcomes such as "The student will, from memory, identify three factors that led to the Civil War" and "Given a list of statements, the student will tell which are facts and which reflect opinions" reflect instructional (behaviorally stated or performance) objectives.

Simply because objectives are phrased in performance terms does not necessarily mean that they are good and worthy of instruction. Rather, teachers must evaluate potential objectives—no matter how they are stated—in terms of (1) their students' ability to achieve them, (2) the goals to which they relate, and (3) their appropriateness.

After you have identified your purpose and your instructional intent, instructional planning becomes a systematic, interactive process—as opposed to a sequence of discrete steps that one must follow. For example, objectives may imply or suggest certain teaching activities, just as activities may suggest or imply certain objectives. In most instances, the unit planning process moves from the "whole," the unit, to one or more of the specific "parts,"—the resources, the teaching activities, or assessment—and then moves back to the "whole."

Suggested Activities

1. Most colleges of education maintain collections of social studies curriculum guides and textbook series. If yours does not, the local school system might loan you copies. Where possible, get two different curriculum guides or texts (preferably the teacher's editions) *for the same grade level.* Compare and contrast them in terms of the following:

    a. the nature and clarity of their goals and objectives

    b. the relationship of suggested activities to the stated goals and objectives

    c. the similarities and differences in format, suggested topics, and suggested teaching approaches

2. Use the Brophy-Alleman framework for instructional activities that appear in the Resource Handbook to analyze the teaching activities that we included in our sample unit in this chapter. Determine whether any, some, or all of the activities should be replaced.

Suggested Readings

Linda L. Levstick & Keith C. Barton. (1997). *Doing history: Investigating with children in elementary and middle schools.* Mahwa, NJ: Lawrence Erlbaum. This book provides detailed examples of activities that engage children in historically related activities.

Stephanie Steffy & Wendy Hood. (1994). *If this is social studies, why isn't it boring?* York, ME: Stenhouse. This collection of first-person vignettes details how fourteen teachers were able to depart from traditional text-based teaching.

11 Assessing Learning

Key Questions

* Where does assessment fit into the instructional cycle?
* How do norm-referenced and criterion-referenced evaluation differ?
* Are assessment and grading compatible?
* How does one evaluate higher-level cognitive skills?
* What is the relationship between objectives and test questions?

Key Ideas

* Assessment is the reciprocal of planning.
* The quality and accuracy of evaluative judgments are a reflection of the quality and accuracy of evaluative data.
* Subjectivity is inherent in all assessment; the goal is to limit and control its influence.
* Every test question has an underlying objective, either implicit or explicit.
* The materials and strategies used to assess higher-level thinking skills may closely resemble the materials and strategies used to teach those skills initially.

Introduction: Revisiting Janet Jacobsen

Developing equitable assessment and grading strategies for inquiry-based learning can be a major roadblock for many teachers. Janet Jacobsen, whom we first visited in the "Pine Tree Shillings" activity (in Chapter 8), had promised she would show us the assessment strategy that she created for her students, no two of whom are necessarily doing or learning the same thing. To learn about Mrs. Jacobsen's approach, we revisited her and her fifth-grade class.

Shortly after our arrival, Janet went over to a bookshelf and picked up a quarter-inch-thick booklet in an orange binder. "This is Jamie Button's report," she said proudly. "Take a look at it."

The first thing we noticed was the title page. In large bold type, it read: "How to Make (Mint) Money by Jamie Button." The next page, half-filled with print, was a combination dedication/copyright page. A portion of it said: "This book is dedicated with pride to my father, Craig Button, who helped me with some of the graphics and illustrations; to my sister Katy, who gave me time on the computer so I could finish this report; to my grandfather, Benton J. (B. J.) Burns (he's my mom's father), who showed me his collection of old coins; and . . ." It was as if Jamie had thanked half the people in the area! We looked quizzically at Janet, who said, "My kids feel this is one of the most important pages in their report, and I'm not about to argue with them." We weren't about to dispute the point, either.

What a dedication!

"Sometimes my students work in pairs, and sometimes I have one or two threesomes, but no larger—bigger groups spend too much time figuring out who is going to do what," Janet noted, "and all of them produced creditable reports, not something they copied out of an encyclopedia." She then added, "The children's reports were on topics like: 'Pirates in Puritan Times,' 'A Comparison of Hawthorne's Written Works,' 'How Do You Make Change in Old English Money?' [where a shilling is one-twentieth of a pound sterling, and a shilling contains twelve pence], and a bunch of others. Everybody did visually based presentations, too. The kids were excited and involved, and they learned more from this activity than I ever imagined. And then," Janet added somewhat dispiritedly, "comes evaluation and grading."

"We're not 'hung up' on evaluation and grades," we indicated, "but in a lot of schools, grading seems to overwhelm everything else."

In some cases, grading seems to drive everything else

"I know," Janet said, nodding in agreement. "Assessment and grading were the hardest things I had to deal with," she added. "And I have both extremes in this class: kids who won't do anything unless it's for a grade, and kids whom grades don't motivate in the least."

"Yeah," we responded. "We've been there."

"One of the first things I had to deal with was the school district's policy. It mandated that all teachers must have at least two grades each week in every subject for each grading period. That policy was O.K. when we used those 'skill builder' worksheets, which we graded and recorded as if they were tests, but that policy is still based on a lot of simplistic assumptions about how learning occurs. Learning is incremental but it doesn't always inch upward, bit by bit; sometimes it grows by leaps and bounds—like when you can see a light bulb go on in a child's expression that tells you, 'Yeah, I finally understand this!' The policy also forced me to spend a lot of time on testing and grading that I could have used for teaching."

Dealing with district policies

"So what did you do?" we asked.

"Well, sometimes if we did an activity that involved both social studies and language arts, for example, I would record the same grade twice, once in each subject area," Janet responded. "But these were coping strategies for what I think was a questionable policy to begin with."

Doubling up

"So what did you do?" we asked.

"I began working to get the district's grading policy changed," Janet responded. "I got my colleagues to begin talking about the policy in their grade-level meetings. Most of them agreed that the policy was often difficult to comply with and that it seemed geared to helping administrators and teachers cover themselves if questions were raised. My seniority in this district probably helped my cause—some of my current students are children of my former students. Anyway, they couldn't dismiss me out of hand."

"Were you successful?" we asked.

"Yes . . . and no," she responded. "What they did was permit exceptions to the policy for teachers who filed an alternative evaluation and grading plan. That was fine with me, except that I had to figure out exactly how I would assess the kids—and this was new territory for me. But then I decided that if I couldn't defend what I wanted to do, and if I couldn't assess my students fairly, I probably shouldn't be doing it.

Goals

"With the kids studying different aspects of events like the 'Pine Tree Shillings' incident, I couldn't very well give them a knowledge-based test—most of the kids were learning different things. And then, it wasn't just knowledge that I was after. I wanted the children to begin taking some responsibility for their own learning, to learn how to inquire about things—to become experienced in using the inquiry process. And I wanted them to become skillful in organizing, interpreting, and presenting information. And I wanted to reward the kids who showed progress in developing those skills, not just give good grades to the kids who already had well-developed skills."

"That's an imposing agenda," we said.

"The more I thought about it, the more I began to wonder what I was getting into," Janet continued. "It's a lot easier to give kids the prepared tests that come with the textbooks series, and let it go at that . . . but I was determined."

"So then . . . ?" we asked.

"I decided to follow my instincts and develop an assessment strategy that reflected my goals." Janet opened a file folder and said, "Remember I'm a novice at this," and gave us a one-page form (shown in Figure 11.1).

"How do you use this?" we asked.

"First of all, at the beginning of the year I give the kids a copy, and we talk about what it means. Then at the end of each grading period, I have a five- or six-minute assessment conference with each student. They complete a copy of the form that they bring to our conference, along with everything they've done in social studies for the period—what I loosely refer to as 'their portfolio.' If they've lost stuff—and some of them always do—that's too bad. I also bring a preliminary copy of the form that I've filled in, based on my anecdotal notes on each child, and then we talk. Together, we complete the form and agree on a grade. The district uses computerized, fill-in-the-bubble grading forms that I fill out for the report cards, but also I send the assessment forms home with the students."

Conferences

"Do you weight each of the elements equally?"

"No," Janet answered. "I almost never give equal weight to the presentation skills, because some kids are naturally shy and some of them are less verbal than others. And sometimes the weightings change based on what we are doing. For example, during the six-week period just before we give the Iowa Test of Basic Skills, a standardized achievement test, we drop the inquiry format and do a teacher-directed overview of the parts of history that we won't get to. It's pretty much awareness-level stuff, but the kids need to be aware of it to do well

Weightings change depending on activities

FIGURE 11.1 Social Studies Assessment/Progress Report

	Unsatisfactory	Satisfactory	Excellent

1. Responsibility for Learning:
    1.1 Demonstrates responsibility for learning.
    1.2 Progress in taking responsibility for learning.

Comments: _____

_____

2. Subject Matter Knowledge:
    2.1 Demonstrates subject matter knowledge.
    2.2 Progress in mastering subject matter.

Comments: _____

_____

3. The Inquiry Process:
    3.1 Ability to use the inquiry process.
    3.2 Progress in using the inquiry process.

Comments: _____

_____

4. Organizing and Interpreting Information:
    4.1 Ability to organize and interpret information.
    4.2 Progress in organizing and interpreting information.

Comments: _____

_____

5. Sharing/Presentation Skills:
    5.1 Ability to present information.
    5.2 Progress in presenting information.

Comments: _____

_____

on the tests. I even give old-fashioned tests, just like I used to. During that period, we use only the 'Subject Matter Knowledge' criterion, because, well, that's all we focus on."

"Doesn't it take forever to have conferences with every child?" we asked.

Time considerations

"Sometimes it seems like it," she responded, "but it only takes three class sessions to do everyone in each of my four classes. But," she continued, "I *really* have to watch my time—five or six minutes per student, no more, otherwise I'd be conferencing all the time."

"What do your other students do while you are conferencing?" we asked.

"Usually I try to schedule them so students are in the research phase of an activity," Janet indicated, "but it almost never works out right. So I give the kids options. While some of us are conferencing they can work on their projects, go to one of the centers I set up around the room, or they can read almost anything their hearts desire. Historical biographies and books like Jean Fritz's *Shh! We're Writing the Constitution* (1987) are really popular. But I will not give my students busywork activities, because that would violate my rule of doing something productive with their time."

"It sounds like you're happy with your assessment system," we observed.

"It's not perfect," Janet responded, "but it's better than what I used to use. And I keep fiddling with it every year to improve it."

"What impresses us about your system is the way you've blended objective and subjective elements and involved your students in the conferencing process. Have you thought about writing this up for a journal article?" we asked.

Janet Jacobsen looked at us a little sheepishly and said, "Maybe when it's perfect."

There is no perfect assessment and grading system, at least none we know of. Yet, Mrs. Jacobsen's assessment system includes some notable aspects: (1) she uses a variety of different (nontest) data forms, including her anecdotal notes and the students' "portfolios," and (2) her assessment process is ongoing, even though the conference itself occurs near the end of the grading period. Too many people hold the mistaken notions that (1) assessment is something that occurs only at the end of the instructional cycle, and (2) the terms *evaluation, testing,* and *grading,* are synonymous. Although evaluation, testing, and grading often go hand in hand, they are separate processes—at least in theory—as we explain in this chapter.

Apparently because so many people lump *evaluation* and *grading* together in practice, some educators sought out a term that referred to "judging quality" but that did not also convey the notion of grading—as *evaluation* so often does. A term that reflects this notion and is being used increasingly is *assessment.* We will use both terms (evaluation and assessment) interchangeably throughout this chapter.

In the first part of this chapter, we look at the roles that assessment can play in the instructional cycle. We then turn to several strategies you might use for gathering assessment information.

Assessment and the instructional Cycle

Assessment is a natural part of the instructional cycle, which is shown in Figure 11.2. In Phase One of the instructional cycle, you decide where you want to go, instructionally speaking, by identifying learning outcomes. In Phase Two, you actually use the teaching activities and experiences with your students, helping them move toward the outcomes you established in Phase One. In the assessment phase of the instructional cycle (Phase Three), the focus shifts to students' performance. The key question in Phase Three is, How well have your students (and you) gotten to where you wanted to get to?

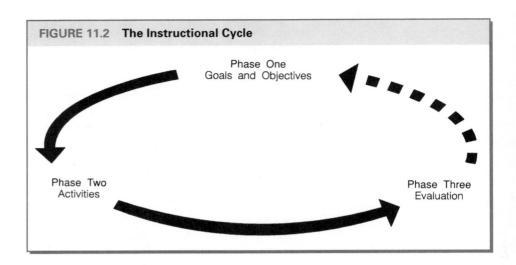

FIGURE 11.2 The Instructional Cycle

Phase One
Goals and Objectives

Phase Two
Activities

Phase Three
Evaluation

The instructional cycle is a series of overlapping and interacting categories, not discrete steps; that is, you can't deal with one phase in isolation from the other phases. The area of the instructional cycle where things sometimes get confusing is shown by the broken arrow in Figure 11.2. That confusion is reflected by two responses to the question, What happens after evaluation? One common response is, "Students receive a grade and then move on to something else." A less common response is, "Students continue to work on unmet objectives until they can demonstrate mastery of them." How you respond will depend on whether you are using mastery learning part of the time, some of the time, or never.

Assessment is a three-part process that consists of (1) identifying criteria or standards (determining what students will be expected to do), (2) gathering data on students' performance with respect to those standards, and then (3) making judgments about the individual's performance (based on the information you have gathered). The first component of assessment—determining what students will be expected to do—occurs during planning. The goals and objectives that you identify during planning should reflect the criteria (or standards) that students will be expected to demonstrate during assessment. For

example, if your objectives indicate that you expect students to identify four of the five Great Lakes, or to distinguish statements of fact from statements of opinion with at least 80 percent accuracy, your assessment criteria are already established. You need only pose the evaluation task to students in an appropriate form.

The second and third elements of assessment can occur during or after instruction. If students seem to be encountering problems during instruction, or even if they are not, it's simply common sense to stop periodically to evaluate how things are going. Evaluating students' progress as learning is "forming up" during instruction, instead of waiting until the end of an instructional episode, is known as *formative evaluation*.

What distinguishes formative evaluation from the commonsense assessment that often occurs spontaneously during teaching is its planned nature. In using formative evaluation, teachers (1) consciously plan to pause periodically to assess how things are going and then (2) use the criteria provided by their objectives to evaluate the situation. In this way, formative evaluation can provide useful information to supplement your intuitive sense of how things are going.

Formative evaluation: a form of feedback

Formative evaluation is one of several forms of assessment, each of which serves a different purpose. The appropriate type of assessment is determined by the kind of information, and the kinds of questions, that you want answers to. The types and phases of assessment are reflected in Table 11.1.

Criterion-Referenced Evaluation

Criterion-referenced evaluation is "referenced," or keyed, to specified knowledge or skills, each of which serves as a criterion that students are expected to demonstrate. If you have decided that each of your students should be able to identify the location of the United States on a world map, for example, that becomes a referencing criterion. But what happens if some of your students are unable to meet that objective? If you use *mastery learning* in your classroom, students who do not meet the criterion must work through additional instructional activities until they can demonstrate mastery. Once your students meet the objective, they (and you) can move on to other objectives and teaching activities. In instances where mastery learning is not used, the student will probably receive a lower grade and then move on to other things.

Evaluation and mastery learning

Criterion-referenced evaluation can be used at any point in the instructional cycle. It can be used (1) as a pretest prior to instruction, (2) to determine student progress during instruction, and (3) to find out whether students have mastered the expected behaviors after instruction. Based on your students' performance on a criterion-referenced pretest, for example, neither you nor your students would need to waste time going over what they already know, and you could then devote your attention to areas where students need additional instruction.

If mastery learning were adhered to in its purest form, students would be expected to answer every question on a test correctly. By doing so, they would be demonstrating mastery of the desired behaviors. However, when several desired competencies are clustered together on a test, the performance standard or criterion is often established as a percentage of questions that must be answered correctly. Thus, to demonstrate mastery, students might be expected to complete at least 80 percent (or another percentage) of the test items correctly.

Alternative criteria

Every question on every test should reflect a corresponding learning outcome. For example, if you expect students to identify the year in which the Magna Carta was signed (1215), you need to have a test question or use some other means to assess that they know that information. Common sense suggests that if a teacher doesn't care whether students know when the Magna Carta was signed, a test question to that effect should not be on the test. However, often we suspect that students sometimes don't discover what they are supposed to know until they actually take the test. This situation exists, we believe, because

Every objective should have a corresponding assessment, and vice versa

Table 11.1   Types and Phases of Assessment as Reflected by Teachers/ Questions

Information Desired (Teachers' Questions)	Type of Programs	Phase of Instruction When Used	Typical Form of Assessment	Comments
"Can the student perform a designated task? Demonstrate a desired behavior?"	Criterion-referenced	Anytime	Teacher-made tests Standardized tests Observations Portfolios	Used to determine a student's skill proficiency. Sole focus is on individual performance.
"How does this student's performance compare with the class's performance as a whole?" or: "How does the performance of my students compare with that of similar students across the state or country?"	Norm-referenced	Anytime	Standardized tests	Used to compare an individual's performance with that of a group, or one group's performance with that of another group.
"How well are students moving toward our goals and objectives?" (How are we doing?)	Formative	During	Observations Journals Student comments	Used to determine progress during instruction.
"How am I doing as a teacher? As a student?"	Self-evaluation	Anytime	Varies	Criteria and results are usually private.
"All things considered, how does the student's overall performance rate?"	Summative	After	Varied measures	May be norm-referenced, criterion-referenced, specific or global, or some combination of all elements.
"Can the student exhibit mastery of important understandings as they apply to real-life problems or challenges?"	Authentic (Applied)	After	Demonstrated performances	Used to demonstrate performance in tasks related to real-life problems or expectations.

some teachers wait until the night before the test to pore over the textbook or some other source, looking for test questions. Only then, *after* they've made the test, do the teachers' real expectations (objectives) become known—to themselves and, later, to students. We are not suggesting that tests are necessarily the preferred way to evaluate one's objectives. Our point is that by identifying clear objectives in the planning phase of instruction, teachers can reduce much of the mystique that is often associated with testing and evaluation.

Testing defined

Vagueness about a teacher's expectations may explain why some students ask that proverbial question, "Will this be on the test?" At other times, the question is simply part of the grading game. In either case, the unfortunate implication is that if something isn't going to be on the test, it's not worth learning. In theory, *testing* is simply a technique for gathering evaluative information, nothing more. Yet no one needs to tell you that, in practice, testing is often a much more potent force.

Let's return for a moment to Janet Jacobsen's assessment strategy. Does she use criterion-referenced assessment? Because each of her students was investigating different aspects of the "Pine Tree Shillings" incident, and thus was learning different things, Janet did not establish knowledge objectives that applied to everyone. Then too, subject matter knowledge was only one of five goals that Janet and her students were working toward. Although each of her goals serves as a kind of criterion, each was stated too globally to meet the strict definition of criterion-referenced evaluation.

Norm-Referenced Evaluation

Norm-referenced evaluation focuses on comparing one student's performance in relation to that of other students. The *norm* in norm-referenced evaluation is usually the average of students' performance—the class average—or, in the case of standardized tests, the performance of students across the school district, the state, or the country. Regardless of how the norm is determined, the purpose is to rate a student's performance relative to the norm.

Norm referenced: comparing students against a norm

Norm-referenced evaluation permits you to say, for instance, that "Johnny did better than 31 percent of the third graders who took this test on map skills." In this instance, Johnny's performance probably isn't very good—indeed, it may be awful—but unless you shifted to criterion-referenced evaluation and analyzed Johnny's performance on each test item, it's doubtful whether you could determine what problems caused Johnny to perform as he did.

Caution

The results of norm-referenced assessment are always stated comparatively—that is, in relation to whatever norm is being used. Thus, to learn that Maria got a 95 on her test might seem impressive at first, especially if you assume it was a 100-item test. However, if it was a 200-item test and the average score was 161, your impression of Maria's performance will probably change considerably. Your impression might change even more when you find that Maria is an average eight-year-old whose native language is Spanish, who has been in this country less than a year, and whose score of 95 was on a test of English vocabulary (or American history). Unless the group that Maria is being compared with (the norm) shares Maria's characteristics (age, linguistic background, etc.), the results of normative evaluation could be misleading.

When school districts or states enter the assessment arena, they use norm-referenced evaluation extensively. School systems select whatever norm they wish to use, depending on the group with whom they want to compare their students. They could, for example, compare students in one class with students in other classes at the same grade level, or the students in one school with students from other schools in the system, or the schools in its system with other schools across the nation.

Norm-referenced evaluation and criterion-referenced evaluation serve different purposes, so it is pointless to say that one is better than the other. In many respects, the comparative nature of norm-referenced evaluation has become one of the conventions of American schooling. But from a purely instructional point of view, criterion-referenced assessment can provide the information that teachers must have to target instruction toward the specific needs of individual students.

Summative Evaluation and Grading

For all practical purposes, *summative evaluation* and *grading* are synonymous. Summative evaluation, which always occurs at the end of an instructional episode, "summarizes" the changes that have occurred as a result of instruction, usually in the form of a grade. Grading, in its technical sense, refers to the process of judging whether someone (or something) belongs in a particular category. The key elements of grading are (1) determining the characteristics of the categories to be used for reporting purposes and then (2) deciding whether the person or object reflects those characteristics. Yet the basic question in both summative evaluation and grading is: All things considered, how would you judge the quality of a student's performance (or product)?

You already know that in most schools summative evaluation and grading are usually reflected by letters (A, B, C, D, F), numbers, descriptive expressions ("Satisfactory," "Excellent," etc.), or some combination of these. The labels we've got! What we lack are consistent descriptions of the categories to which they apply. As a result, almost everyone knows that one teacher's A can be another teacher's B, C, or even worse.

Some teachers use norm-referenced evaluation for grading purposes; that is, the student's grade is based on the individual's performance relative to the class's performance as a whole. That procedure is commonly called "grading on the curve," and is well known to most college students. Other teachers identify grading categories by using a criterion-referenced format. In those instances, the standards—such as "scores of 90 or more are an A"—are commonly established in advance. Things usually work out adequately *if* the pre-established standards are appropriate and *if* there are a limited number of elements that grades are based on. But when teachers say things like "In determining your grade, I'm going to 'count' your test scores, homework, class participation, and group work," expectations can become fuzzy. Other teachers use

mathematical formulas (e.g., "Class participation counts one-fifth") in an apparent effort to make grading more objective. However, the mathematical manipulation of scores does not necessarily make grading more objective and

We have not dealt with self-evaluation in this chapter because it is among the most private forms of evaluation; the criteria are usually private, as are the results—unless, of course, you choose to make them public.

Self-evaluation demands a considerable degree of self-awareness and self-direction. To help our own students develop these qualities, we decided on one occasion to permit them to give themselves their citizenship grades. To be certain that everyone used similar grading criteria, we spent much time talking about what constituted "good citizenship." However, when the children turned in their grades, we found that, almost without exception, their grades were one to two grades lower than we would have given. When we investigated, we discovered that what we had considered trivial incidents, such as the failure to complete a homework paper on time, were blown out of proportion, and students had downgraded themselves accordingly. We ended up spending even more time helping the children to examine their conduct in a broader perspective and trying to convince them that they were being overly harsh on themselves.

On another occasion we permitted college students to use self-evaluation as a basis for determining their course grade. Once again, we attempted to identify mutually agreeable criteria. This time the results were very different; all thirty-four students gave themselves an A.

Our elementary students had taken self-evaluation more seriously than we had anticipated, but by the college level the connection between grading and self-evaluation had apparently become tenuous at best. Interestingly, some students at both levels objected vehemently to basing their grades on self-evaluation. They claimed that grading was the teacher's responsibility, whereas self-evaluation was a private matter—one that should remain private.

teachers who use such devices may be doing little more than objectively manipulating subjectively selected data.

Judgment and subjectivity are currently an integral part of summative evaluation and grading. Subjectivity can be controlled, of course, which explains much of the emphasis on performance outcomes and on establishing clear expectations for students (as well as for teachers, who are also subject to periodic evaluations). To make assessment and grading even more reliable, and thus avoid the wide discrepancies in grading from one teacher to the next, more and more schools are developing assessment rubrics. These are devices that more clearly and consistently identify the characteristics of performances that fit into existing grading categories. We consider the development of rubrics as part of the movement toward authentic assessment in the next section.

Authentic Assessment

Are American schools "test driven"?

A retired British educator of our acquaintance is fond of chiding us that American schools are "test-driven." "Everything in your schools," he claims, "is geared to testing—weekly tests, six-week tests, final examinations; and then there is standardized testing at least once or twice a year. You Americans spend so much time on testing, it's a wonder the students ever have time to learn anything."

There's no question that testing in American schools is a time-consuming business. However, there is also growing recognition that many tests fail to measure learning in important and authentic ways. The problem, as Wiggins (1989) suggests, is that many tests are standardized, but they are not *standard setting*—that is, much of the learning that tests supposedly measure is neither realistic nor is it necessarily worth striving for. Rather, much testing is a perfunctory, bureaucratic checkup designed to put marks in a gradebook instead of posing authentic, challenging tasks that are related to real-life problems and expectations (Parker, 1991).

If much of the testing in schools today is inauthentic, even trivial, it's reasonable to ask what authentic assessment, or what is sometimes called "performance assessment" (Wiggins, 1994), would look like. Most authorities suggest that students engage in periodic performances (hence the term *performance assessment)* that reflect important understandings and abilities (Spady, 1994). Parker (1991, p. 88) recommends the following as attributes of authentic assessments:

Characteristics of authentic assessment tasks

1. Tasks that go to the heart of essential learnings; i.e., they ask for exhibitions of understandings and abilities that matter.
2. Tasks that resemble interdisciplinary real-life challenges, not schoolish busywork that is artificially neat, fragmented, and easy to grade.
3. Tasks that are standard setting; they point students toward higher, richer levels of knowing.
4. Tasks that are worth striving toward and practicing for.
5. Tasks that are known to students well in advance.
6. Tasks that are few in number; hence, they are representative.
7. Tasks that strike teachers as worth the trouble.
8. Tasks that generally involve a higher-order challenge—a challenge for which students have to go beyond the routine use of previously learned information.
9. All tasks are attempted by all students.

Parker (1991) argues that authentic assessment should be incorporated in benchmarks that occur at major academic transition points, such as the end of elementary school and the end of middle or junior high school. Parker (pp. 24–25) cites the following as examples of authentic benchmark assessment activities:

At the End of Elementary School

Assessment benchmarks

* Writing/Civics/History: Students write a summary of a current public controversy drawn from school life and tell how a courageous and civic-minded person they have studied (e.g., Sojourner Truth, James Madison) might decide to act on the issue.
* Geography: Students sketch a physical map of North America from memory and locate (given coordinates) five cities.

At the End of Middle/Junior High School

* Writing/Civics/History: Students write an analysis of a current public controversy facing their community and draw a historical comparison.
* Geography: Students sketch a world landform map from memory with continents labeled and locate (given coordinates) eleven capital cities.

The movement toward more authentic assessment is increasingly working its way into schools. For example, Larry Lewin, a teacher at the Monroe Middle School in Eugene, Oregon, described how he uses performance tasks to help students in his U.S. History/English class understand the events of 1492 (O'Neil, 1996). Larry's students spend several weeks preparing for and writing a short story from the point of view of either a Spanish sailor or a Taino Indian. The story, although fictional, must reveal the student's understanding of historical events.

Preparation

The target audience for the stories that Larry's students write is fifth graders, who are also studying 1492. The students' stories are judged on how realistically they present their fictional characters, the setting, and the other events that occur. In preparation for their assignment, students in Larry's class read several selections of historical fiction to help them understand the genre. Before beginning their final story, they must also write a short expository piece on "A Sailor's Life." The point is that students are not given a performance task and then turned loose to "sink or swim"; several mini-performances serve as building blocks for their final story.

The Use of Rubrics. When Larry Lewin assesses his students' final stories, he uses a rubric similar to the one shown in Figure 11.3. A *rubric* is a device that permits teachers to rate the characteristics of students' performances at various proficiency levels (see also O'Neil, 1994). The sample rubric shown in Figure 11.3 was designed to assess students' writing ability.

Rubrics are an assessment tool

A rubric itself does not eliminate teacher bias. For example, some teachers have difficulty giving a "4" rating to students' stories that contain only one or two mechanical problems, even though the criterion states "Grammatical or mechanical errors are slight and hardly noticeable." Everyone knows that what is "hardly noticeable" to one teacher can be a major problem to another.

Rubrics can serve as diagnostic tools

The development of assessment rubrics reflects a movement to describe students' performance with more precision than is common to traditional letter grading. In addition, giving students the rubric in advance and then using it as the basis for a student-teacher conference can indicate where students are encountering problems and can serve as the basis for additional instruction. In other words, rubrics can sometimes serve as diagnostic tools, not simply grading devices.

Designing assessment rubrics can be a challenging task. Danielson (cited in ASCD, 1996) suggests the following standards:

Rubric design recommendations

1. Use a four-point scale, as shown in our sample, as opposed to a five- or six-point scale. A five-point scale corresponds more closely to the A-B-C-D-F grading system, but the larger number of points can make it more difficult for people to distinguish between the different levels.
2. Use equal distances between levels, as opposed to giant leaps.
3. Use examples of student work at each level. These provide concrete examples of performances at each level.

Proposals for more authentic assessment—and less testing—are consistent with the renewed emphases on active participation in social studies and on being certain that students can perform the tasks required of informed citizens. We

Figure 11.3 Rubric for Assessing Students' Writing

Rating 4 = Excellent Response

Organization: Well-organized paper with a clear beginning and end. Transitions are smooth and clear. Content is logically structured.

Clarity: All information is clearly explained.

Content: Information is thorough enough to provide a clear explanation.

Mechanics: Grammatical or mechanical errors are slight and hardly noticeable.

Rating 3 = Adequate Response

Organization: Paper is organized with a beginning and ending. The structure is logical, and there are no major problems in reading.

Clarity: Most of the information is clearly explained.

Content: There is sufficient information to explain the subject.

Mechanics: The grammatical and mechanical errors that may exist do not detract from the explanation.

Rating 2 = Less than Adequate Response

Organization: Paper is not organized. It may lack a clear beginning and ending. The reader has difficulty moving from one idea to another.

Clarity: Parts of the paper are difficult to understand.

Content: Information is insufficient to provide a clear explanation; some unnecessary information is included.

Mechanics: Grammatical and mechanical errors are frequent enough to create problems for the reader.

Rating 1 = Inadequate Response

Organization: Paper has very little sense of organization. It has no clear beginning and ending. The reader has major difficulties following the explanation.

Clarity: Most of the information is difficult to understand.

Content: Information does not explain the topic. Much irrelevant information is included.

Mechanics: Numerous grammatical and mechanical errors make the information difficult to understand.

believe that authentic assessment should replace much of the norm-referenced testing that goes on in schools today, and not become simply another layer that is added on to, and possibly dwarfed by, existing testing programs.

Gathering Assessment Information

The keys to gathering useful assessment information are, first, identifying the kind of information you want and, second, using an appropriate means to gather that information. The kind of information needed to evaluate social studies usually relates to (1) what children know and are able to do (cognitive domain) and (2) what children believe and how they respond to what they believe and feel (affective domain). We examine assessment in the cognitive and affective domains in the following sections.

Assessing Cognitive Knowledge and Skills

The most common technique for evaluating cognitive knowledge and skills involves a teacher's oral questions. The second most common technique involves paper-and-pencil testing. In this section we examine questions posed in test form.

Instrument is the technical name for an evaluation technique or scale. There are three major categories of instruments: (1) nationally standardized tests and scales; (2) achievement tests developed by local, regional, or state agencies; and (3) tests constructed by teachers themselves.

Standardized Tests.

Standardized achievement tests are often used as part of statewide or schoolwide testing programs. For examples of standardized test items, see the graph for population growth of two cities in this chapter (p. 275), and the Pleasure Island Activity (Figure 13.6), which assesses map skills. The key element about standardized test items is that they almost always provide information for children to work with, a principle that should also be reflected in teacher-made tests for higher-level thinking skills. Consider how you would respond if you were asked to draw a graph of the corn production in Iowa between 1987 and 1997. Drawing a graph is not too difficult, but asking you to memorize Iowa's corn production for a ten-year period would probably elicit justifiable howls of protest. The example may seem extreme, but the point is that, when testing a student's ability to process information, the necessary data should be provided.

Teacher-Made Tests.

Developing good test questions may seem easy enough, but appearances can be deceptive. For example, it is not at all difficult to write a question such as "Abraham Lincoln was born in _____," but this apparently straightforward question places an unfair burden on students, who must figureout which of a multitude of possible answers (place? month? year?) the teacher has in mind. In such cases they may not be able to demonstrate what they know about Lincoln's birth.

Validity. *Validity* refers to the extent to which test questions measure what they are intended to measure. If there is any doubt, the validity of our Lincoln question is very low.

Clarify your intent

The validity of questionable test items can often be improved by adding information that clarifies the teacher's intent. To do this, teachers must first eliminate any fuzziness (from their original objectives) about what they expect of students. Thus an objective such as "From memory, the student will identify something about Abraham Lincoln" won't do, because the word *something* is too vague. Depending on what the teacher really expects students to know, the objective could be "From memory, the student will identify the place (state) in which Lincoln was born." In this instance, a short-answer test item could then be stated as follows: "Abraham Lincoln was born in the state of _____."

Changing the form
of the question

The clarity of test questions can sometimes be improved by changing the form of the question itself. For example, instead of using a short-answer format, the sample Lincoln item could be presented as a multiple-choice or true-false question. In multiple-choice form, the question could be stated as follows:

_____ Abraham Lincoln was born in

  a. Illinois

*b. Kentucky

  c. Indiana

  d. Washington, D.C.

As a true-false item, the question could be phrased as

_____ Abraham Lincoln was born in Indiana. (F)

Both examples clearly reflect the underlying objective, which pertains to identifying the state in which Lincoln was born. At the same time, changing to a multiple-choice or true-false format can also compromise their validity somewhat because it introduces a larger "chance" (or guessing) factor than was true for the short-answer (completion) format. For true-false questions, students have a fifty-fifty chance of guessing the correct answer. This doesn't mean that you should forgo using true-false or multiple-choice test questions, but you cannot be as confident that they validly measure what you are trying to measure.

Considerations

Appropriateness. Regardless of the form in which our Lincoln test item is asked, a crucial question remains, Should students be expected to recall such information from memory? Is it a worthwhile question that everyone should be expected to answer, or does it deal with trivia?

Judging appropriateness: Is it
worth knowing?

A test question such as "List the fifty states in order of their admission to the Union" can be perfectly valid, but it (and the underlying objective it reflects) must be judged in terms of its appropriateness—by whether it tests something that is worth knowing. Unless test items (and the objectives they reflect) are reasonable, appropriate, and worth knowing, validity doesn't even enter the picture. To avoid such problems and to be certain that your evaluation is consistent with your objectives, we recommend that you identify potential test questions during planning, even if you don't plan to use testing as an evaluation technique.

A Sample Nontest

The sample test that follows illustrates some of the common problems teachers encounter in writing test questions. After each "poor" question we suggest ways in which it might be improved.

A Nontest—Colonial America Completion/Short Answer

Fill in the blanks with the correct answer.

1. *Poor:* The _____ ____ _____ were among the first people to trade with the Native Americans. (French fur traders)
Better: The first people to trade with the Native Americans in the Northwest Territory were the French _____ traders. Or: The first people to trade with the Native Americans in the Northwest Territory were fur traders from the country of _____.

   Blanks should be at the end of the sentence

   Analysis: Ordinarily only one key word or short phrase should be omitted, and ordinarily the omitted word or phrase should be near the end of the sentence, so that the student need not continually reread the sentence to figure out the subject. In addition, the blank lines where students write their responses should be of approximately equal length so as not to provide clues to the desired answer.

   Short-answer test items are often clearer if they are phrased as direct questions instead of as sentence-completion items. This is particularly true if the question contains multiple elements. Thus an alternative short-answer format for this test item is:

   What was the nationality of the first people who traded with the Native Americans in the Northwest Territory? _____

2. *Poor:* Manhattan Island was purchased on July ____, _____. (July 14, 1649)
Better: None.

   Omitting words from textbook sentences encourages nonessential memorization

   Analysis: The problem here is not the form of the question but the appropriateness of the underlying objective: of expecting children to remember the month, day, and year of the purchase. This item also resembles the kind of sentence you'd find in a social studies textbook, from which a few words were deleted to create a test item. Omitting key words from the sentences in a textbook and then using the incomplete sentences as test questions encourages memorization, not understanding.

3. *Poor:* At the first _____, the _____ brought _____ and the _____ brought _____ and other wild animals.
Better (if used at all): At the first Thanksgiving, the Pilgrims brought several kinds of food, including _____ and _____.

   Analysis: Whether students should remember who brought what to the first Thanksgiving is questionable to start with, but the original question contains so many blanks that its intent is not clear. Even in restated form, there are many correct answers, all of which should receive credit.

4. *Poor:* The colonists who attended the first Thanksgiving were called _____.
Better: None.

   Do other questions provide answers?

   Analysis: The form of this question is fine, but the answer is provided by the previous question. The validity of a test is compromised when some questions provide the answers to other questions.

True-False (Alternative Response)

Use + for true and 0 for false unless directed otherwise. (Capital T's and capital F's can look very much alike—sometimes intentionally so.)

5. *Poor:* The Puritan religion was best suited for the colonies.
   Better: None.
   Analysis: The question asks the student to make a value judgment in the absence of clearly defined criteria.

Avoid absolute terms

6. *Poor:* Native Americans never helped the Puritans.
   Better: None.
   Analysis: Absolute terms such as *none, never,* and *always* tend to be associated with false statements. Generally, such terms should be avoided in true-false questions *unless you are dealing with situations where they are appropriate*—for example, "Evaluation always requires the identification of criteria."

7. *Poor:* The first Thanksgiving was held over the winter of 1720–1721 and was attended by the Pilgrims, Native Americans, the English, and the Dutch.
   Better: The first Thanksgiving was held during the winter of 1720–1721.
   Analysis: The "poor" question is misleading because the false element, the date,

Is the intent clear?

   is subordinate to the main thrust of the question. In addition, it is not clear whether the accuracy or the completeness of the list of attendees is the concern. True-false questions should avoid statements that could be misinterpreted.
   An alternative technique for handling true-false questions that involve multiple elements is illustrated below:

   French explorers who visited North America included
   (+) 1. La Salle
   (0) 2. De Soto
   (+) 3. Champlain
   (0) 4. Hudson
   (+) 5. Cartier

Multiple-Choice Questions

Select the best answer and write the letter in the space provided.

All distractors should be plausible

8. *Poor:* _____ A red-orange root plant grown by the Indians was (a) corn, (b) yam, (c) pumpkin, (d) asparagus.
   Better: As multiple choice, none; if used at all, the question could be asked in a completion or true-false format.
   Analysis: All distractors for multiple-choice items should be plausible. In this instance, only one root plant is listed.

9. *Poor:* _____ The Puritans
   a. were not the group that founded the Massachusetts Bay colony.
   b. went to southern Georgia.
   c. didn't believe in taking a bath.
   d. left England, went to Holland, and then fled to the North American colonies of Great Britain, where they could avoid religious persecution.
   Better: _____ The Puritans settled in Massachusetts in order to
   a. establish a fur-trading company.
   b. avoid the high taxes they had been forced to pay in England.
   c. practice their religion without interference.*
   d. prevent Spain and France from claiming the area.

Analysis: Where possible, most of the statement should be presented in the intro-duction, or stem, of the question. All incorrect answers should be plausible, of the same general style, and of approximately the same length as the correct answer.

10. *Poor:* _____ The name of the minister who headed the colonial govern-ment in Rhode Island was (a) John Smith, (b) Bunker Hill.

Better: _____ The name of the minister who headed the colonial govern-ment in Rhode Island was

a. John Smith.
b. John Adams.
c. Roger Williams.*
d. Cotton Mather.

Analysis: Multiple-choice questions should have a minimum of three and preferably four or five alternative answers. The fewer the alternatives, the higher is the probability that students may guess the right answer. More im-portant, the correct alternative response must be provided (it is not provided in the "poor" form of this question). Further, alternative answers should be of the same general type—the names of people, the names of places, state-ments, and so on. Mixing different types of alternative responses or provid-ing obviously false distractors should be avoided. Also to be avoided are mul-tiple-choice questions in which the correct answer is revealed by clues in the item itself, such as "Many colonial families used a (a) axe, (b) apple peeler, (c) candle mold, (d) ox." Only item c is grammatically correct. Such questions should be reserved for grammar tests.

Did you notice that for our sample multiple-choice questions the correct answer was usually item c? Because test-wise students often look for such a pattern, the position of correct responses should be distributed randomly throughout the test.

Matching

Write the letter from Column II in the space provided in front of the correct term in Column I.

11. *Poor:*

Column I	Column II
1. _____ Patroon	a. the Native American word for corn
2. _____ Maize	b. a Dutch system for landholding along the Hudson River
3. _____ Mayflower	c. one of the middle colonies
4. _____ Delaware	d. a ship

Better: Instructions: Write the letter for the occupation described in Column II in the space provided in front of the term associated with that occupation (Column I).

Column I	Column II
1. (d) blacksmith	a. barrelmaker
2. (e) chandler	b. hatmaker
3. (a) cooper	c. wheelmaker
4. (g) deacon	d. iron worker
5. (f) teamster	e. ship's supplier
6. (c) wheelwright	f. wagon driver
	g. church official

Analysis: The items in the "poor" example are so few and so dissimilar that almost anyone could complete the exercise, even if they know nothing about "patroons." In addition, guessing is facilitated because Columns I and II have the same number of items. Guessing is minimized if one column contains more items than are required or contains responses that are used more than once.

Matching categories

A fundamental problem in developing good matching questions lies in identifying enough similar items to place in the respective columns without resorting to trivia. Some of the following examples, adapted from Gronlund (1985), could be used for matching purposes. Separate questions would ask students to match a list of people with a list of their achievements, a list of inventors with their inventions, and so forth.

Column I	*Column II*
People	Achievements
Inventors	Inventions
Dates	Historical events
Objects	Names of objects
Terms	Definitions
Places	Geographical locations
Rules	Examples
Principles	Illustrations
Machines	Uses

Whenever your tests begin to look like our "poor" examples, you've got problems. Not only will the form of your test items be questionable, but you may also be guilty of emphasizing the kind of trivia that has given social studies a bad reputation—one that in this case is justly deserved.

Evaluating Critical Thinking Skills

Fewer items are usually needed

Assessing a student's information-processing skills is not inherently more difficult than knowledge-level evaluation, but it is different. For example, assessing critical thinking typically requires fewer evaluation questions or tasks. Instead of a fifty-item test, for example, two or three skill-oriented questions are often sufficient.

Essay Tests. Essay-test items permit teachers to gain insight into how students think and process information. Students and teachers alike know that on essay tests it is nearly impossible to "fake it." At the same time, essay testing is an impossibility if students are not mature enough to express themselves effectively in writing. Because of this limitation, essay tests are not widely used in elementary schools.

Some problems associated with essay-test items are shown next.

Sample Nontest—Colonial America, Part II

Write a good essay on one of the following questions.

1. *Poor:* What crops did the early Pilgrims grow?
   Better: None.

Analysis: Essay questions should ask students to do more than simply reproduce information. In this instance, the question lends itself to a list, not an essay. A short-answer (completion) question would probably be better (e.g., "List five crops grown by the Pilgrims."), but the appropriateness of the underlying objective is still questionable.

2. *Poor:* Discuss Native Americans.
   Better: Describe, with examples, three ways in which the colonists' contact with the Native Americans benefited both groups.
   Analysis: "Discuss Native Americans" is so broad that it is difficult to know (a) where to begin and (b) what the intent of the question is. The improved question clearly conveys what the student is to do.

3. *Poor:* Tell all you know about why people should always be brave and thankful.
   Better: None.
   Analysis: The task in the "poor" question is clear enough, but establishing valid criteria for evaluating students' responses would be almost impossible. This is a common problem in attempting to evaluate students' attitudes, which is what this question seems geared toward. Of course, teachers could gain insight into their students' attitudes by asking them to respond to questions such as "Why do you think some people are thankful?" But using those responses for grading purposes would be inappropriate. Some of the observational techniques suggested later in this chapter may prove to be more valid indicators of students' attitudes than direct or written questions like the ones illustrated here.

As we noted earlier, another difference that separates thinking-skill test items from their knowledge-level cousins is their presentation of information to be interpreted, analyzed, evaluated, and so forth. In evaluating critical thinking, the key element is the student's ability to transfer a process for manipulating information from whatever data they have worked with previously to the information presented on a test.

The following are examples of what we are talking about. Note that in Example 1 the information from *The Works of James I* was rewritten at a lower reading level.

Example 1

Skill Area: Analysis and interpretation of data.

Instructions: Read the following quotations. Explain what they show about the responsibility of individuals and how they control themselves.

Sample 1

Kings are like God. If you think of what God can do, you can think of what a king can do. For example, a king can do anything with his people. He can make them a success or make them a failure. He can judge whether or not what people do is right. But no person shall judge the king. A king's people are like chess pieces and the king is like a chess player. He decides the moves. He decides what the pieces will do. The people should serve the king. No person is to change the government. The government is the king's responsibility.

(Adapted from *The Works of James I* [1603])

Contemporary technology presents opportunities for multimedia presentations by teachers and students. (© *Michael Zide*)

Sample 2
Having taken this trip for the glory of God and to help the Christian faith, we agree to work together for the Glory and the Faith.

(From *The Mayflower Compact* [1620])

Example 2

This example shows how a portion of the previous question can be tested in multiple-choice format.

Skill Area: Translation and comprehension.
_____ Which of the following statements best shows the main idea of Sample 1 (in the preceding question)?
a. People in a democracy have the right to participate in the goverment.
b. Kings rely on the people's support for everything they do.
c. The people keep a king in power.
d. Kings can do almost anything they want to.*

Example 3

Question 1. Skill area: Interpreting data.

Instructions: Use the data in the table about population growth to answer the following questions. (True-False:
Use + for true, 0 for false.)
_____ 1. City A has always been larger than City B. (0)
_____ 2. City A has grown faster than City B. (+)
_____ 3. City A was larger than City B in 1975. (+)
_____ 4. City A is likely to have more city employees than City B. (+)
_____ 5. City B is likely to have more schools than City A. (0)

Population Growth of Two Cities Between 1875 and 1975		
Date	City A	City B
1875	111	72
1900	192	220
1925	1,621	400
1950	11,006	1,890
1975	24,000	2,773

Alternative Assessment Strategies

Testing too often overshadows other equally useful assessment techniques that we deal with in this section.

"I Learned" Statements

An obvious and commonsense way to find out what students have learned is to ask them. Parents have done this for years. Unfortunately, parents often get less-than-satisfactory answers from children, who have learned that a response like "Nothin'" can avoid the additional questions that are sure to follow.

Teachers who use "I learned" statements usually have much better results. The key is to limit the focus that students must deal with. Instead of asking about an entire day or week, teachers can pose the "I learned" question after a single lesson or series of lessons. The question "What did you learn?" forces students to reflect on their experience, and it permits them to self-select the elements of the lesson they think are important.

Children can respond to "I learned" statements in either oral or written form. Teachers of younger children can summarize "I learned" responses on the board or on large chart paper, or they can simply respond to children orally. Teachers of older children may request "I learned" statements in writing or make them a part of ongoing journal-writing activities or what are sometimes called "learning logs." Consider the following example taken from a child's journal:

> Now I understand why Great-Grampa thought ice cream was so special. His ice box was not cold enough to keep the ice cream from melting, so they had to make it fresh.

No matter how teachers gather "I learned" statements, we think that asking students to pause and reflect on a lesson is clearly superior to the common alternative: "Okay, children, put away your books and get ready to go to lunch," and so on.

Limit the focus to something manageable

Portfolios

Putting your best foot forward

The work of artists, photographers, and architects cannot be judged solely by objective criteria. So when those individuals apply for new commissions, they typically take a portfolio of their previous work with them. The samples in the portfolio show the variety and quality of their work—usually their best work—as well as how that work has changed over time. Samples of their poorer work are left behind in the studio, probably chalked up to experience.

When you think about it, a fundamental purpose of teaching is to help students grow and change, socially and intellectually, over time. Grades are one way to reflect growth and change, but grades are only generalized symbols. When a student's grades improve, the area of performance where the improvement occurred is seldom apparent, even to the teacher.

Portfolios use real work, not symbols

Consider using a portfolio, as Janet Jacobsen (from our earlier example) does, that contains representative samples of the student's best work as a basis for assessment. Every student develops a portfolio, which could include projects, papers, homework, tests, assignments, or anything representative of the quality of the student's work. The overall quality of their "best work" would vary from student to student, of course. Each student must also decide which material to include in the portfolio, and be prepared to explain why it is best.

From time to time, the teacher and student (and parents) can review the portfolio together, discussing the quality of the latest work and how it may be different from earlier work. Portfolio reviews are based on tangible samples, not on abstract symbols. Instead of making vague exhortations such as "You need to work on your grades," a teacher might point to several sample assign-

Because interviews with individual students can be extremely time-consuming, some teachers conduct assessment with small groups. (© *Michael Dwyer*)

Permit specific feedback

ments and say "Sarah, you seem to have trouble with the last part of your assignments, like you're rushing to get them finished and don't care what you put down. Tell me about it." We believe that portfolio-based assessment holds more promise for long-term growth than does the grading ritual so common in schools today. Portfolios need not replace grading, but they would certainly be effective complements to it.

Interviewing and Observing

Finding out what students know or are able to do by talking with them or watching them is hardly a new idea. Even Socrates did more than just ask questions! But observing and talking with students has traditionally been a casual affair. When students were obviously having difficulty, for example, teachers just as obviously walked over and talked with them about the problem. What distinguishes interviewing and observing from their more casual cousins is their

Interviews and conferences are systematic

systematic quality. An interview is systematic, though not rigidly so, and it is conducted for a particular purpose: to find out what students know about something and how they feel about it. In other words, the interview, like testing, is an information-gathering technique. We recommend that you resist your impulse to use the interview as an opportunity to correct children's misconceptions or to teach them something.

Time demands

A major deterrent to interviewing is the amount of time it can take, as Janet Jacobsen's conferencing illustrated in the introduction to this chapter. A clear and sometimes preferable alternative to individual interviews is group interviews. Group sessions permit several students to share the teacher's attention. Suggested interview procedures include the following:

Recommended procedures

* Identify sets of similar questions on whatever it is you want to find out so that you don't always ask exactly the same questions.

* Keep your facial expression as "interested" but as unevaluative as possible.

* Do not be put off by an immediate response such as "I don't know." Often it's just the way children gain time while they think about something. Give them time to think; then probe.

Assessing Attitudes and Values

Special strategies are usually not needed

To assess students' cognitive skills, they must do something to demonstrate their ability. This could involve taking a test, participating in an interview, or otherwise proving what they can do. Students' attitudes and values, on the other hand, are typically expressed in the course of their day-to-day activities. Simply by observing students' activities over time, it is possible to infer what their attitudes and values are. This means that setting aside a special time for assessing attitudes and values is usually not required. Evaluators need to know what they are looking for, but attitudinal evaluation usually doesn't require any special behavior on the student's part. In many instances, students' behaviors may more accurately reflect their underlying beliefs and values if students don't know they are being observed; that way they're less likely to behave in ways they think

COMMENTARY: Halos—Negative and Positive

As my wife and I (Welton) were selecting a name for our first child, I suggested Michael. My wife, a former teacher, responded with an immediate "No." Inexperienced as I was, I soon discovered that name choosing is not an entirely rational process.

"What's wrong with Michael?" I asked.

"Well (emphatically), when I was teaching fourth grade, I had a student whose name was Michael. He picked his nose, smelled of garlic, and always needed a bath. There's no way that we're going to name our son Michael!"

It goes without saying that none of our three sons is named Michael. We mention this incident because it illustrates the *halo effect,* a common phenomenon that can influence a teacher's observation of students. Just as my wife's feeling about the name Michael was biased by her former student, it's not unusual for teachers to generalize from a few behaviors to all of a student's actions. In other words, a teacher may base a uniformly negative or positive (but not both) opinion of a student on just a few behaviors. That opinion can extend to almost everything the student does, which is why those with positive halos can sometimes get away with almost anything—the proverbial "teacher's pet"—whereas children with negative halos may be always suspect, even when they are completely innocent.

are expected of them. The point is that observation is an excellent technique for gathering information on students' (or anyone's) attitudes and values.

A major difficulty in assessing students' attitudes and values lies in identifying precise behavioral indicators for tolerance, respect, or whatever attitudes and values you want to focus on. It is equally difficult to identify attitudinal indicators that do not tread on people's personal liberties. For example, as long as someone's behavior doesn't interfere with another person's rights, the individual has the right to believe whatever he or she wants to believe and to like or dislike whatever (or whomever) he or she chooses.

No precise behavioral indicators

The difficulties involved in identifying and stating precise behavioral indicators for an attitude or value, combined with an unwillingness to infringe on personal liberties, may explain why attitudes and values are usually expressed as goals (instead of as behavioral objectives). This lack of precision may also account for the absence of formal instruments to measure the development of attitudes and values. Despite this limitation, when attitudinal measures are used in conjunction with other techniques, they can provide information and a point of departure that would otherwise be denied the teacher. In the following sections we examine several techniques for assessing attitudes and values.

Attitude Scales

Conventional tests usually have correct answers; attitude scales do not. An *attitude scale* is composed of a set of questions or statements, such as "Students should willingly share ideas and materials with others" or "I think cats are smarter than dogs," to which individuals are then asked to respond in terms of their beliefs or preferences. Because those beliefs are personal, even if not always "politically correct," there are no previously established "right" answers on most attitude scales.

Attitude scales usually include several items that pertain to a particular attitude or belief. The individual responds to the items using a scale such as "Strongly Agree," "Agree," "Undecided," "Disagree," and "Strongly Disagree." By analyzing the pattern of responses, it becomes possible to infer the individual's attitude or belief toward the topic in question. The key decision in dealing with attitude scales occurs before you administer one, namely, deciding what you intend to do with the information once you've gathered it.

How will you use the information and for what purposes?

Questionnaires and Inventories

Questionnaires often deal with a wide range of topics, whereas interest inventories are usually restricted to what an individual likes or dislikes. Questions like "What do you like to do in your spare time?" or the familiar "What subjects do you like best (or least) in school?" are typical.

Open-ended questions

Questionnaires and inventories are easy to develop. You simply identify open-ended questions to which the respondent supplies a response. In interview settings, the students' responses are oral. Regardless of how you administer the questionnaire or interest inventory, you once again need to determine what you intend to do with the information after you've obtained it. Determining what your students do in their spare time, for example, can provide insight into your students and the activities they pursue. But only you can decide whether such information will affect the kind of teaching you provide, and whether collecting it is worth the time it takes.

Checklists and Rating Scales

A checklist consists of a series of descriptive statements, such as "Works willingly with others" or "Participates in class discussions," next to which the evaluator makes a check mark when an item is observed. There is no restriction on who should use a checklist; it could be the teacher, other students, or, as in self-evaluation, individual students themselves.

Rating scales require qualitative judgments

Checklists and rating scales often have similar formats. The difference between them usually lies in the kind of marking system employed. On a checklist, the evaluator marks a category, as illustrated on the sample rating scale/checklist shown in Figure 11.4. On rating scales, evaluators usually use a qualitative rating to judge or rate the individual's characteristics or performance.

Remember that what observers report may be colored by their perceptions. Remember also that students' responses may reflect what they think you want to hear, not what they really feel about a topic or issue. And, finally, remember that your evaluation of a shy child's lack of participation in class discussion, as might be identified by the instrument shown in Figure 11.4, may be based on elements that are far removed from the evaluation itself. Observation checklists and rating scales may show that certain children do not participate regularly in class discussions, but they will not identify the cause of that behavior. We are also suggesting that assessing students' attitudes and values, or even their class participation, can be more involved than it appears.

FIGURE 11.4 Sample Rating Scale/Checklist for Class Participation

	Rating		Always	Usually	Seldom
		Checklist Criteria			
Participates willingly/regularly					
Provides relevant ideas					
Respects rights/opinions of others					
Identifies or clarifies problems or questions					

For rating scale, use Outstanding = 4, Above Average = 3, Satisfactory = 2, and

Needs Improvement = 1.

Summary

Teachers have long used evaluation as more than just a basis for grading. However, grading is such a powerful phenomenon it can overshadow everything else. Most teachers know that *evaluation* and *testing* are not synonymous with *grading*, but they don't always act that way. Quite unintentionally, they may find themselves stressing "a very important test on Friday," thereby perpetuating the evaluation-grading mystique.

Assessment, like planning, is an ongoing process. Just as teachers' goals and objectives help to identify *what* they are attempting to do, assessment and evaluation helps them identify *how well* they (and their students) are actually doing it. Testing sometimes becomes a confounding variable, even though simply an information-gathering process, nothing more. Testing, like observations, interviews, checklists, portfolios, attitude scales, interest inventories, and rating scales, is a way of gathering information.

The assessment process consists of (1) identifying (or accepting) assessment criteria, the standards against which evaluative judgments are made; (2) measuring an individual's performance, behavior, or products in relation to those standards; and (3) making judgments about the individual's performance. The form that eval-uation takes is largely determined by the teacher's purpose. If you wish to assess whether a student can demonstrate a certain skill or knowledge, you will undoubtedly turn to *criterion-referenced assessment*. However, if you wish to compare your students' performance with that of another group, you will turn to *norm-referenced evaluation*. In instances when you are interested in determining how things are going during an instructional episode, you may turn to *formative evaluation*. If you are interested in determining the overall quality of a student's performance or product at the end of an instructional period, you will turn to *summative evaluation*. Finally, if your purpose is to figure out how well you are doing, you will undoubtedly turn to *self-evaluation*.

The growing interest in using portfolios for assessment purposes is, we think, a reflection of the broader move toward authentic assessment. Although much of the evaluation in schools today pertains to the knowledge and skills required to get through school it may have little bearing on what it takes to be successful in life beyond schools. Authentic assessment does that; it seeks to assess performance through worthwhile and realistic activities that students will encounter in real life.

Suggested Activities

1. Obtain a copy of one of the standardized tests that deals with elementary social studies (your psychology department should have copies if your education department doesn't). First, take the test so that your attention is not distracted by the content of the questions. Then analyze the items in terms of the skills they are really testing.

2. Assume that the students in your fifth-grade class need help in developing the following skills: (a) classification, (b) inductive reasoning, (c) question posing, and (d) hypothesis development. Using social studies content, develop at least two activities designed to promote skill development in each of those areas. Then, using the same activity format but substituting data different from the data used in the learning activities, develop a way to evaluate student performance in those skill areas.

3. It has been argued that creativity, evaluation, and grading are incompatible, that you can't have one as long as you have any of the others. What do you think? Is it possible to reconcile creativity, evaluation, and grading?

Suggested Readings

If you are interested in pursuing topics related to evaluation or test construction, any of the following books or the journal articles should serve that purpose.

Educational Leadership. (1989, April). A special issue on assessment.

D. Adams & M. Hamm. (1992). Portfolio assessment and social studies: Collecting, selecting, and reflecting on what is significant. *Social Education, 56,* 103–105.

Norman E. Gronlund. (1985). *Measurement and evaluation in teaching* (5th ed.). New York: Macmillan.

Grant Wiggins. (1990). A true test: Toward more equitable assessment. *Phi Delta Kappan, 70,* 703–713.

12 Nurturing Critical and Reflective Thinking

Key Questions

* How does one teach students to process information critically and reflectively?
* What kinds of materials and activities do teachers use to teach reflective thinking?
* What is decision making, and how does it relate to reflective thinking?
* How do teachers decide which questions to ask, and when to ask them?

Key Ideas

* Critical and reflective thinking skills are part of an interactive system of mental activities that we use to interpret and assess different kinds of information and experience.
* Teachers and students can model their thinking processes by talking out loud with each other.
* Metacognition involves thinking about one's thinking processes.
* Underlying every question that teachers ask is a purpose for asking it. These purposes may be as varied as the questions.

Introduction: Reading Between the Lines

Going beyond the printed word

"Reading between the lines" sounds innocent enough, but explaining it to young children can be challenging. Part of the problem is that even beginning readers know that the spaces between the lines on a page are blank. The situation is complicated further because "reading between the lines" is a figurative expression, like "it's raining cats and dogs." Even children who realize that you are speaking figuratively may still have no idea what you are talking about. Of course, you could explain that "reading between the lines" involves taking two or more pieces of information and then relating them in some way to produce a third idea that goes beyond the original information, but don't be surprised if your children still look puzzled.

Despite the complexity of its definition, "reading between the lines" is not that difficult to do, especially if the children have some previous experiences with it. But for children who lack those experiences, "reading between the lines" is likely to be an abstraction, even if you define it for them. Instead of beginning with questions like "What is the author really saying?" or "What does the author really mean?", we recommend that you begin by saying something like "Let's see if we can figure out what this author is really saying," and then systematically modeling (demonstrating) your thinking processes for the children. In other words, questioning alone does not teach children the process, since most questioning strategies are primarily a test of their existing ability. In addition, most authorities (see Beyer, 1987) agree that reading between the lines and most other reflective thinking skills are best taught through modeling and by providing guided practice, not by questioning.

Modeling is the key

Our premise throughout this chapter is that experience should precede analysis. This premise reflects a constructivist approach to learning wherein children (and adults) construct meaning by acting on and analyzing their earlier experiences. For example, we suspect that few people know that a *quark* is the product of a collision between two electrons. You could memorize this definition, of course, but even then it is doubtful that quarks would be meaningful unless you (and we) had more experiences with physics, the properties of electrons, the reasons they collide, and what happens when they do. In more practical terms, we are suggesting that "reading between the lines" and other reflective thinking skills are best taught by (1) modeling the desired behaviors, including talking out loud as you think through the problem, (2) accompanying the modeling with clear explanations, (3) working with students as they practice the skills on related information, and then (4) talking (reflecting) with students about these experiences.

Experience precedes analysis

This chapter is also designed to address three goals. The first is to help you identify the thinking skills that students should develop, including metacognition, or thinking about thinking. Second, we want to illustrate how reflective thinking skills are part of a family of interrelated skills, and third, we will present some exemplary teaching activities that can help students process information efficiently and effectively.

Metacognition: Thinking About Thinking

Helping students become proficient thinkers and decision makers involves providing them with opportunities to process various kinds of information and experience. However, teaching students how to think critically will not necessarily make them self-directed, independent thinkers. The information-processing skills that we deal with in this chapter will certainly provide the basis for independent, self-directed thinking and decision making, but actually helping students to consciously direct their thinking requires going a step further.

Helping students become conscious of what thinking involves

The goal is to help students reach the highest and most sophisticated level of thinking—consciously controlling and directing their own thinking. This means that individuals must think about *how* they are thinking while they think. For example, when you are considering a problem and you say to yourself something like, "I really ought to consider some alternative solutions," you are monitoring or exercising control over how you are thinking. Doing this—thinking about how one is thinking—is called *metacognition*.

Most authorities (Beyer, 1987; Costa, 1984; Bonny, 1984) agree that metacognition develops slowly, apparently paralleling students' ability to think abstractly. Although Beyer suggests that "it is doubtful that most older students will engage in metacognition by the time they leave school" (p. 195), there are still things teachers can do to foster readiness for metacognition. These include maintaining a learning environment where thinking (as opposed to memorization and rote learning) is encouraged and valued. Also important, we think, is directing explicit attention to the components of thinking and problem solving as you model and use them with children. For example, asking "Does it look like we are getting anywhere?" or saying "Let's think about some other possibilities" can stimulate students' awareness of metacognitive behavior.

A thinking environment

Other activities to stimulate readiness for metacognition, cited by Beyer (1985, pp. 196–197), include the following:

Activities to stimulate metacognition

1. *Conscious choosing.* Whenever students have an opportunity to make a choice—determining what to do next in class or what to do for recess, and so on—have them identify at least two options and then identify some possible consequences of each option. By reflecting aloud on the consequences, students can articulate criteria for making the choice and extend their thinking beyond the here and now to the anticipation of future events or ideas.

2. *Categorizing with multiple criteria.* Whenever students have an opportunity to discuss their actions or choices, have them make at least two categories, such as useful/not useful or like/not like or fun/not fun, and so on. Like the preceding activity, this activity extends student thinking and requires thinking about another thinking act.

3. *Paraphrasing what is heard.* Have students restate, put in their own words, or elaborate one another's plans and actions as they engage in them or observe their peers engaging in them. This may take the form of having students state goals, suggest ways to accomplish them, and try to outline exactly what would have to be done to carry out their "plan." They can also restate or paraphrase directions, or rate and discuss their own understanding of something. [Authors' note: This activity and those that follow can be done orally, but they are also excellent topics for students to include in their journals.]

4. *Reflecting on how an answer was derived.* Have the students, on occasion, stop in the middle of a thinking task to discuss whether they are doing it correctly, exactly where they are in the process, whether they skipped anything and/or what to do next (and why) once they resume the process. Students can also predict the results of a thinking task and, when finished with it, reflect on and discuss the extent to which their prediction was accurate, whether or not anything occurred to alter it, and so on.

5. *Engaging in "I think" activities.* After or before engaging in a thinking task, students can write a short paragraph describing how they were thinking

about it. At first, such writing may be a disjointed stream of consciousness, but students can focus eventually on reporting how and why they did or planned to do a task in a specific way.

6. *Making plans.* Students can plan classroom activities and assignments in terms of goals, sequence of activities, and anticipated obstacles; list the plan on the board; and refer to it as they execute it. Upon concluding the activity or assignment, they can evaluate their plan as well as the success of their activity.

To Beyer's list we are inclined to add a seventh element: "Limitation: Despite everything that we think we know, we also recognize that there are things we need to know more about, and that we might also be wrong somewhere along the way."

Modeling attitudes of reflective thinking

Modeling the desired behaviors is the key to teaching readiness for metacognition or any critical thinking skill. Among those behaviors are the beliefs and attitudes that help to create the environment within which any kind of thinking takes place. For example, teachers who try to provide positive reenforcement by always responding to correct answers with an immediate "That's right! Great answer!" may unwittingly be creating an environment that actually undermines reflective thinking. A simple "Thank you, let's think about that" could still provide the desired reinforcement, but without the negative side effect. The point is that attitudes and dispositions such as the willingness to suspend judgment, to consider alternative solutions or points of view, and to revise one's opinions in light of new evidence are as essential to teaching rational thinking and decision making as are the thinking skills themselves.

Teaching Reflective Thinking

When confronted with a genuine problem, most of us follow some variation of the inquiry/problem-solving process that we described in Chapter 9. Briefly, we identify and clarify the problem, identify and gather the necessary data, identify possible solutions (hypotheses), evaluate the alternative solutions to decide which one best fits the situation, and then act appropriately. During that process, we may employ one or more of the following skills:

Information-processing skills

1. describing
2. estimating
3. classifying/categorizing
4. evaluating (judging)
5. interpreting
6. inferring
7. deducing
8. hypothesizing (predicting)
9. analyzing
10. experimenting
11. planning and designing
12. generalizing

The preceding list of thinking skills may seem imposing, but all of them can be taught in some form to elementary and middle-school children. It is not unusual to find children who lack the vocabulary or prior experiences to handle complex forms of analysis, synthesis, or evaluation, yet most children can indicate, for example, if something in a story "fits" or if "something seems wrong." The key often lies in how you present the task to them, and more specifically, in the language you use.

Using language that fits children

Skills that involve measuring, observing, and describing seldom pose unusual problems for students, but you will probably need to translate other skills into simpler language. Your exact translation will depend on the kind of data or experiences you're using, of course, but some examples of what we mean are illustrated in Table 12.1.

Table 12.1 Translating Tasks into Children's Language

Task	Adult's Language	Child's Language
Classifying	Classify these into two categories.	Let's see if some of these go together.
	Can you classify these in different ways?	Can we group these together in different ways?
Hypothesizing and inferring	Develop two hypotheses that might explain this.	How can we explain this? Let's look for some other reasons why this happens.
	Given data, develop three hypotheses.	What is _____ really like?
Analyzing	Given two sources of data, identify possible contradictions.	Let's see if we can find anything "wrong" or unusual (about these data). Is there anything here that doesn't seem to "fit" right?
	Identify relevant or irrelevant information.	Is there information here that we don't need? Which information is most helpful?
Inductive reasoning	Given two or more data sources, develop an inductive generalization.	Let's find an idea that "fits" all these examples.
Deductive reasoning	Given an idea, can you test its validity?	Given this idea, let's think of other examples that it applies to, or examples where it does not apply.
Evaluating	Identify criteria to support your judgment.	Let's figure out why we think one criterion is better than another.

COMMENTARY: What We Know About Thinking

Some of the research on thinking suggests the following:

* Students' performance in classrooms is often more dependent on the strategies they use to get and use information than on IQ.

* Novice thinkers often try to memorize and recall isolated bits of information, whereas more proficient thinkers tend tend to look for larger patterns and relationships within the information.

* Learning thinking skills often involves repetition and practice as well as reworking, organizing, and elaborating on the information.

* Thinking involves intuitive, inductive, inferential, and sometimes even illogical components.

* A key element of thinking involves learning how to apply and use what is known.

The balance of this section is organized to reflect the holistic ways in which we use thinking skills—that is, in relation to the inquiry (problem-solving) process. For example, before students "do" anything with information, they must sense the existence of a problem; they must have something to inquire about. Thus we first examine how we can help students identify problems. We then consider techniques for helping students identify hypotheses and make inferences, for helping students gather information and then do something with it, and, finally, for helping students to generalize beyond their immediate experience.

Identifying Problems

Fact: When the story of Hansel and Gretel is told in some parts of Africa, the witch's house is made of salt, not candy.

Dissonance—when things don't fit

When American children hear about how the tale of Hansel and Gretel is told in Africa, they may sense that somebody has been messing around with a story they know well. For some children at least, the change in the witch's house from candy to salt can be a *discrepant event* that leads to cognitive dissonance—that is, something that doesn't "fit" the world as they've come to know it.

Sensing that a problem exists is the first stage of problem solving. If children choose not to pursue the matter, the process can end there—with an awareness of a possible problem. The turning point comes when a child is sufficiently concerned to say something such as "I wonder why they changed the story of Hansel and Gretel." At that point, the child's awareness of a possible problem is converted into a *real* problem for which they want an answer.

If you are sufficiently interested in why some people in Africa use a different version of "Hansel and Gretel," you've probably moved to the next step of problem solving: speculating (hypothesizing) on possible reasons for an action. Lest we get ahead of ourselves here, consider that among some groups in Africa, wealth is measured by the number of cattle or wives or the amount of salt one has (or some combination thereof).

To reach the hypothesizing stage, you may need to provide activities in which you intentionally create cognitive dissonance among your students, thus providing them with motives for further inquiry. Unfortunately, it is often difficult to translate traditional social studies content into problems that really engage students. Traditional requests such as "Identify the capitals of the Middle Atlantic states" or "Trace the sequence of Roman emperors" are usually teachers' problems that may or may not become the students' problems.

Techniques for
creating dissonance

Even within a fixed curriculum, teachers can use some techniques to enhance their students' involvement and create the feeling that they are dealing with *their* problems. These techniques include (1) creating mystery-type situations, where students must work with unknown elements, (2) providing incomplete (limited) information at the outset of an activity, from which students try to "fill in the holes," and (3) using speculative-heuristic questions, such as "What if you were the fire chief?" or "What if you were a member of the Indian Parliament and were facing a request to . . . ?"

Limiting the
information available

Creating mystery-type situations that evoke a sense of "problem" often involves limiting the amount of information available to students *at the beginning of an activity*. This limitation on information holds for all statistical data, regardless of what kind of situation you are trying to establish. Most children can deal with only limited amounts of statistical data at one time—seven to ten pieces or less—whereas a page or even a half-page filled with statistics can easily overwhelm them (and most adults). The limitation on information is intended to prevent information overload at the outset of a lesson, but once an activity is under way, students should obviously have access to as much information as they want or need.

Adding mystery elements

The following Model Student Activity is based on a teaching device called a *fact sheet*. A fact sheet is a sheet you provide to students that contains a few selected but uninterpreted facts. To enhance the children's interests, we've elected to add some mystery elements by concealing the name of the real country and identifying it only as "Nation X." If we were to provide the name of Nation X, which we eventually will of course, it would eliminate all traces of mystery from the problem, and students would simply rely on their prior knowledge about it. In this activity, students must use the uninterpreted facts to make inferences that describe Nation X. A minor problem here is keeping students' attention focused on *describing* Nation X, because they will want to guess which real nation Nation X is. Permitting students to make activities like this one into guessing games will restrict their usefulness.

Data Suitable for Fact Sheets. Not all "facts" are suitable for fact sheets. On one occasion, for example, some teachers modified the "Nation X" format to apply to states. Their "State X" fact sheets included data such as the state bird, the state tree, the state motto (in Latin), a picture of the state flag, the date of the state's admission to the Union, and sometimes the state insect. This kind of information was so unique and so tied to the individual states that little could be said about it. To be told that the state bird of X is the cardinal or that the state tree is the buckeye tells you that the state has birds and trees, but then all states have birds and trees. The point is that the data on a fact sheet should permit comparisons but should not reflect unique, one-of-a-kind information.

Must use generalizable data

Fact sheets are devices for presenting information that the children then use, and we emphasize *use*—in this case to make inferences about Nation X.

MODEL STUDENT ACTIVITY

Nation X—Using a Fact Sheet

Overview

Using the following data, students are asked to describe Nation X. Like most inferences, these may be modified with additional information. How this activity ends depends on how far you wish to take it. We would follow up with culture cards (see following chapter text) that permit students to validate their inferences and provide additional information.

Procedure

1. Establishing set: "Today we are going to use just a few facts to describe a real nation. Some of our descriptions may be correct and some may be wrong; we'll know that after we get more information. So, let's see what we can tell about Nation X."

2. Distribute Fact Sheet 1 and pose the following task: "Using just this information, let's describe what Nation X is like. What can we tell about the people who live there?"

Fact Sheet 1

	U.S.A.	Nation X
Doctors and nurses (per 2,000 people)	15	1
Literacy (people over 15)		
Males (per 100 people)	92	55
Females (per 100 people)	92	28
Radios per 1,000 inhabitants	750	2
People living in cities (per 100 people)	66	18
Rooms in each dwelling (average number)	5	2

3. List inferences (in terms of key descriptors) on the board or overhead, or have small groups list their inferences on chart paper.

4. Summarize inferences, pointing out those that may be contradictory. For example, the data on doctors could suggest either that Nation X has poor health conditions or that Nation X needs only a few doctors.

5. You may wish to raise some questions such as, How is literacy defined? How big must a city be to be considered a city? Is it fair to say that Nation X is poor?

6. Present the class with the information in Fact Sheet 2 (on an overhead projector).

Fact Sheet 2

Life Expectancy for Males (in years)

USA 72
X 57

Source: Copyright 1990 PC Globe, Inc. Used by permission.

Consider whether this information confirms any hypotheses about health care or the way of life in Nation X.

7. After assessing whether the inferences follow from the data, ask students what other information they think they might want. (Be prepared for a long list.)

8. Present the following information (on an overhead transparency).

Fact Sheet 3

Nation	Population (1995 est.)	Percentage of World Population
China	1,175 million	21
Nation X	931 million	15
United States	260 million	7
Russia	148 million	6
Japan	131 million	3

Some students will use the information from Fact Sheet 3 to guess the identity of Nation X. Or they can check population figures in the atlases found at the back of most social studies texts. In any event, trying to maintain the mystery much longer could prove frustrating, so you can tell the class that Nation X is India. (Knowing that, you can now assess your *own* inferences.)

9. At this point you have the option of pursuing the India study in one of several ways. You might wish to do two things simultaneously: (a) have students use their inferences as research questions to be answered, using whatever resources or references they can garner, and (b) pursue an inference that children often make about Nation X, namely, that it is poor. If they don't infer this, you can always build a case for it. Among reasons that will be suggested for India's poverty are its health and population problems.

10. You can pursue the poverty issue by raising questions such as: If most of the people in a country are poor, what does being poor mean? Is being poor an average condition? If so, would the average Indian be likely to define himself or herself as poor? The following information can then be presented to the class (again, using an overhead transparency may be easiest).

Fact Sheet 4

In many rural villages in India, the poorest families are those in which there are no children.

What does this statement suggest about the Indian value structure?

11. Closure: Using the original list of inferences, determine those about which students are fairly confident and those for which they need more information.

12. Follow up in future lessons with textbook-based passages or culture cards.

Source: Adapted from John T. Mallan and Richard Hersh. *NO G.O.D.s in the Classroom: Inquiry and Elementary Social Studies.* Philadelphia: W. B. Saunders, 1972.

Must focus on using data

The purpose of the fact sheet is *not* to present factual information for children to memorize. Expecting students to understand that India has health care problems is one thing, but we think that expecting them to remember that India has one doctor or nurse for every two thousand people violates the appropriateness criterion we talked about earlier.

You will be pleasantly surprised

Don't let your prior experiences with statistical information stand in the way of trying the fact sheet approach. Students often respond very positively to fact sheets. This is not a sales pitch for fact sheets; we're simply suggesting that you not rule them out until you've tried them.

Culture Cards

The thought of cutting the pictures from a *National Geographic* is more than some people can bear. As a result, many teachers leave one of their most potent instructional resources sitting on the classroom shelf. Since almost every school library has a complete set of *National Geographic* that can be used for reference purposes, there's little reason not to use your copies for teaching purposes.

What you are after in magazines such as *National Geographic* and *Smithsonian* are their spectacular photographs. If you have access to the necessary technology, equally good photographs can be downloaded from the Internet. Whatever source you use, uncaptioned photographs can provide the basis for remarkably involving information-processing activities.

Data-Based Computer Software

It once took hours in the library to locate the data for fact sheets. Today, that information is often just a couple of keystrokes away. Most schools already have computer database programs, like *PC-USA* or *USAtlas* for the United States, and *PC Globe* or *WorldAtlas* for countries outside the United States. Some schools also have one or more editions of *Encarta World Atlases* that contain similar information. If you are interested in developing fact sheets, these resources contain more information than you will ever want or need.

Fact Sheet 2 in the "Nation X" activity was produced by our *PC Globe* program. We merely directed the program to print a graph of the life expectancy data for India and the United States. Creating additional graphs for other countries is simply a matter of telling the program which nations you want to include. Had we wanted maps of the nations on our fact sheet, the programs noted above would print them too. The growing availability of computerized databases, means that locating information for reflective thinking lessons is no longer the time-consuming task it once was.

Captionless photographs can be used with students of any age or grade level, early childhood through graduate school (and not just with students who have reading problems). You could create an alternate activity by mounting the captions on a separate "caption card" and having students match the captions with the appropriate photos.

When pictures or photographs of a particular culture are clustered together, you have what we call *culture cards*. If you organize the photographs on some other basis, such as similar occupations or similar types of homes, you could just as well call them *picture cards*.

Techniques for Using Picture and Culture Cards

1. Prior to studying a culture or area, provide the class with a set of uncaptioned pictures of the people (Inuit, the Japanese, etc.) or the region (the Ukraine, Switzerland, etc.). Using just the pictures, ask students to describe the people or region as best they can. The object is not to guess who the people are or what the region is. You can reduce students' tendency to do that by simply telling the class, "Here are some pictures of "X" that we want to describe as best we can. How do the people live? What kind of area do they live in?"

   Some descriptions (and inferences) that the students provide will be inaccurate because they are working with limited information. Inaccurate descriptions will be corrected as the students move into other materials—the texts, videos, and databases—that describe the culture or region. The students' inferences and descriptions should be treated as hypotheses to be tested as they obtain additional information.

2. After studying a culture, provide students with a set of uncaptioned cards intermingling photographs from two or three cultures. The students' task is

to separate the pictures of the culture just studied from pictures of other cultures.

3. Provide students with a set of randomly assorted culture cards, and ask them to group the cards according to (a) criteria that you supply (family activities, seasons, etc.) or to (b) criteria of their choosing. This type of classifying activity is an integral part of concept building.

4. As a small-group activity, students can write their own captions for the pictures. They can then compare their captions with the original captions (which are mounted on a separate "caption card").

Determining Researchable Problems

Help students determine a problem's researchability

During most social studies activities, students will generate some questions that no amount of research can ever answer. In the previous Model Student Activity, for example, an inference that India is poor because the people are lazy will undoubtedly lead to frustration and discontent should your students attempt to research it. It's simply not a researchable question as long as *poor* and *lazy* are left undefined. The teaching implication in such cases should be evident: you will need to help children examine the researchability of possible problems. To do otherwise could send them on a wild-goose chase.

Some of the following statements and problems are based on Model Student Activities we've considered thus far. Others are not. Decide which of the following statements, as presented here, lend themselves to further student research or study:

Yes/No   *Problems/Statements*

_____ 1. Identify the constitutional requirements for the office of president of the United States.

_____ 2. Ronald Reagan and Franklin D. Roosevelt were two of the best presidents the United States ever had.

_____ 3. The Dutch are an industrious and friendly people.

_____ 4. The introduction of new technology into a culture is likely to lead to other changes.

_____ 5. American farmers today produce more food on larger, more specialized farms than did farmers ten or twenty years ago.

_____ 6. Yuppies are more patriotic than retired people.

_____ 7. Most students in *this* class like Italian food.

Vague terminology poses problems

Remember Mrs. Fleury's class from the "Wearin' of the Green" activity, where the students discovered they had to decide how much green clothing someone had to wear to be considered "wearing green"? Somewhat the same problem influences the researchability of the problems listed here. Researchable problems (hypotheses, inferences, and questions) cannot use vague terms, yet they must be specific enough that one need not spend a lifetime in the quest. As such, Statements 1, 4, 5, and 7 are researchable, but Statements 2, 3, and 6 need to be specified more precisely before students can deal with them. For Statement 3, for example, it might be possible to define *industrious* and *friendly,* but how do you define *the Dutch?* Are the Dutch only those people who live in the Netherlands? Or do they include all people of Dutch descent?

Hypothesizing and Inferring

Based on the "Help Wanted" cartoon shown in Figure 12.1, which of the following might you reasonably infer?

Yes/No

———— 1. Business seems to be good.
———— 2. The cartoon depicts a scene in the United States.
———— 3. The employer has a bias against women.
———— 4. Women are not good workers.
———— 5. The sign reflects a basic societal belief that a woman's place is in the home.
———— 6. The cartoon depicts a scene that might take place today.

It's reasonable to infer that business is good; otherwise there would not be a "Help Wanted" sign. On the other hand, perhaps working conditions in the plant are so bad that employees quit after only a few days. If that were true, the management would continually need additional help just to maintain normal operations. But then perhaps all of the current employees are now women, and they want males so as to satisfy a quota. All of these are plausible inferences.

From inferences to hypotheses

If you have no intention of testing which of these inferences is valid, your inference would remain just that—a plausible inference. But when you set out to test whether business is good, at least as depicted in the cartoon, your inference then functions as a hypothesis. That is, your inference is a testable proposition:

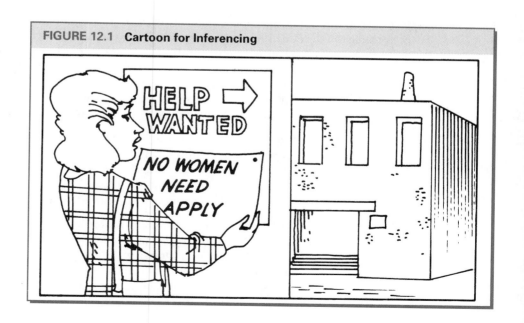

FIGURE 12.1 Cartoon for Inferencing

the reason the plant displays a "Help Wanted" sign is that business is good and the company therefore needs additional employees. To test your hypothesis, you clearly would need more data about the events depicted in the cartoon.

All of us make inferences as we attempt to explain and understand events around us. Because we infer and hypothesize anyway, why then should there be such concern for formal hypothesis testing? The answer is that what we do in informal situations has application in many more formal situations and with many kinds of data sources. In informal situations we might be satisfied using impressionistic data—a hunch, a whim, or a feeling—but formal hypothesis testing requires that all elements of the process be *public*. In other words, in face-to-face relations, we can use whatever information we wish, but in more formal data-validating situations, we are expected to follow the rules of science—hence our distinction between inferences and hypotheses.

Formal hypotheses testing is public

Knowns and Unknowns. When something is known, there's not much left to hypothesize about. A statement such as "Milk comes from cows," for example, isn't likely to lead to any speculation. But if you ask, "Where does milk come from?" you can get some interesting hypotheses:

* From trucks
* From dairies
* From the supermarket

The accuracy of these responses is clearly testable, but you must also assess whether students will gain enough from testing them to make the effort worthwhile. We can test the accuracy of knowns, but we must hypothesize about things that are unknown or that can be explained only in part.

Physical objects can often serve as excellent vehicles for hypothesizing activities, especially when the object and its uses are unknown to students. A colonial bootjack—a forked board used to help remove one's boots—or even a butter churn can lead to creative hypothesizing activities.

Using physical objects for hypothesizing

Coins, stamps, buttons—almost any physical object—can provide the basis for hypothesizing and inferring activities. For coins, for example, the student's task can be stated as follows: "Given a half-dollar, a quarter, a dime, a nickel, and a penny, what do you know about the people who made them, the world they live in, and what things they seem to value?"

"Buildings seem to be important, as well as eagles."
"Except for one, all the coins have a man on them."
"They have a letter and number system."
"They have a god in whom they trust."
"They have a language we don't understand, *E Pluribus Unum*."

In summary, hypothesizing and inferring activities require something that is unknown to students, because otherwise there may be nothing for children to explain. To help children hypothesize and infer, teachers can provide them with unexplained events—unknowns that, through inferring, hypothesizing, and hypothesis testing, can become knowns.

Gathering and Interpreting Data

Before anyone bothers to gather and process data, it's only common sense to have previously identified a purpose for that information. Gathering data is something we do in response to a problem, although in school settings the problems are often imposed on us.

Because students and teachers may perceive data gathering differently, teachers need to ask themselves two questions: What's my motive (as a teacher) for having students study this? and What are my students' motives for dealing with this information? Motivation, then, is a process of identifying the best possible match between your motives as a teacher and the motives of your students.

Conditions for data gathering

Successful data gathering depends on three interacting elements: (1) a precisely stated problem, (2) an awareness of the specific information needed, and (3) the ability to deal with data that are presented in different forms (narratives, charts, graphs, etc.). The most important of these, we think, is stating the problem precisely. This was driven home to us on one occasion when we made our sixth-grade students "ambassadors" and had each of them do a written report on a foreign nation. At the time, we failed to consider that a precisely stated problem provides the criteria for determining what information should be included—*and excluded*. Without those criteria, students put anything even remotely related to the country into their reports. The student who "did" Scotland, for example, brought her report to class in a huge carton. Reading the reports was a nightmare and, like it or not, grading was based on a subjective mixture of quality and weight. Our students were proud of the huge stacks of information they had gathered, most of which we suspect they never read. The next year we spent considerable time narrowing the topics down to a more manageable size.

Using children's experiences

Teachers sometimes equate data gathering with "library research," as we did, and thus neglect data that can grow out of students' experiences. Even primary children can get involved in data-gathering procedures. Conducting surveys to determine children's favorite TV shows or the time at which most students go to bed, for example, are possible topics for data collection.

Using Data from Primary and Secondary Sources.

Some kinds of information (or data) better lend themselves to information processing than do other forms of data. You may recall our earlier comments about information such as the state tree, state flower, and so on. When your purpose is to help children process information, your main focus should be on providing them with unprocessed information—raw data—that they can work with. As a rule that information should be presented in uninterpreted form so that students can do the interpreting.

Social studies programs that emphasize helping students work with information from primary sources often lean heavily on uninterpreted information, some of which (as for surveys) the students may gather firsthand. Note that *primary* in this sense refers to firsthand accounts, whereas *secondary* accounts relate to already interpreted information.

As a kind of self-check, decide which of the following sources are most likely to provide primary (firsthand) accounts (use a P) and which are most likely to contain secondary (previously interpreted) accounts (use an S). Use ? if you are not sure.

Data sources

_____ Aerial photographs	_____ Lectures
_____ Advertisements	_____ Letters (personal)
_____ Artifacts	_____ Magazine articles
_____ Atlases	_____ Maps
_____ Census reports	_____ Paintings
_____ Diaries	_____ Documentary photographs
_____ Directories	_____ Reports
_____ Documents	_____ Survey reports
_____ Encyclopedias	_____ Textbooks
_____ Interviews	_____ Journal articles

The secondary sources on this list include encyclopedias, lectures, magazine articles (and _some_ journal articles), reports, and textbooks. Some sources, such as advertisements, may be questionable, especially since the way data are used in advertisements is often questionable. Interviews might also be questionable, because interviewees sometimes give the answer they think the interviewer is anticipating. Maps could also fall into the questionable category, because someone had to transform (i.e., process) data into map form. However, for all practical purposes, it is safe to regard most maps (and the balance of the items on this list) as primary sources. You can turn to them as some of your best resources for process-based activities.

Using Data Banks.   The problem of keeping track of skills-based teaching materials need not become overwhelming, especially if you either have access to a computer or are willing to develop a data bank. A data bank can take a variety of forms. Some teachers store the information on their personal computers, whereas others prefer 5- by 8-inch index cards, like the one illustrated in Figure 12.2. The data bank should include two elements: (1) sets of data for students to work with, which may include extrapolated raw data, charts, graphs, tables, figures, maps, and, if necessary, hypothetical data; and (2) notations regarding different ways in which students can use the data.

Potential data-based activities

   When potential teaching materials are organized in data-bank form, the following things should become apparent:

★ You need not use all the data at one time. Rather, you can select the kind and amount of data to be included in an activity.
★ When you provide the data for students to work with, students tend to spend less time on data gathering and significantly more time on developing reflective thinking skills.

Generalizing

One of the more challenging aspects of teaching is helping students identify patterns or relationships among otherwise unconnected events or pieces of data. That challenge, expressed in a word, is *generalizing*.

Looking for patterns in the data

The process of making generalizations requires that students move into the realm of abstraction. Yet many students and even some adults may get so wrapped up in the specific details or the content of situations that they tend to consider those details separately. We are not talking about the need to generalize here, for that clearly exists. Our concern is with some people's unwillingness to move into the realm of abstraction, which is something that adults are sometimes reluctant to do.

Working with classes of behavior

Generalizing reduces the disorder and confusion of otherwise isolated bits of experience. That reduction is achieved by organizing data or experiences into classes and categories. Generalizing, then, involves making statements about classes or categories of objects or events. We provide examples of how you can help children do this in the next section.

Strategies for Teaching Critical Thinking Skills

Teaching strategies for helping children think reflectively typically involve (1) the teacher modeling the desired behaviors, or (2) posing a sequence of questions to the whole class or to cooperative learning groups, or a combination of the two, which is (3) followed by a period of reflection on the activity itself—on what worked and what didn't. After providing children with data to interpret, the basic teaching strategy follows a three-element pattern based on What?, Why?, and What does it mean?

We are reluctant to call the What-Why-What does it mean? sequence a questioning pattern because that could be misleading. Each element (What?, Why?, etc.) could be posed as a question, of course, but we recommend that you pose the elements in the sequence as tasks, using them as guides as you model the process. By using the sequence as a general guideline, you can then tailor specific questions that correspond to the data you are using. As an example, we will use the information on the sample data-bank card shown in Figure 12.2.

Question 1: What?

The "What?" task is intended to elicit what students notice about the data, including things that are common or anything unusual. However, if your students lack the prior knowledge to identify Boston, Moscow, London, etc. (as shown on the data card) as large cities, you will need to point this out to them. Young students often have problems distinguishing between the names of cities, states, and countries—they think that London and Paris are countries—so some brief detours may be needed here. Before students can look for patterns among data, they need to understand the data they are dealing with.

Question 2: Why?

Once your students understand that many cities are located along large rivers, you can then move to Phase 2: "Why do you suppose this happened?" The purpose of the "Why?" phase of the sequence is to elicit explanations or inferences that might explain the phenomenon. Accept all reasonable hypotheses. Every community needs a reliable water supply, of course, but large rivers also offer avenues for trade and commerce. Still, the availability of water alone may not explain why some communities are smaller than those on the data card.

Question 3: What does
it mean?

Figure 12.2 Sample Data-Bank Card (5 × 8 Format)

Skill: Generalizing from data

Data	Possible Activities
Boston is on the Charles River	1. Check accuracy of each statement.
Moscow is on the Volga River.	
London is on the Thames River.	2. Identify two variables at work in each statement.
Cincinnati is on the Ohio River.	
Paris is on the Seine River.	3. Make a general statement, about both variables, that would include all statements given.
	4. Identify/locate three other cities that would fit under the broad general statement.
	5. Identify one "major" city that appears to be an exception.
	6. Formulate three possible explanations for the exception in number 5.

After children have explored possible inferences and explanations (about the relationship between cities and rivers), you can move to Phase 3, "What does this mean?" Students often want to generalize hastily and make statements such as "All big cities are located near large rivers because they [the rivers] offer reliable water supplies and opportunities for trading." Accurate as their generalization might seem, they are not finished yet. This is where the issue of probability that we mentioned in Chapter 2 enters the picture. This is also where they will certainly need more data about large cities. Consider that at least two of the ten largest cities in the United States—Atlanta, Georgia, and San Antonio, Texas—are not located on large rivers. The San Antonio River, for example, averages only 2 to 3 feet deep, and certainly cannot support large river craft.

Our points here are several. First, to help children identify patterns among data that will then permit them to develop generalizations, they should deal with a very limited amount of information at first, such as the five statements on our sample data-bank card. At the same time, the tradeoff comes with helping children to understand that they cannot make generalizations based on limited information alone. Teachers need to be ready to provide additional data that may or may not be consistent with the original information and that students can then use to confirm the accuracy of the general statements they make. Taking exceptions into account is part of that process, and students need to understand that failing to accommodate exceptions can cast the shadow of doubt on their overgeneralizations. It is true, for example, that many major cities are located

From time to time, all of us have encountered teachers who ask questions such as "Who can tell me the capital of Alabama?" or "Who can tell me what a body of land surrounded by water is called?" Our problem with questions like these is their phrasing; that is, both begin with "Who can tell me . . . ?" We refer to these as "Queen Bee" questions, because they implicitly suggest that whoever answers them will impress the teacher by doing so. Both "Who can tell me the capital of Alabama?" and "What is the capital of Alabama?" lead to the same answer: Birmingham. However, "Queen Bee" questioning tends to make impressing "me," the teacher, the focal point of the activity. The "Who can tell me?" question format may seem innocuous enough, but using it repeatedly could send powerful messages about the kind of classroom environment you are trying to maintain.

Taking exceptions into account

along large rivers, but saying that "all major cities are located along major rivers" is not true. To take the exceptions into account, students need to alter their original generalization by using "many" or "most" instead of "all." Closure for this activity can come when the teacher says, "Are we accurate if we say that 'many major cities grew up along large rivers because of the reliable water supples and opportunities for trade and commerce that the rivers offered'?" In the next section we examine some of the other purposes that questions can serve.

Questioning Strategies

Is the question really relevant?

Everybody knows that questions are a teacher's stock in trade. Theoretically, a teacher's questions are supposed to lead to something, but this mission sometimes goes astray. For example, some teachers ask a question like "Has anyone ever been to Disneyland?," which they hope will motivate students and pique their interest. But if you are leading into an activity that you are going to do regardless of how your students respond, such questions could be irrelevant. Whether such questions actually engage young students is questionable, and unless students' responses (about Disneyland) are relevant to the lesson that follows, you should consider moving into the activity immediately by saying something such as "Now, we're going to do an activity that . . ."

For Every Question There Is a Purpose

For every question teachers ask, there is (or should be) an underlying purpose, something the teacher is trying to get at. In many respects, deciding what questions to ask, deciding how to ask them, and deciding what answers you anticipate is part of every teaching strategy. The reverse of our statement is equally true— for every purpose there is a question. To illustrate this, we will use the information presented on the data card shown in Figure 12.2, which we used previously.

We noted earlier that if students are not aware that the names listed on the data card (London, Boston, Moscow, etc.) are major cities, the activity could become an exercise in futility. To determine whether students already have this

| Memory-recall questions | or any other prior knowledge in their possession, you could ask a *memory-recall* question, such as "What major city is located along the Thames River?" The main purpose of memory-recall questions is to determine if students can recall specific, factual information. |

Memory-recall questions

or any other prior knowledge in their possession, you could ask a *memory-recall* question, such as "What major city is located along the Thames River?" The main purpose of memory-recall questions is to determine if students can recall specific, factual information.

Descriptive-interpretive questions

If your purpose is to determine whether students can identify patterns among data, you might ask students a *descriptive-interpretive* question. This category of questions asks students to describe, interpret, or otherwise explain what the cities listed on the data card have in common. Asking this question was part of the "Why?" phase of the sequence that we described earlier. In this instance, students' description or interpretation must be in their own words, not a memorized rehash of someone else's description (otherwise it becomes a memory-recall question).

Application-synthesis questions

Once students have concluded that the large cities shown on the data card are located along major rivers, you could follow up by asking them to speculate on why this is the case. Was it simply the availability of water, or did other elements play a role? Although you might be asking another "Why?" question, in this instance it would be an *application-synthesis* question that requires students to identify possible relationships and draw conclusions, bringing in other information as needed. Application-synthesis questions require that students put things together (synthesize) so as to identify relationships or generalizations that go beyond specific events. Note, however, that unless application-synthesis questions are preceded by several lower-level questions, they may seem to come from nowhere.

Evaluative-judgmental questions

If you are interested in determining whether students have internalized the data-card lesson, you might ask an *evaluative-judgmental* question such as "How would you advise colonists as to the best places to locate their settlements?" Evaluative-judgmental questions always contain a "good-bad" or "better-best" element, which is what makes them judgmental. These questions require students to produce an evaluation or render a judgment. A distinguishing characteristic of evaluative-judgmental questions is that students must identify the *criteria* they will use in reaching their evaluation. Thus, an evaluative-judgmental question might be phrased more accurately as follows: "What criteria would you use to decide whether colonists had established their settlements to ensure possible growth?" This might seem a long-winded way to pose a question, but our intent is to emphasize the need to specify clearly and in advance the criteria by which something is being judged. In the absence of such critera, students' responses will be purely personal opinion.

Speculative-heuristic questions

Other potential questions could ask your students to speculate in a hypothetical mode. Examples of such *speculative-heuristic* questions based on our data card include "What might have happened if Boston (London, Paris, etc.) were located 100 miles upstream from their present locations?" The "what-if" form illustrated in this example is characteristic of speculative-heuristic questions. Although speculative-heuristic questions are excellent for generating inquiry, promoting divergent thinking, and getting students to speculate on and analyze alterative courses of action, be cautious here; asking three "what-if" questions in a row may be enough to confuse even your most sophisticated students.

The various types of questions are summarized in Table 12.2.

Table 12.2 Types of Questions by Category and Purpose

Type of Question	Purpose
Memory-recall	To determine whether students can recall previously learned information
Descriptive-interpretive	To describe, interpret, and/or explain events or actions in the student's own words, including reasons (nonspeculative) for why individuals acted as they did
Application-synthesis	To identify relationships and to form and draw reasonable conclusions that go beyond the particular action or event
Evaluative-judgmental	To render an evaluation or judgment as to actions or events in light of explicit, previously identified criteria
Speculative-heuristic	To encourage divergent thinking and to speculate on and analyze alternative courses of action

Wait Time

"Whenever we have a discussion, the same kids participate all of the time and the rest of the class just sits there. Sometimes the students who talk don't have much to say, and it is all very superficial. I don't know. I'm about ready to give up on discussions."

Frustrated teachers have been echoing complaints like this for years, yet they often overlook a potential solution to their problem. The solution takes no special skills and has achieved dramatic results where it's been employed. It is: Doing nothing. Well, almost nothing.

In some now-classic research, Mary Bodd Rowe (1969) examined the relationship between a teacher's wait time and the quality of classroom discussions. Wait time refers to the period of silence between the end of a teacher's question and the teacher's next statement or question. Rowe found that many teachers apparently have difficulty tolerating silence during a discussion; their average wait time was only nine-tenths of a second. No wonder students didn't participate! They didn't have time to think before the teacher went on with another comment or question.

After Rowe informed teachers how short their wait time was, they decided to double it—at least to two seconds. Awkwardly at first, the teachers waited the allotted two seconds, even though it sometimes seemed like an eternity. The results? The number of students participating in class discussions improved dramatically, as did the quality of their contributions. When teachers also

Avoid responding too quickly

What two seconds of silence can yield

Increasing the "wait time" between a teacher's questions and the students' responses often leads to increased student involvement. (© *Paul Conklin/Monkmeyer Press Photo Service*)

lengthened the period of silence between a student's response and the teacher's next comment or question—what Rowe called "Wait Time II"—the results were even more impressive. Even more students responded, including some who almost never participated, and the quality of discussions also improved.

The implication is clear: if your discussions don't go well and the same students participate all the time, try lengthening your wait time. If you do that and your discussions still don't go well, you may need to reexamine the kinds of questions you are asking.

Decision Making

Choosing among alternatives

Decision making is the process of making reasoned choices from among alternatives. In social studies, decision making often has two meanings, one of them broad and the other narrow. In the broad sense, *decision making* describes a total approach to social studies, one that incorporates all the process skills that we deal with in this book. In its narrower sense, *decision making* describes instructional activities that ask students to apply decision-making skills. Our concern in this section is with decision making in the narrower, "activities" sense of the term.

The Model Student Activity, "Returning from the Crusades," illustrates a common model for decision-making activities. A heuristic (what if?) question is posed in the introduction, and students are then asked to select among the various choices provided. This is essentially the same format used in the "Who Is

Returning from the Crusades

Introduction

The year is 1291. You are a knight who has been fighting to win back the Holy Lands—the Middle East—from the Moslems for your king and country, England. After months of fighting, you learn that the battle to win Jerusalem was lost. It has been a long and hard journey, but it is time for crusaders, like yourself, to leave the Moslem lands.

Weary and unhappy because of losing the battle, your thoughts turn toward seeing your family and loved ones once again. However, as you begin your journey back to England, you notice some abandoned Turkish villages that have different things lying about. You lost everything except the clothes on your back, so you decide to pick up some of the things the Turks have abandoned. However, between your backpack and horse you can carry only an additional 50 pounds. Even if you put some things into your pockets (instead of the backpack), your horse may not be able to carry the extra weight.

Below is a list of things you find in the foreign lands. Select the ones you would want to take back to England with you. When you have decided which items to take, rank-order these, with 1 being the most important. But remember, you can carry only 50 pounds.

Group Rank	Your Rank	
_____	_____	Large pouch of Turkish coins (8 lb.)
_____	_____	Small barrel of flour (30 lb.)
_____	_____	Pouch of water—2 gallons (6 lb.)
_____	_____	Your bow and arrows (4 lb.)
_____	_____	A small, live Mulberry tree (9 lb.)
_____	_____	Large, 4-person tent (18 lb.)
_____	_____	20 yards of silk cloth (8 lb.)
_____	_____	One iron cooking pot (13 lb.)
_____	_____	Shovel (4 lb.)
_____	_____	One jar of silk worms (3 lb.)
_____	_____	One camel (No weight, can be led)
_____	_____	Persian rug (24 lb.)

Group Rank	Your Rank	
_____	_____	Arabian math books (20 lb. for all of them)
_____	_____	10 Arabian toys (10 lb. @ 1 lb. each)
_____	_____	Food to last for the journey (33 lb.)
_____	_____	Small pouches of spices (6 lb.)
_____	_____	An elegant silk dress (4 lb.)
_____	_____	Stray puppy (6 lb.)
_____	_____	10 blown glass goblets (5 lb. @ ½ lb. each
_____	_____	Fishing pole (4 lb.)
_____	_____	Small package of apricots (3 lb.)
_____	_____	Arabian artwork—1 piece (9 lb.)
_____	_____	Soap, 1 bar (½ lb.)
_____	_____	Other _____
		(Weight will vary)

Source: This activity was designed by and is reprinted by permission of Ms. Dena Hawley.

Procedure

1. *Individual selections:* Students should rank-order their choices of the goods they propose to take back to England.

2. *Group selections:* If you have not already done so, create small groups of about five members each. Ask each group to create a single list of items they will be taking back to England.

3. *Determining the common ground.* Ask each group to list their items on the chalkboard. Ask groups to explain their rationale for selecting the items they did, and then circle the goods that were common to all groups.

4. *Exploring the exceptions.* Explore items that were selected by only one or two groups and ask them why they selected those items.

5. *Realities:* Display (on the overhead) the following list of items that Europeans actually brought from the Middle East. These items included:

Silk cloth and silk worms

Mulberry trees (to feed the silk worms) [Note: a jar of silkworms would die en route without mulberry leaves for food.]

Blown glass objects

Apricot trees

Arabic system of numbering

Assorted spices for preserving food and for seasoning.

Camels

Persian rugs

Translations of Latin and Arabic literary works

Middle Eastern styles of clothing

Nice-smelling soap

Analysis

This activity asks students to make decisions similar to those made by people over 700 years ago. At the conclusion of this activity, students should be able to see the influence that Middle Eastern nations, especially Turkey, ultimately had on Medieval European cultures. Students should also be able to consider the extent to which their decision might have "changed history," as well as explain the extent to which interchange with nations in the Middle East led to changes in what is sometimes called "the Dark Ages."

Qualified for Presidency?" Activity in Chapter 1, although in this case there are more possible choices. In this and many other decision-making activities, participants must first make decisions individually and then reach consensus in small groups. In addition, and because many decision-making activities do not have previously identified "correct" answers, teachers usually identify the common ground, or the most common choices selected by all the groups.

Developing and Using Decision-Making Activities

Decision-making activities often work well as introductions to areas with which children are unfamiliar, particularly because the activities help to raise questions about what an area is (or was) like. Decision-making problems can be shifted to almost any area or historical period. For example, "If you were Marco Polo . . ." or "If your family was going from Connecticut to California in 1849 . . . what would you bring with you?"

Applications

Decision-making activities must be limited to problems that are both real and manageable for students; otherwise they'll have no basis for considering the alternatives. This means that for most elementary students, a question such as "Which had a better organizational basis, the League of Nations or the United Nations?" isn't a manageable problem for a decision-making format. As a rule, decision-making activities for elementary and middle-school students should afford immediate access to the information on which their decisions will be based.

Maintain a clear focus

Decision-making activities can serve as a focus for information-processing skills, but unless teachers continually stress rational information processing, these activities can degenerate into arguments of "My opinion is as good as yours." Attention should also be focused on the processes that students use in arriving at their decisions, not just on the decisions themselves.

Decision-making activities require students to *use* information, as do other process-oriented activities such as fact sheets, surveys, and problem situations. Decision-making activities can be incorporated into social studies programs at every grade level on a regular basis and should not be relegated to a trivial role—as something "neat" to do on a Friday afternoon or during a rainy recess. As for all critical thinking and decision-making activities, the focus on *using* information and on rational decision making should be maintained.

Summary

This chapter has focused on activities that can help you manage skill-oriented instruction. We suggested that reflective thinking skills are part of a family of skills that cannot be held in isolation for very long. Hypothesizing, for example, cannot end there; once students have hypothesized, they must then do something with those hypotheses. Otherwise they—the students and the hypotheses—will be left hanging.

One key to developing information-processing and decision-making activities lies in limiting the amount of information available to students at the outset of the activity to avoid information overload. After students understand the original information, additional data can (and should) be supplied. Paralleling the limitation on the amount of information, we also suggested that students are not likely to do much thinking about information that already has been interpreted. Thus a second key factor in creating critical thinking activities involves selecting uninterpreted information with which students can work. Finally, we suggested that some process-oriented and decision-making activities can be misused or become gimmicky if a focus on information processing is not maintained.

Throughout this chapter, we have suggested that asking questions may actually be a test of your student's prior knowledge. Our concern is not for the students who can answer the questions you pose, but for the students who sit silently, praying that you will not call on them. The questions and tasks that teachers pose will often determine the way their students use social studies content. We identified five types of questions that teachers might ask—memory-recall, descriptive-interpretive, application-synthesis, evaluative-judgmental, and speculative-heuristic—that are keyed to the thinking skills a students must employ to answer them.

Teachers who ask higher-level questions—that is, higher in terms of their level on the *Taxonomy of Educational Objectives*—are more likely to demand that their students use content. This doesn't make knowledge-level questions "bad," however, because they can be used to determine if students have essential prior information in their possession. However, the goal in most instances is to help children move beyond the knowledge level.

Suggested Activities

1. Design a forced-choice format decision-making activity following the guidelines suggested in this chapter.

2. Following the guidelines suggested in this chapter, develop either a fact sheet that contrasts two states or two countries, or create a set of culture cards.

Suggested Reading

Barry K. Beyer. (1991). *Teaching thinking skills: A handbook for elementary teachers*. Boston: Allyn & Bacon. This handbook provides an excellent overview of thinking skills as well as exemplary lessons to teach those skills. Companion volumes by Beyer include *Practical strategies for the teaching of thinking* (1987) and *Developing a thinking skills program* (1988).

13

Helping Students Use Maps, Globes, and Graphics

Key Questions

* How can students use maps, charts, and other forms of social studies information?

* How can mathematics be used in social studies?

Key Ideas

* Maps, globes, graphs, and charts are specialized forms in which information is presented.

* All maps omit certain information; if they didn't, the information they do present would be lost in a fog of detail (which is also true of other data forms).

* When students have difficulty gaining access to specialized forms of information, part of the problem may be their lack of understanding about how the information got into that form in the first place.

* Some map and globe skills—specifically, latitude, longitude, and scale—are founded in mathematics and should be treated accordingly.

Introduction: Basic Premises

Specialized ways for presenting information

Whenever someone says "social studies," many people think first of history and geography, followed closely by maps and globes. There's no question that maps, globes, and, to a lesser extent, charts and tables are integral to social studies, yet there is nothing inherently "social" about any of them. They are simply specialized ways for presenting information.

Decoding maps, charts, and graphics

The information presented on most maps, globes, graphs, charts, and tables can almost always be presented in other forms. Aerial photographs, for example, can convey at least as much (and probably more) information as many landform maps. Likewise, the information on a chart or table could be presented in a written description. Although a narrative of the income tax tables would probably be hopelessly confusing, it could be done.

Reading a map, chart, or graph demands decoding skills not unlike those required to read information presented in narrative form—as you are doing now. True, the symbols are different: the dots and squares on a map, for example, usually stand for different things. Yet the process of bringing meaning to these symbols is a form of decoding.

Reading plays such an important role in gaining access to the information on maps, graphs, charts, and tables that our approach in this chapter is borrowed from the language-experience approach to teaching reading. That approach reflects the premise that if children can see their speech being encoded into written form, they will be better able to read those symbols.

How encoding and decoding are related

This chapter is also based on the premise that one reason students sometimes have difficulty reading maps or tables is that they don't understand how the information got *into* that form. In other words, students may not understand what the information on a map is supposed to represent. Likewise, when children have difficulty decoding charts and tables, the problem may lie in their inability to understand how information was encoded into the chart or table in the first place. We note this to explain why we place so much emphasis on providing encoding experiences as a necessary balance for the decoding experiences—map reading, table reading, chart reading—that traditionally play important roles in social studies programs.

In the first section of this chapter, we examine map- and globe-related skills and identify exemplary activities you might use to teach those skills. In the following sections, we consider experiences with tables, charts, and other graphic forms.

Maps and Globes

Why maps omit details

No one needs to tell you that maps are among the more abstract devices used in teaching social studies. As Monmonier (1991) noted, we live in a three-dimensional world that is too rich in details to be presented on a complete and yet uncluttered two-dimensional map. As a result, many maps distort the reality they depict by leaving out more information than they include and by using a variety of symbols to describe the information that is included.

The abstract nature of maps is illustrated in Figure 13.1. What to us may look like a random collection of sticks and shells can make perfect sense to mariners from the Marshall Islands. The sticks represent wave patterns, and the shells mark reefs and islands. With maps like this one, the Marshall Islanders navigated their way across empty stretches of the Pacific.

Large-area maps can pose special problems for children, who have probably never seen the real-world elements those maps depict. That many adults may have difficulty interpreting Figure 13.1 reflects the fact that some maps are models of things we have never seen and in many cases never will.

Maps as models

The abstract nature of maps is often compounded by the rapidity with which they lose one-to-one correspondence. For example, many things that children see and know to exist in their immediate environment do not appear on most maps of the area. Trees and buildings are among the first real-life elements to disappear. And as the map scale grows larger, cities often become dots or squares that look nothing like the areas they represent.

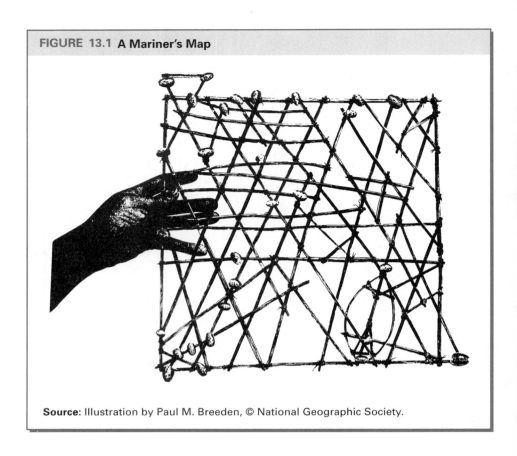

FIGURE 13.1 A Mariner's Map

Source: Illustration by Paul M. Breeden, © National Geographic Society.

Maps also demand that we look at things from a different perspective. Except for astronauts, few of us have had the luxury of viewing the world while suspended in space. (Landsat maps made from satellite photographs have helped considerably in this respect—see p. 315.) Maps require that we assume the perspective of "looking down on" or what, in children's terms, can be described as a bird's-eye view. Because that perspective is not one that most children have experienced in their daily lives, we recommend that you provide activities in which young children look at objects from a bird's-eye view. Here are some suggestions:

1. Draw a picture of your shoe. (If the heel is visible, it's not a bird's-eye view.)

2. Hold a "bird's-eye view contest." Place small objects in a paper bag, where they cannot be seen by others, and have students draw and identify pictures of the objects as they would be seen from a bird's-eye view. Note that doll house furniture works well for this activity.

3. Follow the activity above by having students draw larger objects from their environment from a bird's-eye view. Some examples are pictured in Figure 13.2.

FIGURE 13.2 Common Objects Seen from a Bird's-Eye View

CHURCH UMBRELLA TOASTER BOOK

4. Place a stepladder somewhere in the classroom, and then place various objects underneath it (model cars, etc.). Have children draw only what they see from the ladder.

5. Have students work with an interdisciplinary computer program, such as *The Backyard* (Brøderbund). By clicking on an assortment of objects, the child may be whisked to faraway places. Other scenarios involve locating buried treasure and reassembling animal skeletons.

6. In working with children's stories, draw hypothetical bird's-eye view maps of the area. For a story like Robert McCloskey's (1941) *Make Way for Ducklings*, for example, you could make a map of the area as seen from a duck's-eye view.

Mapmaking

Map copying is not mapmaking

Mapmaking refers to activities in which children actually produce a map. This excludes a variety of map-copying activities (even though they are sometimes called "mapmaking") in which children color in and correctly label outline maps. Copying existing maps may be useful in helping to fix areas in a child's mind, but it teaches little about what maps are or the purposes they serve. In addition, map-copying lessons too often focus on the artistic dimensions of mapping, especially if students use colored glitter or other unusual materials to depict the different areas. Such maps should probably be judged as works of art rather than as ways for displaying certain types of information.

Children seldom omit any details

Mapmaking in the encoding sense requires an area to be mapped. Beginning with bird's-eye views of various objects, students can move to increasingly larger areas, such as their living room or bedroom, their classroom, the school building, the neighborhood around the school, or other areas of the community. Figure 13.3 shows a third grader's map of his home and yard. The map is detailed and accurate, except that the cardinal directions are incorrect (the front of the house faces to the east). The back yard, which looks like a swimming pool, is really grass surrounded by a concrete walkway—to keep the grass from going into the shrubbery. The child has maintained a high level of one-to-one correspondence by showing things that he knows are present in the environment, including the piano keys, the boat in the side yard, and the jungle

FIGURE 13.3 **Third-Grader's Map of His House and Yard**

gym/swing set, which is made from ladders, in the back yard. About the only things not drawn strictly from a bird's-eye view are the trees, which is wholly expected for children of this age. Note that students who live in multi-story houses are usually baffled by the prospect of showing several floors simultaneously; they should map each floor separately.

Specific objectives

Objectives for initial mapmaking activities include (1) helping children to visualize their immediate environment from a bird's-eye (or spatial) perspective and (2) helping them to understand that when anything is reduced in size—as maps are in relation to the areas they depict—some things must be omitted. Children should consider on what basis some things are kept in and others left out.

Relief Maps.   If your school is located on the plains of west Texas, making a relief map of the area is probably pointless; much of the terrain is as flat as a tabletop. In most other areas of the country, relief maps can show hills and valleys, thus illustrating yet another type of mapmaking. But beware! Making accurate relief maps can be a time-consuming and often messy process.

Moving from two dimensions to three

Making Relief Maps.   To build relief maps of small areas such as the neighborhood around a school, you might have students actually measure the changes in elevation. However, because doing that is more difficult than it may seem, we recommend that you use topographical maps from the U.S. Geological Survey. They show changes in elevation while showing buildings and other features not found on many maps.

Relief maps can be constructed from a variety of materials. The least messy but most costly is clay—pound after pound of clay. Several recipes for other relief-map making materials are included in the Resource Handbook.

Computer-Based Maps.   Instead of constructing relief maps, you may wish to draw on the maps included in computer database programs such as *PC-Globe, PC-USA,* and *Encarta World Atlas.* Most such programs contain a variety of maps and other data for any given area: relief maps, political maps, landform maps, population distribution maps, major cities, highways, rainfall—you name it. Most programs also permit you to print the maps.

A superb teaching resource

The *Atlas* software is notable for its ability to focus on small areas of a larger map, creating exploded views. Used with a computer projection system, it permits students to see map details that were previously difficult to see even on large wall maps.

Scale.   In most mapmaking activities, it usually isn't long before a question arises as to whether maps should be drawn to scale. For primary-grade children, the answer is generally no; neatly drawn but not-to-scale drawings will usually suffice. For the intermediate grades, the answer depends on the math program your students are using. The notion of scale, like latitude and longitude, is mathematically based. And scale, perhaps better than anything else, reflects the zenith of representational thought. In this case, one thing is said to equal something else. For younger elementary students, the notion that one inch can equal one foot (or one mile or ten miles) can present some of the same difficulties that algebra students encounter when they find that x can equal anything.

Representational thought

Scale is so integral to maps and mapmaking that it cannot be dealt with casually. By the end of the intermediate grades, for example, Hanna and his colleagues suggest that children have experienced some of the following ideas related to scale (Hanna et al., 1966, p. 25):

Concepts about scale

* Scale is the relation of distance on the map to the distance the map represents on the ground.
* The scale of a map is large or small in relation to the object the map represents.
* Maps that use a large scale can show many details about a small area.
* Maps that use a small scale can show large areas but with fewer details.
* Scale permits the measurement of the distance between any two points on the Earth's surface.
* The scale on one part of a map may be different from the scale on another part (an inset map, for instance).

Correlate scale with your math program

You may have to be satisfied when most of your students can use the scale on a map to calculate the distance between two points. However, many math programs introduce representational thought, and even the notion of scale, much earlier than they used to. Therefore, we recommend that you correlate your mapmaking activities with your math program.

Adding three-dimensional models may help children better understand two-dimensional maps
(© Mary Lang/Positive Images)

Translation Mapping. *Translation* is a major subdivision of the comprehension category of the *Taxonomy of Educational Objectives* and is defined as changing data from one form to another. This is, in fact, what mapmaking is all about—depicting three-dimensional reality in a two-dimensional map form. The following map-related activities involve different kinds of translation. Although some of them may not seem especially thrilling, they are educational.

Scope and sequence

* Produce a written description of information contained on a chart or table (educational, but not too thrilling).

* Produce a map of a nation, such as Japan, from a written or oral description. (This activity is more interesting than it may seem and produces some very interesting maps—inaccurate but interesting.)

* Produce and translate a map. (In this activity, one group of students produces a map and another group uses it to locate an object—interesting, though the instructions are more complex than the activity.) The class is divided into teams of two. Each team places an object somewhere around the school grounds (lavatories are off-limits), returns to the classroom, and provides an oral description to the second team, which produces a map from that description. Finally, the maps are given to yet a third team, which must retrieve the object. As a follow-up, share the various problems the teams encountered in either making or using the maps.

When Should Map and Globe Skills Be Taught?

There is no single established sequence for map and globe skills for the elementary and middle-school grades. Sometimes first graders are expected to know and locate the major continents and oceans, for example, but in other instances, this may not be covered until Grade 2 or later.

From time to time, various individuals and groups have identified a desirable scope and sequence for teaching map and globe skills. A sample scope and sequence for map and globe skills developed by the Joint Committee on Geographic Education of the National Council for Geographic Education and the Association of American Geographers (1984) appears in Table 13.1.

Table 13.1   Suggested Scope and Sequence for Elementary Map and Globe Skills

Grade Level	Recommended Learning Outcomes
Kindergarten	1. Knows and uses terms related to location, direction, and distance (*up/down, left/right, here/there, near/far*). 2. Recognizes a globe as a model of the Earth. 3. Recognizes and uses terms that express relative size and shape (*big/little, large/small, round/square*). 4. Identifies school and local community by name. 5. Recognizes and uses models and symbols to represent real things.
Grade 1	1. Knows geographic location of home in relation to school and neighborhood. 2. Knows the layout of the school campus. 3. Uses simple classroom maps to locate objects. 4. Identifies state and nation by name. 5. Follows and gives verbal directions (*here/there, left/right*). 6. Distinguishes between land and water symbols on globes and maps. 7. Relates locations on maps and globes to locations on Earth. 8. Observes, describes, and builds simple models and maps of the local environment.
Grade 2	1. Makes and uses simple maps of school and home neighborhoods. 2. Interprets map symbols using a legend. 3. Knows and uses cardinal directions. 4. Locates one's community, state, and nation on maps and globes. 5. Identifies local landforms. 6. Differentiates between maps and globes. 7. Locates other neighborhoods studied on maps. 8. Traces routes within and between neighborhoods using a variety of maps and models. 9. Compares pictures and maps of the same area.
Grade 3	1. Uses distance, direction, scale, and map symbols. 2. Compares own community with other communities. 3. Compares urban and rural environments.

(continued on next page)

Table 13.1 Suggested Scope and Sequence for Map and Globe Skills (*continued*)

Grade Level	Recommended Learning Outcomes
Grade 4	1. Interprets pictures, graphs, charts, and tables. 2. Works with distance, direction, scale, and map symbols. 3. Relates similarities and differences between maps and globes. 4. Uses maps of different scales and themes. 5. Recognizes the common characteristics of map grid systems (map projections). 6. Compares and contrasts regions on a state, national, or world basis.
Grade 5	1. Recognizes distance, direction, scale, map symbols, and the relationship of maps and globes. 2. Works with longitude and latitude. 3. Uses maps, charts, graphs, and tables to display data. 4. Discusses location in terms of *where* and *why*. 5. Maps the correspondence between resources and industry. 6. Maps physical and cultural regions in North America.
Grade 6	1. Improves understanding of location, relative location, and the importance of location. 2. Uses maps, globes, charts, and graphs. 3. Readily uses latitude, longitude, map symbols, time zones, and basic Earth-Sun relationships. 4. Gains insight about the interaction of climate, landforms, natural vegetation, and other interactions in physical regions. 5. Maps trade routes, particularly those connecting developed and developing nations. 6. Plots distributions of population and key resources on regional maps.

Source: Abridged and adapted from Joint Committee on Geographic Education (1984).

Using Maps and Globes

Landsat Maps. Satellite photography has made it possible to illustrate the Earth in a manner previously possible only with a globe. Landsat satellites have circled Earth and sent back color photographs of remarkable clarity. The landsat map shown in Figure 13.4 is of New York City, Long Island, and the New Jersey coast. Our sample is reproduced in black and white, but it should give you some idea of the potential this innovation has for map-related instruction. Landsat maps are available from the Educational Programs Office, NASA Goddard Flight Center, Greenbelt, Maryland 20771.

The merits of globes **Globes.** Landsat maps notwithstanding, the globe is still one of the most accurate tools for helping children orient themselves to Earth. It can help them distinguish between land and water areas, and it can also help to correct the common notion that "up" on a map is north and "down" is south. Students may still use those expressions, but at least they will understand that up is away from

FIGURE 13.4 Landsat Map of New York City, Long Island, and the New Jersey Coast

Source: Courtesy of Community and Education Services Branch, Public Affairs Division, National Aeronautics and Space Administration.

the center of the Earth and down is the reverse. With a globe, they can also learn that north is toward the North Pole and south is toward the South Pole, something almost impossible to illustrate clearly on a wall map.

When it comes to locating specific places on the globe, two problems usually emerge. To avoid the problem of having students line up and file past the globe, some schools purchase classroom sets of eight- to twelve-inch globes, which are often kept on a cart and wheeled from classroom to classroom as needed. The second problem is a function of the size of the globe. On a twelve-inch globe, for example, the United States measures approximately four inches from west to east. The average wall map of the United States measures approximately

Size limits the amount of detail

four feet from west to east, thus permitting the presentation of much more detail. Some schools have purchased very large, thirty-six-inch globes—which often serve as focal points for libraries or learning centers—but even such large globes are limited in the amount of detail they can present. The globe is an excellent geographic tool, but when it comes to detail, you'll probably need to turn to a wall map.

Wall Maps.   Getting a round Earth to fit onto a flat map has perplexed cartographers for centuries. The classic example of peeling an orange and then trying to make the peel lie flat illustrates the essence of the problem. In cartographic terms, it is a question of "projection." Projecting rounded surfaces onto a flat map in different ways can yield the images shown in Figure 13.5.

Misleading impressions

The distortion on most wall maps is greatest at the high latitudes, and is largely responsible for the question children commonly ask: "Why is Australia a continent but Greenland isn't?" It's a logical question, because on many maps Greenland appears to be two to three times the size of Australia. Using a globe, students will find that Australia is three times larger than Greenland—Australia has 2,975,000 square miles versus Greenland's 840,000 square miles. Explaining to students how some maps make small things appear larger than they really are is no small feat! For very small areas, the distortion created by different map projections is usually negligible, but for large land masses, we recommend that you use a globe in conjunction with wall maps.

Large-scale maps

To avoid the "north is up" phenomenon, we suggest that you occasionally lay wall maps on the floor. Some schools have gone even further; they paint huge outline maps on the school parking lot or playground. Such large-scale maps should be accurate in direction and as accurate as possible in scale.

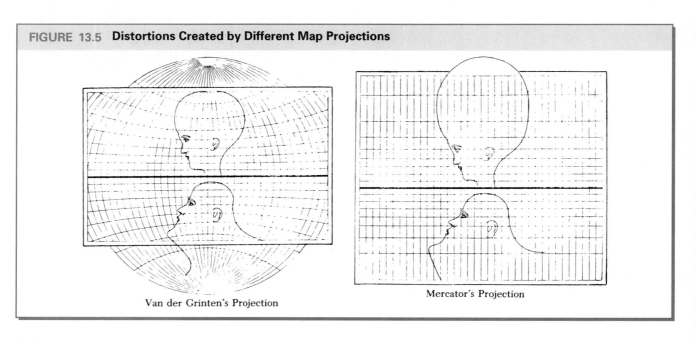

FIGURE 13.5   **Distortions Created by Different Map Projections**

Van der Grinten's Projection

Mercator's Projection

Plotting Earthquakes

Everyone knows that during the 1990s some of the worst earthquakes in the United States occurred in California. What many people do not know is that earthquakes of varying magnitudes are daily events around the globe. Some earthquakes are so weak you can barely feel them, and others are so powerful they cause widespread destruction. The key questions are: (1) Are some places in the world more prone to earthquakes than others, and (2) if so, where?

Overview: This problem-solving activity uses latitude and longitude to plot the location of recent earthquakes on an oversized map of the world. The completed map should resemble the one shown in Exhibit B.*

Materials:

1. A *really* large outline map of the world. (Suggestion: Make an overhead transparency of an appropriate world map by (a) mounting large paper on the wall and then (b) projecting the enlarged image onto the paper. Then (c) have children trace the outlines of continents and countries with markers. They should (d) use small dots to locate the location of parallels of latitude and meridians of longitude. After they (e) remove the map from the wall and lay it on the floor, students can use yardsticks and fine-point markers to draw in the latitude and longitude. Once this is done, they can (f) label the completed map and remount it on the wall.)

2. Earthquake locators. These are 1- by 1-inch squares of clear overhead transparency material with an X drawn on them. (Suggestion: Make a sheet of neatly drawn Xs, and then make three or four transparencies. Cut the individual Xs apart. Since there are many earthquakes, you will need many Xs; start with at least fifty).

3. Download the earthquake locations from the Internet at either URL:

   http://home.synapse.ru/cgi-bin/eq/
   http://wwwneic.cr.usgs.gov/neis/bulletin.

   The data will be similar to the data in Exhibit A:

4. Attach the earthquake locators on the map at the correct locations by using small loops of clear Scotch tape.

5. Identify patterns of the earthquake-prone areas around the world. Follow up with research on what sets these areas apart from other areas.

Exhibit A

Introductory Note: There are often 6–9 earthquakes every day that are above 3.5 on the Richter scale, and countless more tremors of lesser magnitude (Mag). The selected earthquakes shown below were in excess of 5 magnitude, and often caused significant damage and deaths. Because of the large number of earthquakes each day, we recommend that you map only those that exceed a threshold of 3.5 or 4 on the Richter scale; otherwise your map will become cluttered very quickly.

	Date	Time	Latitude	Longitude	Mag.	Region/Comments
1997	May 10	07:57	33.83 N	59.81 E	7.3	Northern Iran: Over 1,500 deaths, 2,300 injured, and 10,500 homes destroyed.
	May 13	05:38	31.82 N	130.28 E	5.7	Kyushu, Japan: 34 injured.
	June 23	19:13	47.60 N	122.57 W	5.0	Washington, Puget Sound Region: Slight damage.
	July 9	19:24	10.59 N	63.48 W	6.6	Near the Coast of Venezuela: Over 80 deaths and 500 injured; extensive damage.
	Oct. 14	09:53	22.10 S	176.77 W	6.7	South of Fuji Islands
	Oct. 15	01:03	30.93 S	71.22 W	6.8	Off the Coast of Chile: Over six deaths, 300 injured, and 5,000 homes destroyed.
	Nov. 21	11:23	22.21 N	92.70 E	5.9	India-Bangladesh Border Region: 23 deaths and 200 injured.
1998	Jan. 30	16:09	23.51 S	69.83 W	6.4	Northern Chile
	Feb. 4	14:33	37.07 N	70.20 E	6.1	Afghanistan-Tajikistan Border Region: 3,000 to 5,000 deaths and thousands injured and homeless.

*Exhibit B appears on page 318.

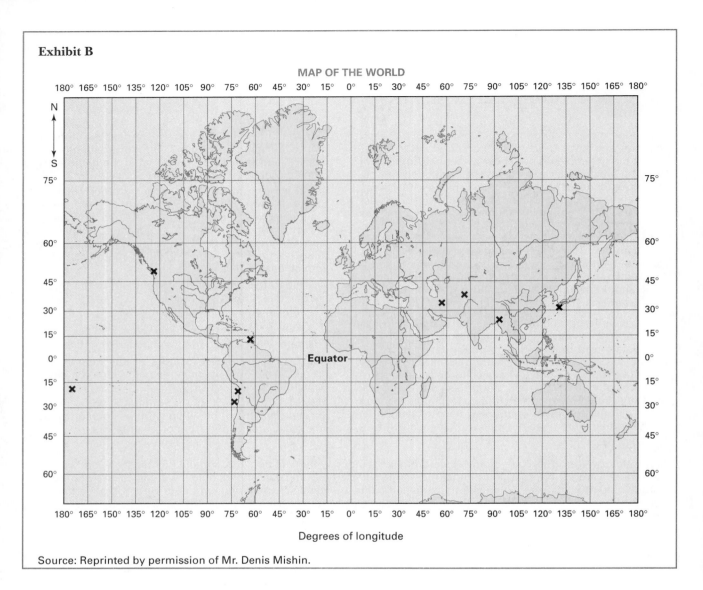

Exhibit B

MAP OF THE WORLD

Degrees of longitude

Source: Reprinted by permission of Mr. Denis Mishin.

Latitude, Longitude, and Other Grid Systems

Latitude and longitude

Most map and globe skill programs from fourth grade upward call for instruction in latitude and longitude. Among the more difficult ideas for children to grasp is the fact that although most parallels of latitude are imaginary lines that appear only on a map, 90 north latitude and 90 south latitude are not lines but are points (or, in mathematical terms, poles). Also difficult is the idea that although the meridians of longitude are of equal length, the parallels of latitude get shorter as one moves away from the equator. We suspect that one reason children find these ideas so hard to grasp is that latitude and longitude are often taught as arbitrary systems rather than as part of circular or spherical measurement. The Model Student Activity, "Pumpkin Geography," shows one way to deal with this difficult topic.

MODEL STUDENT ACTIVITY

Pumpkin Geography

The following illustrations show how you can use pumpkins to teach geography.
Set A: Shows hemispheres, the equator, and the prime meridian.

Set B: Shows how circular measurement is translated into latitude and longitude.

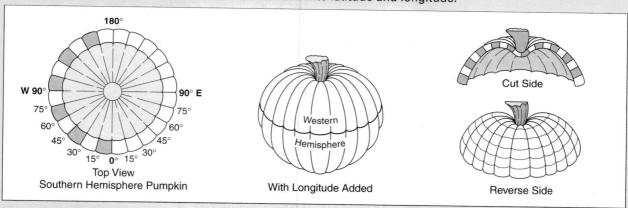

Set C: A pumpkin globe with latitude, longitude, and continental shapes drawn on.

Teaching latitude and longitude in elementary social studies programs can be reduced to three components:

1. Use of a grid system (any grid system)
2. Use of the grid system (longitude and latitude)
3. Understanding the basis for longitude and latitude

Grid-based map games

Even primary children can become adept at using a grid system, especially one involving a combination of letters and numbers. Math texts frequently include an assortment of grid-related activities, sometimes more than social studies texts. Also, many gridding activities can be converted into games that kids love to play. A classic is Battleship, in which a student locates his or her navy on a simple grid and then another student tries to sink the navy by calling out the various squares on the grid. You could also obtain classroom sets of state road maps from one of the petroleum companies or the state highway department and create a version of Cops and Robbers. In small groups, the robbers identify a quadrant on the map and then the rest of the students ask them questions that can be answered only by yes or no, such as "Are you in a square near a large city?" In other words, it is the detective game adapted to a map. This activity serves several purposes: it provides experience in using a grid system for locational purposes; it helps children formulate questions; and it also provides familiarity with state geography. The road map game will prove very popular even after the skills you're teaching are learned.

After your students have had experience using a simple grid system, you can explain the basis for latitude and longitude and its relationship to the globe. In this case, your task will become one of applying to the globe a system that children have already worked with. If you opt to present latitude and longitude through an expository teaching strategy, you will find yourself explaining two things at once: both the system and its application to the globe. Whatever approach you finally use, we make the same recommendation that we did for teaching the concept of scale: correlate latitude and longitude with whatever math program you are using.

Map Reading (Decoding Maps)

Encoding complements decoding

Students who have had rich and varied mapmaking (encoding) experiences are likely to find that map reading is considerably easier to cope with. Realistically, however, children will be expected to read a wider range of maps than most of them will have had experience making.

Map skills

By the time students leave elementary or middle school, they generally are expected to be able to answer the questions on pages 321–322, which are based on the map shown in Figure 13.6. The questions are similar to those found on standardized achievement tests. Note that we are doing two things here: (1) illustrating how map and globe skills are likely to be tested and (2) identifying what those skills are. Accordingly, you should (1) try to answer the questions and (2) identify, in the space provided, the skill or skills required to answer the questions. You may want to use the scope and sequence we presented in Table 13.1 as a guide for identifying the skills needed.

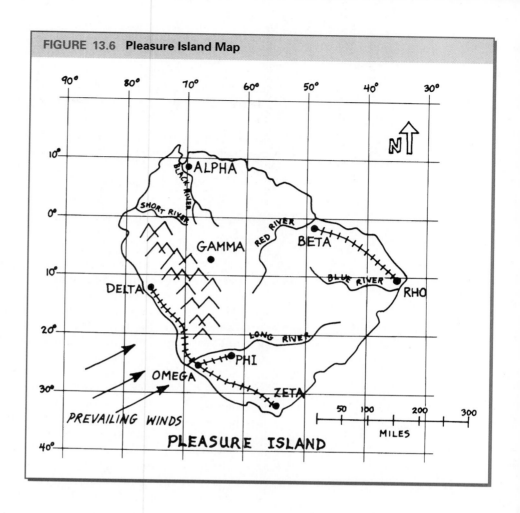

FIGURE 13.6 Pleasure Island Map

Questions

1. What is the northernmost city on Pleasure Island?
   A. Beta   B. Alpha   C. Gamma   D. Zeta
   Skill: _____

2. How far is it from Delta to Rho?
   A. 250 miles   B. 550 miles   D. 900 miles
   Skill: _____

3. Which river flows toward the northeast?
   A. Long River   B. Blue River   C. Black River   D. Red River
   Skill: _____

4. What is the busiest port city on Pleasure Island?
   A. Beta   B. Gamma   C. Omega   D. Phi
   Skill: _____

5. What city probably gets the least rainfall?
   A. Beta   B. Gamma   C. Delta   D. Can't tell
   Skill: _____

6. What city lies closest to the equator?
   A. Beta   B. Alpha   C. Rho   D. Can't tell
   Skill: _____

7. In what hemisphere is most of Pleasure Island located?
   A. Northern   B. Eastern   C. Southern   D. Can't tell
   Skill: _____

(*Answers:* 1. B; 2. B; 3. D; 4. C; 5. B; 6. A; 7. C)

Task Analysis. Most map skills are complex chains of steps that must be followed in sequence. For example, to identify the hemisphere in which Pleasure Island is located (see preceding Question 7), the student must know that the equator is at 0°latitude, and that as one moves southward the degrees of latitude increase in number until one reaches 90°south latitude at the South Pole. The student must then apply this knowledge to the information provided on the map. As a further example of this, identify what you must know to determine whether Pleasure Island is in the Eastern or Western Hemisphere.

Most skills are a sequence of steps

The mathlike nature of map skills makes it possible to determine precisely what students must know and do to achieve success. For example, to determine the distance from Delta to Rho (Question 2), the student must know that (1) all maps have a scale; (2) the scale indicates real distances in shortened form; (3) by using a measuring device (a ruler, etc.), one can convert the distance on a map to the real distance; and so forth. All of these elements must be brought to bear on the problem in the correct sequence; otherwise, failure is almost guaranteed.

Students who have used symbols, scale, and directions to make maps are likely to have fewer problems when they encounter these elements in map reading. But when students encounter problems, we suggest that you plan lessons in which you model the use of the skill in question. For example, to help students find the distance from Delta to Rho, make an overhead transparency of Figure 13.6, and then model the process in a simple, step-by-step fashion. No elaborate questioning procedure is necessary. Because most map and globe skills yield a single correct answer (such as the distance between two cities), showing your students an efficient process for finding that answer will not inhibit their creativity in the least.

Model the process

Map-Related Activities

Some effective and interesting map-related student activities begin with a heuristic question such as "If you were the town council, where would you build the new incinerator (or park, or shopping center, or apartment complex)?" and use maps as the main data source.

Another type of map-based activity involves presenting students with a sequence of maps, each of which adds specialized information. In the following Model Student Activity, students are asked where they would locate a city on a mythical island. Then, in succession, additional information on terrain (landforms), vegetation, and rainfall is provided, each on a separate map.

MODEL STUDENT ACTIVITY

Where Would You Locate Your City?

Overview

The object of this activity is to determine whether students will change their original decision in light of new information.

Procedure

Provide students with a copy of Map 1. Ask where, with just the information they have, they would locate a city if they were prospective settlers. Assume that the area is otherwise uninhabited. Permit students to discuss their choices in small groups, and then have each group present its choice to the entire class. Then provide each group with copies of Maps 2, 3, and 4 (see page 324), one at a time, permitting discussion and explanations (as warranted) after each map is distributed.

Sources/Variation

Making the maps for this activity used to be a major undertaking. However, for any teacher with access to the computer programs we referred to earlier (*PC-Globe, PC-USA, USA Atlas, World Atlas,* and *Microsoft Encarta*), it is now a simple process, and the areas that students deal with are real. The computer programs will usually print whichever maps you need. However, it is usually necessary to remove the name of the area manually, using typewriter white-out, tape, or some other method, if you wish it to remain anonymous. After students have decided where to locate their cities, you can provide them with a computer-generated map showing the actual location of major cities.

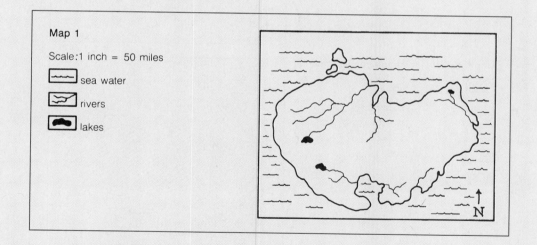

Map 1

Scale: 1 inch = 50 miles

sea water

rivers

lakes

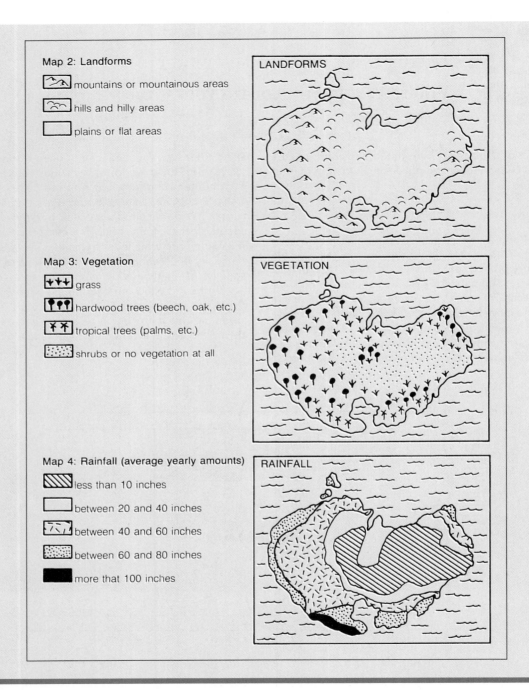

Map 2: Landforms

- mountains or mountainous areas
- hills and hilly areas
- plains or flat areas

LANDFORMS

Map 3: Vegetation

- grass
- hardwood trees (beech, oak, etc.)
- tropical trees (palms, etc.)
- shrubs or no vegetation at all

VEGETATION

Map 4: Rainfall (average yearly amounts)

- less than 10 inches
- between 20 and 40 inches
- between 40 and 60 inches
- between 60 and 80 inches
- more that 100 inches

RAINFALL

Literary Mapping. Remember reading Mark Twain's *The Adventures of Huckleberry Finn,* in which Huck and his comrades travel to various places along the Mississippi? Most of the places Huck visits are real, and most can be located on a map of the area. While reading *Huck Finn* wouldn't it make sense to trace Huck's travels on a map? Such an activity need not be a major undertaking. In fact, it is probably best done almost incidentally to reading the story, yet the activity will show a functional use for map skills.

Mapping hypothetical areas

There is a wealth of children's literature in which the settings are real places and, thus, locatable on a map. There is still more literature in which the settings are fictional but are described in enough detail that it's possible to create a map of the area. Think about Beatrix Potter's *Peter Rabbit* for a moment. The cardinal directions might be amiss, but it is possible to map the relative location of major elements in *Peter Rabbit*—the tool shed, Mr. McGregor's garden, the fence, the watering can in which Peter hides, and so forth. Each child's map might be different, but the idea is to create a tangible map of an idealized literary location. Other children's literature that lends itself to mapmaking includes *Little Black Bear Goes for a Walk,* by Beatrice Freschet (1977); *Rosie's Walk,* by Pat Hutchins (1968); Robert McCloskey's (1941) classic *Make Way for Ducklings,* which we referred to earlier, and *Henry Explores the Jungle,* by Mark Taylor (1968).

Sandra Pritchard (1989) expanded on the notion of using children's literature for teaching geography and map skills by identifying story-related activities that correlate with the five themes for geographic education (Joint Committee on Geographic Education, 1984) that we presented in detail in Chapter 2. Following is an abridgement of some of Pritchard's recommended geography-related activities for Virginia Lee Burton's (1943) *Katy and the Big Snow.*

Location: Position on the Earth's Surface

Activities correlating literature and the five geography themes

* Locate buildings and streets on a map.
* Identify and locate cardinal directions.
* Determine in which direction Katy went from the school to the railroad station; from the police station to the fire station, etc.
* Describe the location of buildings in relation to other buildings and streets.

Place: Physical and Human Characteristics

* Discuss seasonal changes in the little town, and how those changes affect people.
* Describe a walk along First or Third Street.

Relationships Within Places: Human-Environment Interaction

* Tell how the snow affects the lives of people in the town.
* Tell what might happen if Katy had not been able to plow out the town.

Movement: Humans Interacting on the Earth

* Identify and describe the various forms of transportation in the story and on the map.
* Identify and describe the various forms of communication.
* Find symbols for buildings, roads, and airports on various maps.

Region/Neighborhoods: How They Form and Change

★ Identify different kinds of neighborhoods in the little town.

Making maps of idealized locations from children's literature may help sensitize students to the ways in which authors describe the physical setting in which stories are set, especially if you call attention to it. Such a purpose may lack clear relevance to social studies, of course, but by giving tangible meaning to a literary element such as "the setting of the story," it could show up in subsequent stories that children write.

Working with Other Graphic Forms

Some teachers and students seem to regard graphs, tables, and charts as one of the "bad breath" areas of social studies. However, quantitative data are not difficult to deal with if they are approached from a "use" perspective—that is, if students actually do something with the information on a chart, graph, or table.

One instructionally troublesome aspect of graphs, tables, and charts is their efficiency in presenting information. They can present so much information in so little space that students can quickly suffer from information overload. Thus our earlier suggestion to limit the information you provide children at the beginning of an activity prevails here.

Avoiding information overload—limit the amount of data

A second consideration involves the way you present the numbers for statistical information. For example, there were 7,527,152,000 bushels of corn and 2,035,818,000 bushels of wheat grown in the United States in 1990. If you are like us, you probably had to count the number of places in these numbers, which have been rounded some to begin with. Because such large numbers can overwhelm children, we recommend that you round them even more—to 7.5 billion bushels of corn, for example. The idea is that the numbers provide the basis for identifying trends and relationships, such as that the United States grows about three times more corn than wheat. It isn't necessary to have numbers accurate to the last possible bushel to identify such relationships. And certainly the numbers are not something you would expect children to memorize.

Helping students deal with large numbers

To help children deal with large numbers, we suggest that you make them as easy to understand as possible. In addition, because many children have no comprehension of how big a billion or how tremendous a trillion really is, we recommend that you use Schwartz's (1985) wonderful book, *How Much Is a Million?*, before you deal with large numbers.

Fact Sheets

The fact sheet illustrated in Figure 13.7 was produced by a fourth-grade teacher who was teaching a unit on farming in the United States. Although the information on it is limited, it still proved to be too much for her students to process at one time. She then had them fold the paper so that only Part I was visible.

As she used the American Farmer Fact Sheet, the teacher alternated between modeling and questioning designed to help the children (1) read the charts and graphs and (2) determine what this information meant. For example, the

Testing versus teaching

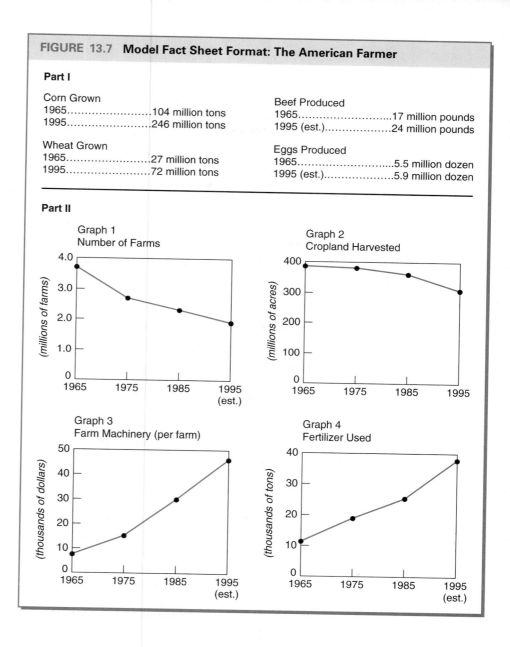

FIGURE 13.7   Model Fact Sheet Format: The American Farmer

Part I

Corn Grown
1965......................104 million tons
1995......................246 million tons

Wheat Grown
1965......................27 million tons
1995......................72 million tons

Beef Produced
1965..........................17 million pounds
1995 (est.)..................24 million pounds

Eggs Produced
1965..........................5.5 million dozen
1995 (est.)..................5.9 million dozen

Part II

Graph 1
Number of Farms
(millions of farms)

Graph 2
Cropland Harvested
(millions of acres)

Graph 3
Farm Machinery (per farm)
(thousands of dollars)

Graph 4
Fertilizer Used
(thousands of tons)

teacher said, "Let's see if we can find out what has happened to the number of farms in this country." "They went down," was the chorus of responses. "Does anyone want to explain how we can figure that out?" After one student volunteered to explain the process for finding that information, the teacher then said, "To find out if the number of farms went down a lot or just a little, we have to look at the numbers." She then modeled the process for showing that the number of farms decreased by almost one-half (50%) and concluded that this seemed like a big decrease.

Working through all the information in a similar fashion, the students concluded that although there are fewer farms in the United States, the amount of food produced on those farms has increased. They also concluded that since fewer farmers (Graph 1) were farming almost the same number of acres as in the past (Graph 2), the average size of a farm is larger today than it was in the past. Furthermore, the students concluded that fewer farmers can grow more food because of the increased use of machinery (Graph 3) and fertilizer (Graph 4). They also suggested that there could be other reasons for this (better weather, etc.), but that they didn't have enough information to be certain of these causes.

Using just the information on the American Farmer Fact Sheet, students developed their own conclusions about the changing nature of American farming. Of course, a teacher could approach the topic by having students read a section in the textbook. That section, in all likelihood, would begin like this: "American farms today are larger than they used to be. Farmers also use more machinery and . . ." In this instance, however, students would be reading *someone else's conclusions* about farming instead of using information to build their own.

Encoding Quantitative Data

Before children can use the information on a graph, table, or chart, they must be able to handle that information at the literal level. For example, if children cannot read Graph 1 on the American Farmer Fact Sheet, then it may be necessary to back up and show them how the information was translated (or encoded) into graph form.

As a general rule, encoding experiences for primary-level students should involve simple examples and small quantities. They can be as simple as tallying the number of girls and boys in a classroom, as illustrated in Figure 13.8. Until students are able to think representationally, it is probably wisest to maintain one-to-one correspondence—that is, where one symbol on a table represents something the child can see in reality. In Figure 13.8, each symbol stands for one classmate. As students grow progressively more able to handle representational thought—as when one symbol equals five classmates, for example—their encoding experiences can become increasingly complex.

Simple surveys can provide a wealth of information for encoding activities. That's what one teacher used when her students had graph-reading problems. Small groups of students surveyed the traffic passing by the school at different times of day. They counted the number of cars and trucks, the number of pickup trucks and minivans, and the number of people who waved back at them. Then, with the teacher's help, the groups put their information onto bar graphs, which were hung around the room to provide a basis for comparison. The result of one group's efforts is illustrated in Figure 13.9.

Making Tables.   Once data have been gathered, they must be presented in a readily understandable form. One such form, a table, is intended to communicate the relationships between the data. General considerations for constructing tables (and graphs) include the following:

FIGURE 13.8 **Sample Table Encoded by Students**

Boys and Girls in Ms. James's Classroom October, 1997		
Boys	⚇⚇⚇⚇⚇⚇⚇⚇⚇⚇⚇	11
Girls	⚇⚇⚇⚇⚇⚇⚇⚇⚇⚇⚇⚇⚇⚇	14
⚇ Boy ⚇ Girl		25

Four characteristics of tables

* Tables should be self-sufficient. That is, a table should give a complete and understandable message: what is being related, the form in which the relationship is established, the source of the information—everything needed to help readers make their own interpretations.

* All rows and columns must have clear headings that follow an identifiable pattern—for example, high to low, alphabetical, geographic—and, where appropriate, indicate the measure being used—percentages, thousands, square miles, and so on.

* The source of the data should be included in a footnote.

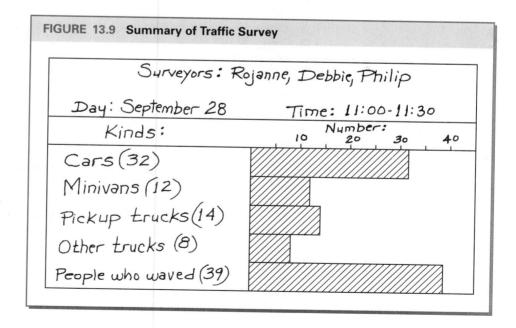

FIGURE 13.9 **Summary of Traffic Survey**

MODEL STUDENT ACTIVITY

Constructing a Table

Temperature and Snow Report, Week of January 9–15

* Monday's high temperature was 30°. Tuesday's high was 25°. Wednesday's high was 28°, followed by 32° on Thursday, 35° on Friday, 37° on Saturday, and 30° on Sunday. The average high temperature for the week was 31°.

* The snowfall for the week totaled 14 inches. It did not snow on Wednesday, Friday, or Saturday. It snowed 4 inches on Monday and 7 inches on Tuesday, for a total of 11 inches for the first two days. Average snowfall was 2 inches a day for the week.

These data were converted into table form, as shown below.

Source: Personal measurements.

Temperature and Snow Report, Week of January 9–15

Day	High Temperature (F)	Snow (Inches)
Monday	30	4
Tuesday	25	7
Wednesday	28	0
Thursday	32	1
Friday	35	0
Saturday	37	0
Sunday	30	2
Average high 31		Total snowfall 14
		Average daily snowfall 2

* The table title should make clear what information is being related and in what terms.

The Model Student Activity, Constructing a Table, follows these guidelines for table (and graph) construction.

Decoding Graphs and Tables

Before children can do anything with the information on a graph or in a table, they must gain access to that information. Fortunately, the process of decoding information presented on a graph or in a table is amenable to task analysis. Probably the easiest way to go about this is to ask yourself two related questions: (1) what must the student know (and in what sequence) to gain access to the information? and (2) at what points might students experience problems?

Modeling is the key

We do not recommend using indirect or discovery strategies for teaching the procedures associated with table or graph reading. There are just too many points at which students might encounter problems. Thus this is another instance where modeling and step-by-step teacher-directed instruction, followed by guided practice, are wholly appropriate.

MODEL STUDENT ACTIVITY

Linear Charting

This technique, which we call *linear charting,* consists of having students attach pictures or short descriptions of a process in the correct sequence on a piece of string or yarn. A linear chart for the production of bread is illustrated below.

This may not sound like an exciting activity, but actually doing it often proves otherwise. Consider, that linear charting can also be used for more than just social studies activities. For example, instead of book reports, students might illustrate the significant scenes or events in a story and then attach those pictures, in the correct sequence, to a piece of yarn. When students present their reports, the rest of the class can refer to a visual representation of the book's events instead of listening to a strictly oral presentation.

Charts

In the days before overhead projectors and copiers became widely available, chart making was probably more common than it is today. With current technology, it is a simple process to make an overhead transparency of a small chart that will be readily visible to everyone in the class. However, once the overhead projector is turned off, the image is gone, whereas a poster-size chart displayed somewhere in the classroom can be viewed repeatedly. An alternative is to use the magnification feature of most copying machines and make enough copies for everyone in the class.

Types of charts

An endless variety of things can be depicted in chart form. If you were to present a schematic drawing of the structure of an organization such as the U.S. Congress, you would have an *organizational chart.* If you were to outline the steps a bill passes through in Congress en route to becoming a law, you would have a *flow chart.* Virtually any process—the production of steel, bread, or whatever—can be illustrated in pictures, in a short narrative description, or in a combination of the two on a flow chart.

Charts, like maps, omit details

All charts summarize whatever they depict. They are like most maps and outlines in that they highlight major points or phrases while omitting details. However, the need to summarize information can be an asset when you have students engage in chart making, because summarizing forces them to identify the main ideas that they should put on their chart. In this context, chart making can be an effective culminating activity for small-group work.

Linear Charting. An alternative form of charting that uses pictures attached to a piece of string or yarn is shown in the Model Student Activity on page 331. This procedure is also useful for highlighting the main elements of a story, in which case it is sometimes called "story mapping."

Summary

This chapter has suggested some approaches for helping children gain access to specialized forms of information—namely, maps, globes, graphs, and tabular data. For each of these forms, encoding experiences—which include map, graph, table, and chart making—can help children understand how information gets into a particular form. Such encoding experiences may provide students with a good basis for decoding or gaining access to information displayed on maps, graphs, tables, and charts.

Unlike some of the other areas that social studies encompasses, map, table, and graph reading (decoding) involves an identifiable sequence of the knowledge and skills necessary for gaining access to information. If any step is omitted, or if the sequence of steps is confused, the student is likely to fail. To avoid failure and the sense of frustration that can accompany it, we recommend that you "task-analyze" what the student is being asked to do by identifying the knowledge and skills required to complete the task. This analysis can provide the basis for step-by-step instruction as you guide your students through the decoding process.

Once students have gained access to information, the next phase is a "natural": they need to do something with it. It becomes almost a circular process when you recognize that what students do with information can provide a reason for them to get (and want) access to it.

Suggested Activities

1. Design a map-based decision-making activity that deals with a problem presently confronting the community you are living in, or, as an alternative, use a hypothetical community.
2. It is sometimes argued that much of the time devoted to instruction in longitude and latitude is wasted and could be better spent on something else. That argument is based on the claim that although *latitude* and *longitude* are concepts many Americans know, they rarely, if ever, use them. Develop a response to that argument.
3. Review the instructional activities presented in this chapter, and identify those that teach and those that test a student's preexisting skills.
4. Design a fact sheet that could serve as the basis for a lesson on any of the following topics: immigration, health care, education, community, industrialization.
5. Obtain two social studies textbooks *for the same grade level* but from different publishers (your curriculum library or learning-resource center should have copies available). Compare the two books in terms of the map-reading skills they require of students. Also compare them in terms of the quantitative-data skills they require, if any.

Suggested Readings

A. K. Ellis. (1997). *Teaching and learning elementary social studies* (6th ed.). Boston: Allyn & Bacon. This text contains an excellent chapter on making and interpreting maps.

Massachusetts Geographic Alliance. (1990). *Global geography: Activities for teaching the five themes of geography.* Boulder, CO: Social Science Education Consortium. We recommend this collection of activities, all of which come with the necessary teaching materials.

Mark Monmonier. (1991). *How to lie with maps.* Chicago: University of Chicago Press. Monmonier explains why "a good map tells a multitude of little white lies" (p. 25).

14 Using Instructional Tools: Print, Multimedia and Community Resources

Key Questions

* What resources are available for teaching social studies?
* What considerations are involved in using those resources?
* What do teachers do when schools lack the resources they want?

Key Ideas

* Instructional tools may lurk in unlikely places.
* Using instructional tools effectively depends on preplanning.
* Identifying community resources is often less difficult than using those resources effectively.
* Resources provide options for teachers in developing teaching activities, individualizing instruction, prompting student interest, achieving social studies goals and objectives, and allowing students to transfer skill and content learning to a variety of contexts.

Introduction: Teaching in the Electronic Age

An abstraction has become real

As more and more schools gain access to the Internet, the number of resources for teaching social studies has grown exponentially. For years we heard about how the reservoir of knowledge was growing by leaps and bounds, but because most of us had no way to tap into the vastness of that reservoir, the so-called information explosion remained largely an abstraction. Today the Internet, combined with other forms of computer-based technology, provides access to more resources than most of us can ever use. The information explosion has become very real.

No longer must teachers rely solely on a textbook, a map, and an almanac to teach social studies. Many teachers still rely on textbooks and maps, of course, but computer-based almanacs and atlases have made life considerably easier. Many teachers also continue to use a variety of noncomputerized resources, especially to teach reflective thinking skills. They recognize that, although the Internet makes available a large amount of information, it does not teach children how to interpret and use that information.

Computerized resources for teaching social studies, along with some older resources like overhead projectors, share a common characteristic: they plug into electrical outlets. However, there is still a wide array of nonelectrical resources available, especially if you know what you are looking for. For example, something as mundane as the Yellow Pages of the telephone directory could provide the basis for a variety of social studies activities:

Activities based on a telephone directory

* For identifying the government services available in the local community.

* For identifying alternative ways in which the Yellow Pages could be organized, and then considering what those organizational patterns would mean for (1) users, (2) advertisers, and (3) the telephone company.

* For finding out what it costs, if anything, to be listed in the Yellow Pages. Is it free? And if charges do apply, speculating on how they are determined and why businesses might pay to be listed. When schools are listed in the Yellow Pages, do you suppose they pay? Or are some listings free and others must be paid for?

* For an activity in which students use the Yellow Pages from the 1960s or 1970s and a current directory to find the location of selected businesses, such as laundromats, florists, hardware stores, video rental outlets (which did not exist in the 1960s), and movie theaters. Plotting the location of each business on a city map, and determining if the number and locations of the businesses have changed over time.

The balance of this chapter is organized in an arbitrary and somewhat eclectic way; it covers print materials and computers, nonprint and visual resources, and finally community resources. Addresses for the teaching resources noted here are included in the Resource Handbook.

Textbooks

Some schools use a multi-text approach

Almost all schools have textbooks, and some classes have access to several different texts. However, some schools—even those with ample financial resources—have elected not to use social studies textbooks. Still other schools may not have enough copies of a single text for all students in the class, but this is usually intentional. Sometimes the number of texts will be limited to no more than ten copies of a particular book. Because there may be as many as forty or fifty social studies texts in a given classroom, it's technically incorrect to say that teachers don't have any textbooks. Teachers in those schools are probably using a *multi-text* approach, in which they select elements from different books as they need them. This approach reduces the pressure that teachers sometimes feel to cover every chapter in a book.

Generalizing about social studies textbooks can be a risky business, but we will venture the following:

* Social studies textbooks for elementary and middle schools today are more similar than they are different, especially in states that have mandated curriculums.

* You can get usable teaching ideas from every social studies textbook or accompanying teacher's guide—no matter how old and decrepit.
* Textbooks have a way of becoming the basis for social studies programs, not a resource to be used with them.

Texts as tools

For teachers who wish to depart from textbook-dominated programs, the first step is to reflect on their perception of the textbook. When they come to regard a text as a tool, as something to use when it suits their purposes, they will have begun the transition from treating the text as a body of information to be learned to treating it as a resource to be used as it is needed.

The following are some alternative ways in which you might use textbooks:

Alternative uses for textbooks

* As a source of background information that students read either (1) prior to studying a topic or concept or (2) after the need for the information has been established.
* As something students read when they need additional information on a topic.
* As a source of potential in-class activities (or test questions).
* As a contrasting point of view or as a source of data for further analysis.
* As a means to confirm or challenge certain hypotheses after group discussion—for example, "India is a 'poor' nation."
* As a vehicle for identifying the main idea of several related paragraphs.
* As a source for establishing the meaning of various terms (so that they need not be dealt with in class).
* As a way of placating people who think that a course isn't worthwhile unless it has a textbook associated with it.
* As an object of study (to determine how the text was organized and constructed).

Supplementary Print Materials

The supplementary print materials available to social studies teachers range from periodicals and current events newspapers through an unbelievable assortment of trade books (children's books) to self-contained teaching kits on almost any topic you can name. We examine supplementary print materials in terms of these categories.

Current Events Publications

If your elementary school was like our elementary school, some of your teachers used a weekly or monthly affairs periodical. These include publications such as *My Weekly Reader, Let's Find Out* (kindergarten), *Scholastic News* (Grades 1–6), or *Junior Review* (Grades 6–9). These publications are still widely available.

Instead of current events periodicals, which must be purchased separately, your teachers may have relied more heavily on daily newspapers. From time to time, they may have asked you to bring in a newspaper article to share with the class for current events time. But unless they put limitations on the kind of clipping you could bring in, a typical assortment might deal with topics such as last Saturday's Little League game or a bank robbery in northeastern Nevada. Seldom do child-selected articles focus on proposed constitutional amendments, changing views of morality, or the problems of international diplomacy—unless a teacher insists on it. Even then, most children will be unable to understand or interpret the significance of such events. Such an assignment reflects the current events problem: much as we might like children to be interested in and aware of events and issues going on around the world that may influence their lives, many of those events and issues can go beyond their current level of comprehension and concern. The fact that some teachers have difficulty explaining things such as inflation or why the Palestine Liberation Organization and Israel have traditionally been at odds illustrates another dimension of the problem. Helping children to understand what is going on in the world at any particular moment is only part of the problem; they also need to understand why these events are occurring.

Current Events or Current Affairs?   As a teacher, you have at least two options for keeping students abreast of happenings going on around them. One option is to maintain an ongoing current events program. In this context, an *event* is anything that has happened or is happening, either trivial or potentially significant. A second option is to establish a current *affairs* program that focuses on continuing issues or concerns. In the absence of realistic limitations, a current events approach can become a warmed-over version of the nightly news, in which case the purposes of the program might be better served if the class actually watched the news on television.

Current affairs programs focus on in-depth studies of ongoing issues—the environment, human rights, conflicts occurring in various parts of the world (the Middle East, Africa, or Bosnia), and so forth. Consequently, current affairs programs are less likely to reflect the piecemeal approach that can occur in current events programs. In a current affairs program, your focus might be on different dimensions of the farm crisis. Or you might use changes in the price (or weight) of bubble gum or candy bars as an entre to the continuing study of rises in the cost of living. The idea of a current affairs program is to tie together the separate events of a continuing problem to help students understand the significance of problems that could remain beyond their comprehension if dealt with on an isolated events basis.

With the Internet and other modern technology, the world has been reduced to the global village of almost instantaneous communications. As a result, you may recall seeing television coverage of people, especially children, running for cover to avoid being shot or killed in hostilities somewhere around the world. Our concern is with the feelings, and sometimes fears, that these images can generate among young children. The purpose of current events and current affairs programs is to help children make sense of events occurring in the world around them, not to frighten them.

Weekly news periodicals, like *Weekly Reader* and *Scholastic,* can furnish the background information essential for interpreting current events. The broad range of events and happenings that the weekly periodicals include may compensate

The current events problem

Current affairs focus on ongoing issues

Seeking common elements among separate events

Depth versus breadth

COMMENTARY: On Helping Children Deal With Terrorism

With the tragic bombings of the World Trade Center building in New York City and the federal office building in Oklahoma City, we can no longer tell children that "terrorism occurs in places that are far far away" and that "such events can't happen here." Adults can take consolation in knowing that their chances of being involved in a terrorist attack are less than one in 100 million (Ellerbee, 1995), but such information seldom offers much comfort to young children. So what, then, is a teacher to do? Ellerbee (1995) offers the following suggestions.

* Let children talk about the event, and let them know it is okay to feel sad or confused—or even scared. However, do so in ways that respect the child's privacy; some children cope by not talking.

* Remind children that it is unfair to judge large groups of people by the actions of a few. You may wish to use words like *cowardly, sneaky,* and *unacceptable,* to reenforce the notion that violence is not the way to get what you want—something that good people already know.

* Understand that in the immediate aftermath of terrorist attacks, many children are more concerned about their parents' safety than their own. Where appropriate, encourage parents to spend extra time with their children.

* Help children to understand that most terrorist acts are isolated events; they do occur, but not often. Also point out the reassuring things that often happen in their aftermath: the rescuers who risk their lives to save others, the communities near and far who lend supplies and support, and the massive outpouring of sympathy for the victims and rage at the perpetrators. People do indeed care about others.

Source: Ellerbee, L. (1995). What shall we tell the kids? *Liberal Opinion Week,* 6 (May 1), p. 7.

---

for their lack of in-depth coverage. Thus the basic decision you face in developing a current affairs or current events program (and in deciding whether to use one of the current events periodicals) is whether to aim for in-depth understanding of relatively few continuing problems or to aim for awareness of a broader range of topical coverage.

In many instances, current affairs can be esoteric for elementary children, even if the events are reduced to their simplest dimensions. This is because it is extremely difficult, for example, to capture the reasons for the traditional animosity that exists between Arabs and Israelis in a single, easy-to-understand publication. Thus you may be better off opting for the broader coverage that you gain with an events approach, especially if you teach at the primary level. However, if you plan to teach at the intermediate or middle-school levels, the possibility of pursuing a current affairs approach becomes much more realistic. Or you can do both; you can use an affairs approach for some issues and settle for broad awareness for other issues.

Newspapers. Daily newspapers provide what the current events periodicals don't, including coverage of local news. But teachers who look to newspapers solely as a source of local news are not looking far enough. In some schools, teachers base much of their instructional program—social studies, math, language arts, and reading—on daily newspapers. Students do comparison shopping using the grocery ads, compute batting averages (math) using the sports page, invest (mythically) in the stock market, examine weather patterns (using the weather map and forecast), realphabetize the newspaper's directory, put

Using the newspaper to teach

scrambled headlines back together again, compare the amount of space devoted to various categories of articles (international news, national news, etc.), use small sections of the paper to compare the amount of factual data (reporting) with the amount of opinion (editorials), or compare the amount of space devoted to ads with the space devoted to news.

Newspaper-based activities

You might give groups of students identical collections of stories clipped from several newspapers and ask them to compose a front page. They should be prepared to explain their reasons for including the articles they did. You could also remove the headlines from various articles and have children create their own based on the content of the story. They can then compare their headlines with the originals. Or they could take several days' accumulation of TV schedules and try to identify patterns in TV programming.

You could do other things with a daily newspaper, but the preceding examples should serve to illustrate the idea. For many newspaper-related activities, it is not necessary for children to be able to read or understand the articles in order to use the newspaper as a learning tool. As with most instructional resources, the essential idea is to consider the newspaper as a resource, as something you can teach *with,* not simply teach *about.*

Trade Books

Criteria for selecting
children's books

In the publishing world, a textbook is a book designed for classroom use. Fiction or nonfiction books intended for sale to the public are *trade books. Mike Mulligan and His Steam Shovel* (Burton, 1939) is a juvenile trade book, as are Kenneth Grahame's (1908) classic, *The Wind in the Willows,* and thousands of others.

Because so many trade books are available, the National Council for the Social Studies reviews only those books considered "most notable" during a given year. Thus, unless the book (1) is written primarily for children (K–8), (2) emphasizes human relations, (3) presents an original theme or a fresh slant on a traditional topic, (4) is highly readable, and (5) includes maps and illustrations where appropriate, it is not included in the listing that appears in each May issue of *Social Education.*

Historical fiction, nonfiction, biography—somewhere there's a trade book that applies to whatever your class is studying. To assess the quality of books for children, McGowan (1987) has recommended the following criteria:

1. Decide whether the book is *developmentally appropriate.* Can the prose be understood by its intended audience, and are the setting, plot, and themes familiar to young readers?

2. Determine whether the book has *literary value.* Is it meaningful and enjoyable to read, and has the author written with attention to character development, dialogue, plot, imagery, and message?

3. Determine whether the book presents *valid information.* Is the story told with reasonable accuracy and in a "true-to-life" fashion?

4. Determine whether the book has *a message of value.* Does the author examine an issue worthy of the reader's attention, or does the story involve values that the reader should eventually assimilate?

Trade books can provide a wealth of information for any social studies program.
(© Elizabeth Crews)

An area of children's fiction particularly appropriate to social studies is ethnic literature. For example, *The Big Push* by Betty Baker (1972), based on a historical incident that occurred when the Hopi Indian children were forced to go to school, is almost guaranteed to generate an active discussion. Likewise, children are likely to enjoy *The Hundred Penny Box* by Sharon Bell Mathis (1975), a poignant story about a young boy who convinces his mother not to throw out all the old things that belong to his great-great-great-aunt, who lives with them.

You might consider using trade books in one or more of the following ways:

* As supplementary reading for children
* As background reading for yourself
* As reference material for children to use
* As a springboard for writing activities
* As the vehicle for units or lessons
* As the basis for an individualized reading program that parallels whatever you are dealing with in social studies

Teaching Kits

Teaching kits are self-contained packages of instructional materials. We have long been fascinated by David Macaulay's wonderful series of books: *Cathedral* (1973), *Pyramid* (1975), *Castle* (1979), *The Way Things Work* (1988), and others. PBS Video (1420 Braddock Place, Alexandria, VA 22314-1698) has now developed multimedia teaching kits based on Macaulay's books. The kits, "Middle Ages" (which combines *Cathedral* and *Castle*) and "Pyramid," cost approximately $200 and include videotapes, teaching modules, and related material. *The Way Things Work* is now available on CD–ROM.

Many museums and state departments of education offer specialized teaching kits on a loan or rental basis. The Institute for Texan Cultures in San Antonio, for example, offers rental kits on "The Indians of Texas." If that topic is not something your students might study, consider the "Mysteries in History" toolbox available from the Indianapolis Children's Museum. Or contact the education coordinator at the nearest historical museum of reconstructed settlement (e.g., Old Sturbridge Village in Massachusetts, Connor Prairie Settlement in Indiana) or your state department of education to find whether they have instructional materials available for loan or rent. Addresses for these sources are in the Resource Handbook.

Self-contained teaching kits can cost upward of $750. As a result, the lower cost of loan or rental kits (approximately $25 plus shipping) often makes them more attractive to cost-conscious administrators. On the other hand, most kits last for years. If four teachers at a grade level share a teaching kit and use it for five years, the per-use cost of a $750 kit would be $37.50, which is not much more than the rental costs.

Workbooks

Most social studies textbook series have workbooks that are correlated with them, but these must be ordered separately each year; they don't just come with the texts. These materials are called *pupil study guides, activity guides,* or something similar, but they are *workbooks* nonetheless. If you teach in a program that demands the kind of reinforcement that workbooks offer, you may find them helpful.

Computer-Based Resources

Computer-based resources

Like many teachers, we use our computers extensively. All our course syllabi, most of our instructional materials (class handouts), and many of our examinations are now created and stored on the computer. If we were teaching in a school where we had to keep lots of student records, we would use a computer-based grade-book program. They can provide up-to-date analyses of students' progress and can provide almost instant grades at the end of the semester. Considering the amount of information and routine paperwork that teachers must deal with, computers have proven to be wonderful tools for managing classroom-related tasks.

A Note About Hardware

In our visits to schools across the country, the computers we see most often are Apple II's. This was an excellent computer in its day, but that day is quickly passing. The Apples are still useful for teaching keyboarding skills, but unless they have been upgraded, they are unlikely to have a CD-ROM player or enough memory to run most of the software available today. Some schools have gotten

Computers on carts

around this limitation by purchasing new machines with multimedia capabilities and placing them on a cart that can be rolled from room to room. If your school is still relying on the old Apples, we recommend that you investigate the "computer on a cart" option.

Instructional Applications

Six modes

The six basic modes of computer-assisted instruction (CAI) are (1) tutorial, (2) drill and practice, (3) simulation, (4) integrated application programs, (5) problem solving, and (6) hypermedia environments (Braun, Fernlund, and White, 1998). We describe each of these briefly.

Tutorial Mode. Tutorial programs were among the earliest forms of social studies software. They are designed to present information to students, usually step by step and in sequential chunks, and are often accompanied by colorful graphics. In a tutorial program, the computer takes the place of the teacher, the textbook, or another source as the provider of information. Most tutorial

Mastery learning

programs also use a form of branching or mastery learning. This means that when the students respond correctly to a series of questions the program will move them into new material. However, if students respond incorrectly, the computer will recycle them until they can demonstrate mastery.

Tutorial programs are available for a variety of topics, including basic economics, introductory history and geography, and, in some cases, nonsubject-related topics. For example, *Kids on Keys* (Spinnaker) is a tutorial program designed to familiarize young children with the computer keyboard.

Drill-and-Practice Mode. Drill-and-practice programs are designed to reinforce prior learning through repetitive practice. If you wish your students to learn the states and capitals or to practice locating places using latitude or longitude, for example, there are several programs that can help them. In fact, most social studies software falls into the drill-and-practice mode.

Drill-and-practice programs have been likened to electronic workbooks. But unlike traditional workbooks, the material is often presented randomly rather than sequentially. This means that students do not interact with the same series of questions and activities each time they use the software. In addition, drill-and-practice programs often use a gamelike format which, when combined with superb graphics, color, and sound, can make them appealing and almost painless.

Immediate feedback   A major asset of drill-and-practice programs is their ability to provide immediate feedback. For example, wherever students enter an incorrect answer, the program typically responds with an encouraging "Try again, Zack." Unfortunately, most computer-based programs do not recognize or give credit for partially correct or misspelled answers, as human graders might. Some drill-and-practice programs avoid this limitation by asking questions in a multiple-choice format, so that students need enter only the letter (A, B, C, or D) for the correct response. Despite these limitations, the interactive nature of drill-and-practice programs can add life to what might otherwise be dull stuff.

Simulation Mode. We described the simulation mode in some detail in Chapter 9, so we will say little more about it here. Using simulations, children can place themselves into lifelike situations in which they must make decisions similar to those that had to be made in whatever real-life situation the simulation depicts. Those decisions may relate to traveling westward on the *Oregon Trail* (or its newer siblings, *Yukon Trail* and *Amazon Trail*, MECC, 1996), building and operating a dinosaur theme park (*DinoPark Tycoon*, MECC, 1995), or operating a school store (*Classroom StoreWorks*, Tom Snyder, 1997).

Beating the computer   Computer-based simulations are very popular but can also be very time consuming. In addition, children sometimes approach simulations as they do video games, where their objective is to outwit the program so they can "win." Such situations may require human intervention—a teacher-led discussion, perhaps—that refocuses students' attention on the content being simulated, and not just the outcome.

Integrated Application Programs. Databases, spreadsheets, and word-processing programs have been available for at least a decade, but integrated application programs incorporate these formerly separate entities into a single powerful program. Examples include *Appleworks* (Claris), *Microsoft Word* (Microsoft), *Clarisworks* (Claris),

Integrated packages

Greatworks (Symantec), and *Works for Windows* (Microsoft). Any one of these programs can be useful for developing and presenting data for teacher-developed instructional activities and for upper elementary and middle-school student's presentations. For example, Janet Jacobsen's students used the *Works* program to create their reports and the graphics associated with them. More appropriate for lower elementary students are programs like *Magic Slate* (Sunburst), *KidWriter* (Spinnaker), or FrEd Writer (Computer Using Educators). Because even most kindergarten children are able to use computers successfully, any hesitancy in this area probably reflects the teacher's misgivings and not the students' capabilities (c.f., Bryant, 1992).

Problem-Solving Mode. Integrated application programs can provide the basis for some fascinating problem-solving activities. For example, consider posing the following question to your students: "How do underdeveloped nations differ from developed nations?" The first step is helping students to decide what characteristics might separate underdeveloped and developed nations. Using a database program, you can easily provide per capita income information for different nations, which students can then use to determine which ones are "developed" or "undeveloped." Once that decision is made, students can use a database program to determine what characteristics are associated with "developed" and "undeveloped" countries.

Figure 14.1, which shows the age distribution data for the United States and Bangladesh, was generated by the *PC Globe* database program (PC Globe, Inc., 4700 South McClintock, Tempe, AZ 85282). By comparing these data for the United States and Bangladesh, students can identify at least one factor, the birth rate, that characterizes the difference between developed and undeveloped nations.

Hypermedia Environments. There are basically two types of hypermedia programs: (1) Internet browsers, such as *Netscape* and *Microsoft Internet Explorer,* and (2) hypertext programs such as *Hypercard* and *Hyperstudio* (for Apple computers) and *Linkway* (for PCs). All of these programs permit users to navigate interactively through audio, video, and text modes. You must have a modem or be wired directly to a network server to use an Internet browser, but hypertext-based programs have no such requirements.

Interactive navigation

Hypertext programs are assembled much like a deck of index cards—each containing certain information—that can be arranged and rearranged in different ways. By pressing a button located on each card, you can move to the next card or, in some instances, start a CD-ROM or other audiovisual device. When a hypertext program is combined with audiovisual equipment, the result is a hypermedia environment, perhaps even a multimedia extravaganza!

Programs for presentation

Hypertext programs are especially well suited for presentations, either by teachers or students. This is because users can easily alter the sequence of presentation. Unfortunately, the description of hypertext programs is often more imposing than the programs themselves. Most middle-school students can learn to use *Hyperstudio* readily, whereas most primary students often feel more comfortable using a somewhat simpler version called *SlideShow.*

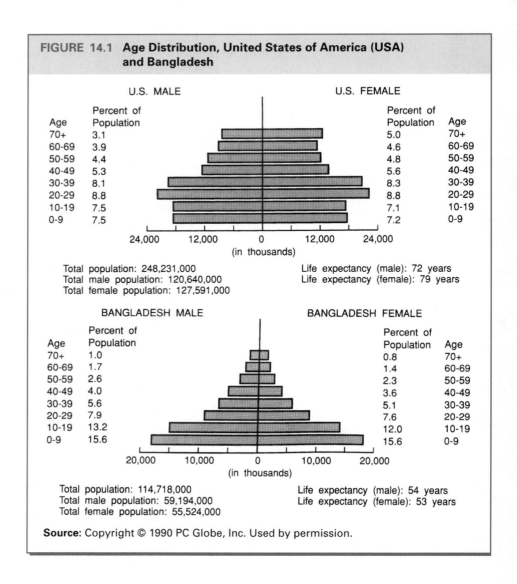

FIGURE 14.1 Age Distribution, United States of America (USA) and Bangladesh

U.S. MALE   **U.S. FEMALE**

Age	Percent of Population (Male)	Percent of Population (Female)	Age
70+	3.1	5.0	70+
60-69	3.9	4.6	60-69
50-59	4.4	4.8	50-59
40-49	5.3	5.6	40-49
30-39	8.1	8.3	30-39
20-29	8.8	8.8	20-29
10-19	7.5	7.1	10-19
0-9	7.5	7.2	0-9

24,000   12,000   0   12,000   24,000
(in thousands)

Total population: 248,231,000
Total male population: 120,640,000
Total female population: 127,591,000

Life expectancy (male): 72 years
Life expectancy (female): 79 years

BANGLADESH MALE   **BANGLADESH FEMALE**

Age	Percent of Population (Male)	Percent of Population (Female)	Age
70+	1.0	0.8	70+
60-69	1.7	1.4	60-69
50-59	2.6	2.3	50-59
40-49	4.0	3.6	40-49
30-39	5.6	5.1	30-39
20-29	7.9	7.6	20-29
10-19	13.2	12.0	10-19
0-9	15.6	15.6	0-9

20,000   10,000   0   10,000   20,000
(in thousands)

Total population: 114,718,000
Total male population: 59,194,000
Total female population: 55,524,000

Life expectancy (male): 54 years
Life expectancy (female): 53 years

Source: Copyright © 1990 PC Globe, Inc. Used by permission.

Interactive Videodiscs and CD-ROMs. Two formats closely associated with hypermedia environments include interactive video discs and CD-ROMs. Videodiscs resemble a silvery, 12-inch LP record, but when they are placed into a videodisc player, they project images and sound on a TV monitor. The two videodiscs that come with the interactive program *GTV: A Geographic Perspective on American History* (National Geographic Society, Education Services, P.O. Box 1640, Washington, DC 20077–9952) contain over two hours of film clips, still images, maps, music, and narration (over 1,600 pictures and 200 maps), which are organized into forty short shows that can be played on any videodisc player. Using a computer, you can make the videodiscs interactive; that is, you can organize the GTV shows in any order and create your own slide presentations or shows, complete with captions, synopses, and scripts. The potential is mind-boggling.

Laser videodiscs should not be confused with the increasingly common CD-ROMs. A CD-ROM is about 4¾ inches in diameter and contains about 550 million characters of information. A laser videodisc, on the other hand, contains five or six times as much data as a CD-ROM and can combine still photographs with continuous video displays. Yet despite the videodiscs' tremendous capacity, the need for special videodisc players may cause this format to fall by the wayside in favor of CD-ROMs.

Telecommunications

More and more elementary classrooms today have computers. However, far fewer classrooms have one or more computers, one or more modems, and one or more telephone lines. All three elements—computer, modem, and telephone line—are needed before your classroom computer can connect to the Internet and the on-line information services such as America Online, Compuserve, and Prodigy. The key and most costly element in connecting your classroom computer to the outside world is a dedicated telephone line.

You may remember Janet Jacobsen from an earlier vignette, whose students use the on-line services (e.g., Compuserve) and communicate via e-mail with individuals around the world. By current standards, her classroom is exceptional, simply because it has its own telephone line. The federal initiative to wire all schools should one day make such facilities commonplace.

Evaluating Software

The quality of social studies software varies tremendously. Sometimes a program's instructions are unclear; in other instances, a program may produce inaccurate stereotypes or require information that students don't have. Such flaws can make the programs unusable or, in the case of inaccurate stereotyping, inappropriate for use with children.

Recommended criteria for evaluating computer software are illustrated in Figure 14.2.

Sources of Information

Resources for computer-based education change rapidly, sometimes almost overnight. We have included many sources of information in the Resource Handbook.

FIGURE 14.2 Computer Software Evaluation Form

Program (title) _____ Grade Level(s) _____

Producer _____ Cost _____

Hardware Required: _____

I. Program Description (describe briefly):

II. General Considerations*:
Does the program promote

1. active social studies learning?   Yes _____   No _____

2. meaningful social studies learning?   Yes _____   No _____

3. a pluralistic perspective on our society?   Yes _____   No _____

4. an integrative interdisciplinary perspective?   Yes _____   No _____

III. Instructional Design
(Briefly summarize any of the following elements that apply; note any problems):

1. Is the content accurate, appropriate, and   Yes _____   No _____
    worthwhile?

2. Is the content appropriately sequenced and   Yes _____   No _____
    free from stereotyping or biases?

3. Does the reading level fit the recommended   Yes _____   No _____
    audience?

4. Does the program make unusual demands of   Yes _____   No _____
    the student, e.g., excessive background
    knowledge, reading lengthy narratives, etc.?

IV. Technical Considerations:

1. Are the instructions/documentation well   Yes _____   No _____
    organized, clearly written, and complete?

2. Are all needed materials included?   Yes _____   No _____

3. Does the program operate as it is   Yes _____   No _____
    supposed to?

Overall Rating _____   *Evaluated by:* _____

*Source: Part II is adapted from Rose & Fernlund, 1997.

Nonprint Materials

Reading and the written word—the print media—have so dominated American schools that nonprint media—videotape, pictures, films, and the like—have a long way to go before they have the educational impact of the printed word. Nevertheless, there have been substantial increases in both the amount of nonprint media available and in the different kinds of nonreading-based materials designed for educational purposes.

Pictures, Films, and Videotapes

The largest and most obvious category of alternatives to the printed word is pictures—those things "worth a thousand words." They come in many forms: collections of study prints, films and filmstrips, videotapes, and paintings and other works of art. Or they can be nothing more than illustrations and advertisements that you have clipped from magazines, calendars, and other sources.

The beauty of photographs as teaching tools lies in their ability to present selected yet uninterpreted data (as we described in the section on culture cards, page 290). Yet educators too often tend to interpret the data for viewers almost immediately. Explanatory captions are provided for most photographs and illustrations, and a narration serves this purpose for films. The intent, traditionally, has been to use the narration or picture caption to convey information. However, *On removing captions and narrations* removing or eliminating the caption or narration increases viewers' involvement with the picture because it forces them to make their own interpretations.

Videos and films are available for almost any topic you can name. There is also a body of educational films and videos that have no narration, only the natural sound of whatever they depict. For example, more than six hours of nonnarrated film or video beautifully portray the life of the Netselik Eskimos (*Fishing at the Stone Weir, Caribou Hunting at the Crossing Place, Autumn River Camp, Parts I and II,* and *Winter Sea Ice Camp, Parts I and II*) and are available from libraries across the country.

Eliminating the narration automatically eliminates any vocabulary problems the narration could present. So the same nonnarrated film or video can sometimes be used by primary students, twelfth graders, and even adults, usually with a different emphasis at each level.

Video cassettes Videotape cassettes have largely replaced traditional 16-mm films in many areas. This has come about largely because of the videotape's availability, lower cost, and, most important, convenience. Because schools or teachers usually own their videotapes, the hassle of scheduling films up to a year in advance is essentially eliminated.

Making your own videos As the cost (and size) of videocamcorders has decreased, more teachers are making their own videotapes. This has been a boon in schools where field trips have been largely eliminated because of policy or budget considerations, or when it would be dangerous to take a large group of students to a site, such as a steel mill. Yet even where field trips are permitted, some teachers videotape them anyhow so that they can call attention to specific elements when they get back to their classroom.

Virtual Touring on the Internet

Unless you teach in the vicinity of Plimoth Plantation in Massachusetts, or Colonial Williamsburg in Virginia, taking your class on a field trip to either place is probably out of the question. And if you are studying the Middle Ages, you probably don't even think about visiting a medieval castle or cathedral, both of which are in Europe. However, by connecting to the Internet, there are hundreds of places your class can visit via a "virtual tour." Some of these places include:

1. The Plimoth Plantation at
   http://spirit.lib.uconn.edu/ArchNet/Topical/Historic/Plimoth/Plimoth.html

2. Colonial Williamsburg at
   http://www.history.org

3. Old Philadelphia at
   http://www.libertynet.org/iha/index/html

4. The Museum of Egyptian Antiquities in Cairo, Egypt, at
   http://interoz.com/egypt/museum

5. The twelfth century Durham Castle and Cathedral in Durham, United Kingdom, at
   http://www.dur.ac.uk/~dla0www/c_tour/tour.html

Virtual touring on the Internet is usually interactive. This means you can determine how quickly to progress through the tour and whether you wish to investigate additional areas of interest. For example, the diagram below is the floor plan of Durham Castle. By clicking your mouse on one of the numbers, you will get a photograph and a more detailed explanation of that area.

Option 2

Option 1

1. The Gatehouse
2. The Courtyard
3. The Entrance, Buttery and Kitchen
4. The Great Hall
5. The Black Staircase
6. The Norman Gallery
7. The Norman Chapel
8. The State Rooms
9. Bishop Tunstall's Gallery
10. Bishop Tunstall's Chapel

Durham Castle Plan in 1 of 2 options.

If you are curious as to whether there is a virtual tour available for a topic that your class is studying, we suggest you contact the on-line collection of virtual tours at http://www.dreamscape.com/frankvad/tours.html.

You can also use one of the on-line search engines that we described in Chapter 2, which is how we located some of these sites.

Source: Reprinted by permission of the University of Durham, Durham, UK.

Realia

Realia: the real thing

Remember when a fellow student brought in his "genuine" Indian arrowhead collection to share with the class? Or when someone's relatives had been to the Orient and brought back an authentic Japanese fan? These things—the arrowheads, the Japanese fan, and other real objects that might be associated with social studies teaching—are all encompassed by the term *realia*.

Most realia are adjuncts to social studies teaching, primarily because the objects are precious to their owners, often part of a collection, and as such the owner would rather not have them handled and possibly broken. Thus they often become things to be displayed—looked at but not used—during a teaching activity, and perhaps rightfully so. Some realia are probably best handled via display and in a passing fashion, such as when a student brings in a World War II bayonet during your study of colonial America.

Options

Using realia unrelated to whatever your class is studying is difficult to justify on almost any grounds. But assume, for a moment, that somewhere in your travels you have acquired a colonial candle mold and your class will be studying colonial America. What are your options? You have several. First, you could display the device and say, "This is a colonial candle mold." You could then describe how it was used.

Second, you might place the mold in a prominent location but say nothing about it. Questions are going to be asked about it, you can be sure. But to the question "What is it?" you could respond, "What do you think it is?" You might mount a large sheet of paper near the mold and ask the children to list what they think it is. At a convenient time, you might display an illustration of someone using a candle mold, again saying nothing about it. Someone will soon notice it, and you may not even need to say anything else at all. Or you might pose the question "How are candles made today?" which will initiate another adventure.

As springboards to inquiry

If the function of the realia is obvious, you might wish to take a different tack. For the Japanese fan mentioned earlier, you might want to ask who uses fans in Japan and why. Are they necessarily to keep Japanese women cool? If you pursue this line of questioning, identify—in advance—some sources the students can use to validate their answers. They may find that fans are a normal part of a Japanese dancer's equipment.

Community Resources

Every community everywhere has someone who has been somewhere or who knows something that can be useful in your social studies program. And almost every community also has places you can visit that will also be an asset to your program.

Resource Persons

Using resource people effectively

Identifying individuals in the community who have specialized knowledge or experience is not especially difficult. The list can go from authors to zookeepers. The more challenging task is using those resource people effectively.

Part of the problem occurs because resource people are, by definition, specialists. As such, they are familiar with the intricacies, the nuances, and the jargon of their specialization. Your students, however, may be at a level where their main concern is with the most fundamental aspects of a specialized area.

Preliminary actions

The local history buff who, for example, gets enmeshed in the minutiae of who married whom in the early 1840s can't count on keeping your students' interest for very long. Once their interest is lost, your students may begin to get restless, and your guest speaker may take their behavior as a personal affront. Therefore, even though it may seem an imposition, clarify in advance exactly what you want the speaker to cover to ensure a successful experience for both the resource person *and* your class.

Lay the necessary groundwork

A related problem arises because resource people are sometimes ill equipped to do more than talk to students. Unless they deal with young children regularly, they are unlikely to have audiovisual aids or other media to enliven their presentations. Even if they have such media, you will need to have worked with your class to establish a need or desire for whatever information the resource person can provide. One of the most helpful things you can do is provide the resource person with a list of questions or topics that your class has developed before the presentation. This helps ensure that (1) the class has at least a passing acquaintance with whatever the resource person will cover (otherwise students won't be able to frame intelligent questions) and (2) the resource person has an idea of the level of the class's concerns and can prepare accordingly.

Caution

A final suggestion about using resource people: be wary of people who *insist* on talking to your class. Among the people who willingly volunteer their services, there are always some who would use the schools as a platform for their special causes. Even if you are sympathetic to the cause, whatever it may be, you may risk your professional future by honoring their offer. Before issuing an invitation, be certain to check school policies and inform the appropriate administrative personnel (principal, etc.) of your intentions.

Oral History

Oral history refers to written histories that are produced primarily from spoken (or oral) sources. When students get involved in oral history projects, they usually do so on a cooperative learning basis. Several students working together develop a written history using data they have gathered by interviewing individuals from the community who have firsthand knowledge of historically interesting events or ways of life. The interviews are tape-recorded and then converted into transcripts that provide the basis for the written history. The resulting document, probably the only one of its kind in existence, is usually placed in the school library.

Using community resources to create history

Oral history is ideally suited to the study of recent local history. The key element is that there must be people around who know something about the period or topic in question and are willing to be interviewed. Grandparents and senior citizens are frequent and often willing subjects for oral history projects.

Plan interviews in advance

A key aspect of oral history activities involves helping students to plan and structure their interviews. If they don't plan carefully, they can easily end up with random conversations of little historic value. Student interviewers must be clear about what information they are after, who is going to ask which questions, and so forth. Their purpose may be to get a local resident's account of the day the old courthouse burned down, someone's views on how population growth has affected the community, or almost anything else that might be of interest. The students' purpose is to conduct an interview *about something*. It doesn't matter so much what that "something" is as long as students understand what kind of information they are after.

Here are some guidelines for conducting oral history activities:

Suggested guidelines

1. The focus should be on one manageable topic, especially in the lower elementary grades.

2. Prepare carefully for the interview, including helping students to "bone up" on the topic by using other sources—wills, diaries, other accounts. On the other hand, don't do so much preparation that your students lose interest.

3. Equipment for the interview may include props like an old photograph or picture, but a tape recorder is essential.

4. Appointments for interviews should be made through official sources so that students don't face the burden of explaining the entire project. Interviews should be restricted to one hour or less.

5. Send students in interview teams of two or three.

6. Contact the computer teacher for possible assistance in putting the transcripts on a word processor.

The logistics of oral history combined with the mechanics of producing transcripts from several dozen tape-recorded interviews can sometimes become so cumbersome that the project may not seem worth the effort. At the same time, students involved in an oral history project are actually creating history. In the process, they can also be developing skills in listening, observing, and asking questions; organizing information; and distinguishing fact from opinion and relevant from irrelevant information. If they do nothing else, oral history activities may lead students to a better understanding and appreciation of the older generation. That alone may make oral history projects worth the effort.

Field Trips and Tours

Some teachers take their students on tours of museums, bakeries, fire stations, and the like, which can provide enriching, hands-on experiences that would be impossible to duplicate in a classroom. Other teachers, however, take their students on field trips to the same places. The distinction between *tours* and *field trips* is based on (1) the activities that take place in the classroom prior to the trip and (2) the students' perceptions about why they are going.

Before scientists "go out into the field," they usually identify their purpose for going. When archaeologists decide to dig at a particular site, for example, their decision is usually based on (1) prior research, (2) a clear sense of purpose (for digging), and (3) previously identified questions or problems that they hope to answer. Likewise, if your students were going on a field trip to a bakery, they should arrive armed with *previously identified* questions that they want answers for: "Do bakeries grind their own flour?" "Do bakeries use the

If taking your class on a field trip is not possible, consider going yourself and videotaping the trip for your class. (© *Gary Walts/The Image Works*)

same kind of flour available in supermarkets?" In other words, because of the students' previous classroom experience, they arrive at the site with a clear sense of why they are there. Students will probably enjoy the experience and learn things they didn't have questions about, but this is simply extra frosting on the cake.

Logistics. Although tours and field trips can add immeasurable value to education, most experienced teachers can also tell horror stories about things that went wrong on a field trip or tour: kids who got lost, children who spent all their lunch money at the souvenir stand, and so forth. The logistical problems can have you tearing your hair out in short order.

In addition, students sometimes assume that rules for classroom conduct don't apply to outside-of-school activities, as on a field trip or tour, which then leads to discipline problems. Although there is certainly no guarantee, the clearer sense of purpose associated with field trips will probably result in fewer discipline problems. Likewise, preplanning can eliminate some of the logistical and discipline-related problems associated with field trips and tours. Consider the following suggestions:

* Obtain administrative approval before announcing the trip to students. (On the application form, always use "field trip," even if you're planning a tour to the zoo—it sounds better and may be easier for the administrator to justify.)

* Avoid going anywhere on Mondays and Fridays. Over the weekend (for a Monday trip), kids often forget to bring their lunches, spending money, and so on. Friday trips deny the opportunity for immediate follow-up.

* Recruit, screen, and instruct parent chaperons so that they can contribute significantly to the trip. Don't wait until just before leaving to tell parents what you expect of them. Send a note home beforehand that outlines (1) what you expect parents to do, (2) rules you have discussed with students, and (3) any other pertinent information.

* Create task groups with specific responsibilities before the trip takes place. For example, there can be recorders (keep records and journals), collectors (obtain necessary items for or from the trip), photographers, public relations people (thank-you-note writers), and maintenance people (clean up).

* If you are taking a tour, select an impressive place. If you were bored on your last trip to the sewage-treatment plant, your students probably will be bored too.

* Take everyone, including your troublemakers. Leaving them behind could lead to deep-seated resentment you can never overcome.

* Send parental permission slips home even if the school uses a blanket permission form covering all field trips for the year.

* Even with signed permission slips, you may be legally liable if you agree to supervise students in too large an area. We're not talking about the

Astrodome here. Trying to supervise students in two large halls of a museum could make you liable if something happened to someone. Err on the safe side, and *take one adult for each group of five children.* If you plan to videotape the trip, take along a parent to do that so you remain free to devote your complete attention to leading the expedition.

Use name tags ★ Use name tags (including the school name). This is essential for young children; for older students it enables chaperons to call them by name.

★ Avoid going in private cars whenever possible; the legal hazards (insurance coverage, etc.) are considerable.

★ Be sure to take a first-aid kit, a summary of students' medical information, especially allergies, and a list of the children's home and emergency phone numbers.

★ Prepare a guidesheet for students to complete while at the museum or other resource.

★ Be certain to debrief the activity. As is true of most things educational, what happens after a field trip is as important as what takes place during or before it.

★ Be sure to send thank-you notes to all parents who assist you.

Don't overlook walking field trips to nearby locations. Supermarkets, banks, bakeries, and those old standbys, the post office and fire station, often welcome visits from schoolchildren. Whether you walk or take a bus, the crucial element is that your students understand why they are going on the field trip. Otherwise, field trips and tours may be seen as a lark or just another day off from school.

Using Community Resources

Using community resources—either resource persons or field trips—involves both a logistical and a substantive dimension. The logistical side includes such things as contacting individuals and arranging for buses (and rest stops, parental approval and assistance, etc.). The substantive dimension relates to the content that you and your class (and perhaps a resource person) will be studying.

Related issues   Many school districts have specific guidelines for the logistical (and legal) considerations concerning resource persons and field trips. Sometimes they also cover substantive questions. Could you, for example, invite an avowed white supremacist to speak to your class? Could you take your students on a field trip to a slaughterhouse or a funeral home? Consider how you would respond if you were an elementary principal and a teacher came to you with such a request. If the teacher could show a clear relationship between the slaughterhouse (or the funeral home) and whatever the class was studying, would it make any difference to your decision? The issues here are far from simple.

Once you have gotten the necessary permissions, the success of the experience will probably depend on the preliminary work you do before a resource person enters your classroom or before your class leaves on the field trip. The basic questions you need to ask yourself include the following:

Basic considerations

* Is a community resource appropriate for the purposes of my group?
* Have I planned preliminary activities that provide a context within which my class can interpret whatever they hear or see?
* Have I identified appropriate follow-up activities?
* Does my class have an identifiable need for the information that the resource can provide?
* Do my students understand what is expected of them—both in terms of their conduct and in terms of what they are to learn?

If you can answer these questions in the positive, you'll be on the way to making effective use of the resources that your community can provide. If you cannot, keep your aspirin handy.

Acquiring Instructional Resources

Determining what is available

Where do teachers get the things they teach with? Many school systems provide teachers with a budget from which they can purchase additional teaching materials. Where such budgets exist, they are almost always small. In acquiring instructional resources, your first step is to identify what is available from commercial publishers or other sources. You can usually find catalogs of educational materials somewhere in the school—the library, the resource center, or the teachers' lounge. The names and addresses of the major teachers' magazines and social studies journals are located in the Resource Handbook.

Evaluate free materials carefully

Many school systems accept teachers' requests for materials in the spring and purchase the materials the following summer. This may mean that you don't have the opportunity to purchase materials during your first year of teaching. In that event, you will be forced to do what hundreds of other teachers do—buy materials yourself. But before doing that, you have a couple of other options. First, find out if there is something you can use that is free (or inexpensive). The quality of free and inexpensive materials can vary tremendously, however, so be selective. Evaluate why various concerns are willing to sell materials inexpensively or give them away. Many schools subscribe to one or more guides to free and inexpensive materials. Sources and addresses are listed in the Resource Handbook.

Second, consider making your own materials. Some of the best teaching resources we've encountered are those that teachers have developed themselves. For example, teachers created most of the student activities in this book. Most of them went through some refining—that is, they were tried out with students and then revised—but once developed, they become a resource to be used in future years.

Procedure

The process of developing teaching materials is not as difficult as you might suspect (a large dose of common sense is about as helpful as anything). Typically, you do the following:

1. Identify (a) the major concept(s) you want to teach and (b) the major question(s), issue(s), or skill(s) you want the children to deal with. (Note: This is sometimes the most difficult step of all.)

2. Decide what kind of format you want to use—a fact sheet, role-playing, limited-choice decision making, and so on.
3. Create the activity (and duplicate as needed).
4. Use the activity with your students.
5. Revise as needed, based on what you found in Step 4.

It's sometimes wise to add a Step 3(a): before you duplicate an activity for students, share it with someone you can rely on for honest feedback—a colleague, a fellow student teacher, or someone else. You are almost certain to find that something you thought was perfectly obvious isn't, and thus you will gain a chance to make appropriate adjustments before using the activity with your students.

Summary

When some teachers think of resources for teaching social studies, they often turn first to those old standbys—maps, globes, and possibly an almanac. Actually there are countless resources you can use, including a can of corn, as we noted earlier, a colonial candle mold perhaps, or even a telephone directory. Determining what is or is not a potential teaching resource is primarily a matter of perception, a matter of asking yourself what you could teach by using "that." The second key is one we have stressed throughout this book; that is, a resource is something you use to teach, as opposed to something you teach about.

The one resource available almost everywhere is the textbook. We have alluded to the problems associated with textbooks throughout this book, but we also understand that using textbooks as your primary resource during your first year of teaching may be understandable and, in some cases, politically expedient. But as you become more familiar with the terrain you are expected to cover, we hope that you will integrate some of the other resources available to you. These may include daily newspapers, children's books—both informational and fictional—and perhaps one of the current events publications. They may also include computer-based resources, such as tutorials, drill-and-practice programs, simulations, integrated application programs that incorporate databases, spreadsheets, and word-processing programs, and, if you have the necessary hardware, programs that allow your students to connect to the Internet or develop presentation materials using one of the hypertext-based programs.

Even if you do not have sophisticated computer equipment, there are other traditional resources that can add to your program. These include individuals in the community who can provide expertise on particular subjects, as well as field trips and tours to places that your students might not otherwise visit. However, we also suggested that the key to using community resource people, field trips, or tours successfully lies in the kind of preliminary work you do before the event occurs. Students who understand why they are listening to a resource person or visiting a particular site are much less likely to regard the event as a lark.

Regardless of what resources for teaching social studies you choose to use, the basic expectation is that they reflect accurate and unbiased, quality "stuff." In addition, the resources must be used in ways that capture the students' attention. Unless they can fulfill that requirement, the quality issue becomes irrelevant.

Suggested Activities

1. Congratulations! Your budget request has been approved and the board of education has authorized $250 per teacher for social studies teaching materials. You can really use some new materials; for example, your textbook carries a 1986 copyright. Your other materials consist of a wall map of the world and one of the United States, a sixteen-inch globe, and an almanac dated 1985. How will you (or your team) spend those funds?
2. In small groups, plan a field trip for an elementary or middle-school class. Then, as a group, go on the field trip you have planned, making certain someone brings a camera. Share your findings with the rest of the class: include your preliminary research, slides of the trip itself, and the way in which you would follow it up.

Suggested Readings

J. A. Braun, Jr., P. Fernlund, & C. S. White. (1998). *Technology tools in the social studies curriculum*. Wilsonville, OR: Franklin-Beedle and Associates. This book provides an excellent overview of the latest technology-related options available to teachers. Also includes reprints of articles.

Mildred Knight Laughlin & Patricia Payne Kardaleff. (1991). *Literature-based social studies: Children's books & activities to enrich the K–5 curriculum*. Phoenix, AZ: Oryx Press. Although we have cited this volume previously, we repeat it here because it contains exemplary units that are based on children's books and that are keyed to topics common to many social studies programs.

Thomas M. McGowan & Meredith McGowan. (1986). *Children, literature, and social studies: Activities for the intermediate grades*. Omaha, NE: Special Literature Press. This excellent publication provides a wealth of information on basing social studies activities on children's fiction.

Epilogue

Remember when you:

* Couldn't understand why Australia was a continent but Greenland wasn't?
* Thought Paris, Boston, and Chicago were states?
* Memorized the Preamble to the Constitution, the Gettysburg Address, or the presidents of the United States in order?
* Were taught that "mail carriers deliver the mail" when you already knew it? . . .

Introduction: Reflecting on Things Past

We began this book by asking whether you remembered some of the things we listed above. We end this book with the hope that you have a better context for explaining and interpreting those things you remembered. We hope you understand, for example, that the perspective from which some maps are drawn makes Australia appear smaller than Greenland (even though it is actually about three times larger) and that young children often have difficulty distinguishing among cities, states, and countries until they gain more experience with their world.

We've seen many changes occur in social studies education over the years, ranging from efforts to teach "history as history" and "geography as geography," through attempts to teach children to use the social and behavioral sciences as they deal with the worlds in which they live. To whatever extent we have an opportunity to influence the direction that social studies education in the future may take, we wish to suggest the following as possible emphases that can take us into the twenty-first century.

Instructional Premises for the Twenty-First Century

* Observation and listening should receive increased emphasis as access skills.
* There should be increased emphasis on helping students become more aware of the thinking processes they use.
* There should be increased awareness of the extent to which mathematics can be a tool for communicating social information.
* There should be an increased use of literature, both fiction and nonfiction, in teaching social studies.

Social studies should provide children with new perspectives on their world. (© *Fredrick D. Bodin/Stock Boston*)

* There should be increased recognition of the power of technology to place a world of data at students' fingertips.
* From the primary grades onward, students should be increasingly involved in designing and conducting their own investigations (their own "social studies," if you will).
* There should be growing recognition that academic values can be addressed as social values, e.g., no cheating, etc.
* Social studies programs and teaching should emphasize systems of relationships among social phenomena rather than the learning of isolated pieces of information.
* In social studies teaching, increased emphasis should be on helping students become skillful in making and testing social ideas.
* Evaluation of student's performance will be increasingly based on portfolios and specific examples of student achievement.
* The trend toward "less is more"—that is, helping students to develop in-depth understanding of fewer significant topics, with correspondingly less superficial coverage—should continue.

From time to time, various individuals and organizations release reports intent on showing what students don't know. Most of those reports are accompanied by claims that we need to teach more of "this" and more of "that" to rectify the apparent crisis. We are not trying to excuse the many problems in schools today, but we reiterate a point that we suggested in Chapter 1: *So long as the reservoir of available information continues to grow, there will always be things that students don't know.*

We think that efforts to teach children everything they might ever be expected to know have contributed to the problem. The time available for teaching has not increased significantly over the last century, whereas the reservoir of knowledge grows larger with each passing day. By trying to cram everything into the limited time available, many social studies (and other school) programs have opted for breadth—for covering large amounts of information in a comparatively short time—instead of focusing in depth on significant understandings, ideas, and skills. The superficial skimming that occurs in "trying to cover everything" has too often resulted in mere exposure and the knowledge of a few facts and names, but at the cost of in-depth understanding.

Clearly all students should know certain basics, certain fundamental ideas and skills. How you identify *which* fundamentals those are depends on the view of the world for which you are educating children. Sometimes this may mean placing more emphasis on information like "Columbus voyaged to America" and "New Delhi is the capital of India," assuming, of course, that social studies programs have ceased emphasizing such information. But also we need to ask ourselves how such information will help students today to function in an increasingly information-rich world—a world of computers and other electronic media. In other cases, the fundamentals can include powerful questions and ideas that are drawn from the human experience—questions like "What makes us human?" and "How did we get this way?" and ideas like "Change begets change" and "All people define the world from their own frame of reference."

In still other cases, the fundamentals can include skills—the process (critical thinking) skills that we identified earlier.

To deal with either the content or process to the exclusion of the other is to deal with neither well. Skills taught in isolation can be forgotten as quickly as facts taught in isolation. Teaching social studies should not be a matter of teaching content *or* teaching process skills, for the two are reciprocal and inseparable. As we move toward a new century, social studies teaching must reflect content *with* process, and process *with* content, for these we think are children's keys to their world.

As a kind of benediction, we share with you an old proverb that we have used since the first edition of this book and that has served us well over those years:

> Give a man a fish
> and you feed him for one day.
> Teach him how to fish, and
> he feeds himself for a lifetime.

In many respects, teaching social studies is indeed like teaching children how "to fish." We also trust that this book will serve as your guide to opening the fascinating world of social studies to the children you teach. Best wishes!

D. A. W.
J. T. M.

Introduction

Introduction

One morning when we first began teaching, the principal (the late Warren Immel) came into our classroom and announced that our class would be getting the newspaper (the *Cleveland Plain Dealer*) free of charge for the next two months. This would be great, we thought, because now all of our students could keep up to the minute on current events. We quickly discovered that spending fifteen to twenty minutes of a forty-five-minute class reading the morning newspaper leaves little time to discuss current events, much less deal with the regular curriculum. As we got further and further behind, we began to wonder whether newspapers were the wonderful resource they were supposed to be. We would have given almost anything for a little booklet called "Using Newspapers in the Classroom," which we didn't know at the time was (and still is) available without cost from the newspaper.

We have designed this handbook to help you address the kinds of problems that we faced when we began using the daily newspaper in our classroom. We have done so from the perspective that a *resource* is useful only when you really need or want it. The Resource Handbook is also designed as something you can turn to when you want or need additional information on a social studies–related topic.

The Resource Handbook has four parts. Part 1 includes materials that are detailed extensions of topics that we discuss in the text itself. If you are interested in the answers to some of the activities in the text, or if you want to examine the national standards for social studies, look in Part 1 of the Handbook.

Part 2 of the Handbook includes (1) an annotated lesson planning guide, (2) Alleman and Brophy's guidelines for designing teaching activities, and (3) a version of the *Taxonomy of Educational Objectives* that is keyed to helping you develop particular thinking and attitudinal behaviors in your students.

Part 3 of the Handbook provides listings of sources for a variety of instructional materials. If you are interested in sources for inexpensive or computer-related teaching materials, for example, look for these in Part 3.

Part 4 of the Handbook provides annotated bibliographies of children's literature. This section has two parts: (1) children's books you might use to teach selected morals and values, and (2) children's literature pertaining to topics commonly taught in social studies. With the multitude of children's literature available for teaching social studies, and considering the broad range of topics that social studies encompasses, we trust that you will find these bibliographies useful.

Part 1   Materials Related to Activities in the Text

1.1 Data Cards for the "Presidency" Activity

Card 1

Data About Benedict Arnold, as of 1801. Before he joined the British in their attempt to defeat the rebels during the American Revolution, Arnold had served George Washington with distinction during military campaigns from 1776 to 1779. Distressed with financial worries and feeling that he was not receiving adequate recognition from the Continental Congress for his services, he abandoned the American cause and became one of the best-known traitors in American history.

Card 2

Data About Franklin D. Roosevelt, as of 1945. The American people elected Roosevelt president four times. Because of his New Deal programs designed to combat the severe financial depression of the 1930s and his leadership during World War II, many historians have classified him as one of the most effective chief executives ever to hold the office. Some of Roosevelt's critics, however, have felt that he misused the power of the presidency by exerting extensive political pressure on Congress to secure passage of the New Deal legislation. He served as president from 1933 until his death in 1945. An attack of polio in the early 1920s left Roosevelt's legs partially paralyzed for the remainder of his life.

Card 3

Data About Martin Luther King, Jr., as of 1968. Before he was assassinated in 1968, the Reverend Martin Luther King, Jr., had become one of the most active champions of the nonviolent civil rights movement. Beginning with his successful boycott of segregated city buses in Birmingham, Alabama, King rose to become leader of the Southern Christian Leadership Conference, one of the most effective organizations to lobby for federal civil rights legislation during the 1960s.

Card 4

Data About Andrew Jackson, as of 1829. According to most historians of American life, Jackson was one of the United States' most forceful chief executives. As president, Jackson asserted the supremacy of the federal government when South Carolina attempted to nullify federal tariff laws. His opposition to any form of monopoly was evident in his veto of legislation to recharter the powerful and half-public Bank of the United States.

Card 5

Data About Alexander Hamilton, as of 1804. Until his death in a duel with Aaron Burr, Hamilton served his country as an adviser to George Washington. His arguments for adoption of the federal Constitution were instrumental in its final approval. His financial genius helped to establish the United States on a firm financial footing during its early years.

Card 6

Data About Eleanor Roosevelt, as of 1949. Eleanor Roosevelt, wife of Franklin D. Roosevelt, became one of America's most active champions of the poor, minority groups, women's labor unions, and civil rights. As Franklin Roosevelt's wife, she was an unofficial adviser for many of his New Deal domestic policies. After her husband's death in 1945, Mrs. Roosevelt was appointed a U.S. delegate to the United Nations.

Card 7

Data About Cesar Chavez, as of 1974. Chavez, the son of poor migrant-worker parents, is the founder and leader of the National Farm Workers Organization (NFWO). He has been especially active in unionizing the

Source: Adapted from Marsha Hobin, "Clarifying What Is Important," in Allan O. Kownslar, Ed., *Teaching American History: The Quest for Relevancy.* © National Council for the Social Studies. Reprinted by permission.

Mexican-American farm workers of Southern California. His most notable success occurred with the NFWO's nationwide boycott of nonunion-picked lettuce.

Card 8

Data About Abraham Lincoln, as of 1865. With the exception of George Washington and Franklin D. Roosevelt, probably no other president ever entered office facing such immense problems as did Abraham Lincoln. Historians of Lincoln's life generally agree that he did as much as any chief executive could have done to lead the Union to victory in the Civil War and to attempt to heal the wounds of that conflict in both the North and the South. On numerous occasions before and during his presidency, Lincoln suffered periods of severe mental depression. His untimely assassination occurred in 1865.

Source: Adapted from Marsha Hobin, "Clarifying What Is Important," in Allan O. Kownslar, Ed., *Teaching American History: The Quest for Relevancy.* © National Council for the Social Studies. Reprinted by permission.

1.2 NCSS Standards for Social Studies (Abridged)

The NCSS standards are organized around ten thematic strands that correspond with one or more relevant disciplines and that span the educational levels from the early and middle grades to high school. The standards are expressed in statements that begin with "Social studies programs should include experiences that provide for the study of"—for instance, culture. The thematic strands are as follows.

Culture

The study of culture prepares students to answer questions such as: What are the common characteristics of different cultures? How do belief systems, such as religion or political ideals, influence other parts of the culture? How does the culture change to accommodate different ideas and beliefs? What does language tell us about the culture? Relevant courses and

disciplines include geography, history, sociology, and anthropology, as well as multicultural topics across the curriculum.

Time, Continuity, and Change

Human beings seek to understand their historical roots and to locate themselves in time. Knowing how to read and reconstruct the past allows one to develop a historical perspective and to answer questions such as: Who am I? What happened in the past? How am I connected to those in the past? How has the world changed, and how might it change in the future? Why does our personal sense of relatedness to the past change? Relevant courses and disciplines include history.

People, Places, and Environment

The study of people, places, and human-environment interactions assists students as they create their spatial views and geographic perspectives of the world beyond their personal locations. Students need the knowledge, skills, and understanding to answer questions such as: Where are things located? Why are they located where they are? What do we mean by "region"? How do landforms change? What implications do these changes have for people? Relevant courses and disciplines include geography and areas studies.

Individual Development and Identity

Personal identity is shaped by one's culture, by groups, and by institutional influences. Students should consider such questions as: How do people learn? Why do people behave as they do? What influences how people learn, perceive, and grow? How do people meet their basic needs in a variety of contexts? How do individuals develop from youth to adulthood? Relevant courses and disciplines include psychology and anthropology.

Individuals, Groups, and Institutions

Institutions such as schools, churches, families, government agencies, and the courts play an integral role in people's lives. It is important that students learn how institutions are formed, what controls and influences them, how they influence individuals and culture, and how they are maintained or changed. Students may address questions such as: What is the role of institutions in this and other societies? How am I influenced by institutions? How do institutions change? What is my role in institutional change? Relevant courses and disciplines include sociology, anthropology, psychology, political science, and history.

Power, Authority, and Governance

Understanding the historical development of structures of power, authority, and governance and their evolving functions in contemporary U.S. society and other parts of the world is essential for developing civic competence. In exploring this theme, students confront questions such as: What is power? What forms does it take? Who holds it? How is it gained, used, and justified? What is legitimate authority? How are governments created, structured, maintained, and changed? How can individual rights be protected within the context of majority rule? Relevant courses and disciplines include government, politics, political science, history, law, and other social sciences.

Production, Distribution, and Consumption

Because people have wants that often exceed the resources available to them, a variety of ways have evolved to answer such questions as What is to be produced? How is production to be organized? How are goods and services to be distributed? What is the most effective allocation of the factors of production (land, labor, capital, and management?) Relevant courses and disciplines include economics.

Science, Technology, and Society

Modern life as we know it would be impossible without technology and the science that supports it. But technology brings with it many questions: Is new technology always better than old? What can we learn from the past about how new technologies result in broader social change, some of which is unanticipated? How can we cope with the ever-increasing pace of change? How can we manage technology so that the greatest number of people benefit from it? How can we preserve our fundamental values and be-

liefs in the midst of technological change? This theme draws upon the natural and physical sciences, social sciences, and the humanities. Relevant courses and disciplines include history, geography, economics, civics, and government.

Global Connections

The realities of global interdependence require understanding the increasingly important and diverse global connections among world societies and the frequent tension between national interests and global priorities. Students will need to be able to address such international issues as health care, the environment, human rights, economic competition and interdependence, age-old ethnic enmities, and political and military alliances. Relevant courses and disciplines include geography, culture, and economics; may also draw upon the natural and physical sciences and the humanities.

Civic Ideals and Practices

An understanding of civic ideals and practices of citizenship is critical to full participation in society and is a central purpose of social studies. Students confront such questions as: What is civic participation and how can I be involved? How has the meaning of citizenship evolved? What is the balance between rights and responsibilities? What is the role of the citizen in the community and the nation, and as a member of the world community? How can I make a positive difference? Relevant courses and disciplines include history, political science, cultural anthropology, and fields such as global studies, law-related education, and the humanities.

Abridged from the Executive Summary of *Expect Excellence: Curriculum Standards for Social Studies Electronic Edition* (1996). 2–4.

1.3 K–4 Standards for Historical Thinking

Standard 1. Chronological Thinking, which includes the following performance indicators: (a) distinguishing between past, present, and future time, (b) identifying in historical narratives the temporal structure of a historical narrative or story, (c) establishing temporal order in constructing their [students'] own historical narratives, (d) measuring and calculating calendar time, (e) interpreting data presented in time lines, (f) creating time lines, and (g) explaining change and continuity over time.

Standard 2. Historical Comprehension, which includes (a) reconstructing the literal meaning of a historical passage, (b) identifying the central question(s) the historical narrative addresses, (c) reading historical narratives imaginatively, (d) providing evidence of historical perspectives, (e) drawing upon the data in historical maps, (f) drawing upon visual and mathematical data presented in graphics, and (g) drawing upon the visual data presented in photographs, paintings, cartoons, and architectural drawings.

Standard 3. Historical Analysis and Interpretation, which includes (a) formulating questions to focus their inquiry or analysis, (b) identifying the author or source of the historical document or narrative, (c) comparing and contrasting differing sets of ideas, values, personalities, behaviors, and institutions, (d) analyzing historical fiction, (e) distinguishing between fact and fiction, (f) comparing different stories about a historical figure, era, or event, (g) analyzing illustrations in historical stories, (h) considering multiple perspectives, (i) explaining causes in analyzing historical actions, (j) challenging arguments of historical inevitability, and (k) hypothesizing influences of the past.

Standard 4. Historical Research Capabilities, which include the following performance indicators: (a) formulating historical questions, (b) obtaining historical data, (c) interrogating historical data, and (d) marshaling needed knowledge of the time and place and constructing a story, explanation, or historical narrative.

Standard 5. Historical Issues—Analysis and Decision-Making, which includes the following performance indicators: (a) identifying issues and problems in the past, (b) comparing the interests and values of the various people involved, (c) suggesting alternative choices for addressing the problem, (d) evaluating alternative courses of action, (e) preparing a position or course of action on an issue, and (f) evaluating the consequences of a decision.

Source: K–4 Standards for Historical Thinking, National Center for History in the Schools (1995). Reprinted by permission.

1.4 The Essential Elements of Geography

The following are the six "essential elements" and eighteen related standards developed by the Geography Education Standards Project (1994).

Element One: The World in Spatial Terms

Geography focuses on the relationships between people, places, and environments by mapping information about them in a spatial context. The geographically informed person knows and understands:

1. How to use maps and other geographic representations, tools, and technologies to acquire, process, and report information from a spatial perspective.
2. How to use mental maps to organize information about people, places, and environments in a spatial context.
3. How to analyze the spatial organization of people, places, and environments on the Earth's surface.

Element Two: Places and Regions

The identities and lives of people are rooted in particular places, and in those human constructs called regions. The geographically informed person knows and understands:

4. The physical and human characteristics of place.
5. That people create regions to interpret the Earth's complexity.
6. How culture and experience influence people's perceptions of places and regions.

Element Three: Physical Systems

Physical processes shape the Earth's surface and interact with plant and animal life to create, sustain, and modify ecosystems. The geographically informed person knows and understands:

1

7. The physical processes that shape the patterns of the Earth's surface.
8. The characteristics and spatial distribution of ecosystems on the Earth's surface.

Element Four: Human Systems

People are central to geography in that human activities help to shape the Earth's surface. Human settlements and structures are also part of the Earth's surfaces that human beings compete to control. The geographically informed person knows and understands:

9. The characteristics, distribution, and migration of human populations on the Earth's surface.
10. The characteristics, distribution, and complexity of the Earth's cultural mosaics.
11. The patterns and networks of economic interdependence on the Earth's surface.
12. The processes, patterns, and functions of human settlements.
13. How the forces of cooperation and conflict among people influence the division and control of the Earth's surface.

Element Five: Environment and Society

The physical environment is modified by human activities, largely as a consequence of the ways in which human societies value and use Earth's natural resources. Human activities are also influenced by the Earth's physical features and processes. The geographically informed person knows and understands:

14. How human actions modify the physical environment.
15. How physical systems affect human systems.
16. The changes that occur in the meaning, use, distribution, and importance of resources.

Element Six: The Uses of Geography

The knowledge of geography enables people to develop an understanding of the relationships between people, places, and environments over time—that is, of the Earth as it was, is, and might be. The geographically informed person knows and understands:

17. How to apply geography to interpret the past.
18. How to apply geography to interpret the present and plan for the future.

Source: Geography Education Standards Project (1994). *Geography for Life: National Geography Standards 1994*. Washington, DC: National Geographic Society. Reprinted by permission.

1.5 Sample Learning Style Inventory

Place the letter that best reflects your preference in the blank provided.

_____ 1. When you really want to study something and learn it well, would you rather (a) work alone, (b) study with others having similar interests, (c) work by yourself but in a setting where there are other people around?

_____ 2. Assuming that each of the following modes is effective and that you have a choice, would you most prefer to learn something by (a) reading, (b) listening, (c) observing?

_____ 3. Learning situations that cause you the most concern are those that appear to be (a) ambiguous, (b) rather closely defined as to the desired outcome, (c) without guidelines, where you are completely on your own.

_____ 4. Do you have most trouble learning things that (a) use abstract symbols, (b) use diagrams and charts, (c) use mathematical numbers and figures?

_____ 5. When you are not really interested in something you are studying, do you find yourself (a) able to discipline yourself to study, (b) easily distracted by other things, (c) going through the motions to look as though you are studying?

_____ 6. When memorizing something, do you find yourself (a) developing a theme within which to relate the parts, (b) creating a pattern that cues the parts, (c) trying to picture the thing in your mind?

_____ 7. Would you prefer to study something that (a) involves some creative effort of your own, (b) calls for you to apply analytical and critical skills, (c) lays out all the points in front of you so you have a chance to understand it?

____ 8. When do you find that you do your best learning? (a) in the early morning, (b) around midday, (c) in the afternoon, (d) during an "all nighter"?

____ 9. When studying, do you find that you (a) create relationships without being told, (b) understand the material but have some difficulty putting it together, (c) must be given the "whole" before the "parts" make sense?

____ 10. In most classes, would you rather be taught by someone who (a) knows the material and can tell it to you clearly and precisely, (b) knows the material and teases and leads you to conclusions, (c) knows the material but primarily raises questions?

____ 11. Do you feel most comfortable when asked (a) to analyze the material studied, (b) to report on the material studied, (c) to summarize the material studied?

____ 12. When studying something completely new, do you (a) need someone around to encourage your efforts, (b) prefer to figure it out for yourself, (c) tend to give up easily even if encouraged?

____ 13. Do you consider yourself as a student who (a) grasps new ideas quickly, (b) goes at a slightly slower pace, yet masters ideas well, (c) deals with new material so thoroughly that you are able to identify new ideas and/or relationships that extend beyond those explicit in the original materials?

____ 14. When studying with a particular instructor, are you (a) very conscious of the teacher's reaction to how you are doing, (b) indifferent to what the teacher thinks about your progress, (c) interested in the teacher's response but only after you have completed the task on your own?

____ 15. If taking a class in which there were no grades or other rewards, would you probably (a) work just as hard as you would if there were grades, (b) end up doing something else you really wanted to do, (c) exert minimal effort?

____ 16. Do you like taking courses where (a) both the objectives and procedures are clearly spelled out, (b) the procedures are fairly clear but the objectives are vague, (c) both the objectives and procedures are vague but there is a lot of excitement and drive on the part of the instructor?

____ 17. When studying something new, would you say your attention span is (a) continuous, (b) irregular, (c) short but concentrated, (d) without a particular pattern?

____ 18. Do you sense the most satisfaction when (a) you've been able to figure out and repair something using your hands and your mind, (b) you've been able to conceptualize or see some meaning in academic work, (c) other people say they think you've done a good piece of work, regardless of what that work is?

____ 19. When you find yourself in a situation determined by the clock, do you usually (a) start making all sorts of mistakes under pressure, (b) slow down and do what you can, (c) speed up and surprise yourself at how much you can do when the heat is on?

____ 20. If you asked those people who know you best, they would probably say that (a) you are usually level-headed and have a lot of common sense, (b) it takes you a long time to get an idea but when you do you hang on to it, (c) you are always coming up with far-out ideas that sometimes work?

____ 21. When bored in a class, do you usually (a) daydream, but of things related to what you are studying, (b) daydream of things seldom related to what you are studying, (c) pay attention even though it doesn't mean very much?

____ 22. Do you find that when something new comes up you (a) adapt rather easily, (b) fight it for a while but are willing, usually, to give it a try, (c) make darn well sure it makes sense and/or is right before making any effort to accept it?

____ 23. When in a classroom with other students and observing a teacher teaching, do you (a) think of other ways to present the material and to teach,

(b) listen to what the teacher is saying rather than watch how he or she is teaching, (c) wonder what the teacher wants and how you can deliver?

_____ 24. If you don't like the instructor, for whatever reason, do you (a) tend not to do well, (b) find reasons for not studying and learning, (c) not let it affect how hard you try?

_____ 25. Do you get upset when studying something that (a) has no immediate and practical application, (b) appears to have some application but you are not sure just what, (c) is too darn practical and immediate?

_____ 26. When a teacher fails to "come across," do you have a tendency to blame (a) the teacher who, after all, is responsible for the class, (b) the subject matter—especially if the teacher tries, (c) both the teacher and yourself for not making it worthwhile.

_____ 27. If you took a course in social studies, would you want it to (a) focus primarily upon the facts, (b) pose some insight into contemporary problems of society, (c) have some payoff in your daily life?

_____ 28. The problem with many teachers is that they (a) overkill, that is, teach too much of the same thing, (b) try to cover too much, (c) do not allow the student to really wrestle with the content.

_____ 29. Do you believe that most students gain confidence through (a) having rather well-established objectives and procedures, (b) being allowed to try different things, (c) psyching out the reward system and playing the game?

_____ 30. When studying, do you prefer (a) absolute silence, (b) low background noise, including music, (c) relative quiet, (d) loud conversation or music, etc., (e) sometimes one way, sometimes another?

_____ 31. Where do you prefer to study? (a) in your own room, (b) in a learning center, (c) at the library, (d) at a media center?

_____ 32. What types of assignments do you most prefer? (a) teacher-directed, (b) projects by contracts, (c) self-directed projects, (d) a combination of these?

_____ 33. How do you most prefer to be evaluated on something? (a) by formal tests, (b) through teacher conferences, (c) on research papers or other written projects, (d) on the amount of your class discussion?

_____ 34. Which of the following is most likely to bring forth your best performance? (a) self-satisfaction, (b) clearly defined teacher expectations and deadlines, (c) public recognition of your achievement, (d) working in a subject area with which you are quite comfortable and familiar?

1

Summary

Instructional modes. Determine your preferred instructional mode from responses to questions 2, 4, 7, 8, 11, 17, 19.

_____

_____

Structure. Determine the degree of structuring from responses to questions 3, 6, 9, 12, 13, 16, 20, 22, 23, and 32.

High   Medium   Low

_____

Social context of learning. Determine the general expectations for the way in which teachers handle their authority from questions 1, 10, 19, and 24.

_____

_____

Group-related activities. Determine your preference for group-related activities from responses to questions 1, 12, 30, 31, and 34.

_____

_____

Physical context of learning. Determine your preferences regarding the physical environment from the responses to questions 8, 17, 30, and 31.

_____

_____

Reward/Praise. Determine preferences for reward/praise from responses to questions 14, 15, 26, 29, 33, and 34.

_____

_____

Goal preferences. Determine your general goal preferences from the responses to questions 5, 18, 25, and 27.

Longer range   Shorter range

_____

1.6 Sources of Commercially Available Learning Style Measures Include:

* Learning Style Inventory, Price Systems, Box 1818, Lawrence, KS 66044-1818
* Learning Style Profile. National Association of Secondary School Principals, 1904 Association Dr., Reston, VA 22091-1598.

1.7 Recipes/Directions

1.7.1. Recipes for Relief Maps

Papier-Mâché. Tear newspapers into strips and soak in water overnight. Mix wheat paste (wallpaper paste) with warm water to the consistency of thin cream. Squeeze water out of the newspaper strips, dip into the paste, remove the excess, and then apply to the map form.

Salt and Flour. Mix four cups flour, two cups salt, and approximately two cups water. Knead thoroughly. Food coloring may be added to the water, or tempera paint can be kneaded into the mixture. The mixture may require from two to three days to dry completely.

Sawdust and Glue. Mix slightly thinned white glue with dampened, fine sawdust until it reaches a workable consistency.

Once the relief maps have dried, they can be coated with a thin mixture of plaster of Paris and water and then allowed to dry overnight. This coating will keep paint from soaking in as much as it otherwise would.

1.7.2 Directions for Making Paper

Introduction. This recipe produces a very rough paper similar to papyrus. Before you begin this activity, you might ask for parent volunteers who will make several, small wooden frames (open rectangles), about 6 by 9 inches, with old window screening attached to the bottom. Old picture frames also work well.

Materials List

One blender, to mix the ingredients
Several clean sponges
A tub or container large enough to hold the screened frames
Grass (or cattails—leaves only, no heads)
Water
One or two old bedsheets
Torn pieces of old, used, lightweight paper (not newsprint)
One bottle laundry starch

Procedure. Place equal amounts of torn paper and the grass or cattail leaves into the blender, and cover with water to make a pulp. Turn blender to high and mix thoroughly. Make several batches, adding about 1 tablespoon of laundry starch to each batch. Put the pulp into a tub that is large enough to accommodate the screen. Add as little water to the tub as necessary to create a fluid mixture, and stir. Insert the screen into the water until it is covered with a layer of the pulp mixture, then pull up and out. Lay the screen on the old bedsheet, and use sponges to soak up some of the excess water from the pulp, but do not let it get so dry that the pulp sticks to the screen. Place a dry area of the sheet over the screen, and then flip so the pulp falls out of the screen onto the sheet. Place on a flat surface, remove the screen, and let the paper dry overnight.

This paper that you produce will be rough, fragile, and difficult to write on. In addition, it may not be even at the edges. Help students to understand that the 8 1/2 × 11 paper we are all familiar with is a convention of modern life and is the result of advanced paper-making techniques.

1.8 Exemplary Simulation—The Holiday Card Factory

The following simulation was designed by a teacher who wanted to teach the elements of mass production under nineteenth-century factory conditions. The entire class will be organized into production areas to produce holiday greeting cards (in this case, for Valentine's Day). To re-create some working conditions from the nineteenth century, the room should be darkened somewhat and students asked to stand at their work stations (desks) throughout the activity. Talking unrelated to work should not be permitted.

The greeting card has a white heart, pierced by a pink arrow, that is placed on a red circle. This subassembly is then mounted on a white paper doily. The completed product should resemble the one below.

Organization

In general, each phase of the card-making process is divided into drawing, cutting, and inspecting. For ex-

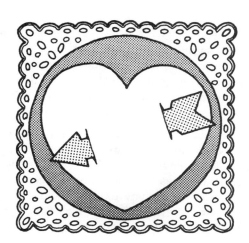

ample, the heart department has teams of heart drawers and heart cutters and a heart inspector. For a class of twenty-five students, you should have the following roles:

Heart Department

   3 heart drawers
   2 heart cutters
   1 heart inspector

Circle Department

   3 circle drawers
   2 circle cutters
   1 circle inspector

Slit Department (for making the hole where the arrow pierces the heart)

   1 slit drawer
   1 slit cutter
   1 slit inspector

Arrow Department

   3 arrow drawers
   2 arrow cutters
   1 arrow inspector

Assembly Department

   3 assemblers
   1 final inspector

If you have fewer than twenty-five students, you can drop some inspectors. If you have more than twenty-five, add them to the drawers in any department.

Cluster the desks into five "departments." Make signs identifying each department (heart department, etc.) in advance. Each student should also make a small sign identifying his or her particular task (e.g., circle cutter). The inspectors are responsible for maintaining quality control and taking the finished products to the assembly area. Provide the following materials and instructions to the appropriate department.

Heart Department

* Heart drawers
  Materials: plain white paper (8½ × 11), pens, rulers
  Instructions: "Draw the largest heart you can that will fit into an 8-inch square."

* Heart cutters
  Materials: scissors
  Instructions: "Cut the heart as accurately as you can."

* Heart inspectors
Materials: a sample heart (which you have made ahead of time)
Instructions: "Make certain that your hearts closely resemble the sample before taking them to the slit department. If anything is wrong with a heart, give it back to the heart drawers or cutters."

Slit Department

* Slit drawers
Materials: ruler and pencil
Instructions: "Your job is to locate the 1½-inch slit where the arrow will pierce the heart. Your inspector has a sample heart to show exactly where the slit should be located."

* Slit cutters
Materials: scissors
Instructions: "Your job is to cut the 1½-inch slit where the arrow will pierce the heart. Cut as accurately and neatly as you can."

* Slit inspector
Materials: sample heart with slit
Instructions: "Make certain that your hearts closely resemble the sample before taking them to the assembly area. If anything is wrong, return them to the slit drawers or the slit cutters."

Circle Department

* Circle drawers
Materials: red paper, pencils or pens, compasses
Instructions: "Your job is to draw an 8½-inch circle on the red paper. It must be exactly 8½ inches in diameter. The circle inspector has a sample you can see."

* Circle cutters
Materials: scissors
Instructions: "Your job is to cut the 8½-inch circle from the red paper. Work as neatly and as accurately as you can."

* Circle inspector
Materials: sample red circle
Instructions: "Make certain that your finished circles resemble the sample before taking them to the as-sembly area. If anything is wrong, return them to the circle drawers or the circle cutters."

Arrow Department

* Arrow drawers
Materials: pink paper (8½ × 11), rulers, and pencils
Instructions: "Your job is to draw a 7-inch-long pink arrow. Your inspector has a sample you can follow. You should get at least four arrows from each sheet of paper."

* Arrow cutters
Materials: scissors
Instructions: "Your job is to cut the 7-inch pink ar-rows. Work as neatly and as accurately as you can."

* Arrow inspectors
Materials: sample arrow
Instructions: "Make certain that your finished ar-rows resemble the sample before taking them to the assembly area. If anything is wrong, return the ar-rows to the arrow drawers or the arrow cutters."

Assembly Department

* Assemblers
Materials: 9- or 10-inch white paper doilies; paste, fast-drying glue, or rubber cement
Instructions: "Your job is to insert the arrow through the slits in the heart and then glue the heart onto the red circle. The heart and the circle should then be glued onto the doily. Your inspector has a sample you can follow."

* Final inspector
Materials: sample completed heart
Instructions: "Your job is to make certain that each finished card resembles the sample. If it does, place it in a pile labeled 'finished'; if not, place it in a pile labeled 'rejects.' "

Remind the students that work is to be done quickly and accurately. Time is money! Also, only the inspec-tors can leave their stations. Wages? One candy heart for every ten minutes of cooperation and work.

Do not stop the activity until students are visibly bored with what they are doing (which, unfortunately, may take longer than you might anticipate).

In the debriefing, consider some of the following questions:

1. How did you like your job?
2. How would you describe what we have done?
3. How would you go about improving conditions in this factory? What would you change?
4. What are some different ways we could produce greeting cards like these?
5. If you were responsible for the workers on an assembly line, what kinds of problems do you think you might have?

Variation

A useful variation is to have one class (or half the class) use the preceding approach while another class (or the other half of the class) uses a cottage-industry approach. In the latter approach, each student constructs the valentine by completing all different tasks—there is no division of labor.

Part 2   Planning Resources

2.1 Alternative Planning Guide

This planning guide is designed to serve different kinds of lessons. Therefore some elements, like motivation and establishing set, will apply to all lessons, but other components may not. At times, you may teach lessons that don't use guided practice or review, for example, or where there is no need to state assumptions. Skip the sections that don't apply to the kind of lesson you are teaching. Note also that because this guide is designed to communicate your lesson to someone else, such as a cooperating teacher or a university supervisor, it is necessarily more comprehensive and specific than the day-to-day plans that most teachers use. Most teachers will have usually thought about the following planning elements, even if they don't write them in their plan books.

I. *Overview/Rationale/Justification.* Provide a brief overview of this lesson *and* why it is something that students should experience or learn.

The key questions here are the following: What's going to happen in this lesson? What is the main idea(s) you are driving at? How will this lesson pertain to something your students will use in the future?

II. State *Objectives.* List at least two objectives for this lesson.

Objectives should be stated in terms of behaviors or knowledge that students will demonstrate at the end of the lesson.

III. *Assumptions.* Identify specific skills or knowledge that students must have *prior* to lesson.

This section of the planning guide pertains primarily to skill- and concept-oriented lessons and may not be relevant to other kinds of lessons. State prerequisite knowledge/skills specifically, such as the ability to count by fives or to identify the symbols used to show cities on a map. Do not identify global skills, such as reading, the ability to multiply, how to use a map, and so on.

IV. Review, Developing Motivation, and Setting the Focus.

In most cases, the following elements can be described in a sentence or two.

A. *Review.* Describe how you will relate this lesson to students' prior learning experiences.

Identify how you will make connections with previous learning in ways that have meaning for students.

B. Develop *Motivation and Setting the Focus* (Establishing Set). This planning element has three components: a description of (1) how you will get students interested in this lesson, (2) how you will introduce the content/skills, and (3) how you will make students aware of the objectives for the lesson.

Your introduction or beginning activity should be content centered and tied to the purpose of the lesson. Be especially cautious about using seemingly obvious questions for "motivational" purposes—that is, "Has anyone ever seen television? or an elephant? etc." (everyone has). Be equally careful about your terminology. For example, a "discussion" involves the identification and assessment of different points of view on an issue; it is not a random sharing of opinions or question-and-answer. Most children can readily tell you about the time they went to Disneyland, for example, but this is more likely to be recitation, not a discussion. Having children share their perspectives on abortion could provide a legitimate (though unlikely) basis for a discussion. The point is that having children share their prior experiences may be desirable—even if no one listens to them—but such activities should not be presented as discussions.

V. Develop the *Lesson.*

A. Provide *Instructional Input.* Outline and describe the content and skills included in the main body of the lesson and how you will present them.

In this part of the lesson you will present content, use manipulatives, give examples, explain, define, read, model, and provide directions for activities, and so on. You may wish to write a script for portions of this section as long as you recognize that scripts can be confining and destroy spontaneity.

B. *Modeling* the Content and Skills. Describe how you will model or demonstrate the content and skills introduced in Part V-A.

Modeling is among the most important parts of the lesson and refers to doing, explicitly demonstrating, talking through, and thinking aloud. Modeling should afford students an opportunity to "see" your reasoning process, to see how you attack a problem. Note that showing the children a completed model, of a narrative story for example, is not modeling.

C. Check for Student Understanding (*Assessment*). Describe how you will assess students' understanding to make sure they have mastered the content and skills introduced in Part V-A.

Use oral, written, or signal responses to check for students' understanding before moving on to application or guided practice. Signal responses can include raising hands, crossing arms, putting a hand on the head, and so on.

VI. *Guided Practice.* Describe the guided practice you will provide relating to the content and skills developed in Part V-A.

This aspect of the lesson cycle is most appropriate, even essential, to certain subjects like mathematics and may be less appropriate to other subjects, like literature. Guided practice is usually called for if you ask students to apply something that you have taught.

VII. *Closure* (and Assign Individual Practice or Homework as Appropriate). Describe how you will close the lesson. Describe the individual practice or homework you will assign, if appropriate, to this lesson.

The purpose of closure is to "lock in" the learning experience. You might summarize the main points of the lesson, or have students do so, explain how the content and skills will be needed in the future, or have students do something "one more time." The closure should have substance; it cannot be a hasty review of the lesson or an administrative end, for example, "Close your books."

VIII. *Follow-up* Activities. Briefly describe other activities or lessons that logically follow from this lesson, or how you would integrate the "big ideas" from this lesson into other subject areas.

Few lessons contain elements that cannot be followed up on. Sometimes it may be the content of the lesson—what it is like to live in different climates, for example. At other times, the process that students used in this lesson can apply to other lessons—practice with a model for writing descriptive narratives, for example. In this section, you should indicate how you will tie this lesson into future lessons. The question to ask yourself here is, How does this lesson tie into other things I might teach?

2.2 Principles for the Design, Selection, and Evaluation of Instructional Activities (Abridged)

Criteria	Response		
A. Primary Principles	**Yes**	**No**	**NA**
A1. *Goal Relevance*			
A1.1 Does the activity address worthwhile curricular goals?	—	—	—
A1.1a Is the activity's primary goal an important one?	—	—	—
A1.1b Is there a clear relationship between what students will be doing and the activity's primary goal?	—	—	—
A1.2 Does the activity deal with (a) powerful ideas that are (b) represented accurately?	—	—	—
A1.3 Is the format of the activity clear and uncomplicated?	—	—	—
A2. *Appropriate Difficulty Level*			
A2.1 Is the activity difficult enough to challenge students but not so difficult that it confuses or frustrates them?	—	—	—
A2.2 Do students have the relevant prior knowledge or skills that the activity requires?	—	—	—
A2.3 Does the activity provide enough structuring that students can complete it with reasonable effort?	—	—	—

2

Criteria	Response			Criteria	Response		
A. Primary Principles (cont.)	Yes	No	NA	**B. Secondary Principles (cont.)**	Yes	No	NA

A2.4 Does the activity *not* combine difficult new processes and difficult new content?   — — —

A3. *Feasibility*

A3.1 Is the activity feasible in terms of (a) normal constraints (space, time, equipment, etc.) (b) the possibility for students to carry out instructions unambiguously and complete the activity with a sense of closure and accomplishment?   — — —

A4. *Cost Effectiveness*

A4.1 Does the activity justify its costs in time and trouble for both teachers and students?   — — —

A4.2 Will the structure of the activity (e.g., closed vs. open-ended, etc.) accomplish the goal directly and without needless complications?   — — —

A4.3 Can students who lack prior knowledge or skills be accommodated?   — — —

A4.4 If the activity cuts across subject lines, does it (a) address major goals in those subjects, and (b) still reflect time allotments for those subjects?   — — —

B. Secondary Principles
The following are desirable but not essential.

B1. *Multiple Goals*

B1.1 Does the activity accommodate multiple goals (e.g., content and process, etc.) as opposed to just a few goals?   — — —

B1.2 Does the activity call for integration across subjects or for inclusion of special topics?   — — —

B2. *Motivational Value.* All things considered, is the activity one that students will enjoy or at least find meaningful and worthwhile?   — — —

B3. *Topic Currency*

B3.1 Does the activity deal with recently taught major ideas (as opposed to minor details or isolated content)?   — — —

B3.2 Are skills incorporated for authentically applying current knowledge (as opposed to isolated skill exercises)?   — — —

B4. *Whole-Task Completion.* Does the activity provide for the completion of a meaningful task (as opposed to isolated skill practice)?   — — —

B5. *Higher-Order Thinking*

B5.1 Does the activity provide opportunities to process information (interpret, analyze, etc.) (as opposed to just locating and reproducing information)?   — — —

B5.2 Does the activity provide opportunities for genuine discourse and discussion (as opposed to recitation)?   — — —

B5.3 If the activity involves writing, does it call for coherent written explanations or arguments (as opposed to filling in blanks or copying)?   — — —

B6. *Adaptability.* Can the activity be adapted to accommodate individual differences among students?   — — —

Source: Abridged from Jere Brophy and Janet Alleman, "Activities as Instructional Tools: A Framework for Analysis and Evaluation," *Educational Researcher*, Vol. 20, No. 4 (May 1991), pp. 15–19.

Part 3   Instructional Resources

3.1 Teaching Materials

1. Social Studies Journals

1. *Social Studies and the Young Learner,* which is available from the National Council for the Social Studies, 3501 Newark Street NW, Washington, DC 20016. This is the only journal that deals specifically with elementary and middle-school social studies.
2. *Social Education,* the K–12 journal of the National Council for the Social Studies. Address: 3501 Newark Street, NW, Washington, DC 20016
3. *The Social Studies,* also a K–12 journal. Published by Heldref Publications, 1319 Eighteenth Street, NW, Washington, DC 20036-1802.

2. Social Studies Publications for Children

Write (or call) the publishers listed here for examination copies of these materials.

2.1 General

> *Calliope: World History for Young People*
> Cobblestone Publishing Inc.
> 7 School Street
> Peterborough, NH 03458
> (800) 821-0115

Calliope is published five times during the school year and is for students in Grades 4–8. Each issue features in-depth information and activities on a single topic.

> *Cobblestone: The History Magazine*
>   *for Young People*
> Cobblestone Publishing Inc.
> 7 School Street
> Peterborough, NH 03458
> (800) 821-0115

Cobblestone is appropriate for students in Grades 4–8 and is published ten times a year. Each issue features an episode of historical interest, such as the Underground Railroad or the Roaring Twenties.

> *National Geographic World*
> National Geographic Society
> Dept. 01090
> 17th and M Streets NW
> Washington, DC 20036

This monthly magazine is appropriate for eight- to twelve-year-olds (or older). Each issue contains articles on a variety of social studies topics.

2.2 Current Events Publications

> *My Weekly Reader*
> American Education Publications
> 245 Long Hill Road, P.O. Box 360
> Middletown, CT 06457

> *Let's Find Out* (kindergarten) or *Scholastic News* (Grades 1–6)
> Scholastic, Inc.
> 730 Broadway
> New York, NY 10003-9538

> *Junior Review* (Grades 6–9)
> Civic Education Service
> 1733 K Street NW
> Washington, DC 20006

3. Resources for Global Education

Two excellent sources of information about global education are:

1. The American Forum for Global Education, 45 John Street, New York, NY 10038, and
2. The Standford Program on International and Cross-Cultural Education (SPICE) Littlefield Center, Room 15, 300 Lassen Street, Stanford, CA 94305-5013.

4. Resources for Law-Related Education

> Center for Civic Education
> 5146 Douglas Fir Road
> Calabasas, CA 91302

Materials include student books (e.g., *We the People,* and *With Liberty and Justice for All*), teachers' guides, and resource materials.

Constitutional Rights Foundation
6310 San Vincente Boulevard
Los Angeles, CA 90048

Materials, primarily for Grades 7–12, include simulations, lesson plans, student resources, a *Bill of Rights Newsletter,* and other materials.

American Bar Association
Special Committee on Youth Education for
    Citizenship
1155 East 60th Street
Chicago, IL 60637

Materials include a newsletter for teachers, *Update on Law-Related Education,* classroom materials, and a catalog of law-related audiovisual materials.

Law in a Free Society
606 Wilshire Boulevard
Santa Monica, CA 90101

Materials include case studies and lesson plans for Grades K–12, and inservice training.

Law in Action Units
West Publishing Company, Inc.
50 West Kellogg Boulevard
St. Paul, MN 55165

Materials include units and lesson plans for Grades 5–9.

National Institute for Citizen Education in the Law
605 G Street NW, Suite 401
Washington, D.C. 20001

Materials focus primarily on teacher training and the development of law-related curriculum materials.

Opposing Viewpoints Series
Greenhaven Press
Box 831
Anoka, MN 55303

Materials offer opposing points of view on a variety of law-related issues.

5. Resources for Character Education

American Institute for Character Education
    A nonprofit educational research foundation that offers a K–9 character education curriculum. Dimension II Building, 8918 Tesoro, Suite 220, San Antonio, TX 78217. Phone: (512) 829-1727 or (800) 284-0499.

ASCD Character Education Network
    Sponsored by ASCD and Boston University's Center for the Advancement of Ethics and Character, its mission is to help teachers and administrators struggling with the ethical and character formation aspect of their work. Kevin Ryan, Boston University, School of Education, 605 Commonwealth Avenue, Boston, MA 02215. Phone: (617) 353-3262.

ASCD Conflict Resolution Network
    Contact Mary Ellen Schaffer, Assistant Principal, Elsie Johnson School, 1380 Nautilus Lane, Hanover Park, IL 60613. Phone: (708) 830-8770. Fax: (708) 893-5452.

The Cambridge Group
    This firm helps school districts develop and implement strategic plans for character education. 5795 Carmichael Parkway, Montgomery, AL 36117. Phone: (205) 279-7150. Fax: (205) 279-7151.

Center for the Advancement of Ethics and Character
    Dedicated to helping schools recapture their role as moral educators, this Center has developed a model that emphasizes the curriculum as the primary vehicle for transmitting moral values to the young. The center publicizes this model through its teacher academies for public school teachers and administrators. A similar program is directed toward college and university faculty responsible for the preparation of future teachers. The center is also involved in researching and developing curricular materials for use by schools, teachers, and parents. Boston University, School of Education, 605 Commonwealth Avenue, Boston, MA 02215. Phone: (617) 353-3262.

Center for Character Education
    An academic alliance of schools and universities that brings together educators interested in implementing the Integrated Character Model for moral education. This model reflects the view that knowledge, affect, and action are integrated in persons of mature character. Duquesne University, School of Education, 410 Canevin Hall, Pittsburgh, PA 15282. Phone: (412) 434-5191.

Center for the Fourth and Fifth Rs (Respect and Responsibility)

Directed by Dr. Thomas Lickona, this center sponsors annual summer institutes in character education, publishes the *Fourth and Fifth Rs* newsletter, and is forming a network of schools committed to teaching respect, responsibility, and related core values as the basis of good character. Education Department, SUNY Cortland, Cortland, NY 13045. Phone: (607) 753-2455. Fax: (607) 753-5980.

Center for Media Literacy

This nonprofit membership organization translates media literacy research and theory into practical information, training, and educational tools for teachers, youth leaders, parents, and caregivers of children. Free catalog of teaching materials. 1962 South Shenandoah Street, Los Angeles, CA 90034. Phone: (800) 559-2944. Fax: (310) 559-2944.

The Character Counts Coalition

This project of the Josephson Institute represents a national partnership of organizations and individuals involved in the education, training, or care of youth. It reflects a collaborative effort to improve the character of America's young people by focusing on the Six Pillars of Character: Trustworthiness, Respect, Responsibility, Fairness, Caring, and Citizenship. It aims to combat violence, dishonesty, and irresponsibility by strengthening the moral fiber of the next generation. 4640 Admiralty Way, Suite 1001, Marina del Rey, CA 90292. Phone: (310) 306-1868.

The Character Education Institute of California University of Pennsylvania

A regional institute that provides character education support to school districts, higher education, businesses, and parents; facilitates research and offers character education courses. Character Education Institute, California University of Pennsylvania, California, PA 15419-1394. Phone: (412) 938-4000.

The Character Education Partnership

A nonpartisan coalition of organizations and individuals concerned about the moral crisis confronting America's youth and dedicated to developing moral character and civic virtue in young people as a way of promoting a more compassionate and responsible society. Activities include a national clearinghouse, community programs, school support, publications, annual and regional forums, and a national awards and media campaign. John A. Martin, Executive Director, The Character Education Partnership, 1250 North Pitt Street, Alexandria, VA 22314. Fax: (703) 739-4967.

The Child Development Project

Reflects a comprehensive approach to translate research knowledge and theory about how elementary-age children learn and develop intellectually, socially, and ethically into practical programs for classroom, school, and home use. Developmental Studies Center, 2000 Embarcadero, Suite 305, Oakland, CA 94606-5300. Phone: (510) 533-0213.

Communitarian Network

This nonsectarian and nonpartisan coalition of individuals and organizations has come together to shore up the moral, social, and political environment. It sponsors an annual conference, produces position papers on family, health care reform, domestic disarmament, character and a civil society, and organ donation, and publishes a quarterly journal, *The Responsive Community: Rights and Responsibilities.* 2130 H Street, NW, No. 174. Washington, DC 20052. Phone: (202) 994-7997. Fax: (202) 994-1606.

Community Board Program

A conflict resolution resource. 1540 Market Street, Suite 490, San Francisco, CA 94102. Phone: (415) 552-1250. Fax: (415) 626-0595.

Educators for Social Responsibility

School Conflict Resolution Programs, 23 Garden Street, Cambridge, MA 02138. Phone: (617) 492-1764.

Ethics Resource Center

This center is working toward restoring our society's ethical foundations by strengthening the capacity of our institutions to foster integrity, encourage ethical conduct, and support basic values. Established in 1977 as a nonprofit, nonpartisan, and nonsectarian organization, the Ethics Resource Center has developed practical and effective programs that address the needs of the education, business, and government communities. Resources include research support, curricular materials, workshops, and conference sponsorship. 1120 G Street, NW, Washington, DC 20005. Phone: (202) 737-2258.

Exploring Ethics Through Children's Literature

This organization offers a literature-based ethics program for Grades 2–6. Critical Thinking Press, P.O. Box 448, Dept. 4, Pacific Grove, CA 93950-0448. Phone: (800) 458-4849. Fax: (408) 372-3230.

The Heartwood Program

This program offers a multicultural, literature-based curriculum that uses classic children's stories to present seven universal values—courage, loyalty, justice, respect, hope, honesty, and love—to students in Grades K–8. The Heartwood Institute, 425 North Craig Street, Suite 302, Pittsburgh, PA 15213. Phone: (412) 688-8570. Fax: (412) 688-8552.

Institute on Media Education

This organization offers a summer institute to help teachers and administrators integrate media literacy into existing subject areas; to develop new teaching methods that help students think critically about what they see, read, and watch; to analyze newspapers and television news and examine press influence on the coverage of the American political process; and to implement media awareness outreach programs in their schools and communities. Programs in Professional Education, 339E Gutman Library, Harvard Graduate School of Education, Cambridge, MA 02138. Phone: (617) 495-3572. Fax: (617) 496-8051.

The Jefferson Center for Character Education

This organization was formed in 1963 to publish and promote programs for schools that teach sound character values and personal responsibility. 202 South Lake Avenue, #240, Pasadena, CA 91101. Phone: (818) 792-8130.

The Joseph and Edna Josephson Institute of Ethics

This nonprofit organization seeks to increase the nation's awareness of ethical issues and to provide people with the skills to make their behaviors more ethical. Activities include research, publications, and skills training workshops; the organization also sponsors the Character Education Coalition. Josephson Institute, 4640 Admirality Way, Suite 1001, Marina del Rey, CA 90292. Phone: (310) 306-1868. Fax: (310) 827-1864.

National Association for Mediation in Education (NAME)

A conflict resolution resource. 205 Hampshire House, Box 33635, Amherst, MA 01003-3635. Phone: (413) 545-2462.

Parent and Child Guidance Center

This agency offers a character education parenting series. 2644 Banksville Road, Pittsburgh, PA 15216. Phone: (412) 343-5698. Fax: (412) 343-8249.

Personal Responsibility Education Program (PREP)

This school-business-community partnership is designed to develop student character, personal responsibility, and achievement. The Network for Educational Development, 13157 Olive Spur Road, St. Louis, MO 63141. Phone: (314) 576-3535, ext. 130. Fax: (314) 576-4996.

WiseSkills

This organization offers a community-based character-building program for Grades K–8. Legacy Learning, P.O. Box 3213, South Pasadena, CA 91031-6213. Phone: (818) 441-7944.

Source Note: This listing is abridged and adapted from "Character Education Organizations and Publications," maintained by the Center for the Fourth and Fifth Rs, Dr. Thomas Lickona, Director, Education Department, SUNY Cortland, Cortland, NY 13045. Used by permission.

6. Other Sources of Materials

Social Studies School Service Catalog (free)
10000 Culver Boulevard, P.O. Box 802
Culver City, CA 90230

Where to Find It Guide (published annually in a fall issue of *Scholastic Teacher*) Scholastic Magazines, Inc., 50 W. 44th Street New York, NY 10036.

6.1 Teachers' Magazines

1. *Teaching-PreK–8.* Address: P.O. Box 54805, Boulder, CO 80323-4805.
2. *Teacher.* Address: 4301 Connecticut Avenue NW, Suite 432, Washington, DC, 20077-3522.
3. *Learning* (the year varies with the current year). Address: 1111 Bethlehem Pike, Springhouse, PA 19477.
4. *Instructor.* Address: 7 Bank Street, Dansville, NY 14437.

6.2 Guides to Free or Inexpensive Materials

Educator's Guide to Free Social Studies Materials, edited by Patricia H. Suttles and William H. Hartley. Educators Progress Service, Inc., Randolph, WI 53956. *Note:* Guides to other free and inexpensive material are also available.

Free and Inexpensive Materials on World Affairs, by Leonard S. Kenworthy. Teachers College Press, 1234 Amsterdam Avenue, New York, NY 10027.

Free and Inexpensive Teaching Aids, by Bruce Miller. Box 369, Riverside, CA 92502.

Free and Inexpensive Learning Materials (updated annually). George Peabody College of Vanderbilt University, Nashville, TN 37203.

Selected Free Materials for Classroom Teachers, by Ruth H. Aubrey. Fearon Publishers, 6 Davis Drive, Belmont, CA 94002.

6.3 Newspaper-Related Materials

Many local newspapers maintain a "Newspaper in Education" department that will provide teaching tips and other aids for integrating newspapers into the curriculum. If your local paper does not offer such a service, contact the American Newspaper Publishers Association Foundation (The Newspaper Center, Box 17407, Dulles International Airport, Washington, DC 20041) for information.

3.2 Sources for Computer-Related Materials and Programs

1. Directories

Directories show what and where computer-based materials are available but do not publish or market the materials themselves.

Educator's Handbook and Software Directory. Vital Information, Inc., 7899 Mastin Drive, Overland Park, KS 66204

Minnesota Education Computing Corporation, 3490 Lexington Avenue North, St. Paul, MN 55126

School Microwave Directory. Dresden Associates, P.O. Box 246, Dresden, ME 04342

Sources for Courses. TALMIS, 115 North Oak Park Avenue, Oak Park, IL 60301

Swift's Directory of Educational Software. Sterling Swift Publishing Co., 1600 Fortview Road, Austin, TX 78704

2. Software Catalogs

Most commercial publishers have catalogs in which they advertise their products. The catalogs listed here are for computer-oriented clearinghouses and evaluation centers.

Educational Products Information Exchange. P.O. Box 620, Stony Brook, NY 11790

Microcomputer Software and Information for Teachers. Northwest Regional Education Laboratory, 300 SW 6th Avenue, Portland, OR 97204

Softswap (for exchanging original programs). San Mateo County Office of Education, 333 Main Street, Redwood City, CA 94063

3. Computer Magazines/Journals

Many computer magazines, of which this list is only a sampling, contain postage-paid cards that permit you to request additional information about the products they advertise. Because these organizations regularly exchange (or sell) their mailing lists, a single request for information can result in a deluge of catalogs.

Electronic Education. Suite 220, 1311 Executive Center Drive, Tallahassee, FL 32301

Electronic Learning. 2280 Arbor Boulevard, Dayton, OH 45439

Classroom Computer Learning. Intentional Educations Inc., 341 Mt. Auburn Street, Watertown, MA 02172

The Computing Teacher. International Council for Computers in Education, University of Oregon, 1878 Agate Street, Eugene, OR 97403-1923

4. Sources of Computer Programs (Selected) and Services

Aldus Corporation
411 First Avenue South, Suite 200
Seattle, WA 98104
Sample Program: PageMaker

American On-Line
8619 Westwood Center Drive
Vienna, VA 22182
On-Line Service

Apple Computer, Inc.
20525 Marianni Avenue
Cupertino, CA 95014
Sample Program: HyperCard

Applied Optical Media
1450 Boot Road, Bldg. 400
Westchester, PA 19380
Sample Program:
Mediasource: Historical Literacy

Broderbund Software
17 Paul Drive
San Rafael, CA 94903-2102
Sample Programs:
Arthur's Teacher Trouble
Just Grandma and Me
Bank Street Writer
Print Shop Deluxe
Where in (Europe; America's Past;
Time; the U.S.A.; the world)
Is Carmen Sandiego?

Castle Software
1228 Powell Avenue North
Merrick, NY 11566
Sample Program: TestWiz

Claris Corporation
5201 Patrick Henry Drive
Santa Clara, CA 95052
Sample Programs:
MacWrite 11 Pro
AppleWorks
ClarisWorks
Culture 2.0

CompuServe Information Service
P.O. Box 20212
Columbus, OH 43220
On-Line Service

Comwell Systems, Inc.
2100 South Rural Road
Tempe, AZ 85282
Sample Programs:
PC Globe-Plus
PC USA

Davidson and Associates
P.O. Box 2961
Torrance, CA 90509
Sample Program: KidCAD

Didatech Software Ltd.
4250 Dawson Street, Suite 200
Burnaby, British Columbia V5C 4B1
Sample Program: Crosscounty USA

Discis Knowledge Research Inc.
45 Sheppard Avenue East, Suite 410
Toronto, Ontario
Canada M2N5W9
Sample Program: Discis Books

The Discovery Channel Multimedia
7700 Wisconsin Avenue
Bethesda, MD 20814-3579
Sample Programs:
Nile: Passage to Egypt
Normandy: The Great Crusade

FredMail Network
Computer Using Educators, Inc.
P.O. Box 2087
Menlo Park, CA 94026
Sample Program: FrEdWriter

Frontier Software
P.O. Box 56505
Houston, TX 77227
Sample Program: Famous Blacks in
   American History

Grolier Electronic Publishing
Sherman Turnpike
Danbury, CT 06816
Sample Program:
New Grolier Electronic Encyclopedia

Hartley Courseware, Inc.
133 Bridge Street
Diamondale, MI 48821
Sample Programs:
The Civil War
Bird's-Eye View

IBM Corporation
P.O. Box 1328-W
Boca Raton, FL 33429-1328
Sample Program: IBM Linkway

Instructional Resources Corporation
1819 Bay Ridge Avenue
Annapolis, MD 21403
Sample Program:
The American History CD-ROM

The Learning Company
6493 Kaiser Drive
Fremont, CA 94555
Sample Programs:
The Children's Writing and Publishing Center
The Writing Center

MECC
6160 Summitt Drive North
Minneapolis, MN 55430-4003
Sample Programs:
Lemonade Stand
MECC Dataquest Series
The Oregon Trail II
Wagon Train 1848
USA/World GeoGraph
MayaQuest
DynoPark Tycoon

Maxis Software
950 Mountainview Drive
Lafayette, CA 94549
Sample Programs:

SimAnt
SimCity
SimEarth
Simlife

Microsoft Corporation
1 Microsoft Way
P.O. Box 97017
Redmond, WA 98052
Sample Programs:
Microsoft Words
Works for Windows
Encarta
Ancient Lands
500 Nations

Mindscape, Inc.
3444 Dundee Road, Dept. C
Northbrook, IL 60062
Sample Program: Dinosaur Dig

National Geographic Society
1145 17th Street, NW
Washington, DC 20036
Sample Programs: GTV: A Geographic
   Perspective on American History
Golden Spike
Picture Atlas of the World

Optical Data Corporation
30 Technology Drive
Warren, NJ 07060
Sample Programs: Powers of the . . .
   President; Congress; Supreme Court
Martin Luther King
In the Holy Land
ABC News Interactive

Pierian Springs Software
5200 SW Macadam, Suite 570
Portland, OR 97201
Sample Program:
Interactive Geography—Digital Chisel

Polarware
P.O. Box 311
521 Hamilton Avenue
Geneva, IL 60134
Sample Programs: The Spy's Adventures
   in . . . South America; North America;
   Europe; Asia; Africa; the Pacific
   Islands

3

Prodigy Services Company
White Plains, NY 10601
On-Line Service

Scholastic, Inc.
730 Broadway
New York, NY 10003
Sample Programs:
Survey Taker
Point of View

Spinnaker Software Corp.
One Kendall Square
Cambridge, MA 02139
Sample Programs:
KidWriter (English or
    Spanish)
KidWriter (Golden Edition)

Springboard Software, Inc.
7807 Creekridge Circle
Minneapolis, MN 55435
Sample Program: The Newsroom

Sunburst Communications
101 Castleton Street
Pleasantville, NY 10570
Sample Programs:
Bank Street School
Filer
High Wire Logic
Magic Slate
Teddy's Playground
Ten Clues

Symantec Corporation
10201 Torre Avenue
Cupertino, CA 95914
Sample Program: GreatWorks

Timeworks, Inc.
444 Lake Cook Road
Deerfield, IL 60015-4919
Sample Programs: Publish It!
Publish It! Easy

Tom Snyder Productions
80 Coolidge Hill Road
Watertown, MA 02172-2817
Sample Programs:
Decisions, Decisions Series
Ancient Empires
Feudalism

Colonization
On the Campaign Trail
Revolutionary Wars
National Inspirer
Classroom StoreWorks

The Voyager Company
514 Market Loop, Suite 103
West Dundee, IL 60118
Sample Programs:
Exotic Japan
Who Built America?

Videodiscovery
1700 Westlake Avenue, N. #600
Seattle, WA 98109-3012
Sample Program:
Small Blue Planet

Ztek Company
P.O. Box 11768
Louisville, KY 40577-1768
Sample Programs:
European Monarchs
U.S. Atlas
World Atlas

3.3 Directory of Living History Museums

Alabama

Constitution Hall Village
404 Madison Street
Huntsville, AL 35801
(800) 678-1819

Constitution Hall Village is located at the site of the drafting of Alabama's 1819 constitution. Both single-day and five-day educational programs are available.

Alaska

Eklutna Village Historical Park
510 L Street, Suite 200
Anchorage, AK 99501
(907) 276-5701

Eklutna is the oldest continuously inhabited Athapaskan site in Alaska. Its cemetery contains spirit houses that were built to protect the spirits of the deceased, and the park has two Russian Orthodox churches built by missionaries in the 1830s.

Native Village of Alaskaland
Fairbanks Native Association
201 First Avenue,. 2nd Floor
Fairbanks, AK 99701
(907) 452-1648

This village contains a variety of different types of housing used by Native American Alaskans, including sod dwellings and plank houses.

Arizona

Pioneer Arizona
3901 West Pioneer Road
Phoenix, AZ 85027
(602) 993-0212

Descendants of the horses that Columbus brought to North America on his second voyage in 1493 are raised at Pioneer Arizona. The museum also includes more than twenty buildings that reflect the influences of Native American, Spanish, and Mexican cultures.

Arkansas

Arkansas Territorial Restoration
200 East 3rd Street
Little Rock, AR 72201
(501) 324-9351

This museum reflects frontier life in Arkansas from 1819 to 1870.

California

El Pueblo de Los Angeles Historic Monument
125 Paseo de la Plaza, Suite 400
Los Angeles, CA 90012
(213) 628-0605

This community, which later became known simply as Los Angeles, has twenty-seven reconstructed buildings.

Mission San Juan Capistrano
31882 Camino Capistrano #107
San Juan Capistrano, CA 92675
(714) 248-2048

Franciscan padres founded the Mission of San Juan Capistrano in 1776. The Serra Chapel is the oldest continuously inhabited building in the state of California. The mission is also famous for the annual migration of swallows each spring.

Colorado

Bent's Old Fort National Historic Site
35110 Highway 194 East
La Junta, CO 81050
(719) 384-2596

This reconstructed frontier fur trading post features blacksmithing and frontier medicine.

Connecticut

Mystic Seaport and Maritime Museum
50 Greenmanville Avenue
Mystic, CT 06355
(203) 572-0711

The Mystic Seaport and Preservation Shipyard is home to nineteenth-century tall ships and schooners. The maritime museum contains antique navigational equipment. The accompanying planetarium has programs explaining how sea captains relied on the stars to determine their location at sea.

Delaware

Delaware Agricultural Museum
866 North DuPont Highway
Dover, DE 19901
(302) 734-1618

Historic activities and demonstrations vary depending on the season. During the summer, children can experience schooling from that period of our history. Lessons are taught from the McGuffey Reader and Noah Webster's Blue Backed Speller with "ciphering" done on a slate. During July and August, children can dress in clothing of the period, churn butter, feed the chickens and cow, and enjoy a storyteller. During the winter months, guides provide interpretations of rural life in the 1850s.

Hagley Museum and Library
P.O. Box 3630
Wilmington, DE 19807
(302) 658-2400

The Hagley Museum and Library focuses on the E. I. du Pont family's role and history in the nineteenth century. Tours include the du Ponts' Georgian mansion and gardens, workers' quarters, and gunpowder mills.

Florida

Historic Saint Augustine Spanish Quarter
P.O. Box 1987
Saint Augustine, FL 32085
(904) 825-6830

Saint Augustine was founded more than 470 years ago and is the oldest continuously inhabited European settlement in North America. Life during the Spanish colonial period of the 1740s is portrayed in restored buildings and gardens.

Georgia

Agrirama
P.O. Box Q
Tifton, GA 31793
(912) 386-3344

This museum consists of almost forty restored buildings that illustrate traditional and progressive farming.

Idaho

Pioneer Village and Idaho Historical Museum
610 North Julia Davis Drive
Boise, ID 83702
(208) 334-2120

This museum village consists of restored and reconstructed log cabins and adobes that may be toured by school groups.

Illinois

Lincoln's New Salem State Historic Site
R.R. #1, Box 244A
Petersburg, IL 62675
(217) 632-4000

Abraham Lincoln first stopped at New Salem when he and a friend copiloted a flatboat down the Sangamon River to the Ohio and Mississippi Rivers. He later returned there to settle and study law. The re-created village provides demonstrations of activities common to daily living during Lincoln's lifetime.

Naper Settlement
210 West Porter
Naperville, IL 60540
(708) 420-6010

This mid- to late-nineteenth-century settlement features historic games and crafts, soap making, and open hearth cooking.

Indiana

Conner Prairie
13400 Allisonville Road
Fishers, IN 46038
(317) 776-6000

Conner Prairie presents three historically accurate areas, each with its own costumed interpreters. Prairietown is an 1836 Indiana village; the second area features the nineteenth-century home of William Conner, a land developer and politician; and the third area is a Pioneer Adventure Area where children are encouraged to participate in dipping candles, soap making, weaving, and wood carving.

Historic New Harmony
506 1/2 Main St.
P.O. Box 579
New Harmony, IN 47631
(812) 682-4488

The Harmonie Society fled Germany because of religious persecution and ultimately developed a utopian community that later failed.

Iowa

Living History Farms
2600 NW 111th Street
Urbandale, IA 50322
(515) 278-2400

This museum depicts agrarian culture from the sixteenth century through to the 1850s.

Amana Colonies
P.O. Box 303
Amana, IA 52203
(800) 245-5465

In 1855 a group of separatists from Germany settled on 27,000 acres in Amana. The community features three furniture factories and several craft shops.

3

Kansas

Old Cowtown Museum
1871 Sim Park Drive
Wichita, KS 67203
(316) 264-0671

This museum features thirty buildings from an authentic cow town of the Old West.

Kentucky

Shaker Village of Pleasant Hill
3500 Lexington Road
Harrodsburg, KY 40330
(606) 734-5411

This nineteenth-century Shaker village has more than thirty original buildings, each furnished with Shaker furniture.

Louisiana

Acadian Village
200 Greenleaf Road
Lafayette, LA 70506
(800) 962-9133

This museum features a general store and houses from nineteenth-century Acadiana.

Maine

Norlands Living History Center
R.R. #2 Box 3395
Livermore Falls, ME 04254
(207) 897-2236

This center has two programs, one that depicts the post–Revolutionary War period and the other that portrays the post–Civil War era.

Maryland

Baltimore City Life Museums
800 East Lombard Street
Baltimore, MD 21202
(410) 396-3279

Six different museums portray life in nineteenth-century Baltimore.

Massachusetts

Hancock Shaker Village
P.O. Box 898
Pittsfield, MA 01202
(413) 443-0188

The Hancock Shaker Village features more than twenty restored buildings, and demonstrations of furniture and textile making.

Plimoth Plantation
P.O. Box 1620
Plymouth, MA 02362
(508) 746-1622

The Plimoth Plantation features a reconstructed village and a replica of the Mayflower.

Michigan

Colonial Michilimackinac
P.O. Box 873
Mackinaw City, MI 49701
(616) 436-5563

This former military outpost and fur trading center has re-created a 1770s Native American encampment, complete with wigwams.

Troy Museum and Historic Village
60 West Wattles Road
Troy, MI 48098
(313) 524-3570

This museum presents a program in which children reenact chores that were common to pioneer families.

Minnesota

Oliver H. Kelley Farm
15788 Kelley Farm Road
Elk River, MN 55330
(612) 441-6896

This farm depicts life in 1860s Minnesota.

Missouri

Arrow Rock State Historic Site
P.O. Box 1
Arrow Rock, MO 65320
(816) 837-3330

Located near the beginning of the Santa Fe Trail, this nineteenth-century village includes a restored church, tavern, courthouse, and newspaper office.

Nebraska

Stuhr Museum of the Prairie Pioneer
3133 West Highway 34
Grand Island, NE 68801
(308) 381-5316

This museum features a Pawnee lodge (replica) and a collection of Native American and Old West artifacts.

New Hampshire

Strawbery Banke
P.O. Box 300
Portsmouth, NH 03802
(603) 433-1100

Strawbery Banke, which was once a colonial seaport, depicts four centuries of history and culture.

New Jersey

Historic Batso Village
Wharton State Forest
Route #9 Batso
Hammonton, NJ 08037
(609) 561-3262

Batso Village was a nineteenth-century ironworking and glassmaking center.

New Mexico

El Rancho de Las Golondrinus
Route 14, P.O. Box 214
Santa Fe, NM 87505
(505) 471-2261

This town was founded by the Spanish as an overnight stop on the Royal Road to Mexico City.

New York

Museum Village
Museum Village Road
Monroe, NY 10950
(914) 782-8247

This village depicts agrarian life in the 1880s.

Old Bethpage Village Restoration
Nassau County Department of Recreation
  and Parks
Round Swarp Road
Old Bethpage, NY 11804
(516) 572-8400

This reconstructed village reflects agricultural, domestic, and trade activities from the pre–Civil War period.

North Carolina

Oconaluftee Indian Village
P.O. Box 398
Cherokee, NC 28719
(704) 497-2111

This village, which is located on the Cherokee Reservation, shows the history and traditions of the Cherokee Nation.

Ohio

Hale Farm and Village
P.O. Box 296
Bath, OH 44210
(216) 666-3711

This living museum depicts life in the 1850s. Demonstrations include glassblowing, candlemaking, blacksmithing, and maple sugaring (in season).

Ohio Village
1982 Velma Ave.
Columbus, OH 43211
(614) 297-2439

This museum portrays problems encountered by African-Americans during the early 1800s.

Pennsylvania

Historic Fallsington
4 Yardley Ave.
Fallsington, PA 19054
(215) 295-6567

This 300-year-old village was founded as a haven for Quakers and features a garden containing plants common to colonial America.

3

South Carolina

Middleton Place
Ashley River Road
Charleston, SC 29414
(803) 556-6020

At this restored eighteenth-century plantation, guides demonstrate woodworking and blacksmithing.

Tennessee

Museum of Appalachia
P.O. Box 0318
Highway 61
Norris, TN 37828
(615) 494-7680

The best time to visit is during the Fall Homecoming, in October, when demonstrations of goat milking, molasses-making, and spinning dog hair into thread are featured.

Texas

Old City Park
1717 Gano Street
Dallas, TX 75215
(214) 421-5141

This city park contains thirty-five restored buildings, from a log cabin to an antebellum mansion.

The Ranching Heritage Center
4th & Indiana
Lubbock, TX 79409
(806) 742-2498

This facility traces the history of ranching from the days of dugout homes to the early 1900s. It features over 20 restored buildings and railroad facilities.

Utah

Ronald V. Jensen Living Historical Farm
4025 South Highway 89-91
Welssville, UT 84339
(801) 245-4064

Interpreters demonstrate how family members on a Mormon farm in the early 1900s did their daily chores.

Virginia

Colonial Williamsburg
P.O. Box 1776
Williamsburg, VA 23187
(804) 229-1000

Among the largest and most famous of the living history museums in the United States, Colonial Williamsburg contains more than 100 restored or reconstructed buildings. A variety of educational programs are available.

Washington

Fort Nisqually Historic Site
Point Defiance Park
5400 North Pearl
Tacoma, WA 98405
(206) 591-5339

This living museum re-creates a former fort and Hudson Bay Company trading post.

Rainier Legacy
Pioneer Farm/Ohop Indian Village
7716 Ohop Valley Road
Eatonville, WA 98328
(206) 832-6300

This museum, which is open between early March and late November, contrasts a Native American settlement with that of European pioneers.

Wisconsin

Old World Wisconsin
South 103 West 37890
Highway 67
Eagle, WI 53119
(414) 594-2116

This living history museum shows nineteenth- and twentieth-century farmsteads for a variety of Scandinavian cultures.

3

4.1 Children's Books for Teaching Character, Morals, and Values

In the following bibliographies, the grade-level designation "P" means the book might be more valuable for the primary grades, kindergarten to Grade 3; the designation "I" means the intermediate grades, 3–8.

A. Self-Esteem

Adoff, Arnold. (1991). *Hard to Be Six.* Illus. by Cheryl Hanna. Lothrop, Lee & Shepard. P, 32 pages.

> On the occasion of his sister's tenth birthday, a six-year-old boy reflects on how tough it is to be just six.

Allinson, Beverley. (1990). *Elfie.* Scholastic. P, 32 pages.

> Elfie has the loudest voice of any ant you will ever meet, so loud, in fact, that all the other ants in the community run away from her. Elfie feels (and is) rejected for a voice that she can't seem to control. When an emergency arises, Elfie's bellowing voice saves the lives of the rest of her family, and they come to accept her for what she is.

Browner, Anthony. (1985). *Willie the Champ.* Knopf. P, 32 pages.

> Willie is a sensitive boy who likes to read, listen to music, and take walks in the park but isn't any good at activities like soccer, swimming, or bike racing. One day when Willie encounters the neighborhood bully, Buster Nose, he doesn't run away as the other kids do. Instead, he defends himself against Buster and is declared a hero by the other children.

Bryan, Ashley. (1989). *Turtle Knows Your Name.* Atheneum. P, I, 32 pages.

> This West Indian tale is about a boy with a very long name, Upsilimana Tumpalerado. He works diligently just to pronounce his name, and when he finally succeeds, he and his grandmother celebrate. Unfortunately, only one of his friends, Turtle, can remember and pronounce his name, but Turtle's effort makes Upsilimana Tumpalerado feel good.

Cameron, Ann. (1988). *Most Beautiful Place in the World.* Knopf. I, 64 pages.

> Abandoned by his parents, Juan lives with his grandmother in San Pablo, Guatemala. During the day he works as a shoeshine boy to earn his keep. Eventually Juan learns to read and realizes that where he lives is the most beautiful place in the world.

Carte, Eric. (1984). *The Mixed-Up Chameleon.* Harper. P, 32 pages.

> Sometimes he is green and sometimes he's brown, but this poor chameleon doesn't know who he is or what color he ought to be.

Cohen, Barbara. (1991). *213 Valentines.* Illus. by Wit Clay. Holt. P, I, 55 pages.

> Wade is an African-American boy who has transferred to Kennedy School to participate in its gifted and talented program. At the new school, Wade feels so unpopular that he is sure he will not receive any valentine cards—except from the one person who drew his name. To avoid this, Wade buys 200 valentines, which he sends to himself and a friend under the names of famous people.

Croll, Carolyn. (1991). *The Three Brothers.* Putnam. P, 32 pages.

> This folktale is about the competition between three brothers who live on a farm in Germany. One day their father indicates that whichever of his three sons can fill the barn to its fullest in just one day will inherit the farm. The oldest son quickly herds the animals into the barn; then the middle son fills it to the rafters with hay. It is evening before the youngest son finally gets his turn. He lights a candle, which completely fills the barn with light, and wins the contest.

Freeman, Don (1964). *Dandelion*. Viking. P, 32 pages.

Jennifer is having a party and Dandelion has been invited. Because this is a special occasion, Dandelion buys new clothes and has his mane curled. When he arrives at the party, no one recognizes him and the door is closed in his face. After a rainstorm, which restores Dandelion's mane to its usual state, he returns to the party and is welcomed with open arms.

Glenn, Maggie. (1990). *Ruby*. Putnam. P, 32 pages.

Ruby, a teddy bear, thinks that the "S" stamped on her paw at the toy factory means "special." The other teddy bears tell her that it means "second" and that she is a mistake. To avoid being thrown out, Ruby escapes from the factory and makes her way to the best toy shop in town. A little girl then selects Ruby because she is different from all the others; Ruby has character.

Graham, Amanda. (1987). *Who Wants Arthur?* Gareth Stevens. P, 32 pages.

Arthur, a dog who has been in the pet shop for what seems like forever, decides that for someone to want him, he will need to act like other popular animals. For example, when Arthur sees that fish are popular, he tries to act like a fish, but to no avail. Only after Arthur becomes himself does someone buy him.

Greenwald, Sheila. (1980). *It All Began with Jane Eyre.* Little, Brown. I, 128 pages.

Franny Dillman is a teenage girl who reads classic novels, like *Jane Eyre,* by flashlight in her closet. Franny's mother tries to convince her to read more "normal" novels, but Franny feels she has little in common with the characters in contemporary fiction books; she much prefers the classics. Franny stands up for her beliefs, even though that may make her different.

Hooks, William H. (1989). *The Three Little Pigs and the Fox.* Illus. by S. D. Schindler. Macmillan. P, I, 32 pages.

In this version of the classic tale, the smallest pig, the female runt of the litter, outwits the fox and saves her bigger brothers.

Isadora, Rachel. (1976). *Max.* Macmillan. P, 32 pages.

On most Saturdays, Max, a baseball player, walks his sister Lisa to her ballet lesson on the way to practice. One Saturday, Lisa invites Max to join the ballet class. Hesitantly, Max joins the group, and to his surprise, he actually enjoys it and performs well. Max then decides that ballet is a great warmup for his baseball games.

Klass, Sheila Solomon. (1991). *Kool Ada.* Scholastic. I, 176 pages.

Ada is a strong-willed girl with adjustment problems. Not only is she new to her northern school, but she has recently moved from a home in the rural, southern mountains. A compassionate teacher finally helps Ada understand that her rough exterior and quick temper are only compounding her problems.

Lane, Megan Halsey. (1990). *Something to Crow About.* Dial. P, 32 pages.

In this predictable book, Randall is a rooster who wants to lay eggs, and Cassie is a chicken who would like to cock-a-doodle-do. They both eventually realize that being different is what they should crow about.

Leaf, Munro. (1936). *The Story of Ferdinand.* Illus. by Robert Lawson. Viking. P, 48 pages.

In this classic story, Ferdinand is a bull who would rather smell the flowers than butt horns with the other bulls. When it comes time to select new candidates for the bull ring, Ferdinand goes off by himself and sits next to some flowers. Unfortunately, Ferdinand sits on a bee, which results in a demonstration of jumping and wild movements that convinces the judges that he belongs in the bull ring. When Ferdinand finally enters the ring for his "big event," all he does is smell the flowers in the ladies' hats.

Levine, Ellen. (1989). *I Hate English.* Illus. by Steve Bjorkman. Scholastic. P, I, 32 pages.

Every non-native speaker of English knows what a hard language it is to learn. This is the case in this story of a young girl who is being tutored in English but sees little need to learn it. Eventually she

4

begins to feel better about speaking her native tongue and about acquiring a second language.

Levinson, Marilyn. (1991). *The Fourth-Grade Four.* Illus. by Leslie Bowman. Henry Holt. P, I, 64 pages.

This is the story of what happens to Alex Burman, a fourth-grader and soccer player, who learns that he needs glasses. Will he be able to continue playing soccer? Will his friends make fun of him? You can see where this is leading.

Lionni, Leo. (1969). *Alexander and the Wind-Up Mouse.* Random House. P, 32 pages.

Alexander is a real mouse who meets Willie, a wind-up mouse. Alexander tries to transform himself into a mechanical mouse like Willie, who is loved by a human, only to find that Willie has been discarded by its owner. Alexander then realizes that being a real mouse isn't so bad after all.

Milhouse, Katherine, & Dalgiesh, Alice. (1990). *The Turnip, an Old Russian Tale.* Putnam. P, 32 pages.

Mice are among the most powerful literary creatures, and so it is in this tale. Everyone who tries to pull a turnip from the ground is unsuccessful until the mouse finally lends a hand.

Peet, Bill. (1986). *Pamela Camel.* Houghton Mifflin. P, 48 pages.

Poor Pamela Camel thinks that she is the dumbest animal in the circus. Pamela feels so bad that she runs away, but in the process she saves a train from destruction. For her heroism, she is given first place in the circus parade.

Polacco, Patricia. (1990). *Just Plain Fancy.* Bantam. P, 32 pages.

Naomi is an Amish girl, one of the plain people. Amid all the plainness, Naomi complains to her little sister that just once she would like to have something fancy. One day as Naomi is collecting eggs, she notices one that is different and fancier than the rest. She places it under a hen, and when it hatches it produces an unusual looking bird. Naomi fears that her fancy bird, a peacock, will be shunned. Instead, the elders view Naomi's peacock as a miracle.

Rodgers, Frank. (1988). *Who's Afraid of the Ghost Train?* Harcourt Brace Jovanovich. P, 32 pages.

Robert is afraid of almost everything and gets teased by his friends accordingly. One day his grandpa, a former lion tamer, gives him an idea for handling his fears. He tells Robert to pretend that the lions are just big babies. Robert tries this technique when riding the Ghost Train at the carnival the next day.

Seuss, Dr. (1990). *Oh, The Places You'll Go!* Random House. P, I, 48 pages.

Like most Seuss books do, the delightful rhyming text of this book reflects optimism personified.

Thomas, Patricia. (1971/1990). *"Stand Back," Said the Elephant, "I'm Going to Sneeze!"* Illus. by Wallace Trip. Lothrop. P, 48 pages.

When an elephant sneezes, all kinds of unexpected things can happen—and do in this story. But once again, a mouse surprises the elephant and keeps him from sneezing, thus saving the other animals from their embarrassing responses to his sneeze. Unfortunately, the elephant ends up laughing, the effects of which are almost as bad as sneezing.

Viorst, Judith. (1972). *Alexander and the Terrible, Horrible, No Good, Very Bad Day.* Illus. by Ray Cruz. Atheneum. P, I, 32 pages.

All of us have bad days from time to time, and this is the case for Alexander. Everything goes wrong, to the point that Alexander decides that he is going to move to Australia to escape his problems. Finally, Alexander's mother assures him that some days are like that, and that it is nothing to worry about.

Waber, Bernard. (1972). *Ira Sleeps Over.* Houghton Mifflin. P, 48 pages.

Should Ira take his teddy bear, Tah Tah, when he is invited to stay over at his best friend Reggie's house? Will Reggie make fun of him for sleeping with a teddy bear? Ira decides against taking Tah Tah, but after they are settled in to sleep, Reggie quietly pulls his own teddy bear, Foo Foo, out of a dresser drawer. Ira then runs home to rescue Tah Tah and bring her to Reggie's for the night.

4

Wildsmith, Brian. (1979). *The Lion and the Rat.* Oxford. P, 32 pages.

> When a lion finds himself caught in a net trap, who is better prepared to save him than a sharp-toothed rat?

Winthrop, Elizabeth. (1980). *Sloppy Kisses.* Illus. by Anne Burgess. Macmillan. P, 32 pages.

> Emmy Lou comes from a family that kisses a lot, and sloppily at that. Emmy Lou's friend, Rosemary, says that sloppy kisses are for babies. For several days, Emmy Lou will only accept pats on the head instead of sloppy kisses, but her family continues to express their affection to one another. One night when Emmy Lou can't sleep, nothing helps her but a sloppy kiss. Emmy Lou realizes that being from a family that kisses a lot is nothing to be ashamed of.

Wood, Audrey, & Wood, Don. (1982). *Quick as a Cricket.* Child's Play. P, 32 pages.

> This is the story of a child who is sometimes as quick as a cricket and sometimes as slow as a snail. Throughout the story there are instances where a child may move quickly at one time, and slowly at another, but all the traits, taken together, reflect the child's total character.

Yashima, Taro. (1955). *Crow Boy.* Viking. P, I, 32 pages.

> Chibi is a shy sixth grader who walks to school from the distant countryside. Although his classmates sometimes make fun of him, Chibi's teacher encourages him to perform in the school talent show. Chibi has learned to reproduce the different calls of crows, which he hears as he walks to school, and this earns him the admiration of his peers.

Yorinks, Arthur. (1988). *Bravo Minski.* Illus. by Richard Egielski. Farrar, Straus & Giroux. P, 32 pages.

> It is difficult to be a scientific genius, especially when your father hauls you around Europe showing off your talents, but this is Minski's fate. But one day, when Minski hears an opera star, he determines to find a way to get the same kind of beautiful voice. Although his father thinks that Minski's musical intentions are impractical and unworthy of a scientific genius, Minski pursues his quest to become a musical performer.

Zolotow, Charlotte. 91972). *William's Doll.* Illus. by William Pene du Bois. Harper. P, I, 32 pages.

> William has a basketball and a train set, but what he really wants is a doll. It doesn't matter that his brother thinks he is a creep, and the boy next door calls him a sissy; they just don't understand. William's grandmother is apparently the only person who understands how he feels and is willing to give him the doll he seeks.

B. Respect for Others

Anholt, Lawrence. (1991). *What I Like.* Illus. by Catherine Anholt. Putnam. P, 32 pages.

> In simple rhyming text, six children share the different things they like to do. They eventually join hands and chant, "What we all like is . . . making a friend."

Brewster, Patience. (1991). *Rabbit Inn.* Little, Brown. P, I, 32 pages.

> Some unexpected guests are coming to Rabbit Inn, so all the other animal guests cooperate to help the rabbit owners to clean up the place. On the last page of the book, they find out who the special guests are.

Bulla, Clyde Robert. (1978). *Keep Running, Allen.* Illus. by Satomi Ichikawa. Harper. P, 32 pages.

> A group of children are running in the hills, but Allen, the youngest, can't keep up. When they reach the top of the hill, Allen offers them something to appreciate; he lies on his back and watches the clouds.

Damrell, Liz. (1991). *With the Wind.* Illus. by Stephen Marchesi. Orchard. P, 32 pages.

> Much of this story focuses on a young boy's thrill of riding a horse. Not until the next-to-last page do the illustrations show that this child has a disability; he has a brace on his leg and is placed in a wheelchair after his ride.

Herman, Charlotte. (1991). *Max Malone Makes a Million.* Illus. by Cat Bowman Smith. Henry Holt. P, I, 64 pages.

> After Max reads about a get-rich-quick scheme, he sets out on one of his own. A six-year-old neigh-

bor volunteers to help him, but Max just scoffs at him. In this instance, the younger child (the six-year-old) is successful and Max is not.

Hoffman, Mary. (1991). *Amazing Grace.* Illus. by Caroline Binch. Dial. P, 32 pages.

This is one of the growing number of books, like Spinelli's *Maniac Magee,* that addresses prejudice and bias directly. In this case, Grace, a truly talented dancer, wants the role of Peter Pan in a school play. But because she is both a black and a female, her classmates decide it would be inappropriate for her to play that role. Fortunately, Grace's grandmother is able to help her deal with her disappointment.

Isadora, Rachel. (1991). *At the Crossroads.* Greenwillow. P, I, 32 pages.

This book is about the children from a segregated South African township who gather at a crossroads to await their father's return from ten months in the mines. The African experience on which this book is based is real, and the underlying emotion—jubilation at the return of a loved one—is universal.

Johnston, Tony. (1986). *Pages of Music.* Illus. by Tomie dePaola. Putnam. P, I, 32 pages.

An artist and her son visit the island of Sardinia, where the poor shepherds share their bread with them. The son, who never forgets the sound of shepherd's pipes, returns years later as a composer and conductor. With him he brings his entire orchestra and an orchestral piece he has composed especially for the shepherds of Sardinia.

Joseph, Lynn. (1990). *Coconut Kind of Day.* Lothrop, Lee & Shepard. P, 32 pages.

This is a collection of poems, told in dialect, about a day in the life of a Caribbean child. Differences between island life and life in the United States are obvious.

Kline, Suzy. (1991). *Mary Marony and the Snake.* Illus. by Blanche Sims. Putnam. P, I, 64 pages.

Mary Marony stutters and her second-grade classmates, especially Marvin Higgins, tease her. Mary earns the respect of her fellow students when

Marvin's father brings a snake to school and Mary rescues it when it gets loose.

Luttrell, Ida. (1990). *Three Good Blankets.* Illus. by Michael McDermott. Atheneum. P, I, 32 pages.

An old woman's daughter buys a new wool blanket for her mother, who lives alone in an old, cold house on a hill. However, the mother gives the new blanket to her faithful donkey who carries her wood. When her son gives her another new blanket, she gives that one to her goat who provides her with rich, creamy milk. And when another son gives her a third blanket, she places it over her trusty dog who gives her protection. The woman also declines an invitation to live with her daughters because her animals depend on her.

Lyons, George Ella. (1991). *Cecil's Story.* Illus. by Peter Catalanotto. Orchard. P, I, 32 pages.

The author asks readers how they would feel if their father left for the Civil War and returned with a missing arm. That is what happens to the child in the story, but even with an arm missing, the child rejoices at his papa's return.

Morris, Ann. (1990). *On the Go.* Lothrop, Lee & Shepard. P, I, 32 pages.

The photographs in this nonfiction book show how people move themselves and things from one place to another in various parts of the world. Children learn that it is normal for people in some parts of the world to carry things on their heads or use various pack animals.

Ringgold, Faith. (1991). *Tar Beach.* Crown. P, 32 pages.

The "tar beach" is the tarred roof of a Harlem tenement on which residents place blankets to sunbathe. It is a special place where Cassie retreats to dream about life. This story was originally written by Faith Ringgold to accompany her story quilt, and a bit of the quilt is seen on each page until at the end you view the completed work.

Schotter, Roni. (1990). *Captain Snap and the Children of Vinegar Lane.* Illus. by Marcia Sewall. Orchard Books. P, 32 pages.

Although everybody is afraid of Captain Snap, an eccentric old sailor, some of the children are curious and visit him periodically. On one visit they find that he is ill, and so they gather a blanket and food for the old man. When he recovers, he turns his junky house into a craft museum for his home-made art, perhaps in gratitude to the community that cared for him while he was ill.

Shelby, Anne. (1991). *Potluck*. Illus. by Irene Trivas. Orchard. P, 32 pages.

Potluck is an alphabet book. For each letter of the alphabet, a child whose name begins with that letter uses an action that begins with that letter to bring a food that begins with that letter to a potluck meal. The illustrations depict children of all racial and cultural backgrounds, and the foods they bring come from around the world.

Spinelli, Jerry. (1990). *Maniac Magee*. Little, Brown. I, 154 pages.

This Newbery Award winner involves a white, homeless school dropout who lives for a time with a black family, then teaches an illiterate former minor league baseball player how to read, and finally makes friends with Mars Bars, the "baddest" black kid in town. The human relationships and the caring are both touching and profound.

Stevenson, James. (1991). *The Worst Person's Christmas*. Greenwillow. P, I, 32 pages.

This book uses a cartoon format to show a Scrooge-like person who refuses to celebrate Christmas until some neighborhood children give him a present. He is ultimately forced to be jovial for the holidays.

Turkle, Brinton. (1982). *Thy Friend, Obadiah*. Penguin. P, 32 pages.

Obadiah's sisters and brothers tease him because a seagull has befriended him and follows him everywhere. At first Obadiah tries to discourage the bird, but that doesn't work. However, when the bird disappears for several days, Obadiah misses the bird and is forced to reflect on his values. When Obadiah finds the bird on the fishing wharf, it has a fish hook caught in its beak. Obadiah helps his special friend, and probably saves its life.

Vagin, Vladimir, & Aseh, Frank. (1989). *Here Comes the Cat*. Scholastic. P, 32 pages.

This book, which was jointly written and illustrated by a Russian and American, is about some fearful mice who are afraid of a cat. But when the cat finally appears, it is pulling a cart containing a huge cheese, a great feast for the mice.

Williams, Karen Lynn. (1991). *When Africa Was Home*. Orchard. P, I, 32 pages.

Peter, a white child, was raised by an African nanny while his parents were working for the Peace Corps in Malawi. Peter has no desire to return to the United States, but he must say good-bye to his African extended family and friends. In the United States, he hates the cold snow and dreams of his former home in Africa. At the end of the story, the family returns to Africa and Peter is happy to be home again.

This bibliography is adapted from *Literature-Based Moral Education: Children's Books & Activities for Teaching Values, Responsibility, & Good Judgment in the Elementary School* by Linda Leonard Lamme, Suzanne Lowell Krogh, and Kathy A. Yachmetz. (1992). Used by permission of The Oryx Press, 4041 North Central at Indian School Road, Phoenix, AZ.

4.2 Trade Books for Reducing and Coping with Violence

The recommended grade levels for the following books, which include both fiction and nonfiction, are intermediate (Grades 3–5), and middle (Grades 6–8). Be certain to review these books carefully; they deal with emotion-laden topics that often have the power to touch readers deeply.

Akin, S. Beth. (1996). *Voices from the Streets: Young Former Gang Members Tell Their Stories*. Boston: Little, Brown. Middle. Nonfiction.

Through the voices of former gang members, this book recounts how they were able to leave their gangs, and who and what helped them to achieve new lives.

Banfield, Susan. (1995). *Ethnic Conflicts in Schools*. Hillside, NJ: Enslow. Middle. Nonfiction.

Ethnic conflict is examined through historic and current examples. Successful conflict resolution programs are featured as models for solving cultural diversity issues in schools and communities.

Carnes, Jim (1996). *Us and Them: A History of Intolerance in America.* New York: Walker. Middle. Nonfiction.

Intolerance is not new in American history. With photographs and text, this book chronicles the darker side of American History from Boston in 1660 to Brooklyn in 1991.

Carter, Jimmy. (1995). *Talking Peace: A Vision for the Next Generation.* New York: Dutton Children's Books. Intermediate, Middle. Nonfiction.

This updated and revised edition, written by the former U.S. president, discusses contributions that individuals, especially young adults, can make to peace.

Clise, Michele Durkson. (1994). *Stop the Violence Please.* Seattle: Allied Arts Foundation in association with University of Washington Press. Middle, Intermediate. Nonfiction.

While playing with a gun, a teenager accidentally kills two children. This book focuses on gun violence and the steps that parents and children can take to stop it.

Cohn, Janice. (1995). *The Christmas Menorahs: How a Town Fought Hate.* New York: Whitman. Intermediate, Middle. Fiction.

This powerful narrative, which is based on true events, tells about how two children, their families, and a community resolve to stand together against bigotry and hatred.

Cooper, Floyd. (1996). *Mandela: From the Life of the South African Statesman.* Philomel. Middle. Nonfiction.

The story of Nelson Mandela's lifelong fight to end apartheid is told compellingly in words and drawings.

Hubbard, Kate, & Berlin, Evelyn. (1985). *Help Yourself to Safety.* Edmonds, WA: Chas. Franklin Press. Intermediate. Nonfiction.

This book is a guide to avoiding dangerous situations with strangers and friends. It includes topics such as "getting to school safely" and "your body belongs to you."

Hyde, Margaret, & Forsyth, Elizabeth. (1991). *The Violent Mind.* New York: Watts. Middle. Nonfiction.

This book looks at the roots of violence, explores the links between violence and alcohol and drug abuse, and discusses ways to reduce violent behavior.

Kyte, Kathy S. (1983). *Play It Safe: The Kid's Guide to Personal Safety and Crime Prevention.* New York: Alfred A. Knopf. Intermediate, Middle. Nonfiction.

This book advises on how to prevent and reduce the risk of burglary, assault, and rape. It also covers home security, the buddy system, and ways to get around cities safely on foot, on public transportation, and in cars.

Lamb, Nancy, & Children of Oklahoma City. (1996). *One April Morning: Children Remember the Oklahoma Bombing.* New York: Lothrop. Middle. Nonfiction.

Healing the emotional trauma of the Oklahoma City bombing is the focus of this book, which uses first-person accounts and illustrations to address the anger, pain, and fear that result from any tragedy.

Levine, Ellen. (1995). *A Fence Away from Freedom: Japanese Americans and World War II.* New York: G.P. Putnam's Sons. Middle. Nonfiction.

The story of the internment of Japanese Americans during World War II unfolds through the voices of young children.

Levitin, Sonia. (1994). *Adam's War.* New York: Dial Books for Young Readers. Intermediate. Fiction.

When Adam and his friends start a war with a rival club over a clubhouse, the conflict ends in violence with an innocent victim. Adam realizes that leadership involves pain as well as pride, and that revenge exacts a terrible price.

Marsano, William. (1985). *The Street Smart Book: How Kids Can Have Fun and Stay Safe!* New York: Julian Messner. Middle. Nonfiction.

This book has short stories of kids getting out of tight spots using street smarts. Survival tactics, as well as how to avoid kidnapping and other dangerous situations, are included.

Mead, Alice. (1995). *Junebug.* New York: Farrar, Straus & Giroux. Intermediate, Middle. Fiction.

Because ten is the age when boys in the Auburn Street projects are forced to join gangs, Junebug would rather remain nine.

Myers, Walter Dean. (1988). *Scorpions.* San Francisco: HarperCollins. Middle. Fiction.

When his jailed older brother wants Jamal to take over leadership of the Scorpions, the situation leads to ownership of a gun and irreversibly unhappy results.

Rinaldi, Ann. (1996). *Keep Smiling Through.* San Diego: Harcourt Brace. Middle. Fiction.

A ten-year-old child tells the truth about an act of violence against her German-American grandfather while adults remain silent. Set in the 1940s, this novel treats the issue of personal responsibility.

Ross, Jim, & Paul Myers (Eds). (1996). *Dear Oklahoma City, Get Well Soon: America's Children Reach Out to the People of Oklahoma.* New York: Walker. Middle. Nonfiction.

This view of the aftermath of the Oklahoma City bombing is based on children's letters and drawings that were sent to survivors and rescuers, and the recollections of these people.

Dr. Seuss. (1984). *The Butter Battle Book.* New York: Random House. Intermediate. Fiction.

In this allegorical fantasy, a simple argument between the Yooks and the Zooks over whether the top or the bottom side of bread should be buttered escalates into a full-scale war.

This bibliography is abridged from Ronald A. Banaszak and Mary K. Banaszak, Trade books for reducing violence, *Social Education,* 61 (1997), 270–271. Reprinted by permission.

4.3 Children's Books for Common Social Studies Topics

A. Biographies of Noted Americans, Real and Legendary

Adler, David A. (1989). *A Picture Book of Abraham Lincoln.* Illus. by John and Alexandra Wallner. Holiday House.

Follows Lincoln from log cabin to the White House.

———. (1989). *A Picture Book of George Washington.* Illus. by John and Alexandra Wallner. Holiday House.

Follows Washington's rise to become the "Father of Our Country."

———. (1989). *A Picture Book of Martin Luther King Jr.* Illus. by Robert Casilla, Holiday House.

Follows King's contributions to civil rights.

Ferris, Jeri. (1988). *Go Free or Die.* Illus. by Karen Ritz. Carolrhoda.

This is the biography of Harriet Tubman, the former slave who became a legendary figure on the Underground Railroad by helping almost 300 other slaves (including her parents) gain their freedom.

Freedman, Russell. (1987). *Lincoln, A Photobiography.* Clarion.

Presents the life of Abraham Lincoln in text and pictures.

Fritz, Jean. (1979). *Stonewall.* Illus. by Stephen Gammell. G. P. Putnam's.

Fighting against Civil War General Thomas "Stonewall" Jackson was like trying to move a stone wall. This biography of his boyhood life tells how he came by his nickname.

Kellogg, Steven. (1984). *Paul Bunyan.* William Morrow.

Presents incidents in the life of this legendary hero.

———. (1986). *Pecos Bill.* William Morrow.

Presents incidents in the life of this legendary Texas hero.

4

———. (1988). *Johnny Appleseed.* William Morrow.

> Presents the real life and legends of Jonathan Chapman, alias Johnny Appleseed, who helped build the orchards of the midwest.

Le Sueur, Meridel. (1947). *Little Brother of the Wilderness.* Knopf.

> This is another of several biographies of Jonathan Chapman (Johnny Appleseed).

Quackenbush, Robert. (1986). *Who Let Muddy Boots into the White House?* Prentice-Hall.

> When Andrew Jackson became President, anyone could enter the White House, and often did. This is a biography of Jackson's life.

This bibliography is adapted from *Literature-Based Social Studies: Children's Books & Activities to Enrich the K–5 Curriculum* by Mildred Knight Laughlin and Patricia Payne Kardaleff. (1991). Used by permission of The Oryx Press, 4041 N. Central at Indian School Rd., Phoenix, AZ 85012, (800) 279-6799.

B. Children and Life in Other Cultures

Aardema, Verna. (1981). *Bringing the Rain to Kapiti Plain.* Illus. by Beatriz Vidal. Dial.

> This African folktale tells how Ki-pat brings rain to end the drought.

Allen, Thomas B. (1980). *Where Children Live.* Prentice-Hall.

> A photoessay of the lives of children around the world.

Daly, Niki. (1985). *Not So Fast, Songololo.* Atheneum.

> A grandmother takes her grandson shopping and buys him a new pair of shoes.

de Paola, Tomie. (1974). *Watch Out for the Chicken Feet in Your Soup.* Prentice-Hall.

> Joey is embarrassed to introduce his friend Eugene to his Italian grandmother but grows to appreciate her when Eugene likes her.

Greenfield, Eloise. (1972). *Honey, I Love.* Illus. by Diane and Leo Dillon. Thomas Y. Crowell.

> A young African-American girl shares poems of activities and people she loves and enjoys.

Haskins, Jim. (1987). *Count Your Way Through Japan.* Illus. by Martin Skoro. Carolrhoda.

> Life in Japan is depicted using the Japanese words and symbols for numbers one through ten.

Levinson, Riki. (1985). *Watch the Stars Come Out.* Illus. by Diane Goode. E. P. Dutton.

> A grandmother tells her granddaughter about her mother's boat trip to America.

Martin, Bill, Jr., & Archambault, John. (1987). *Knots on a Counting Rope.* Illus. by Ted Rand. Henry Holt.

> A Native-American boy and his grandfather recall his birth, his first horse, and an amazing race.

Pomerantz, Charlotte. (1989). *The Chalk Doll.* Illus. by Frane Lessac. J. B. Lippincott.

> Rosa's mother describes her life and childhood in Jamaica.

Rogers, Jean. (1988). *Runaway Mittens.* Illus. by Rio Munoz. Greenwillow.

> A young Eskimo boy continually loses his mittens until newborn puppies find a use for them.

Say, Allen. (1982). *The Bicycle Man.* Houghton Mifflin.

> In postwar occupied Japan, a group of schoolchildren are amazed by an American soldier's bicycle tricks.

Weston, Reiko. *Cooking the Japanese Way.* Lerner, 1983.

> Describes Japanese food habits and recipes.

This bibliography is adapted from *Literature-Based Social Studies: Children's Books & Activities to Enrich the K–5 Curriculum* by Mildred Knight Laughlin and Patricia Payne Kardaleff. (1991). Used by permission of The Oryx Press, 4041 N. Central at Indian School Rd., Phoenix, AZ 85012, (800) 279-6799.

C. The Civil War Era

Beatty, Patricia. (1987). *Turn Homeward, Hannalee.* William Morrow.

> The Union Army forces two children from Georgia to the north. This book describes their escape and return home.

————. (1988). *Walking the Road to Freedom.* Illus. by Peter E. Hanson. Carolrhoda.

> The story of a woman who speaks out against slavery and advocates women's rights.

Johnson, Neil. (1989). *The Battle of Gettysburg.* Four Winds.

> This account is based on photographs from the 125th anniversary reenactment of the Battle of Gettysburg.

Lester, Julius. (1968). *To Be a Slave.* Illus. by Tom Feelings. Dial.

> This collection is based on interviews with former slaves.

Nixon, Joan Lowery. (1987). *A Family Apart.* Bantam.

> This is the touching story of six children who are adopted by farm families in the Midwest because their mother cannot support them.

Reit, Seymour. (1988). *Behind Rebel Lines.* Harcourt Brace Jovanovich.

> This is a story of the exploits of Emma Edmonds, who spied for the Union army.

Turner, Ann. (1987). *Nettie's Trip South.* Illus. by Ronald Himler. Macmillan.

> Nettie is a ten-year-old girl who travels to Richmond before the Civil War and is shocked by the aspects of slavery she has seen.

D. Cultural Uniqueness and Similarities

Baer, E. (1984). *This Is the Way We Go To School.* Scholastic.

> Written in a simple rhyming pattern, this book depicts various modes of transportation that children around the world use to get to school.

Brandenberg, A. (1984). *Feelings.* Greenwillow.

> Text and illustrations present children in everyday situations. Different feelings are portrayed in a manner with which all children can identify.

Friedman, I. R. (1984). *How My Parents Learned to Eat.* Houghton Mifflin.

> In this account, a young girl tells the story of how her parents—a Japanese girl and an American sailor—met and fell in love. One parent had to learn to eat with chopsticks while the other learned to eat with silverware.

Gray, N. (1988). *A Country Far Away.* Orchard Books.

> This account depicts the similar experiences that two young boys share, one of whom lives in an American suburb and the other in a village by the ocean. Through text and dual illustrations, this book contrasts the similarities of growing up in two different cultures of today's world.

Hamilton, Virginia. (1985). *The People Could Fly.* Illus. by Leo and Diane Dillon. Knopf.

> This is a collection of African-American folktales about animals, the supernatural, and striving for freedom.

Heide, F. P., & Gilliland, J. H. (1990). *The Day of Ahmed's Secret.* Lothrop, Lee & Shepard.

> This first-person story tells of one day in the life of a young boy named Ahmed, who lives in a Middle Eastern city. Ahmed works all day to keep a special secret until he arrives home and can share it with his family: Ahmed has learned to write his name!

Kandoian, E. (1989). *Is Anybody Up?* G. P. Putnam's Sons.

> As Molly awakes and starts to prepare her breakfast, many people in other parts of the world are doing the same thing.

Morris, A. (1989). *Bread, Bread, Bread.* Lothrop, Lee & Shepard.

> The photographs in this book show that people all over the world eat bread or something similar to it.

Musgrove, M. (1976). *Ashanti to Zulu.* Dial.

> In a modified alphabet-book format, this Caldecott Award–winning selection shows important customs from each of twenty-six African cultures.

Polacco, P. (1990). *Thunder Cake.* Philomel.

> In this delightful tale of Russian origin, a little girl's Babushka (her grandmother) helps her to overcome her fear of thunderstorms. Together

4

they make a Thunder Cake, which they enjoy eating during the storm.

Rogers, P. (1989). *What Will the Weather Be Like Today?* Greenwillow.

This book uses rhyming verse to describe the day's weather in different parts of the world.

Spier, P. (1980). *People.* Doubleday.

This nonfiction work describes the appearance, customs, food, traditions, and people from all areas of the world in a manner that accentuates similarities in people.

Williams, K. L. (1990). *Galimoto.* Lothrop, Lee & Shepard.

This is an account of how Kondi, who lives in an African village, gathers supplies throughout the day to make himself a toy car.

This bibliography is abridged and adapted from Fry, P. G., McKinney, L. J., & Phillips, K. B. (1994). Expanding multicultural curriculum. *Social Studies and the Young Learner,* 6, 12–15. (© National Council for the Social Studies. Reprinted by permission.)

E. The Environment (Ecology)

Adoff, Arnold. (1991). *In for Winter, Out for Spring.* Illus. by Jerry Pinkney. Harcourt Brace Jovanovich. P, 32 pages.

This book contains delightful poems about a family's experiences during each of the seasons.

Albert, Burton. (1991). *Where Does the Trail Lead?* Illus. by Brian Pinkney. Simon & Schuster. P, 32 pages.

While camping with his family on an island a boy decides to follow a trail he has discovered. In the process, he observes the natural beauty of sand dunes, wildflowers, tidal pools, wild animals, and deserted shanties.

Arnold, Caroline. (1989). *The Terrible Hodag.* Illus. by Lambert Davis. Harcourt Brace Jovanovich. P, 32 pages.

The Hodag is a monster whom lumberjacks fear. In this story, the Hodag "rescues" a group of lumberjacks who have been ordered to clear an entire forest in less than a week. The moral is: always be sure to leave part of the forest for the Hodag.

Aronsky, Jim. (1990). *Near the Sea.* Lothrop. P, I, 32 pages.

This book is a portfolio of beautiful paintings—including fish, birds, tidal pools, a marsh, cave, and boat yard—that document the author's experiences on a small island in Maine.

Ayres, Pam. (1988). *When Dad Cuts Down the Chestnut Tree.* Illus. by Graham Percy. Knopf. P, 32 pages.

Is it more valuable to leave a huge, old chestnut tree standing in the yard, generating leaves that must be raked, or would it be better to cut it down and use the wood for other purposes? This is the question that two children confront in this book. (They decide to leave it standing.)

Baines, Chris. (1989). *The Old Boot.* Crocodile Books. P, I, 32 pages.

Baines describes how insects and other creatures create a miniature ecosystem in a discarded boot.

———. (1989). *The Picnic.* Crocodile Books. P, 32 pages.

This book is similar to *The Old Boot,* only this time Baines shows how different animals and insects use the leftovers from a picnic.

Bash, Barbara. (1989). *Desert Giant: The World of the Saguaro Cactus.* Little, Brown. P, I, 32 pages.

This nonfiction book presents the beauty and character of desert life. It forcefully counteracts the common notion that "nothing lives in the desert."

———. (1991) *Urban Roosts: Where Birds Nest in the City.* Little, Brown. P, I, 32 pages.

This beautifully illustrated book shows how birds, including hawks and falcons, have adapted to urban settings.

———. (1989). *Tree of Life: The World of the African Baobab.* Little, Brown. P, I, 32 pages.

The baobab tree grows on the dry savannahs of Africa. When the rains come, the tree becomes the home for countless birds and insects. For the African people, the baobab is a source of honey, its bark is woven into rope and baskets, its fruit is made into candy, and its roots and leaves are used for medicine.

Burningham, John. (1989). *Hey! Get Off Our Train.* Crown. P, 32 pages.

This book combines fantasy with reality when a young boy dreams that his toy train has come to life and that he has rescued five endangered animals. Each animal begs to remain on the train but for different reasons: the elephant because its tusks will be cut off, the crane because its wetlands are being drained, and so on.

Cherry, Lynn. (1990). *The Great Kapok Tree: A Tale of the Amazon Rainforest.* Harcourt Brace Jovanovich. P, I, 32 pages.

Similar to Ayres's *When Dad Cuts Down the Chestnut Tree,* and Bash's *Tree of Life: The World of the African Baobab,* this story focuses on a man who has second thoughts about cutting down a kapok tree.

Cole, Sheila. (1991). *When the Rain Stops.* Illus. by Henri Sorensen. Lothrop, Lee & Shepard. P, 32 pages.

A young girl and her father are picking blackberries when they are interrupted by a thunderstorm. Afterward they notice many differences that the storm caused in the habitat.

Cowcher, Helen. (1990). *Antarctica.* Farrar, Straus & Giroux. P, I, 32 pages.

This picture book shows how helicopters and visitors from cruise ships are affecting the Adeile and Emperor Penguins in Antarctica.

Cowcher, Helen. (1991). *Tigress.* Farrar, Straus & Giroux. P, I, 32 pages.

When a tigress kills a sheep and a camel to feed her cubs, the local herders get up in arms. They consider killing the animal, but, after talking with a ranger, they decide to frighten it back into the animal sanctuary with firecrackers.

Dewey, Jennifer Owings. (1991). *A Night and Day in the Desert.* Little, Brown. P, 32 pages.

This beautifully illustrated book, like Bash's *Desert Giant: The World of the Saguaro Cactus,* depicts the variety of animal activity that occurs in the supposedly barren desert.

Dobson, C. (1989). *Fred's TV.* Firefly Books. P, 32 pages.

Because Fred spends almost every waking moment in front of the TV, his parents move the set to the backyard. Fred soon becomes engrossed in viewing the birds that nest in the TV set.

Fife, Dale H. (1989). *The Empty Lot.* Illus. by Jim Aronsky. Little, Brown. P, I, 32 pages.

Harry Hale visits a vacant lot that he owns in the country before selling it. During his visit, he finds that the lot is a haven for wildlife and decides not to sell it.

Florian, Douglas. (1990). *Discovering Trees.* Aladdin Books. P, 32 pages.

The nonfiction book focuses on the life cycle of a tree.

George, William T. (1991). *Fishing at Long Pond.* Illus. by Lindsay Barrett George. Greenwillow. P, I, 24 pages.

While Katie and her grandfather are fishing on a pond they are awed by the animal, bird, and plant life they observe.

Giggons, Gail. (1989). *Monarch Butterfly.* Holiday House. P, 32 pages.

This book follows the life cycle and migration patterns of the monarch butterfly.

Ichikawa, Saromi. (1991). *Nora's Duck.* Philomel. P, 32 pages.

In this heartwarming story, Nora takes a sick duck to her family doctor for treatment.

Jeffers, Susan. (1991). *Brother Eagle, Sister Sky: A Message from Chief Seattle.* Dial. P, I, 32 pages.

In words and paintings, this book presents the message attributed to the Native American chief, Seattle: the earth and every living creature on it is sacred.

Lehrman, F. (1990). *Loving the Earth: A Sacred Landscape Book for Children.* Celestial Arts. I, 48 pages.

This book focuses on environmental concepts like air and water pollution and on how children's lives can have an impact on global environmental problems.

Lovel, Anita. (1990). *Alison's Zinnia.* Greenwillow. P, I, 32 pages.

> In this magnificently illustrated alphabet book, each girl (named in alphabetical order) does something to care for a flower for the next child in the book.

McDonald, Megan. (1990). *Is This a House for Hermit Crab?* Illus. by S. D. Schindler. Orchard. P, 32 pages.

> This award-winning story is about a hermit crab who has outgrown his current house and goes looking for a new one. Some of the homes he tries include a fishing net and a discarded tin can.

Melville, Herman. (1991). *Catskill Eagle.* Illus. by Thomas Locker. Philomel. I, 32 pages.

> This is an inspiring story about the endangered eagles that live in the Catskill Mountains.

Mendoza, George. (1990). *Were You a Wild Duck, Where Would You Go?* Illus. by Ann Osborn-Smith. Steward, Tabor & Chang. P, I, 32 pages.

> This book, in which birds speak directly to the reader, is a plea to protect and preserve the wetlands, marshes, and other wildlife nesting sites from human greed.

Orr, Katherine. (1990). *My Grandpa and the Sea.* Carolrhoda. P, 32 pages.

> In *My Grandpa and the Sea,* Grandpa is a fisherman on the Caribbean island of St. Lucia. The Caribbean views in the illustrations are spectacular. The moral here is that we must give something for everything we take.

Paladino, Catherine (1991). *Our Vanishing Farm Animals: Saving America's Rare Breeds.* Joy Street Books/Little, Brown. P, I, 32 pages.

> This photo-essay focuses on eight animals whose genetic traits could hold answers to farming in the future.

Parsons, Alexandra. (1990). *Amazing Spiders.* Knopf. P, I, 32 pages.

> The text and full-color photographs in this intriguing book can help children to appreciate the spider's role in the environment.

Peet, Bill. (1966). *Farewell to Shady Glade.* Houghton Mifflin. P, I, 46 pages.

> When developers build a new shopping center in Shady Glade, the animals are forced to band together and move further into the country to establish new homes. Whether there will always be new places to move to is not considered.

———. (1975). *The Gnats of Knotty Pine.* Houghton Mifflin. P, I, 46 pages.

> At the beginning of hunting season, the animals hold a meeting to plan how they can stop the hunters. The gnats decide to bombard the hunters as they enter the woods, causing them to retreat before they can even begin their hunt. The anti-hunting message in *The Gnats of Knotty Pine* is unmistakable.

Romanova, Natalia. (1985). *Once There Was a Tree.* Illus. by Gennady Spirin. Dial. P, 32 pages.

> This wonderfully illustrated story, which was originally published in Russia, depicts the life cycle of a tree.

Ryder, Joanne. (1991). *When the Woods Hum.* Morrow. P, 32 pages.

> In this story, the woods hum on warm summer evenings with the songs of the seventeen-year cicadas.

Simon, Seymour. (1990). *Deserts.* Morrow. P, I, 32 pages.

> The beautiful photographs in this book follow the common theme of deserts as places full of life and activity. However, this book also presents differences among deserts around the world and can help children to understand that not all deserts are like the Sahara.

Slote, Elizabeth. (1991). *Nelly's Garden.* Tambourine. P, I, 32 pages.

> In this book, Nelly Dragon visits her garden behind her house during all the seasons of the year.

Van Allsburg, Chris. (1990). *Just a Dream.* Houghton Mifflin. P, I, 32 pages.

> This is the story of young Ben, who has bad dreams in which he is transported into an environ-

4

mentally scary future. The dreams get Ben's attention, and he recognizes the need to care for the environment.

Wildsmith, Brian. (1979). *Hunter and His Dog.* Oxford. P, I, 32 pages.

This is another book with a strong antihunting message. In this instance, instead of bringing injured birds to the hunter as he has been trained, the dog nurses them back to health. When the hunter discovers what the dog is doing, he gives up hunting entirely.

This bibliography is adapted from *Literature-Based Moral Education: Children's Books & Activities for Teaching Values, Responsibility, & Good Judgment in the Elementary School* by Linda Leonard Lamme, Suzanne Lowell Krogh, and Kathy A. Yachmetz. (1992). Used by permission of The Oryx Press, 4041 N. Central at Indian School Rd., Phoenix, AZ.

F. Families and Family Life

Aliki. (1979). *The Two of Them.* Greenwillow.

A little girl's grandfather cares for her until she grows up; then she cares for him until he dies.

Blaine, Marge. (1975). *Terrible Thing That Happened at Our House.* Illus. by John Wallner. Parents Magazine.

Things are not the same when Mother goes back to work, and the children may need to accept new responsibilities to help the family adjust.

Blaustein, Muriel. (1988). *Play Ball, Zachary!* Harper & Row.

A little tiger and his father have different ideas about how to have fun but learn to enjoy games together.

Brown, Laurie Krashy, & Brown, Marc. (1986). *Dinosaurs Divorce.* Little, Brown.

The seriousness of the anxieties that children of divorced parents sometimes face is offset somewhat by the humorous illustrations in this account.

Cameron, Ann. (1981). *The Stories Julian Tells.* Illus. by Ann Strugnell. Pantheon.

Julian tells five stories about life in his family and neighborhood.

Clifton, Lucille. (1983). *Everett Anderson's Goodbye.* Illus. by Ann Grifalconi. Henry Holt.

Helping children deal with death is often a problem. In this account, a boy goes through five stages of denial, anger, bargaining, depression, and acceptance after his father's death.

Drescher, Joan. (1980). *Your Family, My Family.* Walker.

This story shows how family units are often made up of different combinations of people.

Fisher, Iris. (1987). *Katie-Bo.* Illus. by Mariam Schaer. Adama.

The touching story of an American family that adopts a Korean child.

Hazen, Barbara Shook. (1979). *Tight Times.* Illus. by Trina Schart Hyman. Viking.

A family living in poverty supports one another even though the father has lost his job.

Hutchins, Pat. (1983). *You'll Soon Grow into Them, Titch.* Greenwillow.

This is the story of how a boy hands down his clothes that are too small to a new baby.

———. (1985). *The Very Worst Monster.* William Morrow.

When her baby brother arrives, Hazel grows increasingly jealous of the attention he receives. This account shows how she overcomes these feelings.

Kraus, Robert. (1980). *Another Mouse to Feed.* Illus. by Jose Aruego and Ariane Dewey. Simon & Schuster.

There are already thirty-one mice in the family, but they find jobs and assume household chores to help their parents raise a thirty-second mouse that was left on their doorstep.

MacLachlan, Patricia. (1982). *Mama One, Mama Two.* Illus. by Ruth Lercher Bornstein. Harper & Row.

This is the story of a little girl who must live with foster parents while her mother recovers from a mental illness.

Moore, Elaine. (1985). *Grandma's House.* Illus. by Elise Primavera. Lothrop, Lee & Shepard.

This account celebrates the delight that children find in going to Grandma's house.

Roy, Ron. (1980). *Breakfast with My Father*. Illus. by Troy Howell. Houghton Mifflin.

David's father and mother are separated. When his father does not take him to their usual Saturday breakfast, David is disappointed.

Rylant, Cynthia. (1984). *This Year's Garden*. Illus. by Mary Szilagyi. Bradbury.

A family's responsibilities for caring for a garden change with the seasons.

———. (1985). *The Relatives Came*. Illus. by Stephen Gammell. Bradbury.

When relatives arrive to visit, the house may be crowded, but it is also a time for sharing stories, laughter, and work.

Smith, Miriam. (1989). *Annie and Moon*. Illus. by Lesley Moyes. Gareth Stevens.

Moon is a cat that must adjust to living in new places, just as do Annie and her mother.

Stock, Cathrine. (1988). *Sophie's Knapsack*. Lothrop, Lee & Shepard.

Susie accompanies her parents on a hiking trip to the top of Purple Cloud Rock.

Viorst, Judith. (1978). *Alexander, Who Used to Be Rich Last Sunday*. Illus. by Ray Cruz. Atheneum.

Alexander is rich when his grandparents give him a dollar, but he gradually spends it all and has nothing left for the walkie-talkie he really wants.

Williams, Vera B. (1982). *A Chair for My Mother*. Greenwillow.

This story chronicles a family's effort to save money to replace a chair lost in a fire.

This bibliography is adapted from *Literature-Based Social Studies: Children's Books & Activities to Enrich the K–5 Curriculum* by Mildred Knight Laughlin and Patricia Payne Kardaleff. (1991). Used by permission of The Oryx Press, 4041 N. Central at Indian School Rd., Phoenix, AZ 85012, (800) 279-6799.

G. Life in Colonial and Frontier Times

Anderson, Joan. (1986). *Pioneer Children of Appalachia*. Illus. by George Ancona. Clarion.

This photo-essay of Appalachian pioneer life between 1790 and 1830 was made at a living history museum in West Virginia.

Brenner, Barbara. (1978). *Wagon Wheels*. Illus. by Don Bolognese. Harper & Row.

Based on a true account, this is the story of a black pioneer family who sought free land offered in Kansas.

Coerr, Eleanor. (1986). *The Josefina Story Quilt*. Illus. by Bruce Degen. Harper & Row.

This is the story of a young girl who makes quilt squares to record her travels west in a covered wagon.

Cooper, Michael. (1989). *Klondike Fever*. Clarion.

This photo-essay with brief descriptions focuses on the founding of the city of Dawson during the gold rush.

Fisher, Leonard Everett. (1987). *The Alamo*. Holiday House.

This book presents the history of the Alamo, site of the famous battle in which Jim Bowie, Davey Crockett, and other famous frontier figures died.

Freedman, Russell. (1988). *Buffalo Hunt*. Holiday House.

This account of the life of Native Americans on the Great Plains, and the importance of the buffalo to their lives, is illustrated with paintings by Catlin, Russell, and others.

———. (1983). *Children of the Wild West*. Clarion.

This account of the role of children in the American West from 1840 to the early 1900s is accompanied by photographs and lithographs.

———. (1985). *Cowboys of the Wild West*. Clarion.

Focuses on the cowboy's day-to-day life and the hardships of the trail drive.

———. (1987). *Indian Chiefs.* Holiday House.

Presents the biographies of six Indian chiefs who resisted efforts to take their tribal lands.

Goble, Paul. (1987). *Death of the Iron Horse.* Bradbury.

Describes the raid on a freight train by young Cheyenne Indians.

Gross, Ruth Belov. (1982). *If You Grew Up with George Washington.* Illus. by Jack Kent. Scholastic.

Presents the way of life of people who lived during Washington's time.

Hall, Donald. (1979). *Ox-Cart Man.* Illus. by Barbara Cooney. Viking.

Follows a New England farm family in the nineteenth-century as the father takes their year's products to sell in the city.

Harvey, Brett. (1988). *Cassie's Journey.* Illus. by Deborah Kogan Ray. Holiday House.

Cassie describes the problems her family encounters traveling by covered wagon from Illinois to California in the 1860s.

Henry, Joanne Landers. (1988). *Log Cabin in the Woods.* Illus. by Joyce Audy Zarins. Four Winds.

Follows the experiences of eleven-year-old Oliver Johnson who lives in a log cabin in Indiana in 1832.

Holling, Clancy. (1942). *Tree in the Trail.* Houghton Mifflin.

This old but fascinating account describes events that occurred around a cottonwood tree in Kansas that eventually became a yoke for a team of oxen.

Hooks, William H. (1988). *Pioneer Cat.* Random House.

The story of a young girl who smuggles a cat on a wagon train going to Oregon.

Jakes, John. (1986). *Susanna of the Alamo.* Illus. by Paul Bacon. Harcourt Brace Jovanovich.

This account focuses on Susanna Dickinson, one of the few survivors of the Battle of the Alamo.

Lawlor, Laurie. (1986). *Addie Across the Prairie.* Illus. by Gail Owens. Albert Whitman.

Describes the problems and adjustments that a young girl, Addie, must make when her family moves from Iowa to the Dakota territory.

Levinson, Nancy Srniler. (1988). *Clara and the Book-wagon.* Illus. by Carolyn Croll. Harper & Row.

Clara learns to read after the first traveling library visits her father's farm.

MacLachlan, Patricia. (1985). *Sarah, Plain and Tall.* Harper & Row.

This is the classic tale of a prairie farmer who orders a wife from New England by mail order.

McCurdy, Michael. (1988). *Hannah's Farm.* Holiday House.

Describes life on a farm in early Massachusetts.

Rounds, Glen. (1983). *Mr. Yowder and the Wind-wagon.* Holiday House.

This delightful book describes Mr. Yowder's fruitless attempt to use windpower to drive a prairie schooner.

Sanders, Scott Russell. (1989). *Aurora Means Dawn.* Illus. by Jill Kastner. Bradbury.

After traveling to Ohio by covered wagon, the Sheldons find they are the first to arrive at the new community.

Turner, Ann. (1985). *Dakota Dugout.* Illus. by Ronald Himler. Macmillan.

A pioneer wife describes her life in a sod house on the Dakota prairie.

Walker, Barbara M. (1979). *The Little House Cookbook.* Illus. by Garth Williams. Harper & Row.

Provides descriptions and recipes for pioneer foods.

Wilder, Laura Ingalls. (1953). *On the Banks of Plum Creek.* Illus. by Garth Williams. Harper & Row.

Describes the life of a pioneer family along Plum Creek in Minnesota.

This bibliography is abridged and adapted from Mildred Knight Laughlin and Patricia Payne Kardaleff. (1991). *Literature-Based Social Studies: Children's Books & Activities to Enrich the K–5 Curriculum.* Phoenix, AZ: Oryx.

4

H. Holidays and Celebrations

1. Christmas

Cazet, Denys. (1986). *December 24th*. Bradbury.

Two rabbits give their grandfather a present after he guesses what special day it is.

Ets, Marie Hall, & Labastida, Aurora. (1959). *Nine Days to Christmas*. Viking.

The story of a young Mexican girl who gets to choose her first Christmas piñata.

Factor, June. (1988). *Summer*. Illus. by Alison Lester. Viking.

Christmas in Australia comes in the summer and is celebrated with special foods and activities.

Kelley, Emily. (1986). *Christmas Around the World*. Illus. by Priscilla Kiedrowski. Carolrhoda.

Descriptions of how Christmas is celebrated in countries around the world.

Robbins, Ruth. (1960). *Babushka and the Three Kings*. Illus. by Nicolas Sidjakov. Houghton Mifflin.

A Russian folktale of an old woman who leaves gifts for children at Christmas.

2. Hanukkah

Nerlove, Miriam. (1989). *Hanukkah*. Albert Whitman.

Follows a boy and his family as they prepare to celebrate Hanukkah.

3. Thanksgiving

Cohen, Barbara. (1983). *Molly's Pilgrim*. Illus. by Michael J. Deraney. Lothrop, Lee & Shepard.

Molly's assignment is to make a Pilgrim doll for the school's Thanksgiving display, but Molly's mother dresses the doll as a Jewish immigrant from Russia.

Gibbons, Gail. (1983). *Thanksgiving Day*. Holiday House.

Describes the first Thanksgiving, and how the holiday was celebrated then and is celebrated now.

Kroll, Steven. (1988). *Oh, What a Thanksgiving!* Illus. by S. D. Schindler. Scholastic.

David wishes he were in Plymouth, but his teacher helps him appreciate his own Thanksgiving.

Prelutsky, Jack. (1982). *It's Thanksgiving*. Illus. by Marylin Hafner. Greenwillow.

Describes Thanksgiving customs in humorous poems.

4. New Year's Day

Anno, Mitsumasa. (1986). *All in a Day*. Philomel.

Pictures of activities on New Year's Day in eight different countries.

Brown, Tricia. (1987). *Chinese New Year*. Illus. by Fran Ortiz. Henry Holt.

A photo-essay of a New Year's celebration in San Francisco's Chinatown.

Kelley, Emily. (1984). *Happy New Year*. Illus. by Priscilla Kiedrowski. Carolrhoda.

Descriptions of New Year's customs from around the world.

5. Halloween

Kunhardt, Edith. (1988). *Trick or Treat, Danny!* Greenwillow.

Danny is ill and cannot go trick-or-treating, but friends help him have fun anyhow.

6. Birthdays

Hill, Eric. (1982). *Spot's Birthday Party*. G. P. Putnam's Sons.

The reader must find all of Spot's hidden friends.

Rylant, Cynthia. (1987). *Birthday Presents*. Illus. by Suzie Steepness. Orchard.

A child listens to descriptions of her birthdays beginning when she was born.

7. Other Special Days

Burns, Diane L. (1989). *Arbor Day*. Illus. by Kathy Rogers. Carolrhoda.

Describes the significance of Arbor Day and how it is celebrated around the world.

Kelley, Emily. (1983). *April Fool's Day*. Illus. by C. A. Nobens. Carolrhoda.

> Describes different theories about the origin of April Fool's Day.

Kroll, Steven. (1988). *Happy Father's Day*. Illus. by Marylin Hafner. Holiday House.

> A family has special gifts for Father to locate.

———. (1985). *Happy Mother's Day*. Illus. by Marylin Hafner. Holiday House.

> As in *Father's Day,* this family has many surprises for Mother.

8. Unspecified Holidays and Celebrations

Baylor, Byrd. (1986). *I'm in Charge of Celebrations*. Illus. by Peter Parnall. Charles Scribner's Sons.

> The author shares celebrations of nature that have special meaning for her.

Polacco, Patricia. (1988). *Rechenka's Eggs*. Philomel.

> Babushka befriends an injured goose and is repaid with two miracles.

Zolotow, Charlotte. (1957). *Over and Over*. Illus. by Garth Williams. Harper & Row.

> Follows a little girl who celebrates various events and holidays from the first snow to her birthday.

9. Related Activities

Ancona, George. (1981). *Dancing Is*. E. P. Dutton.

> A photo-essay of dancing around the world.

Brown, Marc. (1988). *Party Rhymes*. E. P. Dutton.

> Presents the music and directions for folk songs and circle games.

This bibliography is adapted from *Literature-Based Social Studies: Children's Books & Activities to Enrich the K–5 Curriculum* by Mildred Knight Laughlin and Patricia Payne Kardaleff. (1991). Used by permission of The Oryx Press, 4041 N. Central at Indian School Rd., Phoenix, AZ 85012, (800) 279-6799.

I. Transportation

The following are easy reading or picture books designed for students in the primary grades.

Ames, Lee. (1976). *Draw 50 Vehicles*. Doubleday.

> Provides step-by-step illustrations for drawing various vehicles.

Barton, Byron. (1982). *Airport*. Thomas Y. Crowell.

> A picture book that shows a traveler arriving at the airport, boarding the plane, and taking off.

———. (1988). *I Want to Be an Astronaut*. Thomas Y. Crowell.

> Follows a child who wants to go on a space mission.

Brown, Laurie Krasny, & Brown, Marc. (1988). *Dinosaurs Travel*. Little, Brown.

> Dinosaur characters use many forms of transportation as they take short and long trips.

Crews, Donald. (1978). *Freight Train*. Greenwillow.

> A picture book with brief text that shows a steam engine pulling a variety of cars.

Gibbons, Gail. (1987). *Trains*. Holiday House.

> A picture book that shows early and present day trains.

———. (1981). *Trucks*. Thomas Y. Crowell.

> A picture book showing different kinds of trucks.

Hoban, Tana. (1983). *I Read Signs*. Greenwillow.

> Picture book of signs along city streets.

Levinson, Riki. (1986). *I Go with My Family to Grandma's*. Illus. by Diane Goode. E. P. Dutton.

> Follows five families, each using a different mode of transportation, to Grandma's home in Brooklyn.

Livingston, Myra Cohn. (1989). *Up in the Air*. Illus. by Leonard Everett Fisher. Holiday House.

> A strikingly illustrated description of airplane travel.

Lyon, David. (1988). *The Biggest Truck*. Lothrop, Lee & Shepard.

4

Follows a truck driver named Jim who travels all night to deliver strawberries to a town.

McPhail, David. (1982). *Pig Pig Rides.* E. P. Dutton.

Pig Pig and his mother talk about the amazing things he will do that day.

100 Words About Transportation. (1987). Illus. by Richard Brown. Harcourt Brace Jovanovich.

Transportation items are illustrated and categorized.

Scarry, Richard. (1974). *Cars and Trucks and Things That Go.* Gallaudet University Press.

A delightful picture book in which the Pigs see various modes of transportation as they travel to the beach for a picnic.

This bibliography is adapted from *Literature-Based Social Studies: Children's Books & Activities to Enrich the K–5 Curriculum* by Mildred Knight Laughlin and Patricia Payne Kardaleff. (1991). Used by permission of The Oryx Press, 4041 N. Central at Indian School Rd., Phoenix, AZ 85012, (800) 279-6799.

J. World War II

Ahlberg, Janet and Allen. (1981). *Peek-A-Boo!* Puffin.

This picture book provides a delightful account of a day in the life of a British toddler during World War II.

Bergman, Tamar. (1991). *Along the Tracks,* translated from the Hebrew by Michael Swirsky. Houghton Mifflin.

This is the true story of a young Jewish boy who flees Nazi-occupied Poland with his family but is separated from his family and becomes one of the thousands of abandoned children wandering through Russia.

Bishop, Claire Huchet. (1952). *Twenty and Ten.* Viking.

This is an easy-reading story of how twenty Gentile children bravely hide and protect ten Jewish children from the Nazis in occupied France.

Coerr, Eleanor. (1977). *Sadako and the Thousand Paper Crunch.* Dell.

In this easy-reading account, Sadako is diagnosed with leukemia ten years after the Allies dropped the atom bomb on her home in Hiroshima.

Dahl, Roald. (1986). *Going Solo.* Penguin.

This is the true story of Dahl's experience as a fighter pilot in Africa, Greece, and the Middle East.

Degens, T. (1974). *Transport 7-41-R.* Viking.

This story of moderate difficulty describes a thirteen-year-old girl's journey from the Russian sector of defeated Germany to Cologne on a train carrying returning refugees in 1946.

Forman, James. (1970). *Ceremony of Innocence.* Hawthorne.

Until they were executed by the Gestapo, Hans and Sophie Scholl published the "White Rose" leaflets that denounced Nazism. More difficult reading.

Garrigue, Sheila. (1985). *The Eternal Spring of Mr. Ito.* Bradbury.

This is the account of a young English girl who is sent to stay with relatives in Canada and learns about racism and hysteria toward Japanese citizens. Moderate-level reading.

Greene, Butte. (1973). *Summer of My German Soldier.* Dial.

A teenage Jewish girl in Arkansas befriends a German soldier who has escaped from a nearby prisoner-of-war camp. More advanced reading.

Haugaard, Erik Christian. (1967). *The Little Fishes.* Houghton Mifflin.

This story follows three homeless orphans from Naples to Cassino in war-ravaged Italy. Moderately difficult reading.

Haurzig, Esther. (1968). *The Endless Steppe.* Thomas Y. Crowell.

This is the account of a Jewish family that has been exiled from Poland to Siberia and endures bitter hardships to survive.

Innocenti, Roberto. (1985). *Rose Blanche.* Creative Education.

This is an illustrated book about Rose Blanche, who lives in a small German town where the war doesn't seem to cause many changes in her life, at least not at first. Then she discovers a concentration camp outside of town.

Leitner, Isabella. (1992). *The Big Lie.* Scholastic.

In this easy-reading account, Isabella and her family are taken to Auschwitz, but not all of them survive the ordeal.

Levitin, Sonia. (1970). *Journey to America.* Atheneum.

Lisa and her family leave Berlin to escape the Nazis in 1938. After many hardships they are reunited in America. Intermediate-level reading.

Levoy, Myron. (1977). *Alan and Naomi.* Harper & Row.

This easy-reading account is set in postwar New York City, where Alan first befriends and then tries to help Naomi, who is haunted by her experiences in Nazi-occupied France.

Lowry, Lois. (1989). *Number the Stars.* Dell.

A ten-year-old girl and her family use courage and cunning to help their Jewish friends escape the Nazis in German-occupied Denmark. Intermediate-level reading.

Maruki, Toshi. (1980). *Hiroshima No Pika.* Lothrop.

This work chronicles the ordeal of Young Mii, who is eating breakfast at home in Hiroshima when the atom bomb is dropped.

Mochizuki, Ken. (1993). *Baseball Saved Us.* Lee & Low.

This is a touching illustrated account of how Japanese-Americans imprisoned in a desert internment camp build a baseball field to relieve the monotony of their imprisonment.

Murray, Michele. (1973). *The Crystal Nights.* Seabury.

Elly and her family must adjust to the arrival of Jewish relatives fleeing Nazi Germany. More difficult reading.

Noonan, Michael. (1988). *McKenzie's Boots.* Orchard.

A fourteen-year-old Australian boy, Rod McKenzie, is tall enough that he can lie about his age and enlist in the Australian army. Before long he finds himself fighting the Japanese in the Pacific, where he learns about himself, the army, and the Enemy. More difficult reading.

Orlev, Uri. (1989). *The Man from the Other Side.* Houghton Mifflin.

In German-occupied Poland, fourteen-year-old Marek finds himself trapped inside the Jewish ghetto during the Warsaw Uprising. More difficult reading.

Reiss, Johanna. (1972). *The Upstairs Room.* HarperCollins.

Annie must hide for the entire war in an upstairs room, protected by a courageous Dutch family. Intermediate-level reading.

Say, Allen. (1982). *The Bicycle Man.* Parnassus.

In postwar occupied Japan, an American soldier performs bicycle acrobatics at a village school, much to the delight of children, teachers, and parents. Picture book.

Shemin, Margaretha. (1969). *The Empty Moat.* Howard, McCann & Geoghegan.

In this intermediate-level account, Elizabeth must decide whether to help the Dutch underground hide Jewish refugees from the Nazis.

————. (1963). *The Little Riders.* Howard-McCann.

Johanna saves the "Little Riders," which are metal figures that represent the resistance to Germans who occupy the small Dutch town. Easy reading.

Singer, Isaac Bashevis. (1984). "The Power of Light." In *Stories for Children.* Farrar, Straus & Giroux.

This is the account of two starving children who resolve to escape from the Jewish ghetto in Warsaw. Moderate-level reading.

Spiegelman, Art. (1986). *Maus 1: A Survivor's Tale.* Scholastic.

This is an unusual, easy-reading comic book, with Polish mice and Nazi cats, in which an old Jewish mouse tells his son the story of his life during the war.

Taylor, Mildred. (1990). *The Road to Memphis.* Dial.

This story, of intermediate-level difficulty, is part of the continuing saga of the Logans, a close-knit African-American family that must deal with white hatred and bigotry in the South. In this account, Stacy Logan is old enough to join the army, and the war is never far from anyone's mind.

Taylor, Theodore. (1969). *The Cay*. Doubleday.

Young Phillip and an old black man drift to a deserted island after Phillip's ship is torpedoed by a German U-Boat. Intermediate-level reading.

Tsuchya, Yukio. (1988). *Faithful Elephants: A True Story of Animals, People, and War,* translated by Tomoko Tsuchiya Dykes. Trumpet.

A picture book of how the keepers at the Tokyo Zoo must kill the wild animals because the army fears that bombs may hit the zoo and permit the animals to escape.

Uchida, Yoshiko. (1971). *Journey to Topaz: A Story of the Japanese-American Evacuation.* Charles Scribner's Sons.

This is a moving account of how Japanese-American families were moved to internment camps during World War II. Intermediate-level reading.

Westall, Robert. (1976). *The Machine Gunners.* William Morrow.

English children collect souvenirs from enemy war planes that have been shot down, including a machine gun, but their game changes when they capture an enemy flier. More difficult reading.

Yolen, Jane. (1988). *The Devil's Arithmetic.* Viking Kestrel.

During one Passover celebration, Hannah opens the door and finds herself transported to a Polish village during the war. After she is placed in a concentration camp, she understands why no one should ever forget the Holocaust. Intermediate-level reading.

This bibliography is abridged and adapted from John Kornfeld, "Using fiction to teach history," *Social Education,* 58, 281–286. Copyright © 1994. Used by permission of the author. (© National Council for the Social Studies. Reprinted by permission.)

References

Prologue: Reflecting on What's Ahead, p. 1

Alter, J., & Denworth, L. (1990). A (vague) sense of history. *Newsweek,* Special Issue, 31–33.

Newmann, F. M. (1988). Can depth replace coverage in the high school curriculum? *Phi Delta Kappan,* 69, 346.

Parker, W. C. (1990). Assessing citizenship. *Educational Leadership,* 48, 17–22.

Schaps, E., & Solomon, D. (1990). Schools and classrooms as caring communities. *Educational Leadership,* 48, 38–42.

1. The Dynamics of Social Studies, p. 8

Arendt, H. (1961). *Between past and future.* New York: Viking.

Asante, M. K., & Ravitch, D. (1991). Multiculturalism: An exchange. *The American Scholar* (Spring), 60, 267–276.

Banks, J. A. (1989). Approaches to multicultural curriculum reform. In J. Banks & C. McGee Banks (Eds.), *Multicultural education: Issues and perspectives* (pp. 189–207). Boston: Allyn & Bacon.

———. (1997). *Educating citizens in a multicultural society.* New York: Teachers College Press.

Barnicle, M. (1994). Dropping our eyes at true evil. *The Boston Globe,* 25 February, C1.

Bell, D. (1990). Resolving the contradictions of modernity and modernism (Part II). *Society* 27, 66–75.

Boyer, E. L. (1990). Civic education for responsible citizens. *Educational Leadership,* 48 (November), 4–7.

Bradley Commission on History in the Schools. (1988). *Building a history curriculum: Guidelines for teaching history in school.* Washington, DC: Educational Excellence Network.

Brophy, J. E., & Alleman, J. (1993). Elementary social studies should be driven by major social education goals. *Social Education,* 57(1), 27–32.

Chase, Stuart. (1967). *The proper study of mankind: An inquiry into the science of human relations.* Revised ed. New York: Harper & Row.

Dewey, John. (1938). What is social study? *Progressive Education,* 15 (May), 367–369.

Engle, S. H. (1965). Objectives of the social studies. In *New challenges in the social studies: Implications for research.* Belmont, CA: Wadsworth.

Engle, S., & Ochoa, A. (1988). *Education for democratic citizenship: Decision making in social studies.* New York: Teachers College Press.

Gross, R., & Dynesson, T. (1991). *Social science perspectives on citizenship education.* New York: Teachers College Press.

Hirsch, Jr., E. D. (1987). *Cultural literacy.* Boston: Houghton Mifflin.

———. (1996). *The schools we need and why we don't have them.* New York: Doubleday.

Hobin, M. (1974). Clarifying what is important. In Allan O. Kownslar (Ed.), *Teaching American history: The quest for relevancy.* Washington, DC: National Council for the Social Studies.

Kaltsounis, T. (1994). Democracy's challenge as the foundation for social studies. *Theory and Research in Social Education,* 22, 176–193.

MacIntyre, A. (1990). How to be a North American. In J. Quay & J. Veninga (Eds.), *Making connections: The humanities, culture, and community* (pp. 1–25). Occasional Paper No. 1. American Council of Learned Societies and the Federation of State Humanities Councils.

Martin, J. R. (1995). A philosophy of education for the year 2000. *Phi Delta Kappan,* 76(5), 355–359.

National Commission on Social Studies in the Schools. (1989). *Charting a course: Social studies for the 21st century.* Washington, DC: National Council for the Social Studies.

National Council for the Social Studies. (1994). *Expect excellence: Curriculum standards for social studies.* Executive Summary. Washington, DC.

Parker, W. C. (1991). *Renewing the social studies curriculum.* Alexandria, VA: Association for Supervision and Curriculum Development.

Parker, W. C., & Kaltsounis, T. (1986). Citizenship and law-related education. In V. Atwood (Ed.), *Elementary school social studies: Research as a guide to practice.* NCSS Bulletin No. 79, pp. 14–33. Washington, DC: National Council for the Social Studies.

Ravitch, D. (1987). Tot sociology. *The American Scholar,* 56 (3), 343–354.

———. (1990). New York education chief seeks new stress on nonwhite cultures. *The New York Times,* 7 February, B4.

Salins, P. D. (1997). *Assimilation, American style.* New York: Basic Books.

Saxe, D. W. (1992). Framing a theory for social studies foundations. *Review of Educational Research,* 62(3), 259–277.

Taba, H. (1967). Implementing thinking as an objective in social studies. In Jean Fair and Fannie Shaftel (Eds.), *Effective thinking in the social studies.* Yearbook 37, 25–49. Washington, DC: National Council for the Social Studies.

Tocqueville, Alexis de. (1947). *Democracy in America,* ed. Henry Steele Commager, tr. H. Reeve. Oxford: Oxford University Press.

Van Sledright, B. A., & Grant, S. G. (1994). Citizenship education and persistent nature of classroom teaching dilemmas. *Theory and Research in Social Education,* 22, 305–319.

Whelan, M. (1992). History and the social studies: A response to the critics. *Theory and Research in Social Education,* 20, 2–16.

Wiggins, G. (1989). The futility of trying to teach everything of importance. *Educational Leadership* (November), 47, 44–49.

2. History and the Social Sciences: The Knowledge Base for Social Studies, p. 32

Alleman, J., & Brophy, J. (1994). Tradeoffs embedded in the literary approach to early elementary social studies. *Social Studies and the Young Learner,* 6, 6–8.

Arendt, H. (1961). *Between past and future.* New York: Viking Press.

Bednarz, S. (1997). Using the geographic perspective to enrich history. *Social Education,* 61, 139–145.

Brophy, J. E., & Van Sledright, B.A. (1997). *Teaching and learning history in elementary schools.* New York: Teachers College Press.

Brody, R. A. (1989). Why study politics? In National Commission, *Charting a course: Social studies for the 21st century* (pp. 59–63). Washington, DC: National Commission on Social Studies in the Schools.

Bruer, J. (1993). *Schools for thought: A science of learning in the classroom.* Cambridge: Harvard University Press.

Bruner, J. (1986). *Actual minds, possible worlds.* Cambridge: Harvard University Press.

Caine, R. N., & Caine, G. (1994). *Making connections: Teaching and the human brain.* New York: Addison-Wesley.

Commager, H. S., & Muessig, R. (1980). *The nature and study of history.* Columbus, OH: Merrill.

Dawson, E. (1929). *Teaching the social studies.* New York: Macmillan.

Downey, M. T., & Levstik, L. (1988). Teaching and learning history: The research base. *Social Education,* 52 (September), 336–342.

Egan, K. (1979). What children know best. *Social Education,* 43, 130–134.

Elkind, D. (1982). *The hurried child.* Reading, MA: Addison-Wesley

Gardner, H. (1991). *The unschooled mind: How children think and schools should teach.* New York: Basic Books.

Good, T. L., & Brophy, J. E. (1994). *Looking in classrooms* (6th ed.). New York: HarperCollins.

Gray, P. S. (1989). Sociology. In National Commission, *Charting a course: Social studies for the 21st century* (pp. 71–75). Washington, DC: National Commission on Social Studies in the Schools.

Henry, T. (1994). Mapping out geography plan. *USA Today,* 21 October, 4D.

Joint Committee on Geographic Education. (1984). *Guidelines for Geographic Education.* Washington, DC: National Council for Geographic Education and the Association of American Geographers.

Levstik, L., & Barton, K. (1997). *Doing history: Investigating with children in elementary and middle schools.* Mahwah, NJ: Lawrence Erlbaum Associates.

Levstik, L., & Pappas, C. (1987). Exploring the development of historical understanding. *Journal of Research and Development in Education,* 21, 1–15.

Momigliano, A. (1982). History in an age of ideologies. *The American Scholar,* 51, 495–507.

Owen, R. C. (1986). Coming of age in anthropology. In S. P. Wronski & D. H. Bragaw (Eds.), *Social studies and social sciences: A fifty-year perspective,* (pp. 139–152). Bulletin 78. Washington DC: National Council for the Social Studies.

Piaget, J. (1950). *The psychology of intelligence.* New York: Harcourt Brace.

Postman, N., & Weingartner, C. (1969). *Teaching as a subversive activity.* New York: Dell.

Theroux, P. (1997). Letter from Hong Kong. *New Yorker,* 12 May, 54–65.

Thornton, S. J., & Vukelich, R. (1988). Effects of children's understanding of time concepts on historical understanding. *Theory and Research in Social Education,* 15, 69–82.

White, J. J. (1988). Searching for substantial knowledge in social studies texts. *Theory and Research in Social Education,* 16 (Spring), 115–140.

3. The Dimensions of Diversity. p. 59

Banks, J. (1989). Approaches to multicultural curriculum reform. In J. Banks & C. McGee Banks (Eds.), *Multicultural education: Issues and perspectives,* (pp. 189–207). Boston: Allyn & Bacon.

———. (1997). *Educating Citizens in a Multicultural Society.* New York: Teachers College Press.

Barber, B. R. (1992). *An aristocracy for everyone: The politics of education and the future of America.* New York: Ballantine Books.

Berman, S. (1990). Educating for social responsibility. *Educational Leadership,* 48, 75–80.

Dunn, R., & Dunn, K. (1992). *Teaching elementary school students through their individual learning styles.* Boston: Allyn & Bacon.

Elrich, M. (1994). The stereotype within. *Educational Leadership,* 51, 12–15.

Fry, P. G., McKinney, L. J., & Phillips, K. B. (1994). Expanding multicultural curriculum. *Social Studies and the Young Learner,* 6 (3), 12–15.

Gardner, H. (1993). *Frames of mind.* New York: HarperCollins Basic Books.

Gay, G. (1991). Culturally diverse students and social studies. In J. Shaver (Ed.), *Handbook of research on social studies teaching and learning,* (pp. 154–174). New York: Macmillan.

Grant, C. A., & Sleeter, C. E. (1989). *Turning on learning.* New York: Merrill.

Lisack, J. P. (1987). *The changing face of America.* Manpower Report 87–6. (Report No. SO 019521). Lafayette, IN: Purdue University, Office of Manpower Studies (ERIC Document Reproduction Service, No. 304 350).

Ravitch, D. (1992). A culture in common. *Educational Leadership,* 47, 44–46.

Rosenthal, B. (1971). *The images of man.* New York: Basic Books.

Schlesinger, A. M. (1992). *Disuniting of America: Reflections on a multicultural society.* New York: Norton.

Suzuki, B. H. (1987). *Cultural diversity: Increasing achievement through equity.* (Report No. UD 026 281). Los Angeles, CA: Los Angeles Multicultural Conference (ERIC Document Reproduction Service No ED 303 527).

Wish, H. (1952). *Society and thought in modern America.* Vol. 11. New York: Longman, Green and Co.

Children's Literature

Mochizuki, K. (1993). *Baseball saved us.* New York: Lee & Lowe.

Uchida, Y. (1971). *Journey to Topaz: A story of the Japanese-American evacuation.* New York: Scribners.

4. How Social Studies Programs Are Organized. p. 84

Apple, M. (1993). *Official knowledge: Democratic education in a conservative age.* New York: Routledge.

California State Board of Education. (1988). *History—social science framework for California public schools, kindergarten through twelfth grade.* Sacramento: California State Board of Education.

Cornbleth, C., & Waugh, D. (1995). *The great speckled bird: Multicultural politics and educational policymaking.* New York: St. Martin's Press.

Egan, K. (1979). What children know best. *Social Education,* 43 (February), 130–134.

———. (1989). Layers of historical understanding. *Theory and Research in Social Education,* 17 (Fall), 280–294.

Hirsch, E. D. (1988). *Cultural literacy.* New York: Vintage Books.

———. (1991–1993). *What your Kindergarten [through sixth] grader needs to know.* New York: Doubleday.

Johansen, B. (1982). *Forgotten fathers.* Cambridge, MA: Harvard Common Press.

Joyce, W. W., Little, T. H., & Wronski, S. P. (1991). Scope and sequence, goals, and objectives: Effects on social studies. In J. P. Shaver (Ed.), *Handbook of social studies teaching and learning* (pp. 321–331). New York: Macmillan.

Larkins, G., Hawkins, M. L., & Gilmore, A. (1987). Trivial and noninformative content of elementary social studies: A review of primary texts in four series. *Theory and Research in Social Education,* 15 (Fall), 299–311.

Levstik, L., & Barton, K. (1997). *Doing history.* Mahwah, NJ: Laurence Erlbaum Associates.

Marshall, M. (1996). Disadvantaged students narrow gap. *Common Knowledge,* 9, 3 & 5.

National Council for the Social Studies (NCSS), Task Force on Scope and Sequence. (1989). In search of a scope and sequence for social studies. *Social Education,* (53), 380–382.

Pappas, C. C., Keifer, B., & Levstik, L. (1995). *An integrated language perspective in elementary school: Theory into action.* White Plains, NY: Longman.

Peterson, B. (1995). What should children learn? A teacher looks at E. D. Hirsch. In D. Levine, R. Lowe, B. Peterson, & R. Tenorio (Eds.), *Rethinking schools: An agenda for change* (pp. 74–88). New York: New Press.

Starna, W. (1990). Letters to the editor. *New York Times,* 7 March.

Taba, H. (1967). *Teacher's handbook for elementary social studies* (introductory ed.). Menlo Park, CA: Addison-Wesley.

Weatherford, J. (1988). *Indian givers: How the Indians of America transformed the world.* New York: Crown.

5. Weaving Instructional Themes into Social Studies Programs, p. 111

Anderson, C. C. (1980). Promoting responsible citizenship through elementary law-related education. *Social Education,* 44 (May), 383–386.

Backler, A., & Hanvey, R. (1986). *Global geography.* New York: Teachers College Press.

Bigelow, B. (1996). On the road to cultural bias: A critique of the Oregon Trail CD-ROM. *Rethinking Schools.* 10, Milwaukee, WS: Rethinking Schools.

———. (1997). The human lives behind the labels. *Phi Delta Kappan,* 79, 113–119.

Cromwell, M., Flanagan, R., Mitchell, M., Newman, J., Stapp, W., Susskind, Y., Wals, A., & Zogg, G. (1992). *Investigating streams and rivers.* Ann Arbor, MI: Green.

Flynn, V., & Chambers, R. D. (1994). Promoting gender equity: What you can do? *Learning 94,* 22 (5), 58–59.

Hickey, M. (1990). Mock trials for children. *Social Education,* 51 (1), 43–44.

Jenkinson, E. B. (1987). The significance of the decision in Scopes II. *Phi Delta Kappan,* 68 (February), 445–450.

King, E. W. (1990). *Teaching Ethnic and Gender Awareness.* Dubuque, IA: Kendall/Hunt.

Kniep, W. M. (1986). Defining a global education by its content. *Social Education,* 50 (October), 437–446.

———. (1989). Global education as school reform. *Educational Leadership,* 47 (1), 43–45.

Kurshan, B. (1991). Creating the global classroom for the 21st century. *Educational Technology,* 31, 47–50.

Laughlin, M. K., & Kardaleff, P. P. (1991). *Literature-based social studies: Children's books & activities to enrich the K–5 curriculum.* Phoenix, AZ: Oryx Press.

Miller, F. G., & Jacobson, M. G. (1994). Teaching for global mindedness. *Social Studies and the Young Learner,* 6, 4–6.

Schmuck, P. A., & Schmuck, R. A. (1994). Gender equity: A critical democratic component of America's high schools. *NASSP Bulletin,* 78, 22–31.

Simmons, D. (1994). Thinking globally, acting locally. *Social Studies and the Young Learner,* 6 (March/April), 10–13.

Tye, B. B., & Tye, K. A. (1992). *Global education: A study in school change.* Albany, NY: State University of New York Press.

Wasson, D. R. (1994). Real-life scenarios for teaching the Bill of Rights. *Social Education,* 54 (3), 169–170.

Woyach, R. B., & Remy, R. C. (1988). Strengthening world studies: The challenge of conceptualization. *Social Education,* 52 (November/December), 484–489.

Children's Literature

Lyon, G. (1994). *Mama is a miner.* New York: Orchard Books.

Priceman, M. (1994). *How to make an apple pie and see the world.* New York: Alfred Knopf.

6. Developing Character and Values, p. 127

Belenky, M. F., Clinchy, B. M., Goldberger, N. R., & Tarule, J. M. (1986). *Women's way of knowing.* New York: Basic Books.

Bennett, W. J. (1994). *The book of virtues.* New York: Simon and Schuster.

Berreth, D., & Scherer, M. (1993). On transmitting values: A conversation with Amitai Etzioni. *Educational Leadership,* 51, 12–15.

Brogmann, A. (1992). *Crossing the postmodern divide.* Chicago: University of Chicago Press.

Bronowski, J. (1973). *The ascent of man.* Boston: Little, Brown.

Brooks, B. D., & Kann, M. E. (1993). What makes character education programs work? *Educational Leadership,* 51, 19–21.

Canter, L. (September, 1989). Assertive discipline: More than names on the board and marbles in a jar. *Phi Delta Kappan,* 70, 57–60.

Coombs, J. R., & Meux, M. (1971). Teaching strategies for value analysis. In Lawrence E. Metcalf (Ed.), *Values education: Rationale, strategies, and procedures* (pp. 29–74). Yearbook, 41. Washington, DC: National Council for the Social Studies.

Doyle, D. P. (February, 1997). Education and character. *Phi Delta Kappan,* 78, 440–443.

Elam, S. (September, 1990). The 22nd annual Gallup poll of the public's attitudes toward the public schools. *Phi Delta Kappan, 72,* 41–55.

Etzioni, A. (1993). *The spirit of community.* New York: Crown Publishers.

Fabes, R. A., et al. (1989). Effective rewards on children's prosocial motivation: A socialization study. *Developmental Psychology, 25,* 509–515.

Gilligan, C. C. (1977). In a different voice: Women's conceptions of the self and morality. *Harvard Educational Review, 49,* 481–517.

———. (1982). *In a different voice: Psychological theory and women's development.* Cambridge, MA: Harvard University Press, 25–32.

Glasser, W. (1990). *The quality school.* New York: Harper & Row.

Grusec, J. (1991). Socializing concerns for others in the home. *Developmental Psychology, 27,* 338–342.

Hersh, R. H., Miller, J. P., & Fielding, G. D. (1980). *Models of moral education: An appraisal.* New York: Longman.

Himmelfarb, G. (1995). *The demoralization of society.* New York: Knopf.

Kilpatrick, W. (1992). *Why Johnny can't tell right from wrong.* New York: Simon and Schuster.

Kirschenbaum, H., Harmin, M., Howe, L., & Simon, S. B. (April, 1975). *Phi Delta Kappan, 56,* 743–746.

———. (1995). *100 ways to enhance values and morality in schools and youth settings.* Boston: Allyn and Bacon.

Kohlberg, L. (1980). High school democracy and education for a just society. In R. D. Mosher (Ed.), *Moral education: A first generation of research and development.* New York: Praeger.

Kohn, A. (February, 1997). How not to teach values. *Phi Delta Kappan, 78,* 429–439.

Lamme, L. L., Krough, S. L., & Yachmetz, K. A. (1992). *Literature-based moral education.* Phoenix, AZ: Oryx.

Leming, J. S. (1985). Research on social studies curriculum and instruction: Interventions and outcomes in the socio-moral domain. In William B. Stanley (Ed.), *Review of research in social studies education, 1976–1983.* Washington, DC: National Council for the Social Studies, and the Boulder, CO: ERIC Clearinghouse for Social Studies/Social Science Education, and the Social Science Education Consortium, 123–213.

Leming, J. S. (November, 1993). In search of effective character education. *Educational Leadership, 51,* 63–71.

Lickona, T. (March, 1977). How to encourage moral development. *Learning, 5,* 37–43.

———. (1980). Beyond justice: A curriculum for cooperation. In D. B. Cochrane and M. Manley-Casimir (Eds.), *Development of moral reasoning.* New York: Praeger.

———. (November, 1993). The return of character education. *Educational Leadership, 51,* 6–11.

Lockwood, A. L. (May, 1977). What's wrong with values clarification. *Social Education, 41,* 399–401.

———. (1993). A letter to character educators. *Instructional Leadership, 51,* 72–75.

Mussen, P., & N. Eisenberg-Berg. (1977). *Roots of caring, sharing, and helping: The development of prosocial behavior in children.* New York: Freeman.

Raths, L. E., Harmin, M., & Simon, S. B. (1978). *Values and teaching* (2nd ed.). Columbus, OH: Charles E. Merrill.

Rogers, C., & Frieberg, H. G. (1994). *Freedom to learn* (3rd. ed.). Englewood Cliffs, NJ: Merrill/Prentice-Hall.

Ryan, K. (1993). Doing half the job. *Houghton Mifflin/ Educators' Forum,* Fall, 12.

———. (1986). The new moral education. *Phi Delta Kappan, 68* (November), 228–233.

Savage, T., & Armstrong, D. (1996). *Effective teaching in elementary social studies* (3rd ed.). Englewood Cliffs, NJ: Merrill/Prentice-Hall.

Scott, K. C. (1987). Missing developmental perspectives in moral education. *Theory and Research in Social Education, 15* (Fall), 257–273.

Shaver, J. P. (March, 1985). Commitment to values and the study of social problems in citizenship education. *Social Education, 15,* 194–197.

Simon, S., Howe, L. W., & Kirschenbaum, H. (1972). *Values clarification: A handbook of practical strategies for teachers and students.* New York: Hart Publishing.

Sizer, T. (1985). *Horace's compromise.* Boston: Houghton Mifflin.

Williams, M. M. (1992). *How a value is treated in middle schools: The early adolescents.* Michigan: University Microfilms International.

Woolever, R., & Scott, K. P. (1988). *Active learning in social studies.* Glenview, IL: Scott, Foresman.

7. Social Studies: Gateway to Literacy, p. 152

Button, K., Johnson, M., & Furgeson, P. (1996). Interactive writing in a primary classroom. *The Reading Teacher, 49,* 2–10.

———, & Welton, D. (1997). Integrating literacy activities and social studies at the primary level. *Social Studies and the Young Learner, 9,* 15–18.

Chall, J. S., & Conard, S. (1991). *Should textbooks challenge students?* New York: Teachers College Press.

Clay, Marie. (1993). *The early literacy observation survey.* Portsmouth, NH: Heinemann.

Cooper, J. D. (1993) *Helping students construct meaning.* Boston: Houghton Mifflin.

Dickinson, D. (1987). Oral language, literacy skills, and responses to literature. In J. Squires (Ed.), *Dynamics of language learning.* Urbana, IL: National Council of Teachers of English.

Flood, J., & Lapp, D. (1987). Reading and writing relations: Assumptions and directions. In J. Squires (Ed.), *Dynamics of language learning.* Urbana, IL: National Council of Teachers of English.

Henning, D. (1994). *Communication in action.* Boston: Houghton Mifflin.

Hymes, L., & Hymes, J. (1960). *Hooray for chocolate.* Reading, MA: Addison-Wesley.

Irvin, J. L., Lunstrum, J. P., Lynch-Brown, C., & Shepard, M. F. (1995). *Enhancing social studies through literacy strategies.* Washington, DC: National Council for the Social Studies.

McAuley, K., & Wilson, R. H. (1985). *The United States past to present.* Lexington, MA: Heath.

———. (1980). The importance of teaching facts in elementary social studies. *Social Education,* 44 (October), 494–498.

Morrow, L. M. (1989). *Literacy development in the early years: Helping children read and write.* Englewood Cliffs, NJ: Prentice-Hall.

O'Day, K. (1994). Using formal and informal writing in middle school social studies. *Social Education,* 58(1), 39–40.

Pinnell, G. S., & McCarrier, A. (1994). Interactive writing: A transition tool for assisting children in learning to read and write. In E. Hiebert & B. Taylor (Eds.), *Getting reading right from the start: Effective early literacy interventions* (pp. 149–170). Needham, MA: Allyn & Bacon.

Ravitch, D. (1987). Tot sociology. *American Scholar,* 56 (Summer), 343–354.

Routman, R. (1996). *Literacy at the crossroads.* Portsmouth, NH: Heinemann.

Sewall, G. T. (1988). American history textbooks: Where do we go from here? *Phi Delta Kappan,* 69, 552–558.

Short, D. J. (1994). The challenge of social studies for Limited English Proficiency students. *Social Education,* 58(1), 36–38.

Taba, H., Durkin, M., Frankel, J. R., & McNaughton, A. (1967). *Teacher's handbook for elementary social studies* (introductory ed.). Reading, MA: Addison-Wesley.

Welton, D. A. (1982). Expository writing, pseudowriting, and social studies. *Social Education,* 46 (October), 444–448.

8. Strategies for Effective Teaching, p. 180

Brophy, J., & Alleman, J. (1990). Activities as instructional tools: A framework for analysis and evaluation. Occasional Paper No. 132. East Lansing: Michigan State University, Institute for Research on Teaching.

Hawthorne, N. (1870). *Twice told tales.* Boston: James R. Osgood.

Johonnot, J. (1887). *Stories of our country.* New York: D. Appleton.

Lauritzen, C., & Jaeger, M. (1994). Language arts teacher education within a transdisciplinary curriculum. *Language Arts,* 71 (8), 581–587.

Rosenshine, B., & Stevens, R. (1986). Teaching functions. In Merlin C. Wittrock (Ed.), *Handbook of research on teaching* (3rd ed., pp. 376–391). New York: Macmillan.

Schmidt, F., & Friedman, A. (1987). Strategies for resolving classroom conflicts. *Learning 87,* 15 (February), 40–42.

Williams, R. G., & Ware, J. E. (1977). An extended visit with Dr. Fox: Validity of student satisfaction with instructional ratings after repeated exposures to a lecturer. *American Educational Research Journal,* 41 (Fall), 449–457.

9. Additional Strategies for Active Learning, p. 207

Berman, Sheldon. (1990). Educating for social responsibility. *Educational Leadership,* 48 (November), 75–83.

Graves, D., & Hansen, J. (1983). The author's chair. *Language Arts,* 60 (February), 176–183.

Kellogg, S. (1988). *Johnny Appleseed.* New York: Morrow.

Lee, J. R. (1974). *Teaching social studies in the elementary school.* New York: Macmillan.

Lippitt, R. (1958). The auxiliary chair technique. *Group Psychotherapy,* 11 (January), 8 –23.

Shaftel, F. R., & Shaftel, G. (1982). *Role playing in the curriculum.* Englewood Cliffs, NJ: Prentice-Hall.

Silverstein, S. (1964). *The giving tree.* New York: Harper & Row.

Walker, B. M. (1979). *The little house cookbook.* New York: Harper & Row.

10. Planning and Orchestrating Instruction, p. 226

Bloom, B. S., et al. (1956). *Taxonomy of educational objectives: The classification of educational goals, handbook I: Cognitive domain.* New York: Longman.

Brophy, J., & Alleman, J. (1991). Activities as instructional tools: A framework for analysis and evaluation. *Educational Research,* 20 (May), 9–22.

Gronlund, N. E. (1995). *How to write and use instructional objectives* (5th ed.). Englewood Cliffs, NJ: Merrill/Prentice-Hall.

Krathwohl, D. R., et al. (1964). *Taxonomy of educational objectives: The classification of educational goals, handbook II: Affective domain.* New York: Longman.

Olge, D. D. (1989). The know, want to know, learn strategy. In K. D. Muth (Ed.), *Children's comprehension of text: Research into practice* (pp. 205–223). Newark, DE: International Reading Association.

Children's Literature

Bunting, E. (1991). *Fly away home.* Boston: Houghton Mifflin.

11. Assessing Learning, p. 253

ASCD. (1996). Designing rubrics for authentic assessment. *ASCD Education Update,* 38 (December), 7.

Gronlund, N. E. (1985). *Measurement and evaluation in teaching* (5th ed.). New York: Macmillan.

O'Neil, J. (1994). Making assessment meaningful. *ASCD Curriculum Update,* 36, 3–5.

————. (1996). Teaching for performance. *ASCD Education Update,* 38, 8, 1, 6.

Parker, W. C. (1991). *Renewing the social studies curriculum.* Alexandria, VA: Association for Supervision and Curriculum Development.

Spady, W. G. (1994). Choosing outcomes of significance. *Educational Leadership,* 51 (6), 18–22.

Stiggins, R. J. (1994). *Student-centered classroom assessment.* Englewood Cliffs, NJ: Merrill/Prentice-Hall.

Wiggins, G. (1989). Teaching to the authentic test. *Educational Leadership,* 46 (April), 41–47.

Children's Literature

Fritz, J. (1987). *Shh! We're writing the Constitution.* Illustrated by Tomie de Paola. New York: G. Putnam's Sons.

12. Nurturing Critical and Reflective Thinking, p. 282

Beyer, B. K. (Ed.). (1987). *Practical strategies for the teaching of thinking.* Boston: Allyn and Bacon.

Bonny, E. (1984). Thinking about thinking. *Educational Leadership,* 42 (March/April), 234–238.

Costa, A. L. (1984). Mediating the metacognitive. *Educational Leadership,* 42 (November), 57–62.

Rowe, Mary Bodd. (1969). Science, silence, and sanctions. *Science and Children,* 6, 11–136.

13. Helping Students Use Maps, Globes, and Graphics, p. 306

Forsyth, A. S., Jr. (1988). How we learn place location: Bringing theory and practice together. *Social Education,* 52 (November/December), 500–503.

Hanna, P. R., et al. (1966). *Geography in the teaching of the social studies: Concepts and skills.* Boston: Houghton Mifflin.

Joint Committee on Geographic Education. (1984). *Guidelines for geographic education.* Washington, DC: National Council for Geographic Education and the Association of American Geographers.

Mark Monmonier. (1991). *How to lie with maps.* Chicago: University of Chicago Press.

Pritchard, S. F. (1989). Using picture books to teach geography in the primary grades. *Journal of Geography,* 88, 126–136.

Children's Literature

Burton, V. L. (1943). *Katy and the big snow.* Boston: Houghton Mifflin.

Freschet, B. (1977). *Little black bear goes for a walk.* New York: Scribners.

Hutchins, P. (1968). *Rosie's walk.* New York: Macmillan.

McCloskey, R. (1941). *Make way for ducklings.* New York: Viking.

Potter, Beatrix. (1995). *Peter rabbit.* Dover.

Schwartz, D. M. (1985). *How much is a million?* Illustrations by S. Kellogg. New York: Lothrop, Lee & Shepard.

Taylor, M. (1968). *Henry explores the jungle.* New York: Atheneum.

14. Using Instructional Tools: Print, Multimedia, and Community Resources, p. 334

Braun, J. A., Jr., Fernlund, P., & White, C. S. (1998). *Technology tools in the social studies curriculum.* Wilsonville, OR: Franklin, Beedle & Associates.

Macaulay, D. (1973). *Cathedral.* Boston: Houghton Mifflin.

McGowan, T. M. (1987). Children's fiction as a source for social studies skill-building. *ERIC Digest* (No. 37). Bloomington, IN: Clearinghouse for Social Studies/Social Science Education.

Passe, J. (1994). Media literacy in a global age. *Social Studies and the Young Learner, 6,* 7–9.

Rooze, G. E., & Northup, T. (1989). *Computers, thinking and social studies.* Englewood, CO: Teacher Ideas Press.

Rose, S. A., & Fernlund, P. M. (1997). Using technology for powerful social studies learning. *Social Education, 61,* 160–166.

Children's Literature

Baker, B. (1972). *The big push.* New York: Coward, McCann & Geoghegan.

Burton, V. L. (1939). *Mike Mulligan and his steam shovel.* Boston: Houghton Mifflin.

Grahame, K. (1954). *The wind in the willows.* New York: Scribners. (Originally published in 1908.)

Mathis, S. B. (1975). *The hundred penny box.* New York: Viking Press.

Name Index

Kownslar, A. O., 14
Krathwohl, D. R., 238

Lapp, D., 157
Larkins, G., 92
Lauritzen, C., 181
Lee, J. R., 212
Leming, J. S., 131, 134, 142, 146
Levstik, L. S., 38, 40, 104
Lewin, L., 265
Lickona, T., 128, 131–136, 143–145
Lincoln, A., 22
Lippitt, R., 209
Lisack, J. P., 61
Little, T. H., 86
Lockwood, A. L., 134, 141
Lundstrum, J. P., 176
Lynch-Brown, C., 176

Macaulay, D., 340
MacIntyre, A., 19
Marshall, M., 98
Martin, J. R., 21
Mathis, S. B., 340
McAuley, K., 162
McCarrier, A., 157
McCloskey, R., 309, 325
McGowan, T. M., 339
McMullan, K., 138
Miller, F. G., 112
Miller, J. P., 144
Mochizuki, K., 69
Momigliano, A., 39–40, 45
Monmonier, M., 307
Morrow, L. M., 158
Mussen, P., 147

Newmann, F. M., 4

Ochoa, A., 18
Ogle, D. D., 228
O'Neil, J., 265
Owen, R. C., 49

Pappas, C. C., 40, 104
Parker, W. C., 4–5, 18, 264
Parks, R., 68
Peterson, B., 100
Piaget, J., 40, 142
Pinnell, G. S., 157
Piper, W., 138
Postman, N., 34
Potter, B., 325
Pritchard, S., 325

Raths, L. E., 141
Ravitch, D., 20, 165
Remy, R. C., 115
Rogers, C., 129
Rogers, J., 163
Rosenshine, B., 187
Rosenthal, B., 80
Rowe, M. B., 301, 302
Ryan, K., 129, 134

Salins, P. D., 19
Saxe, D. W., 23
Schaps, E., 5
Scherer, M., 134
Schmidt, F., 198
Schmuck, P. A., 123
Schmuck, R. A., 123
Scott, K. P., 147
Sewall, G. T., 165
Shaftel, F. R., 214
Shaftel, G., 214
Shaver, J. P., 129

Shepard, M. F., 176
Sleeter, C. E., 66
Sobel, T., 85
Solomon, D., 5
Spady, W. G., 264
Starna, W., 85
Stevens, R., 187
Susuki, B. H., 61

Taba, H., 28, 107, 174, 175
Theroux, P., 50
Thornton, S. J., 40
Tubman, H., 42
Twain, M., 65, 325
Tye, B. B., 115
Tye, K. A., 115

Uchida, Y., 69

Van Sledright, B. A., 25, 27n, 40
Vukelich, R., 40

Ware, J. E., 185
Wasson, D. R., 120
Weatherford, J., 85
Weingartner, C., 34
Welton, D. A., 161
Whelan, M., 23
White, C. S., 341
White, J. J., 40
Wiggins, G., 264
Williams, J., 226
Williams, M. M., 135
Williams, R. G., 185
Wilson, R. H., 162
Woolever, R., 147
Woyach, R. B., 115
Wronski, S. P., 86

Subject Index

Popular *Model Student Activities* are ready-to-be-used or adapted in the classroom.

MODEL STUDENT AC...
Is It "Made in the U.S.A."

Introduction

Most adults and some children already know that many products are made in countries where manufacturing costs are significantly lower than in the United States. This activity is designed to help children determine an approximate proportion of randomly selected clothing and apparel items that are made elsewhere.

Materials Needed

1. Data Retrieval Chart (as shown)
2. Samples of wearing apparel (in the children's closet) as determined by the child's task group

Procedure

1. Explain that the purpose of this activity is to determine how many of the clothes that the children (and their parents) wear are made in the United States.
2. Explain that small groups will be assigned to different kinds of apparel (shoes, shirts, blouses, etc.), and students will need to read the labels to determine where the objects were made.
3. Do a sample investigation:
   - Ask each student to remove one shoe, place it on the desk, and look for the label indicating where the shoe was made. The label may be inside the shoe, stamped on the tongue, or on the sole. If there is no label or it is unreadable, tell children, "That's O.K., because these are the kinds of problems we may find in our investigation."
   - Record the information for each child's shoe on an overhead transparency of the Data Retrieval Chart. A sample chart with some information filled in follows.
   - After completing the Data Retrieval Chart, do a preliminary analysis by summarizing (counting) the number of shoes manufactured in the various

Your N

Brand
Name

Nike
Hush
Puppy
None
Eddie
Bauer

MODEL STUDENT ACTIVITY
Pumpkin Geography

The following illustrations show how you can use pumpkins to teach geography.
Set A: Shows hemispheres, the equator, and the prime meridian.

Southern Hemisphere Pumpkin — Top View
With Longitude Added
Reverse Side
Western Hemisphere

Part 3 Instructional Resources

3.1 Teaching Materials

1. Social Studies Journals

1. *Social Studies and the Young Learner*, which is available from the National Council for the Social Studies, 3501 Newark Street N.W., Washington, DC 20016. This is the only journal that deals specifically with elementary and middle-school social studies.
2. *Social Education*, the K–12 journal of the National Council for the Social Studies. Address: 3501 Newark Street, N.W., Washington, DC 20016.
3. *The Social Studies*, also a K–12 journal. Published by Heldref Publications, 1319 Eighteenth St., NW, Washington, DC 20036-1802.

2. Social Studies Publications for Children

Write (or call) any other of the publishers listed here for examination copies of their materials.

2.1 General

Calliope: World History for Young People
Cobblestone Publishing Inc.
7 School St.
Peterborough, NH 03458
(800) 821-0115

Calliope is published five times during the school year and is for students in Grades 4–8. Each issue features in-depth information and activities on a single topic.

Cobblestone: The History Magazine
for Young People
Cobblestone Publishing Inc.
7 School St.
Peterborough, NH 03458
(800) 821-0115

Cobblestone is appropriate for students in Grades 4–8 and is published ten times a year. Each issue features an episode of historical interest, such as the Underground Railroad or the Roaring Twenties.

Part 2 Planning Resources

2.1 Alternative Planning Guide

This planning guide is designed to serve different kinds of lessons. Therefore some elements, like motivation and establishing set, will apply to all lessons, but other components may not. At times, you may teach lessons that don't use guided practice or review, for example, or where there is no need to state assumptions. Skip the sections that don't apply to the kind of lesson you are teaching. Note also that because this guide is designed to communicate your lesson to someone else, such as a cooperating teacher or a university supervisor, it is necessarily more comprehensive and specific than the day-to-day plans that most teachers use. Most teachers will have usually thought about the following planning elements, even if they don't write them in their plan books.

I. Overview/Rationale/Justification. Provide a brief overview of this lesson *and* why is it something that students should experience or learn.

The key questions here are the following: What's going to happen in this lesson? What is the main idea(s) you are driving at? How will this lesson pertain to something your students will use in the future?

II. State *Objectives*.
List at least two objectives for this lesson.

Objectives should be stated in terms of behaviors or knowledge that students will demonstrate at the end of the lesson.

III. *Assumptions*. Identify specific skills or knowledge that students must have *prior* to lesson.

This section of the planning guide pertains primarily to skill- and concept-oriented lessons and may not be relevant to other kinds of lessons. State prerequisite knowledge/skills specifically, such as the ability to count by fives or to identify the symbols used to show cities on a map. Do not identify global skills, such as reading, the ability to multiply, how to use a map, and so on.

IV. Review, Developing Motivation, and Setting the Focus.

In most cases, the following elements can be described in a sentence or two.

A. *Review.* Describe how you will relate this lesson to students' prior learning experiences.

Identify how you will make connections with previous learning in ways that have meaning for students.

B. Develop *Motivation* and Setting the Focus (Establishing Set). This planning element has three components: a description of (1) how you will get students interested in this lesson, (2) how you will introduce the content/skills, and (3) how you will make students aware of the objectives for the lesson.

Your introduction or beginning activity should be content centered and tied to the purpose of the lesson. Be especially cautious about using seemingly obvious questions for "motivational" purposes—that is, "Has anyone ever seen television? or an elephant? etc." (everyone has). Be equally careful about your terminology. For example, a "discussion" involves the identification and assessment of different points of view on an issue; it is not a random sharing of opinions or question-and-answer. Most children can readily tell you about the time they went to Disneyland, for example, but this is more likely to be recitation, not a discussion. Having children share their perspectives on abortion could provide a legitimate (though unlikely) basis for a discussion. The point is that having children share their prior experiences may be desirable—even if no one listens to them—but such activities should not be presented as discussions.

V. Develop the *Lesson*.

A. Provide *Instructional Input*. Outline and describe the content and skills included in the main body of the lesson and how you will present them.

In this part of the lesson you will present content, use manipulatives, give examples, explain, define, read, model, and provide directions for activities, and so on. You may

End-of-text *Resources Handbook* includes instructional materials; planning aids; instructional resources; and annotated bibliographies of children's literature